Saltwater Angler's Guide to™

SOUTHERN CALIFORNIA

Fishing Titles Available from Wilderness Adventures Press, Inc.™

Flyfishers Guide to™

Flyfisher's Guide to Alaska

Flyfisher's Guide to Chesapeake Bay

Flyfisher's Guide to Colorado

Flyfisher's Guide to the Florida Keys

Flyfisher's Guide to Freshwater Florida

Flyfisher's Guide to Idaho

Flyfisher's Guide to Montana

Flyfisher's Guide to Michigan

Flyfisher's Guide to Minnesota

Flyfisher's Guide to Missouri & Arkansas

Flyfisher's Guide to New York

Flyfisher's Guide to New Mexico

Flyfisher's Guide to Northern California

Flyfisher's Guide to Northern New England

Flyfisher's Guide to Oregon

Flyfisher's Guide to Pennsylvania

Flyfisher's Guide to Saltwater Florida

Flyfisher's Guide to Texas

Flyfisher's Guide to Utah

Flyfisher's Guide to Virginia

Flyfisher's Guide to Washington

Flyfisher's Guide to Wisconsin & Iowa

Flyfisher's Guide to Wyoming

Flyfisher's Guide to Yellowstone National Park

Best Fishing Waters™

California's Best Fishing Waters

Colorado's Best Fishing Waters

Montana's Best Fishing Waters

Oregon's Best Fishing Waters

Washington's Best Fishing Waters

Anglers Guide to™

Complete Anglers Guide to Oregon

Saltwater Angler's Guide to the Southeast

Saltwater Angler's Guide to Southern California

On the Fly Guide to™

On the Fly Guide to the Northwest

On the Fly Guide to the Northern Rockies

Field Guide to™

Field Guide to Fishing Knots

Fly Tying

Go-To Flies™

Saltwater Angler's Guide to™

SOUTHERN CALIFORNIA

Jeff Spira

Wilderness
Adventures
Press™

Belgrade, Montana

<u>*Dedication*</u>
For Big Joe Spira, my father, who taught me how to fish.

Disclaimer: *All maps in this book are for general reference only and are not intended for navigational use. It is strongly recommended that NOAA and USCG navigation charts be used for all navigation and that all boaters participate in the U.S. Coast Guard Auxilliary's Boating Skills and Seamanship Course before venturing out on the waters covered in this book.*

Published by Wilderness Adventures Press
45 Buckskin Road
Belgrade, MT 59714
866-400-2012
Website: www.wildadvpress.com
email: books@wildadvpress.com

Second Edition - 2007

Printed in the United States of America

ISBN 9-781932-09840-2 (1-932098-40-2)

Table of Contents

Introduction

Fishing has been one of man's favorite pastimes since humans first ventured into the water to see what was there. Primal man probably first caught fish with his hands, emulating many animals. It didn't take long for him to start using tools, most likely spears at first. Archeological sites have yielded hand carved hooks, made from bone and antlers, that are more than 20,000 years old. When you grab a stick for an afternoon's fishing, recognize that you are pursuing an activity more than a thousand generations old. Many of us learned to fish from our fathers or grandfathers. Fishing knowledge has been handed down from father to son (or daughter) down a long, long line.

Ocean fishing is a wonderful hobby. It is relatively inexpensive, as compared to many hobbies, and has the added benefit of providing food. If you love to eat fish, you quickly find out how expensive it has become in the fish markets. Add to this the less-than-fresh fish found in most grocery stores and the persistent barrage of medical information warning us to reduce our consumption of red meat, and we have the perfect excuse to go fishing, but then again, who needs an excuse?

Right next to the bustling cities, crowded freeways, forests of high-density housing, and the fast-paced lifestyle that make up much of California's coastline, there is an ancient, primeval wilderness that flourishes: the Pacific Ocean. Little has changed underwater since the last ice age more than 10,000 years ago. This wilderness is a wonderful place to experience. The breathtaking scenery, almost unbelievable variety of life, and dreamlike relaxation possible only a few hundred yards from freeways jammed with expensive imports and cellular phones is almost impossible to believe.

A number of years ago when I was commercial fishing off the southern California coast, my crewman and I were just returning from several days bottom fishing at the Tanner Bank and decided to anchor in the northwest harbor of San Clemente Island. We set a lobster trap for dinner and pulled up a couple of lobsters within an hour. We fired off the barbeque, roasted the bugs and a big red snapper from our catch and cracked open a bottle of wine. It was one of those picture-perfect, balmy summer days. While we dined on fresh lobster and fish, we watched the most spectacular sunset I think I've ever seen. It was at that moment I realized how much I loved being out on the ocean fishing. The beauty and serenity of the moment will be clear in my mind until the day I die.

Sportfishing can be enjoyed by men, women, boys, and girls. It doesn't matter how young or old, athletic or handicapped, rich or poor you are, there's more fun, excitement, and relaxation to be had than nearly any other sport can offer. There's no minimum skill level to have lots of fun, either. Can you say that about golf, skiing, surfing, motorcycle racing, or about any other hobby you can think of?

For less money than it costs to get into Disneyland, you can get on a party boat and spend the day on the ocean having fun and catching fish—if you have your own boat, so much the better. A day's cruise on the briny will yield you memories to last a lifetime and enough fish for a week's worth of dinners. All of this without telephones, finance charges, loud rap music, or surprise notices from the IRS.

This book is about fishing: It will guide you step by step about how and where to catch fish; teach you methods to catch fish when many other people won't be catching any; and teach you to catch fish in any season anywhere on southern California saltwater, from Santa Barbara to Mexico, from bays to islands. Everything presented here was gained from experience. Many of the techniques are commonly known, and some are almost unique. They may not be the best methods, but they work better than most. Over a span of more than 20 years, they've all been personally tested and found to be the most consistently productive.

The California coast can be divided into two distinctly different zones for purposes of fishing: north and south, and the dividing line for fishermen is the Point Conception/Point Arguello "corner." The coast runs mostly southeast—northwest in the southern zone and mostly north-south in the northern zone. Where the coast turns is the Conception/Arguello corner.

Northern California's ocean is supplied with nutrient laden cold water by a major current flowing south from Alaska. A current of warm, highly saline water flows north from Mexico. The two currents collide at the corner and flow almost directly out to sea. This collision is one of the reasons Point Conception has a reputation for having terrible ocean conditions—it is nearly always choppy and miserable.

These two currents cause all sorts of interesting effects. Many of the fish found just north of Point Conception are never found just south and vice versa. There are plentiful schools of petrale sole in the sandflats off Vandenburg Air Force Base, just a couple of miles north of Point Arguello. But just 5 miles south, just inside Point Conception, there are no petrale sole. The Gaviota coast kelp beds, just south of Point Conception, are alive with calico bass, barracuda, and bonito, yet the kelp found only a few miles north is totally devoid of these species.

Some kinds of fishing, especially deep-water rock fishing, are just as good south of the point as north. In fact, the deep canyons just off the Point Conception/Point Arguello corner probably harbor the biggest and hungriest schools of deep-water rockfish to be found on the coast. The weather is horrible, but on that occasional flat day, you can't help but fill up every hook on a 5-hook gangion within seconds of hitting the bottom.

Throughout my years of fishing the California coast, I have been an experimenter. I've tried lots of spots and techniques that proved to be a joke, but a few proved to be excellent. I've listened to oldtimers, watched successful fishermen, and asked everyone who thought they had something to contribute in order to find the best ways to fish the coast. I'm always open to suggestions, too, so if you have a better way or a secret you want to share—I'm all ears.

Though the fishing is not what it used to be, the fishing tackle, electronic aids, and modern boats make California fishing just as productive as when our grandfathers fished the coast. On the last five party boat trips I've made, I have come home with a limit of fish on four of them. On the fifth, I just fished for lingcod and got two beauties that netted nearly 50 pounds of meat. Maybe the fish weren't as big as my grandfather could have caught, but they were just as fresh and just as good eating. I'll bet the captains of the boats had a far easier time finding the fish than the captains in my grandfather's day, too.

We've all heard the stories of huge schools of yellowtail in a feeding frenzy in Avalon Bay or the albacore run back in the good old days when you could walk across the backs of the fish as they crowded through the Catalina Channel. But how many of these stories do you actually think are true? Time has a way of eroding the bad memories and enlarging the good. Perhaps they were true, but believe me, there were a lot of days back then when granddad came home wet, tired, and skunked.

Saltwater fishing is a sport that can be enjoyed for a lifetime. The better you get, the more the challenge. Whether you want to set a world's record for marlin or just want to pick up a few flatfish for dinner, the southern California coast can provide all of the variety and challenge you could ever hope for.

Before you set out to enjoy fishing on our coast, please get a copy of the "Sportfishing Regulations," published by the California Department of Fish and Game. Just about every fishing tackle store has free copies. Learn and follow the rules. They are intended to make sure our grandchildren have a fun and productive place to fish, too. Let's not ruin the planet for our children—they deserve to have just as much fun as we do. Just think, we can tell them about that great albacore run back when they were jumpin' into the boat even after we put the poles away!

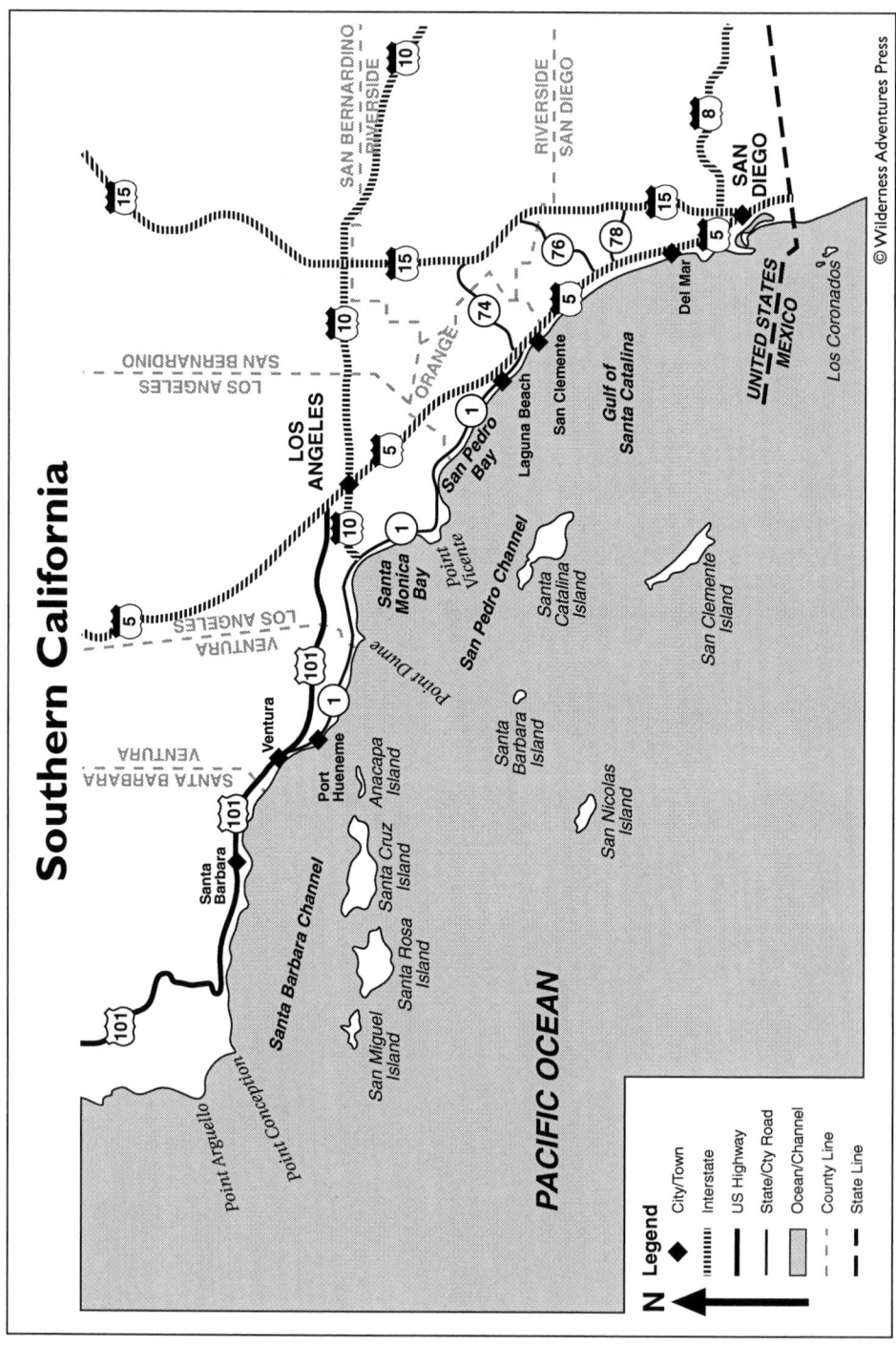

California Facts

California has a land area of about 158,000 square miles. It is the third largest state, behind Alaska and Texas, and is the most populated state in the Union, in excess of 32 million, with the vast majority living within 30 miles or so of the coast. It is also one of the longest, stretching 800 miles from north to south—roughly the equivalent of New York to Florida or Wisconsin to Texas. California is home to the highest mountains in the lower 48, the Sierra Nevada with Mount Whitney, and the lowest valley, Death Valley, only about 90 miles from Mount Whitney.

California's San Joaquin Valley, stretching 50 miles wide and nearly 600 miles long, grows 80 percent of the market vegetables in the United States, more cotton than is grown in all the southern US states, and more wine grapes than all the wine production in the rest of the world combined! With all of these people and all this agriculture, you'd wonder how there could be any room left for wild places, yet California boasts more undeveloped pristine wilderness than any other state with the exception of Alaska. Immense national parks, national forests, state parks, state preserves, and wilderness areas checker the state with thousands of square miles of recreational wilderness awaiting the outdoor sportsman.

California has over 3000 miles of coastline, ranging from wide, sandy beaches to towering cliffs plunging from over 1000 feet high to nearly 1000 feet below sea level. Whereas the East and Gulf Coasts are older and are stretching out as the major tectonic plates shift, the California coast is new, being pushed up from under the Pacific Ocean. Powerful geologic forces are constantly at work. The San Gabriel Mountains, defining the northern edge of the Los Angeles Basin are the fastest growing mountains in the world, climbing at a rate of over 4 inches per year. For these reasons, the undersea environment is highly variable, depending on location. Certain species of fish may be plentiful in one location and may never be caught a mere 200 yards away.

Area	158,693 sq. mi.
Rank	3
Length	800 miles
Width	375 miles
Highest point	Mount Whitney, 14,495 feet
Lowest point	Death Valley, 232 feet below sea level
Capital	Sacramento
Counties	58
Population	32,344,000
Nickname	The Golden State
State Flower	California Poppy

State Bird	California (Valley) Quail
State Fish	Golden Trout
State Tree	California Redwood
State Parks	194
National Parks	6
	Channel Islands National Park
	Kings Canyon National Park
	Lassen Volcanic National Park
	Redwood National Park
	Sequoia National Park
	Yosemite National Park
National Monuments	7
	Cabrillo National Monument
	Death Valley National Monument
	Devil's Postpile National Monument
	Joshua Tree National Monument
	Lava Beds National Monument
	Muir Woods National Monument
	Pinnacles National Monument
National Forests	18
National Scenic Areas	7
and Other Recreational	East Mojave National Scenic Area
Areas	Golden Gate Natinoal Scenic Area
	Kings Range National Conservation Area
	Mono Basin National Forest Scenic Area
	Point Reyes National Seashore
	Santa Monica Mountains National Scenic Area
	Whiskeytown/Shasta/Trinity National Scenic Area

California Saltwater Fishing Regulations

The capture of California game fish is regulated by the California Department of Fish and Game (Cal DF&G). In addition to the issuance of hunting and fishing licenses and the enforcement of fishing and hunting regulations, this active agency is also charged with the scientific research and sensible management of the state's bountiful wild resources. The Cal DF&G is also heavily involved in the protection of wildlife habitat, wildlife education, and a host of other valuable services for the people of California to ensure the protection and conservation of this most populous state's wildlife.

A complete and accurate treatise of the saltwater regulations is beyond the scope of this book and would almost certainly be obsolete by the time of the publication of the book, let alone any time period after the publication date. Laws and regulations change. It is strongly suggested thata before ever venturing out on a fishing trip, you fully familiarize yourself with the latest fishing regulations. Just about every fishing tackle shop, certainly every place where you may purchase a fishing license, has copies of official California state publications detailing the latest fishing regulations. In addition, the Cal DF&G maintains a website on the Internet at http://www.dfg. ca.gov with the full text of all current fishing regulations.

Don't count on the crew of a fishing boat or charter master to know and follow all of the fishing rules. If you have a fish in your possession, it is YOUR responsibility to ensure the fish was taken legally, is possessed legally, and meets the requirements for filleting or dressing in compliance with the law. I personally witnessed a person ticketed and fined for possessing a barracuda fillet slightly shorter than the legal limit when the whole fish itself was legal. The fish was filleted by the deck hand of the fishing boat. While he may have a case to fight the fine in court, the possession of the short fillet was illegal, and the fisherman was responsible for its possession.

This chapter represents an overview of the fishing regulations you are likely to need for fishing southern California's ocean. It does not represent a complete representation of all the laws and is only accurate up to the time this was written.

Licensing

All persons 16 years old or older taking or attempting to take any fish from ocean waters in the state of California is required to have a current, valid California fishing license. Licenses are available at most fishing tackle stores, sportfishing landings, and offices of the California Department of Fish and Game. You may purchase a one-day license or an annual license. The annual license expires on December 31 of the year it was issued. A saltwater-only license or a combination salt and freshwater license are available.

Fishing licenses are required to be worn visibly on the fisherman's clothing above the waist. Landings and tackle shops sell clear plastic holders with pins or clips to attach the license to your hat or shirt. Most sportfishing landings do not allow you to get on their boats without a fishing license, because if you are caught, both of you get tickets.

The only exception of the fishing license regulations is for fishing on public piers. The public fishing piers along the coast are license-free zones. In addition, the Cal DF&G hosts "Fishing Free" days to encourage people to try fishing. On these days, anyone can fish without a license. Consult the Cal DF&G official publications or website for rules, areas, and times.

Prohibited Fish

The following fish are fully protected in California and cannot be kept. They must be released if they are inadvertently caught.

Giant black seabass	Broomtail grouper
Garibaldi	Great white shark
Gulf grouper	

Fish Bag and Size Limits

In general, 10 fish of any species is the limit, with a maximum take of 20 fish of all species in any given day. The exception is for rockfish, which have a limit of 15 fish, only 3 of which can be bocaccio. They can all be of the same species.

If fish are filleted aboard a boat, fillets are required to have at least a one square inch patch of skin so that the species can be determined.

The following fish have no limit:

Albacore	Shiner surfperch
Anchovy	Skipjack
Bluefin tuna	Jack mackerel
Grunion	Pacific mackerel
Jacksmelt	Pacific staghorn sculpin
Topsmelt	Starry flounder
Petrale sole	Round herring
Pacific butterfish (pompano)	Pacific herring
Queenfish	Pacific sardine
Sanddabs	

Kelp Bass, Barred Sand Bass, and Spotted Sand Bass Limits

There is a 10-fish limit on any combination of these bass. In addition, a 12-inch minimum length is required. Any fish less than 12 inches in length should be released immediately. If these bass are filleted on the boat, the fillets must be at least 6½ inches long.

White Seabass

From June 16 to March 14, a 3-fish limit is in effect. Between March 15 and June 15 while fish are spawning, a 1-fish limit is in effect. White seabass can only taken when larger than 28 inches in total length. If the fish is filleted aboard the boat, a minimum fillet length of 19 inches is required. In addition, the fillet is required to have at least a one-inch square patch of silver skin attached in order to identify it.

California Barracuda

The minimum size for barracuda is 28 inches total length. Fillets must be at least 17 inches long.

Pacific Bonito

There is a 10-fish limit, but no more than 5 of the fish can be smaller than 24 inches in fork length or 5 pounds. You may not fillet more than 5 fish on a boat, and these all count toward the smaller than 24-inch quota.

Yellowtail

There is a 10-fish limit, but no more than 5 of the fish can be smaller than 24 inches in fork length.

California Halibut

There is a 5-fish limit on halibut and a minimum size of 22 inches. If the fish are filleted aboard the boat, they are required to be at least 16¾ inches long and may not be cut in half. The entire skin must be intact. Actually, it's best not to fillet any flatfish while on board. Since many of these fish are similar as to meat and skin, a whole fish is required for field identification. Also, if pursuing halibut, it is required that you have a landing net with an opening at least 24 inches wide to ensure any undersized fish are not gaffed.

Lingcod

There is a 3-fish limit on lingcod and a minimum size of 24 inches. Fillets must be at least 15 inches long, with the usual one-square-inch minimum size patch of skin attached.

Leopard Sharks

Leopards have a bag limit of 3 fish with a minimum size of 36 inches.

Rockfish

New regulations have been introduced to regulate the season, fishing depths, and species of rockfish, as well as the size of various species of rockfish allowed to be taken in Southern California. These change on an annual basis based on the Department of Fish and Game biologist's estimation of the health of the groundfish stocks. Consult the Department of Fish and Game's web site at www.dfg.ca.gov for updated information.

Other Species
Some other species and their limits include:

Broadbill swordfish:	2 fish	Thresher shark:	2 fish
Marlin:	1 fish	Shortfin mako shark:	2 fish
Boccacio:	3 fish	Soupfin shark:	1 fish
Surf smelt:	25 pounds	Sixgill shark:	1 fish
Herring eggs:	25 pounds	Sevengill shark:	1 fish
Blue shark:	2 fish		

Salmon
In some years, salmon run in the northern part of the southern California range, especially in the Santa Barbara Channel between the coast and the Channel Islands and in the offshore areas around Point Conception. California salmon regulations vary from year to year and contain specific tackle requirements in addition to size and bag limits. Before you attempt to catch a salmon, you should familiarize yourself with all the current regulations.

Other Fish in California
There are many other fish to be found in southern California, as residents and as occasional visitors. Unless you are certain of the species of fish you catch as well as its possession regulations, please release it. It may end up to be a very expensive catch since the possession of some protected species can result in a fine of up to $10,000.

Southern California Game Fish

Fishes of the Kelp Beds

Yellowtail (*Seriola lalandei*)

Few southern California anglers would disagree that except for the far off-shore species like billfish and tuna, yellowtail is the premier game fish of southern California. The combination of power and aggressive fight along with the excellent table fare of the yellowtail makes it the most desired fish in these waters.

Yellowtail are members of the jack family and are sometimes also called amber-jack, though that name actually belongs to another member of the jacks. In Australia and New Zealand, the term kingfish is used for these fish. Along the Pacific Coast, yellowtail range from southern California all the way south to Chile and on the other side of the Pacific, from New Zealand north to Japan. They can grow to 80 pounds (100 pounds on the other side of the Pacific) but are very rare over about 40 pounds. In the 1960s an annual yellowtail derby was held by the main sportfishing landings in San Diego. The biggest fish of the season could win the lucky angler a new car. Typically, the grand prize for the season was a fish in the 40 to 45-pound class.

Yellowtail are truly handsome, fast, and powerful. After herding bait into tight balls, they sweep through schools of squid, mackerel, or anchovies with ferocity, gorging themselves on their prey. When they strike a fly or lure, the angler knows it instantly and they follow the first vicious strike with punishing, deep diving runs, only yielding when exhausted. The angler's gear and technique needs to be in top form to land these wily creatures. The first Yellowtail I'd ever seen hooked on a fly, about an eight pounder, hit a blue and white streamer fly on a 10-weight graphite rod with 30-pound tippet (some say enough stick for sailfish). The angler, the editor of a flyfishing magazine and no slouch at flyfishing for big fish, had no chance in stopping the fish's first run. That 'tail ran immediately for the kelp paddy we were fishing near, balled the line around the kelp strands and snapped the line like it wasn't even there.

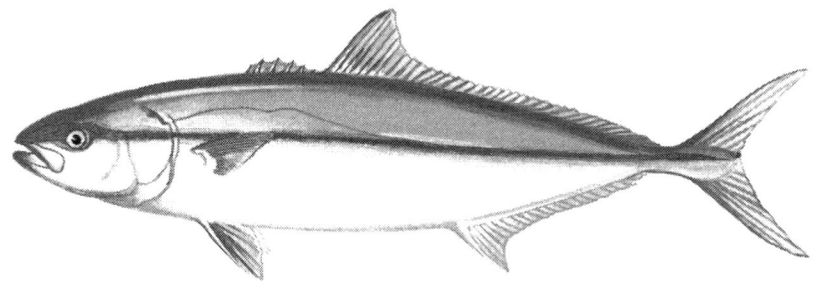

Yellowtail (Seriola lalandei)

The yellowtail populations went into serious decline throughout the 1960s and 1970s. This was due, in no small part, to the decline in the kelp forests from overharvesting. In addition, commercial gill net fishermen followed the kelp cutter ships and set their nets directly into the recently cleared waters killing all of the fish, juvenile and adult alike. In the 1980s, yellowtail fishing in California was an unpredictable affair, restricted to San Clemente Island, far offshore, and the Coronado Islands, just across the Mexican border and off limits to American commercial fishermen.

With the banning of gill nets, the cessation of kelp harvesting, and some early and strong El Niño years (years when the water temperature is warmer than usual), yellowtail have staged a remarkable comeback in the 1990s. Sport fishing harvests in the late '90s have been the highest in 30 years and this magnificent predator is now a staple of the sport fishing industry.

Typically, in early spring when the water temperature rises above about 62 degrees, yellowtail arrive in southern California from Mexico in search of schools of squid. They winter far down the Baja coast in deep reefs. They feed throughout the summer as far north as the Santa Barbara coastline but seem to prefer the offshore islands. By October, they begin working themselves south and seem to disappear during the winter. However, recently, hangers on seem to spend the entire year in California as evidenced by incidental catches throughout the year.

Yellowtail take just about any type of bait or lure. You can catch them on trolling feathers while trolling past kelp beds or floating paddies that break loose from the main body of kelp. You can catch them with blue and white, green and yellow, squid purple, or "pissed off squid" mottled black bone jigs. They'll strike a rubber swim bait, especially when fished deep, in brown herring, blue shad, green sparkle or root beer colors. They'll hit an anchovy, a sardine or perhaps their favorite food, live squid. I've even caught one on a piece of cut squid when flylining for calico bass near the kelp beds. In addition, any fly imitating any of these baitfish can be used to fool yellowtail, particularly when frenziedly feeding on chum.

White Seabass (Atractoscion nobilis)

White seabass are another game fish sought after almost reverently by devotees. This massive member of the croaker family (not a bass at all) can reach 5 feet long and 90 pounds, but they're rare over about 50 pounds. Fish in the 20- to 30-pound range are taken most often. There is a minimum size limit of 28 inches and a daily bag limit of 3 fish in California waters as this book is being written but be sure to consult the latest fishing regulations from the California Department of Fish and Game before going after white seabass.

Contributing to their popularity, white seabass are strong fighters as well as being one of the best eating game fish in the state. Their fight is more one of punishing, deep dives than one of aggressive maneuver. The tenacity and strength of the white seabass makes light tackle fishing certainly not a cinch of landing the fish— the fish probably has at least a 50/50 chance of getting away on 20-pound test line or

White Seabass (Atractoscion nobilis)

smaller. On more than just a few occasions, the angler connected to a white seabass may fight the fish for 45 minutes or more and just when he's bringing the fish to gaff, it will dash away suddenly, snapping the line.

White seabass are denizens of the kelp forest. They feed midway up the water column on baitfish, squid, and red pelagic crabs. The traditional way of fishing for them is with bone jigs yoyoed midway between the surface and bottom. Sardines or anchovies sent down with a bit of lead, or live squid are the ticket for the bait-fisherman. Twin-tailed scampi or mojo-type rubber swim baits in green or purple also produce for white seabass. The best white seabass I've ever taken (55+ pounds) was from a deep reef in northern Baja. It was caught on a green twin-tailed scampi.

White seabass are another comeback success story. This magnificent creature almost disappeared due to kelp harvesting and gill netting in the 1960s and '70s. In the 1950s and before, catching white seabass was easy and the fish were plentiful. By the late 1980s, less than 1000 fish per year were caught by sport fishermen. Since the banning of gill nets and kelp cutting, and the imposition of size and bag limits, these big croakers have staged a comeback. While their numbers are nowhere near the premassacre levels, conservation efforts assure there will be white seabass available for the recreational fisherman for years to come.

A new program of taking white seabass broodstock from the ocean, spawning them in a hatchery in Carlsbad, growing the fingerlings (about 2½ inches long) in pens distributed all up and down the southern California coast, then releasing the fish once they're of a size where excessive predation is reduced (about 8 inches), has been instituted by The United Anglers of southern California. This excellent program has released over 500,000 white seabass to date and with a new pen planned for the Los Angeles harbor area may increase their output to over 400,000 fish per year!

Kelp (Calico) Bass *(Paralabrix clathratus)*

Kelp bass, or more commonly called calico bass, are the mainstay of the southern California inshore recreational fishery. This grouper-like seabass is popular for excellent table fare and skill required to hook and land them consistently. Easily recognized by the squarish white spots all over the fish, calicos are the most numerous fish inhabiting the extensive kelp forests of southern California. Any half-day party boat in the summer months will generally target either calico bass or their cousin, sand bass.

Calico bass have had a commercial ban for over 30 years (it is illegal to sell calicos) and a minimum size limit of 12 inches so these sport fish have been plentiful and will remain so for years to come. A big calico is 18 inches and 8 pounds, but fish over 15 pounds have been caught. Though calicos are predominantly a summer fish, they do not migrate and can be caught all year round near many of kelp beds.

Kelp bass are voracious feeders. Many a fisherman has had the experience of tossing an 8- or 9-inch long brown bait (herring) right into the fringes of the kelp bed thinking he would hook a trophy sized bass, only to have the huge bait inhaled by an 11-incher (too small to be kept). Calicos readily take any of the more common live baits including anchovies, sardines, brown herring, and squid. In addition, they hit rubber swim baits well.

Few southern California fishermen use plugs in salt water (rapalas, poppers, flatfish, and the like), but the bass also take these artificial lures readily. A few private boat fishermen who use tackle and techniques very similar to fresh water bass fishing have some success, but most ocean fishermen seem reluctant to abandon their tried and true salt water techniques.

Kelp bass also take flies. Larger blue and white streamer flies imitating anchovies seem to do the best coupled with a shooting head, sinking line. Though they'll sometimes boil on the surface to feed they usually prefer to stay from a few feet below the surface to the mid water depths. Often the surface action is mostly mackerel, not the preferred catch of kelp bed fishermen.

Kelp (Calico) Bass (Paralabrix clathratus)

Pacific Barracuda (*Sphyraena argentea*)

   The Pacific barracuda, now the most common big predatory fish in southern California, is a success story in conservation efforts. Aside from the banning of gill nets, the only efforts made to return the barracuda to previous common numbers was the imposition of a 28-inch minimum size limit on these toothy game fish. This allowed almost all barracuda to breed. They get up to 4 feet long but are commonly less than 3 feet. A 4-footer will only weigh about 20 pounds, since the fish is so long and thin. Most keepers are in the 6- to 10-pound class.

   Barracuda occur throughout southern California and range from the surface to deep water. Though their main haunt is the fringes of the kelp beds where they stalk unsuspecting baitfish and ambush them as they wander away from cover, they often sweep through inshore flats areas chasing schools of bait. The fertile flats areas where sand bass breed attract many small baitfish and of course, where there's prey, predators won't be hard to find.

   Though the Atlantic (great) barracuda can sometimes be dangerous, the Pacific barracuda is completely harmless in the water. They're not a threat because of their small size and habit of only striking what they can eat whole. However, some caution when handling a landed fish is in order, though. These fish are strong and have long rows of sharp teeth. Many an angler has needed some bandaging when carelessly grabbing a flopping fish on the deck. The best way to pick up a barracuda is by grabbing just behind its head, slipping your fingers under the gill plates and holding its neck. They can be pretty slimy and hard to hold. Some fishermen use a short hand gaff made up of a barbless double trolling hook attached to a 12-inch piece of 1-inch diameter hardwood dowel. This is especially effective for those of us with "office hands."

   Barracuda are primarily a fish of the summer, but of late, they have been nearly a year-round proposition. In the early spring, they move up from their deep-water haunts into the near shore areas. The fishing is spotty in February, March, and April. By May, becomes consistent and carries usually at least until September or October.

   Barracuda are easily caught on bone jigs or bait. They will also hit flies and top-water plugs but only when they are busting the surface in midsummer near kelp

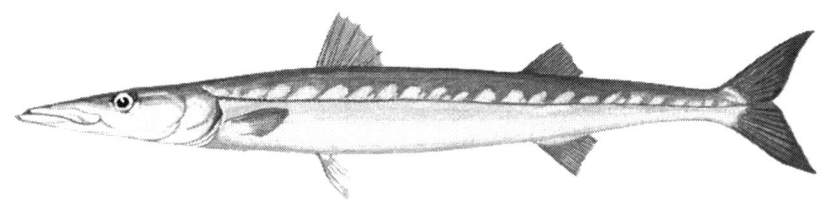

Pacific Barracuda (Sphyraena argentea)

beds or when you catch a school, out in the open, chasing a bait ball. The preferred jigs are blue and white, purple and white and an old favorite of mine green and black—especially for those overcast days. You can also catch them at night when they seem to prefer shiny chrome type jigs. If there are short fish about, later in the season, single hook jigs are preferred. Often, getting a treble hook out will do real damage to the fish's mouth. It's a shame to throw a fish back after you've mutilated its mouth and marked it for sure death. I personally use only single hooks on all my barracuda jigs.

Streamer flies in blue and white to simulate anchovies or in green and white to simulate sardines will be the best bet for the flyfishermen. You'll probably go through lots of flies because when these fish hit, they hit *hard* and are used to killing their prey instantly with their crushing jaws. Their fight is vigorous and strong, making hard turns, shaking their heads, and in general, giving the light tackle fisherman all he can handle. An 8-weight rod is the minimum and a 10 is preferred with a shooting head and sinking line.

Barries also will take bait. Live anchovies or sardines fly lined near the kelp or sent down with a Carolina rig with a sliding sinker, is the hot ticket. Beware, though, their teeth are sharp and will saw through a mono leader with ease. Some fishermen use short wire leaders. This will result in less strikes but far fewer losses.

Barracuda are excellent table fare, too. They do have a strong fish taste like salmon or tuna so they may not be for everyone's palette, but if you like fish, you'll love barracuda. Because of their high oil content, they also are great eating smoked.

Pacific Bonito (*Sarda chilinsis*)

Bonito are another popular southern California kelp bed fish. Related to the tunas, bonito are probably, pound for pound, the fightingest fish in the world. On a 10-weight fly rod, you'll swear you have a 500-pound blue marlin on the end of the line. And after about 40 minutes of sweating, straining, singing drags, and desperate reeling, you'll discover a 3-pound bonito on the end of your leader. A better sport fish on light tackle simply cannot be found.

Bonito can get as big as 3 feet and 35 pounds, but most fish are from 2 to 10 pounds. They feed predominantly near the edges of the kelp forest on the schools of sardines, anchovies, and squid. They're most active during the spawning season from January through May, but can be caught through July or August in the warmer seasons. The last half of the year, they seem to disappear and may migrate to deep-water canyons.

Bonito seem to be willing to take just about any bait or lure. They've been caught on flies, feather lures, top water plugs, bone jigs, spoon jigs, or live bait. They like flashy colors, so white crystal flash streamer flies, chrome spoons, or chrome headed feather jigs all seem to work well. It used to be great sport on the piers to watch for bonito slashing through bait schools and cast bonito feathers (chrome-headed feather jigs) just ahead of their paths. There aren't nearly as many fish now as there were back in the '60s so this technique will result in a lot of waiting and watching.

Pacific Bonito (Sarda chilinsis)

Bonito have experienced a serious decline since the old days when they were usually considered a nuisance fish. The California Department of Fish and Game has instituted new take regulations for bonito. A limit of 10 fish with a maximum of 5 fish under 24-inch fork length or 5 pounds. This along with the gill net ban should result in an increased bonito population and a guarantee that these fish will still be around for our grandchildren to catch.

Bonito are another strong-flavored fish. Some like the taste fresh, but most people, if they keep the fish at all, smoke it. The high oil content makes it an excellent smoked fish. Very fresh, bonito are great barbecued. To do so, make sure you first remove all the dark flesh, and you'll enjoy it more.

Blue Perch or Halfmoon (*Medialuna californiensis*)
Blue perch are a very common fish of the kelp beds. Though they are small (a 12-incher is huge) they are great eating and fun to catch. They tend to school up and often several thousand fish may sweep through an area. On the lee side of Catalina Island, huge schools of blue perch are permanent residents and they are a frequent catch near local kelp beds.

Blue perch have small mouths, so if you're fishing for some other species of fish, using 1/0 hooks and live anchovies or bigger plugs, you may not even know they're there. You have to target these fun fish. I commonly use a #6 hook with eight pound test on a freshwater spinning setup and have a blast catching them for a couple of hours on my trips to Catalina. A tiny piece of cut squid on the hook is attacked as soon as it hits the water. It's a bit like trout fishing in that you can see the fish all over, swarming the bait.

Near the kelp beds, you'll often catch them when fishing for calico bass especially in the mid summer when the anchovies are running small and you're using #4 or smaller hooks. Since they're so easy to catch on bait or fly, I've never tried any

Blue Perch or Halfmoon (Medialuna californiensis)

other types of artificial lures, but there's no reason to believe they won't take minnow imitation spoons or lures.

Blue perch are easily deceived by a fly and seem to be willing to hit almost anything that has the slightest chance of being food. A green woolly bugger on a sinking 5-weight fly line is all you need to catch as many blue perch as you can handle. You'll be surprised at the amount of fight in these tiny titans. In fact, if you've only fished in lakes, streams and rivers, you'll be astounded at the amount of fight all saltwater fish have.

Blue perch are excellent eating. Their light, fluffy white meat is just the ticket for the "I hate fishy tasting fish" palettes. You can bake, broil, saute, or barbecue them all with equal ease.

Pacific Mackerel (*Scomber japonicus*)

Mackerel are the scourge of many southern California fishermen. They are considered a nuisance, snapping up anchovies intended for bass. Most fishermen curse their arrival to a fishing spot. In fact, the Pacific mackerel is a noble fish, with a strong fight and moderately good edibility. Schooling anywhere near kelp forests for the easy accessability of bait, they hunt the sea in packs and are, in turn, preyed upon by larger predators.

Mackerel will eat almost anything, from anchovies to shrimp to small squid, and floating pieces of clam or mussel. For this reason, they'll eagerly snap at almost any bait or lure presented to them. When rock cod fishing with large (5/0) garish flies in blue and white, red and pink, or chartreuse, should the weak link to the sinker break, the floating gangion will be immediately attacked by mackerel.

A mackerel hooked on a fly will be one of the strongest adversaries a fisherman could hope for. Their high speed zig zag runs, deep soundings, and deceptive sur-

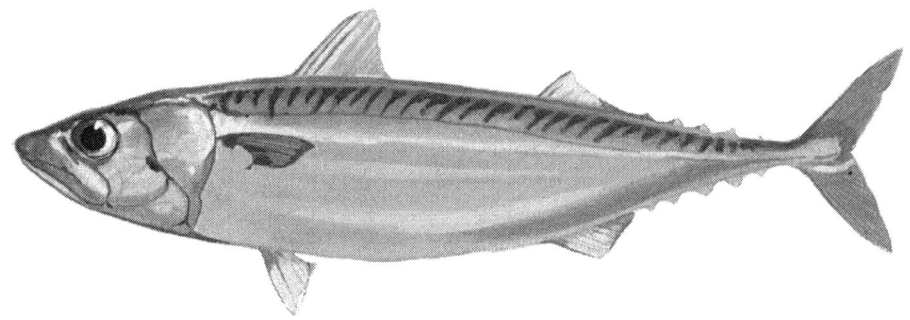

Pacific Mackerel (Scomber japonicus)

vival strategies will convince the sporting flyfisherman that he's found the ultimate challenge on a fly. Likewise, with a small rubber bug on light freshwater spinning tackle, you'll be amazed at how fun catching mackerel can really be.

Smaller mackerel make excellent bait for bigger yellowtail and tuna. They are also excellent bait for sending deep to get huge lingcod. Often five hook "Bait Rigs" are used to catch mackerel for bait. These have yellow and red yarn flies imitating small shrimp. The longer-range boats traveling down the coast of Baja search out bait mackerel to use for tuna fishing.

The bigger the mackerel, the better it is for eating. The higher fat content of the meat allows it to cook up better. Like bonito, when fresh, remove the dark red meat and broil or barbecue. Some people enjoy its strong flavor. You can steam (can) or smoke mackerel also. Another increasingly popular way to prepare mackerel is to pickle it like sushi mackerel, though it is darker meat than the traditional Japanese mackerel.

Near Shore Surf Fish

If you enjoy fishing from piers, jetties, boat docks and the beaches, you'll be fishing for a variety of shallow water surf fishes that all primarily feed on small bottom creatures. They feed on the incoming tide, high tide and first hour or so after the high tide in the surf zone. In the lower tides, they move a bit offshore to feed in the wide expanses of sandy flats just off California's miles of famous beaches.

California Corbina (*Menticirrhus undulatus*)

California corbina are the most esteemed surf fish in the southern half of the State. They have been protected from commercial exploitation since the turn of the century. They grow up to 28 inches and 8 pounds, but are most common under 4 pounds. They feed on small shrimps, crustaceans, and mollusks.

Corbina fishing is primarily a baitfishing proposition. Ghost shrimp, available in most coastal bait shops, makes an excellent bait. In lieu of buying ghost shrimp, they can be caught in the sandy tidal zones at low tide. Professional bait collectors use a suction piston to suck the shrimp out of their holes, but an hour or so with a bucket and shovel should net you enough shrimp for a day's fishing. Another excellent bait is bloodworms. Though there are some available in the mud flats, they are mostly imported from the East Coast and sold through bait shops.

One old time Japanese surf fisherman who fishes the beach near my house nearly every day, buys premium bloodworms from Maine and has them flown in live. He constantly complains about the price (they're over 50 cents apiece) but is never without them—and he catches plenty of corbina.

California corbina will also take clam siphons (frozen razor clams are available), mussels (frozen or pluck your own from under a dock), or cut squid. Attach the bait to a small treble hook (or special mussel holding hook) and cast out into the surf line, using a surf style sinker and wait. It takes patience to surf fish since there are rarely schools of fish that close to shore.

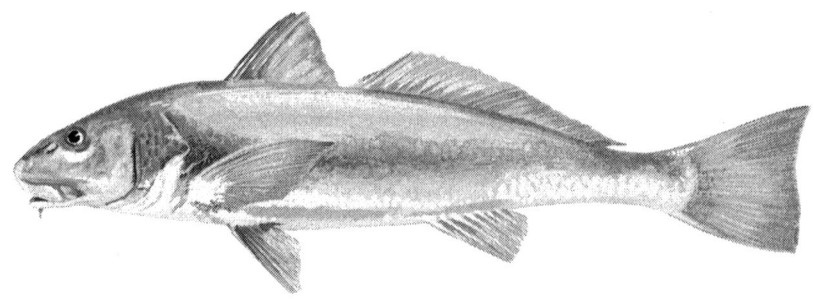

California Corbina (Menticirrhus undulatus)

California corbina are excellent eating. Like many scavenger fish, their flesh is white and mild tasting. They can be prepared any way white meat fish is eaten but true aficionados eat them broiled with a squirt of lemon.

Spotfin Croaker *(Roncador stearnsi)*
Spotfins are the other favorite surf fish in southern California. Like corbinas they frequent the surf line looking for worms, shrimps, and mollusks. They have heavier jaws and have the ability to eat clams by crushing the shells and sucking out the meat.

Spotfins are a heavier bodied fish than corbina and get heavier, up to 10 pounds. Most caught are in the 3-pound range and less than 15 inches long. This doesn't mean they aren't scrappy, fun game fish, though and a real challenge on light tackle. The spotfin is easily distinguished by the dark spot right at the base of the pectoral fins.

The identical baits and methods used for corbina offer the best way to catch spotfins, their close cousins. These fish occur across the same range so you never know which you may have hooked until you actually land the fish.

Yellowfin Croaker *(Roncador unbrina)*
Yet another fish closely related to the corbina and spotfin croaker is the yellowfin croaker. It is aptly named for its distinctive yellow fins. A big yellowfin croaker is 5 pounds and 20 inches long. It ranges throughout southern California along sandy beaches and coastal areas with wide sand flats swept by currents.

The yellowfin croaker eats the same foods as the corbina and spotfin with one notable exception. The yellowfin croaker will also feed on small fish and can be caught on frozen or live anchovies in addition to the shrimps, worms, and shellfish diet of the corbinas and spotfins.

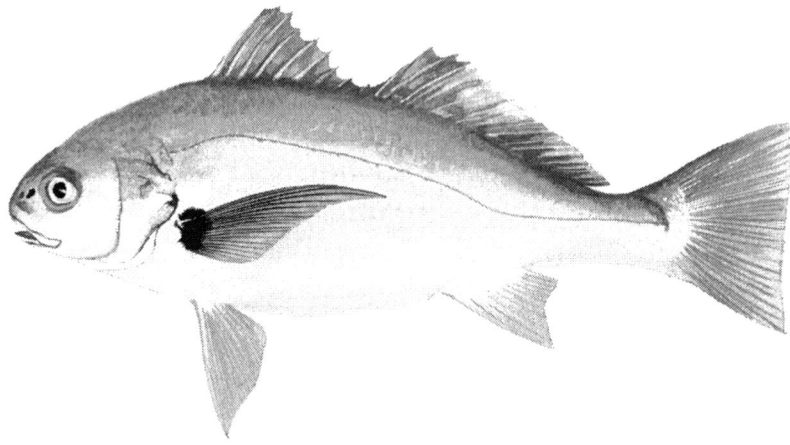

Spotfin Croaker (Roncador stearnsi)

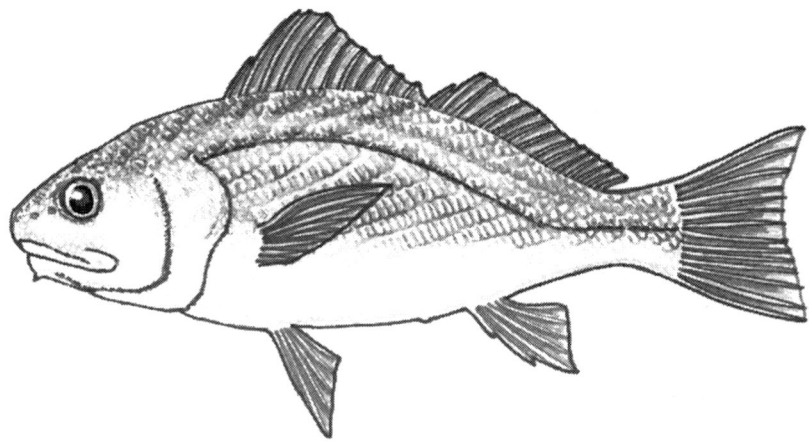

Yellowfin Croaker (Roncador unbrina)

Barred Surfperch (Amphistichus argentus)

White Croaker (*Roncador blanco*)
Also called tomcod, queenfish, and kingfish, white croaker are an abundant fish in southern California. They swim in large schools in shallow water over sandy bottoms grazing the bottom for food. White croaker are the most common fish caught off piers and jetties.

Croaker caught away from harbors and river mouths are good eating but those caught within bays should not be eaten. Though clean up efforts have been successful, pollutants in the silt in the major harbors and bays work their way up the food chain and into the bigger predators, like the white croaker.

You'll usually catch white croaker incidentally, when fishing for corbina or spotfins. The same techniques and bait are used. White croaker are generally smaller than corbina, spotfins or yellowfin croakers, rarely exceeding one foot and about a pound and a half.

Barred Surfperch (*Amphistichus argentus*)
Fishing for barred surfperch is a Christmas tradition for many southern California anglers. The week between Christmas and New Year's when many people have time off work, you'll find the beaches alive with surf fishermen out chasing these tasty little fish. Though they get as big as 17 inches and 4 pounds, most are about half that length and less than a pound in weight.

Barred surfperch tend to school up in the winter so wherever you find one there are sure to be more about. They move into the surf lines from two hours before high tide to one hour after, feeding on small shrimps and worms. The morning tide seems to produce the best results perhaps because they don't feed at night.

Though some fishermen use bait, most avoid the smell and mess and just use rubber lures. Small, green 1½-inch rubber grubs pitched right into the breaking waves are the hot ticket for barred perch. The ideal rig is 24 inches of 4- or 6-pound test leader with a tiny swivel holding a ½-ounce sliding egg sinker on the main line.

It is totally unnecessary to use long, surf types poles and cast way out into the sea to catch barred surfperch. A freshwater casting type pole with bait casting reel and eight or ten pound test is fine for fishing for these perch. They come right up into the white water and the vast majority will be hooked in less than two feet of water. Some even surprise you by striking virtually at your feet in ankle deep water.

Barred surfperch's light delicate meat is delicious. Just head, gut, and scale the fish then pop it into the broiler with a little salt—or into the frying pan with a little olive oil and garlic. Add a dash of lemon or soy sauce and you have a fun, quick meal. I prefer eating them with chopsticks but it does take some acquired skill to navigate the small bones.

Fish of the Flats

Much of the sea floor off the southern California coast consists of broad sand or mudflats. Fishing the flats is a common, productive method to catch a wide variety of delicious, challenging sport fish. Some very famous areas have been sport fished for years and are still fished on a daily basis by party boat, charter boat, and private boat fishermen, and these areas still produce well. In fact, since heavy commercial pressure has been taken off these sport fishing areas, catches are increasing every year. The resources of the sea are proving to be resilient and renewable if sensible controls and conservation efforts are followed.

California Halibut (*Paralichthys californicus*)

California halibut are the most famous of all sandflat fish. Everyone loves to catch and eat halibut. This is not the species that grows to 300 pounds or more in Alaska (Pacific halibut), but a home-grown, southern California only, species. They're just as tasty as their bigger cousins, though. Halibut start out their lives more or less like other fish, swimming vertically in the water with one eye on each side of their heads. As they pass from this juvenile stage into adulthood, one eye migrates from its original position around the nose of the fish and ends up on the other side. The blind side then turns white and the fish begins swimming horizontally over the bottom with the white, blind side down. Halibut are members of the left-eyed flat fishes, however, 40 percent of them are actually right-eyed (the left eye migrates to the right side.)

California halibut can grow to 5 feet long and 60 pounds, but most are far smaller. In fact, throughout most of the 1980s and 1990s, it was very unusual to find a halibut that was large enough to keep—22 inches. Twenty would be thrown back for every fish that measured up. Now, since conservation efforts and heavy restrictions on where trammel nets (the commercial nets used for flat fish) can be set, the halibut population is increasing, and the size of halibut that are caught by sport

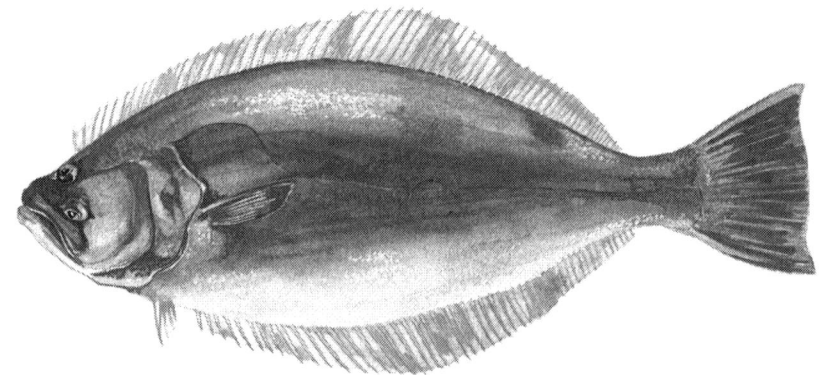

California Halibut (Paralichthys californicus)

fishermen is also increasing. By 1997, about half of all halibut caught were breeding adults (bigger than 22 inches), so the comeback of this popular game fish is well on its way.

Halibut are masters of ambush. They sit partially buried on the bottom, waiting for prey to wander by and then leap out, grabbing the unsuspecting forage fish. Halibut usually prefer live bait. In the past, scientists believed halibut were more like sole or sanddabs—grubbing for food and scavenging anything that came by, but now they're known to be aggressive predators. They eat sardines, anchovies, squid, and any other smaller baitfish.

Halibut are found anywhere from in-shore beaches, harbors, and river mouths, all the way to deep, deep water. They can live in over 1000 feet of water, and halibut caught in deep water are the best eating.

Pacific Sanddab (*Citharichthys sordidus*)

Sanddabs are a very popular local delicacy. Looling like miniature halibut, they are flat fish, lying on one side at the bottom of sandy or muddy areas with only their eyes showing. Sanddabs can be small, but they have a well-deserved reputation as being fine table fare. Typically, these flat fish are in the 8- to 12-inch range.

Sanddabs are opportunistic feeders, taking nearly anything that happens by, either dead or alive. They'll hit live bait, dead whole bait, cut fish, cut squid, rubber lures, or shrimp flies. Sanddabs will take nearly anything you throw at them. Like halibut, sanddabs are found in a broad range of depths.

One day while rock fishing in deep water off Anacapa Island, I discovered that sanddabs hit brightly colored shrimp flies. We were fishing in deep water (800 to 900 feet) and there was a lot of wind and current, so staying over the undersea reef was difficult. Every time we drifted off the reef and over the sand and mud bottom, our squid-baited rock cod shrimp flies were hit by small sanddabs.

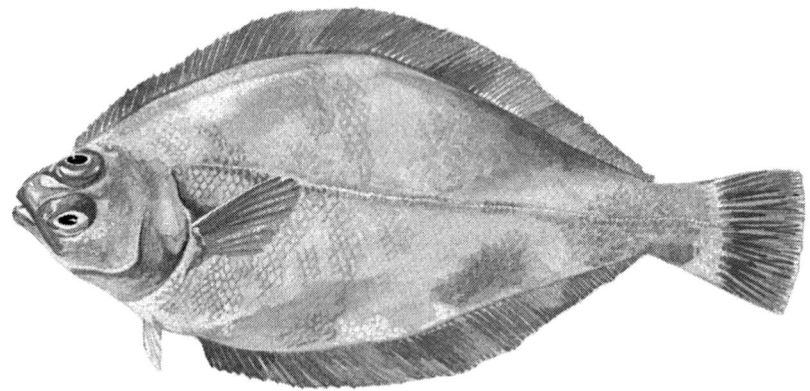

Pacific Sanddab (Citharichthys sordidus)

Barred Sand Bass (Paralabrax nebulifer)

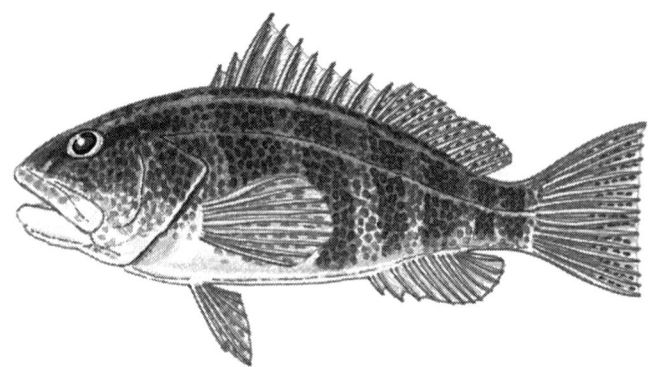

Spotted Sand Bass (Paralabrax maculatofasciatus)

Sculpin or California Scorpion Fish (Scorpaena guttata)

Barred Sand Bass (*Paralabrax nebulifer*)
The two different types of sand bass occurring in southern California are the barred sand bass and the spotted sand bass. In addition, there is a third type that rarely occurs in southern California, called the gold spotted sand bass, but is fairly common in Baja California (Mexico.) Except for coloration and markings, there is almost no difference in these three species as far as body shape, diet, habits, or taste. I am continually amazed at the many species that occupy the exact same habitat yet remain distinctly different.

In spring, sandies move from their deeper water haunts to spawn on the broad sand and mudflats just off the California beaches. They become sedentary, not moving around much, and begin feeding voraciously. The season extends throughout the summer and finally in the fall, they seem to disappear, moving off into deeper water. They have been caught year-round but are far easier to catch in the summer months.

Like calico bass, sand bass have a 12-inch minimum size limit. This assures that any fish taken have had a chance to breed. They don't get extremely large—the record is just over 13 pounds, held by a friend of mine. The fish was caught in the Huntington Flats, probably the most consistent sand bass spot anywhere.

Sand bass seem to prefer very active live bait that is sent to the bottom with a sliding sinker, which prevents them from feeling any resistance when they hit. Like sea gulls, they appear to grab the bait, swim a short distance to make sure they're not being followed, then stop to eat it. They'll eat sardines, anchovies, and squid or cut bait if properly fished. In addition, they'll strike rubber lures, hard, bone-type jigs, and baited shrimp flies.

Sand bass are excellent eating. They can be prepared any way that white, mild fish can be prepared, however, many people like them fried in beer batter.

Spotted Sand Bass (*Paralabrax maculatofasciatus*)
Spotted sandies are nearly identical to their barred cousins except in coloration. They respond to the same fishing techniques and baits as well as living in the same habitat.

Sculpin or California Scorpion Fish (*Scorpaena guttata*)
While not truly a sculpin (see the description of cabezon), the scorpion fish is really related to the rockfish group (*Sebastes*). Nonetheless, if you were to say, "I just caught a California scorpion fish," most fishermen wouldn't have a clue as to what you were actually talking about. If you showed them the fish, they'd insist it was a sculpin.

Anyway, sculpin exhibit vastly different behavior than most rockfish. Though it does live near reefs, rock piles, and wrecks, it is probably most commonly caught on the wide mud and sandflats just offshore on the miles of southern California beaches. It sits alertly in one spot, propped up on its fins, looking just like an algae-encrusted rock, awaiting the passage of a careless browser. It ambushes its prey with an aggressive, sudden attack.

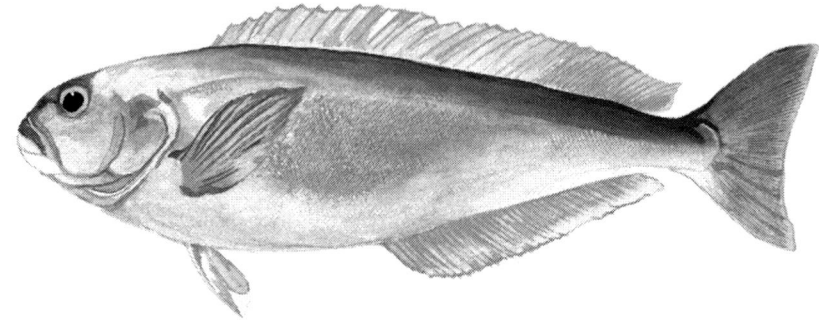

Whitefish (Caulolatilus princeps)

In springtime, hordes of sculpin move from their reef homes out into the flats to spawn. At times, the bottom is littered with adults tending their nests and awaiting a meal to swim or crawl by. The flats just offshore from Los Angeles International Airport and the famed Huntington Flats in Orange County are prime sculpin breeding grounds. Sculpin can be caught year-round, but during winter seem to favor a bottom with more structure than they do during summer.

Be careful handling California scorpion fish, because its sting is venomous and it sharp dorsal fins can cause considerable pain and swelling if touched. Like bee stings, some people are much more susceptible to the venom than others due to an allergic reaction. One person might only experience minor pain and discomfort after being poked by one of the spines, while another might experience excruciating pain and a great deal of swelling—sometimes doubling the size of the hand. In addition to the dorsal fin spines, scorpion fish have spines on their pectoral fins, anal fins, gill covers, and heads.

Sculpin are excellent to eat and are revered by the Japanese as prime sashimi (raw fish). With firm, light, and mild flesh it can also be prepared in many different ways.

Whitefish *(Caulolatilus princeps)*

In the past, whitefish were not very common in the southern California ocean, however, over the past few years, a population explosion seems to have taken place. While it is not known for certain why this has happened, some speculate that the ban of near-shore gill nets or the disappearance of other, competing species has caused a shortage of some types of predators in the habitat that whitefish have begun to fill. Years ago, whitefish were reef dwellers, but more recently, they have begun to scour the flats for food, especially in the winter when other predatory species move away.

Whitefish can get large—specimens up to 3½ feet have been caught—but most are a foot long or so. The first one I ever caught was in the rocky reefs just north of

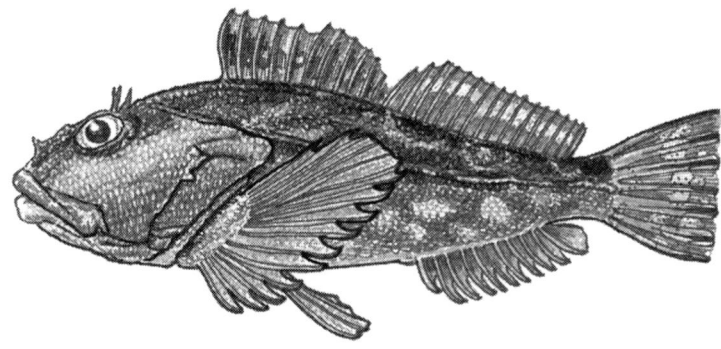

Cabezon (Scorpaenicthys marmoratus)

San Clemente Island. I didn't know what it was at first, thinking it was some sort of deformed yellowtail. It probably weighed 15 pounds. That was in the early 1970s, and I didn't catch another one until the early 1990s during an El Niño season.

Whitefish are caught near the bottom and reefs on live bait or squid-baited shrimp flies. The techniques used for sand bass fishing are the primary effective technique for taking whitefish.

Cabezon *(Scorpaenicthys marmoratus)*

The cabezon is a true sculpin, a member of the *Cottidae* family, and is highly prized as table fare. Like lingcod or greenling, the cabezon meat can have a blue or green tint but cooks up fluffy white and delicious. Cabezons can grow as big as 39 inches and 25 pounds, but normally, a 10-pound, 18-inch fish is a big one. Cabezon inhabit the mudflats and hard bottoms in the northern part of southern California and especially like bottoms with lots of shells. They are quite common in central and northern California.

Cabezon are opportunistic feeders, eating shrimp, small fish, clams, crabs, and just about anything else they can ambush and gobble up. They have huge jaws and cavernous mouths that can create enough suction when opened to draw in many of their prey. Their rough skin and mottled pattern serves as a perfect camouflage—they look more like an algae-encrusted rock than a fish when viewed underwater.

Like many fish of the flats, cabezon don't move much, preferring to lie in wait for their prey to pass by. So drifting the flats with bait is the most effective way to catch cabezon. Keep the bait moving along the bottom and cover as much territory as possible.

If you enjoy fish roe, steer clear of cabezon roe—it is toxic and can cause violent illness. This is one of the only fish in southern California with any toxic parts. Cabezon meat is completely safe to eat—only the eggs have the toxin.

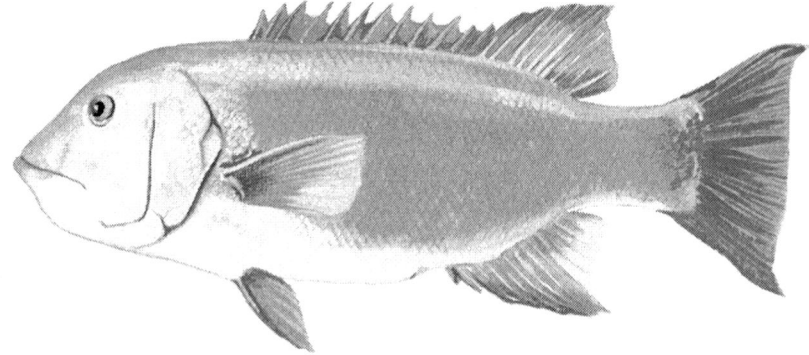

Female Sheephead (Semicossyphus pulcher)

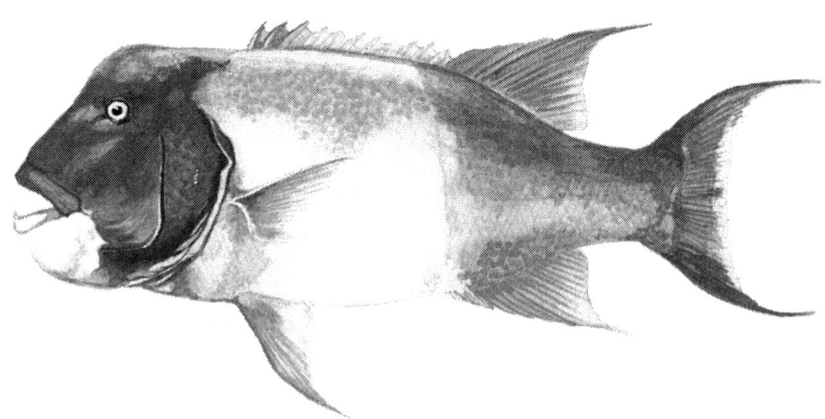

Male Sheephead (Semicossyphus pulcher)

Shallow-water Rockfish

Along the southern California coastline, many fish inhabit shallow rocky out-croppings, reefs, and rock piles. In addition, manmade reefs and breakwaters provide cover for these species and handy underwater surfaces to which many and varied life forms attach themselves. Crabs, shrimp, starfish, lobsters, sea urchins, and other shellfish find homes here, as do abalone, limpets, chitons, barnacles, and other mon-ovalve shelled creatures. Plenty of marine plants, along with stationary animals such as anemones and mussels, encrust any submerged hard object. All of these stationary species attract small fish and the fry of larger fish, which, in turn, attract larger spe-cies. And the larger species are what attract fishermen, the top of the food chain.

Sheephead (*Semicossyphus pulcher*)

The sheephead is a member of the wrasse family, an unusual group of fish with an almost unbelievable life cycle. All wrasse grow up to be female and reproduce as females by laying eggs. Later, the bigger and more successful female wrasse undergo morphosis, changing into males, which then reproduce again as males. Why some females, but not all, experience nature's sex change operation is still a mystery.

Sheephead have substantial teeth that look more like a cat's set of fangs than those of a fish. They use these stout teeth, along with heavy, powerful jaws, to crack open clams, crabs, sea urchins, and abalone, as well as shrimp. Probably because of this gourmet diet, sheephead is something of a gourmet treat and is one of the best white meat fishes found in the southern California ocean. The thick, heavy center bone (spine) is ideal for making chowders, soups, and court bouillon for poaching other fish. The meat itself can be cooked in a variety of ways, but poaching, baking, and other simple methods of cooking bring out its light, delectable flavor.

Sheephead are fairly large—big males can weigh up to 50 pounds and grow to 3 feet. These huge examples are getting more rare because divers, fishing with spears, have been after these magnificent fish for years. Taking "only the big ones" elimi-nates many of the breeding males. Males commonly run under 18 inches and about 8 pounds, while females are generally a foot long and 5 pounds.

The classic method for catching sheephead in the shallow rocks is to use a some-what large bait hook (4/0 or 5/0 size) with a head-on uncooked shrimp as bait. You can buy these shrimp in grocery stores, particularly oriental stores, to use as bait, and if you don't catch anything, you can cook up the leftover bait for dinner! Send the shrimp down with a weight into rocky reefs or to the bottom near kelp beds. I find it is better to keep the bait moving than to keep it in one spot. I've also caught them on live anchovies sent down into the rock piles.

Though I've tried, I've never hooked a sheephead on a shrimp fly, even one baited with a strip of cut squid. I'm planning to keep at it, though and expect to perfect a technique or at least a fly pattern that will hook sheephead on a regular basis—I'm convinced it's possible.

Treefish (Sebastes serriceps)

Olive Rockfish (Sebastes constellatus)

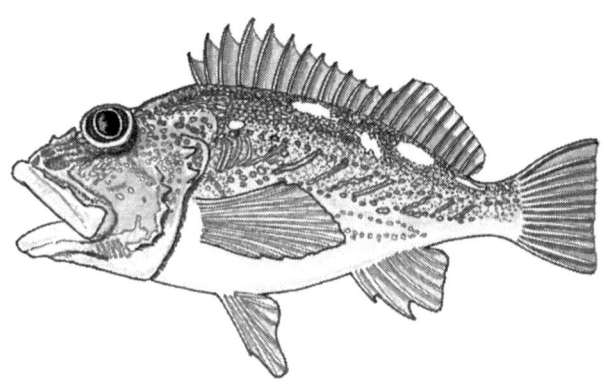

Starry Rockfish (Sebastes constellatus)

Treefish (*Sebastes serriceps*)

The treefish is probably the most outlandishly colored fish in the ocean. It has a yellow and black bumblebee-striped body and looks like it's wearing bright red lipstick. A member of the rockfish genus, the treefish is a bottom-dwelling, heavy-bodied fish. They eat a wide variety of available food, from shrimps and crabs to live baitfishes to scavenging other dead fish.

Treefish are common in shallow, rocky reefs and are often found living on the rocky bottom under kelp beds. They are usually less than 12 inches in length and average 1 to 2 pounds. Kelp anchors itself to rocks, so the bottom is home to many of the shallow water reef and rock pile dwellers.

They eagerly snap at live anchovies, dead anchovies, cut fish bait, cut squid, or baited shrimp flies sent down with sinkers into their rocky homes. Treefish are good eating, whether fried, sauteed, broiled, or baked.

Olive Rockfish (*Sebastes constellatus*)

The olive rockfish is one of the few members of the *Sebastes* genus not red in color. This fish looks far more like a green perch-type fish than the normal bass-looking profile of most rockfish. Though small, it is active and hungry most of the time. Most people do not target olive rockfish because of their small size. They are generally caught incidentally while fishing for bigger shallow water rockfish species and using the same tackle and techniques.

Starry Rockfish (*Sebastes constellatus*)

A beautiful, although usually somewhat small, member of the rockfish family, the starry is a great eating, brightly colored, and welcome catch. Many anglers immediately think "fish tacos" when they see a starry. A fillet is just the right size to fry up in beer batter, wrap in a warm tortilla, douse with salsa, and gobble down. Starry rockfish are shockingly bright, almost bright orange in color.

Like the olive rockfish, starry's are an incidental catch using the same tackle, bait, and techniques as used to catch other reef or rockfish.

Deep-water Rockfish

Deep-water rockfish are often called rock cod or red snapper. Neither snapper nor cod, they are one of a large family of bass-like fish that are perhaps the most numerous (at least in variety) along the Pacific Coast. Their genus name, *Sebastes*, means magnificent, and they truly are. There is a huge variety of deep-water rockfish along the California coast—69 separate species have been identified to date and more are being found on a continual basis. Most inhabit deep, rocky reefs from about 300 feet to about 1500 feet down. Most fishermen prefer to stay shallower than 600 feet because of the heavy, specialized fishing tackle and strenuous work required to fish deeper. True fanatics (and I have fished with that crowd extensively), however, like to fish from 600 to 1000 feet deep.

Rock cod are excellent table fare, having firm, white meat with a mild taste. They are ideal for many ethnic dishes—Japanese revere them for sashimi (raw fish), Chinese for steamed whole fish, Mexicans for the best cevechi (pickled fish) and fish tacos, and the locals for the best fish and chips. Nearly all fish and chips sold in coastal restaurants in California are rockfish.

It seems unusual that fish of the deep reefs should be so brightly colored. It would seem logical that the mostly bright red coloring of deep-water rockfish would draw the attention of predators to feed on this plentiful bounty. However, light only penetrates about 300 feet down, so in the eternal darkness of the deep reefs, red is the ideal camouflage color. Red has the lowest frequency in the visible light spectrum, so to the eye, it turns darkest under subdued light. Consider your own eyesight—as light subsides, your eye changes from a receptor of color to a receptor of black and white with shades of gray. What color appears darkest at night? Red!

Deep-water rockfish are spiny and should be handled with care. The fin spines and some of the body spines are mildly venomous, and handling these fish can cause painful punctures if you're not careful. For this reason, many people use a small hand gaff, made by attaching a barbless (or barbs squashed flat) double trolling hook to a short length of 1-inch hardwood dowel, to serve as a handy device for picking up fish without touching them.

Since there is no light, it is somewhat surprising that rock cod take a fly so well. In fact, you'll catch more rock cod on a baited fly than any other way! The brighter and more garish the fly is colored, the better—probably because rock cod eat many different types of shrimp and are always on the lookout for a shrimp-like meal. It's best to bait the fly with thin strips of squid, about 3/8-inch wide and as long as you can cut. This gives them an odor and initial taste when hit that fools a fish long enough to get hooked. Chunks and bigger pieces of bait defeat the purpose of the fly. They may still get hit but not with the consistency of thin bait strips.

It is common when deep-water rock fishing to get several species on the same gangion at the same time. For instance, it's not unusual to drop a 5-hook gangion and catch one cow, two reds, a boccaccio, and a chilipepper. Other times, you'll only get one species. Apparently, the schools mix and separate at different times and at different locations.

Red Rock Cod or Vermillion Rockfish (Sebastes miniatus)

In addition to baited flies, rockfish take jigs well. Chrome bar jigs, kite jigs, and bigger, heavier bone jigs are popular as are heavy spoons. Often, a teaser fly is tied above the jig as an enticement, but don't be surprised if the teaser fly gets hit before the main jig.

Red Rock Cod or Vermillion Rockfish (*Sebastes miniatus*)
The most sought-after rockfish, reds are the probably the best eating of all the rock cod. They grow up to 3 feet long and 15 pounds, but are far more common in the 15-inch and 4-pound range. In shallower water (300 feet), they are smaller yet— usually around 10 inches and 1 pound. They eagerly snap at shrimp flies and seem to prefer blue and white or pink and red colors. The green and yellow patterns don't work nearly as well on reds as on other, less desirable species.

Cowcod (*Sebastes levis*)
Cows are the biggest of the rock cod. They have huge heads and can weigh upward of 30 pounds. When fishing the outer banks in 600- to 800-foot deep holes, it isn't unusual to catch plenty of fish in the 20-pound class. I've been on charters with 24 people aboard when everyone got at least one 20-pound cow and some people got four (along with many other varieties.) The cowcod is tops as table fare.

Bosco, also Aurora Rockfish (*Sebastes aurora*)
A truly deep, deep-water rockfish variety, bosco are rarely caught in water shallower than about 600 feet. The plump body and solid pink coloring make boscos readily identifiable. They are esteemed as sashimi because the meat is firm, clear, and tasty.

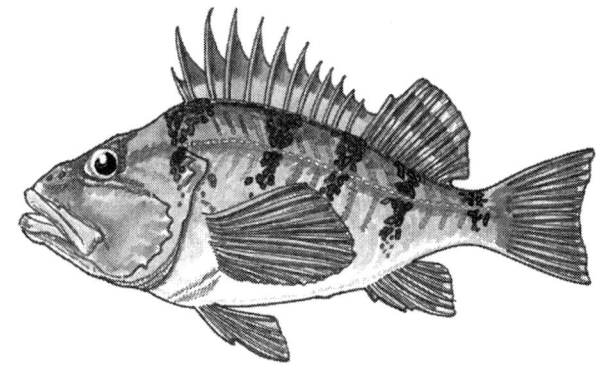

Cowcod (Sebastes levis)

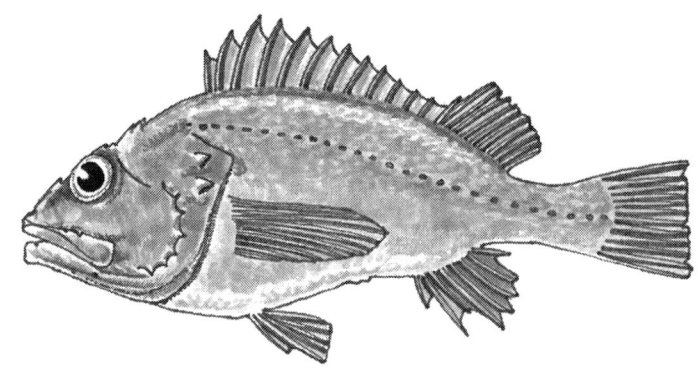

Bosco, also Aurora Rockfish (Sebastes aurora)

Boccaccio, also Salmon Grouper (Sebastes paucispinis)

Boccaccio, also Salmon Grouper (*Sebastes paucispinis*)

Boccaccio, meaning "big, ugly mouth" in Italian, lives up to its name. It's unrelated to cod, salmon, and grouper, yet has been graced with these noble sounding names. It is a big fish, often exceeding 18 inches, and can be caught in shallower water, making it more popular than the really deep-water fish for the occasional fishermen. It is, however, not one of the top-rated fish for the table. Boccaccio are excellent when cleaned promptly and cooked fresh, but the meat doesn't keep well and takes on an odor if it is not skinned within a half-day or so of being caught. To keep, the meat should be immersed in water and frozen to keep it from getting rubbery and gamey tasting.

Boccaccio sometimes rise upward in the water column over the deep reefs—probably chasing food. They can come as much as 150 feet off the bottom. At such times they take live bait well—anchovies or sardines, even preferring them to shrimp flies and cut squid.

Barberpole Snapper, also Flag Rockfish (*Sebastes rubrivinctus*)

Barberpoles are very distinctive for their bright red- and white-striped color pattern. Though they are often small (a 12-incher is big), they have a distinctive taste and are rated by many to be the best eating of all the rockfish.

Florida Snapper, also Bank Rockfish (*Sebastes rufus*)

A very common deep-water rockfish, Floridas are distinctive for the pink stripe along the lateral line. They are usually small to moderate sized. They're good eating, but not rated up there with reds, cows or barberpoles. Smaller Floridas are eaten by big cows and can be used as bait. A good technique is to fillet the Florida snapper, keeping the tail and skin attached, then use the entire fillet as bait on a 16/0 circle hook sent down into cow country.

Speckled Rockfish (*Sebastes ovalus*)

Probably the most common near-shore, deep-water rockfish in the heavily fished banks off the Los Angeles area, speckles are usually fairly large, some over 16 inches, and good eating.

Chilipepper (*Sebastes goodei*)

Chilies are a common catch when pursuing other, usually bigger, rockfish. They are small to medium sized and look more like perch than rockfish. They're good to eat but not as desirable owing to their smaller size.

Lingcod (*Ophiodon elongatus*)

The only non-rock cod (*Sebastes*) you're likely to encounter in deep rock piles, wrecks, and reefs is the huge lingcod. Lingcod, like many southern California fish, are not properly named. They are more closely related to the true sculpin fishes than to cod. They grow to 5 feet and 70 pounds but are typically less then 40 pounds and

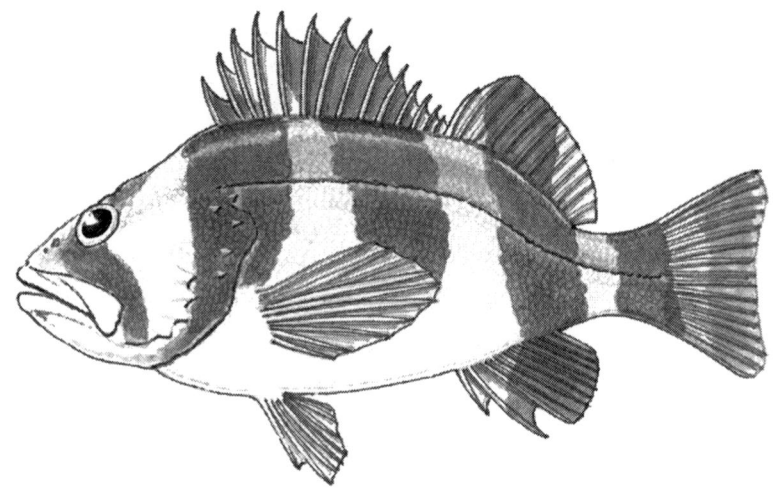

Barberpole Snapper, also Flag Rockfish (Sebastes rubrivinctus)

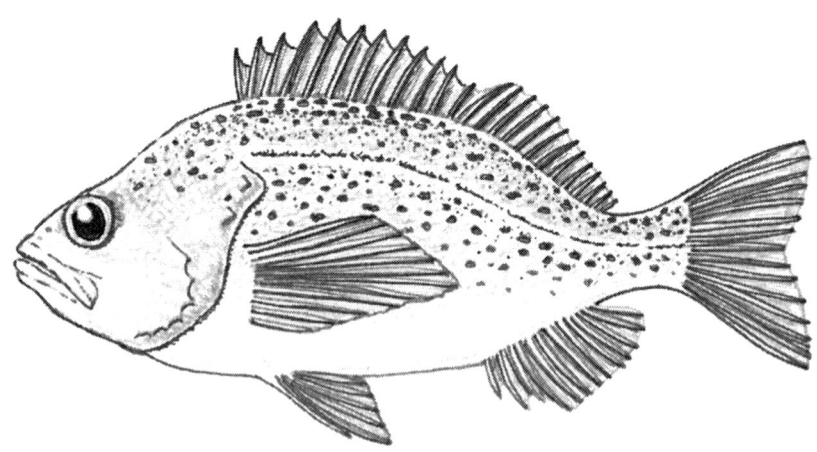

Speckled Rockfish (Sebastes ovalus)

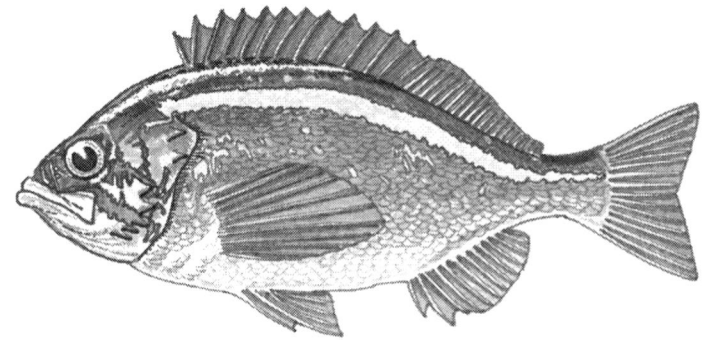

Florida Snapper, also Bank Rockfish (Sebastes rufus)

Chilipepper (Sebastes goodei)

Lingcod (Ophiodon elongatus)

40 inches. There is a minimum size limit of 28 inches for lings. Denizens of underwater caves, lingcod seek shelter wherever they can find it and ambush their prey from rocky lairs, inhaling them into their huge, toothy jaws.

Lings are esteemed as a food fish, having mild, firm, and moist meat. In some cases, the meat has a decidedly green or even bluish cast. Many a fishermen has thrown away the meat thinking it was somehow tainted. This is entirely normal. In fact, those in the know sometimes prefer the green meat. Once cooked, the flesh turns immediately to an appetizing white.

Lings are sought eagerly by fishermen, not only for their meat but also for their fight. The first few minutes of a lingcod battle are a real challenge. This fish immediately dashes for its hole or cave, and if it makes it inside, the fight is over and the ling has won. The fisherman's job is to turn the fish and get it moving upward. This requires strength, finesse, and a smooth, well-adjusted reel drag. Once turned, the ling keeps fighting all the way to the surface, running, diving, and throwing curves to the fishermen. This could take a substantial amount of time considering you're fighting a 40-pound fish upward, sometimes from a thousand feet of water.

In the late winter and early spring, lings move from their deep-water haunts to shallower water, taking over many of the southern California shipwrecks and the shallower rock piles and reefs. At this time, they can be enticed to strike shallower species, such as live mackerel, and will hit chrome or shiny jigs well.

Sharks and Rays

Once considered the garbage fish of the ocean, sharks now hold a prized position as being both excellent eating and scrappy fighting game fish. How this has changed over the past 20 years or so has been both a blessing and a curse to the many types of sharks calling the southern California coastal ocean their home. The curse is that so many more fishermen are targeting these fish, and the blessing is that new efforts have been made to conserve this valuable natural resource and to stem the decline in the numbers of breeding fish.

There is a huge variety of sharks inhabiting the coastal waters, very few of which pose even a moderate danger to man. Most couldn't harm a person if they wanted to, and those with the ability to actually inflict wounds spend more time avoiding contact with man than searching him out. There are a few species in the southern California waters that have actually attacked humans, though, and anyone venturing out into the sea should be aware of their presence.

The most famous of the dangerous sharks, and rightly so, is the great white shark. It has a taste for sea lions and other marine mammals. Actual attacks on humans are extremely rare—you're more likely to die being struck by a meteor than by being bitten by a great white. Based on studies performed at the Farralon Islands in northern California, shark attacks on humans commonly involve kayaks and surfboards. Researchers believe that the sharks mistake the shadow cast by these craft for a big sea lion. Remember, just like King Kong or the creature from the Black Lagoon, "Jaws" is strictly a fictional character with fictional behavior.

These huge creatures are very rare throughout the oceans of the world, but southern California has a population of these sharks. They prowl the offshore islands in search of unwary marine mammals and fish. Killing great white sharks is now forbidden by law in the state of California, and stiff fines and possible prison time await those flaunting these laws.

A common and potentially dangerous shark found in southern California waters is the blue shark. This small, slender shark can grow to 10 feet long but may only weigh 50 pounds or so. They have impressive teeth and are capable of inflicting a damaging bite. Blues are inedible—or at least bad tasting—because of an ammonia or urine odor the skin and meat give off. Most blue sharks feed at night, but do eat during the day at times. If you ever have your game fish stolen off the hook, bringing up only the head, you've probably been picked clean by a blue shark. One of their favorite tricks is to hang around fishing boats, waiting for a helpless meal to be dragged by on the end of a line.

A blue shark cruising around the surface near a fishing boat will shut down the bite as the game fish either move away or head for cover. For the fisherman, it means time to move. If you hook one, catch it if you must, but it would be far better off for the shark, your buddies, and the productivity of the rest of the day if you just clamp your thumb on the reel spool and break it off intentionally.

Be careful handling any shark. All can inflict painful bites, though the smaller, toothless ones might only result in a bad bruise. They are flexible creatures and most

Leopard Shark (Triakis semifasciata)

can turn around and bite your hand while you hold them up by the tail. If you insist on taking a shark home, dispatch it with a sharp blow to the head, or cut its head off. There are cases on record where the severed head of a shark has bitten off a man's hand—so you can't be too careful. If you're planning to release it, cut your leader close to the shark's mouth without removing it from the water. The hook will corrode away in a few days, and the fish will be no worse for the wear.

Of the dozens of varieties of sharks and rays inhabiting the coast, only a few have a reputation for edibility and occur in sufficient numbers to be considered game fish.

Leopard Shark (*Triakis semifasciata*)

Leopards are considered one of the best eating sharks in southern California. Their firm, white meat cooks up tender and tasty. Leopards are bottom-feeding sharks common in bays and estuaries. In broad, flat bays, they are sometimes stranded on mudflats by the outgoing tide. They can also be caught along the beaches and flats where they browse for food. They have no teeth, only hard, rasplike gums used to grind up the bits of food they dig up out of the sand and mud. Leopards eat a wide variety of foods, which accounts for their mild flesh.

Dead bait is generally used to catch leopard sharks. Cut strips of mackerel, dead anchovies, cut squid, and other similar baits are the best. Since they browse the mud, the bait's smell is usually more important than its appearance. Fish the incoming tides in the shallower areas of bays and river mouths or the high tides of beaches for best results.

Leopards can grow to 6 feet or more but are most common in the 3- to 4-foot range. Like the blue shark, they are very slender, and a 5-footer might weigh only 18 pounds. Leopards are partially protected—see the section on fishing regulations for the minimum sizes and bag limits.

Thresher Shark (*Alopias vulpinus*)

Thresher sharks were the first sharks to be commercially exploited for food. Threshers are large, big-bodied sharks with a long, scythelike tail used to herd and

Thresher Shark (Alopias vulpinus)

stun their prey. They are strikingly beautiful in appearance, with brightly colored skin and eyes. In addition, they have a mild, meaty flesh excellent for broiling or barbecuing.

Threshers have substantial mouths and teeth and are efficient, fast predators. Their fight is active and strong, consisting of powerful runs and dives. They rarely break the surface or jump, preferring to dive for deeper water. They'll take live bait or hooked smaller fish, especially sardines and mackerel. They hunt in the midwater column or near the bottom looking for unwary fish.

It is difficult to target threshers because they are simply too scarce, fast moving, and unpredictable. You may catch one while fishing for halibut, barracuda, or other species.

Mako Shark, also Bonito Shark (*Isurus oxyrinchus*)

Mako sharks are the kings of the game fish sharks. They are blue-water, wide ranging fish fairly common in southern California and esteemed not only for their tasty meat but also for their wild leaps and acrobatic marlin-like fight. Mako sharks can get over 12 feet long and 1100 pounds. These are big, dangerous blue-water sharks.

Mako fishing is best done at night and relies heavily on chumming and trolling. A special Mako shark trolling jig is used that has an unusual head shape to simulate the vibrations made by wounded, thrashing fish. Their sense of vibration is acute, and sonic vibrations in the water attract cruising sharks from miles away. In addition, large quantities of fish guts or blood are distributed behind the boat to attract sharks. In addition to being very sensitive to vibration, surface-feeding sharks can smell blood in the water in amazingly tiny quantities. Some say they can smell blood from a mile away. New research on hammerhead sharks shows just how acute a shark's senses can be: Hammerheads can detect the electrical impulses that a small flounder's brain sends causing the heart to beat even when the flounder is buried in the sand.

If you're interested in catching one of these denizens of the night, your best bet is to select a guide experienced in Mako shark fishing. This is not a sport for the careless amateur.

Shovelnose Guitarfish (*Rhinobatos productus*)

Fishing the piers, harbors, or sandflats, you may catch an unusual fish that looks like it's half shark and half ray—this is the shovelnose guitarfish. There are actually several species, and all are good to eat and fun to catch. Guitarfish inhabit the sandy coastal stretches and compete with all the other sandflat fishes for baitfish passing through the area. Their hunting tactics are similar to a halibut laying partially buried in the sand, sometimes with only their eyes exposed, awaiting any incautious prey that wanders by. With a fierce leap, they ambush and devour their meal, then settling motionless on the bottom once again. Guitarfish are usually caught incidentally when fishing for other flats, harbor, or surf fish.

Mako Shark, also Bonito Shark (Isurus oxyrinchus)

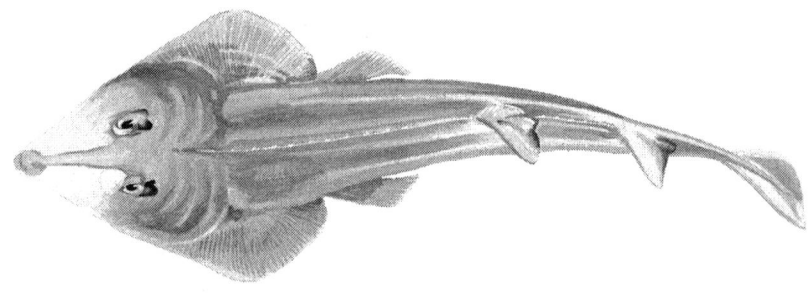

Shovelnose Guitarfish (Rhinobatos productus)

Harbor and Pier Fish

The many bays, harbors, and piers of southern California are home to a host of different fish species. Many fish from the surrounding areas come into the harbor. It is not unusual to see kelp bass, barracuda, bonito, and mackerel that have come from their surface haunts into a bay on top, Sand bass, sculpin, and halibut come in on the bottom, and the occasional yellowtail breezes through to feed on the bounty. Even the surf fish wander into bays, so you have the largest variety of fish of any habitat along the coast.

Most bays and harbors in southern California offer boat rentals, so this is one of the easiest places to fish. Navigation is uncomplicated because of the plentiful landmarks, and there is plenty of scenery to keep even the slightly bored, occasional angler occupied.

Use the same techniques in bays and harbors as you would to target the fish in the open ocean.

In addition to the fish mentioned above, two other fish are commonly targeted in bays and on piers along the southern California coast. As a poor college student, I credit these fish for a good percentage of my protein back then. They were the easiest to catch and edible fish were available for most of the season in the bay where I lived back in the early 1970s. I often took my trusty old 8-weight fly rod, attached a #12 trout hook, pulled a couple of mussels off the dock floats, and in only 20 or 30 minutes caught all the jack smelt and jack mackerel I could handle. Both of these fish also take small, brightly colored shrimp flies.

Jacksmelt (*Atherinopsis californiensis*)

Not truly a smelt or a jack, this is actually a type of fish known as a "silverside." They grow large for this type of fish—sometimes nearly 18 inches. The recent El Niño years have brought an abundance of jack smelt to southern California. Like jack mackerel, they seem to prefer feeding at night. Pier and dock fishermen usually catch them with clams or mussels baited on tiny hooks. Their mouths are very small, so a hook size of 6 or smaller is preferred. For best results, fish near a well-lit area with heavy shadows.

Jack Mackerel (*Trachurus symmetricus*)

Yet another misnamed fish, the jack mackerel is actually a jack but not a mackerel. The name would be more correct if it were "mackerel jack," which is the term used on the can labels of this fish in the grocery store. Jack mackerel get to be over 2 feet in length, but most are under a foot. These jacks are better eating than jack smelt and run in the same company.

Jack mackerel are a prey fish for many predators, including barracuda, bonito, and yellowtail, and consequently skittish to catch at times. One of their favorite tactics is to wait in the shadows of a brightly illuminated dock or pier at night and watch the lighted water for possible passage of something edible. When something is spotted, they dash out into the light, gobble it up, and run quickly back into the shadows before they can be preyed on themselves. This should give you plenty of ideas for locations near marinas and in harbors where you can catch them. They'll take most cut baits and will also attack a wet fly if it is allowed to drift into the light from a dark shadow.

Jacksmelt (Atherinopsis californiensis)

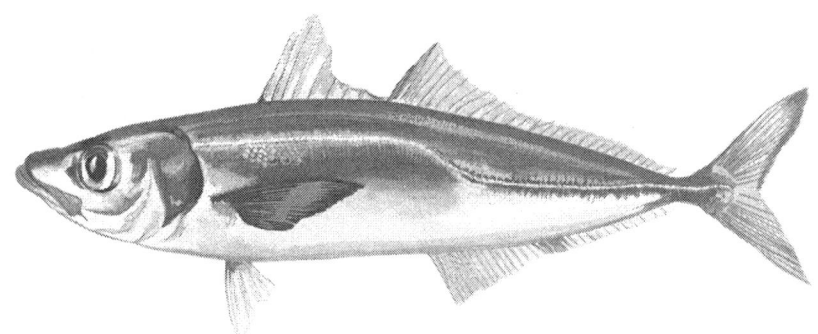

Jack Mackerel (Trachurus symmetricus)

Blue-water Fish

Once you get a mile or two off California's shoreline, the water changes from a greenish or brownish color, filled with particulate matter and living organisms, into a crystal clear offshore condition most anglers call "blue water," blatantly suggesting this ocean's nickname: the blue Pacific. Actually, the water here is very clear and colorless, but with California's crystal clear skies that occur over 300 days per year, the icy blue sky reflected in the ocean makes it shine with an intense blue color. This is the home of the fastest, most powerful, and aggressive fish to swim the seas: the offshore species.

Every summer, wandering bands of these predators arrive at California's shores to feast on the bounty of huge baitfish schools. Some of these fish travel from thousands of miles away (as far as Japan) to summer in the California sunshine. Still others move north from Mexico to feed because there is less competition from the densely populated schools off Mexico's Baja peninsula. These big, fast offshore species fight aggressively and are voracious feeders. The slightest hint that they have arrived causes local fishermen to drop whatever they're doing, call in sick, grab their heavy gear, and head offshore for a chance to do battle.

Several species of tuna and one kind of dolphin visit California nearly every summer. Cooler summers bring schools of albacore and the occasional bluefin tuna. Warmer years bring yellowfin tuna, skipjack, bigeye tuna, and dorado. One thing's for sure: When these fish are in town, you're in for a fight.

Albacore Tuna (*Thunnis alalunga*)

The fastest, most wide-ranging and least corrallable of all the tuna, the albacore is one of the most welcome visitors to southern California. In southern California, albacore arrive only in years when the water temperature remains in the low 60s until mid-July. In warmer years, they go only as far as the central and northern California coasts. Albacore are the best table fare of any tuna. They are the only fish that can be sold as white tuna in cans. When fresh, the meat is light and delicious with a decidedly meaty texture.

Because of their habit of moving in very fast, very loose schools, it's nearly impossible for net boats to catch albacore in commercially viable numbers. Nearly all albacore are caught on hook and line, either trolled lures or by jackpoles from commercial boats chumming with bait. This means there are always plenty of albacore around for the sport fishermen to hook up.

Albacore are sometimes called "longfin tuna" for their distinctive, extra long pectoral fins. They can get as big as 90 pounds or so but are commonly in the 20-pound range. They'll eagerly snap at almost any silvery object (even bare hooks) in the water when in a feeding frenzy, and once on the line, put up a classic, powerful tuna fight. Just because you get an albacore on the end of your line, it doesn't mean you'll land one. Its dogged determination to get loose and seemingly herculean endurance make it a favorite among southern California anglers.

Albacore Tuna (Thunnis alalunga)

Something like 90 percent of all albacore are taken in water between 62 and 67 degrees F. Although I recently discovered this fact, my personal experience has taught me that if the water wasn't within a degree or two of 65, there weren't going to be any albacore caught. I first realized this when trolling commercially for albacore in central California in the early 1970s. I was washing the deck using a hose that was supplied with seawater from a pump in the hull of the boat. Suddenly, I felt the water change from cold to warm, indicating we'd just passed a thermocline. Immediately, all 18 of our trolled jigs had fish on! After that, I had a remote reading seawater temperature gauge installed in my boat. From then on, I checked the water temperature when we ran into albacore and found it was always very near 65.

Bluefin Tuna (*Thunnis thynnis*)
Bluefin tuna are another of the bluewater species that sometimes summer along the southern California coast. Their classic tuna shape and delectable meat make them one of the most recognizable and famous fish in all the oceans.

In the Pacific Ocean, bluefin only get to about one-third the size of their Atlantic kin. They are hunted relentlessly by commercial net seiners and have experienced a serious decline in numbers over the past few years. Recent regulations regarding the capture and exploitation of wild stocks have been successful, and a gradual comeback of these magnificent creatures is currently happening. Continued conservation efforts should assure that catching a bluefin tuna will continue to be an experience our grandchildren can enjoy.

Bluefin, like albacore, are esteemed both for their aggressive fight and excellent table fare. They can grow to 300 pounds, but in southern California, a bluefin larger than 100 pounds is a rarity. They eat all manner of baitfish, and when a group has corralled a school of baitfish into a tight ball, individuals slash through the bait ball and gorge themselves. When these fish hit bait, lure, or fly, they hit HARD! There's

Bluefin Tuna (Thunnis thynnis)

little doubt you've got one aggressive critter on the end of your line when a bluefin takes your bait!

Yellowfin Tuna *(Thunnis albacares)*

Yellowfin tuna are the most welcome visitors in warmer seasons. Few people will dispute the tenacity and fighting spirit of a yellowfin tuna. Down in Baja, especially at the Islas Revillagigedos, a volcanic chain of islands beginning some 220 miles southwest of Cabo San Lucas, huge yellowfin tuna can grow to 400 pounds. Battling one of these fish makes fighting marlin seem like child's play. Anglers new to yellowfin tuna are simply astounded at how much fight these fish have in them.

Yellowfin are also excellent table fare. Their meat is lighter than the dark red bluefin but darker than albacore. Like other tuna, their diet consists of the many baitfish found along the coastline. Bigger fish take on California mackerel, too, a member of the tuna family. Yellowfin are beautiful fish with dusky yellow fins, growing to extra long length in mature individuals, and colorful bars and spots on the fish's sides and belly that quickly fade to a dull steel gray when the fish dies.

Bigeye Tuna *(Thunnis obesus)*

Thunnis obesus, the scientific name for bigeye tuna, means "fat tuna." Well, they certainly are big and fat. Some individuals get in the150-pound range in southern California, making them the largest of the tunas to visit California. Often traveling in the company of yellowfin tuna, bigeyes arrive in California at the same time as their smaller cousins. Bigeyes are generally difficult to find—it's usually just luck that you run into them.

On many typical overnight tuna trips to the offshore banks, the ratio of bigeyes to yellowfins is usually about 1 in 50. The best time to hook a bigeye is at dawn or dusk, since they usually travel deep during the day. I've seen huge schools of bigeye

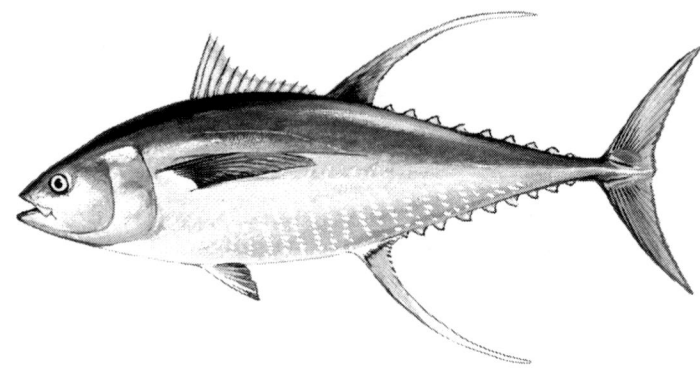

Yellowfin Tuna (Thunnis albacares)

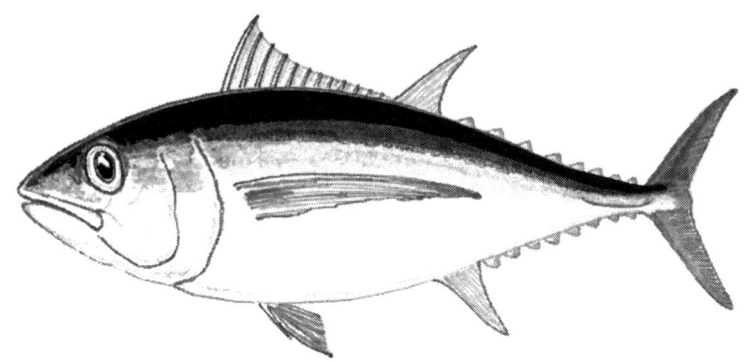

Bigeye Tuna (Thunnis obesus)

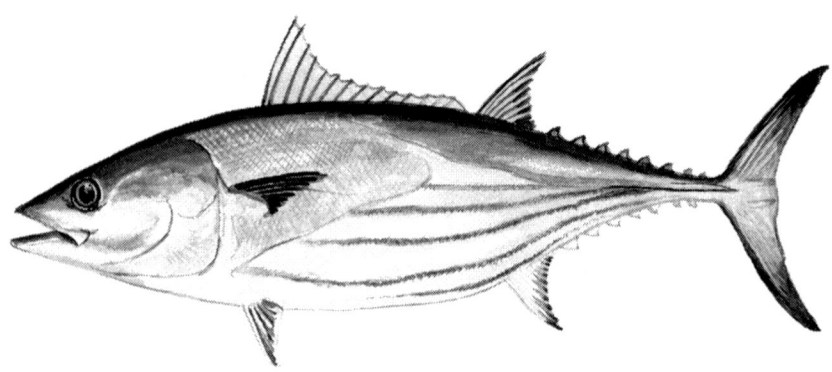

Skipjack Tuna (Katsuwonus pelamis or Euthynnus pelamis)

jumping and feeding for hours, but nothing we could do would entice them to take a bait or lure. They're that clever in identifying which sardines have hooks in them. Probably the best way to hook a bigeye is by trolling. I guess they have to hit the trolled feather so fast they don't have time to think about whether it has a hook or not.

Bigeyes are typical tuna fighters, powerful and capable of incredible endurance. Bigeyes don't have as violent a fight as an albacore or yellowfin, but their tenacity is nonetheless incredible. Once I was aboard a party boat less than 35 miles south of Point Loma when we ran into a school of 100- to 150-pound bigeyes. Four were hooked on the troll with tuna feathers. Two broke off immediately, one was landed (mine) in about an hour, and the last was finally broken off by the deck hand after an hour-and-a-half fight. The fisherman swore the fish was a harder fighter than a 500-pound marlin he had landed in Mexico.

Skipjack Tuna (*Katsuwonus pelamis* or *Euthynnus pelamis*)

Skippies also travel in the company of yellowfin and bigeyes. Considered a pest by many fishermen, this almost regal tuna is anything but. It's an aggressive fighter and, although small (usually 5 to 8 pounds), they give the light tackle fisherman a real run for his money. Skipjack are the ideal tuna to fish with a fly rod and can be both challenging and exciting.

One of the bad raps given to skipjack is that they aren't good to eat. This also isn't true. The Japanese esteem the tuna's dark flesh for a variety of dishes, including sashimi (raw), tataki (cooked medium rare and served with flavorful ponzu sauce), and fully cooked. Dried, shaved skipjack tuna is used as a seasoning and as a soup base. If you've ever had traditional Japanese miso soup, you've had skipjack soup. It's used as the soup base in many Japanese dishes.

Skipjack will only eat anchovies. If you're in a mixed school of fish and want to avoid catching skipjack, just fish with a sardine, a green jig, or green and white streamer fly. Skipjack only hit blue jigs, blue flies, and live anchovies.

Dorado, also Dolphinfish, Mahi Mahi (*Coryphaena hippurus*)

Dorado are a summertime visitor to southern California in the warmer years, along with the skipjack, bigeye, and yellowfin tuna. They are highly esteemed, both for their aerial, acrobatic fight when hooked and for their delectable table fare. Though they can grow to be as big as 5 feet and 80-plus pounds, most of the southern California specimens are less than 2 feet and under 20 pounds.

Dorado put on a spectacular fight when hooked. They dodge, weave, leap, and really put on a show. They hit trolled feather jigs, live bait, cast jigs, and flies with equal ferocity. The angler has to be right on top of the fish to recognize when it is running toward him and never allow slack in the line. The slightest slack is all this skilled escape artist needs to spit the hook and get away.

A fishing buddy of mine tells a tale of fishing dorado down in Mexico, when one especially frisky fish leapt out of the water directly at his forehead. Although he ducked, the flying fish still managed to give him a decent slap on the head with its

Dorado, also Dolphinfish, Mahi Mahi (Coryphaena hippurus)

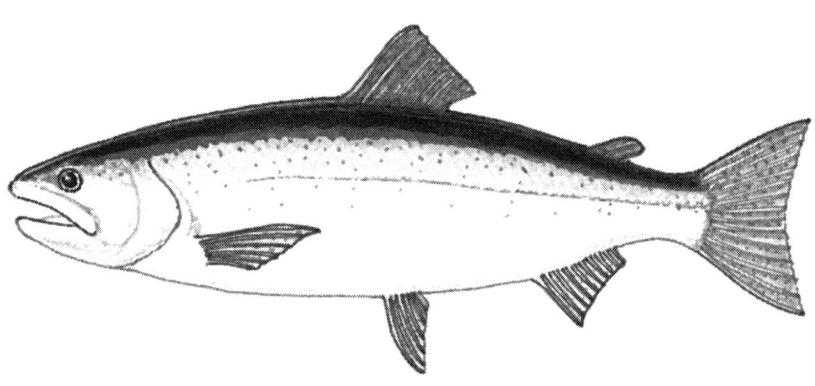

Coho (Silver) Salmon (Oncorhynchus kisutch)

tail. While in the air, the dorado spit the hook and was gone. I wasn't there to verify the facts and it may be pure fiction, but I rather believe the story since I've seen these fish run directly at a fisherman in order to get slack, and then leap 8 to 10 feet out of the water, twisting and writhing to get free.

Coho (Silver) Salmon (*Oncorhynchus kisutch*)

Southern California gets a substantial springtime run of silver salmon in the Santa Barbara Channel. Several other species, including chinook salmon, sometimes appear with the silvers but not in appreciable numbers. These fish can get up in the 15-plus pound range, but the majority are in the 3- to 6-pound range.

Most southern California salmon are taken by slow trolling, but there are the occasional instances almost every year that people catch them with bait while fishing off the piers. The primary months to catch salmon are from the opening day in February until late June or early July.

Like all salmon, silvers are anadromous, spending their lives in saltwater and returning to rivers and streams to breed and then die. This means that every salmon taken in the ocean is a juvenile that has not yet had a chance to breed. The wisdom of doing this is questionable. Since excellent farm-raised salmon is now available for those who want to eat salmon, I believe the wisest course is to release sea-caught wild salmon in the interest of preserving the breeding population.

Fishing Tackle for Southern California Saltwater

No one will admit faster than I that all sorts of tackle are used for fishing. No one setup or combination of tackle is perfect for a particular situation, and a wide variety of possible combinations of rods, reels, and terminal tackle can be used for a specific type of fishing. Some fishermen like to use very light tackle for a particular situation, believing, and rightly so, that the undersized gear will draw more strikes and represent a bigger challenge when landing a fish. Having hooked and landed a 5-pound yellowtail on 80-pound test stand-up trolling gear suitable for a 200-plus-pound tuna, I understand this theory. It really wasn't much of a challenge, and the poor yellowtail never had a chance. Still other fishermen believe heavier tackle results in surer, quicker landings that are less stressful for fish if you plan to release them and more certain to bag the fish if you plan to keep it.

My personal preference is somewhere in the middle of the two extremes. Depending on the type of fishing you plan to do, I believe you ought to use tackle sturdy enough that you have a good chance to land a fish but light enough to get hit often, that makes landing a fish a challenge, and that allows the especially tenacious fighter a chance at freedom. As it turns out, most fishermen use approximately the same weight tackle as I do, and I assume that they are operating on the same theory. The recommendations I make throughout the text are middle-of-the-road approaches to having sensible tackle light enough that it won't scare fish away but heavy enough to land a fish even if you make a few mistakes.

Types of Ocean Fishing and Fish Habitat

KELP BED FISHING

Of all the different types of southern California ocean fishing, few get fishermen more excited than surface-fishing the kelp beds. During summer, the action is almost always good, the fish have a lot of fight in them, and the warm sunshine and breathtaking coastal and island scenery all combine to make this the favored sport for many fishermen.

The California coast is well endowed with kelp beds. This fascinating seaweed is extremely tall and fast growing—kelp can grow 6 feet in a single day. It's common for kelp to grow all the way to the surface in 150 feet of water, making it the giant among seaweeds. Being algae, it is a favorite food of a variety of small sea species. Microscopic shrimp and other small, free-swimming creatures congregate in kelp beds to graze on both live kelp and bits of kelp broken loose from the main forest. On the bottom, sea urchins, clams, and abalone also feed on kelp. Kelp forests grow so fast that even though great amounts of it are eaten, it is replaced faster than it is depleted.

Schools of small fish come into the kelp forests to reap the bounty. Herring, sardines, and anchovies move in to eat the shrimp, and sheephead move in to eat urchins, clams, and abalone. Naturally, wherever small baitfish proliferate, game fish are sure to be found. Bonito, barracuda, mackerel, bass, and yellowtail join in and feast on the proliferation of small baitfish.

Halibut, sole, sculpin, crabs, and lobsters move into the area as scavengers to clean up any food passed up by the others. Kelp provides shelter for the eggs of these fish, too. Eggs and hatchlings provide yet more food for small baitfish. This great circle of life in a single kelp bed means one thing to a fisherman: this is the place to fish!

The easiest ocean fishing for the average angler is kelp bed fishing. Commercial party boats and privately owned boats travel to kelp beds for outstanding fishing all summer. Fishing is best when the water temperature is above 62 degrees, making kelp bed fishing best from about mid-June until well into October for most of southern California.

To fish a kelp bed, anchor the boat outside but nearby dense kelp. Don't go into the surface kelp with a powerboat—there's a good chance you'll foul your prop or rudder. Many areas around visible kelp beds have kelp down below that hasn't reached the surface. These are ideal places for surface fish.

Baitfishing the Kelp Beds

There are several ways to fish kelp beds, but by far the most productive is baitfishing. Any and all of the different varieties of fish found in kelp beds can be caught on bait. Baitfishing the kelp beds of southern California has been the mainstay of the huge local party boat fleet. Productive kelp beds are located within a couple miles of every port or harbor in the area. Just outside the huge harbor of San Diego, with its enormous Navy presence, are the Point Loma kelp beds, a productive place to bait-fish ever since the harbor was discovered and still productive today. Just outside the busy port of Los Angeles lie the horseshoe kelp beds, probably the most consistent fishing spot in the entire area. If you're planning to fish southern California, plan to baitfish the kelp beds.

Rods and Reels

Rods and reels for baitfishing the kelp have been decreasing in size over the past few decades. This is perhaps because the fish are getting smarter and more line shy. It may also be because of advances in technology from bamboo to fiberglass and now to graphite, with improved reels and their high-tech drag systems. I suspect it is a little of both. If you were to survey line weights of kelp bed bait fishermen in the 1960s, you'd find the majority used 20-pound test. Today, it would probably average about 12-pound test. Some use as light as 8 and a few use up to 15-pound test. I carry 10-, 12-, and 15-pound rigs when fishing the kelp with bait or rubber lures.

The most useful light rod for baitfishing the kelp is a longish graphite rod (7 to 9 feet) with a long, ocean-type grip. Length choice is a matter of personal preference. Some fishermen like a longer rod for its ability to pitch an anchovy a good distance away from a boat into the kelp forest. While this may be useful on party boats, where elbow-to-elbow anglers compete for small patches of water, it may not be as effective in many other, less competitive, fishing situations. In fact, tossing a hooked live anchovy a good distance tends to stun it and isn't nearly as effective in luring a big predator out for an ambush. A lively, swimming anchovy is far more effect, so the less shock it receives in catching, hooking, flying through the air, and landing on the surface of the water, the better it will swim.

Graphite rods tend to be less than friendly to the kind of bumps, scrapes, and general rough treatment awaiting any fishing tackle on party boats, which is why so many anglers prefer fiberglass rods. The excellent blanks made by Calstar have been a very popular base for building custom rods for party boat use. Their 196 series, 215 series, and 270 series fit the bill for a durable kelp bed bait stick. These are fairly fast taper rods with a light, sensitive tip, easily deflected but with lots of backbone in the midsection to handle heavy fish. The sensitive tip allows an angler to feel the dif-ference between the bait running for its life and the actual strike of a game fish—a common confusion made by novice kelp bed bait fishermen.

Match the rod with a heavy-duty freshwater type, or light-duty saltwater type baitcasting reel. The two most popular are the Shimano Calcutta and the Pen Squidder, but many others are suitable for this type of work. Of course, there are many anglers who wouldn't ever give up their spinning reels for this type of fishing. They have a point, and a spinning reel will cast out an anchovy with minimal stress. They're easy and simple to use without requiring an angler to level-wind the line on his retrieve, and modern saltwater-type reels are plenty durable enough for this type of use. The preferred baitfishing reel holds no less than 250 yards of whatever pound test line an angler chooses.

Terminal Tackle and Bait

The vast majority of kelp bed baitfishing is done by "flylining," that is to say, fishing with only a bare hook tied directly to the fishing line. The hook is baited with a live anchovy that is allowed to swim wherever it likes. Live bait hooks in #4 or #2 are used for flylining. The size of the hook is more dependent on the size of the bait than the size of the intended quarry. A #4 hook is perfectly suited to catch anything from a small blue perch to a 40-plus-pound breezing yellowtail. If you're carrying sardines or live squid in the bait tank (both excellent kelp bed baits), switch hook sizes to 2/0, 3/0, or 4/0, depending on the size of the bait.

Rubber swim baits, both the traditional twin-tailed "Mojo" or "Scampi" types or the more modern single-tailed baits in green, blue, or brown colors have always been and will continue to be excellent kelp bed lures. On the surface or just below, calico bass hit these lures with élan. Fished in mid to deep water, they'll entice bigger white seabass or yellowtail from the depths when the water is cool and the surface bite slow. These are especially effective when sweetened with small strips of squid to give that special scent that seems to drive game fish wild.

In addition to hooks, the bait fisherman needs sinkers on occasion—sinkers with rubber twist-on cores work well. Three sizes of sinkers will do the job: ½-, ¾-, and 1½-ounce sizes are enough to account for any current and drift conditions.

A sinker is used when fish are not on the surface or when wind or current tend to tangle the lines. Whether or not to use a sinker can be determined by first "flylining," that is, baiting the hook and allowing the bait to swim free without a weight. If nothing is caught, the line just keeps the bait floating. If only mackerel are hitting the bait, add the smallest weight to get the bait to sink toward the bottom. If this gets the same results, add more weight.

To rig up for baitfishing, use a clinch knot to tie the hook directly to the line without a swivel. If the fishing or drift conditions call for a sinker, twist it on the line about 18 inches above the hook.

Fishing the kelp beds calls for live bait, specifically anchovies. Anchovies are a small, active baitfish that are very common in the southern California ocean. They are caught and kept alive by bait-seining boats. Anchovies are available for sale at bait barges in just about every harbor on the California coast. They are sold to fishermen by the "scoop." Just how many anchovies are in a scoop varies from place to place, as does the size of the bait. For two fishermen in a small boat, a half scoop will provide plenty of bait for a full day of action on the kelp beds.

Many fishermen just select the biggest bait, thinking they'll catch the biggest fish with it—this doesn't work. To select a baitfish in a large, crowded bait tank, look for the liveliest bait. Also look for a green back on an anchovy. If it's green, the fish still has most of its scales and will swim in the most natural manner. The most active bait is the most effective. Game fish prefer a struggling, squirming bait to one barely moving.

Keep the idea of active bait in mind while you're fishing, as well. The fishermen who catch the most fish are the ones who change their bait most often. If a strike doesn't occur in 5 minutes or so when sport fishing the kelp beds, pull in the bait and change it for a livelier one—don't wait until you're sure the bait is gone. If you get a strike and don't hook the fish, change the bait immediately, because the fish will be dead or at least injured enough to stop wiggling.

There are a number of ways to hook an anchovy or sardine, shown in the diagram. The best but most fragile is the gill-hooking method. Using this method, you'll probably lose more bait, but the bait will stay livelier and catch the most fish—that is, if you can get it to stay on the hook. If the bait just won't stay on the hook using the gill-hooking method, use the nose hook method. This stays on the best, but the tradeoff is that the bait will only last a few minutes before it quits squirming and becomes useless. The tail-hooking method should be used when flylining and you want the bait to swim downward. Like the nose-hooking method, you'll only get a few minutes of life out of the bait.

Once the bait is on the hook, toss it out in the general direction of the thickest part of the kelp and let it swim. Most likely, it will take only a few moments for a strike. When a surface fish hits, its first reaction is to run away with the bait before eating it. Watch sea gulls beg bits of French fries or bread from tourists at a seaside

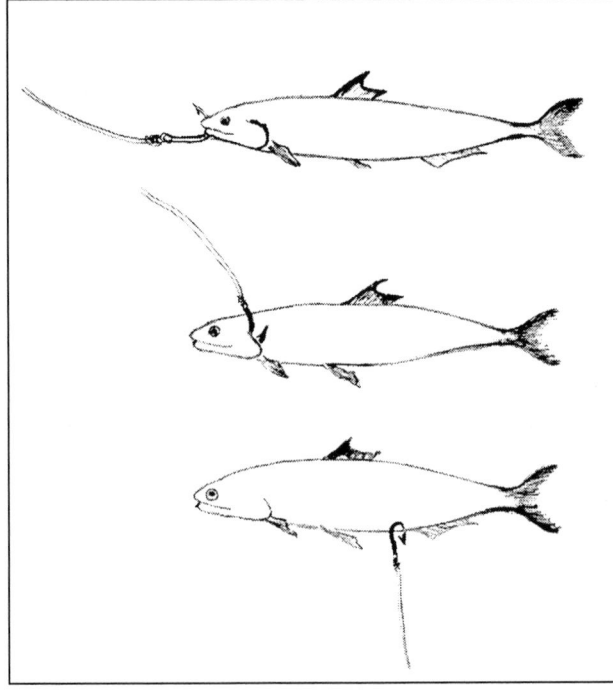

Common methods for hooking an anchovy or sardine.

cafe. The gull grabs the food, runs a short way with it to make sure no other birds have claim to it, and then swallows it. Surface fish react much the same way, grabbing the bait, running with it, and then eating it.

To catch surface fish, keep in mind that the fish's first reaction is to dash with the bait and that it is essential, although difficult, not to react at the first sign of a strike. Keep the reel declutched so the fish can freely take all the line it wants for the first dash. From one to three seconds later, the fish will stop—that's when to clutch in the reel and set the hook with a jerk. The rod's flexibility prevents jerking the bait out of the fish's mouth and allows the hook to be set with authority.

Once the fish is hooked, it will make its first run. The drag on the reel should be set for about one-half the test strength of the line. For 20-pound test line, set the drag so that line will come off with about a 10-pound pull. Don't worry about the fish pulling line off—that's the way reels are supposed to work. Let the fish take whatever line it wants on its first run. Once it stops, begin to pump and reel retrieve, always keeping tension on the line.

At times, a hooked fish runs toward the boat. If this happens, retrieve line as fast as the fish is running, never allowing slack in the line. Keep the rod tip bent. If the fish decides to run away from the boat again, stop the retrieve, maintain tension, and let the fish take line. When it stops, begin retrieving again. Keep at it until the fish is up to the boat, then gaff it or bounce it aboard, depending on how big the fish is.

A large variety of fish can be taken by bait fishing the kelp beds. Yellowtail are a favorite due to their size, fighting ability, and table fare. Calico bass are next, mostly for their eating quality. Bonito offer the most fight per pound of just about any fish in the ocean. They rate right up there with tuna as a fast, powerful fish. California barracuda fight well, are good eating, and are plentiful all over southern California.

When bait fishing is slow on the surface, don't miss out on the bottom action. Using the same methods but with a heavier sinker, many fish that make excellent table fare can be found near and around kelp beds. Big sheephead, an excellent fish to eat, are often found around kelp beds. Sculpin, one of the most prized eating fish, are also common. Whitefish, treefish, blue perch, and rockfish are to be found hanging around the kelp, as well.

Jigfishing the Kelp Beds

Hardware, bone jigs, or candy-bar jigfishing (all three familiar names for the same lures), have been effective ways to fish kelp beds for as long as there have been fishermen venturing out into coastal waters. Bigger fish (the more aggressive predators) often hit the jigs. It isn't unusual for a yellowtail breezing by a kelp bed, stopping just long enough to gulp down some readily available bait, to be enticed into hitting a jig cast just in front of its path. Yellowtail, barracuda, calico bass, and white seabass will all take a jig. For an angler who wants some action, a jig is an essential item.

Jigfishing is probably the least understood fishing method. Good jig fishermen are rare, but when you see one, you'll be impressed by the size and quantity of fish that are caught. Jigs catch fewer but bigger fish. To understand why this is so, it's necessary to understand the basic psychology of predators. Watching a common house cat as it plays and hunts is a good way to understand predator behavior. To a predator stalking and killing are refined instincts that are separate from the urge to eat. A cat will attack when it sees the right motion even if it is not hungry.

You can scare away African lions simply by running at them and clapping your hands. If you turn and run away, there will be an entirely different reaction from the big cats that could put you on the lunch menu. If you've ever played with a house cat, you might have noticed that the cat backs away if you make a funny noise and move your hand toward it. However, if you just make small motions and no noise, the cat gets interested; and if you make motions and pull your hand away, the cat pounces.

Like cats, big game fish are predators. Their instincts call for them to strike when the right combinations of motion and vibrations invade their space. They do this whether they're hungry or not and strike any time the right vibrations, flashes of color, and motion occur. Fishing jigs are designed to provide these three things. It's not that the fish thinks the jig is food—like the kitten that pounces on your hand, the fish strikes because the jig stimulated its strike instinct. Check out a few jigs, and you will notice that ocean-fishing jigs don't look anything like a baitfish.

Fish have a unique organ called a lateral line that senses vibrations in the water somewhat like land animals' ears sense vibrations in the air. Motion in the water, such as a baitfish struggling, can be sensed from quite a distance due to the lateral line. The commonly held notion that sharks can sense a struggling swimmer is true—sharks have an acute sense of vibration. Fish rely far more on their sense of vibration than most people suspect.

Because man is such a visual creature, relying on sight so heavily, we tend to think other animals do the same. This is not so. I have astounded more than one boatload of fishermen by catching fish on a jig painted flat black—just for fun. It settled a number of arguments about which color jig works best for each type of fish. Fish are far more sensitive to vibration and the direction of motion than to the appearance and color of the jig.

Rods, Reels, and Line

Jig sticks are long—often 8 to 9 feet—in order to provide enough leverage to really throw the jig out far enough. They usually have a parabolic or medium taper with a heavier tip. This allows all of the rod's flex to be used for propelling the jig. Calstar's T90, 6480H, and 270/8H are the three most popular of the Calstar line. These are sold as blanks to be used as bases for custom-wrapped rods. Most ocean fishing rod manufacturers make one or more rods suitable for jig fishing. They are rated by the breaking test of line to be used. Typical jig sticks for kelp bed fishing are sized for use with 20- to 40-pound test line, with 30-pound probably the most popular.

Many people favor a grip/reel seat area on the jig stick so that it can be simply cork tape-wrapped instead of hypalon-gripped with a reel seat. This allows an angler to adjust the reel location either farther up the rod toward the tip or farther back toward the butt to get just the right feel for his or her particular casting preference. While this is less expensive and possibly slightly lighter than traditional grips and reel seats, it lacks a comfortable grip for many. For those who know their preference, a custom rod can be built to accommodate arm size and casting preferences.

Reels for jigfishing have several things in common: They have to have a light, low inertia spool for casting, and they require a fast retrieve—4.5:1 to 6:1 (the number of times the spool turns for every turn of the reel handle) for most effective use. The Penn Jigmaster is the prototype reel for this type of work, having revolutionized jigfishing when it first came out back in the early 1960s. Since then, almost all major reel manufacturers have come out with models specially designed for jigfishing.

Another important consideration for a good jig reel is a light spool. Most newer reels come equipped with anodized aluminum spools, but many still have chrome-plated brass spools. Either aluminum or plastic spools should be used for a jig stick. Brass spools have too much inertia to really throw out a jig. With a brass spool, either the cast will be short or you'll find yourself contending with a horrible "bird's nest" snag on the reel after a power cast.

Few anglers use spinning tackle for jigfishing, because the gear tends to be heavier, with 25- to 40-pound test line the rule. With lighter line (when targeting barracuda, for example), spinning tackle works fine, but when using heavier line weights, most anglers elect to use conventional reels. This is not to say that spinning gear isn't usable or effective for this type of fishing, because with modern, high-tech reel designs having bigger and better drag systems, spin jigfishing tackle can be used and should be more popular than it is. With some practice, though, a conventional reel jig fisherman can cast equally far and with just as much, if not more, control than a spinning reel. This means the choice is strictly personal. For the occasional fisherman who doesn't fish enough or practice enough on conventional reels, spinning reels offer an easy-to-use alternative.

Jigs

Jigs for kelp bed fishing have been getting smaller over the past 30 years. This is probably because the fish have been getting smaller. Back in the late 1960s, a 20-pound yellowtail was a normal size, with a 40-pounder really big. Now an 8- or 10-pound yellowtail is normal and a 25-pounder considered something to brag about. Today, jigs 4 to 5 inches long in the body are the most common, effective size for general use around kelp beds. Of course, kelp beds on the far side of San Clemente Island, where there is almost no fishing pressure, demand a completely different jig than the heavily-fished Horseshoe Kelp, just minutes from the Port of Los Angeles harbor entrance. I still have plenty of the 6- to 7-inch long jigs from my old days back in the late 1960s and 1970s to use on offshore island trips, but almost all of the new jigs I buy are of the smaller variety.

Jigs come in two weights, determined by the material from which the jig is cast. Heavy jigs are cast in zinc—what many people call pot metal, used for matchbox cars, carburetors, and automobile nameplates. The majority of the jigs seen gracing

Trolling jigs
(top to bottom):
jethead feather jig,
plastic head artificial
material jig, soft head
feather, a handmade
"bamboozler" feather
jig by the author, and
a cedar plug-type
trolling jig.

the pegboard racks of tackle stores are this heavy variety. Some jig manufacturers offer a "professional" or "tournament" jig. These are cast from aluminum. Light jigs are more difficult to cast and don't sink as well as the zinc ones. It is a rare day when the fish hit jigs right on the surface more often than they hit jigs running a few feet below the surface, so unless you're a pro and really want a light jig for some particular fishing locale or method, stick to the heavier jigs. If the rare occasion arises, you can make a heavy jig skim the surface with a retrieve technique in those rare instances when fish are only taking a surface-running jig.

By far the most popular jig is a blue and white. This color simulates a crippled anchovy and is taken by almost all game fish found in kelp. The second most popular color is green and yellow. This simulates sardine colors to a game fish. Another popular color is mottled purple, simulating squid. One of my favorite colors is green and black. I also used to have an excellent red and white jig that would really perform in the bright sunlight. There are literally dozens of color combinations on display in most tackle shops. Most of these colors are designed to hook fishermen, not necessarily to hook fish. It is far more important how you fish the jig than what color it is. Stick with the three or four basic colors, and you'll never be left out in a good jig bite.

Another type of jig that's still as effective as ever, though it has fallen from favor with many fishermen, is the heavy spoon jig. These are heavy, stamped steel jigs, often chrome- or nickel-plated, sometimes with bright reflective panels of mackerel green or blue translucent markings. These jigs are excellent for bigger predatory fish, such as yellowtail or big bonito, and are most effective in the bright sunlight, something that southern California never seems to lack. Many experi-

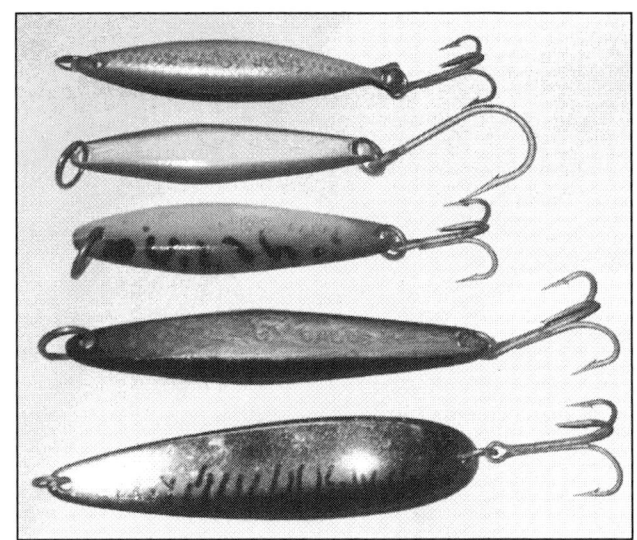

Metal jigs (top to bottom): sea striker, Tady #9, Salas 6× Junior, Salas 6×, and crocodile spoon.

enced jig fishermen like them because they have lots of action and don't require quite as intense a retrieve to generate the appropriate "come eat me" vibrations that all jigs produce.

To jigfish, tie the jig directly to the line without any weights, swivels, or leaders. Using a swivel on a jig kills the jig's action—remember those vibrations. A swivel generates the wrong kind of vibration, and fish generally avoid them. I tested this one summer day many years ago while fishing the La Jolla kelp beds. Using the same jig, four times as many casts were needed to catch fish when the line was attached with a swivel and snap than were needed when it was tied directly to the line. (By the way, that day I took the jackpot on the party boat with a 24-pound yellowtail. I caught two other yellowtail that day, the only yellows on the boat. All were taken on a green and yellow 6X jig.)

To jigfish, you must first learn to cast. While casting is not really all that difficult, you might get the mistaken notion that it is a very strenuous, Herculean task when watching some fishermen. I often chuckle to myself when watching some people cast. They take three steps, grit their teeth, throw their arms forward with all of their might, and usually blow the cast. Casting involves a simple flick of the wrist, letting the flexibility of the rod do the real work.

Try it out and practice, practice. Nothing is more frustrating than being at a wide-open hot spot where yellowtail are jumping out of the water and you have to spend 20 minutes unwinding a backlash while your fishing buddies are hauling them in.

While putting the jig where you want it provides the chance to catch a fish, whether or not the fish strikes the jig is all in the retrieve. Many fishermen just point the rod tip at the water and crank in the jig at a constant rate. This might be fine when fish are boiling out of the water, but those days are rare and becoming rarer. Remember the cat example: moving your hand in exactly the same way soon causes the cat to lose interest. But by moving your hand in a variety of ways and alternating the speed from slow to quick and sometimes stopping completely, the cat remains curious and interested.

Present a fish with a variety of motions to keep it interested and arouse the fish's strike instinct. Often, you'll get hits when the jig is floating down before you've started your retrieve. This should give you a clue: declutch the reel and let the jig flutter at times. Give it a few jerks, retrieve slowly, retrieve quickly, and declutch. Give the jig some action, not just the same old boring retrieve. Your job as a jig fisherman is to get the fish to pounce.

Don't be afraid the fish might get scared if it sees the jig take off. It might if the jig comes right toward it, but game fish are used to their quarry darting off at times. This is what predators expect from their prey. It stimulates their strike instinct.

Really effective jigfishing near the kelp beds requires some chumming. Toss some live bait into the area you plan to cast and watch for boils—fish splashing the water on the surface. This means feeding game fish. Pitch the jig right in front of the boil. When bigger game fish cut through a school of bait, they slash and eat voraciously—sometimes eating dozens of small fish. When you see a boil, it means a big fish is eating there.

Often, game fish are lurking in deeper water and are not on the surface. I've pulled yellowtail and white seabass up from several hundred feet deep on a jig. The technique is similar. Cast out, let the jig sink, clutch in, give it a few jerks, declutch, let the jig sink, clutch in, etc. Sometimes, you'll find the fish right near the bottom.

Jigfishing is a challenging, fun way to fish. You'll catch bigger fish and spend more time fishing because you won't have to spend time rebaiting hooks. If you're an active person, you will probably enjoy the fishing more because there are simply more things to do when jigfishing. Give it a try.

Surface Plug-and-Swim Bait Fishing the Kelp Beds

One of the newest techniques for catching fish near kelp beds is with the use of plugs. Calico bass seem especially fond of surface and diving plugs. The same types of plugs used for freshwater bass fishing, except larger, are becoming the new rage for ocean fishing and seem to work quite well.

Lighter tackle than jigfishing tackle can be used. Freshwater-sized reels with 8-, 10-, 12-, and 15-pound test, coupled with long, flexible (by ocean standards) poles, usually graphite, are the plug fisherman's choice for fishing in kelp.

It's a bit unusual to see bass boil the surface, although they'll do that in the dog days of summer when the famous southern California sun has been warming the surface layer to a balmy 70-degree-plus temperature. This means a diving, or subsurface, running plug usually attracts fish better than a surface running plug.

Swimming plugs, such as this Rapala Magnum, are gaining in popularity for both slow trolling and casting.

Be careful to avoid the kelp when casting. It is a sturdy, tenacious plant and will eat your expensive tackle far more predictably than the fish it harbors. Try to cast your lures to the edges of the kelp for best results and minimal losses.

Rubber swim baits have also been used with some success near kelp beds. Use them with the same tackle and techniques as described for plugs. It has been only in the last couple of years that fishermen have even tried swim baits and plugs, so by doing a bit of experimentation, you could be in for a surprise. I've seen big bull calicos inhale Rapalas like they'd never eaten. Both the rubber swim baits and plugs should be tied directly to the line for best results.

Trolling the Kelp Beds

Trolling is a fun, productive way to catch surface fish. Surprisingly few people ever try it out. This isn't possible when fishing on a party boat, but on a charter or on a private boat, it's tops for finding great spots and picking up some nice fish when out cruising on a nice summer day.

Trolling for surface fish can be done anywhere. Although the areas near kelp beds are often the most productive, many areas that are farther from kelp beds can be just as good. The main skill needed for successful trolling is being able to find schools of baitfish. Where there are baitfish, there will be game fish.

Finding schools of baitfish is easier than you might suspect. The secret is watching the birds. When looking across the water, pay particular attention to the direction that sea birds are traveling. If you spot a good percentage heading in a particular direction, follow them. Crowds of birds can often be seen hanging around a particular patch of ocean, some diving, and some circling overhead. Sea birds have an excellent sense about where to find schools of small fish—their survival depends on it. Where birds are feeding, so are game fish. When you find where birds are feeding, stay with them, trolling in lazy figure eights right through the center of the bird activity, where the fish concentration is heaviest. Trolling is usually done between 6 and 10 miles per hour. While some fishermen troll faster, I doubt they catch any more fish, but they certainly burn a lot more fuel.

Trolling can be done with a wide variety of fishing rods and reels. I commonly use a heavy baitfishing rod and reel with 30-pound line. I have a fishing buddy who always uses a spinning rod and reel. The best setup when trolling for surface fish is a tuna stick with 50-pound line. It might be a bit heavy for many of the fish you'll catch, but if you happen to hook into a big one, you'll be ready to fight it.

To achieve the best results, use trolling feather or vinyl-skirted jigs with special double hooks. Trolling jigs come in a number of sizes, shapes, and colors. Which ones work better is a personal choice—they all have their days. In fact, some jigs produce better on a particular day and even a particular time of the day. It depends on the angle and amount of sunlight hitting the jig. I lean toward purples and greens when the sky is overcast and bright colors, such as red and white or Mexican flag (red, white, and green) in the sunshine. The smartest thing to do is to troll a number of lines, one for each person aboard, each with a different type and color of jig. If one color or type outperforms the rest, switch to that type or color of jig. The diagram illustrates the a typical trolling jig with double hooks.

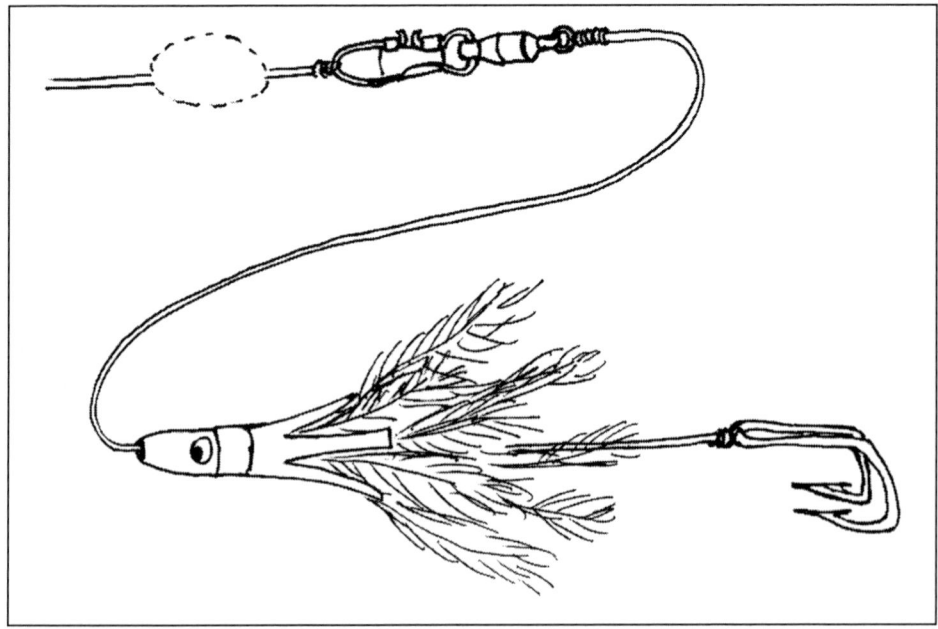

Trolling rig with double hook.

Unlike bone jigs, trolling jigs are usually rigged with a leader, about 6 feet long, attached to the main line with a swivel. If the jig rides high in the water and the fish are running deeper, a sliding egg-shaped sinker can be used on the main line between the swivel and the rod.

Yellowtail, bonito, and barracuda will all hit trolling jigs. When a fish hits the jig, grab the pole and stop the boat immediately. It is important to maintain some tension on the line at all times. Let the fish run if it wants to, then use the pump and reel retrieve to land the fish.

Once you find a spot where trolling gets fish, stop and use jigs or bait to get in on the hot surface action. The style and method of fishing is just like kelp bed fishing. Remember that you are fishing a moving school of baitfish being followed by game fish. Keep your eyes on the birds: if they start to move away, follow them and you won't be disappointed.

Trolling to find the fish and stopping for the action is one of the most enjoyable ways of surface fishing, since action is almost guaranteed.

Flyfishing the Kelp Beds

Flyfishing the kelp is a new sport in southern California that is gaining in popularity because of its challenge and outright fun. Bass, barracuda, bonito, and yellowtail all take a fly. The lee side of Catalina is an ideal place in the summer to flyfish. Because the kelp beds are very close to the island, the towering cliffs shield them from nearly all the wind. Here, the fish are less wary than their coastal cousins because of lighter fishing pressure. In addition, the water is generally glassy calm, so you can watch your flies being struck—just as in a clear mountain stream.

Plan on catching more than a few mackerel for every game fish you may encounter when flyfishing the kelp. Macks are quickly attracted to bright colors and will snap at almost anything in the water. Their tenacious, acrobatic fight will really sharpen your fish-fighting skills. The vast majority of people release mackerel after catching them.

Rods, Reels, and Line

An 8-weight fly rod should be considered minimum for this type of work. A 10 is preferable and a 12-weight wouldn't be overgunning it, especially if yellowtail are around. I've seen many an angler convinced that a 10-weight would land any yellowtail in southern California only to come home with broken leaders, sizzled drags, and a blistered palm.

I know some of you are scratching your heads in disbelief thinking about how you landed a 9-pound largemouth bass on Lake Whatsit with an 8-weight and I'm only talking about a 5-pound fish or so. Trust me—if you've never caught ocean fish, you have no concept of how tenaciously they hang onto life and what lengths they're willing to take to get off that hook. I watch the good ol' boys bass fishin' the lakes on TV. They pump that 12-pound bass over to the boat on 6-pound line with barely a squeak out of the drag. Then they reach over, grab the fish by the lip, and hold it up for the camera to see its fat belly. Try that with a 12-pound yellowtail or bonito! First, it would snap 6-pound line as though it wasn't even there. Second, if you did manage to keep the line from snapping, the drag would be screaming so loudly, your buddy would have to dump buckets of water on your reel to keep it from melting down. And third, if you did manage to get it to the boat and reach down to grab the fish on the lip, it would toss you into the water while taking off your thumb at the elbow! In other words—don't undergun yourself or you'll be replacing plenty of lost line.

A sinking line is necessary for getting at game fish unless you're fishing in the dog days of summer when fish are busting the surface. You'll get far more hits a few feet down, though, and by getting the fly lower, you'll avoid catching only mackerel. A shooting head is also wise to get farther out from the boat and target particular clumps of kelp. Often, fish are waiting just under clumps of surface kelp to ambush anything that approaches unwarily.

Fly Patterns

Blue and white (anchovy pattern) or green and white (sardine pattern) streamer flies always produce consistently. These can have considerable amounts of crystal flash in their bodies. You'll never scare away a southern California ocean game fish by having too much flash. All white streamer patterns with pearlescent threads also produce well, especially for bonito, a highly sought-after kelp bed native. If you get them deeper, all white streamer flies also attract white seabass. Another producing streamer pattern for the kelp is a purple squid pattern. The most effective kelp bed flies are tied on 1/0 to 4/0 hooks.

FISHING THE FLATS

Southern California is well endowed with flat sandy or muddy bottoms fringing the coastline. Practically every area has thousands of square miles of flat areas. All of these flats contain fish. Though overlooked by most, they can be the source of some excellent fishing.

It is said that 90 percent of all sea life lives within sight of land. This is quite believable, since the shallower areas contain the one thing necessary to most sea life—sunlight. Where there is sunlight, there is also an abundance of plant life. Where there are plants, there are animals grazing on the plants. Where there are grazers, there are predators. It's that simple.

Clams, mussels, limpets, barnacles, and other shelled creatures are the grazers of the flats. They anchor or bury themselves in one spot, then just sift through the water to pick up plant matter swirling through water kept in constant motion by the sea's waves, tides, and currents. Predatory fish scour the bottom to find young, dying, or simply incautious grazers. Nature's great circle of life and death works in the sea as it does on land.

Keeping the bottom clean are the scavengers. While humans generally think of land scavengers as dirty and repulsive creatures, sea scavengers are among our favorite food items. Crabs, shrimp, and lobsters, the main sea scavengers, are considered delicacies. This illustrates the folly of assigning man's morality to nature's creations.

Unlike land creatures, sea scavengers are the prey of numerous fish. Crabs, shrimp, and lobsters aren't only a delicacy to man—many fish also dine on these delectable creatures. These are generally tough-skinned, big-toothed fish having delicious meat that is the result of their diet of mild-tasting crustaceans.

In the flats, halibut, sole, and flounder scour the bottom for bits of food. Sculpin in the south and cabezon in the north patiently wait on the bottom, propped up on their fins, for a meal to swim by. Croaker zip around in great schools to pick off anything passed over by the others. In many areas, sand bass and whitefish add to the variety of good eating fish available throughout the coast.

Also lurking in the flats are a wide variety of sharks and rays scavenging on any food they can find. Most of these are bottom-dwelling creatures, basically harmless to man except for protective spines and barbs. Almost all are great fun to catch and good to eat.

When I crewed on a rock cod boat in San Diego, the crewman of another boat and I used to go leopard shark fishing in the evenings after work. We found the best place to catch them was the shallow, sandy flats just off the swimming beaches. They moved in after most of the people left to forage for food as the tide came in. We used to let them bite our fingers, just for fun. They really don't have teeth, just hard, rasp-like gums that could do some damage if you aren't careful. They are great eating and lots of fun to catch but hardly a threat to anyone.

Fishing the flats is one of the more relaxing ways to fish. Party boats often travel to the more productive areas to fish, but just about anyone with an outboard skiff can enjoy the bounty of the flats. Fishing the flats is not dissimilar to fishing lakes, so displaced freshwater fishermen might find sand and mudflat fishing the easiest form of saltwater fishing to master.

If you look at a chart of your area, you'll see lots of flat areas indicated by widely spaced depth lines and marked with legends such as Gmd, Bmd, and Sdy. These stand for Green Mud, Brown Mud, and Sandy, respectively. The fishable depths can range from 6 feet to nearly a thousand feet—all produce fishing action.

Fishing the flats is almost exclusively a baitfishing proposition. There are some lures that produce but only if the lure hook is baited. I suspect this is because fish in these areas rely heavily on their sense of smell. Most of the fish are relatively slow swimmers as compared to surface fish and spend much more time poking around the bottom, swirling up clouds of silt and sand. This makes their eyes much less effective for finding food. I'm just speculating about this, but for whatever reason, bait seems to be a near necessity for catching fish in the flats.

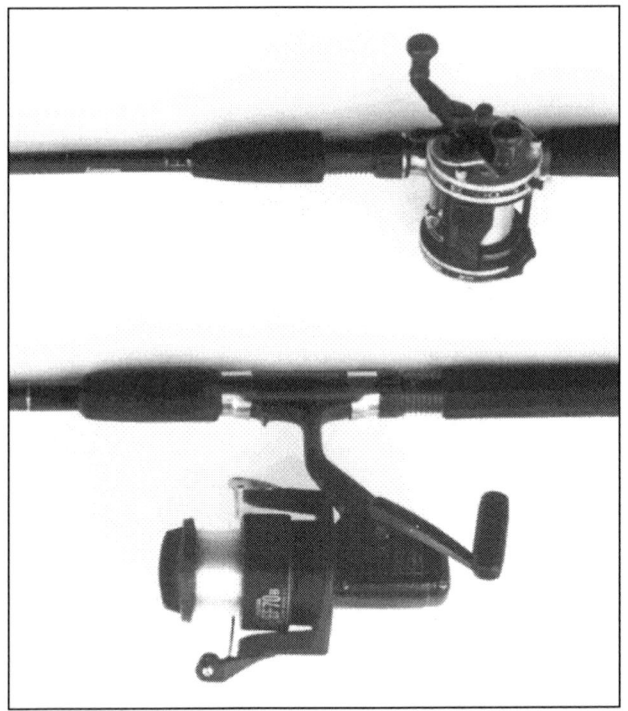

Author's rods and reels for pier, surf, and shore fishing. Top, a Berkley Lightning 7-foot graphite, heavy-action rod with Mitchell 200 reel and 10-pound test. Bottom: an 8-foot, no-name, graphite spinning rod with a Silstar EF-70 spinning reel and 15-pound test line.

Rods and Reels

For baitfishing in the flats, a typical boat rod in the 15- to 30-pound line class should be selected. There's no particular advantage in having a long rod, so rods in the 6- to 6½-foot range are most popular. Most people favor a more parabolic action, since fairly heavy weights (3 or 4 ounces) are used at times and a soft sensitive tip only makes setting the hook more difficult. These rods are inexpensive by saltwater tackle standards, ranging from $10 to $100. Calstar's 6460 or 6465 blank has been used as the base to build many effective custom rods for this use. All saltwater rod manufacturers make suitable rods for flats fishing.

Any of the many traditional conventional spool reels are fine for flats fishing. A high-speed retrieve is seldom, if ever, needed so the simpler, less expensive models usually perform just fine for this type of fishing. Spinning reels are rarely used for flats fishing by experienced anglers.

Terminal Tackle and Bait

There are many popular methods for rigging up gear to fish the flats. I've tried just about every one of them and have found the Carolina rig to probably be the most used and most effective rig for baitfishing the flats. The sliding sinker allows

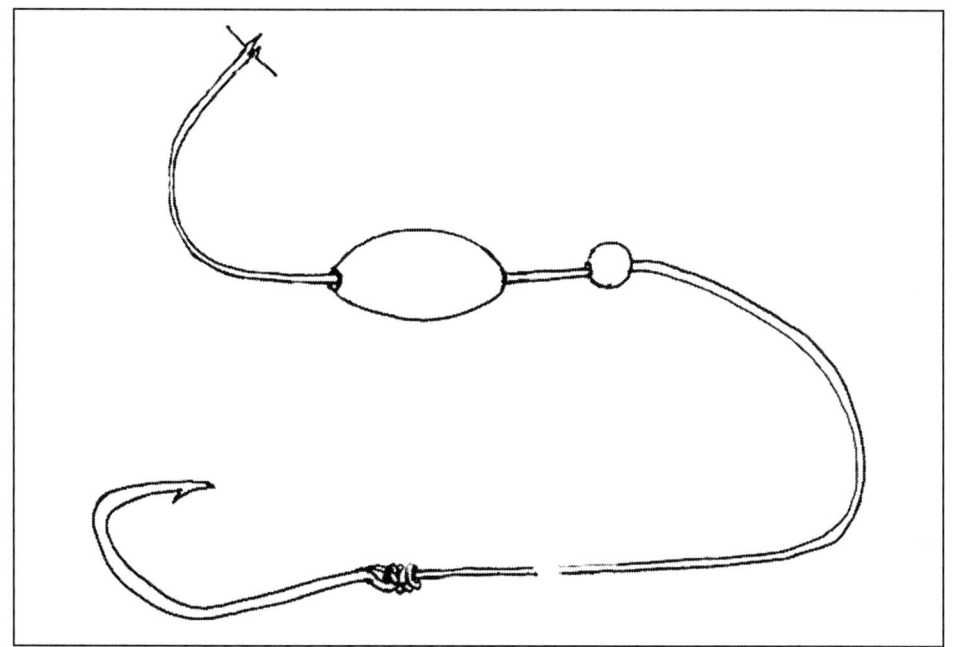

Carolina Rig.

the fish to take the bait and run with it, taking line without feeling the sinker until the angler sets the hook. Letting the fish run with the bait in its mouth is a significant way to improve your bite-to-land ratio. A swivel, split shot, or new "Carolina Keeper" bead keep the sinker away from the hook. With the hook tied in place, slide the sinker from 18 inches to 24 inches up the line and install a split shot sinker to prevent the larger egg sinker from getting close to the hook.

On occasion, especially when fishing with 2 ounces or more in a swift current, the Carolina rig doesn't work as well as a simple dropper loop for tying on torpedo-shaped sinkers. While this doesn't have the advantage of allowing the fish to run before setting the hook, it does get the hook reliably on the bottom in a swift current.

Live bait hooks should be sized according to the bait you are using. Small, mid-summer "pinhead" anchovies call for a hook as small as #4 or even #6, while larger anchovies call for #2. Preferred hook size for small sardines is #2/0 and #3/0 for larger sardines and squid. Whole, head-on shrimp call for hooks as large as #5/0, while squid heads are best fished with a #2/0. Dark-finished live bait hooks seem to work better in the flats than the shiny, chrome-plated ones.

Some fishermen use treble hooks when chasing halibut and sole. These fish have somewhat soft mouths, so you can pull a hook out of the fish's mouth if you have a heavy hand. If you find yourself losing fish, switching to #4 or #6 treble hooks will usually get them aboard.

For bait, just about anything can be used. Anchovies are one of the favorites, with live ones the best, but frozen or salted work also. Clam or mussel strips work well. Squid is an excellent bait, live or dead, whole, or cut in strips. Sometimes squid heads with the tentacles work the best, especially for sculpin and cabezon.

To fish the flats, just find a flat area—no chore for even the most novice navigator—and shut the boat off to drift. Bait the hooks and drop them to the bottom. Fish with the reel declutched so that the fish can take line. Just as surface fish do, fish in the flats tend to grab the bait and run before eating it, so give the fish line for a few seconds before setting the hook.

One of the secrets of fishing the flats is to keep the bait moving. I don't mean wiggling, since many of these fish are used to eating dead or unmoving food, I mean covering ground. Many flats fish aren't actively swimming around looking for food; most merely squat in one place and wait for food to come by. If you anchor the boat, drop a line in, and don't move it, the bait could be inches from the tail of a huge halibut and it would never see it. On the other hand, if a boat is slowly drifting, the bait is dragging along the bottom for a few feet, then stopped for a minute or so, then moved, etc., every fish in the area would quickly become aware of it. Some will come to investigate, and one will surely bite it.

This technique is easily performed with the thumb on the reel spool. With the reel declutched, put your thumb on the spool and pull the bait along for a few feet, staying alert for a strike. Then let it sit with all the slack out of the line for a minute or two. You may have to let line out if the boat is drifting along. Then, pull the line ahead again. If you get a strike, let the fish take line for three seconds or so, then set the hook. If you feel the fish hit when pulling the line forward, as they often do, immediately release pressure on the spool to let the fish take line. Keep your thumb slightly on the spool to prevent a backlash. As long as you keep the bait moving, you'll soon be landing a lot of different types of fish.

Some lures also work well in the flats, the most notable being the rubbery shrimp-tail swim baits. The single-tailed, shad shaped swimbaits in the 4 to 6 inch range are the most popular. These have thin, soft, silicone rubber tails attached to a lead-headed single hook. They work best baited with strips of squid or full squid heads. The colors that produce very well when drifted over the bottom include shad (blue and silver), sardine (green and yellow), and brown (brown and gold). The twin-tailed scampi or mojo rubber baits that were used in the past still perform well, though most fishermen have abandoned their use for the single-tailed (probably because they're "in"). Green sparkle and root-beer-colored twin-tailed baits seem to be the best in the flats.

To fish with swim baits, tie the lure directly on the line, bait up the hook with a long, thin strip of squid or a squid head, and drop it to the bottom. Once on, lift the jig and pull it forward a short way, then let it settle back to the bottom. Lift, pull, and settle, lift, pull, and settle: that's the sure way to catch them. I've hooked an incredible number of different types of fish with this technique and these lures.

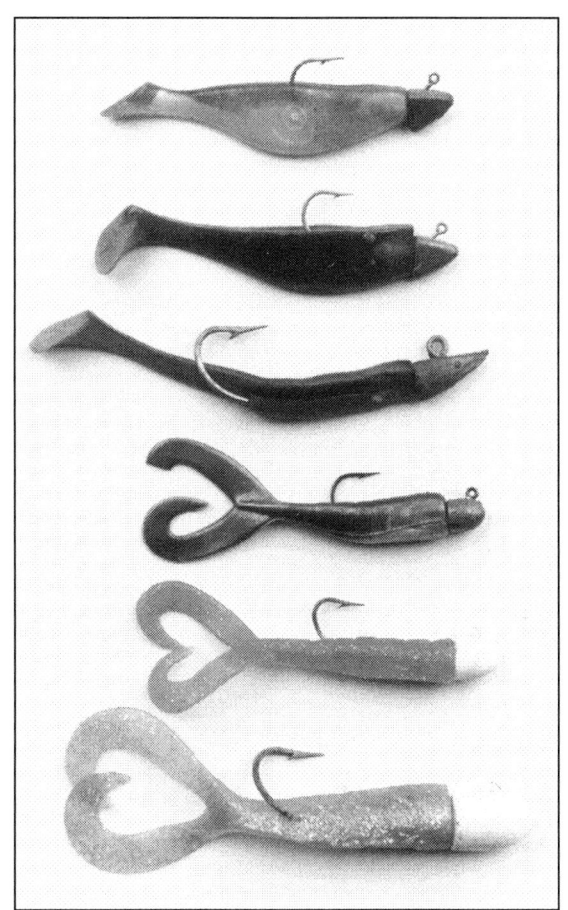

Rubber swimbaits come in a wide variety of shapes, sizes, colors, and head styles.

Fly Patterns for the Flats

On a conventional light tackle rod and reel arrangement along with a Carolina rig and sinker, you can tie on a shrimp fly and have extremely good luck. I may be one of the very few people in the area who have experimented much with this. When I've tried it, even when I was the only one catching fish, I was the only angler using anything even resembling flies. I discovered this technique quite by accident. A group of friends and I were fishing on a charter boat near Anacapa Island for deep-water rockfish. The currents were fairly strong that day, and we were drifting fairly rapidly. We were using standard (for fanatical deep-water rock fisherman) rock fishing gear with six or eight 5/0 bucktail shrimp flies on long gangions and 3 to 4 pounds of lead to keep the gear on the rock pile. Every time we drifted off the pile and over the sand and mudflats, our huge rock cod flies were being snatched up by sanddabs.

This got me to thinking, so I after that trip, I tied up a bunch of 1/0-sized bucktail flies to fish the flats. The very next trip I went on, the weather turned bad so the skipper elected to stay local and fish the flats instead of heading to Catalina. Well, I pulled out those 1/0 bucktail shrimp flies and started catching flatfish and sculpin. I was the only one on the boat catching fish. On the next trip, a buddy and I went out on a half-day boat out of Redondo Beach. It was still winter, so there was no surface action. They headed to the Scattergood anchorage, where oil tankers anchor up to unload fuel for the power plant, situated right off the coast from Los Angeles International Airport. The sculpin were there in good numbers. I pulled out my shrimp flies loaded on a short, three-hook gangion and started hauling them in two or three at a time. I gave my buddy a gangion and he did likewise. We both limited out with 10 fish in an hour and a half or so, while the most anyone else had in the boat was two fish! I could have auctioned those flies off for lots of money that morning.

Ever since then, I've carried flies for the flats in my tackle box for every trip I suspect might be near the flats. Try out bucktails baited with squid, anchovies or clam strips. I have found strips of cut squid about 3/8-inch wide and as long as I can cut them to be the most productive. Green and red bucktail flies really get their attention, but don't forget yellow, purple, orange, blue, and combinations of colors. You never know what color the fish will like until you try them all out every time.

To fish with bucktail flies, tie up a three-hook gangion with flies. Use a 2- or 3-ounce sinker on the bottom of the gangion depending on the depth, current, and winds. Try a rubber twist-on sinker, about one-half ounce, or so just above the gangion. Cast the works out as far as you can, then use the same technique as you'd use when fishing with a Mojo. The smaller weight on top makes the gangion lay down on the bottom. When you move it, it will swirl up a little mud. When the fish see that mud swirling and the flies dancing, they're all but in the bag.

Once you master the flats, you'll want to go back for more. It's a relaxing, productive place to fish, and most of the species are great to eat.

ROCK FISHING

From the Oregon border to Mexico, from the coldest February to the hottest August, one type of ocean fishing is always good—rock fishing. Rockfish are found everywhere on the California coast, easily within the range of any small boat capable of being on the ocean. Rockfish are also one of the finer eating fish of California. The firm white meat is ideal for many excellent seafood recipes. The low oil, mild taste of rockfish is acceptable to just about every picky fish eater.

You may not think you've ever had rockfish, but most likely you have eaten lots more than you think. Ever had fresh Western red snapper in a restaurant? If not, how about fish and chips in a seacoast town? If so, you've eaten rockfish.

Rockfish are sometimes called red snapper or rock cod by many California fishermen. What they are referring to is a wide variety of deep- and shallow-water, bottom-feeding fish, generally red, orange, or pink in color. The chapter on fish species covers only the most common fish in southern California. These will give you an idea of just some of the huge variety of fish just off the coast waiting to be caught.

Many fishermen consider rock fishing just something to do in the off-season. Still others refuse to fish for rockfish, saying they'd rather buy fish in the market than fish for those ugly things. For a whole group of anglers, however, rock fishing is the most fun, most challenging, most consistent fishing they could ever do.

There's one thing that can be said for rock fishing: It's a rare, rare day anyone gets skunked, because these fish are plentiful. The skill is in catching big ones and in consistently catching quality species.

Rockfish are found in areas (you guessed it) with rocks on the bottom. Anywhere with a rough, rocky bottom profile has an abundance of rockfish. One of the reasons rockfish are so plentiful is because commercial trawler boats, dragging wide nets across the bottom, can't pull their nets through rocky areas because their big, expensive nets would be damaged or lost if they tried. Perhaps in the past, rockfish were also found over muddy or sandy bottoms, but these days, underwater rocky crags are a safe haven for rockfish.

A quick glance at a nautical chart shows dozens of rocky bottom areas near any port on the California coast. Rocky bottom areas are marked with a small "Rky" legend on the charts. Just locate these spots and you've found a rockfish hole.

A charting-type or video-type bottom meter is very helpful in locating rough bottoms. Once you've found the area, slowly survey the rocky area looking for schools of fish over the rocks. It won't take long to spot schools. Rockfish always seem to be hungry and show up in clouds over the bottom on a typical bottom meter.

Rock fishing can be roughly broken down into two categories. The first is shallow-water rock fishing and includes fishing from near the surface down to about 50 fathoms (300 feet). The second is deep-water rock fishing, usually 100 to 200 fathoms deep (600 to 1200 feet!), although fishing much deeper than about 150 fathoms (900 feet) is much more work than most fishermen care to do.

Shallow-water Rock Fishing

A lot of fishermen put down shallow-water rock fishing, thinking it's just for sissies. They insist all of the quality fish are deep. Well let those deep-water snobs keep fishing deep, because the shallow-water rocks are just the ticket for an afternoon of fishing action and fun.

There are a huge variety of fish found in the shallow-water rocks. Just about every time I go, I see a new type. There are treefish that you'd swear are wearing red lipstick and a bumblebee black and yellow striped Halloween costume, big black and red sheephead with huge dog-like teeth, bright blue rock cod, and dozens of others that are both fun to catch and good to eat.

Shallow-water rock fishing doesn't take exotic tackle, long-range boats, specialized lures and jigs, or much skill for that matter. It's great for the new fisherman just getting started in the ocean or the freshwater fisherman wanting to try out the sea.

Southern California's rock fishing action is usually for sculpin, cabezon, starry rockfish, barberpole snapper, treefish, sheephead, boccacio, chilipeppers, and whitefish. There's even a species of rock sole that's an excellent eating flatfish.

Rods and Reels

For rock fishing in very shallow water, use the same gear that is used for flats fishing. I see fishermen using everything from jig sticks to tuna sticks. The poles that just about every landing rents for a couple of bucks work just fine. Often, shorter boat-type rods with 15- to 30-pound test are common. For deeper water or bigger fish, a stiffer, 40-pound test rod is needed. A shorter rod is often handiest and easiest on the back when it comes to cranking gear up off the bottom.

For lighter, shallow work, a typical flats-type fishing reel is fine. In fact, most fishermen use their flats tackle for the shallow rocks. For deeper water, in the 300-foot range, a 4/0-sized reel is necessary.

My favorite shallow-water rock and reef gear, especially in the winter when the possibility of hauling in a bigger lingcod is pretty good, is the same rod and reel I use for local, shallow-water trolling. It is a 5-foot 6-inch heavy, parabolic trolling rod with a Penn 4/0 Special high speed Senator equipped with a Tiburon frame and spooled with 40-pound test monofilament. With it, I have had no trouble cranking up a 40-pound lingcod from wrecks or reefs at times when allowing the fish to run into a hole or cave would have meant a lost fish and broken line.

Terminal Tackle, Fly Patterns, and Bait

For terminal tackle, weights from 4 ounces to a pound are generally used attached to simple bait gangions or shrimp fly gangions. You can fish with anywhere from 1 to 10 hooks on the gangions with ease. Swivels on the top and the bottom of gangions keep the works from getting balled up. If you have more than four or five hooks, an intermediate swivel is helpful on the gangion line.

Lighter gangions, normally three-hooked, are the most useful for shallow-water rocks—30-pound test main lines work well. On each gangion station, you have a choice of a smaller bucktail shrimp fly or a bare hook to be baited with live or cut bait. Hooks in the #2 to 5/0 range can be used, depending on the type of bait used. The shrimp flies for this type of fishing mirror the deep-water rock cod "magic buck-tails," except they're scaled down to a 1/0-long shank hook size.

When chasing bigger lingcod, especially in the reefs and wrecks in the early winter, a special arrangement using live mackerel is the secret to catching these brutes. The illustration shows how a double-hook rig can be used to make sure you hook up the fish no matter which end of the bait it elects to grab.

Rockfish aren't too picky about what size hooks they'll take. Just about any bait-hooks work well, from 2/0 size to over 8/0. To really do well in most places, a smaller and less obvious hook is better for enticing rockfish to bite. Shrimp flies on 1/0 to 4/0 hooks baited with strips of squid work well. Whole, salted anchovies on 4/0, 5/0,

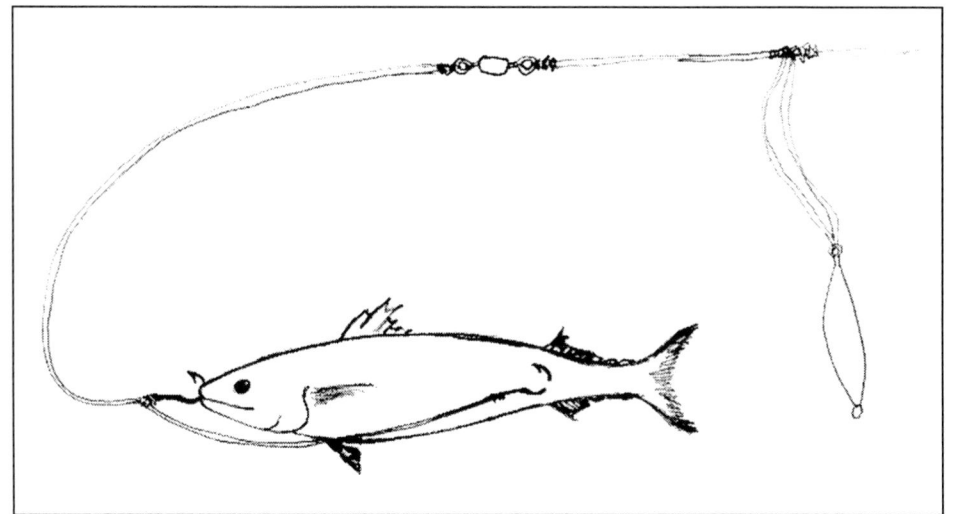

A double-hook rig using live mackerel for chasing lingcod.

or 6/0 long shank hooks, depending on the size of the bait, seem to be about right. Whole squid or squid heads on 5/0, 6/0, or 7/0 hooks usually get the big ones, too.

Be sure to use a breakaway link between the sinker and the gangion in case the weight gets stuck in a rock. Usually, a line is used with about half of the breaking strength of the gangion line, and the main line is used to attach the weight. This allows you to break the sinker free, and thus, not lose the fish. The diagram shows a typical setup for fishing shallow-water rocks.

For bait, just about anything can be used. Salted anchovies, squid strips, mussels, clam strips, and salted mackerel strips all work fine and bring in lots of fish. To fish, simply bait up the gangion, toss it in and let it drop to the bottom. Once you're sure it's on, crank it up a foot or so to keep yourself from getting hooked on real estate and wait for the fish to bite. Nothing could be easier or more relaxing.

Since most of these fish aren't large, you don't have to be much of an expert at landing them. Just don't be in a huge hurry—there's no race to get the fish in. Once it's hooked, it won't come off the hook as long as you keep even tension on the line. People sometimes get excited about catching fish and end up cranking on the reel for all they're worth. Hunters call this "Buck Fever." This seems inappropriate for fishing, so let's invent a new term, and just call it "Jackpot Fever." It's more likely that you will lose many more fish by pulling them in too fast than you would pulling them in too slowly. Take your time and you'll fill up your bag.

Even though I run with the "real men fish deep" gang of rock fishermen, I hesitatingly admit that on some afternoons I'd just as soon kick back with my bait stick

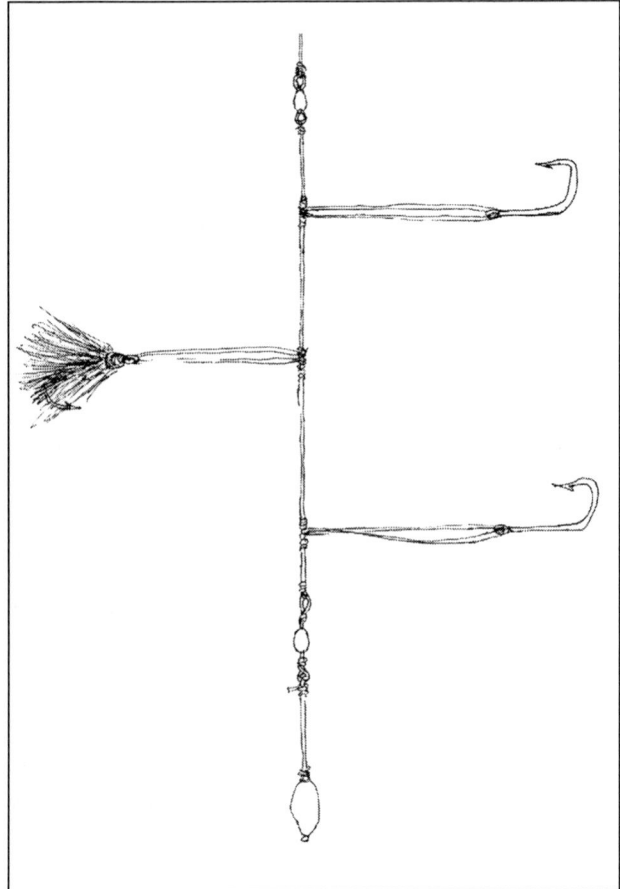

*A typical shallow-
water gangion*

and a six-pack for some relaxing shallow-water rock fishing. It always reminds me
why I'm out there—to enjoy the sun and sea and relax.

Fishing the Rocks from Shore

In many areas, prime shallow-water rock fishing areas are within casting distance of the shore. I even know a location in central California where it's possible to
fish for deep-water rockfish in 400 to 600 feet of water, from shore! Look for rocky
points and deeper areas between offshore rocks. The Palos Verdes peninsula and
Point Mugu are two of the many excellent areas where this kind of fishing is productive. Here, you'll be able to cast out a baited shrimp fly right into a reef teeming
with life. Use traditional shallow-water rock fishing methods for best results.

Deep Water Rock Fishing

Important Note: In 2001, new laws to protect Cow Cod, and other deep-water rockfish were put into effect. This has essentially closed deep-water rock codding in Southern California. These fishing techniques can no longer be used in California waters, however, during the winter months, boats from San Diego have been fishing Mexican waters for deep water rock cod, where these techniques are still legal and allowed, so long as the angler and boat has the appropriate Mexican fishing licenses.

The tackle is big and heavy, the reel cranking strenuous, and after a good, productive day, you feel like you've just moved a houseful of furniture. Deep water rock fishing has its rewards, though. Bringing up a limit of reds, cows, and boscos means enough fish to eat for weeks. It's delicious eating, too. You can sashimi it, fry it, sauté it, bake it, broil it, poach it, make it into soup or cioppino—just about anything you can do with fish, you can do with deep-water rockfish.

My commercial fishing career started off on a rockcod boat out of San Diego. Since then I've crewed and skippered several other commercial rockcod boats out of central and northern California. When commercial fishing, we used 50 hooks at a time, all baited, and dropped them deep, usually 100 fathoms (600 feet) with 10-pound weights. When they'd fill up, it was backbreaking work hauling those lines in. Nothing was a more welcome sight to a commercial fisherman, though, than seeing 50-foot long gangions floating to the surface with bright red rockcod popping up on the surface. As the fish are pulled up from so deep, their swim bladders swell up enough to make the fish float and even lift the 10-pound weight.

Finding spots like that requires extensive knowledge of the various fishing areas. Most of the spots capable of producing that well are a long, long way from any port. It's not the kind of place you can easily sport fish. Sportfishing in the deep rocks usually means going to a well-fished spot and working it with the tackle and techniques that commercial hook-and-line guys can't afford to mess with.

Fly and Bait Fishing the Deep Rocks

While about as far different as any two techniques could possibly be, deep-water rock codding is really flyfishing. I know of no combinations of traditional flyfishing gear that can reach down into 600 to 900 feet of water and present a fly to the inhabitants of deep, rocky reefs, so very specialized gear has been developed to pursue this interesting sport.

Rods and Reels

Rods for deep-water fly and baitfishing are very specialized. They're generally huge, 9- to 12-feet long and stiff, sometimes 1¼ inch in diameter at the butt and 3/8 inches at the tip. They are often made from gaff blanks—fiberglass poles intended for use as gaff handles rather than for use as fishing poles. The rods have either all roller guides or roller stripper and tip with intermediate guides and hard ceramic inserts. Most rod makers shun the use of handles and reel seats and simply wind the handle and reel seat area with cord, sometimes adorning their work with Turk's head knots and other ornamental marlinspike handiwork.

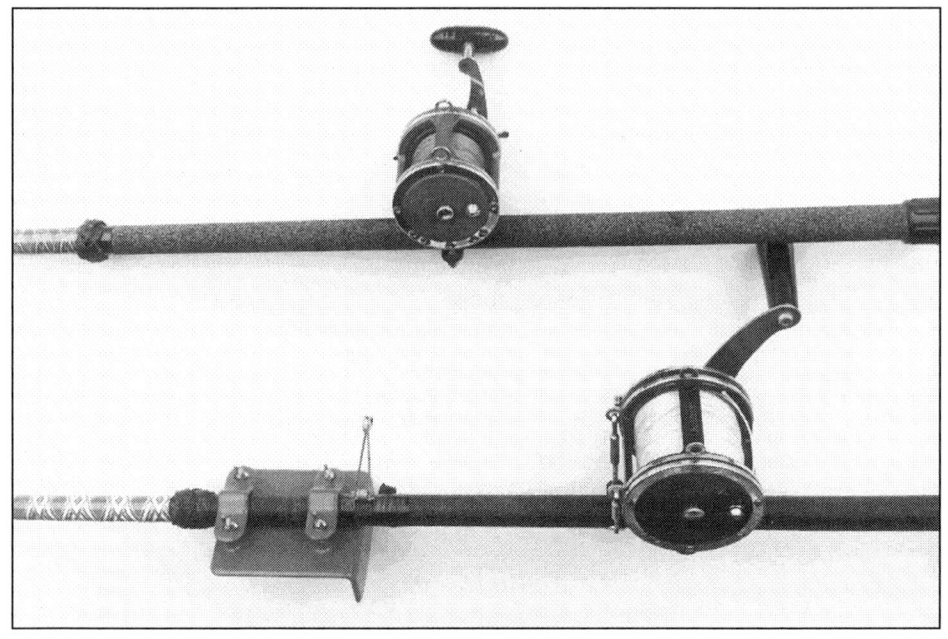

Author's deep-water rock codding gear:
Top: a custom-wrapped Calstar T-90, 9-foot heavy jig rod wearing a Tiburon-
framed Penn 113H 4/0 size, high-speed Senator filled with 50-pound Spectra
super braid line (that's a lotta line!);
Bottom: Gangion fishing rod, a custom-wrapped Saber 9-foot gaff blank with an
Accurate-framed Penn 114 9/0 Senator and extended cranking handle filled with
80-pound test Dacron line. Note the rail plate and line level winder.

For reels, the bigger, the better is the rule. A few people use reels as small as 6/0 with 60-pound test line, but the majority use 9/0 spooled with 80-pound test, and some even use 12/0 reels! Aftermarket extended handles are almost a must, since the short, factory-installed handles make it painful to bring in one drop from deep water. The perfect combination is a Penn 9/0 Senator with an extended handle and an Accurate aftermarket frame to maximize the reel stiffness.

Dacron line is a must. Monofilament line, while very useful on the surface, is far too stretchy for real deep-water use. The preferred line for most deep-water fly and baitfishing is 80-pound test. Some people use 100-pound test, but a 9/0 reel doesn't hold quite enough for some deep use, especially when it's a bit windy or the drift is high. A good friend of mine uses a 12/0 reel with one-quarter pound of 130-pound test on the reel first, with one-quarter pound spool of 80-pound test on top. He claims to have fished in 1100 feet of water fairly easily with this rig. For a 6/0-sized reel, 60-pound test line is best to get enough line on the reel to reach down into cowcod country.

There are two important extras needed for successful rock cod fishing. The first is a rail plate attached just ahead of the foregrip of the rod. These rods are heavy by themselves, and once you add the weight of a 4-pound sinker, 900 feet of wet Dacron line, and a gangion load of fish, not even Arnold Schwartzenegger would be strong enough to hold it up all day. The rail plate allows you to balance the rod on the rail of the boat while fishing and cranking up. The second feature, especially useful to those of us who spend most of our lives sitting in an office, is a line guide. This handy gadget allows an angler to level-wind the line onto the reel without touching the line. Wet Dacron line is abrasive and has no trouble slicing through skin. Unless your hands are pretty tough, you'll lose plenty of skin after a day of deep-water rock codding.

Terminal Tackle, Flies, and Bait

For fly or baitfishing deep down, a rock cod gangion is needed. While you can buy rock cod rigs at any tackle store, it is better to tie your own. This allows the judicious use of swivels in the gangion to keep it from getting all balled up once a couple of fish get on and start struggling to get free. Anywhere from 3 to 10 hooks can be used on the gangion—the most common is probably 5 or 6.

Store-bought gangions use a dropper loop for each hook, but tying flies or hooks with special extra stiff leader materials improves the performance of the flies. The diagram on page 76 shows my favorite arrangement using three-way swivels tied with 80-pound test monofilament. The flies or bait hooks are attached with hard leader material, and the sinker is attached with 30-pound test mono as a weak link— I'd rather lose a sinker than a gangion full of fish.

An important thing to remember when tying up the gangion is to make sure the branch loops are at least 3 or 4 inches long. If not, some bigger fish will feel the main line and won't hit. Also, make sure the hooks are spaced enough that they don't touch each other when you pull the lower one up and the upper one down. If not, they'll tangle too often.

The photos on the following pages show how to tie the Magic Bucktail flies out of marabou feathers, bucktail hair, and rooster neck feathers.

On some gangion stations, a bare hook can be substituted and the hook baited. In the past, the classic method was to use a 7/0 long shank hook and bait it with a salted, dead anchovy. While this method has caught many fish, nowadays the fish tend to be pickier and aren't fooled as easily. A 16/0 or 12/0 circle hook is the modern method. These tend to set themselves, so an angler doesn't need to make a strong "jerk" to keep a fish on the line. For bait, use a whole squid, squid head, or even a fillet of a smaller rock cod with the skin and tail attached.

When I fished commercially, anchovies were the best bait; squid and mackerel strips just didn't produce. Of course, we were using 7/0 and 8/0 bare hooks. I thought I had deep-water rock fishing down cold. I experimented some when I was a skipper but always came back to salted anchovies as the best producer. This was a number

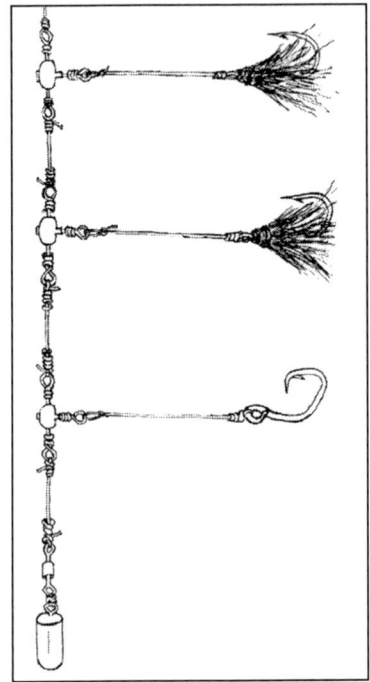

Deep-water
rock cod gangion.

Author's award-winning
deep-water rock cod
"Magic Bucktail" shrimp
flies tied on 4/0 hooks.

TYING THE "MAGIC BUCKTAIL"

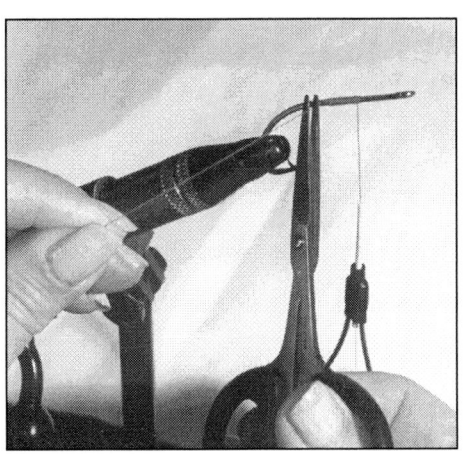

Step 1:
Begin with an underwrap of
"A" nylon thread in about the center
of a 5/0 stainless steel fly tying hook.

Step 2:
Add the first layer of maribou,
the tips of two feathers.

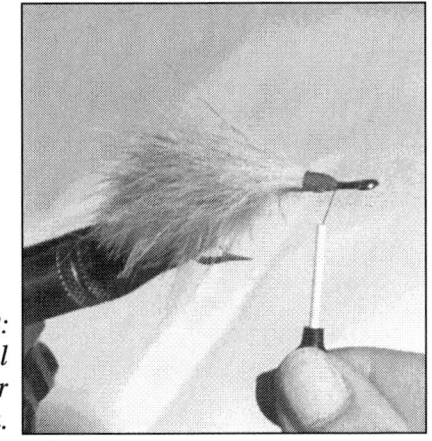

Step 3:
The first layer of bucktail material
should be approximately the same color
as the maribou.

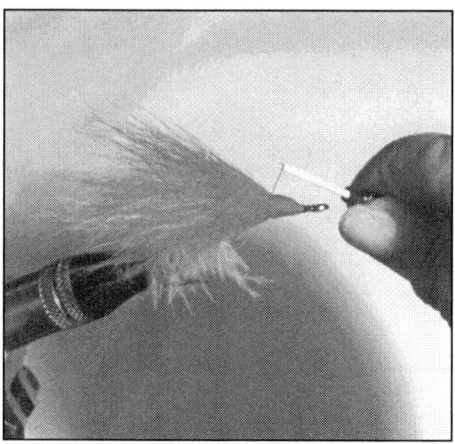

TYING THE "MAGIC BUCKTAIL"(CONT.)

Step 4:
The main fly color goes on next.

Step 5:
Finish with a darker color
(in this case, black).

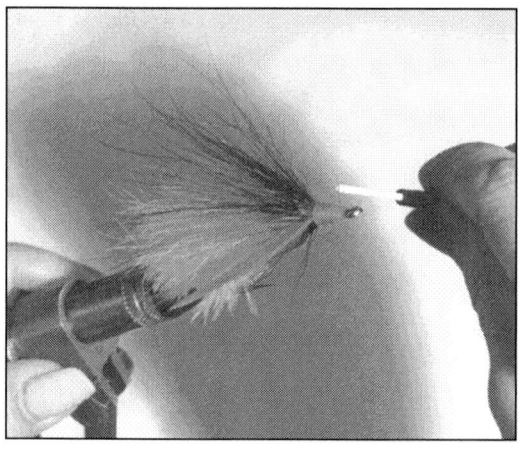

Step 6:
Add the rooster feather "pectorals".

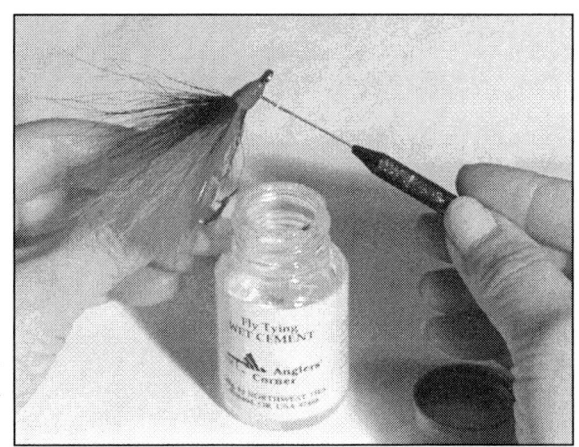

Step 7:
Finish the head off with wet
cement. Note the bullet shape.

The finished fly, ready to catch
a deep water rockfish.

of years ago, and I didn't really do much more deep-water rock fishing until a few years ago when I met a group of hard-core sport rockcodders.

These fellows introduced me to a deep-water fishing fly they called the "magic bucktail." They even taught me how to tie them. I started out making them just as they had shown me, but over the last few years, I've refined this fly even more and now use marabou, bucktail, and cock feathers to make an improved version—one that has since won fly tying awards. These flies can't be bought anywhere—I've never even seen anything close. One thing I do know is that they catch more fish than you'll believe is possible. Even on slow days, these will fill your gangions. Tie them on stainless steel fly tying hooks in 4/0 or 5/0.

Not only is the size, shape, and winding technique vital, the colors are important. Green colors seem to attract chilipeppers and blues. Bright reds and oranges get sucked up by boccacios. Darker purples, browns, and Indian red colored flies seem to find favor with reds and boscos. Here's a secret—cowcod go mad over blue and white flies with black hairs on top.

If you make up some of these flies and try them, attach them to the gangion loops just as you would bare hooks. Bait them with long, thin strips of cut squid, about 3/8 to 1/2 inch wide and as long as you can cut. I sometimes cut a slit in the bait so it looks like two thin tails; the diagram shows this arrangement. For weights, a 3- or 4-pound sinker is the best bet. Make sure the sinker has a rounded or pointed bottom so that it sinks straight.

If you have your own boat, locating a deep-water school of rockfish is just like finding a school of shallow-water rockfish. Run over rough, rocky areas looking for feeding fish on the bottom meter. Once you find them, quickly determine how much and which direction the boat will drift. Go up-drift, generally but not always, upwind, enough so that the gangions will fall into the school. It takes precision underwater bombing to hit the school. Don't stop the boat directly over the fish because by the time the boat actually stops, the gear is thrown out, and the lines sink 600 or 800 feet down, the lines won't be anywhere near the fish. The key is to calculate the drift correctly in order to hit the fish.

Bucktail fly with split-tailed bait attached.

When the lines hit the bottom, you'll be able to tell if you're on the rocks or on a muddy bottom by the feel. If you feel the bottom is soft, you probably missed the rock pile. Pull up the lines and start again. If you feel the hard bottom, just wait for the strikes. One thing's for sure, if you hit the fish and you're using Magic Bucktail flies, you'll fill up the gangion pretty quickly.

One technique, especially if using bucktails, is to keep the tails moving. One reason rockcod sticks are so big is that it is easier to produce a bobbing motion to the gangion when it is down deep. If the ocean's swell is more than a foot or so, the boat bobbing up and down will help. Magic Bucktails, like any other bait, must be kept moving to really produce. Bait has to move to catch fish. If it just sits there, the fish won't find it unless it practically lands in their mouth.

It is dark and cold in 300 feet or more of water—99.8 percent of all the water in the oceans is 33°F. This explains why deep-water rock fishing is a year-round sport. The temperature, salinity, and darkness simply do not vary from winter to summer. The fish are always out there waiting to be caught—just show them moving bait. Vibrations are what it's all about for a fish.

When you're ready to haul in the gangion, give it a couple of good (6-feet or so) pulls before cranking. It's hard to jerk on 800 feet of wet 80-pound Dacron with a bunch of fish and a 3-pound sinker on the end, but if you do it once or twice, any poorly hooked fish will either get hooked better or will be pulled off the line. After hooking the fish, start the retrieve—slow, steady cranking will get the gangion up in the best shape. Remember, don't get jackpot fever when you're cranking, just keep that line coming in evenly.

JIGFISHING DEEP

Fishing with jigs catches some of the bigger fish to be found in the deep-water reefs and rock piles. Big cowcod, lingcod, and most of the other species will attack a well-presented jig. This sport is for those anglers who aren't afraid of a workout while fishing because it takes some real energy output to be a good deep-water jig fisherman.

Rods, Reels, and Line

Standard jig sticks, especially heavier ones like Calstar's 6480/H or T90, are the best choice for deep-water jigging. Some fishermen use shorter sticks since it takes a lot of work to keep that jig moving when it's 800-plus feet down, but the longer (8- to 9-foot) rod will give the jig more action and will result in more catches.

Probably the most common reel size for this kind of work is 4/0, since a considerable line capacity is needed. However, smaller reels will work with the new, high-tech, thinner lines. My personal favorite is the old Penn 349 Master Mariner reel. It has 6/0-sized sideplates with a fairly high speed retrieve but is only about 1¾ inches wide, so it's easy to level-wind the line on as you retrieve. I fill mine with 30-pound test Dacron. Others prefer the 50-pound test, "Spider Wire" type lines for low stretch and small diameter.

A good overall choice for jigfishing the bottom is 40-pound test monofilament, especially if you don't have a dedicated rockfish jigging reel. The only problem with mono is that it is somewhat stretchy. This isn't usually a problem for surface fish when you have a fairly light jig and only 100 or so yards of line out. When jigging the bottom with a heavy jig and 300 or more yards of line out, the stretch becomes significant, and it's difficult to give the jig much action. If you get hooked on jigfishing for rockfish and elect to get a reel to dedicate to this technique, load it up with 30-pound test Dacron line. Dacron won't stretch nearly as much as mono, and you'll be able to give the jig plenty of action.

Jigs and Rigs

The larger bone jig style hardware (8X and 12X) in blue and white, red and yellow, or green and yellow is commonly used and is a very effective deep-water jig. In addition, heavy kite-shaped, round bar or hex bar style jigs in chrome and iridescent reflective finishes are also effective when fished deep. Heavy spoon jigs in chrome and reflective finishes are another excellent choice and provide lots of action down deep. They'll often catch fish when nothing else will.

The illustration below shows the most popular deep-water jigfishing arrangement.

When targeting rockfish with a jigfishing setup, the terminal tackle setup is different from surface fishing. Often a teaser bucktail is used above the jig. A swivel is used on a long (6- to 8-foot) leader of 40- or 50-pound test monofilament. This isn't necessary if you're using mono on the reel but important if Dacron line is being used.

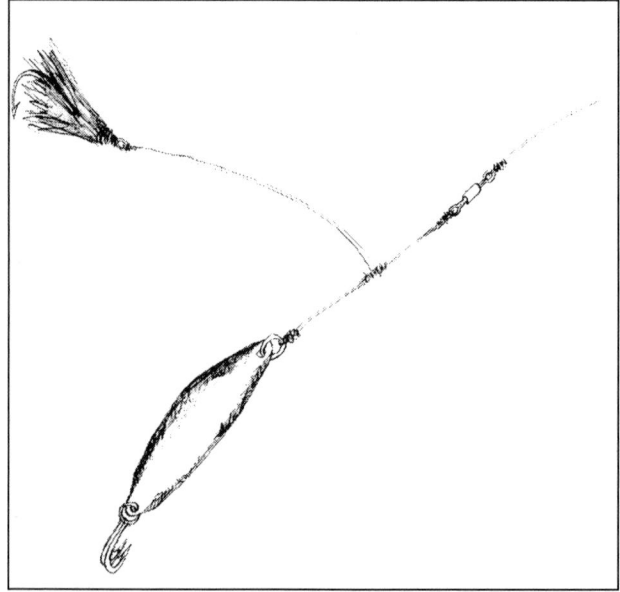

Deep-water jig set-up.

Bait can be used on both the jig and the teaser—this isn't mandatory but it helps. In my mind, the best bait is squid cut into long strips. I have a fishing buddy, though, who swears by mackerel strips. He outfishes me on this type of fishing, but I can't seem to get the same results he does with mackerel. One of these days, I'll get the secret out of him, but until then I'm sticking with squid.

On many occasions, I've caught two fish at a time using a jigging setup like this, one on the teaser and one on the jig. This is especially true if the jig gets hit first, because the struggling fish really gives the bucktail lots of action.

When the rig is tied, drop the jig and let it fall all the way to the bottom. Then reel in just enough line to pick it up a foot or so. Start jigging—jerking the jig up at least 6 feet, then relax the tension and let it flutter down. Up down, up down, up down, keep that jig bouncing. One thing about jigfishing in deep water: your arms and back will get a good workout. It's a whole lot more fun than going to the gym, though.

Periodically, let the jig fall back to the bottom to make sure you're not drifting upward. When bottom fishing, the boat just drifts. If there's even a little current and/or wind, the jig tends to drift upward and away from the bottom. Declutching every couple of minutes and letting the jig fall to the bottom will help ensure that the jig is down where the fish are.

Jigfishing for rockfish is a good way to get big fish. I've tried it from the northern California coast well into Mexico, and it seems to work great everywhere. It's a good workout for the fisherman who likes to stay active while fishing and often results in the jackpot, especially if everyone else is fishing with bait.

BIG FISH ROCK FISHING

You can bet that wherever there are rockfish, there are big rockfish. Big lingcod hang around schools of smaller rockfish. They love rough, erose bottoms with lots of caves and crevasses in which to hide. Big lings can go over 60 pounds, but ones in the 20- to 40-pound range are common. Lings occur from border to border in rocky spots on the California coastline. They can be fished year-round with no preference for season.

Most fishermen consider it just luck to latch onto a lingcod. The main reason is that they are not fishing for lings, they just happen to catch one now and again when fishing for smaller rockfish. In truth, they're not that hard to catch. On a recent trip on a southern California party boat to a very well-fished shallow-water rock fishing hole, I hooked up and landed three lings, the smallest being 28 pounds. The only other ling caught on the boat was an 8-pounder caught incidentally by a young lady fishing for smaller rockfish. Of course, I was fishing only for lings and everyone else was fishing for small rockfish.

To catch big lings, a heavy bait stick should be chosen. I use a parabolic taper, heavy, 6½-foot long bait stick with 30-pound test line. Some of my friends use jig sticks, but I find the control of a shorter stick important in that first few critical seconds after hooking into one of these monsters of the rocks.

Mackerel is the preferred bait for lingcod. They need not be alive, but they should be whole. A double hook setup works best, using 6/0 or 7/0 bait hooks. With single hooks, the bait (or half of the bait) can be pulled out of a lingcod's mouth as the fish grabs it and dashes for its home cave. If the fish succeeds in getting in its cave, you'll never pull it out but you will break the line.

Usually an 8-ounce to 1-pound sinker is adequate in all but the heaviest current and wind conditions. If using live mackerel, it's sometimes necessary to cut off the lower lobe of the bait's tail to get it to descend. A big, lively mackerel can keep an 8-ounce weight up near the surface for quite a while.

Drop the baited hook in among the rocks on the bottom and wait for the strike—it's that simple. When you get a strike, let the ling run with the bait for a couple of seconds with the reel declutched. Like surface fish, lings tend to make a quick dash after grabbing the bait. If you try to set the hook too soon, you'll jerk the bait out of its mouth. When you feel that the fish has the bait firmly, clutch in the reel and set the hook with authority.

You can't let the fish get wedged into its cave or you'll lose it. To make sure it can't run, keep the drag set fairly tight (but still less than the breaking strength of the line.) Keep even, heavy pressure on the fish and get it moving upwards. You won't need to retrieve line the first minute or so when fighting a ling. Once the fish is moving upward, use the pump and reel retrieve technique to keep constant pressure on the fish.

Lings sometimes run, especially when they're still near the bottom. If this happens, let it run only as much as needed to prevent the line from breaking. It is necessary to stop the fish from finding a nice cave to wedge itself into. Generally, once the fish is moving upward, it keeps coming with a minimum of struggle. It is a big, heavy fish, so keep alert for a possible run and keep consistent, heavy pressure on the fish.

Nothing is quite as satisfying as hauling up a big, ugly lingcod from the depths. You'll get your share of jackpots with lings and keep your freezer full of delicious fish.

SURF CASTING

Ahhhh, the southern California beaches, where oiled, bronzed teenagers with just enough on to keep from getting arrested make their almost religious daily pilgrimage. It's here at the interface between sea and land that some of the most relaxing, enjoyable fishing experiences are awaiting the casual or frequent angler.

The intertidal zone (the zone that is sometimes submerged at high tides and exposed at low tides) is an area teeming with life. Shrimps, mollusks, and other sea life congregate here as a survival mechanism, where they are safe from deep-water predators that are afraid of being stranded and from land animals afraid of being drowned. Nature has a way of adapting life to take advantage of almost every condition, and specialized predators for the intertidal zones have sprung up to feed on these creatures. On any beach, sandpiper birds can be seen scurrying out in the wake of retreating waves to grub in the sand, and then scurrying back as the next wave rolls in. Conversely, on the ocean side, specialized fish follow the waves up the beaches looking for food, only to turn back and make a run for deeper water as the wave retreats from the land.

Most of the fish feeding in the surf are croakers. They have adapted to eat small mollusks and shrimps common in the shallow-water intertidal zone. Sometimes these fish can be seen feeding in only a couple inches of water, even having their backs exposed to the air as they chase their prey.

Other types of fish find the surge and currents of the surf zone to their liking. Many of the sandflat fish (see the section on fishing the flats) come near shore to feed on the sometimes-bountiful pickings in the surf. In addition, a whole group of fish, known as surfperch, frequents this area and finds life here to their liking.

Surf fishing is very popular among saltwater anglers. For one thing, it doesn't take a boat, and many find boat fishing unpleasant. It also doesn't take much time. The early riser can run down to the beach and get in an hour of surf fishing before work or stop by after work for a few pleasant minutes in the sunset. For still others, the beach environment is a magical place where sea, sky, and sand combine to make an Eden-like setting. For whatever reason, surf fishing always has been and will continue to be a favorite pastime for many anglers.

Unlike surf fishing on the East or Gulf Coasts, surf fishing in southern California does not require specialized surf casting rods and reels. This is because the West Coast has a far faster dropoff than the East Coast. One never hears about a continental shelf in the Pacific. There are areas 200 fathoms deep (1200 feet) within 100 yards of the coast in some parts of California, whereas on most of the Atlantic Coast, you have to go out many miles to find water deeper than 100 feet or so. Fish on the West Coast feed in the breaking surf or closer, which is rarely more than 50 yards or so from dry beach. I've caught fish literally at my feet while standing in water about halfway between my ankles and knees.

Flyfishing the Surf

Flyfishing in the surf is a productive, enjoyable technique that local fishermen have only recently employed as a viable fishing method. My guess is that it was discovered accidentally. The beach is an excellent place to practice flycasting. There's water nearby, lots of open space to prevent an errant line or hook getting hung up in a bush or tree, and the soft sand is much friendlier on lines and tippets than the hard asphalt of a parking lot. Imagine the surprise when a local angler came out to test his new 5-weight trout rod on the beach and hooked up a spotfin croaker!

Now the river mouths and stream outlets are the most popular places for surf flyfishermen to ply their sport. Whether this is more or less productive than the open beaches is anyone's guess. Some swear by it, others feel it's just easier to cast crosswind than into the breeze that commonly blows onshore at the beaches. The wide-open beaches are prime territory for fishing, though, and you shouldn't pass up a beach just because there isn't any structure there.

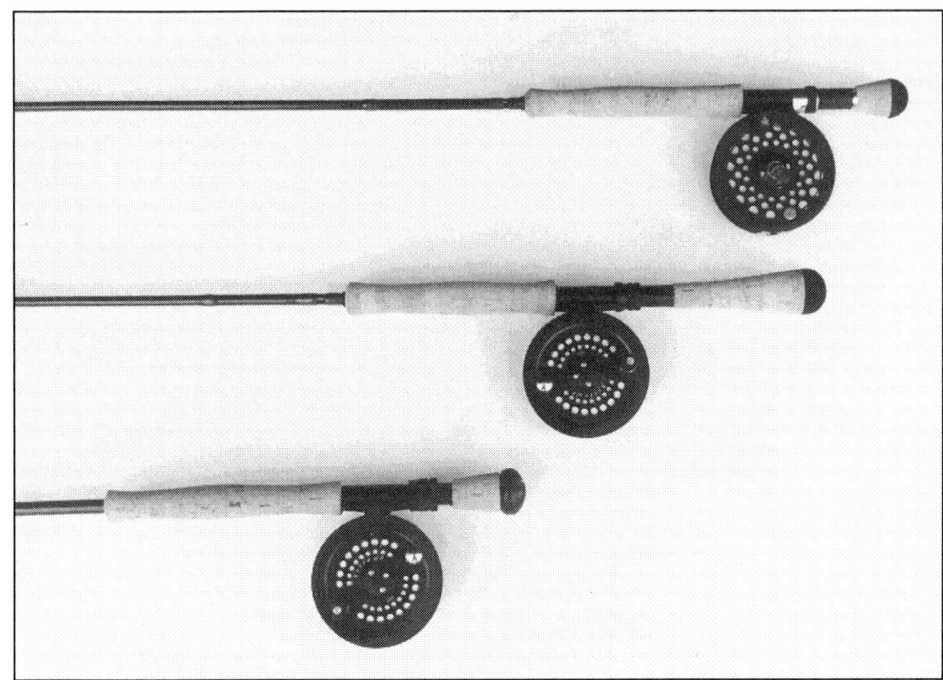

Author's flyfishing rigs for southern Califormia (top to bottom): a 9-weight Pflueger graphite rod with STH reel for light use; a 10-weight Pflueger graphite rod with Scientific Anglers System 2 1213 reel; and a 12-weight Sage graphite rod with Scientific Anglers System 2 1213 reel. All three have as much backing as possible (at least 400 pounds) and shooting head, fast-sinking lines.

Rods, Reels, and Line

Probably the best overall fly rod for the surf is an 8-weight. A 10 can be used, particularly if you plan on using the rod when fishing kelp beds from a boat, as well. An ocean-type reel with an anti-reverse and an adjustable disc drag is almost a must. There is a good possibility of hooking a pretty large, tenacious fish, such as a leopard shark or halibut, so spend the extra money and get one of the better aluminum bar stock-type reels.

A weight-forward sinking line is a good choice, but an even better one is a shooting head. You can cast it farther, it sinks faster, and is less affected by breaking waves. A floating line is next to useless in the surf since waves will ball it up into a tangled mess. Although you could use a floating line when fishing a short way upriver, where there isn't any surf and fish are busting the surface for food, this is more like freshwater fishing, which is beyond the scope of this book.

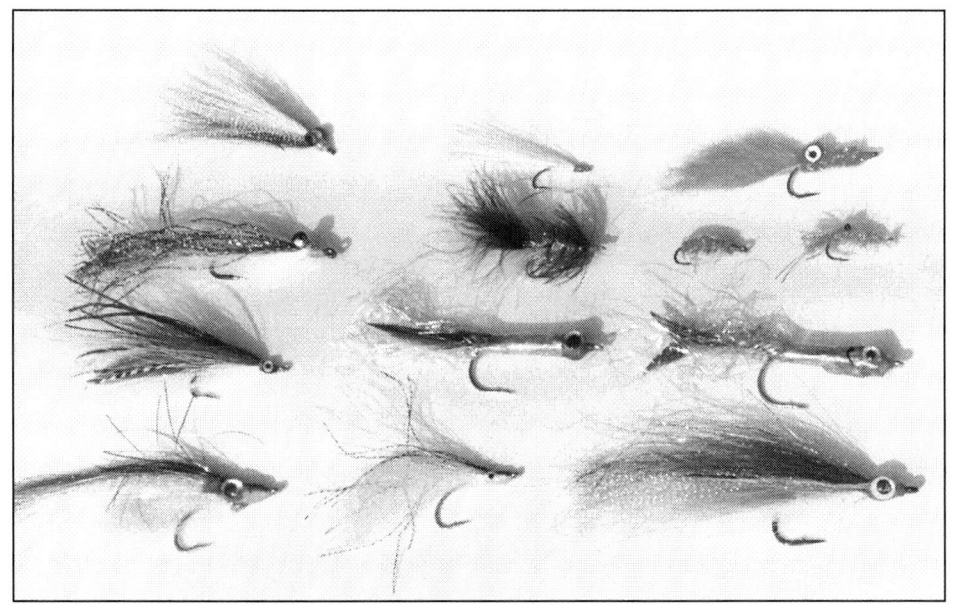

Saltwater fishing flies for southern California (left to right):
Row 1: Clouser minnow for bay use, mackerel magic, squid;
Row 2: Clouser minnow for offshore use, salt bugger, sand crab, shrimp;
Row 3: Deceiver, saltwater epoxy fly, Mosca Espanol;
Row 4: Alf, bonito magic, epoxy whistler.

For a tippet, most saltwater fishermen abandon the delicately tapered trout leaders in favor of 10 feet of a standard mono leader. Most successful fishermen seem to prefer 4- to 10-pound test, with 6-pound being the favorite.

Fly Patterns

Fish venturing into the surf are looking for sand creatures being churned up by the high tide. These include ghost shrimp bloodworms and clam siphons (the little neck that sticks out of the sand that the clam uses to draw in and expel water.) Any fly that simulates these food items is a wise choice in the surf. A green woolly bugger does a moderately good job at simulating a small bloodworm and should get inhaled quickly, especially by surfperch. Also, any shrimp or crawfish-imitating fly will be taken as a ghost shrimp and snapped at eagerly by croakers and other feeders in the surf zone.

Fishing the Surf with Bait and Lure

Rods and Reels

There is a wide choice of rods and reels available for surf fishing. Ideally, the line weight class should be from about 8-pound test to a maximum of 20-pound line. Generally 10-, 12-, or 15-pound test is the ideal range. In a conventional reel arrangement, 10- or 12-pound test line on a heavy freshwater baitcasting reel, such as that used for bass fishing, coupled with a long (7- or 8-foot), medium to heavy graphite rod is about ideal. In fact, a good freshwater bass fishing setup is just about perfect for the surf fisherman with a preference for conventional tackle.

There is much debate as to the merits of spinning vs. conventional reels for surf fishing, and I don't really want to enter into the discussion here. The truth is that the fish just don't care what you're using. You'll get just as many hits on the same

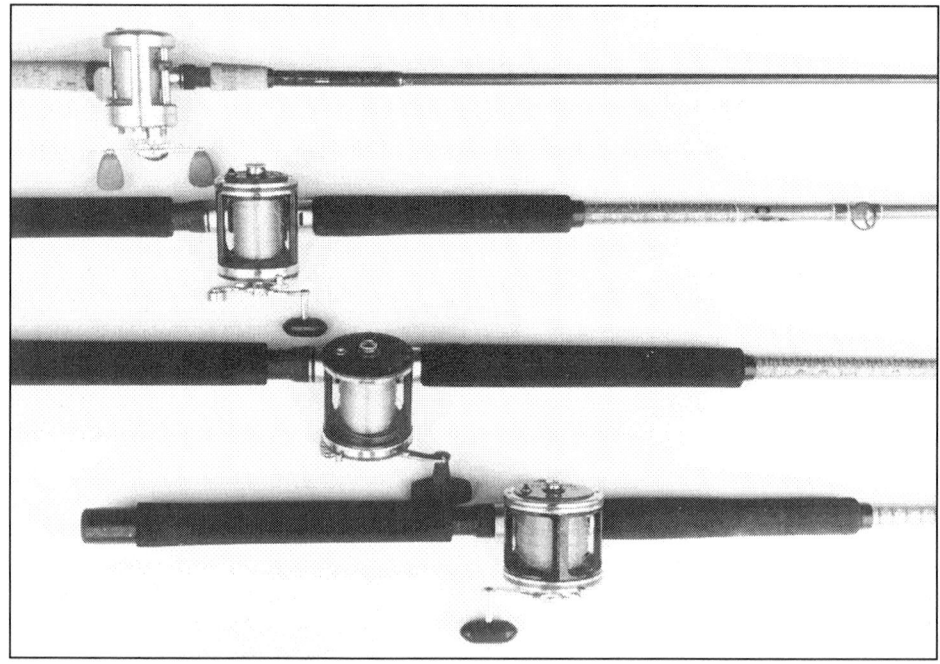

Author's arsenal for kelp, flats, and shallow reef fishing (top to bottom): An All Star 7-foot "Flipping Stick" with a Banax Sounion reel wound with 10-pound test mono for light bait fishing; a custom wrapped Calstar 270 with a Tiburon framed Penn 140 Squidder and 15-pound test for all-around bait fishing; a custom wrapped Calstar 270/8-H rod with Tiburon framed Penn 500 Jigmaster wound with 25-pound test mono for pitching jigs; custom wrapped Calstar 6465 with an Accurate framed Penn 112H 3/0 High Speed Senator wound with 30-pound test mono for heavier flats, bottom, and shallow-water rock fishing.

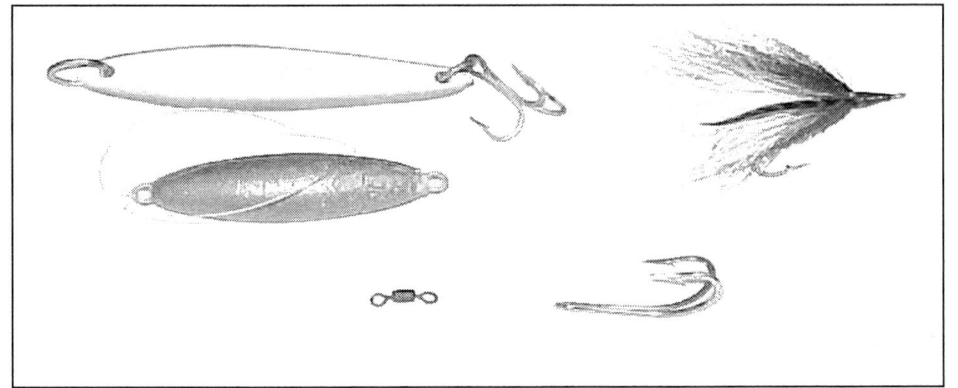

A collection of useful terminal tackle for southern California.

leader/hook/bait combination when fishing with a spinning reel as you will with a conventional one, so pick the one you're more comfortable with and use it. Light saltwater spinning reels coupled with medium to long (7 to 9 feet) matched rods seem to do fine. Most anglers who use spinning tackle use slightly heavier lines, with 12-, 15-, and 17-pound test being the popular range.

Terminal Tackle

The classic surf fishing terminal tackle for baitfishing, a light leader, usually 6-pound, is tied to a swivel, and the main line from the reel attaches to the other end of the swivel. A dropper loop is then tied in the main line to attach the sinker. A somewhat small (#4 or so) bait hook should be on the leader. Some fishermen use treble hooks, especially if they're fans of using mussels for bait. This terminal tackle arrangement is ideal for the fisherman who likes to cast it out, plop it down in the sand, and open a good book. Use a surf type, anchor-shaped weight of about 2 or 3 ounces for this type of fishing.

For more active fishermen who like to cast, retrieve, and move, a more modern approach consists of using a Carolina rig with a sliding egg sinker of 3/4 to 2 ounces. This is slipped on the main line before a tiny swivel is tied on. Follow this with about 3 feet of 6-pound test mono and a small (#4 or #6) hook or tiny treble hook for best results. This very same rig with a small worm hook and a 10-½-inch green rubber grub named "Perch Killer" has earned its name and is a highly effective, trouble-free rig when surfperch are running, especially in the winter months.

Surf fishing is an active sport that requires the bait to be kept moving—a cast out into the surf followed by a slow retrieve works best. You may have to retrieve rapidly when the waves are surging toward you and stop when the surge is retreating to keep a constant current pressure on the bait, but this is important to preset the bait to as many possible passing fish as is possible. In the surf zone, water visibility is minimal,

Flyfishing in Southern California Saltwater

While there has been a core of hardcore saltwater flyfishermen in southern California for many years, the recent explosion of flyfishing has taken the sport from somewhat of an oddity here in southern California, to commonplace. More and more anglers take their fly rod to the beach, bays, and open ocean to practice their hobby. Every different type of habitat in southern California with the possible exception of deep rock fishing can be successfully fished with a fly rod. The surf, kelp beds, offshore banks, the flats, the back bays and river mouths all hold a host of new possibilities for the beginning saltwater flyfisher or traveling angler. Shooting heads and sinking lines like Rio Density Compensated or the Teeny line series are needed for most situations but some exciting flyfishing can be had on everything from yellowtail, bonito and barracuda to mackerels, makos and white seabass.

The best place to start is at a fly and tackle shop specializing in flyfishing or with an experienced guide. Specialized tackle is offered along with many classes, tours, and outings designed specifically for saltwater flyfishers. Flyfishermen generally love to talk about their sport and asking lots of questions at any fly shop should land you all the information you'd ever need to get started.

Following are the major southern California flyfishing shops:

Bob Marriott's Fly Fishing Store
2700 W Orangethorpe Ave
Fullerton, CA
(714) 525-1827

Rocky Point Marina
At the Portifino Hotel
Redondo Beach, CA
(310)374-9858

Mike Scott's Hackle Tackle & Flies
1892 N. Tustin Avenue
Orange, CA
(714)998-9400

San Diego Fly Shop
4401 Twain Ave. Suite #6
San Diego, CA
(619) 283-3445

His & Her Fly Fishing Store
1666 Newport Blvd
Costa Mesa, CA
(949) 548-9449

In addition to the above shops, there are also several guides that specialize in flyfishing the southern California coast. These guides all handle light tackle anglers as well. They focus primarily on fishing from boats, although they can help with surf fishing needs also. The following is a short list of established guides that cater to flyfishers:

Fly Time Guide Service
Capt. Bill Matthews
310-540-3539

Malibu to Dana Point and Catalina Island (Covering most of the L.A. area) Inshore, island, bays and harbors and near offshore.

Capt. Ray Chandler
Pecaando con Mosca's
800-914-4094
L.A. harbor to San Diego
(Dana Point area as well)
Ray lives in San Clemente.
Inshore and the bays.

Capt. Conway Bowman
619-286-4625
San Diego area, great with shark fishing. Inshore and near offshore.

Capt. Peter Picone
619-275-5158
San Diego and Mission bay,
great on the inshore.

Another great place to start is the Federation of Fly Fishers (FFF) The newest chapter is in San Diego, the San Diego Fly Fishers. They may be contacted at:

San Diego Flyfishers Headquarters
Stroud Tackle
1457 Morena Blvd
San Diego, CA 92110
(619) 276-4822

or check out their website at: http://www.sandiegoflyfishers.com/

with all sorts of stirred-up sand and silt, so keeping the bait moving relative to the volume of water it's passing through is essential for success.

Fishing the Stream and River Mouths

Though southern California is basically a desert, there are streams and rivers flowing from the mountains to the sea, bringing snowmelt and natural spring water to renew the great water cycle of sea, sky, land, and again sea. Where these streams and rivers enter the ocean are excellent places to fish. Many species of fish inhabit these areas, waiting for edible items to pass in the nonstop flow of all the different things the stream has picked up in its passage from the mountains to the sea.

The one caveat to all this is that between the pristine mountains and the sea lay the very heavily populated coastal plains. These streams aren't great rivers—most are mere trickles throughout most of the year, so significant amounts of industrial and commercial pollutants contribute to a proportionally high percentage of undesirable chemicals in the water. For this reason, fish in the stream mouths take on a definite taste of oil and pollutants and should be considered inedible. They are still fun to catch, but I caution anyone who catches a fish within a few hundred yards of a river mouth to practice catch and release.

The same techniques used from shore when surf casting or used from boats when flats fishing can be used when fishing stream mouths. Often rocky jetties are built around these mouths to keep erosion down, so there are plenty of places to stand or sit and fish. Some prefer longer rods for this kind of work so that they can cast farther into the center of the channels, but wise fishermen know the edges of the channels are just as productive, sometimes more so, than the centers of the channels.

Halibut, sand bass, and sculpin wander up into the river mouths in search of food. In addition, white croaker come in from the sandy beaches to browse. Even mackerel and jack smelt come to the river mouths to take advantage of the bounty available there.

Both live bait fishing and flyfishing are popular in the river mouths. At certain times of the year, fish boil the surface while feeding on insects. At these times, fishing the river mouths is more like fishing a trout stream. A dry fly presented upstream from the fish feeding surface activity and allowed to drift into the commotion will get hit just as it would in a mountain river. A shrimp fly or grub-imitating fly, such as a woolly bugger, can produce quite well.

For bait and lure fishing, again, baitfish-imitating lures (plugs and spoons) do poorly, while grub-looking swim baits, especially squid, produce better. The best ones are dead bait, such as cut anchovies, cut squid, clams, or mussels. A very light weight that allows the bait to work its way down the current looks the most natural to underwater inhabitants of the area.

Pier Fishing

The one place in California you're allowed to fish without a license is from the many wonderful piers and boardwalks. Most piers have a carnival atmosphere, and many have restaurants and eateries, but all have fishing. Nearly all fishing from piers is done with bait. Whether you're fishing off the end of the pier for pelagics or the shore break for surf type fish, light saltwater or heavy freshwater tackle is generally needed.

Rods and Reels

A wide variety of common tackle is useful on piers. While walking many piers, you'll see tackle intended for freshwater fishing, saltwater, surf, deep-water, trolling, and even for tuna and offshore species. While you can fish on the piers with any of this tackle, you'll have the best luck with lighter tackle. Actually, heavier freshwater gear is ideally suited for pier fishing. Longer graphite or fiberglass bass-type rods and reels are ideal.

Terminal Tackle, Fly Patterns, and Bait

For pier fishing, suitable hooks for holding bait include everything from #4 or #6 for smaller ghost shrimp and bloodworms to tiny treble hooks for mussels to bigger bait hooks when fishing live bait near the end of the pier. Cut anchovy, squid, mussel, or clam all work well.

Whenever fishing the piers, remember that fish tend to be very picky. They have to be because incautious fish simply end up on the dinner table long before they're able to breed. For this reason, fish tend to be line shy. If you're fishing with anything heavier than 8-pound test line, make sure you have a light leader. Usually, 6-pound test leaders are the most common. I often see unknowing pier fishermen using typical 20-pound test saltwater gear who don't understand why the fishermen on either side of them seem to be catching fish while they sit there hour after hour without a bite.

Also, always use the lightest sinker possible that will keep the bait on or near the bottom without drifting excessively. If the fish picks up the bait and starts to run with it but feels the weight, it will drop the bait immediately. If you accidentally hook it in this process, it is pure luck. A Carolina rig will ensure the fish can run a bit without feeling the weight. I've tried to identify the major fishing piers in southern California throughout the text with a description of where along the pier's length is most productive, but don't just camp out in one spot. If the fishing near the end for flats type fish isn't productive, move back toward shore and fish the surf line for surf-type fish. Keep at it and you'll figure out how to take fish consistently.

FISHING THE BAYS AND INLETS

Numerous bays and inlets in southern California make this a very popular fishing pastime for recreational anglers. Flats-type fish are just as likely to be in the flat bottom bays as out off the beaches. In fact, Los Angeles Harbor has one of the largest concentrations of big California halibut in the area.

Most harbors have rental boats for the occasional fisherman. In the majority of cases, these boats may not be taken from the harbor out to sea. One harbor in particular, King Harbor in Redondo Beach (Los Angeles County), specializes in flyfishing. The boats and tackle shops are all geared toward flyfishermen. Bonito are the favorite catch in King Harbor and frequent the harbor year-round. It's just the thing for the new ocean flyfisherman to cut his teeth on before venturing offshore for bigger and more aggressive prey.

For bait fisherman, the tackle and techniques described in the "Fishing the Flats" section of this chapter cover the bay fishing habitat well. Use these methods for best success.

TUNA AND BLUE WATER SPECIES

Tuna! The very thought of those strong, powerful, wide-ranging fish make fishermen forget everything in their lives and grab their poles and head to sea. With the possible exception of billfish, tuna is the biggest, most powerful fish most ocean fishermen will ever get a chance to catch. The long-ranging fish hit the coast of California in midsummer and sometimes stay until the end of fall.

Bluefin, yellowfin, skipjack, and dorado are generally fished near offshore kelp paddies. Kelp paddies are patches of kelp broken free from the kelp forests and floating free. Often only a few strands of kelp can harbor a huge school of fish. Kelp paddies over about 20 feet across are extremely rare; so don't keep looking for big paddies if you're out looking for yellowfin.

Flotsam and jetsam found floating in the ocean provide another likely place to find tuna. Baitfish in the open sea congregate near anything floating in the water. Of course, tuna know this, too, so they also congregate near anything floating in search of food. If you ever see a piece of plywood floating in the water, be sure to try it out for hidden tuna.

Terminal Tackle, Fly Patterns, and Bait

The best way to locate tuna schools is trolling. Tuna trolling requires specialized trolling jigs. A good assortment of different colors is helpful. On some days, nothing can beat the good old standby red and white feather. Still other days, the tuna ignore the red and white and go nuts over some other color. At a minimum, you should have a red and white, zucchini (green and orange), a black and purple, a Mexican flag (red, white, and green), a blue and white, and an abortion (a green and blue vinyl—don't ask me why, I didn't name it!). These trolling lures are designed to ride

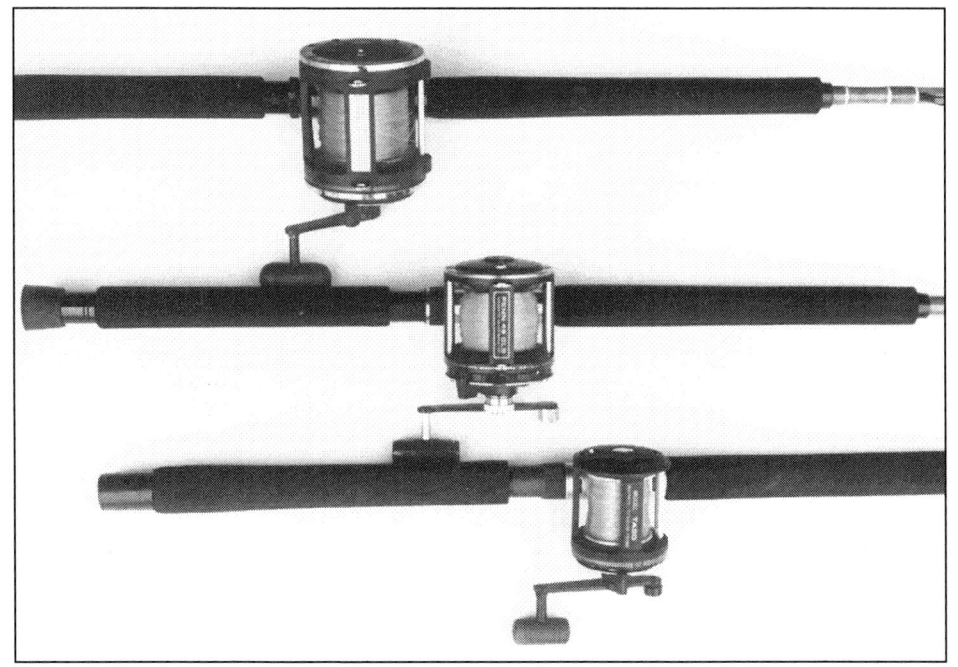

Author's offshore arsenal:
On top is a heavy trolling rig with a custom wrapped Calstar 6455XXH blank
with all Aftco roller guides wearing an Okuma 100 lever drag graphite reel with
80-pound test. In the middle is a heavy bait rig, a custom wrapped Calstar 665H
with heavy Fuji guides wearing a Penn 45GLS lever drag reel with 40-pound test.
On the bottom is the light bait rig, a custom wrapped Calstar 670 with light Fuji
guides wearing an Okuma 25 lever drag graphite reel with 25-pound test.

on the trolling leader or line, and they generally come unrigged. To use, simply slip them on the line, then tie a double trolling hook on the end of the line. The skirted trolling feather rides down over the hook and helps conceal it.

Recently, many people have returned to an old-fashioned trolling lure that still works as good as it ever did—the cedar plug. In addition to good old natural cedar, some companies, such as Sea Striker, are offering these painted to look like common baitfish with extra large eyes. These trolling lures are very effective, and no offshore tackle box should be lacking in cedar plugs.

When baitfishing for tuna and offshore species, you really don't need much tackle, just a handful of different live bait style hooks of different sizes to match different sizes of bait. Smaller anchovies call for #4 hooks, larger #2. Small sardines call for 2/0 or 3/0 hooks and larger, about 4/0. If fishing with smaller live mackerel, a 7/0

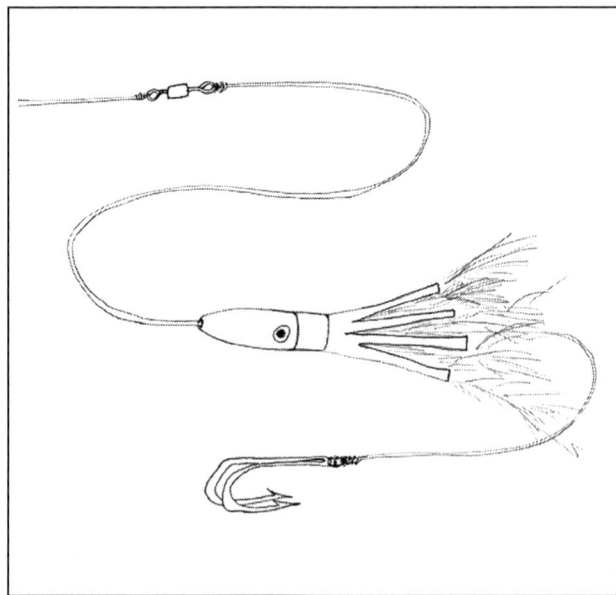

Typical trolling rig set-up for tuna.

is needed. Chunk bait tuna fishermen in Mexico use as big as 16/0 bait hooks. The hook is always tied just to the end of the line, and no swivels or leaders are necessary.

To troll, tie up the trolling rig as shown in the diagram. The leader should be at least 3 feet, 4 feet is better, and some like leaders 6 feet long. Let the line out about 100 feet behind the boat. Troll off to the side of the wake of the boat but don't forget the bubble stream right in the center of the wake. Tuna sometimes mistake the agitation made by the propeller for the agitation made by a terrified school of baitfish.

Troll with the boat moving between 8 and 12 knots (10 to 15 miles per hour). Don't be overly concerned if the jig occasionally skips along the surface out of the water. If you've ever seen tuna rip though a school of baitfish, you probably noticed how the bait leaps from the water in an attempt to escape the big predators. A jig bouncing out of the water very likely excites the fish into thinking the bait is trying to escape its jaws. There is a very famous series of photographs commonly seen in tackle shops in southern California. The photos are a sequence of a mackerel jumping from the water about 3 feet in the air. Just as the mackerel's leap peaks, a huge bluefin emerges from the water and catches the bait in midair, snapping it cleanly in half and leaving only the head and gills flying through the air. It is a masterful job of photography. It is well worth cruising tackle shops just to see the photos, but they illustrate why it is all right to let your jig skip along the surface.

The jig doesn't have to be a long distance behind the boat. For example, one time when I was trolling for tuna with a friend on his boat, I had picked up three fish with a jig and he had hooked none. He was trying everything, including switching to the same color feather as mine, trying to get a hit. Suddenly, he spotted my lure less than 50 feet behind the boat. "Is that your jig right there?" he asked. After answering him in the affirmative, he brought his up from about 150 yards back and almost immediately lit up with a nice yellowfin. Someone had told him that the boat scares the fish, so he always tried to get his jig a long way back. This may be true in lakes, but in the ocean, agitated water is a sign of struggling bait.

While trolling, keep your eyes peeled for signs of floating kelp paddies, floating logs, or lumber. Troll as near as possible to these without fouling your lines. Also keep your eyes peeled for diving birds—if they're diving, they're eating baitfish. Keep your eyes peeled for jumpers, too. If you've ever noticed elevated flying bridges on some boats made of pipe, you've seen what fishermen call "tuna towers." They give the skipper the advantage of being up a bit higher so he can scan the horizon for jumping fish. Jumpers are always feeding when they jump; they never jump just for the fun of it.

While discussing jumping for the fun of it, it is no secret that dolphins often shadow schools of tuna. Commercial seiners have known this for years. Dolphin schools, unlike tuna schools, are easy to spot. Don't worry about possibly hooking a dolphin. In all my years of fishing, I've seen all sorts of critters inadvertently hooked while fishing, including seals, birds, sharks, rocks, boats, kelp, logs, even lost fishing poles, but I've NEVER seen a dolphin hooked. I've fished in the middle of schools of dolphins with at least 2000 individuals jumping, diving, and darting all around and never seen one hooked. It is true that net boats have to work to keep dolphins out of their nets, but don't worry about hook and line fishing around dolphins. They're too smart to get caught.

When tuna are found in feeding schools of dolphin, a special technique often referred to as "Runnin' and Gunnin' " is used. Since the schools in this case are fluid and moving rapidly, head the boat right into the melee of leaping tuna and dolphin, shut it down, and get lines in the water within the first few seconds of arriving. If no hookups occur within just a few seconds to perhaps as much as 15 seconds, fire off the boat and move to the center of action again. This type of fishing is often frenzied but is sometimes the only way to land tuna, particularly in the latter part of the season.

If you're trolling and you pick up a fish, especially if you pick up two or more within a few minutes, you've probably located a school and can try baitfishing. If you are in the main school and haven't just picked up a few "scouts," the school will rise to bait. Throw some chum out and look for boils (fish breaking the surface as they attack the bait). If you see boils, break out the baitfishing sticks and flyline. Flylining is fishing with live bait on a hook tied directly to the main line without swivels or weights. The spool of the reel is kept declutched. Apply only enough thumb tension to the edge of the spool to feel if the bait gets hit. Otherwise, just let the bait swim and take as much line as he likes.

When you're in the fish it won't take long to get a hookup. The anchovy or sardine will suddenly take off. Don't be overanxious at this stage. Let the tuna run with the bait for at least 2 seconds, then clutch in the reel and set the hook. You need not be gentle when setting the hook. Tuna have hard mouths, so don't worry about pulling the hook out or through the fish. The flexibility of the rod will take care of softening the impact.

If you've never hooked a tuna before, you will likely be shocked at the power of the fish's first run. Even if you hook into a 12-pound skipjack, the speed and determination of the first run will strip yards and yards of line off even a hefty reel, and you'll be convinced you've hooked into a world record bluefin.

After the first run, begin a pump-and-wind retrieval. Most likely, the fish will make one or two more runs before you're able to reel him in. Tuna run in three-dimensional patterns, unlike many other surface-type fish. Tuna often do vertical loops, especially when tiring. Experienced fishermen call these circles the tuna's "death circles." It takes concentration at this point to make sure the fish never gets any slack. The experienced fisherman will use these death circles to winch the fish in. With heavy tackle and big fish, the better long-range skippers tell their fishermen to set the rod on the rail and crank for all they're worth at this stage. One thing is for sure, when fighting a tuna, you're fighting a fish, not just playing him. It's a war and sure to test your skill at fishing techniques.

If you've found the fish, change your bait often. If you don't get a hit in about 2 or 3 minutes, change the bait. Like most surface fish, tuna like their bait lively. Once hooked on the line, most bait lasts only about 3 or 4 minutes before it can no longer pull the line out from the reel while swimming in a seminatural manner. When you're in the fish and have a lively bait on the hook, you won't have to wait long.

If you are bluefin, yellowfin, skipjack, or dorado fishing, most likely you'll be near a kelp paddy or floating flotsam, be sure to keep track of the paddy as the boat drifts. Once you quit getting bites, you'll want to find the paddy again. Believe me, this is not as simple as it may seem when you're out of sight of land. Remember, the key part of the word landmark is "land." As the boat starts drifting, note the direction on the compass so you can find it again.

While you're at it, consider this: If you are looking for floating lumber, floating kelp paddies, or other cover for bait fish with schools of fish beneath and are drifting around in the boat, guess what the boat becomes after a very short time with the engine off. Give yourself three points if you said it is just another piece of flotsam for the fish out there. When you're ready to move on after bait fishing, fire up the engine, shift the engine into gear for just a moment, then shift it back into neutral. This will chase the tuna out from under the boat. Keep your lines in the water with fresh bait when you make this maneuver, too. This is just the trick to pick up a couple more big ones after the bite has died down. The better party boat and charter boat skippers do this regularly.

Another potentially productive way to catch tuna is with jigs. Generally, sticks that are a bit heavier than standard surface fishing jig sticks are used. Standard bone jigs work well for tuna. In addition, the chrome, spoon-type jigs tend to be effective, as well. As with all jigfishing, the best colors change from day to day. Blue/white, green/yellow, chrome, all white, angry squid patterns, mackerel patterns, and injured sardine color schemes are all effective on one day or another. Keep changing jigs until you find the best one for the day. Brighter, shinier colors and patterns with chrome tend to attract bigger offshore fish.

Be sure to read the information on jigfishing in the section on surface fishing. The theory of jig fishing will give you key hints on how to jigfish productively. It's the action of the jig that is the key. Remember also, you'll probably catch bigger fish when jigging than on bait. This isn't an absolute, but it does often occur. Though I've never heard a confirmation of this, I believe it is because the more daring, aggressive fish tend to eat better and thus become bigger in the first place. The more cautious fish won't grow as big.

Rods and Reels

Big tuna and other bluewater species require specialized tackle. They put serious demands on tackle, and anything less than top quality equipment lowers the chances of landing your intended quarry. Modern materials and manufacturing techniques have produced equipment far lighter yet far more capable than the old standbys our fathers and grandfathers carried.

To do serious bluewater fishing, you'll need three rods: The first is a trolling stick, traditionally a 5- to 5½-foot long, stiff, parabolic rod with rod gimbal butts, long foregrips, and heavy duty roller guides. The classic, and my personal favorite, is the Cal Star 6455 XXH. This is probably the most popular rod carried to Mexico on long-range trips. The Cal Star blank needs to be custom wrapped for those interested in crafting their weapons themselves or can be built by almost any of the many southern California saltwater tackle stores. An equivalent rod is made by many different makers and is available off the rack. Make sure the rod is rated for 80-pound test minimum.

This trolling rod should wear a reel at least 6/0 wide. While long-range captains prefer two-speed reels, single-speed reels are adequate for close range. The Penn 6/0 Senator is the classic tool for this type of work. Many fishermen replace the reel's crossbars with a solid, machined aluminum frame for extra heavy use. These are made by two companies: Tiburon and Accurate Fishing Products. These are great for absorbing the heavy torque loads applied when a big fish takes the jig, and 80-pound test line is a must. Other reels made by different manufacturers are available and are equally suitable. My own favorite is the Okuma size 90, lever-drag graphite reel. It's a moderately priced big reel, and I've had no trouble subduing 100-plus-pound bigeyes and plenty of midsized yellowfin with it.

If you want to go first class, a two-speed reel is nice. The Penn International 50 SW is the most popular of these for an 80-pound test, trolling rod. Fin-Nor's new two-speed Ahab series would be my first choice if cost were no object. Just turning the crank of one of these reels in the tackle shop makes you yearn to go night chunking for big bull yellowfin at Clarion Island. A number of other manufacturers make two-speed reels in this size.

The second tuna stick you'll need is a bait stick. A stiffer, 7-foot rod coupled with a stout reel for 30-pound test class line is a good primary baitfishing tool for most southern California offshore situations. My personal favorite is a Cal Star 670 rod. Like all of my rods, this one was personally custom triple-wrapped with the finest Fuji ceramic line guides and reel seat. An extra long hypalon foregrip graces the rod, also. Many other manufacturers have similar rods, and just about any fishing tackle store in the area can get you set up with a 30-pound test tuna stick from as low as about $60 up to several hundred.

My 30-pound test rig holds an Okuma lever-drag graphite reel in size 25 and is very similar to a Penn 25 GLS lever-drag reel. I've landed plenty of 40-plus-pound yellowfin with it. I have a 25-pound test line on it, but most elect to use the sturdier 30-pound. Other suitable reels include Penn's Jigmaster, 3/0 and 4/0 high speed Senators, the Daiwa Sealine series, smaller Fin Nor Ahabs, Newell reels, and numerous others—too many almost to list.

A third rod I like to carry when tuna fishing, especially in El Niño years, is a 40-pound test rig. When the tuna fishing is hot, they'll bite on 40-pound just as well as 30, and it gives you a bit more power to get the fish in faster and with less stress. This is especially important when fishing in a crowded party boat, with people running every direction following their fish, or when you intend to release the fish. Tuna sometimes fight until they're completely exhausted. My favorite rod for this use is a Cal Star 665H, a 6½-foot long, moderately tapered rod ideally suited for tuna on 40-pound test.

This 40-pound rig uses a Penn 45GLS graphite lever drag reel. I like graphite reels for their high strength and light weight. The lever-drag feature is a breeze to operate with one thumb, an especially important feature when fighting a tough, tenacious tuna.

If you'd like to try your hand at flyfishing for tuna, don't even attempt it with anything lighter than a 12-weight rod with a matching reel having a disc or drum drag. Less stick would be pure folly. A shooting head-sinking line is needed, along with leaders of at least 25-pound test. Most people use straight monofilament line as leaders for this type of fishing instead of the tapered, trout-type tippets. There's no need to present the fly gently because tuna like splashing on the water surface. Flies tied to imitate small baitfish, especially anchovies or sardines, are most effective. I like sizes from 3/0 to 7/0. Some newer epoxy-bodied bucktail-haired flies are becoming available as more and more flyfishing shops recognize that many of their customers are fishing in saltwater. Before you pitch a fly at a hundred-pound bigeye tuna, at least tune up on some skipjack. They're usually plentiful, and if you're in the area with them, pitch a blue and white anchovy-imitating fly to gather some (trust me) much-needed experience in subduing these tough fish.

Though the opportunities to fish tuna in California aren't as abundant as the opportunities for most other species, fishing for tuna is an experience not to be missed. Tuna fishing is both a challenge and a lot of fun. They'll give you a good workout and test your fishing skill while filling the freezer with delicious, healthy meat.

SALMON TROLLING

Last, but certainly not least, southern California sports a productive salmon run every spring in the Santa Barbara channel. The silver or coho salmon range well into the channel beginning about February and stretching into the early summer.

Unlike other local predatory fish, particularly the free-swimming pelagic species, salmon are careful eaters. They are somewhat picky and don't attack bait until they've eyed it over a bit and decided it's OK to eat. This can be extremely frustrating to fishermen who are used to the frenzied action of barracuda, bonito, yellowtail, tuna, and dorado that come out of the water and inhale bait as they hit the water. By contrast, salmon fishing is a slow, methodical process.

Since southern California represents the southern fringe of salmon habitat, the high densities of fish that are found farther north in California, Oregon, Washington, British Columbia, and of course, Alaska, just aren't present. This means that stillfishing or mooching are simply not productive enough to be considered here. All southern California salmon fishing is done by trolling.

Again, to contrast styles, trolling for pelagic species involves surface-swimming jigs, some actually even skipping out of the water, and can be done at speeds up to 18 knots. Salmon, on the other hand, have to be trolled very slowly—less than 2 mph if dodgers are being used and only up to about 4 mph if flashers are used. They can also be trolled in the midwater, usually about halfway from the surface to the bottom. Ideally, the bottom should contain fish-holding structure, such as rocky reefs, and have deep water north and west of the reefs. This attracts bait for several reasons: One is that there are plenty of places in which to hide from marauding predators. I can't imagine what it would be like to be a baitfish, but you can bet I'd be looking for a hideout. The second is that it creates upwelling from the north to south current that moves water down the coast of southern California. This nutrient-laden water from the deep sea attracts hordes of tiny diatoms and plankton, themselves the grazing fodder of small fish. Here again, small fish go where the grazing is good, and where the small fish go, the predators, such as salmon, surely follow.

The rocky reefs on the northwest sides of the Channel Islands are perfect places to fish for salmon. If salmon are in the area, they can be enticed to strike by either artificial lures or dead bait on bait-holding hooks sent down to within 50 feet or so of the bottom and moved slowly in "S" patterns. A downrigger is a great help in getting lures or baits down into productive salmon water. In the absence of a downrigger, a dropaway sinker rig or diving planer can be substituted.

Rods and Reels

Thirty-pound test line and a parabolic taper rod are required for salmon trolling. A rod with very similar characteristics to shallow-water rock fishing is ideal. I use one for both types of fishing: a custom wrapped Cal Star 6465. It has the heavy tip important for a rod used with heavy weights and plenty of backbone for encouraging big fish to come around to your way of thinking. I also use this rod for coaxing big lingcod out of their caves in rockpiles and wrecks. The majority of rods gracing the racks of local tackle stores are more oriented toward surface fishing with light, sensitive tips. These aren't ideal for salmon trolling, so keep looking if you want to buy something suitable.

My salmon rod is fitted with a Penn 3/0 High Speed Special Senator. The original crossbars have been replaced with a machined aluminum, twist-free Accurate Fishing Products frame. Other reels are suitable, including the famous Newell 300 series of reels. These lightweight, high-speed reels are ideally suited for this demanding requirement. Many other reels are equally suited for this task, as well.

Terminal Tackle, Lures, and Bait

Salmon trolling requires a very specialized setup. A quick-release is tied to the end of the line that carries the cannonball sinker of 2 to 4 pounds. You can either sacrifice the sinker each time you get a hit or you can hook the sinker to a downrigger line so that the downrigger reel is used to retrieve the sinker after a strike. Tied to the quick-release is a dodger or flasher. The old dodgers wobble side to side and require trolling to be very slow, usually less than 2 mph. Modern trolling uses a flasher, similar in size and shape to a dodger, but the action is very different. It is designed to rotate about its trolled axis, enticing the salmon to strike. This allows the troll speed to be a bit higher and certainly allows greater latitude in speeds over the traditional (some feel superior) dodger. I don't care to get into a debate, but when I troll, it's with a flasher.

Salmon have excellent eyesight, and for the flasher to be a good attractant, it must be highly reflective. Silver chrome flashers are most common, but prismatic, hammered texture, half-and-half silver- and brass-colored, or the especially exciting, new holographic flashers all outperform the straight chrome ones. Tagging behind the flasher is the bait or lure. The entire arrangement is supposed to look like a single bigger baitfish chasing a small school of smaller baitfish. The salmon, of course, targets the trailing fish.

Somewhere between 1 and 3 feet behind the flasher is the main bait—the lure. Some devotees say it should be placed exactly 14 inches behind, while others prefer different distances. Rubber "Hootchies" are common and work well, especially in lighter colors, including beige, yellow, and light green. Newer, brightly painted wooden plug lures can also be used successfully and are now really catching on in northern California—it won't be long before they'll catch on in the south. Spoonlike lures are also producers on salmon. These fish are more wary than the hard-hitting tuna that snap at anything passing by, slow or fast, and a careful, slow presentation will always get you more fish than a fast-moving, flashy lure.

In addition to lures, some salmon fishermen use dead bait to troll. Anchovies and herring are the most popular trolled baits. Frozen bait is available everywhere and is very useful as a salmon attractant. Special bait-holding hooks, sometimes called crowbars, are sold for this purpose. Other inventions abound to keep bait on the hooks while trolling. Some are useful, others are junk.

While trolling for salmon, it's common to catch other species, as well. Halibut have been known to rise up 70 feet or more off the bottom and take a trolled hoochie. Lingcod also often end up on the end of salmon gear, as does the occasional white seabass.

There are no southern California party boats that fish for salmon. It's too complex an operation and simply not productive enough. Party boat skippers look for the numbers to publish in the paper every day. If 25 passengers picked up 5 salmon (an exceptional day in this part of the range), it's not nearly as impressive as if 25 passengers picked up 200 rock cod, 12 lingcod, 3 rock sole, and 2 cowcod, a good but not exceptional early spring three-quarter day trip out of the northern ports in southern California.

For these reasons, it's necessary to charter a boat or fish from your own boat if you want to fish for salmon. A number of charter boat skippers out of Santa Barbara, Ventura, Channel Islands, and Port Hueneme are successful salmon fishermen—others are not. If you're set on catching a salmon from a charter boat, interview your prospective guide carefully to make sure he fits in the former group.

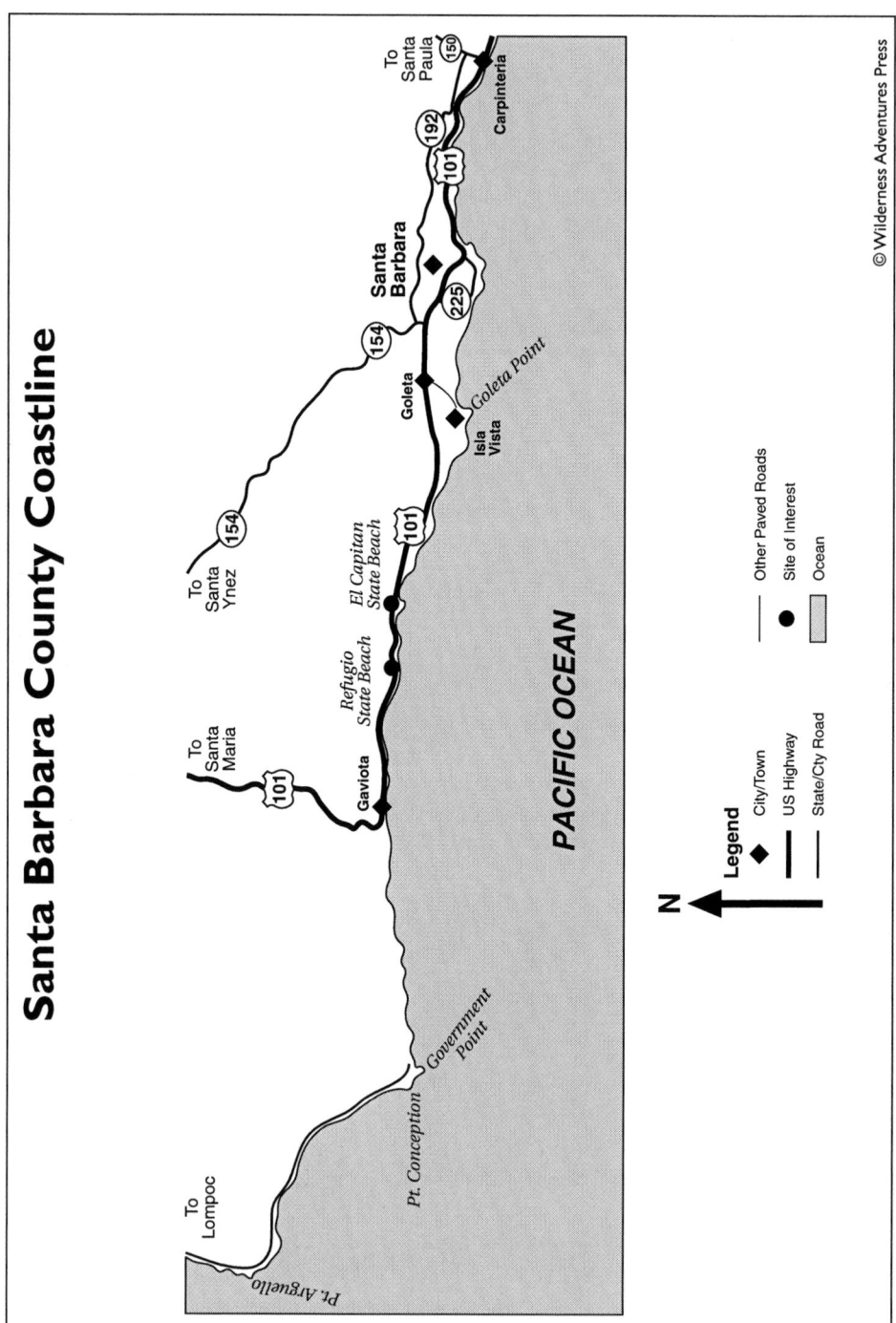

The Santa Barbara County Coastline

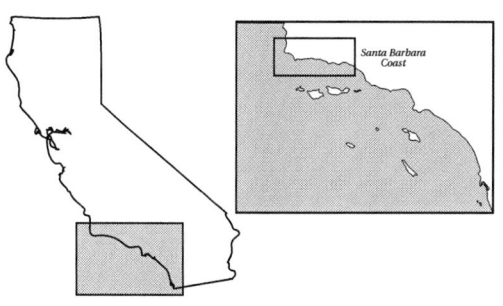

Santa Barbara County is arguably the most beautiful stretch of southern California coastline, with 4000-foot high mountains that plunge into the sea in just a few short miles. I lived for a time in Goleta and used to help some hang-gliding friends by driving the recovery truck. We used to drive to the top of the mountains, some as high as 4600 feet. They launched their gliders and I took the truck down the mountains and picked them up on the beach. I always beat them down and had to wait as they lazily circled like raptors in the gentle breezes framed against the crystal blue sky and rugged mountains. Santa Barbara is a place of stunning vistas, crystal clear air, and year-round beautiful weather. Few places in the world can offer such a combination of relaxed lifestyle, rich cultural heritage, and stunning natural beauty.

Prior to the arrival of white men, Santa Barbara was originally populated by Chumash Indians who were seafarers and fishermen. They paddled their 28-foot long wooden canoes, called *tomols*, across the Santa Barbara Channel to Santa Cruz and Santa Rosa Islands. Juan Cabrillo, generally considered the discoverer of the California coast, came next in the late 1500s and found the area to be a pleasant anchorage along his journey of discovery. The area was named later by explorer Sebastian Viscaino, who sailed into the channel on December 4, 1604. December 4 is supposed to be the day of remembrance for Santa Barbara, always referred to as a virgin and martyr.

Father Junipero Serra, the famous monk who founded a string of California missions, established the Presidio, a military fortification, in 1782, followed by the mission of Santa Barbara in 1786. These structures still stand today. A small *pueblo* (town) grew up around the presidio on small land grants first offered in 1797 for soldiers and their families and became known as Santa Barbara. In 1822 following Mexico's war of independence, the people of Santa Barbara swore their allegiance to Mexico, having previously been subjects of Spain.

Richard Henry Dana, the author of *Two Years Before the Mast*, a classic of American literature and textbook for historians studying the days of wooden ships and iron men, landed in Santa Barbara in the 1830s. Then it was a land of ranchos and farms, spread over such a large area that the land was very little changed from the days when only the Chumash tribe called Santa Barbara home. Dana's description of what Santa Barbara was like before the gold rush reads somewhat like the descriptions of Shangri-La in James Hilton's *The Lost Horizon*.

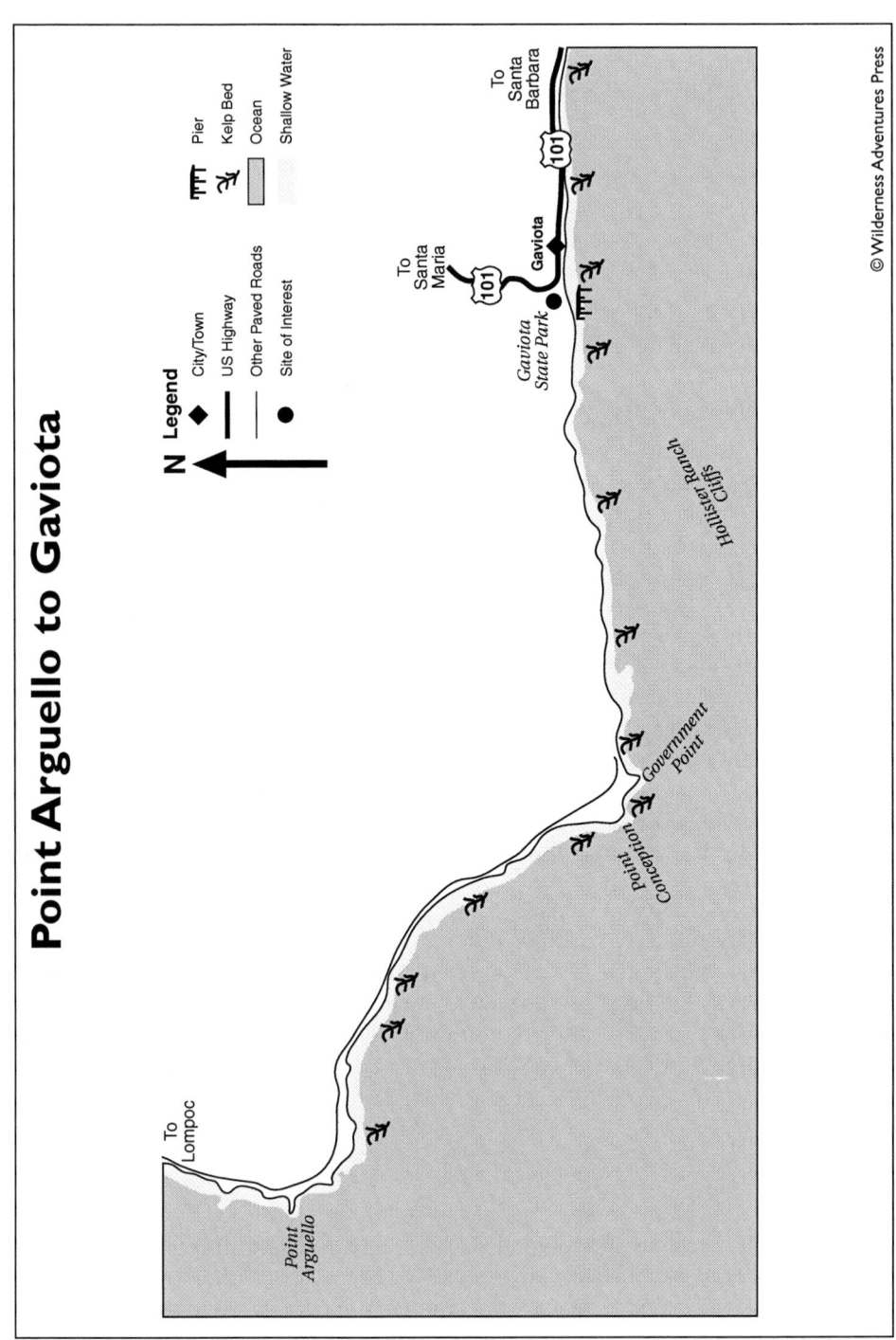

Point Arguello to Gaviota

© Wilderness Adventures Press

When Mexico ceded Alta California to the United States after the Mexican-American War in 1848, Santa Barbarans again were required to switch their country of allegiance from Mexico to the United Sates. Just a year later, with the discovery of gold at Sutter's Mill, the great rush of people to California turned Santa Barbara from a sleepy little pueblo to a booming city of 100,000. California went from territory to state in 1850, and what is now Santa Barbara County was separated out of a bigger county that originally included Ventura County in 1877.

The 1900s have brought prosperity to Santa Barbara. It has always been a playground for the wealthy, where celebrities in the early days of the movie industry sought an escape from the hustle of Hollywood and the recognition of excited fans. Gorgeous resort getaways are clustered in Santa Barbara, originally serving only the wealthy but today within the realm of all budgets. Today, the city is a vacationer's dream with a wealth of nightlife, shopping, sightseeing, and recreation opportunities.

Santa Barbara has always had a close association with the sea. Since the land is situated on a narrow coastal plain near the confluence of the two great currents that feed the Pacific Coast of North America, it is situated in an incredibly fertile sea and is home to many species of both northern and southern fishes. Commercial fishing has been a major enterprise in the area since the Chumash Indians lived here, and the bounty of the seas has not gone unnoticed by sportsmen who fish for challenge and fun. Plenty of diving opportunities are a trademark of this area, as well. Commercial abalone and urchin diving has been an important industry to the area, and these days, sport divers come from all over the world to dive in the clear Pacific and enjoy the stunning undersea topography, brimming with sea life of all sorts from tiny plankton to great whales.

Point Arguello to Gaviota

The Corner, as the Conception to Arguello coastline is called, is the classically defined separation point between southern California and central California. Most people think of Point Conception as the separation, but Arguello is really the more clearly defined transition between a north/south coastline fed by the cold, nutrient-rich Alaskan current to an east/west coastline warmed by a huge eddy of water bringing warm, highly saline water up from Mexico.

Point Arguello and much of the coastline between Arguello and Conception is owned and managed by Vandenburg Air Force Base. Vandenburg is an important test base for missiles and is also home to the western base of NASA. Vandenburg has a much wider launching angle than Cape Canaveral and can launch satellites in many different orbits, including polar ones. Because the Air Force Base restricts access by land, these excellent fishing areas are accessible only by boat.

Along the coast from Point Conception to Gaviota is the Hollister Ranch, a very exclusive, gated community of small ranches. The lots are 100 acres, so you can be certain that no high-density housing is likely here for a long while. Even though California law states that all beaches are public property, access to these beaches is only available by water, also.

The coastline is typical of Santa Barbara County, with mountainous ridges plunging into the sea creating plentiful rocky reefs separated by sand and pebble beaches. The shallower (150 feet or less) rocky reefs generally wear garlands of thick kelp forests that lure plenty of sea life into their protective cover. With so much kelp, resident and seasonally migratory fish abound in the kelp beds. Plenty of rugged, deep-water canyons and reefs provide homes for the deep-water rock dwellers, as well. In all, this area is an excellent place to fish.

Some of the better places to fish along the Arguello to Gaviota coastline include:

Point Arguello Canyons

If there's a deep-water rock cod fisherman's heaven, it's certainly the Point Arguello canyons. The weather here is terrible—I have been on the hook in the Point Arguello anchorage while 60-mile-per-hour winds whistled offshore, trying to drop gangions in 15-foot seas with little or no luck. But I've also fished here on days when it was flat calm, the bite simply never ended, and gangions filled with 5- to 8-pound reds within seconds of hitting the bottom. This remote area is a long way in a boat, especially in a displacement type boat, from either Santa Barbara to the east or Port San Louis to the north, so that those on multiple day trips are the only ones who visit.

A series of deep cuts in the coastal plain between Point Conception and Point Arguello form a very erose, rugged bottom structure. The rough canyon bottom area covers thousands of acres of ocean bottom and is rather extensive in scope. The bottom is too rough for commercial trawlers with expensive bottom-dragging nets, so the rock cod find this a terrific spot where they can live and breed practically unmolested, except for the very few hook-and-line commercial boats and the occasional sport boat.

To fish the canyons, a good charting or video bottom meter is needed. Begin by following bottom contours—the 100-fathom line (600 feet) is a good place to start. You'll usually find fish stacked up downcurrent of obstructions. For instance, on southfacing canyon walls, they'll arch up in a feeding school sometimes 50 to 80 feet off the bottom. Drop squid-baited bucktail/maribou shrimp flies on multiple hook gangions with 3 to 4 pounds of sinker right into these schools. If you hit the school, the gangion should be filled by the time you realize it's on the bottom. Haul 'er in and repeat until you have a limit of nice fat reds on the deck.

In addition to reds, Arguello has great cowcod fishing. I believe there are plenty of world record and California state record cowcod living here at the Point Arguello canyons. One of the better techniques to catch big cows is to fillet a Florida snapper (bank rockfish) and leave the skin and tail intact on the fillet. Make sure the pink stripe is visible and impale the big end on a 16/0 circle hook, leaving the tail to wave about in the current. Send this down with low-stretch Dacron or Spectra line with a 1-pound sinker and start jigging up and down. I have a 9-foot jigfishing-type rod for this and use 50-pound test Spectra on a 4/0-sized reel. With this arrangement, you'll not only nail big cowcod but also lingcod. If a bank rockfish isn't available, try double hooking a live mackerel.

There are two anchorages near the Point Arguello Canyon. The best is Cojo Anchorage behind Government Point near Point Conception. It offers good protection and usually mild weather. Farther north behind Point Arguello, only moderate protection is available in the southfacing shoreline. These anchorages are only good during normal northwesterly conditions. If a southerly storm blows, these can be downright dangerous. Travel to Point Arguello is not for the inexperienced sailor or unproven craft. This is open sea with frequent fog, strong blows, and heavy seas that make this area unforgiving to blunderers. Confidence in your seamanship, navigation, and boat come from lots of experience in the ocean, best gained in the more protected, near-port areas of southern California. It was here at Point Arguello in the 1920s that seven US Navy destroyers were dashed upon the rocks and lost, along with most of their crews, on a single fateful day.

Point Arguello Kelp

Nestled between Point Arguello and Point Conception are some kelp beds worth mentioning. They're almost never fished since they're so far from port. Commercial crab fishing boats are about the only visitors to this rocky shoreline. Because these kelp beds remain so undisturbed, they harbor some of the biggest, fattest calico bass available in southern California.

In addition to calicos, white seabass frequent these kelp beds and live here in good numbers. Live squid is always the best choice for these big croakers, but they'll also gobble up well presented, rubber swimbaits or jigs yoyoed deep. Sometimes they'll also hit a live anchovy or sardine. Spring is the best time to fish this stretch of kelp forest for either white seabass or calicos.

Point Conception

Tucked just behind Government Point (often confused with Point Conception) is a snug anchorage called Cojo. I first visited here while ferrying a sailboat from Santa Barbara to Morro Bay. While pulling in, I noticed a great, thick kelp forest and thought how good the fishing must be there but was unable to drop a line at that time. Several years later while fishing the Arguello canyons, I decided to try out the kelp beds here. I wasn't surprised when I found the fishing excellent. Plenty of fat calicos lived in the kelp beds and circling the fringes was a hungry school of barracuda. On the bottom were rockfish and sculpin—in all, an excellent place to fish.

Use live bait for best results, but rubber swimbaits, flies, and swimming lures are also very enticing to resident bass. Cast to the edge of the dense kelp canopy and slowly retrieve to get the fish to break cover and pounce on your offering. For barracuda, the trusty old blue and white jigs seem to work best. Cast them out, let them flutter at least to midwater, then rapidly retrieve. I didn't catch any white seabass on that trip, but I see no reason why this excellent kelp stand shouldn't support strong numbers of these game fish. Late winter and spring should be prime times for whites.

Hollister Ranch Cliffs

A mere 2 miles off the Hollister Ranch coastline, the bottom drops from 150 feet to nearly 1000 feet in a steep cliff. It certainly must be a dramatic underwater sight.

Like cliffs on land, these aren't smooth walls—they are studded with outcroppings, cracks, caves, and other excellent cover for the bottom-dwelling reef species of fish, the rock cod.

Fishing these cliffs can be tricky. It takes precise positioning to drop a gangion down through moving water from a drifting boat and into metered fish. Ideally, the wind and current should be minimal, but as long as both are running in the same direction, it should be all right. When the wind and current are opposite, it's nearly impossible to place your bait where you spot the fish. Fortunately, most often the current and winds cause drift along this part of the coast. This tends to keep hooks at a constant depth and makes the fishing both easier and more productive.

Typical deep-water rock cod fishing techniques work best here. Maribou and bucktail shrimp flies baited with thin strips of cut squid are the best producers. Other effective bait combinations are cut mackerel or salted anchovies on long shank bait hooks and strips of cut rock cod on circle hooks. Each has its advocates, but on my personal rig, you'll always find bucktail flies.

Gaviota Kelp Beds

Gaviota means "sea gull" in Spanish, and this beautiful stretch of beach is aptly named for its bountiful population of these sea birds. Just offshore from the Gaviota State Park and pier, a large, rocky reef supports a thick kelp forest. This provides habitat for all kelp species. Surrounding this reef is a sandy bottom supporting the main flats species of this area, as well. Three different types of fishing—kelp, shallow water rock, and flats fishing—can be done here, resulting in excellent mixed bags of fish.

I generally save the kelp bed surface type fishing for sunny afternoons and begin in the flats or rocks. Drift the sandflats with live bait, rubber swimbaits, squid-baited shrimp flies, or cut squid for halibut, sanddabs, and a great eating refugee fish from farther north, cabezon. When this gets boring, drop into the rocky reefs with cut squid, shrimp flies, live bait, or head-on uncooked shrimp from your local oriental market for great rockfish, sheephead, and in the winter, lingcod fishing.

When the sun comes out, work the outer edges of the kelp bed for calico bass, barracuda, and sometimes bonito in the summer, or white seabass in the winter. Bait, jigs, rubber swimbaits, and swimming lures can all be effective at different times. If there's no luck with one, simply switch to another. The fish are there—just having the right thing on your line to stimulate their pounce instinct is the key.

These kelp beds are a fun place to flyfish, also. Because there are some windy days, I suggest taking your conventional tackle along in case the wind makes fly casting difficult. Clouser minnows in blue, green, and yellow, in combination with white, seem to be the most popular here and are often very effective on the local populations of bass and barracuda.

Gaviota State Beach

Along Gaviota State Beach, some very interesting shore fishing can be done. This beach is located just as US 101 turns inland from its coastal track south and east

The pier at Gaviota, an excellent place to fish,
is now undergoing a major renovation.

of Gaviota, passing through the coastal range mountains to the valleys of central California only to reappear on the coast more than 50 miles north. The state park encompassing this beach includes campgrounds, a fishing pier, and other facilities for the traveler.

Much of the beach is sandy, but some rocky outcroppings serve as alternatives to the usual surf species. Some rockfish come in close enough to the beach to approach with a good cast. For the rocky portions, I like anchovies or cut squid cast out near the offshore rocky reef formations that are clearly visible from the shore. Squid-baited shrimp flies are another possibility.

For sandy beaches, mussels, bloodworms, sand crabs, clam siphons, and ghost shrimp are the best baits. Barred surfperch are the most common catch, but spotfin croakers can also be enticed, especially with clams. If you cast out farther, you have a chance at a halibut or shovelnose guitarfish when using squid or anchovies. You get more attention if you rip the anchovies into chunks rather than cutting them into pieces. When you rip them apart, tiny pieces break loose and offer a kind of chum slick that makes a scent for fish to follow.

Gaviota Pier

Right in the center of Gaviota State Park, one of the most interesting fishing piers in all the southern California range stretches out into a kelp bed. The Gaviota pier is the most remote of any pier in southern California, so it doesn't get any huge fishing pressure. The fact that it covers all sorts of bottom (sand, rocks, and kelp forests) means that you can probably catch more species of fish here than anywhere else in southern California.

The surf zone has the usual barred surfperch and spotfin croakers. Ghost shrimp or bloodworms are an excellent choice for fishing here. Mussels are also good bait that can attract different species of perch. As the pier stretches into deeper water, the kelp clusters get thicker and support a wide variety of fish, including several species of rockfish, kelpfish, jacksmelt, and of course, calico bass. On the bottom are white croaker, halibut, and sandy bottom sharks, such as leopard sharks, shovelnose guitarfish, and thornbacks. Near the end of the pier, mackerel, barracuda, and the occasional bonito are on the menu.

This pier also has quite a reputation as a nighttime shark fishing destination. Campers staying overnight at the state park have access to the pier all night. Often, groups and families cluster near the end of the pier to try their hand at bigger shark fishing. Cut mackerel is a popular bait, and quite a few different types of sharks can be caught here, including thresher sharks, bat rays, and spiny dogfish, in addition to the usual shovelnose and leopards.

Access to the Point Arguello to Gaviota Coast

US 101 turns inland to pass through the coastal mountain range and into the Santa Maria valley beyond, so only the beach at Gaviota State Park itself is accessible to the shore fisherman. Gaviota has minimal facilities, and reservations are on a first-come, first-served basis and must be made by calling Gaviota State Park at 805-968-1033.

The balance of the coast is only accessible by water. Santa Barbara is the closest port, some 30 miles or so to the east. Santa Barbara features excellent launch ramps, charter boats, and party boats. The trip from Santa Barbara is relatively uncomplicated but can be hazardous if foggy conditions or a southerly wind and weather pattern are prevailing. Numerous offshore drilling rigs and oil production equipment stud the offshore banks off the coastline between Santa Barbara and Point Arguello, so make sure you have the latest charts and a way to navigate should the fog roll in. The prevailing winds are from the northwest, so the entire coastline is protected from the weather. However, blows from the south can spring up and turn the seas from flat calm to downright nasty. There are ample anchorages that offer protection from the north and northwesterly winds, but none save the Santa Barbara harbor offer protection in southerly winds, unless you attempt to cross the channel and anchor up in the lee of one of the Channel Islands, a chancy and very rough experience in foul weather.

Refugio to Goleta Coast

Just east of Gaviota, the coastline opens up to a narrow coastal plain between the mountains and the sea. Most of the coastline consists of cliffs to narrow, rock strewn beaches. There are a number of places where there is beach access. The subsea topography is also fairly flat for several miles offshore, with a flat plain averaging

Refugio to Goleta Coast

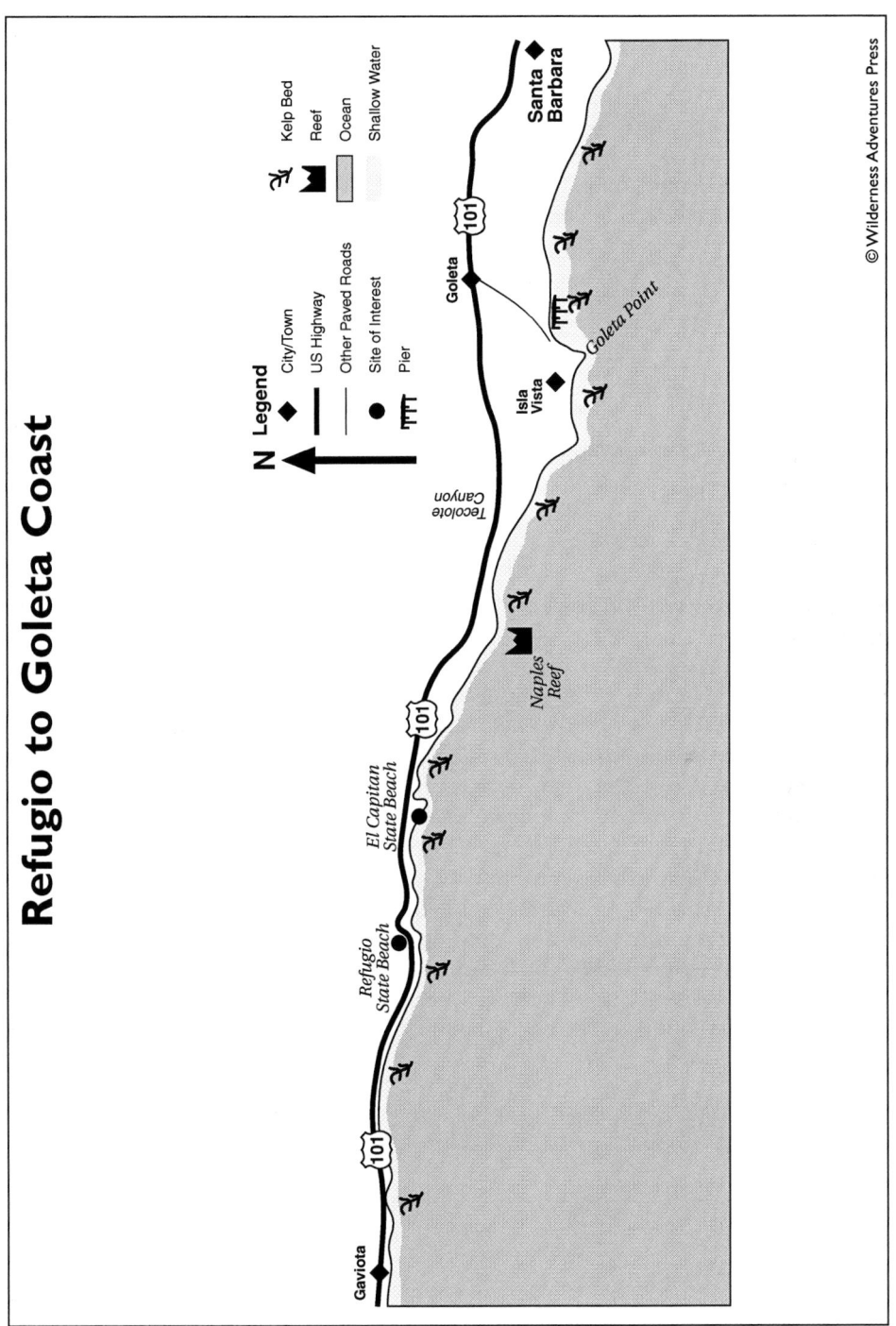

Legend

N

◆ City/Town

— US Highway

— Other Paved Roads

● Site of Interest

⊤⊤⊤ Pier

⬛ Kelp Bed

◆ Reef

▢ Ocean

Shallow Water

Gaviota

Refugio State Beach

El Capitan State Beach

Naples Reef

Tecolote Canyon

Isla Vista

Goleta

Goleta Point

Santa Barbara

101

about 150 feet deep before encountering a sharp dropoff to the bottom of the Santa Barbara Channel. Rocky reefs stud the shoreline, nearly all covered with thick stands of kelp.

Plentiful surface fishing, shallow water rock fishing, and flats fishing locations stud the coast. Actually, there are few places along this coast that stand out because the fishing is relatively good anywhere along the coast. In addition, the dropoff on the outside edge of the shallower near-shore flats area has a number of cracks and gorges offering good habitat for the many deep-water rock cod species. The shore angler is somewhat limited, since much of the coastline has no access due to the tall cliffs characteristic of the shoreline. In all, this coastline is a fisherman's paradise.

Some of the better places to fish in this area include:

Refugio Kelp

Another near-shore kelp bed hugging the Santa Barbara western coastline is the thick kelp forest off Refugio State Beach. Gripping a rocky undersea reef, the thick kelp canopy is refuge for a wide variety of kelp-dwelling species and is frequently visited by bigger pelagic species during their annual summer migrations to the coast.

The king of the kelp-dwelling game fish is the calico bass. Here at the Refugio beds, calicos are both common and large. Fish the edges of the kelp beds with live anchovies for best results. The livelier the bait, the better chance you'll have of fooling a big bull calico into darting out from under cover to engulf the offering. In addition to live bait, a variety of artificial lures, including metal jigs, rubber swimbaits, or bigger swimming lures worked around the edges of the kelp canopy will also entice these fish to strike.

Calicos are a fun flyfishing sport, and Refugio is a great place to flyfish. Present baitfish imitation flies to the edges of the surface kelp and retrieve with an erratic ripping action for best results. When bigger pelagic fish, such as barracuda or bonito, are here, they will also attack a well-presented fly, so make sure you don't undergun yourself. I have a 9-weight that's the minimum I'll use—and that's only if I'm fairly sure there are no big bonito or yellowtail around. If so, I step up to a 10 or 12.

Barracuda, bonito, and occasionally yellowtail are warm summer visitors to Refugio, and if conditions are right, fishing for these species can be quite good. Keep a jig stick handy with a blue and white, green and yellow, or one of my favorites, a green, black, and white jig rigged. If you spot any boils—fish breaking the surface after bait—pitch them a jig.

The bottom of these kelp beds can be quite good for rockfish of various types, sheephead, and the occasional cabezon and white seabass. Fishing deep with cut squid, squid-baited shrimp flies, live anchovies, or rubber swimbaits with a thin strip of cut squid, or for sheephead, head-on shrimp, should yield some interesting varieties of fish to round out your catch.

Refugio State Beach

This is one of the smallest state beaches in California but one that should not be passed up as a potential fishing spot. The sandier areas get their runs of barred surf-

The many rocky points along the Santa Barbara coast, such as this one at Refugio State Beach, are revered by fishermen for their ability to produce many different fish species.

perch and the occasional spotfin croaker. Refugio Beach is easily accessible via the US 101 west of Santa Barbara.

The beach is fairly steep, dropping off quickly to 100 feet within a few hundred yards from the shore. If you are targeting surf species, the biggest mistake most neophytes make is to think they have to cast a long way off. Surf fish feed in the white water inside the breaking waves. You can literally catch them in ankle deep water, so if your bait is 100 yards offshore in 20 feet of water, you have no chance. I like a shorter, bass-type rod and reel for these fish. Use green rubber grubs for barred perch, or if you prefer bait, try bloodworms or mussels. The best time to fish is within an hour or two of high tide.

Refugio is an interesting place because you can cast out into deeper water where there are some submerged rocks. Use cut squid or squid-baited shrimp flies in these areas to target brown rockfish, kelp rockfish, and occasionally, a cabezon.

El Capitan State Beach

El Capitan State Beach is a popular surfing spot for many young Santa Barbara water sportsmen. They have excellent facilities and parking and it's only a short drive from the city. A stairway leads you down to the shoreline from the bluffs above. It's also a wonderful fishing beach. Like many of the beaches west of Santa Barbara, El Capitan offers both sand beaches and a rocky shoreline, complete with tide pools, providing an interesting variety of species for any fisherman.

To fish the rocky areas, try cut squid, squid-baited shrimp flies or torn apart anchovies for best results. Cast between the shore and one of the many exposed or intertidal rocks easily visible from the shoreline. Rockfish, an occasional cabezon, and several other possible species of fish are on the menu here.

The sandy beaches also host barred surfperch in really fine numbers. These fish are year-round visitors to nearly all the California beaches and offer a great way to break into surf fishing. They are fun and easy to catch, good to eat, and great sport. The best baits are bloodworms or mussels on tiny hooks cast right into the breaking surf. Use light leaders, 4- or 6-pound test mono on a Carolina rig for best results.

El Capitan Coastal Kelp

Just offshore of the El Capitan area, an excellent stand of kelp forest covers a wide, rocky reef. Like all kelp-covered reefs, this one attracts southern California's most popular game fish, calico bass. Resident bass can be caught here year-round, but the summer is always more productive than the cooler months. This is because the fish become more active and feed closer to the surface. Live bait is always the most productive, but cut squid, swimming plugs, and rubber swimbaits all produce well here. Cast just to the edges of the kelp; then, if using live bait, let it struggle to be free while giving it all the line it wants, or if using an inanimate lure, begin making it look animated.

From the spring months through summer, schools of barracuda frequent this coastline and often stop at the El Capitan kelp to feed. Blue and white lures are the most enticing for barracuda, but other colors and other baits work well, too. If using live bait, a short section of wire leader will keep you from getting your mono bitten through by these sharp-toothed predators.

Occasionally, yellowtail or bonito visit these kelp forests as well. Keep your eyes peeled for big boils around the outsides of the kelp beds and cast a green and yellow, blue and white, or shiny chrome spoon or jig in front of the boiling fish to land one of these great fighting game fish.

The El Capitan kelp is an excellent place to flyfish for calico bass, barracuda, yellowtail, as well as bonito. The summer months usually bring very calm conditions and a glassy water surface, perfect for sight-casting to submerged kelp strands waving in the currents. Here, kelp-dwelling fish hide to ambush bait, and the bigger, bluewater fish, such as yellowtail, constantly scour places like this attempting to trap their prey out in the open where they are more vulnerable. A baitfish-imitating fly, such as a Clouser minnow, is the ideal enticement for these species.

Don't forget to try out the bottom here, also. The sandy flats around the kelp stands hold halibut, sand bass, and sanddabs, while the rocky bottom areas can offer up sculpin, sheephead, and several species of rockfish. In the winter, and especially when the squid spawn is on, big, fat white seabass cruise the area as well, so be prepared when fishing the bottom at these times.

Naples Reef

Situated at the edge of the El Capitan kelp beds are a series of submerged, rocky reefs extending over a mile offshore. This structure comprises Naples Reef. It's an excellent habitat and gathering point for both bottom-dwelling resident species and migratory game species. Naples Reef is a year-round producer of fine fishing.

In summer, Naples offers some of the finer pelagic game species fishing in the Santa Barbara area. Barracuda, bonito, and in the warmer months yellowtail, pass through the area and stop at Naples to feed on the schools of baitfish that the area seems to attract like a magnet. Trolling, jigfishing, and live bait fishing are all productive here. I recommend trolling to find the schools, unless there happens to be a lot of diving bird activity, then bait or jigfishing once the main body of the school is located. Live anchovies (sardine if yellowtail are in the neighborhood) or even small mackerel baits are preferred. As for jigs, blue and white is hard to beat, especially in the sunshine. If the skies are overcast, a green or dark color sometimes improves the hookup ratio.

Don't forget the bottom—Naples reef provides year-round action for calico bass, rockfish, and sheephead. Occasionally, cabezon, rock sole, and several other rock-dwelling species can be caught, too. Just run your baits down to the rocky reef after metering the rocks for the presence of fish.

The sandy bottoms surrounding the reefs are another area not to be missed. Some excellent California halibut fishing, along with sanddabs and white croakers, can be done by keeping live bait moving along the bottom. In lieu of bait, bounce rubber swimbaits along the bottom to drive the bottom predators wild. In addition, some excellent shark fishing can be had among these reefs. Shovelnose guitarfish, leopard sharks, some thresher sharks, skates, and rays can all be found near the reef.

Tecolote Canyon Kelp

Where the Tecolote Canyon mouth cuts through the coastal mountains just ashore of this part of the Santa Barbara coastline, a great kelp bed grows just offshore. This is a calico bass haven, and plenty of excellent fishing exists nearly all year, although it is best in summer.

The Tecolote Canyon kelp should be fished, just as any other kelp bed area, with live bait, swimming plugs, or rubber swimbaits to entice resident bass out of their hiding places among the kelp fronds and get them to strike. In addition to bait and lures, flies are yet another fine attraction for calicos while adding a new dimension in challenge and fun for the fisherman. Be sure to use a fast sinking fly line. It is a very rare day when bass rise all the way to the surface to snatch a floating meal.

Barracuda are the other main game fish at Tecolote, visiting only in late spring and early summer. They are such voracious predators that they can be caught many different ways. The challenge of yet another technique to convince these strong fighting game fish is always a fun study.

Isla Vista Shoreline

The University of California at Santa Barbara sits on a stunning promontory point called Isla Vista. From the point, the sun rises out of the ocean and sets into the ocean. It is truly a unique place with fascinating beaches, both rocky and sandy.

*Goleta's productive fishing flats are literally in the shadow of the famous
University of California at Santa Barbara (UCSB).*

I learned to surf on the waves off Isla Vista and spent many enjoyable hours fishing
there, as well.

For the surf fisherman, first decide whether you wish to pursue sandy bottom
species, such as barred surfperch, halibut, sand sharks, or spotfin croakers, or if you
would rather fish the rocks and try for starry rockfish, cabezon, and other types of
surfperch. If you choose the former, select a sandy beach area and use mussels or
bloodworms, or if you cast way out, use cut squid. The barred surfperch and spotfins will inevitably be caught right in the whitewater, whereas halibut and sharks are
generally farther out.

If you like rocky bottom fishing, tear dead anchovies into hunks or fish with strips
of cut squid. You'll need to drag the bait along the rocky bottom to keep it moving and
present it to as many potential fish as possible. You'll probably lose a lot of tackle in the
sharp rocks before mastering the technique of dragging a sinker over the rocks without allowing it to hang up. I generally use a short, "weak link" of mono line (about half
the breaking strength) to my main line and attach the sinker to the end of the leader.
This ensures that if the sinker fouls, the sinker line will break and allow my main line,
complete with hook and bait, to float free. Another wise idea is to use torpedo-shaped
sinkers. These foul much less easily than a surf- or pyramid-shaped sinker.

Goleta Kelp

Right offshore from the Goleta Beaches there is an excellent rocky bottom that supports a healthy stand of kelp. This is an interesting kelp bed to fish since it's so close to the Goleta Beach and Pier where small aluminum skiffs can be rented. This makes these kelp beds an easy jaunt for even novice boaters. The kelp beds cover several acres, so even with the relatively heavy fishing pressure they receive, they still support a strong population of resident species and attract plenty of bait. This means plenty of fast swimming pelagic species in the summer months. All things considered, there are few more convenient, highly productive fishing spots in southern California.

Start at the Goleta kelp bed with live bait if you can get it. Calicos can be easily convinced to emerge from their leafy hiding spots to chase well-presented live bait. For a different challenge, try swimming plugs, especially the deep diving variety. Another hot lure is lead-headed rubber swimbaits. Blue and white, green and white, or all green bait are the favorites. These days, the single-tailed, shad-shaped body swimbaits are the rage, but I find the twin-tailed swimbaits just as effective as they have always been.

If you are looking to try out ocean flyfishing, you can't find a better place to develop your skills. A blue and white Clouser minnow or similar baitfish-imitating fly on a shooting head, sinking fly line is just the thing for getting calicos to take notice. Look for breaks in the kelp, where you can drop the fly with a clear channel out of the kelp, and use a twitchy but moderately fast retrieve.

In the warmer months, barracuda and occasionally bonito and yellowtail frequent the Goleta kelp beds. They are found on the seaward side, so it might be a bit far to take a rental skiff. Trolling or metal jigfishing are the two preferred methods to catch these species, but they will also hit live bait and swimming plugs. They will take a well-presented fly, also, but prefer a fast, ripping retrieve to the slower technique you might prefer for calicos and kelp-dwelling species.

The bottom here is also an excellent place to fish. The sandy bottom around the reef is active with browsing halibut, bigger sand sharks, and rays. Sand bass make their home in these flats, as well. Live bait, cut squid, or rubber swimbaits, especially sweetened with a small strip of cut bait, are all excellent choices for the flats.

The rockier-bottomed areas feature smaller rock cod, cabezon, and sheephead. They'll eat squid-baited shrimp flies, live bait, cut squid, or perhaps best of all, shrimp. Keep your wits about you, especially when fishing with squid, because white seabass are returning in more and more numbers and the chance of hooking one of these big croakers, while fishing with squid above a rocky bottom near standing kelp, keeps getting better and better every year. Fifty-pounders are not all that unusual.

Goleta Beach

The Goleta Beach recreational area is a great playground for families. Plenty of barbecue pits, shelters, and facilities make it an excellent beach for people of all ages to enjoy. The fishing here is also among the best places in all of southern California

The fishing pier at Goleta Beach near Santa Barbara.

for sandy-bottomed species. Barred surfperch, spotfin croakers, and occasionally halibut are caught here in good numbers.

The best baits for surf casting here are bloodworms. In addition, mussels, sand crabs, ghost shrimp, and clam siphons are all productive baits. The surf here is generally quite mild, so keeping bait in the whitewater means having them exposed and laying on the beach much of the time. A flip cast, not too far out, is all you need to get bait into the prime feeding area. Keep the bait gently moving, either by sidling down the beach, or by casting out, slowly retrieving and casting out anew. The trick here is to cover as much bottom as possible. Surf species are on the lookout for roiled mud. It usually means something is crawling around on the bottom, so give them what they want!

Goleta Beach is one of the best shark beaches in the county, also. Giant bat rays, leopard sharks, and shovelnose guitarfish are all plentiful here. At sunset or just after high tide is the ideal time to fish. Some ground-up anchovies in an old sock with a rock in it, tossed out as far as possible on a long string, makes a bait slick that will attract both baitfish and sharks. Cast your torn-in-half anchovy baits out near the chum and hang on.

Goleta Pier

This is perhaps one of the finest fishing piers in southern California. There's nearly always something biting here—usually the species that are most desirable. The pier itself is a 1450-foot long wooden structure that is well maintained. It is open

24 hours a day and features lights at night and a convenient fish cleaning station. There is a sling to launch small boats here and also a boat rental facility to take aluminum boats out into the protected water nearby.

On the pier, the fishing is generally very good. Near the shoreline in shallow water, plenty of barred surfperch can be caught on bloodworms, ghost shrimp, or mussel baits. The sometimes-good runs of spotfin croakers can give the angler using clams a real treat. Shovelnose guitarfish, especially at night, are another treat this pier offers near the shoreline. In the pier's middle area, white croakers and other types of perch are on the menu. Anchovy chunks, mussels, or cut squid are the hot ticket for white croakers. Halibut are also found in the middle pier area. This is one of the better halibut piers in southern California, and many bigger fish are caught here. Cut squid that is kept moving or anchovies are the preferred baits for these flatfish, but a rubber swimbait, expertly walked along the bottom will also certainly get noticed by any big halibut in the area.

Out near the end of the pier, calico and sand bass hide in the sometimes thick kelp paddies that get trapped among the pilings. In addition, mackerel, barracuda, occasionally bonito, and even yellowtail visit the pier. When the pelagic species are around, a small feather jig, shiny spoon, or metal jig seem to be the lures of choice.

If you have the time and interest, renting an aluminum skiff and taking it out into Goleta Bay is a great and inexpensive way to spend a very enjoyable day fishing. I once hooked a huge bat ray on 8-pound test spinning tackle here. The big fish towed the boat around for almost two hours as I gave and took line. Three times I had the fish up to the boat to gaff, and each time it somehow found renewed strength and sounded again. When it finally managed to hide in the kelp, I broke it off. Though I lost the fish, it still remains one of my most memorable fish battles.

The pier is located in the Goleta County Beach and managed by the County of Santa Barbara. Excellent parking, restrooms, a snack and bait and tackle shop, as well as a picnic area await the traveler arriving at Goleta. It's a great place for family fun. Unlike the beaches farther south, Goleta Beach, like most Santa Barbara beaches, has little, if any, pounding surf. This makes them exceptionally safe.

Access: Refugio to Goleta Coast

US 101 passes right through the area and is the only main thoroughfare in the entire area. Beach access turnoffs are clearly marked. Throughout the western end of the area, US 101 looks out over the ocean and is a spectacular drive.

Refugio State Beach operates from dawn to dusk. Picnicking and beach use are the main activities available here (besides fishing, of course!). And a bike trail runs from Refugio to El Capitan to the east. To get there, take US 101 west from Santa Barbara for 23 miles and follow the signs to the beach. Call 805-968-1033 for the latest conditions at Refugio.

Traveling east from Refugio, El Capitan State Beach is only 19 miles from Santa Barbara and offers overnight camping in addition to day use. It's a lovely place to spend the day for the whole family. For information, call 805-968-1033.

The Isla Vista coastline is readily accessible from US 101 by following the signs to the University of California at Santa Barbara. Both the university coastline and the residential portion of the coast are available for public access, although a permit is needed to park in the University grounds.

To reach the area by boat, Santa Barbara is the only convenient port. Excellent launching facilities are available next to Stearns Wharf. For smaller boats, a sling launch facility is available at the Goleta Pier. To get to Goleta Pier and Beach, take US 101 to the CA 217 airport exit. Follow it to Sandspit Road and the Goleta Beach Park turnoff. Follow this to the park and the pier.

Santa Barbara and Carpinteria Coast

Just east of Goleta, the coastal plain widens to form the main part of the city of Santa Barbara. Some of the better places to fish in this area include:

Arroyo Burro State Beach

A small beach situated near the posh, exclusive Hope Ranch section of Santa Barbara, Arroyo Burro State Beach is a great place to fish. It's usually fairly uncrowded and offers a great stretch of sandy coastline for a surf angler to ply his sport. Surf species, particularly barred surfperch and sometimes spotfin croaker, compose the bulk of the catch off Arroyo Burro, but bigger game, such as halibut and shovelnose guitarfish, are another option that makes for interesting fishing.

For surf species, the preferred baits are mussels, bloodworms, ghost shrimp, or, if available, sand crabs. Don't cast the bait too far out into the surf. The hour or two on either side of high tide are the best times. In the winter, you can also try small (1½-inch) green rubber grubs, called surfperch killers (I wonder why) for barred surfperch. These are especially effective during the Christmas spawn.

Cast farther out to get at the guitarfish and halibut. Cut squid, dead anchovies, or torn-apart anchovies are probably the better baits. Use more weight and a slow retrieve to keep the bait moving unless you're lucky enough to have a strong current parallel to the beach to help you out in this department.

Santa Barbara Kelp

This is one of the smallest but nicest patches of kelp along the coast. Its proximity to Santa Barbara Harbor means it is fished rather heavily, however, it is still a very productive place to fish and one that shouldn't be overlooked if you're in the area. It is predominantly a calico bass spot, but it also gets its share of barracuda in season and, like most kelp beds, has a strong bottom-dwelling population of reef fish. Few fishermen ever check out the bottom when kelp bed fishing, preferring the surface or midwater species. This is a shame because most kelp beds harbor plenty of smaller game species, such as rock cod of various types, halfmoons (blue perch), opaleye, and several others. These are all very good eating and lots of fun to catch on light tackle.

Work the outside edges of kelp beds for the best results on calicos. Live bait is, as usual, the best producer. For a change of pace and fishing style, try switching to

Santa Barbara to Carpinteria Coast

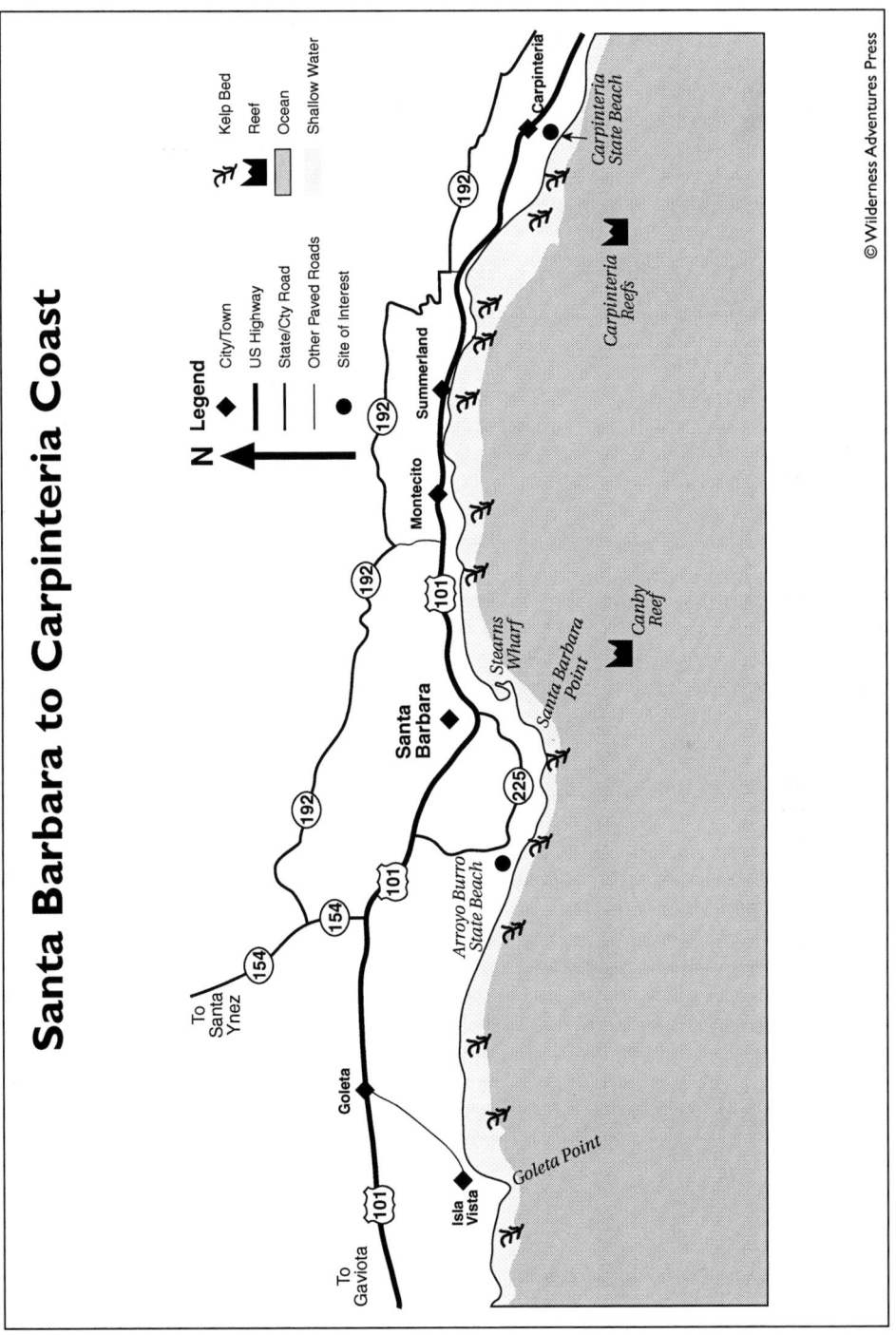

Legend

◆ City/Town
━━ US Highway
━ State/Cty Road
━ Other Paved Roads
● Site of Interest

Kelp Bed
Reef
Ocean
Shallow Water

To Gaviota

To Santa Ynez

Goleta

Isla Vista

Goleta Point

Arroyo Burro State Beach

Santa Barbara

Stearns Wharf

Santa Barbara Point

Canby Reef

Montecito

Summerland

Carpinteria Reefs

Carpinteria

Carpinteria State Beach

© Wilderness Adventures Press

diving plugs, just like the freshwater bass fishermen use. You'll have a blast pitching the lures to the edges of kelp and luring the bigger bass out of their hiding places. Rubber swimbaits are another old standby and work quite well here.

To fish the bottom, use just enough sinker to get to the bottom. Once again, live bait is one of the preferred methods, but cut squid can be almost as effective (sometimes more). I like a strip, squid-baited shrimp fly tied on a stainless 1/0 hook for this kind of fishing. It will attract a wide variety of small game and the occasional bigger fish, such as a sheephead or even white seabass.

If halfmoons are schooling, step down to a #6 or #8 hook and bait up with tiny pieces of cut squid or mussel. These tasty little fish have very small mouths, so only a tiny hook and bait will result in a hookup. While you can use bigger chunks that elicit aggressive attacks, you'll get very few hookups. I carry a graphite freshwater spinning rod and reel rigged with 8-pound test for just such occasions as this. Let all those other guys scratch and scrimp for calicos, I'll be having a blast hauling in the blue perch.

Canby Reef

Right off Santa Barbara Point, just about 2 miles offshore, is a series of submerged rocky reefs in about 215 feet of water, which is too deep for a stand of kelp. These are called the Canby Reef and are an interesting habitat for many resident and a few migratory species.

Canby is known for its calico bass fishing. I know there isn't any kelp, but nonetheless, calicos seem to like the underwater structure and are often on the reef in strong numbers. Here, a Carolina rig with at least a ¾-ounce (usually more) sinker is needed to get bait down to the bottom in this depth. Live bait is the best bet, but rubber also brings them up from the deep. It's too deep to fish with plugs, but metal bone jigs can be used successfully if you prefer fishing with hardware.

In the winter months, lingcod move into shallower water, and quite often, a big ling can be dragged up from Canby. I like a whole, live mackerel sent down with 8 ounces of lead in a double hook arrangement, but some people prefer chrome jigs and spoons. A deck hand once told me the giant crocodile spoons were the best for this type of work since they tended to produce lots of action with minimal motion, but I found my hookup ratio improved once I switched from mono to braided line when jigfishing deep. The nonstretch characteristics of Dacron, or my preferred line, Spectra, give jigs plenty of action and lure the big lings in.

Of course, the usual shallow water rock cod species also inhabit Canby. You'll catch them incidentally using the same techniques as for calicos. If you're really feeling lucky and the season is right, try a whole live squid for a possible white seabass or a shrimp for a big sheephead.

Santa Barbara Flats

Just offshore of the Santa Barbara Harbor is one of the finest near-shore halibut flats anywhere. Some mighty fine halibut are often taken within a stone's throw from

The beautiful Santa Barbara coastline is a great place for surf fishing.

the Santa Barbara channel entrance. In addition, shovelnose guitarfish, sanddabs, and often sand bass inhabit these flats and make fishing here a real experience.

As with all flats fishing, drifting is the most productive way to get bait covering the ground in order to present it to the most game fish. Be careful, though, Santa Barbara Harbor can be a busy place, with everything from jet skis and kayaks to nearly ship-sized commercial boats passing back and forth through this area while entering and leaving port. Live bait is the halibut fisherman's staple and rubber swimbait is a close second. If all else fails, use long strips of cut squid and keep them slowly fluttering to imitate a swimming motion on or near the bottom. Keep covering ground and the bait is bound to pass something hungry. There are plenty of other types of bottom-dwelling sharks and rays here, as well, so be prepared. It shouldn't be a shock to hook into a 100-plus-pound bat ray in this area.

Stearns Wharf

In the main Santa Barbara Harbor district is a 130-year-old shipping pier called Stearns Wharf. Though the original structure is long gone through rot, fire, and general deterioration, it has been replaced with modern materials and building techniques while retaining its original design when piers were used as loading and unloading docks for ships in the days before semi-trucks and paved super highways.

This very popular pier is a giant, comparable in size to the huge Santa Monica Pier. You can drive out onto the pier and park there. Seafood restaurants, tourist shops, a museum, and other commercial businesses call Stearns Wharf home.

While not primarily a fishing pier, you can still fish on Stearns Wharf and enjoy considerable success. Santa Barbara Harbor is an excellent place to catch halibut, and these big flat fish are the most desired target on the pier. They're best caught on live anchovies, but dead bait or cut squid, if kept moving, will also entice them. Some anglers also fish with rubber swimbaits. Long, single-tailed green baits on smallish hooks seem to be preferred by halibut in this area. I'd sweeten the rig with a very thin strip of cut squid for that special aroma that drives fish wild. Keep the bait moving for best results.

White croaker, jacksmelt, surfperch, and shovelnose guitarfish are also caught on this pier in good numbers. Use small baits or bait-catching rigs for the perch and jacksmelt, cut squid or anchovy pieces for the croaker and guitarfish.

One day when I was visiting this pier, I saw someone catching plenty of spider crabs using a large crab net baited with the center of a filleted fish. The crabs were covered with seaweed as a sort of camouflage. Dozens of tourists gathered around to see these large moss-covered crabs sidle along the pier as the crab fisherman let them creep along on their own before the crowd of astonished tourists.

Stearns Wharf has parking both on the pier and in the lots at the base of the pier. It's open 24 hours a day and features lights, benches, restrooms, and many eateries and snack bars. It's an experience not to be missed when traveling to Santa Barbara, whether you actually fish there or not.

Santa Barbara/Montecito Beach

From the Santa Barbara Harbor to the posh residential neighborhoods of Montecito, a long, sandy beach with occasional pebble-covered stretches graces the coastline. This beach is very accessible, quite enjoyable, and is productive to fish. The water is generally fairly calm and the beach slope gradual, more like the wide beaches of Orange and San Diego Counties.

Two types of fishing can be done from these beaches: the usual sand species, including barred surfperch, spotfin croaker, yellowfin croaker, and the occasional corbina; or deeper water surf casting, more like flats fishing for halibut and sand sharks of various types.

If you're after surf species, bloodworms, sand crabs, ghost shrimp, or mussels are your best bet for bait. Cast out with very light leaders (6-pound test) and small hooks (#6 or smaller) not too far out into the surf for best results. Since these species are used to finding food in mud swirls, they can be stimulated by slowly retrieving the bait, which works well because it kicks up the mud a bit as the sinker scrapes along the bottom. In winter, try switching to single-tailed green rubber grubs instead of live bait. When the surfperch run is on, it saves you lots of time rebaiting hooks.

If you want to try for a big flat fish, switch to live bait, cut squid, or anchovy chunks cast out as far as possible, then slowly retrieved toward the beach. Do this at night or even in the early evening, and a big shovelnose guitarfish or leopard shark might be on the menu. Even big bat rays (up to 150 pounds or more) can be enticed to strike this way.

For a very fun and unique experience, bring a 10-weight fly rod to the beach with a shooting head, sinking line. Red and orange flies simulate shrimp and other sand-dwelling critters, while blue and white streamers imitate anchovies. If all else fails, a green woolly bugger will get surfperch downright frantic to strike. This is a fascinating place to fly cast from the beach. You'll probably draw a crowd of curious onlookers who are wondering what you're doing with that funny looking pole, so keep an eye on your backcast or you might hook a 150-pound tourist.

Summerland Kelp

The coastline by the small community of Summerland features a rocky point extending out into the channel. Just offshore this rocky characteristic continues, and an excellent stand of kelp forest graces this undersea reef. Here, calico bass inhabit the area year-round. Sand bass and halibut love the sandy and muddy edges of the reef, and sculpin, sheephead, and rockfish are also year-round residents. In summer, the abundance of life here attracts the bigger, pelagic species, such as barracuda and the occasional bonito or even yellowtail.

Fish the Summerland kelp as you would just about any kelp bed by working the edges at different depths until you find what's biting. Some people refuse to try deeper and insist on only flylining live bait. This can be a mistake—you'll miss out on some excellent action and a wider variety of fish species if you stick to one depth only.

In warmer months, keep an eye peeled for breezing fish (pelagic fish like barracuda or yellowtail) passing through. They'll probably be following bait, and the birds will have noticed as well. I like to keep a jig stick rigged and within easy reach just in case a big yellowtail comes through. Often, these fish are very transient, and if you see them and aren't prepared, they'll be a mile or more away by the time you rig up, and you'll have missed your chance.

Carpinteria State Beach

Hailed as "The World's Safest Beach," Carpinteria is one of the nicer family beach recreational areas in the county. While not a "world class" fishing beach, Carpinteria is nonetheless a fine fishing destination and one that easily accommodates fun family excursions when not all the family members are devout anglers.

The primary catch at Carpinteria is barred surfperch. These are best caught two hours before to one hour after high tide. Use bloodworms, mussels, or green rubber grubs, don't cast too far out, and allow them to drift with the wave-induced surges. Occasional spotfin croaker catches can liven up the action, as well. If you cast farther out from the beach, you have a chance at halibut by using cut squid or anchovy pieces. The best technique is to cast out as far as possible, then slowly retrieve the bait in toward the shore. When using this technique, be alert for the slightest bump on the line. Some of these fish do not hit hard. Once felt, set the hook with authority to snag your prey.

Santa Barbara's boat launch ramps: in the background is Sea Landing, one of Santa Barbara's sportfishing landings, and farther in the background is Stearn's Wharf.

At night especially, Carpinteria State Beach can be a good to excellent shark beach. Shovelnose guitarfish, bat rays, and leopard sharks make up the bulk of the catch. Cut mackerel, torn anchovies, or cut squid are all good shark bait. An early evening high tide is often a sign of a good shark run. An even better time is when a grunion run is predicted. Sharks seem to know when the grunion are planning to run and congregate near the beaches to feast on the little fish.

Carpinteria Reefs

Lying just offshore of the Carpinteria coastline are a series of submerged reefs in 90 to 110 feet of water. On occasion, these rocky bottom areas wear kelp crowns, but most years, they do not. Nonetheless, they're still excellent places to fish for shallow reef-type fish, such as calico bass and sheephead. In the spring and summer months, barracuda are attracted to this area, and in some years, bonito and yellowtail frequent the site.

Fishing the reefs requires going into deeper water than the usual kelp bed fishing. Send live bait down on Carolina rigs for the best results with calicos. Lead-headed rubber swimbaits, particularly blue and brown shad patterns and green and white patterns, also seem to work well here.

If barracuda are present, metallic jigs are the best choice. Cast them to the reef, let them sink all the way to the bottom, and then begin a fast retrieve. Keep alert because barracuda often hit the jig as it flutters down. If barracuda are running small, I prefer single hooks. You may not get as many hookups, but it prevents mangling the mouth of a short fish while trying to get the treble hook out with the realization that it's going to die anyway. That's a real shame.

During fall and winter months at dawn, a whole, live squid on the bottom is sometimes just the breakfast a big white seabass is looking for, particularly in the dark of the moon. Here's a good place to stalk one of these big croakers. You might also find there are some really good-sized sheephead along this reef. A whole, head-on shrimp on the bottom among the rocks will find out for sure.

Access to the Santa Barbara and Carpinteria Coast

From the south, Hwy 101 follows right along the beach past Rincon Point, the separating line between Santa Barbara County and Ventura County. From the north, US 101 is again the main artery into Santa Barbara County, which hosts a wide variety of facilities for travelers. Two visitor centers that are open to the public serve Santa Barbara:

The Santa Barbara Tourist Information Center
1 Garden Street
Santa Barbara, CA 93101
805-965-3021
Hours
Monday through Saturday, 9AM to 5PM
Sunday, 10AM to 5PM
Hours may vary according to season

Santa Barbara Hot Spots
36 State Street
Santa Barbara, CA 93101
800-793-7666
Hours
Monday through Saturday: 9AM to 9PM
Sunday: 9AM to 4PM
Coffee bar and lobby open 24 hours

In addition to driving by car, Santa Barbara has commercial and private airport service located in Goleta. United Airlines (805-967-7427), Alaska Airlines (800-426-0333), American Airlines (800-433-7300), America West Airlines (800-235-9292), Northwest Airlines (800-225-2525), and US Airways (800-428-4322) all have service to Santa Barbara. Amtrak has train service to Santa Barbara from either Los Angeles to the south or the bay area (San Francisco, Oakland) to the north. Amtrak can be reached at 800-872-7245.

COMMON GAME FISH AVAILABILITY BY MONTHS
SANTA BARBARA COUNTY

Species	Jan	Feb	Mar	Apr	May	Jun	Jul	Aug	Sep	Oct	Nov	Dec
Yellowtail												
Barracuda												
Bonito												
Calico Bass												
Sand Bass												
White Seabass												
Halibut												
Lingcod												
Shallow-water Rockfish												
Deep-water Rockfish												
Sheephead												
Sculpin												
Blue Perch												
Salmon												
Whitefish												

Not Available   Fish Possible   Good Fishing   Excellent Fishing

Santa Barbara Charters

Santa Barbara has an excellent harbor with a wide, well-maintained launch ramp. It is located right next to Stearns Wharf. There are several full service sportfishing landings located in the harbor. These landings offer a variety of trips, from 4-hour local half-day trips to multiple day island fishing cruises. Six-pack charter boats can also be booked at these landings:

Stardust Sportfishing
SEA Landing
301 W. Cabrillo Boulevard
Santa Barbara, CA 93101
(805) 963-3564
http://www.stardustsportfishing.com/

Wave Walker Charters
301 W. Cabrillo Blvd.
Santa Barbara, CA 93109
(805) 964-2046
http://www.wavewalker.com

Santa Barbara Tackle Shops

Plenty of fishing tackle shops grace Santa Barbara County. Here's a listing of the major shops:

Harbor Tackle
117 Harbor Way
Santa Barbara, CA 93109
(805) 962-4720

The Bait Shop
232 Stearns Wharf
Santa Barbara, CA 93101
(805) 965-1333

Hook Line & Sinker
4010 Calle Real
Santa Barbara, CA 93110
(805) 687-5689

Santa Barbara County Accommodations

The following list is a sampling of lodgings that are close to port in Santa Barbara. These range from basic to luxury, and you should keep in mind that nothing along the southern California coast, particularly anything close to the water, is inexpensive.

Country Inn by the Sea
128 Castillo Street
Santa Barbara, CA 93101
805-963-4471

Franciscan Inn
109 Bath Street
Santa Barbara, CA 93101
805-963-8845

Eagle Inn
232 Natoma Avenue
Santa Barbara, CA 93101
805-965-3586

Mason Beach Inn
324 West Mason Street
Santa Barbara, CA 93101
805-962-3203

Travelodge, Santa Barbara Beach
22 Castillo Street
Santa Barbara, CA 93101
805-965-8527

Best Western Beachside Inn
336 West Cabrillo Boulevard
Santa Barbara, CA 93101
805-965-6556

Marina Beach Motel
21 Bath Street
Santa Barbara, CA 93101
805-963-9311

West Beach Inn
306 West Cabrillo Boulevard
Santa Barbara, CA 93101
805-963-4277

Ocean Palms Resort
232 West Cabrillo Boulevard
Santa Barbara, CA 93101
805-966-9133

Harbor View Inn
28 West Cabrillo Boulevard
Santa Barbara, CA 93101
805-963-0780

Beachcomber Inn
202 West Cabrillo Boulevard
Santa Barbara, CA 93101
805-965-4577

Fess Parker's Doubletree Resort
633 East Cabrillo Boulevard
Santa Barbara, CA 93103
805-564-4333

Blue Sands Motel
421 South Milpas Street
Santa Barbara, CA 93103
805-965-1624

Santa Barbara Inn
901 East Cabrillo Boulevard
Santa Barbara, CA 93103
805-966-2285

Old Yacht Club Inn
431 Corona Del Mar
Santa Barbara, CA 93103
805-962-1277

Radisson Hotel
633 Est Cabrillo Boulevard
Santa Barbara, CA 93103
805-963-0744

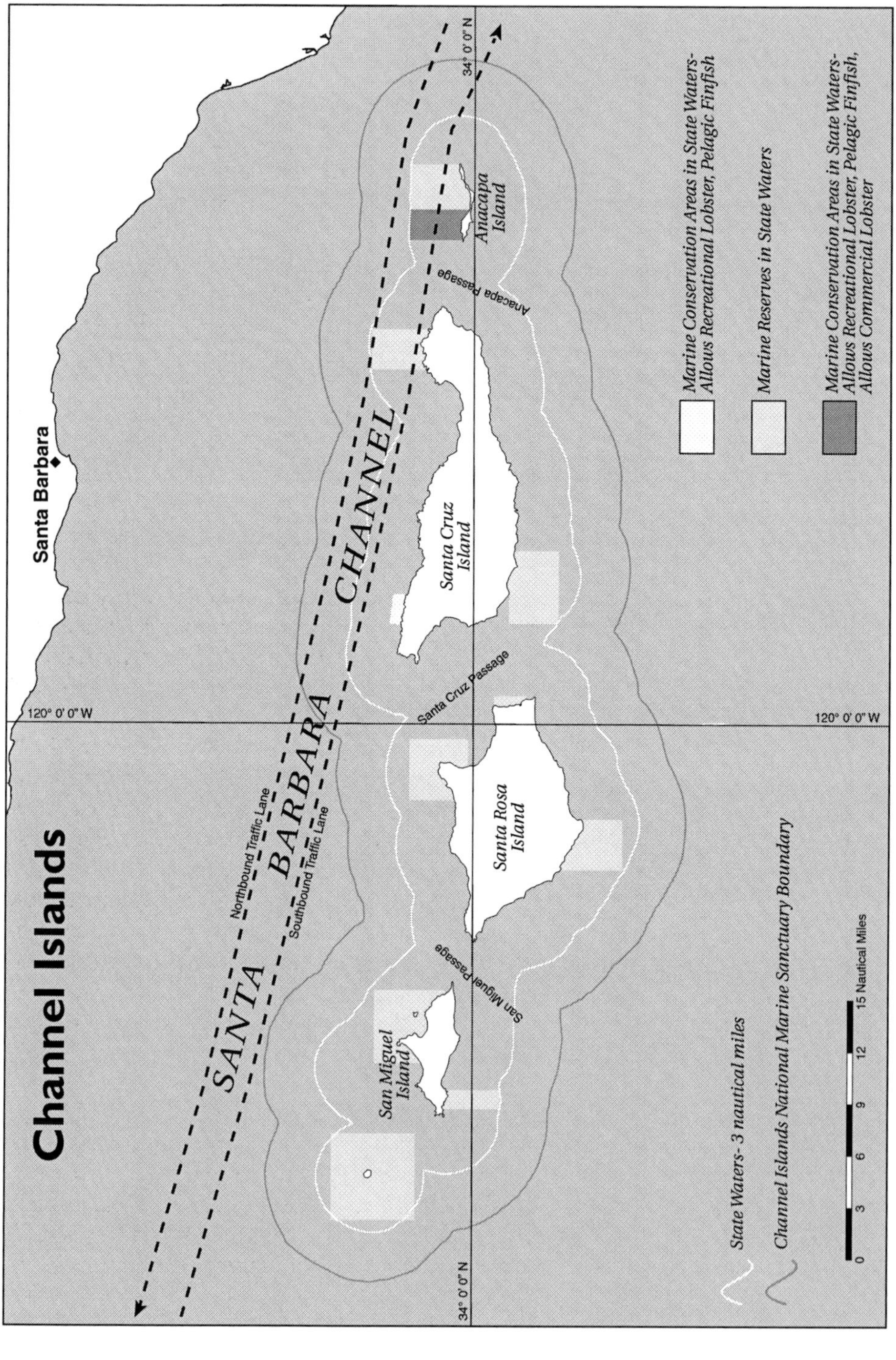

Channel Islands

Santa Barbara

Santa Barbara Channel

SANTA BARBARA CHANNEL

Northbound Traffic Lane

Southbound Traffic Lane

Anacapa Island

Anacapa Passage

Santa Cruz Island

Santa Cruz Passage

Santa Rosa Island

San Miguel Island

San Miguel Passage

120° 0' 0" W

120° 0' 0" W

34° 0' 0" N

34° 0' 0" N

Marine Conservation Areas in State Waters– Allows Recreational Lobster, Pelagic Finfish

Marine Reserves in State Waters

Marine Conservation Areas in State Waters– Allows Recreational Lobster, Pelagic Finfish, Allows Commercial Lobster

State Waters– 3 nautical miles

Channel Islands National Marine Sanctuary Boundary

0   3   6   9   12   15 Nautical Miles

© Wilderness Adventures Press

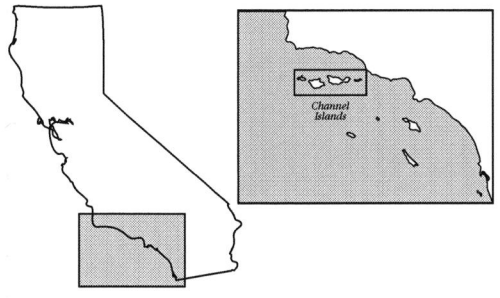

Channel Islands

The Channel Islands, one of California's wild treasures, are now National Parks, but not so many years ago, that wasn't the case. The two biggest islands, Santa Rosa and Santa Cruz, were in private hands. Santa Rosa was mostly a cattle ranch, and Santa Cruz was held by as many as seven different owners. San Miguel, the farthest west of the chain of islands, was always in the hands of the government but didn't get added into the national park until recently.

The Channel Islands are not only rich in natural beauty, they also harbor an amazing variety of wildlife, both in the sea and in the islands' diverse habitats. San Miguel Island is home to what is probably the largest pinniped (seal and sea lion) rookery on the West Coast of the lower 48 states. The islands have a species of fox that is found only here. All four islands offer nesting grounds and refuge for huge populations of dozens of species of sea birds.

In addition to all these natural wonders, the islands share a bounty of both ancient and modern historical artifacts. Collections of pygmy mammoths fossils from the Pleistocene age are found on several of the islands. It is thought that full-sized mammoths swam to the islands after smelling the scent of rich grazing land that was carried to the mainland on prevailing westerly breezes. Upon arrival, a breeding colony survived, but due to the limited resources, only smaller individuals survived on the islands. Over a period of not very many generations, the mammoths shrunk to less than half the size of their cousins on the mainland. This works much the same way as breeding toy poodles from full-sized poodles—it can be done in less than the life span of one human.

The Channel Islands were also home to ancient Native Americans. Archeological digs on the islands have identified settlements in excess of 11,000 years old. A continued occupation of the island from these times through the rich Chumash Indian culture and through the Spanish exploration period, combined with the islands' remoteness, helped keep artifacts undisturbed and make this area one of the most significant archeological sites in the western United States.

In 2003, California Governor Gray Davis signed into law the Channel Islands Marine protection bill, that banned sport fishing in certain areas of ocean adjacent to the Channel Islands to allow these areas to recover from heavy fishing pressure. The law is intended to have these areas eventually open up while other areas close to have an ever-changing patchwork of sanctuaries and open areas. While this will do little for pelagic species whose migratory habits keep them moving, many reef species should rebound in the closed areas.

San Miguel Island

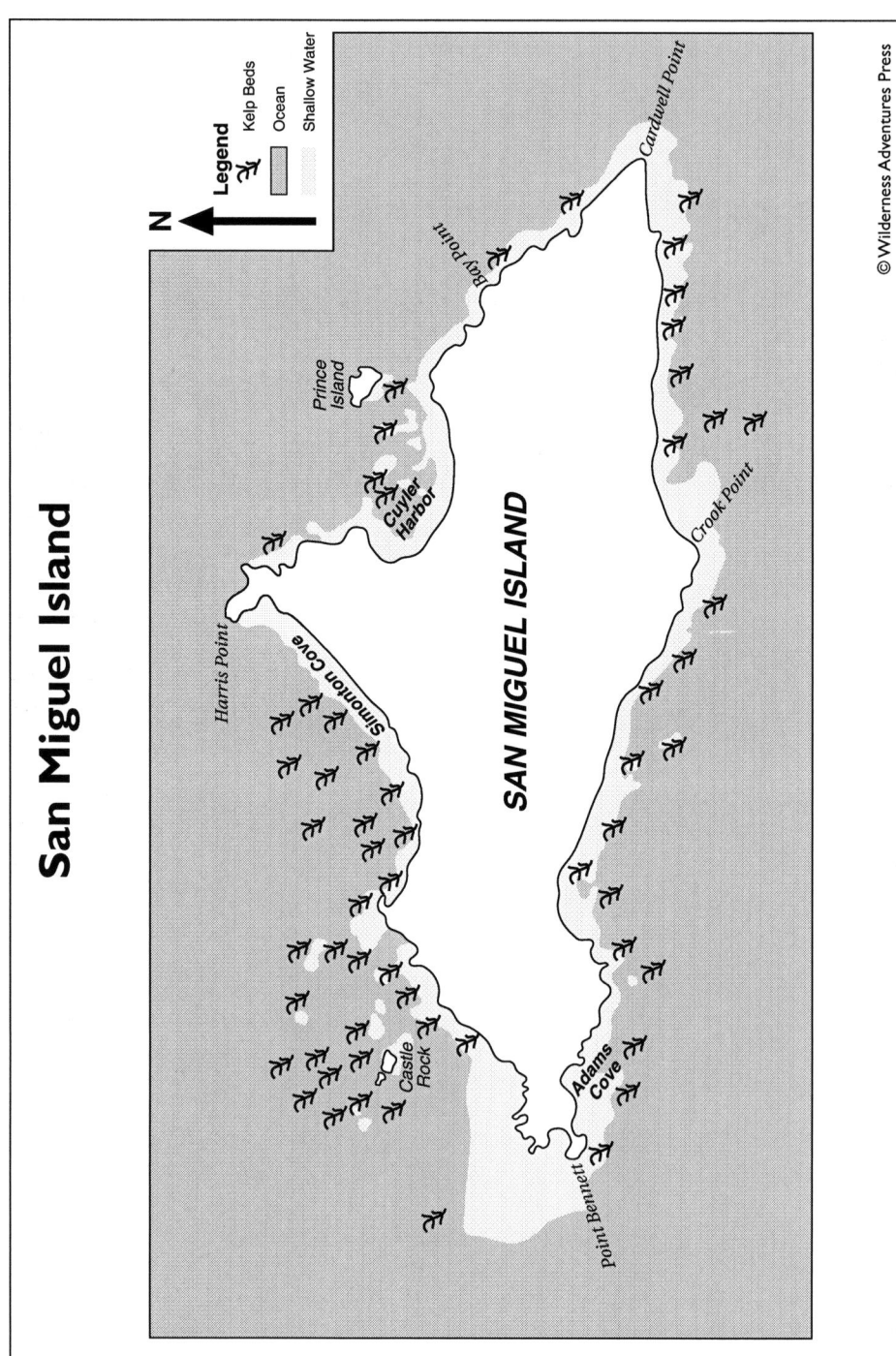

San Miguel Island

San Miguel Island is located 55 miles west of Ventura and is the westernmost of all the offshore islands of southern California. San Miguel is exposed on its western and northwestern shores to the open ocean, with prevailing westerly winds that bring high winds, heavy surf, and plenty of fog. The island covers 9,325 acres and has 27 miles of coastline, mostly jagged and rocky but also dotted with white sandy beaches. The island has a tall, mesalike structure with lush grassy plains exploding with the colors of wildflowers at certain times of the year because of the abundant fog and moisture.

The westernmost point of San Miguel Island is Point Bennett, the only place in the world where up to six different species of sea lions and seals come ashore to breed and have their pups. In the winter, up to 20,000 individuals call Point Bennett home.

The rugged shoreline is filled with cliffs and caves, making San Miguel a haven for sea birds of all types. Another fascinating geologic feature of San Miguel Island is called the caliche forest. In prehistoric times, caliche sand made perfect castings of prehistoric tree roots and plants. Exposure over time has eroded the molds to reveal an eerie ghost forest.

All of these spectacular natural wonders bring adventurous ecotourists to the island to experience this remote wilderness. A primitive campsite and naturalist-led hiking tours make the island accessible to the public.

For fishermen, San Miguel Island represents a sort of transition from the warm, southern California calm ocean fed by the Mexican current to the rough and colder central California coast fed by the Alaskan current. Species from both sides abound here, and the Island's remote location makes it an excellent destination, both for fishing and enjoying the wild, natural beauty. San Miguel is probably the finest scuba diving destination in southern California, having a huge variety of undersea life, including what is probably the biggest population of abalone, sea urchins, and other exotic sea life.

Fishing San Miguel Island

What makes fishing at San Miguel Island so interesting is that, although there isn't a huge population of any one species of fish, it has the potential to produce catches of an enormous variety of species. The island experiences light fishing pressure due to its remoteness and the rugged rocky bottom that discourages commercial net boats from exploiting the fish stocks.

In the summer months, surface fishing action is decent, with good catches of calico bass and occasional bonito and barracuda runs. Salmon appear in the area in spring and can be fished throughout the summer. All year, excellent catches of flatfish in the flat-bottomed areas, shallow water rockfish in the shallow reefs, deep water rockfish in the deep rockpiles, and near-shore variety sport fishes, such as surfperch, sheephead, sculpin, corbina, opaleye, and other reef fishes, are abundant. In winter, excellent white seabass and lingcod fishing adds some heavyweight variety to the fisherman's bag.

*Randy Lacko is all smiles
while showing off his feisty
white seabass, while Tiffany
Bacon, the deckhand of the
Wave Walker charter boat out
of Santa Barbara, looks on.
Photo courtesy
Captain Dave Bacon—
Wavewalker Charters.*

San Miguel is also a good base of operation to troll offshore for such fish as salmon and albacore, or in some El Niño years, yellowfin tuna, bluefin tuna, and dorado. Its anchorages offer an overnight stay on the hook before or between offshore jaunts to chase the heavyweights.

Some excellent fishing can be found all around San Miguel, but some of the more famous spots and areas are as follows:

Northwest Reefs

North and west of San Miguel Island is a broad expanse of shallow, highly irregular, rocky, reef-encrusted bottom. Though difficult to fish because of its numerous exposed and boiler rocks, it is one of the most productive shallow water rock fishing areas in southern California. In the summer, plenty of sheephead, whitefish, and sculpin can be found here. The best action is usually available with live anchovies for most species. Fish with a sliding sinker in the holes and undersea caves and a #4 to #1/0 hook depending on the size of the bait.

Often, this area is plagued with considerable drift, so staying in one area can be a problem. If this is the case and you find yourself losing lots of gear, switch to a three-way rig with the sinker tied to a three-way swivel with a weak link (a piece of monofilament line with about half the breaking strength of the main line). This feature allows the sinker to break free in the event a fish grabs the line and the sinker saws against any jagged rocks.

Switch to other types of bait, such as abalone trimmings, whole, head-on shrimp, or cut squid, to test the waters for other species in the area or in the event you lose too much live bait amid the erose bottom features. Marabou and bucktail shrimp flies in #1/0 size, fished on conventional tackle, also perform well here, especially when sweetened with thin strips of cut squid.

In winter, this area is prime white seabass and lingcod hunting ground. These big predators prowl the reefs in search of prey. The most successful technique is to fish with live squid, bigger sardines, or even live, smaller mackerel. In the absence of these baits, jigfishing using heavier metal jigs in all white, chrome, or blue/white also produces. Larger rubber swimbaits sent down into the rocks work well, also. And just like anywhere else, baiting them with cut squid can boost their effectiveness. Try green sparkle, blue shad, green sardine, or root beer colors.

Pure flyfishing here is difficult because of the high winds, considerable drift, and because most of the species are bottom dwelling reef fish. There are plenty of good days, though. I'm reminded of my first trip around Point Conception. I'd been warned it was like going around the horn and expected to see 25-foot seas and high winds. Sailing a 19-foot O'Day sailboat, I crossing to the north in March—the worst of the worst times to be there. Well, that day the sun was out, the sea was as flat as a millpond, and there wasn't even enough breeze to keep the sails full. We ended up motoring around the point with the outboard.

On those calm days, I fish with my 10- or 12-weight fly rod, a shooting head, sinking line with shrimp flies or white sparkly streamer flies, and let them sink almost to the bottom before giving them an erratic but not rapid retrieve. The fish found here don't chase down their prey like open water pelagic types—they're ambushers, so give them a chance to notice the fly and pounce on it.

Northwest Inshore Flats

An excellent flats area is located just west of Harris Point, the northernmost outcropping of the main island. With kelp beds near shore and a flat bottom, this area is excellent for sand bass in the late spring and early summer, sculpin in the winter, and flatfish year-round. Drift the flats with a Carolina rig and live anchovy baits or with rubber swimbaits in any season, and you'll quickly discover what's on the menu. On good days, let flies sink all the way to the bottom, then rip them home in large, rapid stop-and-go retrieves to get the bigger flatfish to pounce. In addition to halibut, there are plenty of sanddabs in this area, and although small, they are one of the best eating fish in our ocean.

Northeastern Flats

This is probably one of the best halibut areas in all of southern California. Best fished in the fall, winter, and early spring, these flats have the capability to produce a world record California halibut. Bigger halibut are ferociously aggressive and rise up off the bottom a considerable distance to ambush prey. Use typical halibut baitfishing techniques. You can also slow troll for halibut, and although not many people try it, it is effective. Using a downrigger, send down a rubber swimbait within 10 to 15 feet from the bottom and just move the boat fast enough to barely cover ground.

I believe the flyfisherman willing to put in the time could break several line class records for halibut in this area. Any baitfish-imitating fly should do the trick here, with color selection dependent more on sunlight than imitating the most common food of that particular season.

East End Kelp

Along the eastern side of San Miguel Island, between Cardwell Point and Bay Point, lies a well-protected string of kelp beds. These beds can be fished relatively free of the stiff breezes that plague the northern and western sides of the island. This area is prime bass country in spring, summer, and fall. Typical bait, lure, or flyfishing for calico bass is effective here. When here, make sure to try out the bottom, also. There are plenty of hefty bull sheephead on the prowl for shellfish along with the usual mix of shallow water rockfish and kelp bed bottom feeders. Strangely enough, white seabass also frequent the area in the late summer, fall, and winter seasons, which is fairly concurrent with the squid spawn.

South Side

The best surface fishing at San Miguel Island is along the numerous shallow water reefs and kelp forests that line the southern face of the island. The rising mesas of the island serve to protect the area from high winds and northwesterly swells. Don't take this to mean you can be off guard when navigating these waters, though. Plenty of exposed and partially exposed rocks dot the area, and the fog can move in very quickly.

The usual mix of calico bass, barracuda, and bonito visit the island chasing schools of baitfish into the kelp. Live anchovies are always the best bait, but "pitching iron" is also a consistent performer, especially if targeting barracuda. In warmer summers, yellowtail breeze through the kelp areas herding bait, and in winter, white seabass prowl the midwater column and shallow reefs.

Access to San Miguel Island

San Miguel Island is not a popular spot for party boats. Check with local landings for trip information. Some overnight six-pack boats travel to San Miguel from Santa Barbara. High-speed twin turbo diesel sportfishing boat charters can make it

Gary Quon of Lakewood, California, with a nice calico bass. Photo courtesy Gary Quon.

to the island and back for one day trips, but expect to pay a healthy premium since these boats guzzle the fuel at an astounding rate. San Miguel Island is best fished from private boats.

San Miguel Island is one of the most remote of southern California's offshore islands. There is plenty of ocean to cross outside the normal shipping and boat traffic lanes. Once there, the island is fully exposed to the brunt of the prevailing westerly winds, weather, and swells. Boating in this area can only be described as treacherous. All around the island, there are many exposed and partially exposed (boiler) rocks. At San Miguel fog can move in suddenly. This area has claimed many an experienced seaman. Navigating San Miguel Island is for the very experienced only. Every time I come across a boater with that "it-can't-happen-to-me" attitude, I relate a story a crewman of mine used to tell when I fished commercially out of Morro Bay.

One of his good friends was crewing on an albacore troller out of Morro Bay. The captains of these boats, when offshore, normally shut down and just drifted at night. In the morning, they awoke to a dense fog. Their loran put them 35 miles offshore of Point Arguello, so the skipper fired off the engine, put the boat on autopilot, headed it toward his intended fishing grounds, and went to awaken the crewman and get going for the day. Moments later, *smack*, the boat ran into one of the massive exposed rocks northwest of San Miguel Island. Apparently, the loran had been mistaken or the captain had misread its readout. The boat broke up immediately and went down. Both the captain and the one crewman managed to struggle ashore injured and battered by the swells on the sharp rocks. They spent the next four days in pain, cold and wet, in only their underwear, eating whatever sashimi they could pry off the rocks, until a passing abalone diver noticed them frantically signaling from the rock. This isn't an attempt to scare you off from fishing at San Miguel Island, just a warning to heed the dangers inherent in being a long way from shore in a small boat near rough rocky shorelines.

COMMON GAME FISH AVAILABILITY BY MONTHS
SAN MIGUEL ISLAND

Species	Jan	Feb	Mar	Apr	May	Jun	Jul	Aug	Sep	Oct	Nov	Dec
Yellowtail					P	P	G	E	E	G		
Barracuda			P	P	P	G	E	G	G	P		
Bonito		P	P	G	G	E	E	E	E	G	P	
Calico Bass	P	P	G	G	G	E	E	E	E	G	P	P
Sand Bass	P	P	P	E	E	E	E	E	E	G	P	P
White Seabass	E	E	G	G	P	P	P	P	P	G	E	E
Halibut	G	G	G	G	G	G	G	G	G	G	G	G
Lingcod	E	E	E	G	G	G	P	P	P	G	G	E
Shallow-water Rockfish	E	E	G	G	G	G	G	G	G	G	E	E
Deep-water Rockfish	E	E	G	G	G	G	G	G	G	G	G	E
Sheephead		P	G	G	G	E	E	G	G	P	P	
Sculpin			P	P	G	G	G	G	E	E	E	E
Blue Perch	P	G	G	E	E	G	G	G	P	P	P	
Opaleye		P	G	G	G	E	E	G	G	P	P	
Whitefish	E	G	G	G	G	P	P	G	E	E	G	G

	Not Available		Fish Possible		Good Fishing		Excellent Fishing

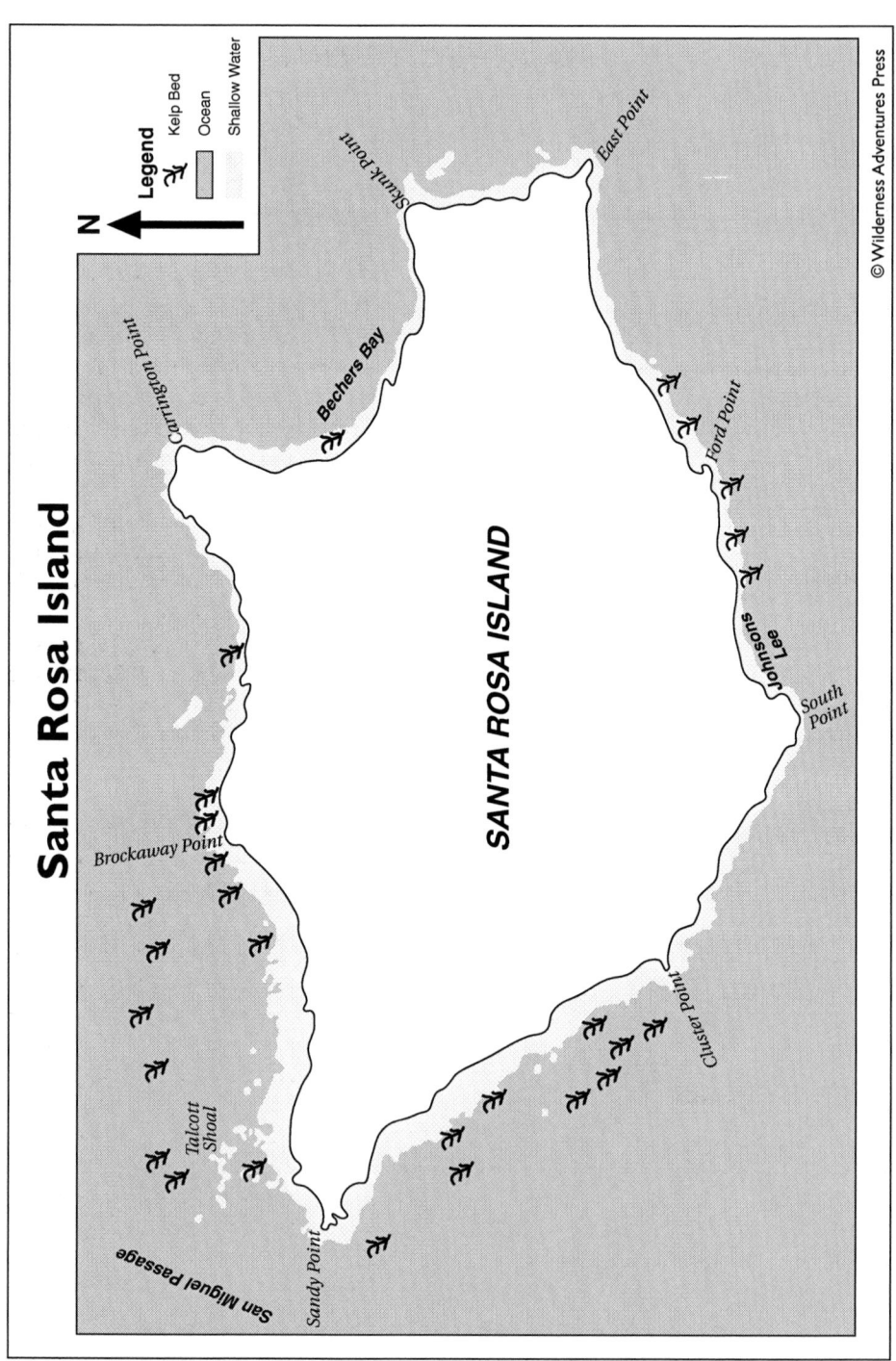

Santa Rosa Island

SANTA ROSA ISLAND

Legend

Kelp Bed
Ocean
Shallow Water

N

Carrington Point

Skunk Point

East Point

Bechers Bay

Ford Point

Johnsons Lee

South Point

Cluster Point

Brockaway Point

Talcott Shoal

Sandy Point

San Miguel Passage

© Wilderness Adventures Press

Santa Rosa Island

Santa Rosa Island is one of the larger of the Channel Islands, covering nearly 53,000 acres. Not so many years ago it was a cattle ranch, and boats would shuttle lowing cattle herds across the 30-odd miles of channel to Santa Barbara. It was a fascinating sight, seeing a rough looking, foul smelling cattle boat arrive amidst the expensive yachts of Santa Barbara's marina and discharge its cargo in a scene far more appropriate for California's San Joaquin Valley than the wealthy seaside resort of Santa Barbara.

Santa Rosa Island is now a national park, although the former owners retain lease rights for certain areas until the year 2011 for wild boar and other imported exotic wild game on the island. There's a ranger station just ashore of Bechers Bay, along the northeast shoreline. If you plan to explore the island on foot, check with the ranger station for the latest closed areas. There's no sense stumbling into a big game hunt when out for a hike, and please leave your Christmas reindeer hats at home when exploring the island. The island's main campground is a short jaunt south of the ranger station.

Santa Rosa Island has very diverse features, including mountains, steep canyons, rolling grass-covered hills, springs, creeks, rocky tide pools, sandy beaches, and steep cave-studded cliffs. The island is home to many unique species of animals, and huge flocks of sea birds call the island their breeding ground.

In addition, Santa Rosa has many paleontological and archeological sites. The most complete skeleton of a pygmy mammoth was discovered here in 1994, and the area is very active with paleontologists searching for more clues to the past. This is a fascinating and remote chunk of land just 40 miles west of Ventura.

Fishing Santa Rosa Island

Santa Rosa Island is more "southern California" than San Miguel Island. It's far enough east in the Santa Barbara channel to be afforded more protection from the prevailing northwesterlies by the south-facing California coastline. Santa Rosa gets most of the pelagic fish in warmer summers, such as yellowtail, bonito, barracuda, and the like. In addition the bigger, migratory species, such as dorado, skipjack tuna, and bluefin tuna, visit the island in the warmer water years. Surrounded with rocky reefs and kelp beds, there are also plenty of resident species to fish here. Its proximity to deep undersea canyons and dropoffs make it a deep water rock fisherman's dream place to fish. The island also sports excellent harbors and anchorages for boaters to drop the hook for the night. In all, it's an excellent, year-round fishing spot. Like the other offshore islands in California, it receives fairly light fishing pressure as compared to the heavily fished near-shore banks and reefs.

Just about anywhere around Santa Rosa Island can be successfully fished—especially areas with kelp beds nearby. Here are some of the best areas to target and methods for the best results:

Talcott Shoal Area

The Talcott Shoal area offers excellent shallow water fishing with good variety. It consists of numerous rocky reefs—some within 8 feet of the surface. Care should be exercised here, especially with a moderate or high sea running and low or minus tides. Keep your eyes peeled for breaking surf where it shouldn't be. Otherwise, scouring the bottom features with a video fish finder should reveal plenty of schools of olive, starry, and blue rockfish, sculpin, sheephead, opaleye, whitefish, and calico bass near any patches of kelp. In the flatter-bottomed areas mixed in between the rocky mounds and spires, you'll find sand bass, sculpin, sole, sanddabs, and halibut. Prowling these reefs, especially in the winter months, are white seabass, giant black sea bass (illegal to take), and lingcod, up from the depths in late fall.

If I were forced to use only one technique in the Talcott Shoal area, it would be to pitch rubber swimbaits. Nearly every species occurring in this area eagerly snaps at a twin-tailed scampi or mojo lure or a single-tailed shadbelly lure or grub-shaped bait. If you've read this book up to here, you'll know I like using a bit of squid on the hook of a swimbait to add to the scent of the lure and to keep up the deception even after the fished has snapped at the manmade hunk of plastic.

Live bait is, of course, always an excellent way to fill your sack, and this area is no exception. Anchovies in the summer, flylined or sent down with just enough lead to sink, produce results on all the target species. In winter bigger sardines, live squid, or even smaller mackerel produce for the bigger predators. If live bait is unavailable, you can always try cut squid, shrimp, or abalone trimmings to entice even the pickiest of the rocky bottom dwellers.

Since much of this area is shallower, it lends itself to flyfishing. Shrimp flies retrieved slowly but erratically with a shooting-head, sinking line on a 10- to 12-weight rod seem to fool more of these species than a baitfish-imitating fly. Fish them as if they were fleeing a bluewater cheetah. Of course, there are the occasional bonito, barracuda, or yellowtail that prefer the terrorized anchovy-imitating tackle and technique, but this area is more prized for its local residents.

Brockaway to Sandy Point Reefs

Brockaway to Sandy Point Reefs, along Santa Rosa's north shoreline, is an area very similar to the Talcott Shoal area with a minor exception. Here, there seems to be an abundance of giant black sea bass. Make sure you are able to recognize this highly protected species, including the brick red, sand bass-looking juveniles, and release any you might catch—OK, you have time for a quick photo, but make sure you don't stress the fish too much. Remember, California law includes up to a $10,000 fine and 6 months in jail for taking one of these huge, beautiful groupers.

Northern Flats

Just outside the near-shore rocky reefs lie excellent flats fishing all along the northern shore of Santa Rosa Island. Halibut abound here, as well as sanddabs, sculpin, and in the springtime, sand bass.

This big bull sheephead shows off its formidable set of teeth. Photo courtesy Kevin Rea—Holly B Sportfishing.

The most effective way to fish these flats is to drift, that is, do not anchor your boat. By keeping the bait moving, you'll cover more ground and present your bait to more potential fish. You could literally drop your bait inches from the tail of a huge halibut that is undercover and waiting for a meal to come by, and it would never know it was there unless the bait started moving. Live anchovies, if available, squid-baited shrimp flies, or baited or natural rubber swimbaits bounced slowly across the bottom are the hot ticket.

Carrington to Brockaway Reefs

The Carrington Point to Brockaway Point stretch also has some excellent reef fishing areas. Rodes Reef to the west and an unnamed rocky area to the east, along with the shallow water rocks in the center of the broad cove, make for an interesting area to explore with a good fish-finding bottom meter. Fish this area just as you would the Talcott Shoals.

Bechers Bay

Bechers Bay is a prime, though moderately fished, halibut area. The southern part of the range, near Southeast Anchorage, is a broad, sandy, and muddy flats area. Drift the area as you would the northern flats and you won't be disappointed for long. Bechers Bay is a great place to fish when the wind kicks up from the west because the massive bulk of Santa Rosa Island protects you from the weather, and you're also very close to excellent anchorages to spend the night.

East Point Pinnacles

About one and a half miles due south of East Point lay the East Point Pinnacles. There are exposed and boiler rocks here, so be careful approaching the area, especially in times with limited visibility. This is a very good reef fishing area, though not quite the caliber of the northern shore reefs. The Pinnacles are a great place to fish if the weather begins to turn poor because the area is protected from the northwest swell and wind.

Fish this area just as you would the north coast reefs, and you'll have no trouble filling your sacks with fish. This is also a great flyfishing zone because of the protection from the wind.

Southeastern Kelp Beds

The southeastern coastline of Santa Rosa Island from Johnson's Lee anchorage all the way to East Point is dotted with kelp beds attracting all the major kelp bed fish of southern California, including calico bass, bonito, barracuda, and, in the warmer months, yellowtail. White seabass, whitefish, and sheephead are found in the midwater depths.

The southeastern kelp beds are quite close to the island and high cliffs adorn this stretch of the island. This means the area is nearly always calm, with minimal winds, making it an excellent place to flyfish. Be careful of southerly storms, and although rare, they could turn your visit here into a nightmare.

Southwestern Kelp Beds

The southwestern coastline of Santa Rosa Island, from Johnson's Lee anchorage to Sandy Point, is probably the most productive all-around area with plenty of surface fish action and some variety of reef fish if fishing along the bottom. At times, it is best to explore this area by trolling and looking for the best bird action. There is no shortage of sea birds here, and following their lead often results in locating the best feeding schools of fish.

From their aerial vantage points, birds locate schools of baitfish, primarily anchovies, by spotting the schools boiling on the surface and then dive in to feast on the bounty. Baitfish boiling on the surface means only one thing: Bigger, predatory fish have herded them into tight balls, using the surface of the water as one wall of a box canyon to hold the school while they gorge themselves on their trapped prey. The fish literally attempt to leap out of the water to avoid being eaten from below, only to find they've leapt into the waiting open mouths of cormorants, pelicans, sea gulls, and other sea birds.

After you've limited on calicos and barracuda here (or at least got bored with catching a fish every cast), be sure to check out the midwater and bottom for exciting reef fish action and the possibility of nailing a big white seabass or lingcod prowling amid the rocks and kelp forest floor.

Access to Santa Rosa Island

One way to reach Santa Rosa Island is by overnight party boats out of Santa Barbara, and occasionally out of Ventura, Oxnard, or even Port Hueneme. Check at the landings to see which boats are headed in that direction. Often, trips are advertised as Channel Islands trips. In these cases, the captain of the boat decides which is the best place among the three closest islands (Santa Rosa, Santa Cruz, or Anacapa) to find fish at that time. Southern California party boat skippers are very conscious of fish counts, and head to wherever their experience tells them they'll get the most fish. Fish counts are published every day in the paper and on the Internet, and avid fishermen check the counts often. Boats with better counts get more business—it's that simple.

Six-pack charter boats also visit Santa Rosa Island frequently. Overnight boats offer fishermen more time to fish the island, but often, all-day trips that leave before dawn and return after dark are also available and offer enough time to enjoy the island's bounty.

By far the most reliable way to get to Santa Rosa Island is by private boat. It's not a simple trip by any stretch of the imagination. Navigating the wide Santa Barbara channel is tricky. Both bad weather and fog can appear quickly and without warning, so the continual stream of big ships moving oil and cargo through this passage pose a real problem to small boats. With about as much chance of coming out on top in a confrontation with one of these ships as a bicycle would have on a freeway filled with Kenworths and Peterbilts, it is necessary to check weather conditions regularly. Santa Barbara is the nearest port to Santa Rosa Island.

The two best anchorages at Santa Rosa are Bechers Bay, especially the Southeast Anchorage area, and Johnson's Lee. Becher's Bay has a pier that was once used for cattle boat loading. As the island changes over to National Park Service jurisdiction, the availability of facilities for private use is changing. The best way to be certain is to contact the visitor's center (see the list of contacts at the end of this chapter). Santa Rosa Island has a campground available and a small airport, with service from Camarillo Airport by Channel Islands Aviation. There is also a ranger station on the island.

COMMON GAME FISH AVAILABILITY BY MONTHS
SANTA ROSA ISLAND

Species	Jan	Feb	Mar	Apr	May	Jun	Jul	Aug	Sep	Oct	Nov	Dec
Yellowtail					Possible	Good	Good	Excellent	Excellent	Excellent	Possible	
Barracuda			Possible	Possible	Possible	Excellent	Excellent	Excellent	Good	Good	Possible	
Bonito		Possible	Possible	Good	Excellent	Excellent	Excellent	Excellent	Excellent	Excellent	Good	
Calico Bass	Possible	Possible	Good	Good	Good	Excellent	Excellent	Excellent	Excellent	Good	Possible	Possible
Sand Bass	Possible	Possible	Good	Excellent	Excellent	Excellent	Excellent	Excellent	Excellent	Good	Good	Possible
White Seabass	Excellent	Excellent	Excellent	Good	Possible	Possible	Possible	Possible	Possible	Good	Excellent	Excellent
Halibut	Good	Good	Good	Good	Good	Good	Good	Good	Good	Good	Good	Good
Lingcod	Excellent	Excellent	Good	Good	Good	Good	Good	Possible	Possible	Good	Good	Excellent
Shallow-water Rockfish	Excellent	Excellent	Good	Good	Good	Good	Good	Good	Good	Good	Excellent	Excellent
Deep-water Rockfish	Excellent	Excellent	Excellent	Good	Good	Possible	Possible	Good	Good	Excellent	Excellent	Excellent
Sheephead		Possible	Possible	Good	Excellent	Excellent	Excellent	Excellent	Good	Possible	Good	Good
Sculpin	Possible	Good	Possible	Good	Good	Good	Good	Good	Excellent	Good	Good	Excellent
Blue Perch	Possible	Possible	Good	Excellent	Excellent	Excellent	Good	Good	Possible			
Opaleye			Possible	Possible	Possible	Good	Good	Good	Good	Possible	Possible	
Whitefish	Excellent	Excellent	Excellent	Good	Good	Good	Possible	Possible	Excellent	Excellent	Excellent	Excellent

	Not Available		Fish Possible		Good Fishing		Excellent Fishing

Santa Cruz Island

Santa Cruz Island is the largest of the Channel Islands at over 60,000 acres. It's only about 20 miles from either Ventura Harbor or Santa Barbara, so it receives fairly heavy boating traffic and fishing pressure. It is an island of great scenic beauty and diverse habitat for both land and marine life. The island has two parallel mountain ranges with a wide central valley between. Deep canyons cut through the mountains carved by year-round springs and streams. There are grassy plains, steep cliffs, and many rolling hills here. The 77 miles of coastline offer sandy beaches, craggy rock coastal features, pristine tide pools, huge cliffs, and enormous sea caves. It is a favored destination for sea kayakers as they are able to paddle into the enormous vaults and grottos lining the island's rocky south shore.

The eastern 10 percent of the island is owned by the National Park Service and is open for visitation, while the balance, the western 90 percent, is owned by the Nature Conservancy and is closed for public use. The island also holds considerable important paleontological and archeological finds and has been almost continually inhabited by Native Americans from over 10,000 years ago up until the 1800s. Pygmy mammoths also called Santa Cruz home.

Fishing Santa Cruz Island

Santa Cruz Island is a great fishing destination, supporting all the major species of native southern California game fish, such as calico bass, sand bass, halibut, sculpin, sheephead, rock cod, lingcod, and many others. Though the island receives moderate fishing pressure, its great size and erose, craggy bottom mean plenty of native fish are here for the angler to tempt. Pelagic fish also sweep though here because the reefs, kelp forest, and rocky bays provide only temporary sanctuary for the huge schools of baitfish attempting to avoid the marauding predators.

Like Santa Rosa Island, the fishing varies widely from the north shore to the south. The north shore faces the Santa Barbara channel and the southern California mainland, while the south shore is protected from the prevailing westerly winds but exposed to nothing but the vast Pacific Ocean—the next major land mass is Antarctica.

Santa Cruz is easier to fish than many of the other offshore islands. Its proximity to ports, excellent anchorages, mild currents, and protection from the northwestern wind and weather make travel to Santa Cruz and fishing less complicated than many of the prime offshore island spots around the area.

Just about anywhere around Santa Cruz Island is a good fishing spot—especially areas with kelp beds nearby. Following are some suggested areas to target.

San Pedro Point to Sandstone Point

This is an area of extreme beauty and sparkling clear water. Three excellent anchorages are found here, and the seas are nearly always calm and the weather clear and sunny. One evening while anchored in Smuggler's Cove, I witnessed an amazing sight: Several thousand skate- or ray-shaped fish were gathered in the depths of the cove like migrating geese in a cornfield. Once organized, they moved

Santa Cruz Island

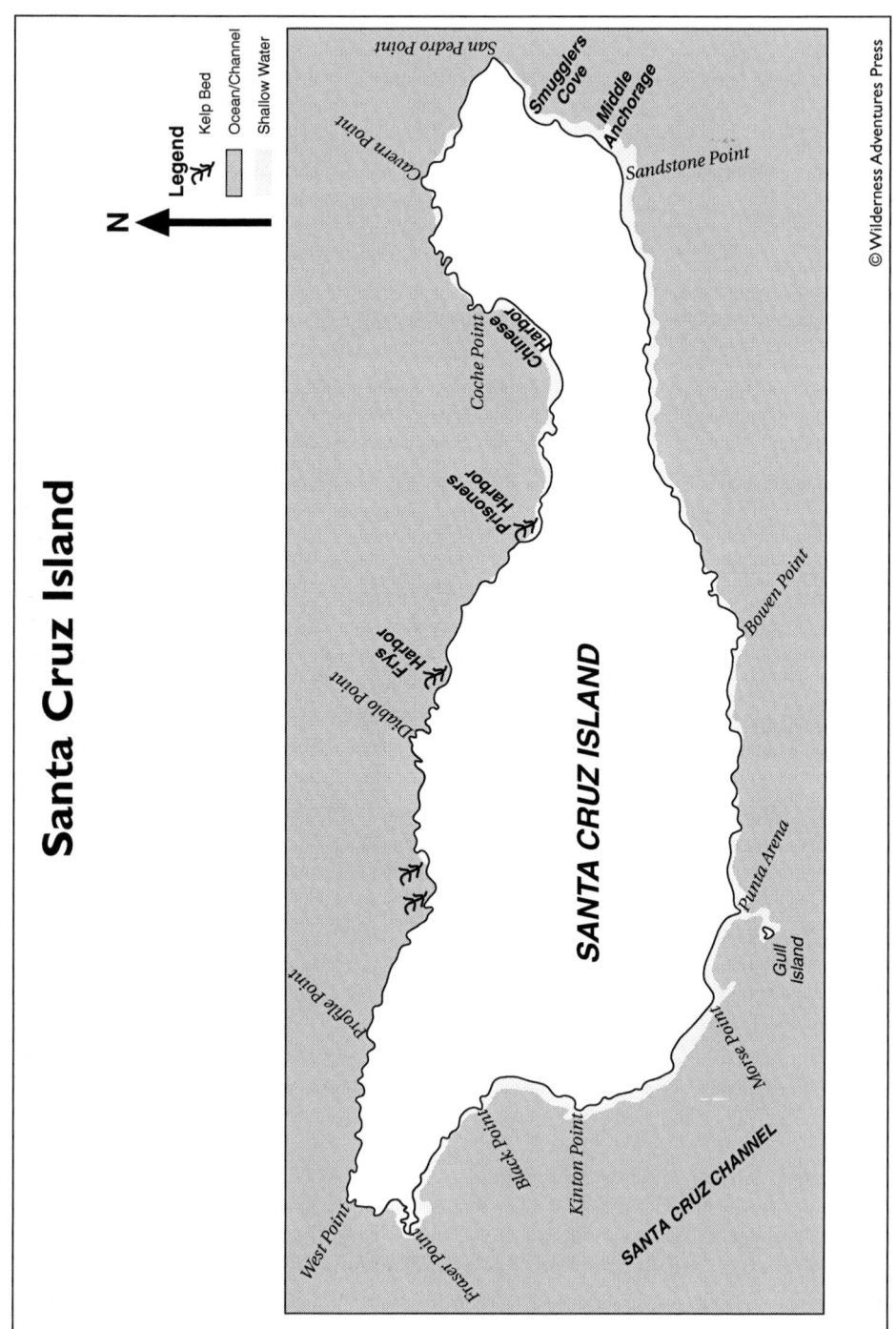

Legend

Kelp Bed

Ocean/Channel

Shallow Water

N

San Pedro Point

Smugglers Cove

Middle Anchorage

Sandstone Point

Cavern Point

Chinese Harbor

Coche Point

Prisoners Harbor

Fry's Harbor

Diablo Point

Bowen Point

SANTA CRUZ ISLAND

Punta Arena

Gull Island

Profile Point

Morse Point

Kinton Point

Black Point

West Point

Fraser Point

SANTA CRUZ CHANNEL

© Wilderness Adventures Press

off in silent flight as a huge school flapping their fish wings in harmony. They were all over 2 feet across and at least 60 or 70 feet down in the crystal clear water of the cove. It was a breathtaking sight and one I'll remember if I live to be 100.

This area is bristling with kelp patches. All harbor calico bass, and in the warmer months, barracuda and bonito. Fish these areas much as you would any kelp area by anchoring beside the kelp and pitching live anchovies, hard jigs, rubber swimbaits, or surface poppers and baitfish-imitating lures to the edges of the kelp. The warmer the water is the closer to the surface you can fish. At certain times of the year, yellowtail breeze through the area chasing baitfish and fall prey to either live bait or any of the above artificial lures.

Don't forget the bottom and midwater column, especially in the cooler months, for a variety of fish, such as sculpin, sheephead, whitefish, opaleye, blue perch, and flatfish, near the bottom. You never know when you might run into a huge white seabass here—50-pounders are not uncommon in this area.

This stretch of southeast-facing coast is one of the most ideal places for saltwater flyfishing. The protected calm water and the shelter from all the normal winds in this area (except the very occasional southerly breeze) make it easy to cast and comfortable to fish in this manner. Use a 9- to 13-weight sinking line, shooting head flyfishing rig, and cast blue and white streamer flies or white crystal flash streamers for best results. I feel you can go as low as a 9-weight, but you'd better hope a yellowtail or bigger bonito isn't in the area since you'll have little or no chance of landing one should it take a fancy to your delicately presented fly. If barracuda are around, you'll probably lose lots of leader and flies due to their annoying habit of sawing off mono leaders in their toothy grins. Some fishermen tie long, double-hooked streamers for barracuda, with the two hooks attached to each other by a short section of steel cable. This way, especially if the fish hits short (and barracuda often do), they get the trailing hook and the steel cable is the only part passing through their teeth.

Footprint Reef

Southeast of Middle Anchorage, this small rocky reef is located just three and a half miles offshore. This is a prime, shallow water rock cod area with year-round action. Baited shrimp flies or rubber swimbaits, sweetened with thin strips of cut squid, are the hot ticket. In winter, big lingcod climb up from their deep water haunts to forage here. Heavy bone or hex-bar-type jigs are often the best bet for big lings, but don't discount the effectiveness of bigger twin-tailed rubber swimbaits for attracting lingcod. Using jigs here in the winter also holds the possibility of catching white seabass.

Southeast Seamount

Rising up from an undersea bottom nearly 3000 feet deep is a huge undersea mountain coming up to within 150 fathoms (900 feet) of the surface. This feature lies about 5 miles off the southeastern side of Santa Cruz Island. Northern currents moving down the coast of California force deep, nutrient laden water up to the sur-

A big bonito is a real workout for a saltwater fly rod, even a 12-weight. This 10-pounder, caught by Mike Scott of Mike Scott's Hackle, Tackle, and Flies flyfishing store in Orange, took considerable skill and patience to land.
Photo courtesy Mike & Regina Scott— Mike Scott's Hackle, Tackle & Flies.

face along undersea structure such as this. It works in the same way that coastal mountain ranges force air currents up, dropping most of the moisture on the coastal plains and creating the desert conditions on the other side of the range. In the sea, the nutrient-rich deep water is a bounty for tiny, free-swimming animals and plants, which in turn, attract huge schools of baitfish—and where there are baitfish, there are predators.

Whenever passing near this seamount, keep a sharp eye open for bird action. If you spot sea birds diving and hovering in an area, go fish it. It means that something big is chasing the baitfish to the surface. You'll find all the major pelagic species, including tuna and dorado, when the water temperature is right. If bird action is spotted, it's best to troll first to find out what's there. To find out if you've found a school of mackerel or something more interesting, you can usually entice one of the feeding fish with a black and purple lure for heavy overcast skies, zucchini color (orange and green) for light overcast, Mexican flag (red, white, and green) for partly cloudy to hazy days, or a red and white trolling feather on at least 50-pound test (80 if conditions are ripe for tuna) dragged only 100 feet or so behind the boat.

The Southeast Coast

The southeast coast of Santa Cruz Island, between Sandstone Point to the east and Bowen Point near the center, is rife with kelp paddies. Here, you'll find the usual mixture of calico bass, barracuda, and bonito on the surface, the occasional white seabass in the midwater, and on the bottom, sculpin, sheephead, and shallow water rockfish. The weather is almost always beautiful, and the stunning vistas of the huge island rising from the sea, with its towering cliffs and giant sea caves, make this a fascinating place to visit as well as a productive fishing locale.

The southeast coast should be fished like any kelp bed with live bait, lures, or flies. Resident species predominate, but the occasional yellowtail visits the area in summer. The very well protected nature of this stretch of coast makes it a great fly-fishing destination, having plenty of action and breathtaking scenery.

The South Coast

Santa Cruz Island's south coast, between Bowen Point and Gull Island, is virtually identical to the southeastern coast described above. It does have one difference, however: an abundance of boiler rocks and very shallow rocky reefs. In the kelp bed areas the usual mixture of calico bass, barracuda, and bonito are found on the surface, while on the bottom there are plentiful and aggressive fighters. White seabass prowl the shallow rocks near shore in the winter, while huge, dog-toothed sheephead search for unwary abalone. In addition, a common central California fish, the cabezon, is found in good numbers in these shallow rocky reefs. They will snap at anything other shallow water rockfish go for.

Like the southeast coast, the south coast has the protected waters, light currents, and minimal winds that make it an excellent flyfishing locale. If you can keep your eyes off the island's natural beauty as you fish the area, there is the potential to catch several species of world-record-class fish on a fly.

Southwestern Seamount

Just south of Punta Arena, along the southwestern coast of Santa Cruz Island, there is a rocky islet called Gull Island where huge flocks of sea birds rest to survey the broad expanse of ocean below them. Running below the surface southwest of Gull Island is the deep chasm named Santa Cruz Canyon. This steep underwater ravine stretches down over a half mile in some places. On the far side, now just 2 miles offshore from Gull Island, the undersea landscape again rises and forms a flat-topped undersea mountain coming up to a depth of 48 fathoms (less than 300 feet). Like the seamount on the southeastern side of Santa Cruz, this undersea mountain also forces up water from below, attracting huge, dense schools of feeding microorganisms that attract the baitfish that attract the larger predators. There is even more action because the seamount lies directly in the Santa Cruz Channel that separates Santa Cruz and Santa Rosa Islands.

This southwestern seamount is legendary for its ability to attract tuna when they are in season and is probably one of the very few spots in southern California where you can fish for tuna in sight of land. In addition, yellowtail frequent this seamount to feed in its bountiful conditions. The top and sides of this undersea mesa are excellent rock cod fishing grounds, and one should never pass up an opportunity to drop a line to the bottom and see what's on the menu that particular day.

Considerable schools of bocaccio rock cod call the flat-topped seamount home. These are some of the biggest and most active of the rock cod family. They'll eagerly snap at baited shrimp flies, live or dead bait, or deep-fished plastic lures with equal vigor.

Fraser Point Bay

Between Fraser Point and Kinton Point, a wide, flat-bottomed bay forms the western shoreline of Santa Cruz Island. The northern part of this bay has a rocky bottom and is known to be one of the better barracuda fishing areas at Santa Cruz. The open nature of the fishing is far more like fishing the near-shore flats areas, like the Huntington Flats in Orange County, for sand bass, barracuda, and the occasional halibut.

This is definitely a drift-fishing proposition, but it's wise to be cautious here, because the sometimes-strong currents can be a considerable hazard, and plenty of jagged shoreline means an out-of-control drifting boat can surely come to some harm among the rocks. The best results come from "walking" a live anchovy along the bottom using a Carolina rig. Pick up the anchovy and set it down, pick it up and set it down, making steps along the bottom as the boat drifts. If you prefer jigs, let them sink all the way to the bottom before beginning your retrieve. Occasionally, declutch and let the jig flutter down, then resume the retrieve. This will assure that you cover plenty of ocean with your jig and give it maximum exposure to your prey.

West End Reefs

Just west and northwest of West Point there is a rocky-bottomed area not unlike the bottom on the northwestern corners of Santa Rosa and San Miguel Islands. This is the bottom fisherman's paradise, with rough reefs, undersea gorges, and rockpiles studded with caves and plenty of cover in which big reef dwellers can hide.

Looking for monster white seabass? Here's the most accessible place to nail a big one. Though this area receives plenty of fishing pressure, there are still plenty of fish out here to catch. Very little commercial fishing is done here because of the potential of losing gear in the rough, erose bottom features. Commercial crab and lobster boats set traps for the delectable crustaceans around here, but the game fish stay relatively unmolested.

Big lingcod frequent this area, and plenty of shallow and deep water rock cod species can be found in the rough undersea terrain. Fish the bottom with jigs, rubber lures, live bait, or flies, and you'll have no trouble getting a good mixed bag of great eating game fish.

Northern Kelp

This small but usually productive kelp bed area holds calico bass. Anchor up just outside the densest portion of the kelp and pitch live anchovies right to the edges of the kelp. This is a good area for crippled minnow type lures, such as Rapalas, and other diving or surface lures. These are especially effective in the warmer summer months when fish boil the surface with little provocation. For flyfishers, flies that mimic baitfish are also effective for these kelp dwellers.

Frys Harbor Kelp

Another good calico spot, these north-facing kelp beds receive the heaviest fishing pressure from charter boats and party boats based in Santa Barbara, Ventura, Channel Islands Harbor (Oxnard), and Port Hueneme. Nonetheless, it's far less pressure than someplace like Horseshoe Kelp just outside the channel entrance of Los Angeles Harbor, and plenty of anglers take a limit of calicos there.

Prisoners Harbor Kelp

Another well-fished but productive calico spot, these kelp beds are within casting distance to deeper water, where many bigger, bottom fish come up to the life-supporting kelp forest to nab their prey before returning to the safety of the depths. These conditions offer the combination of excellent bottom fishing and very productive kelp bed fishing. Some of the bigger, pelagic surface fish visit the Prisoners Harbor kelp beds in the summer, also. Barracuda, bonito, and the occasional yellowtail round out the catch.

Chinese Harbor

Chinese Harbor is probably one of the most appealing places to fish at Santa Cruz Island. It has a well-deserved reputation for being an excellent barracuda spot. In addition, plenty of shallow water rockfish prowl the reefs. These are often overlooked in favor of the more glamorous surface feeders, but as you can tell by now, I love to catch them all. I can haul in a sheephead, sculpin, or bocaccio just as enthusiastically as a bonito or calico bass.

It is best to fish Chinese Harbor by starting on the surface and gradually probing deeper, all the way to the bottom if necessary, until you find your prey. A good bottom meter, able to distinguish major bottom features, is a necessity. Always fish near submerged structure for best results.

Chinese Harbor Flats

The broad, flat-bottomed area, from 200 to 400 feet deep just outside the nearshore rocky reefs about a mile north of Chinese Harbor, is one of the most famous California halibut grounds in the state. Huge flatfish abound in the area. Drift fishing is usually the best method, but trolling is also proving to be productive. That's right, I said trolling for halibut, much as you would troll for salmon. Moving very slowly and keeping the bait or lure near the bottom ensures that you are always prepared for the first massive strike. Breakaway devices to drop the lead sinker or undo a downrigger line are a great boon to this type of fishing. This allows you to fight the fish without being impeded by the weight and water resistance of a sometimes 2-pound sinker.

Access to Santa Cruz Island

Party boats, operating out of Santa Barbara, Ventura, Channel Islands Marina, and Port Hueneme landings, visit Santa Cruz Island often. Check with these landings for schedules, cost, and special requirements. Many six-pack charters are available out of these same ports, and most operators are happy to ferry you to the largest and, by many people's account the most beautiful, of the Channel Islands.

A moderately sized and seaworthy private boat is an excellent way to fish Santa Cruz. The generally mild sea conditions at the island and the abundance of good anchorages offer boaters the ability to enjoy multiday trips there. Be aware that the Santa Barbara Channel isn't a millpond and has the reputation for building a tough chop in a hurry when windy conditions move in. It takes a proven craft and plenty of experience to venture offshore across crowded shipping lanes in an area with a reputation for wind and fog. Still, every year, many private boats, some as small as sea kayaks (only for the very experienced, and then only in groups with a support boat) make the short jaunt across the channel to visit this wildlife haven for its magnificent scenery and, most of all, its challenging and productive fishing.

COMMON GAME FISH AVAILABILITY BY MONTHS
SANTA CRUZ ISLAND

Cell values: N = Not Available, P = Fish Possible, G = Good Fishing, E = Excellent Fishing

Species	Jan	Feb	Mar	Apr	May	Jun	Jul	Aug	Sep	Oct	Nov	Dec
Yellowtail	N	N	N	P	P	E	E	E	P	P	N	N
Barracuda	N	N	P	G	E	E	E	E	E	G	P	N
Bonito	N	P	G	G	E	E	E	E	E	E	G	N
Calico Bass	N	G	G	G	E	E	E	E	E	E	G	G
Sand Bass	N	G	G	E	E	E	E	E	E	G	G	G
White Seabass	E	E	E	G	G	G	P	P	P	G	G	G
Halibut	G	G	G	G	G	G	G	G	G	G	G	G
Lingcod	E	E	G	G	G	G	P	P	G	G	G	G
Shallow-water Rockfish	E	G	G	G	G	G	G	G	G	G	G	G
Deep-water Rockfish	E	G	G	G	G	G	G	G	G	G	G	G
Sheephead	N	P	G	G	E	E	E	E	G	G	G	G
Sculpin	G	G	P	P	G	G	G	G	E	E	G	G
Blue Perch	P	G	E	E	E	E	G	G	P	P	N	N
Opaleye	N	P	G	P	G	E	E	E	E	G	G	G
Whitefish	E	E	E	G	G	G	P	P	E	E	G	G

Not Available	Fish Possible	Good Fishing	Excellent Fishing

Anacapa Island

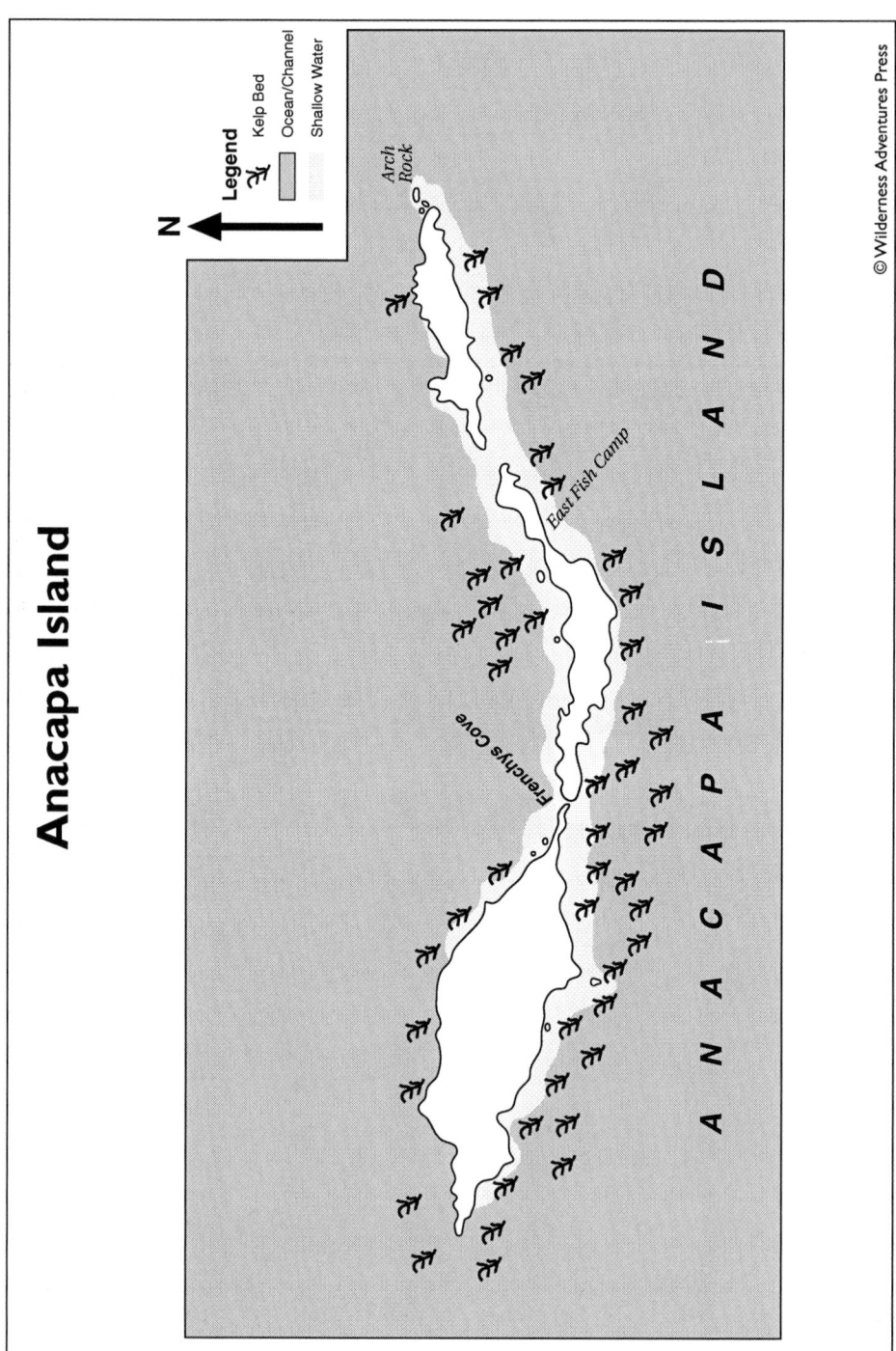

Legend

N

Kelp Bed

Ocean/Channel

Shallow Water

Arch Rock

East Fish Camp

Frenchys Cove

A N A C A P A   I S L A N D

© Wilderness Adventures Press

Anacapa Island

Anacapa Island is the smallest of the Channel Islands, having only about 700 acres. It's only about 14 miles from Ventura Harbor and about 20 from Santa Barbara. This long, thin strip of land is just barely large enough to support land plants and animals. This is the only of the Channel Islands to retain its original Indian name, "Eneepah," originally a Chumash word meaning isle of deception or mirage. The rest of the Channel Islands were renamed by Spanish settlers for their patron saints, and the original Chumash Indian names lost forever.

Anacapa was the first of the Channel Islands to be named a national park. It has an established visitor center, museum, campground, and hiking trails. Many people visit Anacapa Island every year. Its natural beauty and abundant sea life and birds make it a favorite spot for those who want to visit an accessible but unspoiled piece of wilderness near heavily-populated and bustling southern California. Unusual plants, such as the *Coreopsis* (tree sunflower) found only on the Channel Islands, and the island's famous natural bridge, Arch Rock, make Anacapa the symbolic gateway to the Channel Islands.

For those fascinated by the undersea world but unable or unwilling to get wet, a facility at the Anacapa Visitors Center offers the opportunity to watch television monitors while rangers scuba dive with video cameras into the fascinating reefs and kelp forests of the island's coastline. Spring and summer are the best times to visit Anacapa. Just a short boat ride away from the mainland, visitors are able to take a step back in time, forgetting cell phones, traffic jams, computers and the Internet, and glimpse a place virtually unchanged since the Chumash held their campfire gatherings and sang of simple pleasures and the bounty of nature.

Fishing Anacapa Island

With the exception of Santa Catalina Island off the Orange County coast, Anacapa Island is probably the most visited of California's eight major offshore islands—for good reason: The island is an excellent place to fish. All the major game fish species in southern California make a showing at Anacapa. Year-round, resident schools of calico bass, sheephead, white seabass, and shallow water rockfish are plentiful. In the warmer months, bonito, barracuda, and yellowtail appear at Anacapa to the delight of local anglers. The deep water rock cod fishing is excellent, with plenty of deep submerged reefs and rockpiles that provide excellent habitat for the fish while discouraging commercial fishermen.

Plenty of party boats come across the channel to fish Anacapa, and the island is more accessible to smaller private boats. The warm summer months bring bright and clear weather to Anacapa, and the protected location assures minimal trouble with heavy seas. The channel crossing, however, can be hazardous in the event of a blow and can get downright uncomfortable even in a bigger boat with an experienced crew.

Just about anywhere around Anacapa Island is a good fishing spot—especially areas with kelp beds nearby. Following are some suggested areas to target.

North Shore

Like many of the Channel Islands, a broad, flat bottom distinguishes the north shore of Anacapa with very shallow rocky reefs right next to the bottom. This means kelp beds near the island and flats fishing just offshore. The calico action is almost always good in these dense kelp forests near the shore. You can anchor up just outside the beds and cast toward the edges of the kelp using flylined anchovies, small artificial lures including swimbaits (especially green ones), smaller hard jigs, surface or diving plugs, or baitfish-imitating flies.

When you get tired of hauling in all those fat bass, just move offshore a bit and drift for flats fish. Here, you'll find sand bass, sculpin, halibut, and sanddabs. The best results are obtained by sending down squid-baited shrimp flies and "walking" them along the bottom. Use two to four ounces of lead on the bottom of a three-hook gangion, run it down to the bottom, and then, when the fly gets caught, lift the rig off the bottom a few feet, and let it drift back down (a few feet down-drift of where it was). Move the rig about once per minute or so, and eventually, you're bound to trip across feeding game fish.

South Shore and West End

The south shore and west end of the island have a more rocky, irregular bottom and tend to house more shallow water rockfish instead of the flats fish of the north. Calico fishing is the same, with plenty of schools of fish finding refuge in the kelp, but running down to the bottom in this area results in more rockfish on the menu, especially big bull sheephead making sure the abalone populations don't get out of hand. Fishing the west end and south shore requires more alertness for possible submerged obstructions and boiler rocks.

East End

The east end of Anacapa boasts some of the best fishing on the island. More species appear here and in better numbers than anywhere else around the island. It's possible to catch as many as 10 different species of fish in a single day. This area is famous for its population of giant black seabass—some over 300 pounds. Remember, in California all black seabass must be released alive—so make sure you can recognize the brick red juvenile fish and stay out of trouble.

Flyline the kelp for calico, bonito, and barracuda. Live anchovies are always good here. If the fish are biting, switch to metal casting jigs, swimming plugs, or rubber swimbaits and have fun!

Dropping bait, especially live squid to the middepths, entices big white seabass or perhaps blacks, and might get a yellowtail interested, as well. On the bottom, you'll find sheephead, sculpin, shallow water rockfish, and the occasional halibut.

The east end of Anacapa Island is a premier flyfishing destination for anglers interested in pursuing this challenging endeavor. A minimum of a 10-weight or 12-weight (preferred) fly rod with a shooting head, sinking fly line is the hot ticket. The preferred flies are baitfish-imitating streamers in blue and white (anchovy), green and white (sardine), or brown and white (herring), in that order. I once met a fly tier and fisherman who had an intriguing squid pattern, and since then, I've seen several in fly tackle shops. One of these days, I plan to try out that pattern, either here at the east end of Anacapa or on the backside of Catalina. My instincts tell me this should be an excellent pattern here, but I have no experience to back up that claim yet.

Access to Anacapa Island

Anacapa Island is often visited by party boats operating out of Ventura, Channel Islands Marina, and Port Hueneme landings. Check with the landings for schedules, costs, and special requirements. In addition, many six-pack charters are available out of those ports, and most operators are happy to ferry you to the closest and most famous fishing destination of the Channel Islands.

A good sea boat with an experienced ocean sailor at the helm can easily reach Anacapa for a day's fishing and fun from Ventura, Channel Islands Marina, or Port Hueneme. Even moderately sized (under 20 feet) trailer boats can make the passage, especially during the calmer summer months. Beware, however, that you're crossing a very heavily traveled shipping lane in the channel, and in one of the common spring fogs, massive ships are steaming unseen across your path on your way out or back. In the spring, fall, and winter, sudden storms can churn the Santa Barbara Channel into a major swell. If venturing out in a smaller boat, stick to the summer months.

COMMON GAME FISH AVAILABILITY BY MONTHS
ANACAPA ISLAND

Legend: — = Not Available · P = Fish Possible · G = Good Fishing · E = Excellent Fishing

Species	Jan	Feb	Mar	Apr	May	Jun	Jul	Aug	Sep	Oct	Nov	Dec
Yellowtail	—	—	—	P	G	E	E	E	E	G	P	—
Barracuda	—	—	P	G	E	E	E	E	E	G	P	—
Bonito	—	P	G	E	E	E	E	E	E	E	G	—
Calico Bass	P	P	G	E	E	E	E	E	E	E	G	P
Sand Bass	P	P	G	E	E	E	E	E	E	G	P	P
White Seabass	E	E	G	P	P	P	P	P	G	G	E	E
Halibut	G	G	G	G	G	G	G	G	G	G	G	G
Lingcod	E	G	G	G	G	G	P	P	P	G	G	E
Shallow-water Rockfish	E	G	P	G	G	G	G	G	G	G	E	E
Deep-water Rockfish	G	G	G	G	G	G	G	G	G	G	G	G
Sheephead	—	P	P	E	E	E	E	E	G	G	G	G
Sculpin	G	P	P	P	P	P	P	P	E	E	G	G
Blue Perch	P	P	E	E	E	E	G	G	P	P	—	—
Opaleye	—	—	P	P	P	E	E	E	G	P	P	—
Whitefish	E	E	E	G	G	G	P	G	E	G	G	E

Not Available   Fish Possible   Good Fishing   Excellent Fishing

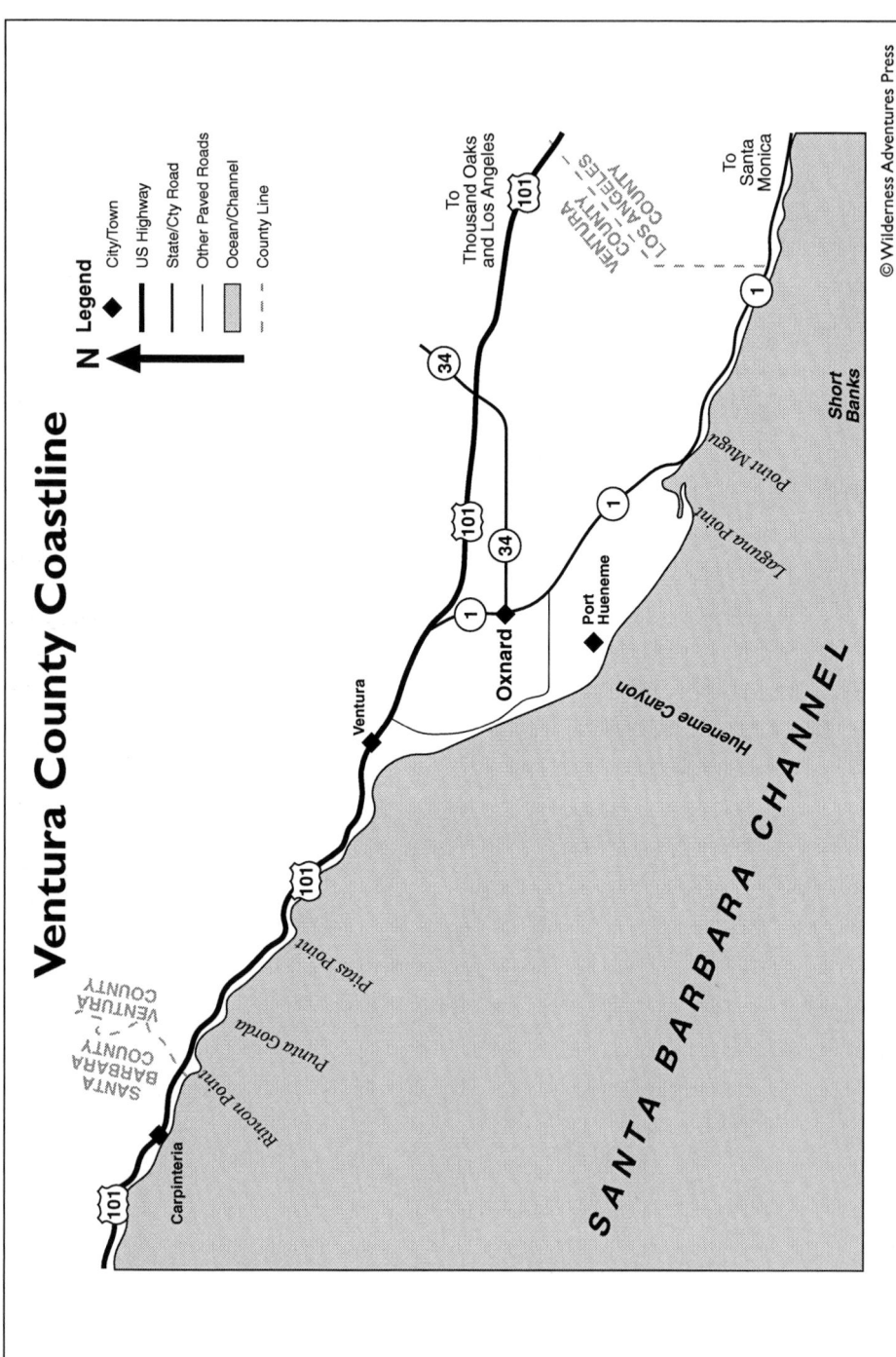

Ventura County Coastline

Ventura County Coastline

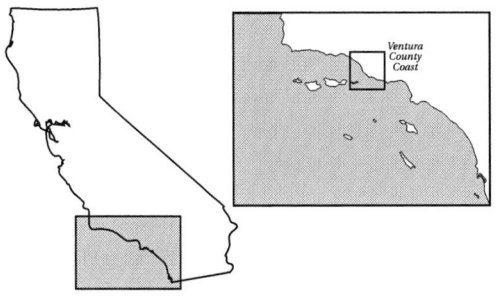

Ventura County has the least coastline of any of the four major southern California counties, with only about 35 miles of seacoast. Nonetheless, it is a rich resource with many excellent fishing opportunities and boasts three harbors, more than Los Angeles or Santa Barbara, on a par with San Diego and Orange Counties.

Before western man came to the California coast, this part of California was also home to the Chumash. Ventura originated as the small mission settlement of San Buenaventura, one of the original missions established by Father Junipero Serra in his early crusade to bring Christianity to the indigenous people of the California coast. Originally under Spanish, then Mexican rule, California was claimed by the United States in 1850.

In the 1850s, a man named T. Wallace More obtained title to 30 miles of coastline and established a ranch with 10,000 head of cattle. Slowly, settlers were drawn to the tiny coastal town near the mission, and in 1864, the city of San Buenaventura was incorporated. At that time, the Ventura area was actually part of Santa Barbara County. Businesses began to grow, and eventually, the citizens of the southern part of Santa Barbara County began a tax revolt, refusing to send taxes to Santa Barbara because of the perceived lack of services given to this part of the county. In 1872, the California State Assembly and Senate passed a bill establishing Ventura as a new county.

In the 1880s, two brothers named Oxnard built a sugar beet factory in the fertile Santa Paula River valley, and another agricultural boom sprouted up. This is one of the most fertile places on the planet due to the thick topsoil formed by the silt that was deposited in the valley as the water slowed down before reaching the ocean. Most of the market vegetables in the United States come from this valley. It's not unusual to turn the fields 8 times per year (6 weeks per crop, year-round), and celery, onions, cabbage, green beans, carrots, and other everyday salad ingredients are hauled out by the semi truckload.

In the 20th century, the Ventura coastline has become famous for something else. The proximity of Ventura (only an hour's drive) to the fast-paced life in the nearby Los Angeles Basin has made the Ventura coast one of the closest places to get away from the bustle of the city and enjoy pristine beaches, as well as a relaxed resort setting offering everything from cozy bed and breakfasts to full blown beach resort hotels. The restaurants range from fast food to five star dining, and things to do range from golf to treasure hunting in antique shops.

Ventura County is a fascinating study in topography, featuring high mountains, rocky shorelines, rolling hills, coastal plains, wide sand beaches, and jagged

Northern Ventura County Coast

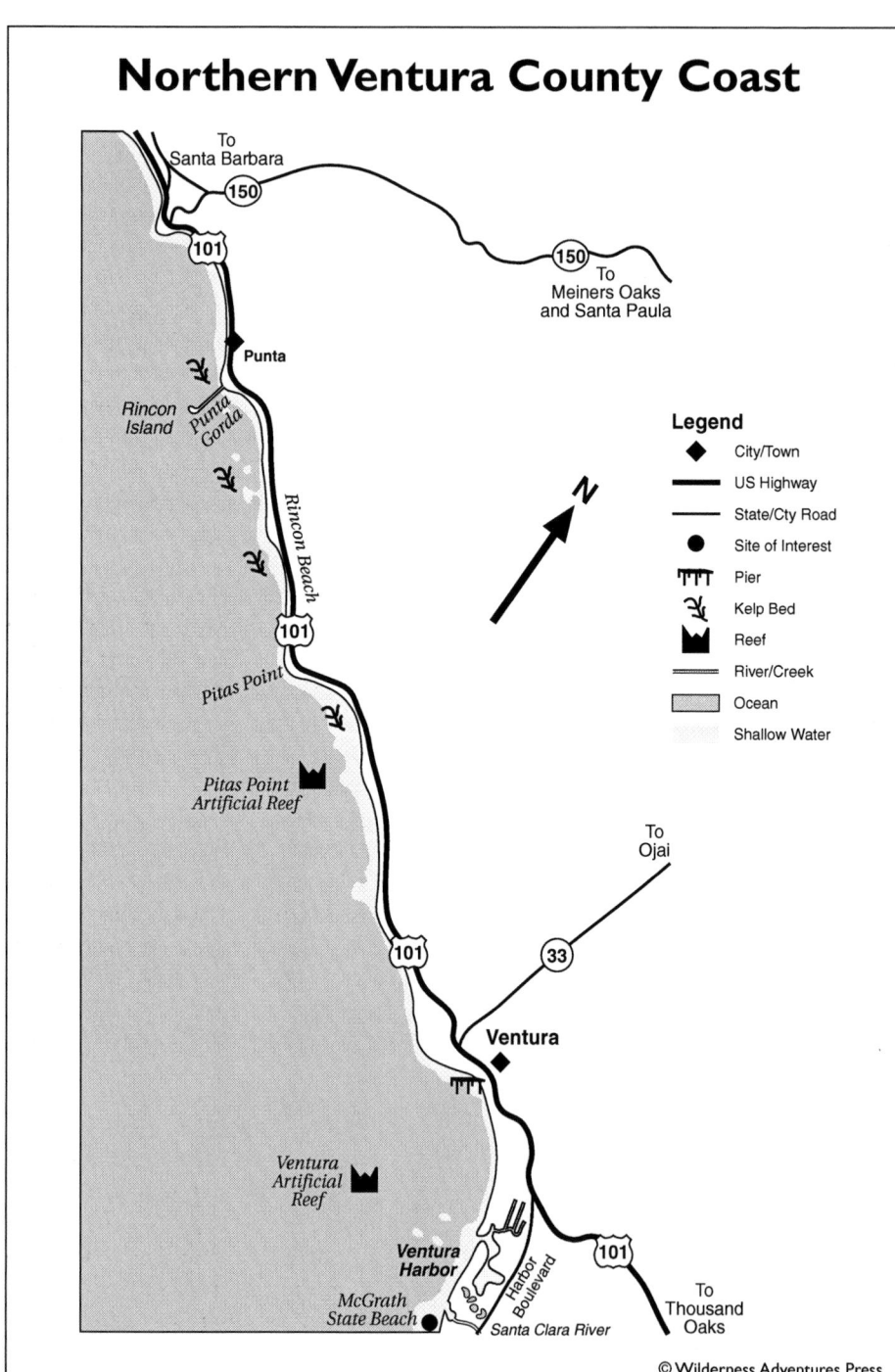

To Santa Barbara

150

101

150

To Meiners Oaks and Santa Paula

Punta

Rincon Island

Punta Gorda

Rincon Beach

101

Pitas Point

Pitas Point Artificial Reef

101

33

To Ojai

Ventura

Ventura Artificial Reef

Ventura Harbor

Harbor Boulevard

101

To Thousand Oaks

McGrath State Beach

Santa Clara River

Legend

◆ City/Town

━━ US Highway

── State/Cty Road

● Site of Interest

⊤⊤⊤ Pier

🌿 Kelp Bed

▰ Reef

══ River/Creek

▦ Ocean

▦ Shallow Water

© Wilderness Adventures Press

columns of once fiery volcanos. The incredibly varied landscape also has interesting variations in weather patterns. There can be snow in one part of the county, while you can bask in the sun on the beach with minimal attire in another part. Generally, though, the weather is typical of the California beach: very mild and lots of sunshine. The coastline is well protected from northwest winds, so the ocean is nearly always mild. This isn't always the case, however, and southerly storms can bring severe ocean conditions to this area. As it can anywhere, the ocean can turn nasty and should always be respected.

As for fishing, the Ventura County coastline offers a wide variety of fish habitat, from rocky reefs to sandy flats, kelp beds, and deep undersea canyons. Nearly every species of fish occurring in southern California can be caught along the Ventura coast, however, the area excels in its habitat for resident, as opposed to pelagic, species. White seabass, halibut, and deep water rockfish are the three most sought-after species in this area. Plenty of sculpin, calico bass, and sand bass frequent the area as well. As a bonus, the pelagic species, such as barracuda, bonito, and yellowtail, make their summer migrations to this coastline and add variety. Low fishing pressure, as compared to the more heavily populated southern counties, mean there's generally plenty of fish to catch, too.

The Ventura County coastline begins with Rincon Point to the north, one of the most famous surfing spots in southern California, and extends to just past Point Mugu to the south (much of this point is a major Navy missile test base and home of the famous P3 Orion submarine hunting aircraft that scour the western Pacific keeping track of any unfriendly submarine activity). Always keep an eye on the NOTAMS (Notices to Mariners) if you plan to do any boating in this area. Intruders are seriously frowned upon, and punishment can be severe for inadvertently wandering into a missile test range. Know before you go.

Northern Ventura County

The northern Ventura County coast, encompassing Rincon Point to the north to Ventura Harbor to the south, is characterized by the steep coastal mountain range, ending almost in cliffs, and a fast-sloping subsea coastal shelf. The bottom is primarily sandy and shalelike, but numerous outcroppings support smaller but very productive kelp forests.

Some of the better places to fish along the northern Ventura County coastline include:

Rincon Beach

If you can find a spot (or at least a time) when surfers aren't thick at this beach, it is one of the better surf fishing beaches in the south. I tend to like it because it offers a combination of sandy and rocky habitats for fish, so you can catch a wider variety of fish here than the usual sandy beaches or rocky points. You can work either the wave zone for surf species or cast out to the quieter, rockier areas for rock-dwelling species. In addition, many different varieties of surfperch are available at this beach—in all, an interesting place to fish.

The best place to start is by using bloodworms, casting into the wave break-ing zone. This should attract the attention of barred surfperch and spotfin croakers. Mussels or clam siphons also work well for these species. If you have no luck there, work farther and farther out using these baits—if that doesn't produce, switch to cut squid or torn pieces of anchovy. Cast these as far as possible in the rockier areas. This should entice any rock-dwelling fish in the area.

Rincon Kelp

Just off Rincon Point, an undersea rocky reef supports a thick growth of kelp. This is prime habitat for calico bass, and the Rincon kelp beds offer perhaps the best calico fishing in the county, short of venturing offshore to Anacapa Island. In addition, the kelp beds offer barracuda fishing in season and should be prime white seabass country when squid are running in late winter and early spring. More and more of these big croakers are returning to their once common haunts, due in part to the banning of gill nets in southern California and as well as the excellent job the UASC (United Anglers of Southern California) have done with their croaker hatch-ery, grow-out, and release program.

For calicos, work the edges of kelp forest using live bait, rubber swimbaits, or swimming lures. Occasionally chumming live anchovies helps keep fish that are hiding interested. If that doesn't produce, work progressively down the water col-umn, starting just under the surface, then midway down to the lower column, and finally, to the bottom rocks. Sometimes, medium depth canopies of different kelp species harbor bait schools, causing predators to shift depth and work the deeper water for their daily requirement of fast moving sushi.

If live squid are available, you would be remiss if you didn't have a line down deep, especially first thing in the morning as big white seabass wake up and start scouring the bottom for breakfast. This is especially true on new moon nights, though the squid are harder to come by. It seems that during a full moon, white sea-bass can see squid at night and feed accordingly. Without a moon, they're hungrier when light finally dawns.

Of course, on warm summer days, work the surface for barracuda, bonito, and occasionally, yellowtail cruising the surface near these kelp beds. Jigs, trolling, or simply flylining live bait are all effective techniques to use at Rincon. On calm days, it's also a good place to try out your ocean flyfishing techniques. A blue and white Clouser minnow and a 10-weight shooting head, fast sinking fly line should net you all the action you could want in the warmer summer months.

Pitas Point Beach

Like Rincon Beach to the north, Pitas Point Beach is also a combination of sand and rocks, making it a fishing beach with good variety. This beach is especially good for surfperch. I have some of the best luck using strips of cut squid, clams, or mus-sel. Natural bait seems to emit a scent trail that makes them easier to locate in the murky surf zone, where bottom silt is constantly stirred up. Of course, all bets are off during the midwinter barred surfperch run, when almost anything in the water gets snatched (watch out for your toes!).

Actually, the beach here is quite steep, so little or no wading is needed to get a good cast out and begin picking up fish. When fishing here, I like an 8-foot surf rig to pitch baits out into deeper water and get into rockfish habitat. A 3-ounce pyramid sinker taking out a #4 hook baited with a piece of cut squid should get you all the action you could want.

Pitas Point Kelp

Pitas Point has yet another thick kelp forest—even larger than the one at Rincon. It also offers a wide variety of fish, including excellent nearby bottom fishing. Sheephead, whitefish, brown rockfish, and in the sandy flats near the edges of the kelp, halibut, sanddabs, and sculpin frequent the area.

When fishing these kelp beds, concentrate on surface fishing. Pitas Point supports a very strong population of calico bass, and fishing for these typical southern California kelp dwellers is as good here as just about anywhere in the area.

The usual kelp techniques, such as live bait, jigs, rubber swimbaits, or swimming lures, are the preferred methods. Also, be sure to fish deeper with these techniques if the action right on the surface isn't producing as well as expected. If all else fails, drop down into the rocky bottom area with a Carolina rig and live bait for year-round action on rock-dwelling fish. In all, this is a great spot to fish the whole year. Don't forget to bring a fly rod if you're so inclined. Baitfish-imitating flies retrieved quickly should drive the resident species bonkers and provide anglers with plenty of action.

Pitas Point Artificial Reef

Constructed in 1984, the Pitas Point Artificial Reef consists of four separate rockpiles totaling 7200 tons of quarry rock. The site covers 1.1 acres and is located 5.8 nautical miles from the Ventura Harbor entrance along a 298-degree magnetic course at 34° 18' 08" N × 119° 22' 06" W.

A considerable amount of kelp has taken hold on the Pitas Point artificial reef, and the project has been very successful as a fish habitat. Calico bass, sand bass, and a number of different species of rockfish, particularly olive and brown rockfish are year-round dwellers. In the winter, surfperch flock here as well as some of the bigger species, such as rubberlip and black surfperch. During summer, barracuda and bonito are also visitors to the reef, and at times, action for these species can be quite brisk.

Fishing the Pitas Reef depends on the season. Most of the action from late fall through early spring is on the bottom. Besides the giant kelp that is common throughout southern California, another species, called feather boa kelp, also grows here. This feather boa kelp forms a deeper surface canopy than giant kelp, providing good, deep holding cover. During winter, when resident species tend to hover down in these depths, a live baitfish with a sliding sinker, Carolina rig gets down where fish are feeding. I also like to use a three-hook, 1/0 shrimp fly gangion with a 3- or 4-ounce torpedo sinker on the end. Baited with strips of squid, this rig not only

Ventura's pier features several restaurants at its base.

attracts rockfish and bass, but also sanddabs, halibut, sculpin, and some surfperch. It's a great way to fish this reef.

In summer, much of the action shifts to the surface. Calico bass tend to move up the water column and feed in the upper kelp canopy. Flylined anchovies are the top producers, with rubber swimbaits, top-water plugs, and metal jigs also producing, especially when barracuda or bonito are around.

Ventura Pier

Set right in the heart of the city of Ventura, this pier is a prominent coastline feature that is easily visible from US 101. The pier was built in 1872 and, like many coastal piers, was once used commercially for unloading ships before trucks became the primary mode for transporting goods. This pier, like many others in southern California, was heavily damaged in the 1983 El Niño storms. The outer one-third of the pier has been closed for quite a number of years. Reconstruction has been delayed while awaiting funds, but as this is being written, work is under way to restore the pier and reopen the last third. I suspect it will again be open by the time this is published.

The last few times I visited this pier, I haven't seen anyone fishing the surf zone. All have been clustered near the end of the public section, which seems odd since most of the species available at this pier are of the surf variety, such as barred surfperch and spotfin croakers. I suggest a stroll through the area where there are the most fishermen to check out their buckets—if they're empty or nearly empty, do the opposite of whatever they're doing. If they're casting away from the pier, cast under it. If they're fishing the end, fish the surf. That's how you find out if it's simply a bad day or if the fishermen are simply using the wrong bait or techniques.

In addition to surf species, this pier also has the usual assortment of sandy-bottom fish, such as halibut, sanddabs, and shovelnose guitarfish. Occasionally, calico bass or sand bass are caught here, as well. With the pier being so short, it really doesn't get into deep enough water for mackerel, barracuda, or bonito, but once the restoration is complete, these species should be available, too.

Ventura Pier has a snack shop and nice restaurant with bar at its foot. There are lights, benches, and a fish cleaning station. In addition, if you're interested in the area's history, there are interesting educational placards spaced out along the length of the pier. This pier also has a fascinating sea water-powered time and tide mechanism. Be sure to check it out if you fish there. The best place to park is in the San Buenaventura State Beach parking lot surrounding the foot of the pier.

Ventura Artificial Reef

The Ventura Artificial Reef is made up of quarry rock and tires. Though it covers a substantial area, it has a fairly low relief and doesn't get the kind of action some of the other, more structured spots receive. Nonetheless, it often produces well and shouldn't be overlooked if in the area. The Ventura Artificial Reef sits in 54 feet of water, 2.0 nautical miles from the Ventura Harbor entrance along a 262-degree course. It can also be reached from the Channel Islands Marina, 7.0 nautical miles out along a 304-degree course. The coordinates are 34° 14′ 30″ N × 119° 19′ 00″ W.

A good bottom meter is important here to survey the bottom and find out where schools of fish are holding. Sometimes they're along the northwest edge, sometimes the center, and sometimes, not at all. Once you scope out the conditions, drop live bait, shrimp flies, or rubber swimbaits into the schools.

Olive rockfish can be found here all year. In winter months, sculpin are frequent visitors along with surfperch. In spring, the barred sand bass fishing can be very good at times. Occasionally, a white seabass passes through the area and could end up on your line, particularly if fishing with live or freshly dead squid. Sanddabs and halibut are quite common in the sandflats along the reef edges.

Ventura Flats

Just south of the city, this coastal shelf widens to a broad, shallow-sloped flats area. This is one of the more famous halibut flats in the area. Opportunities for other sandy species, such as sanddabs, barred sand bass, and sculpin, are also very good. In addition, sandflat sharks and rays are common here and make very sporting targets for the angler looking for a variety of thrills.

Like many flats areas, the Ventura flats are ideally fished from a drifting boat. The only possible exception is late winter or early spring sculpin fishing. At these times, it's best to fish where you've caught other fish because sculpin cluster together and don't budge, even to chase bait. All other times, cover ground. Keep those baits or lures skipping off the bottom, and sooner or later, they're bound to pass within striking distance of a hungry predator. I like green rubber swimbaits, baited with a thin strip of squid, for best results in flats such as these. Halibut, sanddabs, sculpin, or sharks can't resist the lifelike wiggle of the long tails as they bounce along.

The Ventura flats are very conveniently located just outside Ventura Harbor or the Channel Islands Marina. The close proximity to good ports with excellent boat launching facilities and the uncomplicated navigation needed to fish these areas make them popular for both experienced and novice saltwater fishermen.

McGrath State Beach

McGrath State Beach and State Park lie along the coastal road between Ventura and the city of Oxnard. This area holds a creek outlet and a salt marsh trapped behind the sand dunes. Creek outlets tend to make great places to fish, since rivers and streams add many organic nutrients and other potential food into the ocean from the land. Unfortunately, the mechanism that is so efficient at sweeping healthy excess organic matter from the land into the sea is also efficient at bringing man's refuse into the sea. The area around McGrath State Beach is quite clean in comparison to some of the stream mouths farther south.

Sandy species, such as barred surfperch and spotfin croaker, can be caught at McGrath. Sand crabs, ghost shrimp, bloodworms, and mussels, in that order, are the best medicine for these species. In late afternoon and evening, sand sharks of various types scour the beaches, also. These are best caught on cut squid or anchovy chunks. Occasionally, a halibut wanders near shore and can be caught using any of these techniques.

Access to the Northern Ventura Coast

US 101 runs right through the north coast of Ventura, in most cases hugging the coastline. Rincon Point and Pitas Point both have exits from the freeway and adequate parking along the old coast road. Access to the Ventura Pier is from the US 101 California Street Exit in the center of downtown Ventura. Follow the signs to the Saint Buenaventura State Beach for pier parking. Farther south, exit at Seaward Drive from 101, Ventura Freeway, turn left on Harbor Boulevard and take it south—it passes Ventura Harbor.

For the trailer boat enthusiast, the best place to launch a boat to fish the northern Ventura coastline is Ventura Harbor. The launch ramps are very well maintained and have plenty of parking. They're located on the right side of the main road into the harbor.

For the party boat fisherman, Ventura Harbor offers two excellent landings. Half-day, twilight, three-quarter day, all-day, overnight, and multiple-day fishing trips are offered. The type of fishing, availability of trips, fishing locations, and other pertinent information are seasonal and subject to change on short notice. Call the landings for

*Ventura Harbor's launch ramps can handle just
about any boat that can be trailered.*

current offerings, prices, and reservations. Both of these landings offer fishing boat
charters for six-pack trips as well as larger groups.

Captain Hook's Sportfishing
1500 Anchors Way Drive
Ventura, CA 93001
805-644-2500

Ventura Harbor Village Sportfishing
1591 Spinnaker Drive #117B
Ventura, CA 93001
805-658-1060

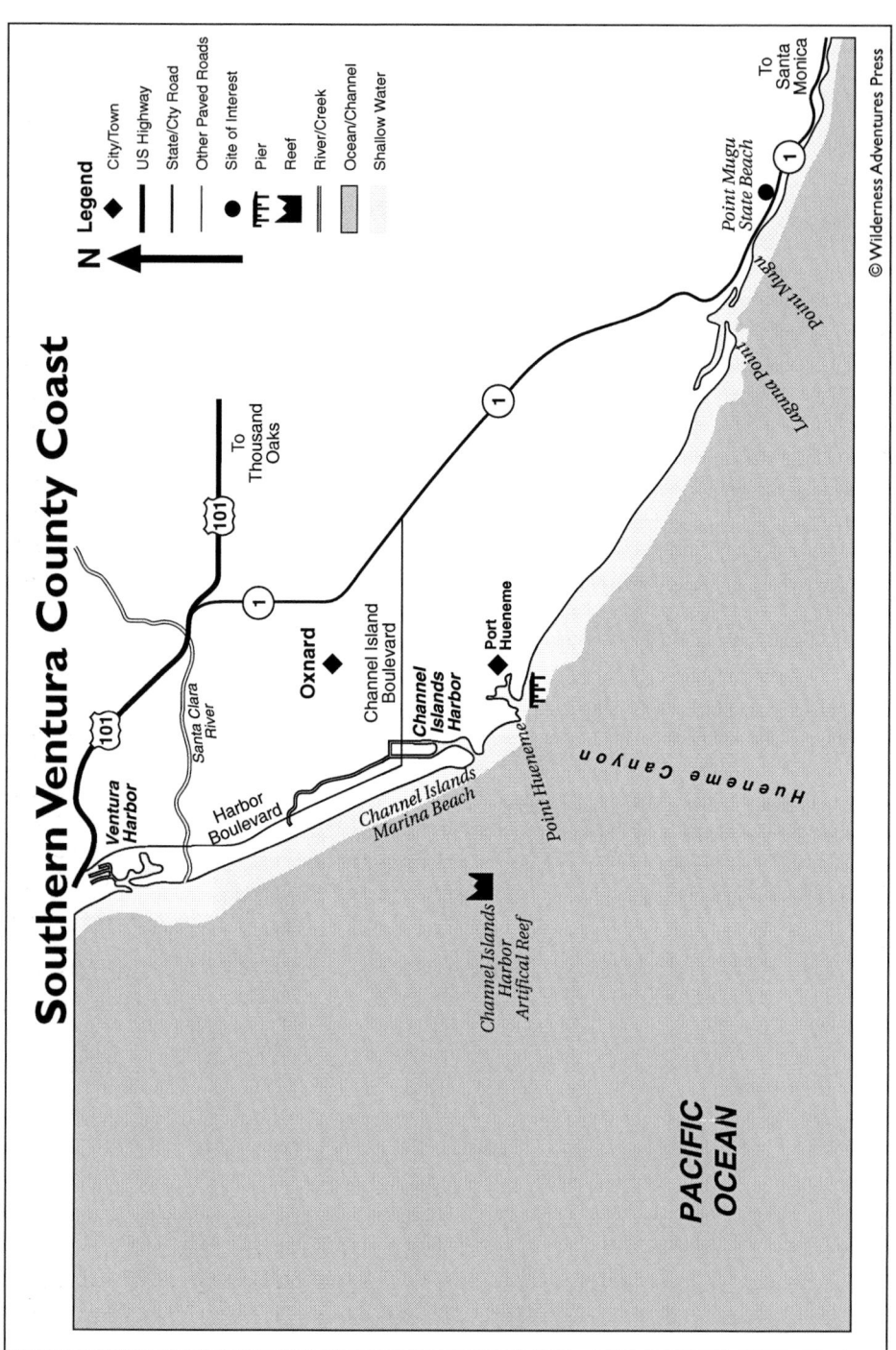

Southern Ventura County

Except for the rocky Point Mugu State Beach area, most of the southern Ventura County coastline is an extension of the broad Santa Paula River valley delta. Geologically, this delta is fascinating and has exceptionally rich farmland. Three cities lie in this area: Oxnard, named after the Oxnard Brothers, early settlers of the area; Camarillo, a predominantly residential community along US 101; and Port Hueneme, a small city but one that features an international shipping port, a strong industrial base, plenty of agriculture, and is home to many military personnel who work at both Point Mugu and the Navy Construction Battalion (Seabees) home base.

The ocean off southern Ventura County has about every different kind of deep sea fishing available anywhere along the coast, with near-shore rocky reefs offering kelp bed fishing, broad sand and mudflats, excellent beach and pier fishing, offshore banks fishing, and deep canyon fishing for rockfish. Whether you like to relax on the pier with a line in the water or want to troll offshore for big game fish, there's a pretty good chance the southern Ventura coast has it.

South Ventura County has two harbors: Port Hueneme and Channel Islands Marina in Oxnard. While both have sportfishing operations, Port Hueneme is predominantly a commercial port, so it isn't equipped to handle the small boater. The best bet for the trailer boat fisherman or the power boater coming north from the Los Angeles area is the Channel Islands Marina.

Some of the better places to fish in this area include:

Channel Islands Marina Beach

Just west of the Channel Islands Marina, actually on the sand spit lying between the marina and the ocean, several rows of homes are built. The beaches facing the ocean along this peninsula are both beautiful and productive for surf casters, whether casting bait, lures, or flies. This is a typical southern California sandy beach area. Barred surfperch are the most common fish caught here, followed by spotfin croakers, yellowfin croakers, and the occasional corbina, halibut, or white croaker.

For best results, work the breaking wave area with bloodworms, mussels, clam siphons, or ghost shrimp. In winter, I like to use green rubber grubs here. Surfperch go wild for them, and you don't have to use messy bait. You don't have to get too far out, since the beach is fairly steeply sloped as opposed to some of the wider beaches farther south. A short cast into the whitewater should be sufficient to get into the feeding zone of surf fish. From two hours before until one hour after high tide are the most productive times for fish to bite.

Channel Islands Harbor Artificial Reef

This is one of the smaller artificial reefs built along the California coast. It was built in 1976 of quarry rock in what is generally considered very shallow water for a reef—only 6 fathoms of water (36 feet). Scuba divers visit this reef frequently, so bigger resident species generally don't last too long after taking up residence. It does attract lots of surfperch, sand bass, and sculpin, each in their respective seasons. It can be located by taking a 257-degree magnetic course from Channel Islands Marina for 2 nautical miles. It sits at 34° 09′ 19″ N × 119° 16′ 02″ W.

To fish the Channel Islands Artificial Reef, you need to get to the bottom. Whether using a rubber swimbait, baited shrimp flies, or live bait, the key to doing well here is to fish as close to the rocks as possible. If you can anchor up, drift from the reef, and allow the boat to ride at anchor directly over the reef, you'll have the best luck getting on and staying on the fish. This is sometimes easier said than done because the currents in this area aren't always as predictable as some other spots along the coast. You may have to set the anchor several times to get your boat into the ideal position.

When fishing here, I like my trusty shrimp flies baited with cut squid. I generally make up three-hook gangions with 30-pound test and tie a 4-ounce torpedo sinker on the bottom with 15-pound test to make sure I have a weak link below the hooks in the event the sinker gets fouled among the rocks.

Hueneme Canyon

A deep undersea gorge cuts through the coastal shelf, from about 2000 feet deep halfway to Anacapa Island through the 100-foot deep coastal plain, literally right to the mouth of Port Hueneme. Like many of the subsea canyons along the California coast, this is the realm of rock cod. While commercial trawlers have scoured the flat depths of rock cod schools, the rugged, erose bottom in these deep canyons is inaccessible to nets, so big schools of these deep water denizens thrive and prosper.

The deeper you fish in places like this, the larger and higher percentage of quality fish you'll catch. I've personally fished in 1100 feet of water in this canyon and can tell you it's full of excellent quality, deep water rockfish of all sorts. My personal best drop here was a six-hook gangion with marabou/bucktail shrimp flies baited with thin strips of cut squid, and a 4-pound sinker sent it into 900 feet of water. Less than a minute after it hit the bottom, I winched it in and had two 25-pound class cowcods, three 6- to 8-pound reds (vermillion rockfish), and a 7-plus-pound bosco (aurora rockfish and probably the best sashimi of the bunch). That was some haul. Needless to say, I limited that day (15 fish) with no fish less than about 5 pounds. Come to think of it, I don't recall ever fishing here when I didn't limit. The secret is to fish deep.

Hueneme Flats

Just offshore of the naval base at Point Mugu, lies a broad sand and mudflat. This area is prime halibut country but also boasts sand bass, whitefish, sculpin, and shark fishing of various types. Certain areas are dangerous at times since the Point Mugu base's rifle and pistol range is oriented so that shots drop into the ocean in this area. And the Navy tests missiles here of all types, warning boaters by use of the Coast Guard NOTAMS (Notices to Mariners), which are available by calling the Coast Guard or on the Internet. Before venturing into these waters, it's important to review the NOTAMS. The Navy will not look kindly on a fisherman wandering into a live missile test.

Port Hueneme's excellent fishing pier.

Fish the Hueneme flats in the usual drifting manner, exposing live bait or rubber swimbaits to as much bottom as possible to get at halibut. If you happen to locate a productive nest of sand bass or sculpin, you can anchor up and fish one spot, but for best results on the flat fish, keep moving.

Port Hueneme Pier

Situated in a great beach area, the Hueneme pier is one of the better fishing piers in southern California. It was originally built in 1871 for commercial use. The current pier was built in 1968 and doesn't project straight out from the beach. It doglegs to the left following an older submerged seawall built to prevent sand migration down the coast. The end has a "T" shape that allows more room for fishermen. This feature takes advantage of the submerged wall, which acts like an artificial reef and gives resident fish structure to lie in ambush and retreat from predators. The pier extends 1400 feet out into the Pacific into water over 20 feet deep.

The Hueneme Pier is noted for its abundance and variety of perch. Blue perch, actually not perch at all but more properly called halfmoons, are a common catch. In addition, opaleye and pile perch are some of the other perch species likely to be found here. Halibut are not uncommon, and shovelnose guitarfish can be common on certain days. The best way to fish this pier is with mussels or bloodworms, and the best spot is probably the right side, right at the bend. On nice summer days, free-floating kelp strands often get caught up in the pilings, sometimes getting quite thick. This is a great sign because it tends to attract plenty of baitfish. If you see this near the end of the pier, small flashers, spoons, or baitfish-imitating swimming lures can really do the trick. There may be bonito, mackerel, barracuda, or calico bass scouring the paddy for a possible lunch.

Hueneme Pier is open 24 hours per day and has a very convenient parking lot at its foot. The pier features restrooms, a bait and tackle shop, lights, benches, and fish cleaning stations.

Point Mugu State Beach

Where the Pacific Coast Highway (CA 1) intersects the beach at Point Mugu, a rocky series of outcroppings, separated by stony, jagged beaches, is the coastline's main feature. Here, some very different and interesting shore fishing can be had. Different species from sandy beach areas frequent the rocks. Shallow-water rockfish, in addition to opaleyes, halfmoons, and sculpin, can be caught here. It's very convenient to stop in one of the many turnouts along CA 1 and drop a line for a few minutes or hours of fun.

Squid is one of the better baits here—I like a long, thin strip on a #4 dark-finished hook. Cast it out with an ounce or two of bait and let it lie on the bottom. I also use 1/0 shrimp flies baited with squid. Sometimes these are the hot ticket, especially for starry rockfish and sculpin. I tend to only allow the bait to sit in one spot for a few minutes. If there's no action, cast in a different place. Because the bottom is so erose, the bait might settle in a good spot and get hit or it might fall into a crack and go unnoticed by passing fish. By the way, bring plenty of extra tackle. The sharp rocks and rugged bottom will claim plenty of hooks, line, and sinkers on most days.

There are several campgrounds in the area, accommodating everything from Class 1 RVs to tents, one on the beach side and the other across the highway at Sycamore Canyon. These are part of the Santa Monica Mountains National Recreational Area. This is a visually stunning place, with tall mountains plunging into a beautiful blue and green sea that crashes into the shore rocks, looking like a scene from a picture postcard. In fact, I'm certain you'll recognize many places along this coast from the movies. So many have been shot here they'd be hard to list.

The Short Banks

Offshore from Point Mugu State Beach and about 4 nautical miles out, a flat-topped mesa sits in 2500 feet of water and reaches up to about 270 feet below the surface. This unusual structure is called the Short Banks. This structure is fascinating, not just geologically but also in terms of fishing. It is probably the farthest spot south where you can reliably catch salmon. The Santa Barbara Channel has regular coho salmon runs in late spring and early summer. Here at the Short Banks, quite a few fish are taken every year, but farther south fishermen have only rare hit-or-miss catches.

*Point Mugu's rocky coast-
line is a great place
to stop and fish while
traveling the famous
Pacific Coast Highway.*

Aside from trolling for salmon, the Short Banks is a great place to fish for halibut along the broad, flat top of the mesa. Also in these flats are sand bass, whitefish, and sculpin. Drift the flats just as you would any flats area, by bouncing live bait, rubber swimbaits, or shrimp flies along the bottom.

Occasionally, especially in August or September, schools of yellowtail visit the Shorts Bank on their migration in search of food. Most often, fish are chasing schools of bait deep down, but they sometimes drive a baitball to the surface. Use a meter, and if you find schools of fish hugging the top of the undersea mesa, try casting out a jig and allowing it to sink to the bottom, then pick it up and begin a rapid retrieve. If yellowtail are in the area, you should be able get one to go for the iron. Naturally, if fish are on the surface, you should resort to surface fishing techniques with bait, jigs, and flies, or by trolling.

The edges of the short banks are also great rock cod habitat. It's a bit tricky to fish since the sides are steeply sloped. You have to pay attention to the drift so that the boat doesn't move too quickly into shallower water. This will undoubtedly foul your lines, and if you have five bucktail flies, a 4-pound weight, and a custom-tied gangion down there, it represents a substantial investment in both time and money. If your drift is into deep water, your lines may only have several seconds near the bottom before drifting into the abyss. I like to search areas where the drift will move the lines along a constant depth line. This provides a good chance to cover ground, even if you miss the main feeding school first spotted on the bottom meter. The 600-foot

(100-fathom) line is probably the best place to start, then work deeper or shallower depending on what you read on the meter.

Access to the Southern Ventura County Coast

From the south, the Pacific Coast Highway (CA 1) runs right along the mountainous coast from Malibu. After passing Point Mugu, the highway cuts inland through farms to join up with the Ventura Freeway (US 101) in Oxnard. From the north, exit the freeway at Seaward, and turn south on Harbor Boulevard, which passes Ventura Harbor, then McGrath State Beach, and finally to Channel Islands Marina. At this point, Harbor Boulevard becomes Channel Islands Boulevard. After passing the Seabee base turn right on Ventura Boulevard to reach the main part of Port Hueneme. A right turn on Eureka will take you to Hueneme pier.

The best place to launch a boat in southern Ventura County is at the Channel Islands Marina, where there is an excellent boat launching facility in the harbor. It's only a short distance to the channel entrance, so fishermen are spared the long, slow boat ride through speed-restricted water that they have to endure in many small craft harbors.

Port Hueneme offers a full service sportfishing landing, with all the different types of local and offshore island fishing trips, including six-pack and larger boats available for charter. In addition to offering local trips, this is an excellent landing to catch a fishing boat to the Channel Islands, particularly Anacapa, for some offshore island fishing action you'll not soon forget. The landing is:

Port Hueneme Sportfishing
105 E. Port Hueneme Road
Port of Hueneme, CA 90344
805-488-2212
www.porthuenemesportfishing.com

In the Channel Islands Marina, the sportfishing landings are:

Capt. Hook's Sportfishing
3600 S. Harbor Blvd #1150
Oxnard, CA 93035
(805) 382-6233
www.captnhooks.com

Channel Islands Sportfishing Center
4151 S. Victoria Avenue
Oxnard, CA 93035
(805) 382-1682
www.channelislandssportfishing.com

Ventura County offers the ocean fisherman a wide variety of species, fishing conditions, and techniques. In addition, Ventura is an excellent tourist destination. From simple tents to luxury resort hotels, Ventura has just about everything for the traveling fisherman. In addition, restaurants ranging from fast food to home cooking to exotic to gourmet dining abound here.

COMMON GAME FISH AVAILABILITY BY MONTHS
VENTURA COUNTY

Species	Jan	Feb	Mar	Apr	May	Jun	Jul	Aug	Sep	Oct	Nov	Dec
Yellowtail												
Barracuda												
Bonito												
Calico Bass												
Sand Bass												
White Seabass												
Halibut												
Lingcod												
Shallow-water Rockfish												
Deep-water Rockfish												
Sheephead												
Sculpin												
Blue Perch												
Opaleye												
Whitefish												

Legend:

☐ Not Available ▨ Fish Possible ▦ Good Fishing ■ Excellent Fishing

Ventura County Tackle Shops

Basswidow Products
6446 Ralston Street
Ventura, CA 93003
(805) 644-2662

Eric's Tackle Shop
2127 East Thompson
Ventura, CA 93001
(805) 648-5665

Fishermans Industry Supply House
3695 Harbor Boulevard
Ventura, CA 93001
(805) 642-2522

Toms Wholesale Tackle
1895 North Ventura Avenue
Ventura, CA 93001
(805) 653-0147

Ventura County Accommodations

The following list is a sampling of lodgings that are close to port in Ventura County. These range from basic to luxury, and you should keep in mind that nothing along the southern California coast, particularly anything close to water, is inexpensive.

Sheraton Four Points Ventura
  Harbortown
1050 Schooner Drive
Ventura, CA 93001
805-658-1212

Holiday Inn Ventura Beach Resort
450 East Harbor Boulevard
Ventura, CA 93001
805-648-7731

Inn on the Beach
1175 South Seward Avenue
Ventura, CA 93001
805-652-2000

Ventura Beach Hotel
2055 Harbor Boulevard
Ventura, CA 93001
805-643-2509

Casa Sirena Hotel and Marina
3605 Peninsula Road
Oxnard, CA 93035
805-985-6311

Channel Islands Inn and Suites
1001 East Channel Islands Boulevard
Oxnard, CA 93033
805-487-7755

Casa Via Mar Inn
377 West Channel Islands Boulevard
Port Hueneme, CA 93041
805-984-6222

Country Inn and Suites
377 West Channel Islands Boulevard
Port Hueneme, CA 93041
805-986-5353

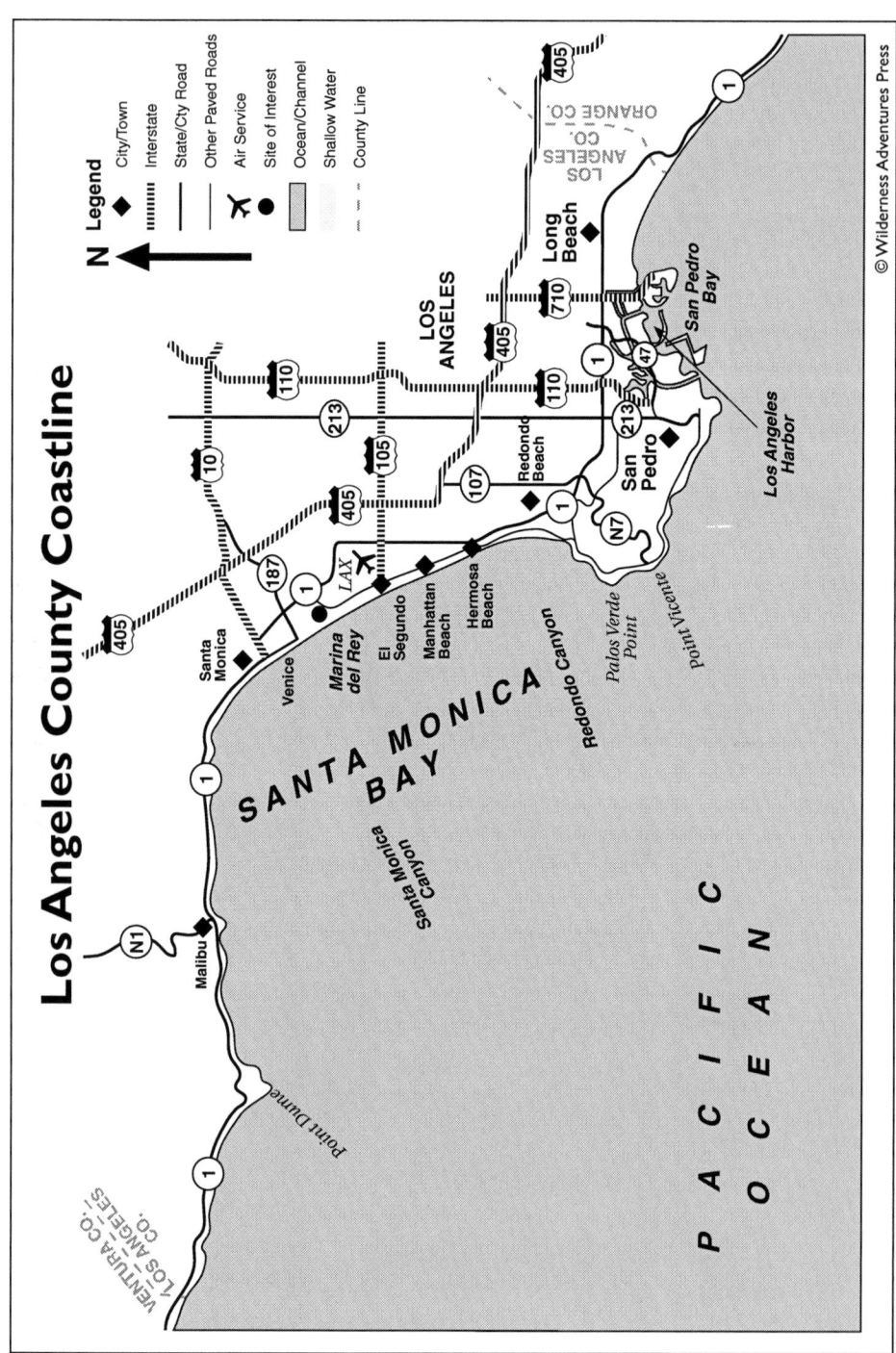

Los Angeles County Coastline

© Wilderness Adventures Press

Los Angeles County Coastline

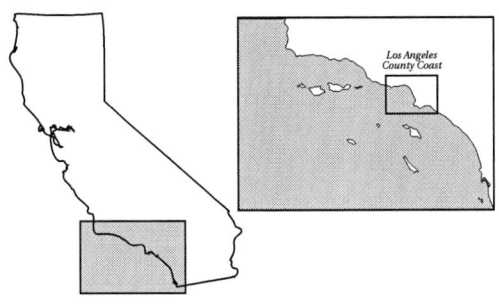

Los Angeles County, one of the most populous places in the United States with over 9.6 million people, is also one of the most diverse in population, ethnic makeup, wildlife habitat, and geological features. Los Angeles County covers an area of about 4000 square miles and includes coastal plains, 10,000-foot high mountains, marshland, deserts, dense pine and fir forests, and hilly chaparral country. It has a national forest, a national recreational area, two islands, and a long Pacific Ocean coastline.

The county encompasses 87 different cities in addition to its largest city, Los Angeles, with a population of about 3.6 million, only about a third of the total number of people who call Los Angeles County home. Ethnically, Los Angeles County is 44 percent Hispanic, 33 percent Caucasian, 13 percent Asian, and 10 percent African-American. This gives the area a rich cultural diversity and lends an international flavor to this major Pacific Rim port city.

The Port of Los Angeles is the busiest cargo port in the United States, with almost 80 billion dollars worth of cargo on over 2500 ships passing through every year. The port alone supports almost 300,000 jobs. Los Angeles International Airport is the fourth busiest in the world, servicing over 58 million passengers every year. There are four other airports in the county serviced by major airlines.

Just about anything a traveler could possibly desire, including recreation, cultural events, the arts, fine dining, great shopping, a wide variety of sports and other outdoor activities, is right here in Los Angeles. In fact, tourism in Los Angeles County is a 14 billion dollar per year business supporting nearly 125,000 jobs.

In 1781, Don Felipe de Neve, the governor of California under Mexican rule, was traveling between San Diego and San Francisco, the two major settlements in California at the time, and named the area, "El Pueblo de Nuestra Señora Reina de Los Angeles de Porciuncula." Translated from Spanish, this means, "The Town of Our Lady the Queen of the Angels of Porciuncula." Well, since that's such a mouthful in either language, the locals just shortened it to Los Angeles (the angels).

Los Angeles remained a sleepy little village until the United States claimed California in 1846. Then a trickle of hearty souls from the East began to seek their fortunes in the West. The California gold rush of 1849 turned that trickle into a torrent, and even the southern part of the state, where there was no gold, grew with the huge influx of people. Los Angeles became a lawless Western town with robberies and gunfights, just like in the movies. In fact, it was so rough, people began calling the town "Los Diablos" (the devils) instead of Los Angeles. Eventually, the Wild West was tamed and the area became safer for settlers and farmers.

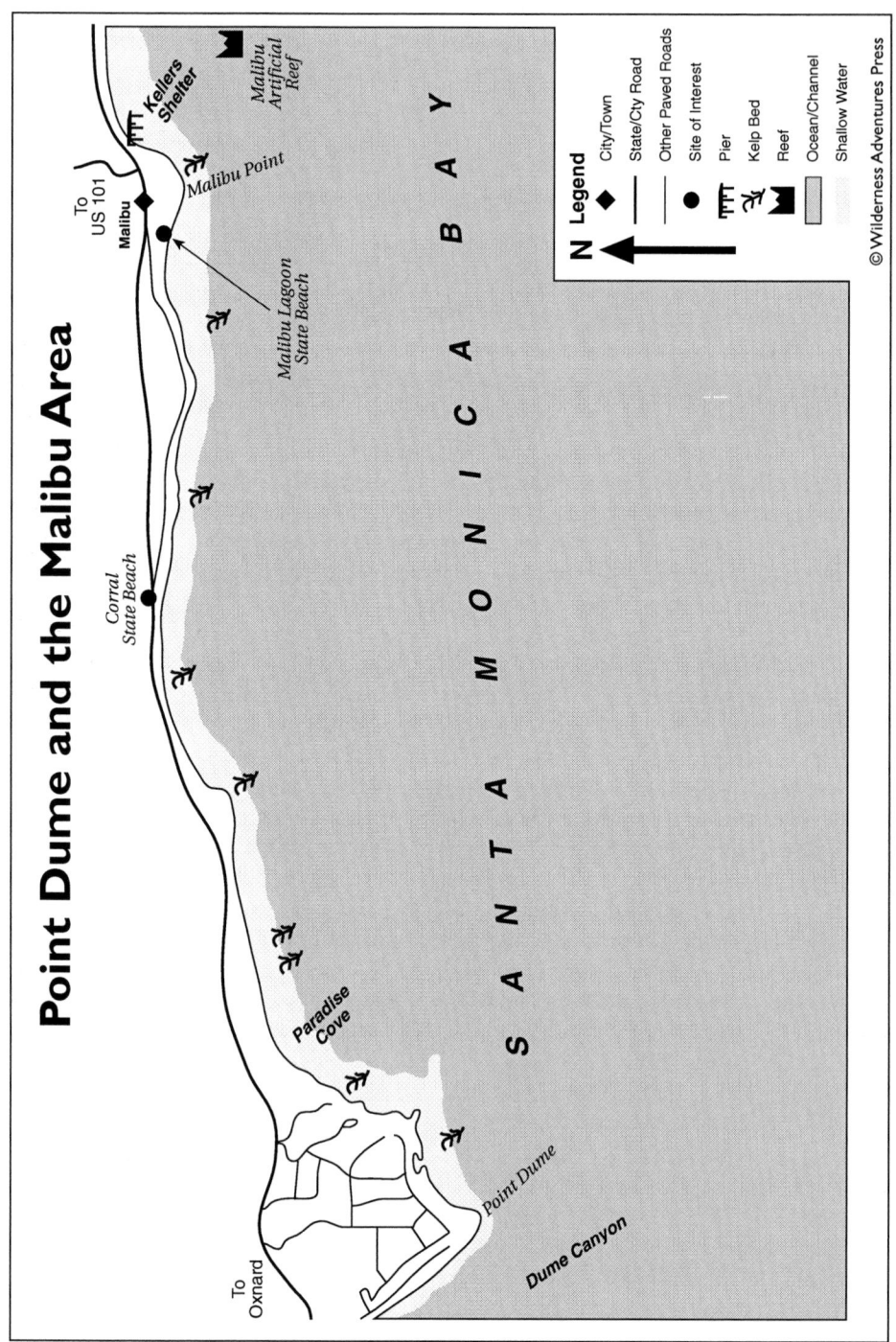

Point Dume and the Malibu Area

Kellers Shelter

Malibu Artificial Reef

Malibu Point

To US 101

Malibu

Malibu Lagoon State Beach

Corral State Beach

Paradise Cove

Point Dume

Dume Canyon

To Oxnard

SANTA MONICA BAY

Legend

N

- City/Town
- State/Cty Road
- Other Paved Roads
- Site of Interest
- Pier
- Kelp Bed
- Reef
- Ocean/Channel
- Shallow Water

© Wilderness Adventures Press

In the 1860s, railroads connected Los Angeles to the rest of the country. This encouraged even more settlers to move to the land of sunshine. Around the turn of the century, oil was discovered in southern California, and a new type of gold miner arrived seeking black gold. The California Aqueduct was built early in this century, bringing the only remaining scarce commodity in southern California needed to support a large population: water.

By the 1920s, the fledgling movie industry had evolved in Los Angeles, and several major aircraft builders had also gotten their businesses going. This established Los Angeles as the capital of both the movie and aerospace industries, almost from their inception, and helped Los Angeles become one of the high-tech and emerging industry centers of the world.

World War II brought additional growth to Los Angeles as both a major wartime aircraft-producing area and as a staging area for many of the men and materials used in the Pacific theater. Many servicemen returning from the war elected to stay in warm, sunny Los Angeles, with its laidback lifestyle, rather than return to their Eastern and Midwestern pre-war lives.

Los Angeles continues to draw people from colder areas to its warm, sunny climate. Today, the entertainment industry, aerospace industry, and high-tech industries still call Los Angeles home, and the prospects for continued growth look good.

One of the area's finest recreational activities is, of course, saltwater fishing. Fishing around Los Angeles County offers all the variety anyone could want—literally hundreds of different species. A wide variety of tackle, techniques, and types of fishing are available, for the occasional saltwater fishing tourist to the fishing fanatic.

Point Dume and the Malibu Area

The beautiful Malibu coastline, made famous in so many movies and TV shows, is home to many wealthy and famous personalities. This area is actually the end of the San Gabriel Mountain range, where earthquakes are one of the most common geological events. This doesn't deter the many quite wealthy people who build their dream homes along this stunning stretch of coastline.

The ocean around Malibu and Point Dume has all the variety you could want for deep sea fishing. There are shallow water reefs, artificial reefs, kelp beds, sandflats, and a canyon perfect for deep water rock fishing. Surprisingly, it isn't fished that much because the nearest ports, either north or south, are a few miles away. It is accessible from Redondo's King Harbor (24 miles) and Marina Del Rey (18 miles) to the south or from Port Hueneme (8 miles) or Channel Islands Marina (9 miles) from the north. This makes it a very productive stretch of coastline for the boater who has attained the level of experience and expertise to navigate the open ocean but still prefers not to venture too far offshore.

Some of the better areas to fish along the Point Dume and Malibu coastlines include:

Dume Canyon

Just offshore of the Point is a deep, steep-sided undersea canyon named Dume Canyon. This structure is prime habitat for deep water rock species of all sorts, such as reds, cowcod, bocaccio, chilipepper, Floridas, and lingcod. There tends to be a good current flowing up from this canyon that brings nutrient laden water with it. This causes microorganisms to flourish and provide prime fodder for grazing bait-fish.

Drop bucktail shrimp flies baited with strips of squid among the holes and crevasses for best results. I like a bit of extra weight here because of the strong currents. Fish as close to the bottom as you can without fouling your gear. If you can catch a mackerel in winter or early spring, send it down whole with a double hook arrangement, and you might find yourself on the fighting end of a big lingcod—it's one of the prime inshore areas for these toothy monsters.

Paradise Cove Kelp

Paradise Cove is home to many famous movie, television, and recording stars for good reason: This stretch of coastline is stunning. The Santa Monica Mountains in the background frame a lush green slope covered with multimillion dollar homes, tennis courts, horse trails, and tree-covered glades. The craggy, erose coastline accentuates the breaking waves sending showers of spray skyward in a show that can only be nature's own. Fishing here brings the serenity that can only happen on the ocean with a stretch of beautiful shoreline in front of you.

Thick, healthy kelp forests choke the coastline in the cooler water years. Like most somewhat remote kelp beds, this is a haven for an abundant variety of sea creatures. Plenty of game fish live or pass through here, and the kelp bed edges are home to many fat resident calico bass. Springtime brings schools of barracuda, and summer brings bonito and yellowtail. When squid arrive in winter, white seabass can be caught prowling the midwater. Sculpin, sheephead, whitefish, halfmoons, and opaleye all live near the kelp year-round.

For a fishing destination, there are few other spots in the county that offer as much possibility of catching so many species in a single trip as Paradise Cove. Work the edges of the kelp forest, shallows, midwater, and the bottom for certain action nearly every day of the year. Live bait, cut squid, shrimp, rubber swimbaits, hard jigs or flies all have days when they seem to work like magic. When one technique, bait, or lure doesn't produce, all you have to do is switch to another—it shouldn't take too long to figure out which one works on a particular day.

Surrounding the kelp beds are some productive flats with good numbers of halibut and sand bass. If the kelp is slow, drift the flats for even more year-round fishing action.

Malibu Kelp

Where there is a rocky shoreline, there is generally a rocky ocean bottom, and this stretch of the Malibu coast is no exception. Much of the near-shore bottom is rocky and provides a good footing for giant kelp plants to grow. This area is

The small, private fishing pier at Paradise Cove is a popular spot.

famous for smaller, patchy kelp beds with sand or mud bottoms in between. Like the Paradise Cove kelp beds, these can produce an incredible variety of species, and any one of many techniques can be productive on different days.

Don't forget to fish the bottom here, especially between the patches of kelp forest, for some sand bass, sculpin, and halibut action. There are also quite a few varieties of shark here, most of which are edible. Leopards and shovelnose guitarfish are just two of the many available here.

In the warm summer months, keep your eyes open for "breezers"—bigger game fish breezing through while hunting for prey. They can often be seen breaking the surface as they feed on the area's baitfish. I keep a jig stick, rigged with a good-casting blue and white or green and yellow jig that I can pick up and cast in front of any breezers I happen to see. I've gotten the only yellowtail on a crowded boat that way and shocked those who were concentrating on calico bass.

Corral State Beach

Situated along Malibu's rugged coastline, Corral State Beach has not traditionally been much of a surf fish beach, instead featuring shallow water rockfish. At some places, you can almost cast out to the kelp beds and boiler rocks. I like to fish this area with cut squid and have been rewarded at times with good catches of starry rockfish and different types of surfperch. This is one of the few beaches where a long, 10- to 14-foot surf rod can be used. On most sandy beaches, a 7-foot bass rod is all that's required.

Mussel baits are also good at times. To keep them on the hook, I like to catch the mussels the day before (reach under docks and pull them off or pull them from pier pilings with a pier gaff), remove them from the shells, spread them out on a cookie sheet, then salt them with coarse-grained salt, sometimes called kosher salt. Let them sit overnight and then rinse. This toughens them up so they stay on the hook much better than when fresh. It can be frustrating to cast the bait off the hook a few times in a row.

Malibu Lagoon State Beach

Just to the west of Malibu Point, Malibu Lagoon State Beach is a surfer's paradise. It's probably the second most famous surfing spot in the world behind Hawaii's Pipeline. If you find yourself at Malibu on a bad surfing day, and there aren't really that many, you'll find very productive surf fishing here. There seem to be plenty of corbina, spotfin croakers, and yellowfin croakers here to go around. In the evening, this is a good halibut and shark beach, as well. Corbina tend to prefer beaches where there are plenty of shovelnose, because these sand probers keep the bottom stirred up and kick the various prey that corbina prefer out of the sand. Corbina often follow shovelnose guitarfish and get a free lunch in the wake of the big sharks.

Keep this in mind when fishing for corbina. If you don't actually see the fish, look for sand and mud swirls where either a bottom-grubbing shark or wave action tends to loosen the bottom. The preferred baits are sand crabs or ghost shrimp, but mussels or bloodworms can also result in good strikes. In the evenings, cast out as far as possible using cut squid or defrosted anchovies torn (not cut) in half to entice shovelnose and bat rays—they really do the trick.

Malibu Pier

This famous pier is very popular for tourists and fishermen. Like many piers, this one has been lost to storms several times. It was built in 1903, rebuilt in 1940, rebuilt again in 1945, and almost destroyed in the big El Niño storm of 1983. Since being sold to the state in 1980, it has been completely renovated. It's fairly short as piers go, only 700 feet or so, but it does stretch into some deeper water. There are several parking lots adjacent to the pier, but they tend to fill up quickly (especially in the summer), so arrive early unless you want to cruise back and forth along the Pacific Coast Highway searching for a parking spot. The pier has lights, benches, a fish cleaning station, restrooms, a snack shop, and a bait and tackle store on the end. In all, it's a well-equipped fishing pier.

Malibu Pier is noted for its ability to attract pelagic species. Mackerel, bonito, barracuda, and even white seabass are caught on this pier in good numbers. This is partially because of the availability of live bait. The fishing sometimes "turns on" for a short period, then "turns off" for the same mysterious reason.

The Malibu Pier, star of many movies, is now undergoing major restoration.

The pier also has good catches of barred surfperch, yellowfin croakers, and corbina when fished with sand crabs, mussels, or bloodworms right in the surf zone. In addition, this is prime halibut country, and since live bait is available, the midpier area is the scene for some nice flatfish action on occasion.

Malibu Artificial Reef

Built in 1961, this artificial reef, along with the Santa Monica Artificial Reef and Hermosa Beach Artificial Reef, were called "replication reefs" and were all built of 330 tons of quarry rock, 44 concrete shelters, 4 automobile bodies, and 1 streetcar. The steel automobile bodies and streetcar didn't last long in the heavily oxygenated saltwater, but the quarry rock and concrete shelters remain as fish-holding habitat. It's located in about 58 feet of water along a 293-degree magnetic course, 10.5 nautical miles from the Marina Del Rey channel entrance at 34° 01' 49" N × 118° 38' 59" W. The relief of the rocks is only two feet above the surrounding sandflats.

The primary game fish caught these days at the Malibu reef is sculpin. They appear in the early spring, sometimes as early as February, and continue through early summer. A squid-baited shrimp fly is one of my favorite baits, but a cut squid strip or live anchovy also produce.

Drifting the flats adjacent to the reefs is the best technique to catch the sculpin as well as bigger halibut. Either live bait or rubber swimbaits, especially when

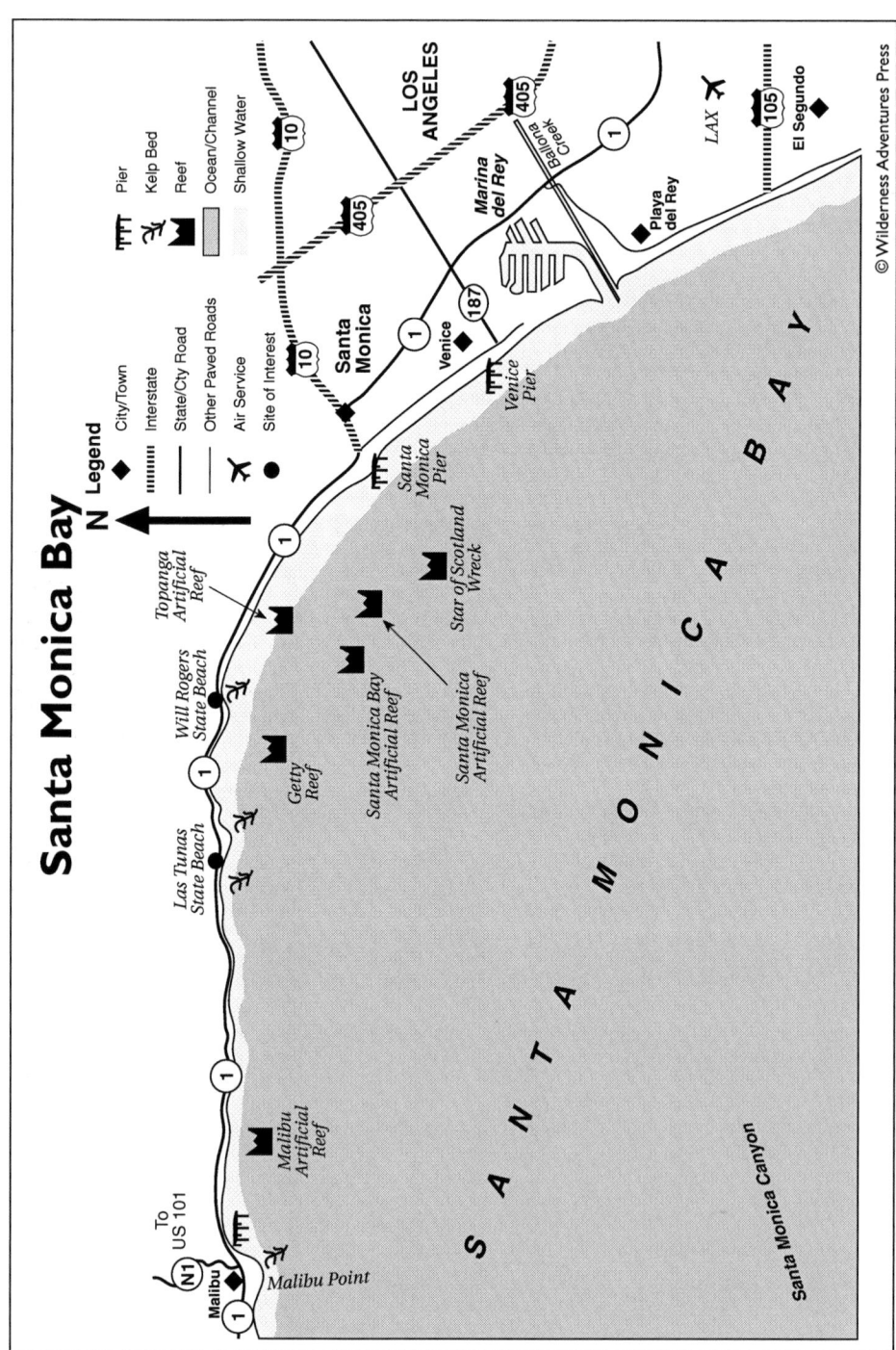

© Wilderness Adventures Press

sweetened with a thin strip of cut squid, produce well. When using swimbaits, select darker colors on more overcast days or when the water appears less clear. Lighter colors do better in the hard sunshine and when the water is very clear.

Access to the Malibu and Point Dume Coastline

From Oxnard in the north to Santa Monica in the south, the Pacific Coast Highway is the main (really, only) road that provides access to the coast. The state beach entrances and pier turnoffs are clearly marked along the highway.

For the private boater, the best harbor to use for access to this coastline is Marina Del Rey. There are excellent boat ramps, good parking, fuel, bait, boat service, and everything the private boater could desire to make a trip more enjoyable. However, this ocean crossing should not to be taken lightly. Though the weather is normally quite fair, there are miserable days, and anyone contemplating this trip should have experience in handling boats in a storm along with a seaworthy vessel. If you have doubts, don't go. There are plenty of far safer places to fish for the inexperienced boat handler.

Santa Monica Bay

Ask any group of fisherman what kind of fish is caught in Santa Monica Bay, and you'll get an instant, unanimous response, "Halibut!" Well, it's true, halibut are the mainstay of the Santa Monica Bay fishery, but that doesn't mean you can't catch plenty of other species than just the flatties. All of the popular game fish inhabit Santa Monica Bay, in addition to some of the best near-coast halibut fishing, making it an excellent destination for the local or traveling fisherman. I've caught great barracuda there, been wide open on sand bass, and hooked more than a few bonito. For those who fish it regularly, yellowtail also make an appearance in the bay.

There are three distinctly different techniques for fishing Santa Monica Bay, each targeting different species, but all three effective. Most people drift the sand-flats for halibut and pick up sand bass and sculpin, as well. This is a proven, effective technique, and one that will result in plenty of fish in the bag. Generally, this is done with live bait, but more and more, artificial lures, such as rubber swimbaits, are employed. The most effective method is to cover ground, so just let the boat drift while lowering fresh, lively bait to the bottom on Carolina rigs.

The second technique is trolling. In the warmer summer months, marauding bands of surface-feeding game fish herd schools of bait into tight balls to gorge themselves on the prey. This does not go unnoticed by the huge population of sea birds living in the area, and when a baitball is formed, you can count on every gull and pelican in the area to take advantage of the game fishes' excellent wrangling job and do a bit of gorging themselves. Keep your eyes on the birds and make sure you troll right through anyplace you see a bird dive. Sooner or later you'll find a school, and once you get a hookup on trolling feathers, chum to keep the school near and break out the bait or jigs. This is fishing at its finest and perhaps one of the most fun techniques for the private boater.

Yet another popular technique for fishing the open Santa Monica Bay is to fish the artificial reefs. There are many in Santa Monica Bay offering good to excellent fishing for any skill level. A person could fish the reefs for a decade and still not know all the fish-holding areas and their subtleties or all the techniques to use here.

Last, but certainly not least, is fishing the Santa Monica Canyon. Plenty of excellent eating, deep water rockfish inhabit this immense undersea structure. In the winter, deep water lingcod move up into the shallower rocks just waiting for a well-presented bait or jig, while year-round, other species of rock cod inhabit the deep craggy sanctuary.

Every year, the Marina Del Rey Anglers sponsor a halibut derby weekend in which all fish must be caught in Santa Monica Bay. For over 25 years, this event has sponsored the Los Angeles youth fishing program. Other proceeds are used for hatchery and grow-out pens to maintain a halibut brood stock to be released into the wild for recreational fishermen. In all, this is a very worthy cause and a lot of fun. The winner in 1999 came in with a 33.7-pound brute. Donated prizes, ranging from a pickup truck to fishing vacations in Alaska and Mexico to fishing tackle, are given for first- to tenth-place finishers. An awards party with drawings and door prizes caps off the festive weekend. To find out more, call 310-827-4855.

Some of the better areas to fish in Santa Monica Bay include:

Las Tunas State Beach

With a name like "the tunas," how could this beach not be a great place to fish? Actually, "las tunas" is a Spanish word meaning the fruit of the prickly pear cactus, not the big ocean fish. Tuna (the fish) in Spanish is "atun." Anyway, Las Tunas is a really fun and productive place to fish. Located just at the end of the Pacific Palisades coastline just south of Malibu, Las Tunas is an interesting place to fish. The main feature of this beach is what's referred to as "groins," built in 1929 in an effort to stop the migration of sand. These partially buried steel and concrete walls extend anywhere from about 80 to 450 feet out into the ocean, making the beach alternately sandy and rocky. This makes the beach dangerous for swimmers and surfers but provides good structure for fish habitat and places to rest out of the main surge of the surf.

Fish the surf here just as you would anywhere else but be prepared to catch other species of fish in addition to the usual surf species. Many species of fish can be taken here, from blue perch to small starry rockfish. Shark fishing can also be good, especially at night, or at least the evening high tide. Squid is one of the better baits in addition to chunks of anchovy, mackerel, or sardines for shovelnose, leopard, or other sand sharks.

Will Rogers State Be ach

Named after Will Rogers, the famous humorist of the 1920s and 30s, this beach is narrow but long (nearly 3 miles) and is situated at the base of Pacific Palisades. The northern parts feature rocky inlets and are great places to fish. A small section at the mouth of Santa Monica Canyon receives storm drain runoff from Brentwood and Pacific Palisades, so it's better not to eat any fish caught here. These days it's called "nonpoint specific" pollution. That includes anything from automobile oil leaks to doggie doo finding its way into the storm drains and ending up in the ocean. Two blocks on either side of San Vicente Boulevard is the primary area. Any fish caught outside this area, though, should be no problem at all to eat.

The beach's northern area is great for surf species, such as yellowfin croaker, spotfin croaker, and corbina. Spotfins seem to be one of the more numerous of these fish and take surf clams or razor clam siphons with gusto. Mussels also provide an alternate bait if clams are unavailable. Sand crabs, ghost shrimp, and bloodworms also work well for these species.

In the winter, especially, plenty of barred surfperch visit these beaches. They're a lot of fun to catch and great to eat. My favorite technique is to use small green rubber grubs, but bait or even flies are other great ways to catch these plentiful surf-dwelling fish.

Getty Reef

The J. Paul Getty Museum lies along the beautiful Pacific Palisades coastline. Named for famous industrialist J. Paul Getty, the museum is part of his philanthropic efforts to give something back to the community. He started the museum personally in 1953 as a display of Greek and Roman antiquities. In 1982, when he died, much of his fortune passed into trusts that funded such things as the expanded Getty Museum, the Getty Research Institute for the History of Art and the Humanities, the Getty Conservation Institute, and the Getty Education Institute for the Arts, which are all wonderful organizations helping to preserve world arts, cultures, and history for all future generations to enjoy.

A natural reef sits just offshore from the museum in 48 feet of water. It lies along a 294-degree magnetic course, 6 miles from the Marina Del Rey channel entrance at 34° 01' 50" N × 118° 33' 40" W. The Getty reef is famous for its ability to attract big halibut. Work the edges of the reef and especially any sand ridges or dropoffs you encounter in the shifting sandy bottom. The big predators love these areas, because they can conceal their bulk while waiting to ambush unsuspecting prey.

Topanga Artificial Reef

The Topanga Artificial Reef is located 5.25 miles from the Marina Del Rey channel entrance along a 302-degree magnetic course at 34° 01' 38" N × 118° 31' 57" W. It was built in 1987 of 10,000 tons of quarry rock. These were placed in three distinct piles, oriented roughly along a northwest-southeast line. The whole site is about 13 acres, but the total acreage of the rockpiles alone is only 2 acres. It was built to encourage kelp growth and has been quite successful in this aspect. It sits in only 28 feet of water. California spiny lobsters are attracted to this reef, especially early in the season, which makes it a popular diving site.

As far as the fishing goes, it is generally very good. Calico bass and barred sand bass inhabit the reef in good numbers, and in some summers, particularly those

You can bring your fly rod along on a party boat but expect some unusual looks from the beer and bait crowd as you ply your craft.
Photo courtesy Mike & Regina Scott—Mike Scott's Hackle, Tackle & Flies.

with cooler water, limits of legal-sized bass are not uncommon. When there is kelp present at the surface, the best bet for calicos is to fish the midwater, 10 to 20 feet deep. When fishing for sand bass, you need to get to the bottom. The sandy flats between the main rockpiles are the best places.

In addition to bass, these rockpiles also attract sculpin, the occasional sheep-head, and some smaller game fish, such as blue perch, white croaker, and starry rockfish. Since kelp attracts baitfish, bigger halibut patrol the nearby sandflats, as well. On occasion, schools of barracuda or bonito can be found feeding on schools of bait near the kelp. All in all, you couldn't ask for a better summer haunt to catch a variety of fish, using a variety of techniques.

Topanga Reef is a good place to flyfish, also. To coax the shy calico bass out of their protective canopies, use shooting-head, sinking fly lines to present an anchovy-imitating streamer fly right on the edge of the visible kelp. Normally, early morning is the best time to break out the fly tackle, since the wind occasionally kicks up in the afternoon and makes flyfishing difficult. If you're not allergic to using both types of tackle on one trip (I say why not?), get your flyfishing in early then move on to meat fishing.

Santa Monica Flats

Just off the coast from the city of Santa Monica, wide sand and mudflats surround the three major reefs. The flats are great places to catch halibut, the most famous of the Santa Monica Bay game fish. Sand bass, sculpin, and several types of sharks are also on the menu. This is classic southern California flats fishing and probably the second most productive area outside Huntington Flats.

Drifting with live bait is generally considered the best way to catch fish here. Unless a "nest" of sculpin or sand bass is located, it isn't usually wise to anchor up, at least not unless the wind or current make it difficult to get a line to the bottom. By drifting with an active bait, there is a far better chance to catch the eye of a halibut waiting in ambush.

I also really like rubber swimbaits here, using a tiny piece of cut squid for scent and yoyoing a green or root beer-colored twin-tailed scampi or mojo down near the bottom with slow, gentle rod sweeps. This seems to drive big halibut wild, and sand bass are also attracted to the struggling, crippled baitfish.

Anytime you're fishing these flats in the warmer months, there is a chance for schools of pelagic fish to move through. In late spring and early summer, plenty of barracuda congregate over the flats to feed. Keep an eye on the birds for best results, but simply trolling around (if you happen to like boat rides) is also a fun, productive, and easy way to pick up fish and locate schools in which to fish with bait, lures, or flies.

Santa Monica Bay Artificial Reef

Offering excellent fishing, the Santa Monica Bay Artificial Reef is a huge site, covering 250-plus acres, although there are really only 7 acres of actual rockpiles. Actually, it isn't one big structure but rather 22 pairs of rockpiles laid out in a gridlike pattern in water ranging from 42 to 72 feet deep. The center of the reef is located 5 nautical miles from the Marina Del Rey channel entrance on a 290-degree magnetic course at 34° 00′ 47″ N × 118° 32′ 33″ W. It was built in 1987 of 20,000 tons of quarry rock and has been a very successful fishing reef design. Like the Topanga Reef, this reef attracts lobsters, and of course, plenty of scuba divers.

In March and April, sculpin arrive in force, offering fishermen plenty of opportunities to catch these tasty, although slightly dangerous to handle, bottom dwellers. In addition, sand bass frequent the reefs throughout the year and are easily caught during late summer and early fall. In spring and early summer, the prime season for halibut, be sure to check out the sandy areas between rockpiles.

A good bottom meter is important when fishing this reef. Survey the site first to see where the main schools of fish are hanging out. Sometimes they're all stacked up in the deeper rockpiles, at other times the tide pushes them to the northern or southern edge. You'll find the best areas to fish by making a survey first.

Santa Monica Artificial Reef

One of the original "replication reef" structures built in the early 1960s, this reef was constructed of 330 tons of quarry rock, 44 concrete structures, 4 automobile bodies, and one streetcar in 1961. It was augmented in 1971 with the addition of 100 tons of concrete pier pilings. Since its construction, the streetcar and car bodies have long since vanished due to the corrosive effects of seawater, but the pilings remain. The reef lies in 60 feet of water, 4.5 nautical miles from the Marina Del Rey channel entrance along a 295-degree magnetic course. Its coordinates are 34° 00′ 34″ N × 118° 31′ 47″ W.

While this reef is often passed up in favor of the larger and newer Santa Monica Bay Artificial Reef, it is nonetheless a very good fishing hole and still produces good catches of sand bass and sculpin in their respective seasons, fall and spring. The outer edges tend to attract halibut, as well, and often, impressive catches can be the result of some diligent fishing efforts directed around the edges of the reef.

Star of Scotland Wreck

Originally the *Star of Scotland* was a 262-foot-long steamer cargo ship built early this century. In the 1920s it was converted to a gambling ship. After leaving port and anchoring 3 miles or more off the coast (outside the state's jurisdiction), these ships could legally proceed with the gambling. The era of the gambling ships came to a close in 1931 by the passage of new, more restrictive laws. The Star of Scotland was retired as a luxury gambling ship and converted to a fishing barge, anchored off the coast and its fishermen ferried back and forth to its decks. It sank in 1942.

The *Star of Scotland* lies in 70 feet of water and is located 3.4 nautical miles from Marina Del Rey on a 286-degree magnetic course at 33° 59′ 52″ N × 118° 31′ 27″ W. Divers still visit the wreck, but it is deteriorating and festooned with fishing nets and lines and is not safe to enter. Nonetheless, since the wreck is so well publicized, people try every year and some never make it home.

Like all artificial reefs, the *Star of Scotland* attracts plenty of fish seeking shelter in its many nooks and crannies. The wreck offers some sand bass and calico bass fishing that is often quite good, the occasional white seabass, sculpin that are often near the wreck, and some excellent halibut fishing in the sand around the ship.

Fish the bottom, both near the wreck and atop the structure, for best results. Live bait is always the best, but cut squid, rubber swimbaits, and metal jigs can produce well, too. There are also rockfish here, so sometimes a shrimp fly gangion sent down into the wreck will attract starry rockfish, treefish, and other shallow water rock-dwelling species. Occasionally, schools of surface fish congregate around the wreck when bait tries to take refuge there. Barracuda and the occasional yellowtail can be found feeding on these schools. Jigs fished midwater or live baits on their way up or down help find them if they're present.

Santa Monica Pier

Located at the foot of Interstate 10, the Santa Monica Pier is actually two piers, one built in 1909 and the other in 1916. The Santa Monica Pleasure Pier was added onto the first part of the pier, the Santa Monica Municipal Pier, in 1916. Later, it was again expanded to its current size, 270 feet wide and 1080 feet long. A huge ballroom was constructed in 1924, and severe storms forced closure of the famous

The Santa Monica Pier features lower tiers just for fishermen in addition to its restaurants, arcades, amusement park rides, and fascinating street vendors.

roller coaster in 1930. In 1981 a full restoration program was begun that lasted until 1990. Today, Santa Monica Pier is one of southern California's most famous. It has appeared in countless movies and TV shows. It sports several nice restaurants, an amusement park, shops, and snack bars. A new, multilevel section is specially reserved and dedicated to fishermen. In addition to its other traits, it is also one of the only readily accessible piers for wheelchairs.

The Santa Monica Pier is open 24 hours a day and features lights, fish cleaning stations, benches, restrooms, and snack shops, but no bait and tackle store. An excellent fee parking lot is located at the foot of the pier, and you can drive right onto the pier and park. There is additional metered parking on the streets at the foot of the pier.

The pier extends out into deep water, so some good fishing is available at the middle and end sections. The surf zone is mostly filled with shops on one side and a restaurant on the other, making it difficult to fish for surf species. White croaker and

Two deep water reef fish, a lingcod on the left and bocaccio on the right, both great eating fish. Photo courtesy Gary Quon.

queenfish are the most common catches, but many other species, up to and including yellowtail, are occasionally caught there. There are also quite a few sharks taken here. Some of the better areas to fish are the right side, where a rocky-bottomed area is located not far from the pier, or under the pier, which is quite easy to do with the tiered fishing areas. Good numbers of several varieties of surfperch can often prevent a good skunking while fishing this pier.

Santa Monica Canyon

The major deep water fishing spot in the Santa Monica Bay is Santa Monica Canyon. Like the Redondo Canyon a few miles south, the Santa Monica Canyon is a major geologic feature of the seabed. Cutting across the coastal subsea plain is a deep gorge, ranging from the near-shore bottom to as deep as 2500 feet (half a mile!).

The canyon's edges are where to fish for the plentiful red rock cod, bocaccios, and chilipepper rockfish.

While some people fish as shallow as 300 feet for these species, I like to fish really deep here. There are more and larger fish at the 800- to 1000-foot depth as opposed to scratching out a few fish in the heavily fished shallower water. Send 5-hook magic bucktail (shrimp fly) gangions, baited with thin strips of squid, to the bottom with at least 3 to 4 pounds of lead. If you're in an area with feeding fish, you won't have to wait long for the gangion to fill up with tasty rock cod.

Venice Fishing Pier

Recently resurrected from years of dormancy, the Venice fishing pier is finally back after being nearly destroyed and sitting condemned since the big El Niño storms of 1983. This pier is entirely new and is a virtual duplicate of the old pier, except that it is made of concrete. The pier itself is nearly a quarter mile long (1310 feet), getting into deep enough water to be a good pier for pelagic species, such as mackerel, bonito, and even an occasional barracuda. There's an artificial reef, made of 4000 tons of quarry rock, surrounding the last 700 feet or so of the pier. This attracts plenty of bait and makes it one of the better piers to fish.

The surf zone has plenty of such surf species as corbina, yellowfin croakers, barred surfperch, and some spotfin croakers in the proper seasons. Fish it as you would any surf zone, with sand crabs, ghost shrimp, mussels, or bloodworms for best results. In the winter, green rubber grubs, known as "surfperch killers," do just that.

Out near the ends, cast out to the artificial reef with live anchovies, dead anchovy bait, or cut squid to get in on the sand bass, sculpin, and occasional calico action. Fish the midwater with live anchovies, spoons, or bonito feathers for the pelagic species in the warmer summer months.

The Venice pier is not known as a fisherman's pier. However, it is a beach-goer's delight with a constant parade of fascinating people, from bikini-clad beach bunnies to muscle beach Mr. Universe wannabes to tourists, hippies, artists, street musicians, street preachers, and just about any other form of humanity you can imagine. If you're a hermit and don't like to be around people, don't bother with this pier.

Access to Santa Monica Bay

The Santa Monica Bay is the closest beach area from downtown Los Angeles and can be reached by taking Interstate 10 (Santa Monica Freeway) west until it ends and becomes the northbound Pacific Coast Highway. Follow this north to the Santa Monica beaches. The last turnoff before the freeway becomes the Pacific Coast Highway is Ocean Boulevard South. Take this off-ramp to go to Santa Monica Pier, Venice Beach, or the Venice Pier.

If going by boat, Marina Del Rey is the closest small craft harbor to the Santa Monica Bay. It has an excellent launch ramp facility (see the Marina Del Rey section)

Marina Del Rey, Playa Del Rey, and LAX

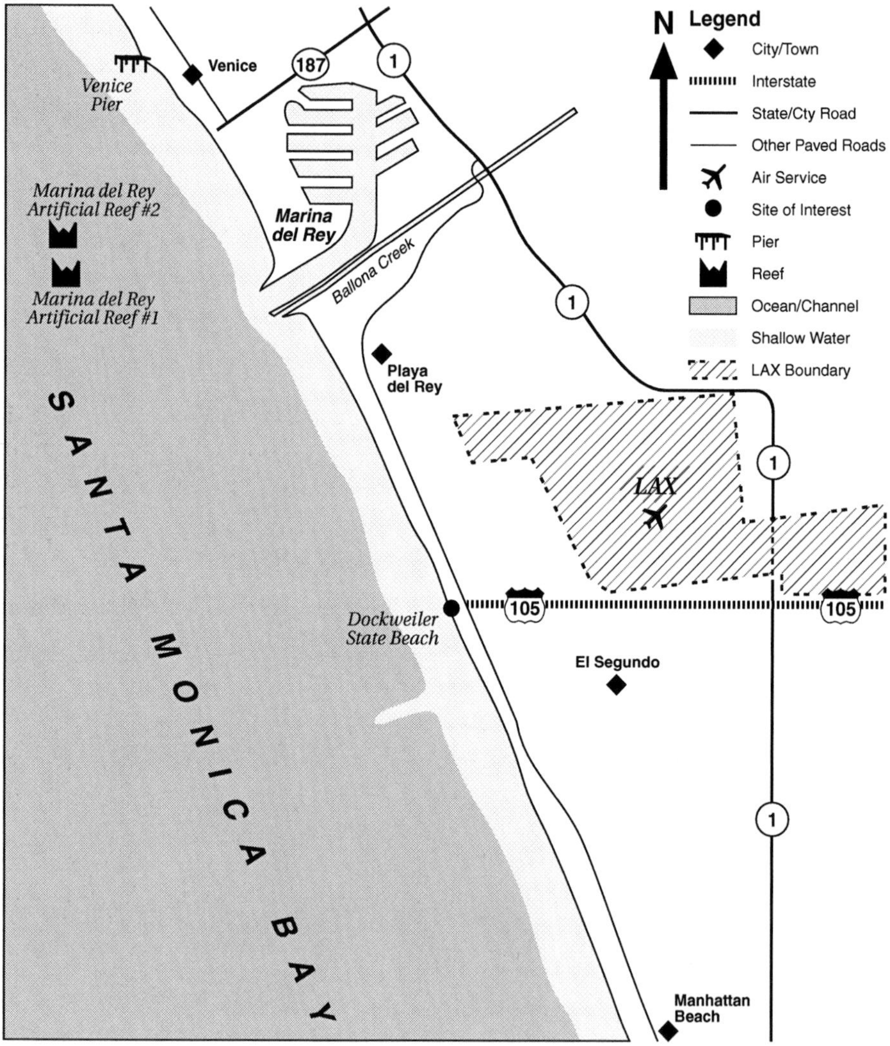

N

Legend

◆ City/Town

⊪⊪⊪⊪ Interstate

—— State/Cty Road

— Other Paved Roads

✈ Air Service

● Site of Interest

⊤⊤⊤ Pier

♕ Reef

▨ Ocean/Channel

Shallow Water

▨▨▨ LAX Boundary

Venice Pier

◆ Venice

187 1

Marina del Rey Artificial Reef #2

Marina del Rey Artificial Reef #1

Marina del Rey

Ballona Creek

1

◆ Playa del Rey

1

LAX ✈

S A N T A   M O N I C A   B A Y

Dockweiler State Beach ●

105 ⊪⊪⊪⊪⊪⊪⊪⊪⊪⊪⊪⊪ 105

El Segundo ◆

1

Manhattan Beach ◆

© Wilderness Adventures Press

and complete marine fuel, service, and marine supply services. A live bait barge sits prominently in the center of the harbor.

Marina Del Rey, Playa Del Rey, and LAX

The Marina and LAX areas of Los Angeles are at the center of the huge curve of Santa Monica Bay, which is the greater portion of coastline in Los Angeles County. Sandy beaches and a gentle undersea slope having a sand and mud bottom characterize this area, because originally, it was the outflow of the Los Angeles River (there really is such a place—it's not a joke). Marina Del Rey is considered to be *the* small craft harbor servicing the majority of the Los Angeles area, particularly the northern half. This includes the communities of Beverly Hills, Bel Aire, Brentwood, Encino, and many of the other posh neighborhoods. There's no shortage of expensive yachts here, either.

The fishing in this area isn't world class, but it is productive and fun. It's close to many of the residential neighborhoods and tourist destinations, so it can be worked in with a minimal investment in time. Some good flats fishing and surf casting are the mainstay of this area, along with visiting the excellent artificial reefs.

Some of the better areas to fish in this stretch include:

Marina Del Rey Beaches

A small section of beach on the peninsula separating Marina Del Rey from the Pacific Ocean, the Marina Del Rey beaches are actually an extension of famous Venice Beach. This is the less visited section with fewer tourists and more locals, reflected in its less fancy and more casual atmosphere. This has always been and should continue to be a good overall fishing beach for most surf species. In winter, barred surfperch congregate in the breaking surf. Beginning in late spring and stretching into summer, spotfin croaker, yellowfin croaker, and corbina all come here to feed in addition to the little perch.

Marina Del Rey Artificial Reef #2

From the success of the first reef, a second reef was built in 1985 of 10,000 tons of quarry rock spread out over a nearly 7-acre site. It lies in 65 feet of water at 33° 58′ 06″ N × 118° 29′ 11″ W and can be reached by traveling 1.25 miles from the Marina Del Rey channel entrance on a 270-degree magnetic course.

Reef #2 tends to attract more sculpin than the other Marina Del Rey reef, and fishing the edges can often result in picking up a few of these great eating fish. More often, sand bass and a few rockfish are on the menu. For best results, fish the bottom as close to the structure as you can (without fouling the lines) with live bait, cut squid, or rubber swimbaits.

Marina Del Rey Artificial Reef #1

The first artificial reef was originally built in 1965 with 2,000 tons of quarry rock, then augmented in 1976 with 120 concrete dock floats, and augmented again in 1978

206 — SALTWATER ANGLER'S GUIDE TO SOUTHERN CALIFORNIA

Big halibut inhabit sand flats areas. George Orozco of Chino shows off his "barn door"' halibut. Photo courtesy Captain Dave Bacon— Wavewalker Charters.

with 4,000 tons of concrete rubble. It also lies in 65 feet of water, 1.25 miles from the marina entrance along a 252-degree course at 33° 57′ 54″ N × 118° 29′ 10″ W. It's a smaller site than the second reef, covering only about 3 acres, but has a somewhat higher relief than the newer reef.

This original reef is renowned for its sand bass fishing. Spring through fall, it's a very predictable place to pick up a few sandies. Just drop rubber swimbaits or live anchovies down into the reef structure and hang on. In the absence of live bait, cut squid strips work just about as well.

If fishing this reef on the bottom, keep your eyes peeled for surface action. Bigger pelagic fish, such as bonito, barracuda, and even yellowtail, often follow schools of bait moving through this area. I always keep a rigged, flylining bait stick at the ready, along with a jig stick, when fishing in places such as this for when the surface bite suddenly turns on. You can see the bait schools move through and, occasionally, the game fish attacking the schools. Usually, birds will be the first indication, but sometimes they're off somewhere else and haven't noticed the school, so don't use birds as your only indicator.

El Segundo Flats

Some very productive fishing flats are found right off Dockweiler State Beach and the city of El Segundo. Halibut, sculpin, sand bass, and occasionally, barracuda frequent the area, with the latter two being more available in late spring and summer. This area is in some ways similar to Huntington Flats down in Orange County, a nursery for several types of spawning fish.

I like to drift these flats with live bait. In addition to being the most productive way to nail big halibut, it also lets you cover some territory to find pockets of nesting sculpin and sand bass. Keep the bait or lures very near the bottom on Carolina rigs with just enough weight to keep the lead on the bottom. Periodically, lift the weight, crank it in a bit, then free-spool it back to the bottom. This keeps it moving, covering territory, and possibly right into the mouth of a waiting halibut. Using this technique, you'll also run into all sorts of other fish, including white croaker, guitarfish, sharks of various types, and of course, barred sand bass and sculpin—in all, a real mixed bag.

Surface fish sometimes cruise these flats, as well. Keep your eyes open for baitboils and bird action. Occasionally, try a jig, yoyoed near the bottom, to see if barracuda or yellowtail are around, especially in the warm summer months. This is an excellent place to fish, just a bit noisy what with the jets from LAX taking off every minute or so.

LAX Beaches (Dockweiler State Beach)

When jet transport aircraft appeared on the scene in the early 1960s, most major airports went through extensive enlargement to accommodate the big jets. LAX was no exception, and the new, longer runways were completed in 1961. The somewhat exclusive oceanfront homes that were located between the end of the runway and the beach became undesirable and were gradually bought up by the city throughout the 1960s and early 1970s. By the mid-1970s, when wide body jets began to appear, this area was unlivable due to the noise and downright danger in the event of an aborted takeoff. Eventually, all the land was bought back by the city, and the only sign that this was ever a residential area are the aging, cracked, and weed-ridden streets.

The beach's sand migrates from north to south due to the normal rip currents running down the beach. Back when this was a fancy residential area, many short breakwaters were built perpendicular to the beach to stem the flow of sand south so that residents could enjoy the sandy beaches year-round. This causes the sand to be deposited in a sawtooth pattern and creates plenty of fish holding structure. Surf

The short breakwaters at Dockweiler State Beach serve to stop sand migration and offer excellent habitat for surf species as a bonus.

feeding species find this area particularly appealing because they can feed along the beach at high tide and grub along the bottom near the rocky breakwater structures in between tides. This makes it not only a productive place to surf fish but an interesting one as well, where different techniques and experimentation often reign over traditional surf fishing tactics.

Fishing this area depends on the tide. When the tide is high, fish the centers of the beaches between breakwaters in the traditional manner with sand crabs, ghost shrimp, mussels, clam siphons (especially good here), or bloodworms. With the outgoing tide, fish the north sides of the breakwaters right where the sandy bottom reaches the rocks. At low tide, fish the ends of the breakwaters and cast out as far as possible to get into the sandy bottom species (halibut, sand bass, sanddabs, sculpin, etc.). With the flooding tide, switch to the south sides of the breakwaters to get into the deepest water with the most structure. Just about any time of day, this area is fishable and tons of fun.

Access to the Marina Del Rey and LAX Area

Marina Del Rey is readily accessible from Interstate 405 (San Diego Freeway) by taking the exit for the CA 90 (Marina Freeway) west until it ends. Admiralty Way circumnavigates the marina and passes all major hotels, restaurants, and marine supply stores. The launch ramps for trailer boats are located at the end of Admiralty Way. In the center of the channel is a bait barge that sells live anchovies and sardines (seasonally) by the "scoop" for boats with live bait tanks.

To get to the LAX area beaches, go west on Interstate 105 (Century Freeway) from any of the major north/south freeways in the Los Angeles area (Interstates 405, 110, 710, 5, 605) until it deadends on Vista Del Mar. Turn right to Dockweiler State Beach and the Playa Del Rey area.

Marina Del Rey Sportfishing is a top-flight landing that features half-day, twilight, three-quarter-day, full-day (overnight), and multiple-day fishing trips to local fishing spots and the offshore islands. In summer, the target is primarily surface fish, and in winter, it is the deep water rock cod spots. They also have charter boats available. The address and contact information is:

> Marina Del Rey Sportfishing
> Dock 52, Fiji Way
> Marina del Rey, CA
> (310) 822-3625
> www.mdrsf.com

Boats may be rented in Marina Del Rey at:

> Fisherman's Village
> Marina Del Rey Harbor
> 13763 Fiji Way
> Marina Del Rey 90292
> 310-823-5411

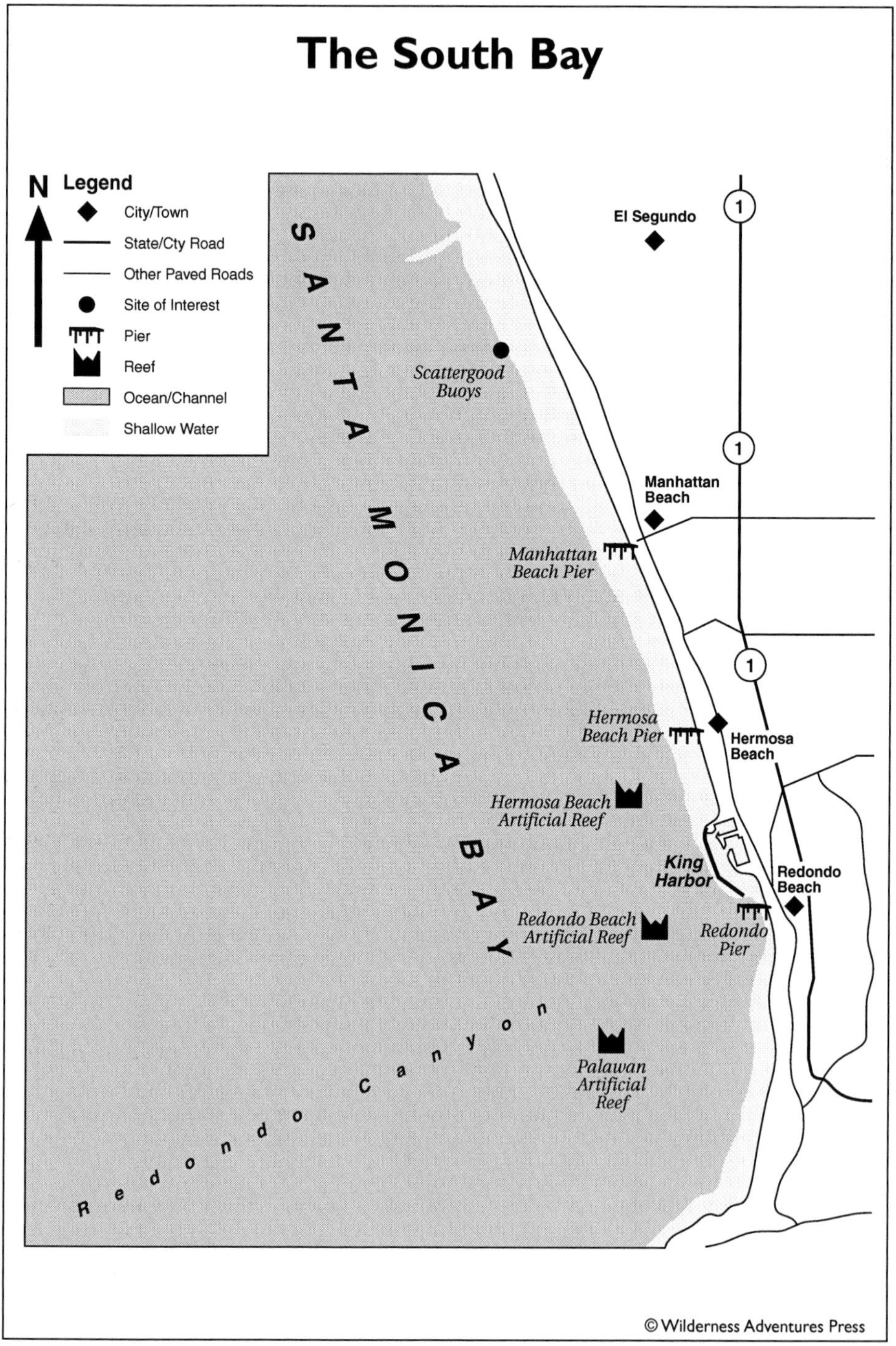
The South Bay
N
Legend
City/Town
State/Cty Road
Other Paved Roads
Site of Interest
Pier
Reef
Ocean/Channel
Shallow Water
SANTA MONICA BAY
El Segundo
1
Scattergood Buoys
1
Manhattan Beach
Manhattan Beach Pier
1
Hermosa Beach Pier
Hermosa Beach
Hermosa Beach Artificial Reef
King Harbor
Redondo Beach
Redondo Beach Artificial Reef
Redondo Pier
Palawan Artificial Reef
Redondo Canyon
© Wilderness Adventures Press

The South Bay

Known for its party life atmosphere, the South Bay has traditionally been one of LA's main singles haunts. This is due, in part, to the area's proximity to Los Angeles International Airport and the large number of airline and related travel industry personnel who live in the area. Back in the '70s, this meant singles. With today's rising real estate prices, much of the area is priced out of the range of most young people and has become far more family oriented than it once was.

Plenty of hotels, restaurants, and night spots fill the beach area, attracting tourists from across town to across the world. Along its beaches, some very famous personalities can occasionally be spotted. The South Bay is a wonderful place to visit or live if you like high-density places. While it isn't anywhere nearly as crowded as Tokyo, it is one of the higher density places in all of southern California.

The fishing in the South Bay is good most of the year. Some of the better flats fishing in all the county is found here, along with some good deep rock fishing and good wreck and artificial reef fishing. It has three excellent piers—all very fine fishing piers capable of yielding some fine catches.

The beautiful white sand beaches offer fishermen the chance to be out on a nearly empty beach (a few surfers and beach joggers) for an early morning high tide, casting for breakfast. I, for one, love the sights and smells of that time of the day when most of the rest of the city is still in bed or only just waking up.

Some of the better places to fish in the South Bay include:

Scattergood Buoys

The buoys right offshore from the Scattergood power plant between Manhattan Beach and El Segundo provide an excellent artificial reef that attracts several species of game fish. In late winter and early spring, this is where huge schools of sculpin come to nest and breed. I fished there one early March day several years ago and discovered they can't resist bucktail shrimp flies. In fact, I was using three-hook gangions of 1/0-sized marabou and bucktail shrimp flies in three different color combinations (pink/red, blue/white, and green/yellow), and it was a rare drop when all three hooks weren't full within a couple of seconds after hitting the bottom. I was on a half-day boat out of Redondo and had no trouble limiting out in a matter of a few minutes. I lent the rig to my friend, and he also limited in a short while. The most caught by anyone else was two fish by someone using squid heads.

This area also has its share of barred sand bass in late spring and early summer. They take live anchovies best but also fall to a rubber swimbait, especially one with some bait attached for that special scent. While sand bass fishing, occasionally try a jig on the bottom. Schools of barracuda or breezing yellowtail can often surprise you here.

Keep your eyes peeled for bird action, too, especially in the warmer summer and fall months. Birds are usually the first to locate baitfish. Troll or just "run and gun"— make a dash into the center of the baitball, toss out live bait immediately, and wait for hits. Chances are the baitball will move away from your boat, making your hooked bait look like stragglers—choice pickings for a game fish. Once the

The Manhattan Beach Pier is excellent for fishing, strolling, or watching people.

commotion moves away from your boat, pull in your lines and make another dash to the center of the frenzy. Bonito, barracuda, and yellowtail all fall for this tactic.

Manhattan Beach Pier

This pier was originally built in 1920 and has been a popular fishing and strolling pier ever since. Situated right in the middle of the bustling beach community of Manhattan Beach, it attracts plenty of locals and tourists. The pier could use an overhaul, but nonetheless, the fishing is very good. It's a good pier for pelagic species, especially because of the artificial reef made of 2000 tons of quarry rock that was installed about 65 feet (an easy casting distance) from the end. The balance of the pier is situated over a gently sloping, sandy beach.

Near the surf line, plenty of barred surfperch inhabit the area, so the fishing for these species is very good, especially during winter months. The midpier area gets its share of halibut as well as the usual pier species, and at night, plenty of guitarfish and other rays cruise the coast.

To find the real action at this pier, cast out to the artificial reefs for calico bass, sand bass, bonito, mackerel, and even barracuda. The best choice is live bait, which isn't available here. You have to catch bait by using a bait-catching rig or bring live bait along in an aerated bucket, purchased from another area where live anchovies are available. In addition to live bait, smaller jigs, feathers, spoons, and rubber swimbaits sometimes produce well on these species.

The pier is open 24 hours a day and features lights, benches, fish cleaning stations, restrooms, and just about anything an angler could want, except, of course, a bait and tackle shop. Be prepared to take anything you might need to fish here. A fee parking lot and streetside metered parking are available, although parking can be scarce, especially on hot days and summer weekends. Be prepared to get there early and fish the morning high tide or late to fish during the evening and night.

Hermosa Beach Pier

Lying just south of Manhattan Beach is Hermosa Beach. In Spanish, hermosa means beautiful, and this beach community is just that. It's a hilly shore area with wide sandy beaches. Aside from being a bit far from the nearest freeway, it is nonetheless one of the area's most desirable beach towns in which to live. The Hermosa Beach Pier is probably one of the best fishing piers in the entire Los Angeles area.

The pier is renowned for its abundant supply of halibut—keeper-sized flatfish are frequently caught there. Larger pelagic fish, up to and including yellowtail, can be caught on this pier in the warm summer months.

The pier extends over 1100 feet into the Pacific, and the last 650 feet is surrounded by an artificial reef made up of quarry rock. The reef is 60 to 70 feet away from the pier (an easy casting distance) and accounts for much of the pier's excellent reputation as a place to catch game fish. The reef structure provides lots of nooks and crannies where small baitfish hide, and consequently, gets picked at continually by marauding bands of bigger fish. For best results, fish this reef in the summer, although winter can have its surprises. Year-round bass fishing can often be good at this pier.

The midpier area is the major place for halibut. The artificial reef tends to trap halibut along the bottom, so that the best place to fish for them is often inside the reefs. The best bait and lures, in order, are live anchovies, cut squid, squid-sweetened rubber swimbaits, and shrimp flies. If you can cast over the artificial reefs to the sand flats beyond, you should be in prime halibut country. They like using structure as a blind to ambush passing prey.

The Hermosa Beach Pier is open 24 hours a day and features lights, restrooms, fish cleaning stations, and even a bait, tackle, and snack shop on the pier. Parking is limited to a somewhat small fee lot and some on-street metered parking. Keep those meters full, too, because the area is well patrolled and parking tickets are issued to violators. On warm summer days, weekends, and holidays, Hermosa Beach is a popular place, so parking can be a problem if you like to fish in the midafternoon at these times.

Hermosa Beach Artificial Reef

Lying right between the Hermosa Beach Pier and King Harbor in about 60 feet of water is the Hermosa Beach Artificial Reef. This reef was one of the first of the original artificial reefs built in 1960. It was comprised of 300 tons of quarry rock, 44 concrete shelters, 44 automobile bodies, and 1 streetcar. It's located 1 nautical mile from the King Harbor entrance along a 302-degree magnetic course at 33° 51' 13" N × 118° 24' 48" W. This is a small site, covering only about a half-acre. The car bodies and streetcar disappeared long ago, leaving only the concrete building parts and quarry rock to provide fish holding structure.

Both larger and smaller game fish seem to congregate at this reef, especially in late summer and early fall. In addition to the usual bass, sculpin, and rockfish found at this and nearly every other reef, schools of halfmoons (blue perch) and opaleye frequent the area in the fall. In recent years, plenty of whitefish have also been spotted and caught at this reef.

As with most flats or bottom fishing, baits or lures held very close to the bottom, or even dragged on the bottom, produce better than those suspended higher in the water column. I prefer live anchovies, cut squid, or rubber swimbaits sweetened with squid for optimum results.

King Harbor

The outer harbor at Redondo Beach's King Harbor is a famous fishing place. Though fairly small, this is where the Redondo Beach power plant releases water, so it tends to be a few degrees warmer than the nearby ocean. This attracts many game fish, especially during fall as the water is cooling. King Harbor tends to be dominated by flyfishermen. I don't know why this is, but nearly everyone you see fishing in the harbor from boats fishes with fly gear. From the breakwater, more conventional tackle is used, but not so in the bay. You can rent small outboard-powered skiffs at Rocky Point Marina, which also has a well-equipped flyfishing store, offering the latest in saltwater fly gear.

The bay gets well flushed from tidal action and is one of the cleanest marina areas in the southland. Bonito, hiding from cooling waters in the fall, are the most popular target at Redondo, since they're plentiful and often quite large. These fish really go after anchovy-imitating streamer flies. All white with crystal flash seems to be the most popular, with blue and white streamers a close second. I like to add Mylar flash to the ones I tie.

In addition to bonito, outer King Harbor holds mackerel, calico bass, and sand bass. The best place to fish is within casting distance to the bait barge, particularly when the parade of sportfishing boats are loading their bait tanks for offshore trips in the early morning. Many frisky baitfish are inadvertently released while bait tanks are loaded, and often, dead bait is skimmed off by the bait barge crew and dumped overboard, making the bait tank a feeding trough for fish. They soon learn to wait patiently around the tank for their morning "feeding." This is when you should give them what they want: a live anchovy, an anchovy-imitating lure, or a fly—you'll soon have a frenzied game fish on your line.

Very few anglers try (except those fishing from the breakwater), but the bottom of outer King Harbor is an excellent flatfish and bottom-fishing area. At night, plenty

For those who hate to back up a boat trailer, the launch facility at Redondo Beach's King Harbor features a drive-through facility with a sling crane to pluck your boat off and on its trailer.

of sand sharks are on the prowl, and during the day, halibut await passing food to ambush. While you're there, you should try fishing the bottom as well as the surface.

Whether fishing from a boat or the breakwater itself, the place to find bass is near the breakwater. Calicos find sheltered caves amid the rocky structure, and sand bass love the sandy and muddy bottom right near the rocks. Work this juncture for the best results. It amazes me to see most breakwater fishermen trying to cast as far from the wall as possible. The best fish are close to structure, such as piers or breakwaters, because of the fish holding structure, so why does everyone think they should cast as far away as possible? Fish close to the structure and come home with the bacon.

The short Redondo sportfishing pier is another great place to fish at King Harbor. While most people don't think of fishing here, favoring either the main Redondo pier or the breakwater, don't count this pier out as a good place to fish. Near the surface with spoons, plugs, or swimbaits, you can catch any of the pelagic fish described above, while the bottom produces many of the sandy-bottom species. Near the pilings, herring and surfperch are available for those interested in using these techniques.

Redondo Beach Artificial Reef

Another in a string of artificial reefs created by the Department of Fish and Game, the Redondo Beach Artificial Reef is located just three-quarters of a mile from the King Harbor marina entrance along a 242-degree magnetic course. It lies in 72 feet of water at 33° 50′ 14″ N × 118° 24′ 32″ W. This reef covers 1.5 acres and was originally built in 1962 with 1000 tons of quarry rock and was augmented several times, beginning in 1974 with the sinking of a barge on the site, in 1975 with 300 tons of concrete pipe, in 1976 with 700 tons of concrete pilings, and yet again in 1978 and 1979 with 1700 concrete dock floats. The profile is quite complex and provides excellent habitat for many species of fish.

Like the Palawan site, this reef is quite a draw for scuba divers. Because of its relatively shallow depth and close proximity to a major recreational port, it is often one of the first ocean dives for newly registered scuba divers.

Many surface fish congregate here due to the generally plentiful bait attracted to the reef. In the warm summer months, the presence of feeding bonito, barracuda, and yellowtail is obvious from the bird activity and surface baitboils. These are prime times to fish the reef. In addition, sending bait or lures deep into the structure yields not only the pelagic species, but also bass, sculpin, sheephead, whitefish, and the occasional white seabass (more and more every year as the hatchery and grow-out program becomes more and more successful).

Don't forget the sandflats just around the reef. These are ideal halibut and sand bass bottoms, sandy but near structure. Many a fisherman has missed some prime fishing opportunities by only fishing the craggy parts of the reefs. Try it! You won't be disappointed.

Redondo Pier

One of the more interesting of all the southern California piers, the Redondo Pier attracts not only fishermen but tourists as well. Festooned with shops and restaurants, it offers fun for the entire family. The fish market and restaurant on the lower level is famous among locals who come out in droves on warm summer days to eat fresh boiled crabs, lobsters, and fish of all sorts, while sitting on the patio and watching the world go by. At night, the area is alive with dancing, drinking, and eating places open until the wee hours of the morning.

This pier had a serious fire and almost burned down completely in 1989. It was rebuilt quickly, though, and now provides one of the most festive atmospheres of any southern California pier. It has plenty of room for fishing and for strolling. An excellent parking structure, capable of handling the huge number of tourists and visitors the pier attracts, is available for the fishermen. Plenty of services, including lights, restaurants, fish cleaning stations, bait and tackle shops, and benches, surround the massive pier structure to ensure that the fisherman has a great time. The only negative thing you can say about this pier is that sometimes it has too many people. If you like socializing, this is for you. But if you like to fish alone and quietly, don't go to Redondo. You'll likely get lots of questions fired at you about how you're doing, especially by the many children enjoying summer afternoons and evenings.

The Redondo Pier is famous for its halibut fishing. Of course, live bait is the best bet, but they'll also hit artificials and cut bait on occasion. The usual surf species fishing is not very good here since the bottom is not as sandy near the shore as it is at

For all-around family fun, the Redondo Beach Pier has shops, restaurants, arcades, and even a fish market in case you don't want to admit you were skunked.

other beach type piers. However, bigger pelagic fish often pass by on their way into and out of King Harbor, so fishing for bonito, mackerel, and an occasional barracuda or yellowtail is often much better than at sandy beach piers. Keep your eyes open for any surface action and cast feathered jigs, metal jigs, or live bait with no sinker into the fish's path for best results. You can fish with flies here, also, but I leave my fly rod home. If you wish to give it a try, use a casting bubble on a spinning rig to present a fly to these fish.

Redondo Canyon

Just outside the channel entrance to King Harbor, a deep submarine canyon slices its way from the deep abyss across the near-shore continental shelf. This huge gorge is over 2000 feet deep in places. This is an incredible structure, and if the sea were suddenly completely transparent, it would be an awe-inspiring sight.

Redondo Canyon is the place to fish for rock cod. Lots of the quality species, such as reds, boscos, cows, and bocaccios, inhabit the deeper recesses of the canyon. Chilipeppers, Floridas, and bank rockfish abound here. This canyon also has sablefish awaiting the fisherman willing to put the effort into fishing sufficiently deep to get to these tasty, black-colored fish.

I prefer to fish deep here—800 to 1100 feet. A 9/0-sized reel filled with 60- to 80-pound test Dacron is necessary to get gangions down that deep. Shrimp flies in

4/0 or 5/0 tied with 40-pound test leaders to the 60- or 80-pound test main gangion line are the best bet. Send them down with 3 to 4 pounds of lead, depending on the amount of drift. I bait the hooks with thin strips of squid, usually cut from fresh squid I buy at the oriental markets. It tends to get hit better than the frozen squid most everyone else seems to use (oops, I just let out one of my fishing secrets!).

Once you let the line sink to the bottom, grab the line ahead of the reel and give it a few good shakes while the sinker sits on the bottom. This will impart some action to the flies and might hook the first fish. Once one fish is hooked, the struggling action of the fish gives plenty of action to the other flies. Periodically, declutch the reel and make sure you're staying right on the bottom, but don't leave your sinker in the rocks or you'll probably lose it in the rugged bottom structure—just one or two cranks up is plenty.

Letter Street Beaches

South of the Redondo Pier, the streets in Redondo Beach are lettered (A, B, C, etc.). Some of the best surf fishing in the area can be found here. These beaches generally face directly into the prevailing swells and get washed off well by the surf. These are good surf species beaches. Just cast sand crabs, ghost shrimp, mussels, or bloodworms into the breaking surf for good action on corbina, spotfin croaker, yellowfin croaker, or barred surfperch.

Probably the best time to fish these beaches is from two hours before high tide until an hour after. Pick new moon morning tides for the best action of all. Look for areas with churned up sand, because this is where surf species are usually prowling.

Palawan Artificial Reef

The Redondo Beach area has several artificial reefs, but the Palawan Artificial Reef may be one of the more interesting, at least historically. It's actually a sunken Liberty ship. Liberty ships were built during World War II as cargo carriers. They were 447-foot long ships designed by the British. Right after the war started, it became necessary to build lots of ships to get war materials and weapons from the safe industrial haven of the United States across the sea to the front lines, both in the Atlantic and Pacific. Of course, the German and Japanese submarines and surface navies had very different ideas.

Famous industrialists, like Henry Kaiser of automaker fame, figured how to make ships in record times. What once took years to build, they could do in weeks without the skilled shipbuilders who had been recruited to build warships. With over one-third of the workforce consisting of women, another one-third too old to be drafted, and the remainder men who were classified 4F (having a physical problem that prevented them from being drafted), over 2700 Liberty ships were built in just a few years to replace the ships that were being sunk at an alarming rate. Over 600 of the Liberty ships never survived the war. Most were used for many years after the war and later scrapped in the 1950s, '60s, and '70s.

The *Palawan* was such a Liberty ship. It was intentionally sunk in 120 feet of water in 1977 to serve its last duty as an artificial reef to attract and hold fish. It is located 2.5 nautical miles from the King Harbor entrance along a 209-degree heading at 33° 49′ 25″ N × 118° 24′ 53″ W. Since its sinking, the superstructure has collapsed. Palawan gets its share of scuba divers and is a popular diving destination.

While fishing the wreck, you'll encounter plenty of local bass, both the calico and sand bass varieties. These are best caught by sending live anchovies on Carolina rigs down into the wreck. Plastics also do well on the old ship.

Occasionally, runs of barracuda develop over the ship. During these times, there is generally plenty of bird action marking the spot where barracuda are herding baitfish to the surface to feast on them at their leisure. The terrified baitfish sometimes jump clear of the water, often into the mouths of waiting birds.

Fishing the sandy flats around the ship for halibut could be one of the most overlooked and productive fishing techniques to use at this reef. Big flatfish hang around the structure to ambush unsuspecting prey cruising the wreck. Live bait, cut squid, rubber swimbaits, shrimp flies, and several other techniques work well on these game fish.

Access to the South Bay Area

From the north, the best way to get to the Manhattan Beach area is to take Interstate 105 (Century Freeway) from any of the major north/south freeways in the Los Angeles area until it deadends at Vista Del Mar. Turn left on Vista Del Mar and follow it into the beach towns. The Manhattan Beach Pier is at the foot of Manhattan Beach Drive. The Hermosa Beach pier is at the foot of Pier Avenue. The Pacific Coast Highway and Sepulveda Boulevard are the same through much of the South Bay. From the south, the coast highway is accessible from the Interstate 710 or 110 freeways. King Harbor and the Redondo Beach Pier lie within sight of the boulevard. Follow the well-marked signs along the boulevard in Redondo Beach.

King Harbor is a fully equipped small craft marina. Instead of a boat launch ramp, a sling/crane arrangement lifts small boats off trailers and lowers them into the water. A straight-through driveway allows boat launching without having to back up the trailer, a difficult task for some people. Ample parking is available at the boat launch ramp.

For those wishing to fish on party boats, Redondo Beach Sportfishing is located at King Harbor. This full-featured sportfishing landing offers a choice of trips, from half-day excursions to the local flats and kelp beds to offshore islands overnight trips. There are also several six-pack charter boats and larger charter boats for groups of up to 60 anglers that can be booked through this landing. For information:

Redondo Sportfishing
233 North Harbor Drive
Redondo Beach, California 90277
(310) 372-2111
www.redondosportfishing.com

For those interested in fishing King Harbor, boats can be rented from Rocky Point Marina in Redondo Beach.

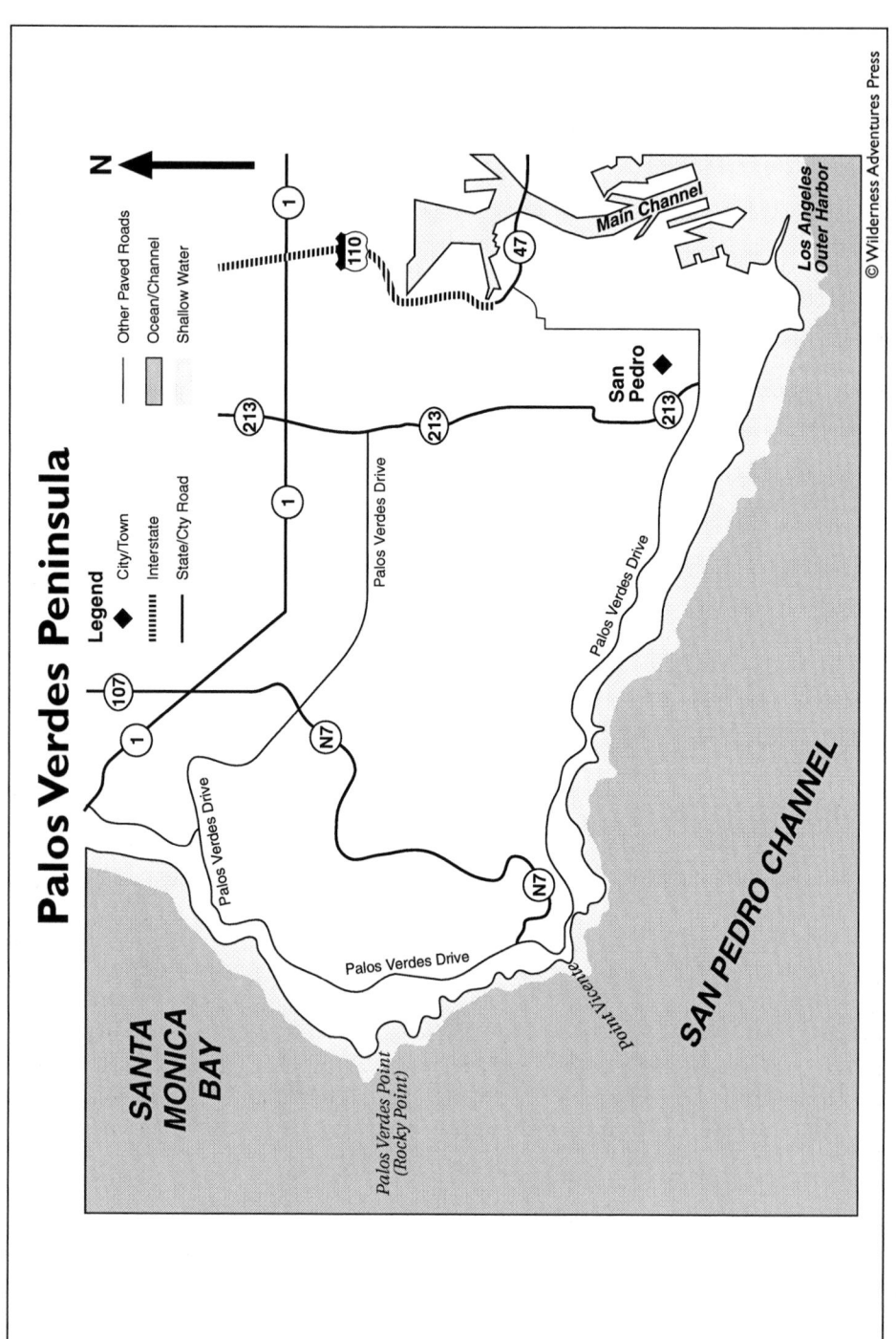

The Palos Verdes Peninsula

Right in the center of the otherwise fairly flat Los Angeles basin, the Palos Verdes peninsula juts up against the skyline and out into the sea. Once considered worthless land, suitable only for cattle grazing, the mountainous peninsula was a part of the Vanderlip Ranch, named after the ranch's owner. A visionary promoter named E. G. Lewis bought an option on 3200 acres of land for development in the early 1920s. Gradually, building lots were sold off, although no massive developments were ever made in this area. Nearly all of the homes were custom designed and built. Now it is one of the most desirable places to live in Los Angeles County, with beautiful homes and stunning vistas of the Pacific Ocean, Catalina Island, and of the entire Los Angeles basin.

Since the subsea environment generally mimics the coastline it abuts, at Palos Verdes Peninsula, you can expect undersea mountains, canyons, and rocky outcroppings. Heavy kelp forests ring the peninsula, where rocky reefs reach close enough to the surface for kelp to grow (usually 30 to 120 feet or so). In cooler years, the area is choked with kelp, making it prime game fish habitat. In areas where you are able to get to the water's edge, the shore fishing is very good, more similar to shallow water rock fishing than to the kind of fishing you'd normally expect from the shore. However, the vast majority of this coast is comprised of cliffs, so it is inaccessible except by boat.

Some of the better places to fish around Palos Verdes include:

Rocky Point (Point Palos Verdes)

When the half- and three-quarter-day boats are having trouble scratching up action in the South Bay, they almost always head for Rocky Point. These excellent kelp beds have been nearly as well fished as the famous "Horseshoe Kelp" near Los Angeles harbor, but a more erose, craggy bottom and thicker kelp forest, as well as a lack of tanker and freighter traffic, ensures that resident species have plenty of places to hide. Here you'll find an abundance of resident kelp bed species, particularly calico bass, sheephead, and whitefish. White seabass are also returning to these haunts now that their numbers are increasing. The bottom also has plenty of shallow water rockfish for your fishing pleasure, and schools of blue perch are common here. In the warmer summer months, yellowtail move up from Orange and San Diego Counties to take advantage of the excellent bait-holding capability of these undersea forests. Schools of barracuda crisscross the point in the spring and summer months, and bigger bonito are also frequent visitors. In all, Rocky Point provides an excellent all-around game fish habitat and should be on the list of anyone contemplating fishing the South Bay coastline.

A short, uncomplicated jaunt from King Harbor and not too much farther from San Pedro to the south, Rocky Point is a simple place to fish. The mild southern California weather and seas make it easy to fish, also. Fish Rocky Point as you would any kelp bed, by working the edges of the surface-floating kelp paddies with live bait to lure calicos out of their haunts. While catching bass, be sure to check out the bottom to pick up more variety.

For bigger pelagic fish, trolling is always my first choice for locating schools, followed by jigging or live bait fishing once a school is located. I always jigfish for barracuda. I don't generally like to fish with wire leaders, and the toothy critters seem to have no trouble at all biting through my mono line if I don't use wire. If you suspect yellowtail are around, use bigger sardine baits for best results. If you happen to pick up bonito on the troll, either live bait (anchovies) or flashy chrome spoons are the hot ticket.

Rocky Point is an excellent place to flyfish. A well-presented anchovy-imitating fly can easily fool calicos, and in some years, especially when red pelagic crabs are in town, a red and orange fly is often irresistible to many of the area's game fish. If you see that the fish have tiny lobsterlike critters in their mouths and stomachs, pull that blue and white off and switch to a red and orange—you should see the results instantly.

Point Vicente

Point Vicente is located at the end of the exclusive Palos Verdes Peninsula, with its posh, expensive neighborhoods perched high on the steep cliffs. This rocky outcropping has been the cause of many a sea disaster before the days of radar. Pieces of modern ships are still visible, dashed on the rocks and offering mute evidence of the area's potential for claiming incautious boats. The rough, rocky, and craggy coastline is an indication of the rough, rocky, and craggy bottom lying just below the surface. Near the point, thick stands of kelp spread into dense kelp forests, farther down, the numerous rocky lairs make this a bottom fish's dream home.

During summer, fishing the kelp beds is particularly productive, especially for calico bass. Fishing the fringes with bait, artificial lures, or flies is sure to produce action. In fact, this kelp is one of the most predictable bass fishing spots in the Los Angeles area. Occasionally, especially in spring, schools of barracuda frequent the point. Trolling and looking for bird action or pitching jigs are both very effective techniques to check if a school has been located. Occasionally, bonito and even yellowtail visit the point to make things interesting.

At the edges of kelp beds near the bottom, prowl the reef fish, such as sheephead, sculpin, and white seabass. The rocky reefs plunge down 2400 feet, and all manner of rockfish, ranging from shallow water treefish to deep water cowcod, can be caught depending on depth and tackle. In 100 feet or less, simple bait rigs work for the shallow water species. Farther away from the point in up to 1000 feet of water, heavier duty bottom-fishing gear is called for, along with squid-baited 5/0-sized bucktail and marabou shrimp flies.

On a recent trip to this area in early spring, I was fishing for barracuda and had let a blue and white jig flutter down to about 160 feet to find out if fish were feeding deep when the jig was whacked by a really decent-sized fish. Cranking it up, I discovered a really good-sized (maybe 4 pounds) red rock cod. (vermillion rockfish). I'd never caught a big red in water that shallow before, most coming

Deep rocky reefs sometimes hold monster red rock cod (vermillion rockfish), such as this 8-pounder caught by Captain Dave Bacon. Photo courtesy Captain Dave Bacon— Wavewalker Charters

from depths of 600 feet or more. After gutting, gilling, and scaling the fish, I tossed it right on my barbecue after stuffing garlic in cross slits in the meat, painting it with olive oil, and sprinkling it with Italian seasoning. Three of us feasted in grand style that night, after popping open a nice bottle of real Italian chianti. Rest assured, I have never gone to Point Vicente since then without at least checking the bottom action.

Marineland Coast

Back in the 1960s and early 1970s, a theme park named Marineland was situated along the protected coast of Palos Verdes. This park closed down in the early

1970s, but the area never lost its familiar name. It is characterized by rocky cliffs, outcroppings, reefs, subsea canyons, and a mostly craggy bottom. In spots, excellent kelp forests dot the coastline and provide habitat for all the major kelp-dwelling species. This excellent bottom structure also provides homes for a variety of rock-dwelling fish, both in shallow and deep water. In all, this is an excellent place to fish: It's close to port, fairly well protected from northwesterly winds and swells, and has the benefit of being one of the more beautiful stretches of coastline in the county.

The area is known for its good calico bass fishing. Work the edges of the kelp beds for action with bass. Barracuda are also frequent visitors to this area, particularly in spring. You have to scan the horizon for bird action to locate the schools, but once spotted, either bait or metal jigs provide the best results.

Don't neglect the bottom rocks when fishing here. In shallow water you'll find sculpin, sheephead, treefish, and various perch species. In deeper water, lingcod (particularly midwinter) and red rock cod are on the menu. In winter, I like to fish a whole, live mackerel in the hope of tempting a huge ling into making a mistake in judgment and ending up in my smoker.

There is also some great white croaker fishing in the deeper holes. Many of you are probably turning up your noses due to the DF&G warning against eating white croaker that have come out of Long Beach Harbor because of the high levels of pollution and toxins in their bodies. It's true that these fish are pollution tolerant and shouldn't be eaten if caught inside the harbor, but miles away from the harbor in deep water, they're perfectly safe and a fine eating fish. Sending live anchovies down into areas where you meter fish will yield interesting results in this area.

Access to the Palos Verdes Peninsula Area

There is virtually no land access to coastal fishing in this area, because much of the coast is comprised of steep cliffs. Fishing here is predominantly done by boat. For private boats, charter boats, or party boats, the closest port to the north is Redondo Beach's King Harbor, and from the south, the San Pedro side of Los Angeles Harbor. Any of the landings in either harbor offer peninsula fishing trips, and a private boat launched in either area has full and easy access to this section of coastline.

Navigation here isn't a piece of cake, though. There are many boiler rocks, surface kelp paddies, and obstructions near the coast. In addition, the northwesterly slope of the peninsula is exposed to the brunt of the prevailing winds and sea, so on some stormy days, this stretch of coastline can be quite hazardous. Most summer days, however, have good visibility and mild seas—check conditions before you go.

LA Harbor and The Horseshoe Kelp

Los Angeles Harbor is the busiest commercial harbor in the United States. This huge complex turns around tankers, bulk carriers, container ships, and RoRo (car carrier) ships by the dozens every day, carrying cargo to all corners of the globe. The brisk Pacific Rim trade relies heavily on the Port of Los Angeles, which is also the third busiest cruise ship port in the United States with nearly one million passengers boarding annually.

The combined San Pedro Bay, Port of Los Angeles, and Port of Long Beach complex is about 10 miles long and has a water area of about 8000 acres. It is well flushed by tides and currents, so the bay's water quality is excellent for a major industrialized port. A diverse marine habitat, ranging from sand and mudflat bottoms to rocky reefs as well as both natural and manmade structure, make it a thriving and active home for great schools of fish and other marine organisms. Just outside the harbor lie excellent kelp beds and sandflats that offer the recreational fisherman a wide diversity of species and techniques. In spite of being in the center of one of the largest major metropolitan areas in the United States, Los Angeles Harbor has remained clean and supports a wide variety of marine life. This is possible because of its favorable ocean topography and undersea currents as well as diligent enforcement of environmental laws and regulations.

Some of the better places to fish around Los Angeles Harbor include:

San Pedro Kelp

Just outside the harbor along the San Pedro coastline, a series of thick kelp beds provide some quite good fishing at times. The bottom fishing here is often excellent, with shallow water rockfish galore. Occasionally, white seabass and big bull sheephead are known to browse the rocks, too.

The surface fishing isn't as good as at the Horseshoe Kelp Beds, but for a place that's quite close and very accessible from the Cabrillo Beach launch ramps, it's nonetheless a good surface fishing destination. This is especially true if you have a smaller boat that isn't designed to be used very far out in the ocean. Generally, the weather is mild, the navigation uncomplicated, and the water is well within the capabilities of a less experienced blue-water sailor.

This is a good area to prowl or just poke around, perhaps trolling, perhaps not. Look for bird action, baitboils, and jumping fish. When you find a likely spot, drop the hook and put in live bait. If nothing is happening on the surface, just add a sinker (or better yet, keep another rod rigged with a Carolina rig) and try out the bottom action. If nothing happens there, move on to the next likely spot. It's a fun and often productive way to fish this coast on a fine summer day.

Cabrillo Beach Pier

Offering a very nice park with trees, picnic benches, a swimming beach, and a small store at its base, Cabrillo Beach Pier is one of the nicer places for a family outing, especially one that includes fishing. The pier is low and extends into Los Angeles

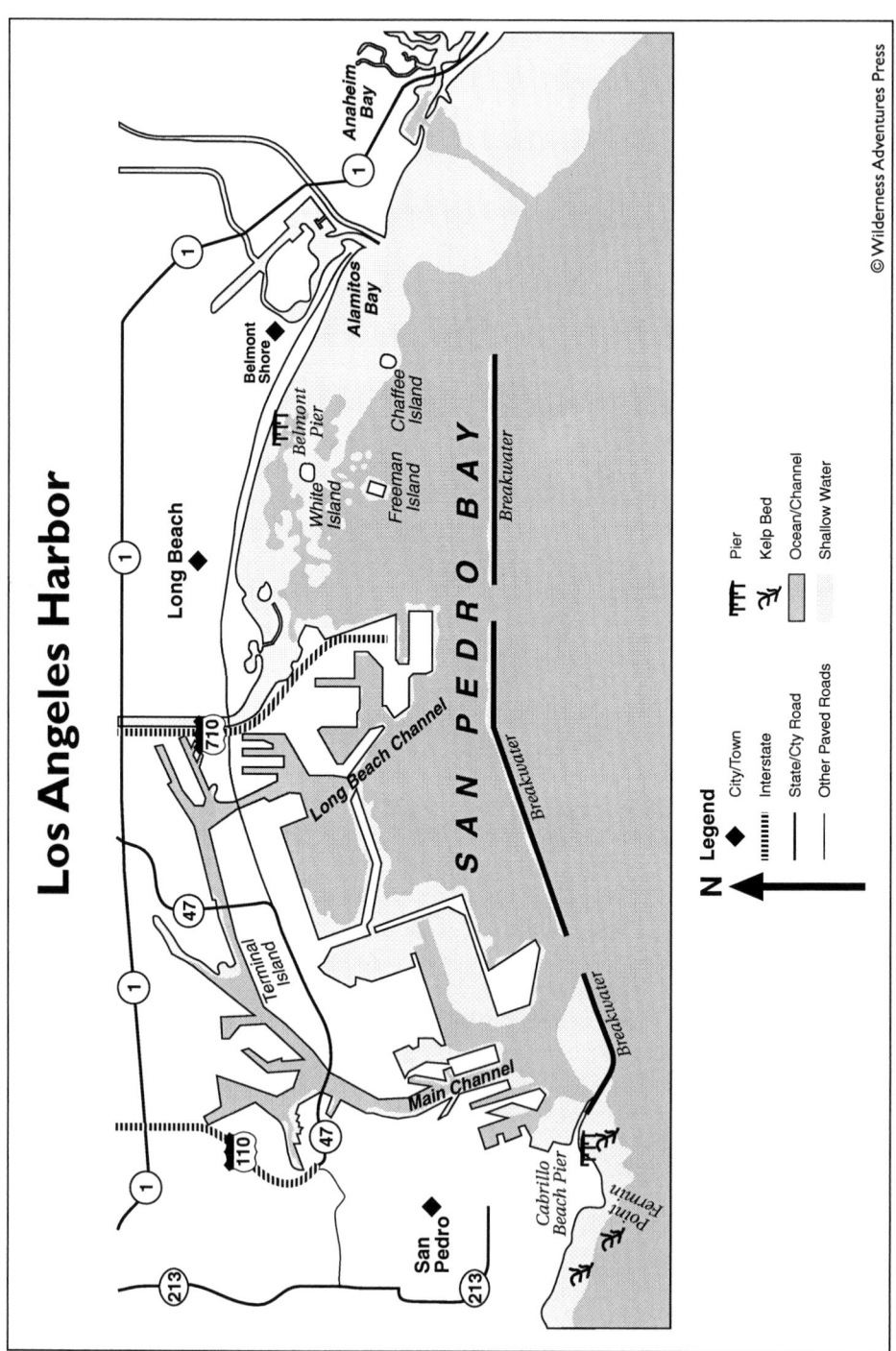

© Wilderness Adventures Press

The launch facility at Cabrillo Beach in San Pedro is well maintained and very convenient to the harbor entrance.

Harbor parallel to the outer breakwater. This shields the pier from poor weather and damaging surf. An automobile tire artificial reef was built under and to the south of the pier to help attract resident reef fish.

This pier is not noted for excellent fishing, but nonetheless draws many fishermen on summer afternoons and evenings. By far the most common species caught here is white croaker. California DF&G has posted a public health advisory that white croaker caught at Los Angeles Harbor should not be consumed because they are pollution-tolerant fish that do not range very far while foraging. Fish that forage over a wider range, foraging on the surface or midwater, such as mackerel, are not a problem.

Because of the artificial reef and the pier's proximity to the rocky breakwater, spotted sand bass, barred sand bass, and calico bass can often be caught from the pier's south side. Live bait cast right into the rocks works best, but many bass have fallen victim to a well-presented rubber swimbait, either a twin-tailed scampi type or a single-tailed, shad-shaped lure.

Around the pier pilings at certain times of the year, surfperch are fairly common. They eagerly snap at a bait-catching rig, such as a Lucky Joe or Lucky Laura. On the bottom, especially when fished at night with squid, various types of sand sharks, especially shovelnose guitarfish, can be taken here, also.

Don't forget about the breakwater on the opposite side of the sand spit. This faces the ocean and can be just as productive as the pier on certain days. I am fond of the winter surfperch fishing here. Use caution when doing this because the rocky wall is low to the water and exposed to the brunt of the crashing surf. Many an incautious fisherman has been swept off the rocks by the surf, with some never coming home.

The pier features restrooms and lights at night. Built-in rod holders (angled holes in the top rail) are a nice feature at the Cabrillo pier. The pier is open from 5:00am to 10:30pm. Ample parking is available in the park at the foot of the pier.

Point Fermin Rocks

Point Fermin lies just at the foot of the city of San Pedro. This is a rocky outcropping with many boiler rocks just off the point. This is a popular as well as fun and productive area to fish. Casting out into the rocks with mussels or cut squid can often result in catches of an interesting variety of shallow water rockfish. Some surf species, such as surfperch, are also available here. For a real thrill, fish with a green rubber grub on ultralight tackle in winter. You'll have tons of fun pulling scrappy little perch out of the surf.

You can also cast out into the kelp beds that sometimes choke the near-shore rocks. This is fishing at its finest with all manner of surface fish available, up to and including yellowtail and white seabass. Plenty of calico bass can be caught in this manner as well as barracuda, and sometimes, if you're lucky, a big bonito or even a yellowtail. Rubber swimbaits can be productive here as well as bonito feathers, swimming lures, cut squid, or best of all, live anchovies (though you'll need an aerated bucket to keep them alive). If you can get yourself situated to allow enough space for a backcast, you can even toss flies into the kelp bed edges for some real interesting flyfishing.

Access to the Point Fermin rocks is through the Cabrillo Beach Park entrance. Plenty of parking is available in the park on all but the hottest summer Sunday afternoons, but there is an entrance fee. After parking as close to the entrance as possible, simply follow the rocky shoreline as far as you can to the southwest until you come to the point.

Outer Breakwater

A long outer breakwater that protects San Pedro Bay meets the shore at Cabrillo Beach in San Pedro. Access to the breakwater is available by walking out all the way to the light at the Angels Gate (San Pedro) entrance to the harbor. This is a hike of well over a mile, but it isn't really necessary to walk that far—the fishing is far better in the first half of the breakwater before it turns toward the east.

Be careful when moving around in this area—a big surf can roll in and surprise you, and people have been whisked off the rocks never to be seen again. When wet, the footing can be quite treacherous, also and it's a long walk back if you happen to slip and sprain an ankle. On warm summer days, though, the area is absolutely stunning. The cool ocean breeze can provide a wonderful break from the usual inland desert heat of late summer.

San Pedro Outer Harbor

The huge, protected San Pedro Bay is a great place to drift-fish. Plenty of barn-door-sized halibut inhabit the flat-bottomed bay, along with mackerel, barracuda, spotted sand bass, white croaker, and an occasional bonito. Remember: don't eat white croaker caught in the bay.

Because there is so much activity in this harbor, boating (especially for smaller craft) can be hazardous. While it's true that you have the right of way when anchored and fishing, don't count on big ships in the harbor going around you. A 600-foot long, 20,000-ton tanker doesn't have a lot of maneuverability. Steer clear of the commercial traffic and check the harbor around you often. This is a *busy* port and all sorts of ships, tugboats, barges, and commercial vessels are constantly on the move. The San Pedro side has the most traffic.

Drifting with live bait on the bottom is the most popular fishing method, but I've had loads of fun here trolling a Rapala or other swimbait. Mackerel and barracuda eagerly snap at the passing lure, and lots of hookups can result. Working near the insides of the long breakwater with swimbaits or live bait can produce bass action, with spotted sand bass being the most common, although calicos are not unusual.

Horseshoe Kelp

The famous Horseshoe Kelp Bed is probably the most fished kelp bed in the entire southern California range, having been heavily fished for over a hundred years. Nonetheless, it remains one of the better places to fish, and excellent catches of many kelp-bed-dwelling species are still possible. It was here several winters ago that I caught an 18-plus-pound yellowtail on a piece of cut squid in January—an almost unheard-of feat!

The kelp at Horseshoe tends to be deeper, and it has been many years since the surface kelp had a visible "horseshoe" shape. With the increased ship traffic in and around this area, it's rare to see much of the kelp breaking the surface as it does in kelp forests closer to shore. Even though you can't see it doesn't mean it's not there! Excellent catches of calico bass in the warm, summer months attest to this.

In addition to calicos, this kelp bed has its share of barracuda and can also attract bonito and, as mentioned above, yellowtail. Fish this area as you would any kelp bed, although you can also jigfish more freely since you don't have to worry as much about fouling a treble hook in surface leaves of kelp.

There are plenty of fish on the bottom, as well: sculpin, sometimes sheephead, and even white seabass are all frequent visitors, in addition to the usual shallow water rockfish found here. Another interesting occurrence here is the plentiful white-fish run in winter, a relatively new phenomenon. Obviously, whitefish have replaced some other species of fish that used to be more common here. It isn't unusual to catch the limit in winter. Live anchovy bait sent to the bottom, or cut squid bait on a Carolina rig with just enough sliding sinker to keep the bait on the bottom, are both very productive for these bottom species.

White Island

White Island is known as "Halibut City" to locals. This is where many a huge flatfish has given itself up to the fisherman with a combination of luck and skill. Being a predator of the sandy bottom, halibut like to find any situation where they have more places to hide, and White Island is just the ticket. Radiating out from this small, manmade oil production island are dropoffs, shelf formations, and sand ridges, which are just the kind of structures halibut seek in order to get a high ground advantage for ambushing prey.

Drifting is the key to fishing White Island—the secret is to fish the crests of underwater ridges. Halibut often sit on the downcurrent side of a crest or dropoff, waiting for a tasty morsel to float by. My advice if you want to fool a halibut into striking is to do what a halibut expects its prey to do: drift over the ridges in an upcurrent to downcurrent direction. The easiest way to do this is to shut off the motor and just let the current take the boat in whatever direction it wants while you work bait near the bottom.

The best bait is live anchovies or smaller sardines. These attract the big flatfish with their struggling motion as you lift the bait, let it sink, lift, let it sink, and so on until it comes under the watchful eye of your unlucky prey. In lieu of live bait, rubber swimbaits work very well for big flatties. Other swimming lures that can dive near the bottom, along with well-presented, baitfish-imitating flies, are all big temptations for halibut.

Belmont Pier

Belmont Pier lies within Los Angeles Harbor and is protected from the brunt of heavy storm seas. It is 1650 feet long and T-shaped, with a restaurant, restrooms, and a bait and tackle shop located in the crossbar of the T. Boats from Belmont Pier Sportfishing pick up and drop off passengers on this pier. It is open from 5:00AM until 10:00PM and features lights, benches, and fish cleaning stations. A big parking lot is located at the foot of the pier, and street parking, both metered and free, is available in the area.

Near shore is the best place to fish Belmont Pier. In warmer summer months, corbina, yellowfin croaker, and barred surfperch are the mainstay of the catch. Fishing near high tide in less than 3 feet of water yields the best results. Most days there is so little surf you can't really say where to fish in relation to the breaking surf. Sand crabs, mussels, ghost shrimp, and bloodworms are all top baits for this type of fishing.

In the middle of the pier or the outer part of the T, jacksmelt and occasionally schools of Pacific sardines, move though the area, and a jigged Lucky Laura or other baitcatching rig can really produce. At night, fishing squid along the sides of the pier can often entice a sand shark into picking up a tasty snack at the end of your line. Shovelnose guitarfish are the most common, but several different types of rays (even stingrays) can also be caught here at night.

Belmont Shore

One of the premier surf fishing spots in the south, particularly for surf flyfishermen, is Belmont Shore. In 1998 and 1999, Cecil Gamble caught 4 world-record

The Belmont Shores Pier that extends out into Long Beach Harbor is a fishing pier and a sportfishing landing. In the background mist, White Island is visible. This manmade oil production island is known as "Halibut City" to fishermen.

halibut on 6-, 8-, 10-, and 12-pound tippets using a Clouser minnow. During the summer months, there is also quite a cult of fishermen who challenge themselves by trying for corbina on a fly, especially when early morning high tides are at their peak.

Of late, quite a number of light tackle fishermen have been spooled and lost their fish when something really big took off with it. These incidents were a mystery at first but were soon solved after a number of white seabass were landed here. The spawning and grow-out operation in southern California has helped these once-threatened game fish to return in excellent numbers, enough that they're once again feeding along Belmont Shore beaches.

While bait fishermen can be found here, Belmont Shore seems to attract far more light tackle enthusiasts. A bass type rod and 8- to 10-pound test are considered ample here. The usual surf fishing bait, such as sand crabs (considered the best), ghost shrimp, mussels, and bloodworms, are all top producers here. There is usually no surf here whatsoever, since it is well protected by the Los Angeles Harbor outer breakwater. Because of this, a Carolina rig is seen more often on this beach than the heavier surf rig used on beaches with pounding surf.

By all means, try your hand at flyfishing the surf at Belmont Shore. Look for feeding fish and present a sandcrab-imitating fly or a green woolly bugger to feeding corbina or yellowfin croaker. For halibut, the same flies or an anchovy-imitating fly (blue and white Lefty's deceiver or other long streamer fly) are your best bet. You'll do better by getting a bit farther offshore when targeting halibut on a fly than when trying to entice corbina to bite.

The only drawback to fishing here is the tough parking situation. Even though there is parking along the street, the high-density pack of houses and lack of garages and driveways cause local residents to use up nearly all of the street parking. If high tide is in the morning, and especially if you're fishing on a weekday, you can time your arrival just as the commuters are leaving for work. On a sunny Sunday, forget it. One option is to use the metered parking at the east end of Ocean Boulevard and walk back along the beach to the prime fishing section—from 67th to 68th Place. Take plenty of quarters, because the meters are limited to two hours and will need more coins if your stay lasts longer.

Long Beach Outer Harbor

For a more relaxing and fun place to fish, Long Beach Harbor also has a wide outer harbor that is less crowded with ships than the San Pedro side. Schools of pelagic fish storm through the bay chasing the plentiful bait found here. Plenty of halibut, sand sharks, white croaker, and other species are found on the bottom.

During the morning rush when party boats are loading bait, many anglers like to fish near the area's several bait barges, using shiny spoons, bait, or flies. In fact, the last three or four times that I was getting bait at the main barge, fishermen on at least two private boats were casting right up to the corners of the barge where morning freeloaders were snatching the overspilled bait.

Trolling here can also be loads of fun; use small trolling feathers or swimming lures. The wide sandy flats at the bottom or near rock walls, moorings, and other structure are all excellent places to catch bottom-dwelling species. Rubber swimbaits work very well, in addition to the usual live bait and feathers.

This part of Long Beach Harbor is great for flyfishing. The water is nearly always flat calm, so standing is no trouble, and the action can be very good. Fish near the bait barges, the inside of the outer breakwater, or cheat and do what many people in Redondo's King Harbor do, troll a fly slowly to locate schools.

Access to Los Angeles Harbor

The port of Los Angeles is very conveniently located at the foot of two of the major north/south crosstown freeways: US 110 (Harbor Freeway) ends in San Pedro, the huge harbor's western end, and Interstate 710 (Long Beach Freeway) ends up right in downtown Long Beach, the bay's eastern side. From the south on the Pacific Coast Highway, turn left on 2nd Street. The Long Beach Marina, one of the bigger, nicer yacht basins in the harbor, is right at the corner. Follow 2nd Street through the community of Naples to Belmont Shore, where surf fishing, pier fishing, and the Belmont Shore Sportfishing landing are located. Turn left at Ocean Boulevard and follow it into downtown Long Beach to reach the heart of the harbor.

There are a number of excellent sportfishing landings in the Los Angeles Harbor/San Pedro Bay/Long Beach complex. They offer trips from half-day jaunts, fishing just outside the harbor in the local kelp and flats, to overnight trips to the outer islands and tuna banks, and even multiday trips to Mexico when the bite is hot. In addition, many six-pack and larger charter boats, up to massive yachts, are available. These boats can be booked at the landings. Nearly all the landings also offer dive charter trips if you like to do your fishing with a spear. The sportfishing landings in Los Angeles Harbor are:

22nd Street Landing
141 West 22nd Street
San Pedro, CA 90731
(310) 832-8304
www.22ndstreet.com

Pierpoint Landing
200 Aquarium Way
Long Beach, CA 90802
(562) 983-9300
www.pierpoint.net

LA Harbor Sportfishing
1150 Nagoya Way
San Pedro, CA 90731
(310) 547-9916
www.laharborsportfishing.com

Long Beach Marina Sportfishing
180 Marina Drive
Long Beach, CA 90803
(562) 598-6649
www.pierpoint.net/lbmsf

Long Beach Sportfishing
555 Pico Ave
Long Beach, CA 90802
562-432-8993
www.longbeachsportfishing.com
562-432-8993

There are two excellent boat-launching facilities in Los Angeles Harbor: From the Long Beach side, the Long Beach Marina Ramp is capable of launching and recovering literally hundreds of boats in a day. On the opposite side of the harbor and closest to open ocean, Cabrillo Beach Recreational Area offers another excellent, multilane launch ramp. It's ideal for anglers planning to head out to Catalina or the outer islands.

COMMON GAME FISH AVAILABILITY BY MONTHS
LOS ANGELES COUNTY

Species	Jan	Feb	Mar	Apr	May	Jun	Jul	Aug	Sep	Oct	Nov	Dec
Yellowtail	NA	NA	FP	FP	FP	GF	EF	EF	EF	FP	FP	NA
Barracuda	NA	FP	GF	GF	GF	EF	EF	EF	EF	FP	FP	NA
Bonito	NA	FP	GF	GF	GF	EF	EF	EF	EF	GF	GF	FP
Calico Bass	FP	FP	GF	GF	EF	EF	EF	EF	GF	GF	FP	GF
Sand Bass	FP	FP	GF	EF	EF	EF	EF	EF	GF	FP	FP	GF
White Seabass	EF	GF	GF	GF	GF	FP	FP	FP	FP	FP	EF	EF
Halibut	GF	GF	GF	GF	GF	GF	GF	GF	GF	GF	GF	GF
Lingcod	EF	EF	GF	GF	GF	GF	FP	FP	FP	GF	GF	EF
Shallow-water Rockfish	EF	EF	GF	GF	GF	GF	FP	FP	FP	GF	GF	EF
Deep-water Rockfish	EF	EF	GF	GF	GF	GF	FP	FP	FP	GF	GF	EF
Sheephead	FP	GF	GF	GF	GF	EF	EF	EF	EF	GF	GF	FP
Sculpin	EF	GF	FP	FP	FP	FP	GF	GF	GF	EF	EF	EF
Blue Perch	FP	GF	GF	EF	GF	GF	GF	GF	GF	GF	NA	NA
Opaleye	FP	FP	FP	GF	GF	GF	GF	GF	EF	GF	FP	FP
Whitefish	EF	EF	GF	GF	GF	GF	FP	GF	EF	EF	EF	EF

	Not Available		Fish Possible		Good Fishing		Excellent Fishing

Los Angeles County Traveler's Information and Fishing Tackle Shops

The number of accomodations, restaurants, and points of interest in Los Angeles County are many and varied. Everything a traveler could ever need is found here.

Following are some of the tackle shops in the area offering saltwater-compatible fishing tackle:

Conejo Custom Tackle
666 East Thousand Oaks Boulevard
Thousand Oaks, CA 91360
(805) 373-6974

Malibu Fishing Tackle
3166 East Thousand Oaks Boulevard
Thousand Oaks, CA 91362
(805) 496-7332

Sport Chalet
1350 North Moorpark Road
Thousand Oaks , CA 91360
(805) 494-5048
www.sportchalet.com

Sport Chalet
39180 10 Street W.
Palmdale , CA 93551
(661) 266-3232
www.sportchalet.com

Sport Chalet
940 South Grand Avenue
Glendora , CA 91740
(626) 335-3344
www.sportchalet.com

Sport Chalet
25560 The Old Road
Valencia , CA 91381
(661) 253-3883
www.sportchalet.com

Turner's Outdoorsman
19329 Vanowen St.
Reseda, CA 91335
(818) 996-5033
www.turners.com

Wylies Bait & Tackle
18757 Pacific Coast Hwy
Malibu, CA 90265
(310) 456-2321

Lincoln-Pico Sporting Goods
2017 Lincoln Boulevard
Santa Monica, CA 90405
(310) 452-3831

Sport Chalet
920 Foothill Boulevard
La Canada , CA 91011
(818) 790-9800
www.sportchalet.com

Sport Chalet
201 East Magnolia #145
Burbank , CA 91501
(818) 558-3500
www.sportchalet.com

Turner's Outdoorsman
835 S. Arroyo Pkwy.
Pasadena, CA 91105
(626) 578-0155
www.turners.com

Sport Chalet
400 South Baldwin Ave., Suite 910-L
Arcadia , CA 91007
(626) 446-8955
www.sportchalet.com

Martin's Fishing Tackle
2821 1-2 S Western Av
Los Angeles, CA 90018
(323) 731-5549

Sport Chalet
100 North La Cienega Boulevard
Los Angeles , CA 90048
(310) 657-3210
www.sportchalet.com

Sport Chalet
5057 S. Plaza Lane
Montclair , CA 91763
(909) 624-1372
www.sportchalet.com

Turner's Outdoorsman
11336 Firestone Blvd.
Norwalk, CA 90650
(562) 929-4056
www.turners.com

Turner's Outdoorsman
357 N. Azusa Ave.
West Covina, CA 91791
(626) 858-8948
www.turners.com

Turner's Outdoorsman
12615 Colony St.
Chino, CA 91710
(909) 590-7225
www.turners.com

Sport Chalet
13041 Peyton Drive
Chino Hills, CA 91709
(909) 627-8996
www.sportchalet.com

Sport Chalet
12449 Foothill Boulevard
Rancho Cucamonga, CA 91739
(909) 987-4321
www.sportchalet.com

Turner's Outdoorsman
491 W. Orange Show Rd.
San Bernardino, Ca. 92408
(909) 388-1090
www.turners.com

Turner's Outdoorsman
10246 Indiana Ave.
Riverside, Ca. 92503
(951) 351-1190
www.turners.com

Sport Chalet
3700 Tyler St., #12
Riverside , CA 92503
(951) 688-8047
www.sportchalet.com

Sport Chalet
13455 Maxella Avenue
Marina Del Rey , CA 90292
(310) 821-9400
www.sportchalet.com

Purfields Pro Tackle
12512 W Washington Blvd
Culver City, CA 90066
(310) 397-6171

Mr Chum
1204 South Pacific Coast Highway
Redondo Beach, CA 90277
(310) 316-0641

Redondo Coffee Shop & Bait & Tackle
141 Fishermans Wharf
Redondo Beach, CA 90277
(310) 318-1044

Turner's Outdoorsman
2323 Hawthorne Blvd.
Redondo Beach, CA 90278
(310) 214-8724
www.turners.com

Just Fishing by Pete
2427 190th St
Redondo Beach, CA 90278
(310) 376-7035

Southbay Fishing Tackles
2304 Redondo Beach Blvd
Torrance, CA 90504
(310) 515-1170

Art's Fishing Tackle
1451 W Artesia Blvd # 14
Gardena, CA 90248
(310) 327-4171

Yo's Custom Rods & Fishing Tackle
16120 S Western Ave
Gardena, CA 90247
(310) 532-1376

Baja Fish Gear
24603 Narbonne Ave
Lomita, CA 90717
(310) 517-9897
www.bajafishgear.com

Rusty Hook
245 N Gaffey St
San Pedro, CA 90731
(310) 832-2429
www.rustyhook.com

Fishermans Hardware
2801 E Anaheim St
Long Beach, CA 90804
(562) 434-8311

Rick's Tackle
4107 Viking Way
Long Beach CA 90808
(562) 496-1870
www.rickstackle.com

Sport Chalet
7440 Carson Street
Long Beach, CA 90808
(562) 429-9560
www.rickstackle.com

Turner's Outdoorsman
2201 E. Willow St.
Signal Hill, CA 90755
(562) 424-8628
www.turners.com

Performance Tackle
4288 Katella Ave
Los Alamitos, CA 90720
(562) 430-7671

Los Angeles County Accommodations

The following list is a small sampling of lodgings that are close to port in Los Angeles County. These range from basic to luxury, and you should keep in mind that nothing along the southern California coast, particularly anything close to the water, is inexpensive.Basswidow Products
6446 Ralston Street

MARINA DEL REY

Marina Beach Marriott Hotel
4100 Admiralty Way
Marina Del Rey, CA 90292
310-301-3000

Best Western Jamaica Bay Inn
4175 Admiralty Way
Marina Del Rey, CA 90292
310-823-5333

Courtyard by Marriott
13480 Maxella Avenue
Marina Del Rey, CA 90292
310-822-8555

Marina Del Rey Hotel
13534 Bali Way
Marina Del Rey, CA 90292
310-301-1000

Marina International Hotel
4200 Admiralty Way
Marina Del Rey, CA 90292
310-301-2000

The Ritz Carlton—Marina Del Rey
4375 Admiralty Way
Marina Del Rey, CA 90292
310-823-1700

Foghorn Harbor Inn
4140 Via Marina
Marina Del Rey, CA 90292
310-823-4626

REDONDO BEACH

Crowne Plaza Redondo Beach and Marina Hotel
300 North Harbor Drive
Redondo Beach, CA 90277
310-318-8888

Best Western Sunrise
400 North Harbor Drive
Redondo Beach, CA 90277
310-376-0746

Portofino Hotel and Yacht Club
260 Portofino Way
Redondo Beach, CA 90277
310-379-8481

SAN PEDRO (PORT OF LOS ANGELES)

Best Western Sunrise
525 South Harbor Boulevard
San Pedro, CA 90731
310-548-1080

Sheraton Los Angeles Harbor Hotel
601 South Palos Verdes Street
San Pedro, CA 90731
310-519-8200

Hilton Port of Los Angeles Hotel
2800 Via Cabrillo Marina
San Pedro, CA 90731
310-514-3344

Holiday Inn- San Pedro
111 South Gaffey Street
San Pedro, CA 90731
310-514-1414

Vagabond Inn
215 South Gaffey Street
San Pedro, CA 90731
310-831-8911

**LONG BEACH DOWNTOWN
MARINA AREA**

Hilton Long Beach
Two World Trade Center
Long Beach, CA 90831
562-983-3400

Hyatt Regency Long Beach
200 South Pine Street
Long Beach, CA 90802
562-597-4401

Westin Long Beach
333 East Ocean Boulevard
Long Beach, CA 90802
562-436-3000

The Rennaisance Long Beach
111 East Ocean Boulevard
Long Beach, CA 90802
562-437-5900

Westcoast Long Beach Hotel
700 Queensway Drive
Long Beach, CA 90802
562-435-7676

Travelodge Convention Center
80 Atlantic Avenue
Long Beach, CA 90802
562-435-2471

LONG BEACH MARINA AREA

Best Western Golden Sails
6285 Pacific Coast Highway
Long Beach, CA 90803
562-596-1631

Long Beach Marina Hotel
4430 Pacific Coast Highway
Long Beach, CA 90803
562-597-4714

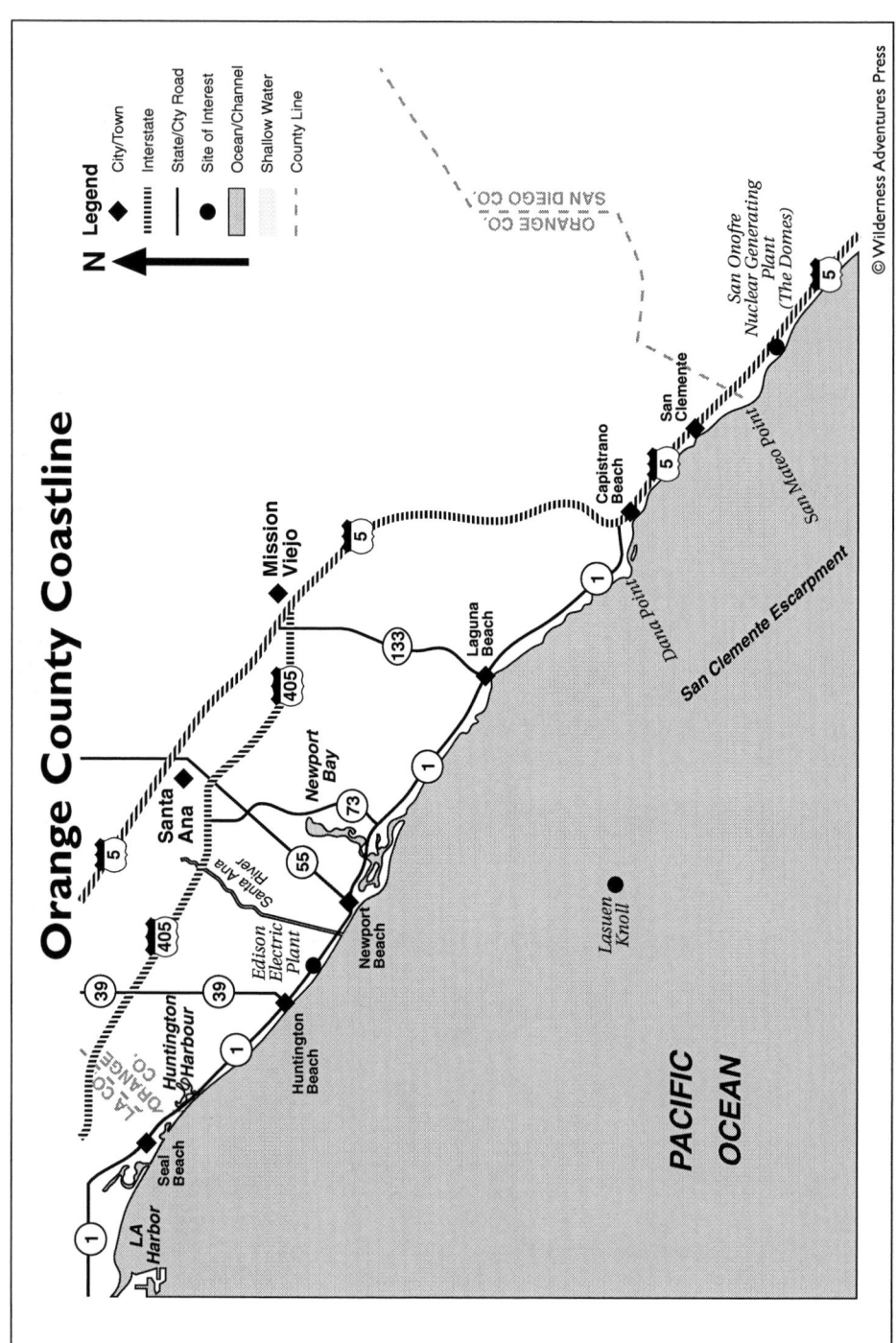

Orange County Coastline

Legend

N

- ◆ City/Town
- ▓ Interstate
- State/Cty Road
- ● Site of Interest
- ▓ Ocean/Channel
- ▒ Shallow Water
- - - - County Line

ORANGE CO.
SAN DIEGO CO.

San Onofre
Nuclear Generating
Plant
(The Domes)

5

San Clemente

San Mateo Point

5

Capistrano
Beach

5

San Clemente Escarpment

Dana Point

1

Mission
Viejo

5

Laguna
Beach

133

405

Newport
Bay

1

Santa
Ana

73

55

5

Santa Ana
River

405

Newport
Beach

39

39

Edison
Electric
Plant

1

Huntington
Harbour

Huntington
Beach

Lasuen
Knoll

L.A. CO.
ORANGE CO.

Seal
Beach

1

LA
Harbor

1

PACIFIC
OCEAN

The Orange County Coastline

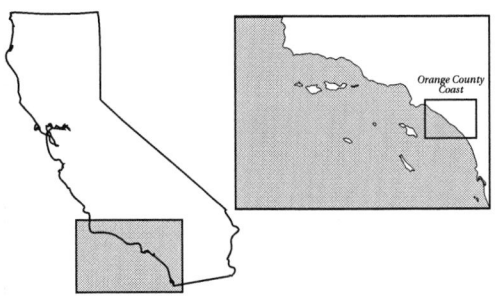

Orange County, a triangle of land only about 40 miles per side, lies between the heavily populated Los Angeles and San Diego Counties. At one time, Orange County was the center of citrus farming in California, but there are almost no orange groves remaining in the county. The only orange trees remaining are in people's yards. Originally, the county was both an agricultural center and a bedroom community for neighboring Los Angeles County, but urban sprawl and terrific growth from the 1950s to the 1990s has transformed it into a major metropolitan area in and of itself. It supports the booming high tech, medical, and aerospace industries and has an industrial manufacturing base, along with banking, financial services, and even some major restaurant chains.

Orange County has a reputation as being conservative, Republican, and intolerant of cultural diversity. While it may be true that much of Orange County votes Republican and the area is conservative, the cultural diversity is amazing for such a small area. Residents of Santa Ana, the second largest city in Orange County behind Anaheim, are 70 percent Spanish speaking. Westminster has the largest population of Vietnamese outside of Vietnam, and it contains a city within a city, called Little Saigon. Garden Grove, another of Orange County's major cities, is one of the major homes for Korean immigrants in the United States. In addition, many South and Central American, Middle Eastern, Indian, Chinese, and European immigrants call Orange County home. Just touring the restaurants and sampling the different ethnic cuisines could take decades.

Orange County also boasts plenty of family entertainment. Disneyland is here, as well as another famous southern California theme park, Knott's Berry Farm. The California Angels baseball team and the Mighty Ducks call Orange County home. From rock to country to classical to jazz, Orange County has an abundance of wonderful music concerts in literally dozens of concert halls attracting top names in the business. The golf, tennis, and other outdoor sports facilities are topnotch. The shopping is fabulous, and the sheer number of things to do is awe-inspiring.

One of Orange County's biggest attractions is its share of the Pacific Ocean coastline. The fabulous beaches that line the coast are a major attraction for many people from all over the world. Whether you come to surf, kayak, scuba dive, skimboard, sailboard, play beach volleyball, roller blade, or just sit in the sun and watch the world go by, you'll never be disappointed in Orange County's miles of beaches.

Most of all, the western edge of Orange County offers the saltwater fisherman a wide variety of fishing to pursue right near home. You can surf cast, laze away the hours on a pier, drift the flats, fish the deep water rocks, troll, fly cast, rock fish from

Seal Beach to Huntington Beach

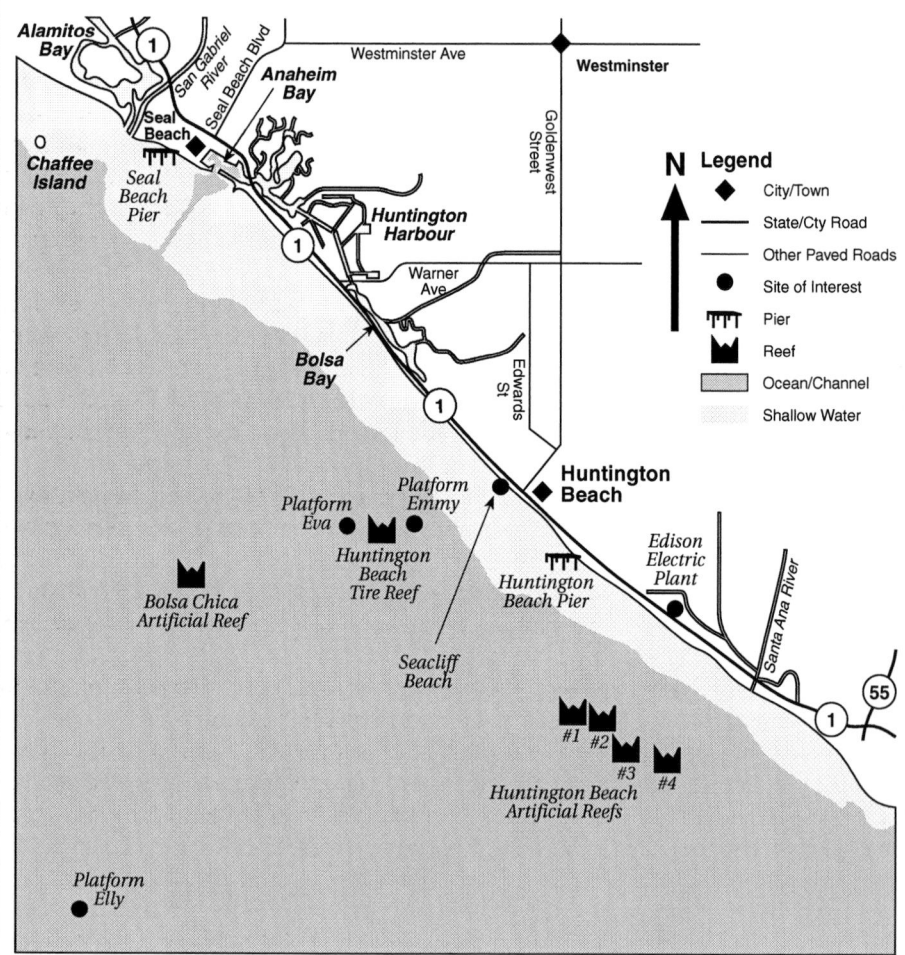

Legend

◆ City/Town
— State/Cty Road
— Other Paved Roads
● Site of Interest
TTT Pier
▲ Reef
▒ Ocean/Channel
░ Shallow Water

© Wilderness Adventures Press

shore, or cast jigs into a kelp bed, all within a fairly short coastline and just about all with excellent results. And with good weather and fish available throughout the year, Orange County's coast is fishable year-round.

Some of the major areas are detailed below:

Seal Beach to Huntington Beach

Nestled between the surfer's paradise of Huntington Beach and the metropolitan area of Long Beach is the small, quaint community of Seal Beach. How it maintains its friendly, small town ambiance in the shadow of Los Angeles is a mystery, but it's more like Mayberry than Beverly Hills. There's a friendliness and charm to Seal Beach unmatched by just about any other place along the southern California coast.

Going south from Seal Beach on the Pacific Coast Highway, a bridge passes over the entrance to Huntington Harbor and into Sunset Beach, which lines both sides of the highway and offers the passing motorist excellent restaurants, antique shops, and other unique and interesting businesses. Expensive houses ring Huntington Harbor, many equipped with a boat dock, which is more likely occupied by an expensive yacht than a simple fishing skiff.

South of Sunset Beach, the Bolsa Chica wetlands form a wild and natural enclave in the mostly densely populated coastline. An excellent, wide beach invites many travelers to this area, and RV camping and fire rings make this one of the favored "party" beaches. On any given day, many people visit the Bolsa Chica wetlands to enjoy its sunshine and its natural attractions. Keep in mind that no fishing is allowed in the salt marshes from the Warner Avenue Bridge south.

South of Bolsa Chica is Huntington Beach proper, a wildly mixed community of people from all walks of life. From surfers to poor immigrants to business people to the wealthy, all find the easy lifestyle and excellent quality of life in Huntington Beach to be attractive enough to call this place home. Huntington Beach consistently rates as one of the top 10 safest cities in the United States, a tribute not only to the excellent city government services and management (Huntington Beach's Police Department is perennially a model department studied not only by the rest of the nation but by the whole world), but also to the relaxed, friendly environment of the city.

The Seal Beach/Huntington Beach coastline is a great place to fish. With an excellent harbor and two different launch ramp facilities, along with its close proximity to the Long Beach Port of Los Angeles Harbor and Newport Harbor, it's very accessible as well. Some of the better places to fish include:

Seal Beach Pier

Built in 1906, the Seal Beach Pier offers very good fishing. Located at the foot of Main Street, the pier is 1865 feet long, and its design, particularly out near the ends, is great for fishermen because of the built-in benches. Take something to sit on since the benches often have bird droppings and bait remnants left by inconsiderate anglers. Nonetheless, the pier is generally clean and well maintained by the city of Seal Beach.

The Seal Beach Pier, a popular fishing destination,
also has a sportfishing landing at the end.

Probably the most productive part of the pier is the northern side at the surf line, where a submerged concrete footing forms a sort of artificial reef. In late summer and fall, spotfin croakers are plentiful here, and the best bet for these fish are clams and mussel bait. In the midpier area, where halibut and white croakers are the most common, use anchovies or cut squid. Queenfish (herring) can sometimes be plentiful at this pier and are best caught with a multiple hook bait rig, such as a "Lucky Laura" or "Lucky Joe." Simply jig these up and down to entice herring to bite. If you catch a smaller, lively herring, you can sometimes use it on a halibut rig with excellent success. Herring seem to be a favorite cuisine for these big flatfish.

The Seal Beach Pier has a restaurant at the end, restrooms, fish cleaning station, and a bait and tackle shop for the convenience of fishermen. It attracts a considerable number of strollers, especially during warm summer evenings. The downtown part of the city begins right at the foot of the pier, where plenty of excellent restaurants, shopping, snacks, and drinking establishments are available. There's a good-sized parking lot at the base of the pier, accessible from a driveway just north of the pier. There is also free on-street parking, but it's usually limited to two or three hours and is well enforced.

Bolsa Chica Artificial Reef

Lying about 4 miles offshore in a broad mudflat, the Bolsa Chica Artificial Reef was built in 1986 of 10,000 tons of concrete rubble and eight steel and concrete barges. Since its creation, several fish species have been attracted to the structure, and at certain times of the year, the fishing is excellent. The reef is 4.5 nautical miles from the entrance of Anaheim Bay (Huntington Harbor) on a 170-degree magnetic course. It lies at 33° 39' 02" N × 118° 06' 05" W.

As it happens, the day before I wrote this paragraph, I was on a boat searching for a barracuda bite that never materialized. Late in the day, after many hours on the boat, we decided to "meat" fish and went directly to the Bolsa Chica Artificial Reef, where sculpin hanging around the reef were thick and ready to bite. We loaded up with limits within an hour and a half and were headed home. It turned a skunk day into a productive one.

Sculpin inhabit the reef all year but are particularly thick during the spring months. This gradually tapers off over the summer. In addition, white croaker (tomcod) and sand bass can be caught at the reef, especially in summer. Whitefish and the occasional sheephead are found here year-round. Starry rockfish migrate here in the winter, too.

Fishing at the reef is strictly a bottom affair. Live anchovies, cut squid, or squid-baited shrimp flies are all good, productive baits here. Heavier sinkers (about three ounces) are needed, particularly in winter and spring when the currents tend to be fairly high. It is best to place the sinker on a dropper loop above the bait as opposed to being on the bottom with hooks above, which is more common for most bottom fishing situations. This allows the bait to sit right on the bottom, the sculpin's preferred feeding place. After reaching the bottom, lift the sinker just slightly, allowing you to feel the fish taking the bait. Don't be too quick on the trigger when setting the hook for sculpin—let it chew on the bait for a few seconds. Some people have switched to circle hooks for this type of fishing, especially when using cut squid. The fish hook themselves, so a hook "set" isn't really necessary.

Seacliff Beach

The area of Huntington Beach known by surfers as "the cliffs" is one of the finer places along the southern California coast to surf fish. Plenty of barred surfperch are available in the winter months, and corbina and croakers are regular summer visitors. Seacliff begins about a mile north of the Huntington Beach Pier, where Goldenwest Street meets the Pacific Coast Highway. The beach is about three-quarters of a mile long and stops at the south end of the low, flat Bolsa Chica State Beach.

Typical surf techniques are used at Seacliff. Light leaders and smallish hooks with bloodworms, sand crabs, ghost shrimp, mussels, and clam bait all produce well. One of the regular fishermen in this area is an older Japanese gentleman. He prefers bloodworms, but not the local type—he buys them mail order and has them flown in from Maine. I've never been that fussy, but then again, I never catch as many fish as he does.

In winter, particularly between Christmas and New Year's, the barred surfperch run begins. Then I switch from bait to a 1½-inch long dark green rubber grub, fished on a tiny rubber worm-type hook. Tie about 24 to 36 inches of 6-pound test leader to a tiny swivel holding up a ¾-ounce sliding egg sinker on the main line. I usually use my bass rod (7-foot graphite rod with a level wind, bait casting reel) wound with 10-pound test line. It's not necessary to cast way out past the surf to get these fish—they usually bite in the whitewater between the breakers and the sand. For best results, fish from two hours before until one hour after high tide.

In summer, I use clams and switch to an 8-foot spinning rod with 15-pound test and 8-pound test leader. Clams are the favorite food of spotfin croakers, one of my favorite eating surf fish. Corbina and yellowfin croakers also frequent the surf line in this area. Again, the hour or two on either side of high tide is always better for surf fishing than any other time.

Two metered parking lots on the west side of the Pacific Coast Highway make it very convenient to stop by for an hour or so before or after work when the tides agree. In addition, you can gain access to the cliff area from the north via the Bolsa Chica State Beach, which has snack bars, parking, camping, fire rings, and restrooms. Enter at the main entrance and go as far south as possible to park.

Huntington Flats

Probably one of the most consistent flats fishing spots in all of southern California, the Huntington Flats continue to be a great place to fish in spite of heavy year-round fishing pressure. Known as the sand bass capital of the world, Huntington Flats produced the world's record barred sand bass at over 13 pounds. Having personally fished with the record holder, Bob Halal, I can say there's a combination of luck and experience that goes into consistently catching big fish. In addition to sand bass, plenty of barracuda prowl the flats in spring and summer. Halibut, sculpin, and the occasional yellowtail can be caught here. In all, Huntington Flats is an excellent place to fish.

Sand bass tend to be hook and line shy, so using the lightest line possible always results in more strikes. About the maximum weight line needed to get consistent strikes is 15-pound test, and 12-pound test is even better, although I often use 10. I tried 8-pound but found it simply abrades or gets bitten off too quickly. If I suspect that barracuda, halibut, or sculpin are mixed in with the sandies at Huntington, I always use 15-pound. When sand bass seem to be the only action, I step down to 10-pound.

I use a dark-finished light wire #4 live bait hook, tying it in a terminal loop so that the hook is free to move easily. This allows the bait the most freedom in movement and most natural struggling action. A sliding egg sinker, held at least 24 inches above the hook with a plastic "Carolina Keeper" bead (or tiny split shot) completes the rig. Nosehook the anchovies, gingerly cast them out so that the shock of slapping into the water is minimized, and let them sink to the bottom. For best results, fish with the reel declutched and wait for the strike, letting the fish run with the bait a bit before setting the hook.

When barracuda are around, they go for smallish metal jigs, generally near the bottom or midway in the water column. I use Cuda Killer jigs and Tady #9 in blue and white or green and black. I also especially like Sea Strikers with their green, black, and red pattern and lifelike scales. It isn't necessary to cast out for barracuda, which can actually be somewhat dangerous due to all the hardware flying around,

Bob Halal and his world record-breaking barred sand bass. Photo courtesy Bob Halal.

especially on a crowded party boat. All that's necessary is to drop the jigs straight down, let them flutter to the bottom, then yoyo the jig—wind it up, let it drop, wind up, let it drop, etc, which minimizes tangles.

Most of the time at Huntington Flats, you'll release from one-quarter to three-fourths of the barracuda caught because of shorts. I always replace the treble hooks on my jigs with a single hook, which causes the least amount of damage to the fish's mouth when removing the hook. Most people prefer not to get their hands too close to a barracuda's mouth for obvious reasons, and pulling a treble hook out of a barracuda with pliers can seriously mangle the fish's mouth. If this happens to a short fish, it will surely starve to death. There's nothing worse than throwing back a fish that you're certain will die anyway.

Swimbaits are often just the ticket at Huntington because you never know what you'll catch. Sand bass, halibut, barracuda, and even yellowtail eagerly snap at a well-presented rubber swimbait, especially one sweetened with a thin strip of cut squid. One of my personal best Huntington Flats yellowtail went for a brown single-tailed, shad-type swimbait with a squid scent enhancer.

When barracuda are in the midwater zone, they can be reached on a fly line by using a shooting head, fast sinking line. They'll eagerly snap at a blue and white or green and white streamer fly, but be prepared to lose a few flies in their toothy grasp.

Huntington Beach Tire Reef (Platform Eva)

Along the north edge of Huntington Flats, just to the north of a line between the closest oil rig platform (Emmy) and the next farthest one out (Eva), a whole slew of automobile tires were sunk in 1975 to form one of the early attempts at an artificial reef. The reef lies in 8 fathoms deep (48 feet). This is often one of the more productive zones of the Huntington Flats area. Sand bass especially seem to love nesting here. It provides cover for ambushing bait and caves and crevasses to hide in. Fish it just as you would the Huntington flats, except it's best to anchor up because drifting the bottom can often result in lost gear.

Platform Elly Rock Cod Banks

Just inside of Platform Elly, one of the major offshore production oil rigs lying off Huntington Beach, lies a canyon that cuts into a steep slope from the edge of Huntington Flats to the deep water of the Catalina Channel. This undersea gorge is excellent habitat for rock cod. While not as productive as some of the farther offshore banks, this area nonetheless continues to produce good catches of reds, bocaccio, and bank rockfish.

This area is generally fished from 240 to 600 feet deep, because the fish are bigger and the catch is greater. These fish tend to be more line-shy than their outer banks cousins, so I often tie a gangion using 50-pound test instead of 80-pound. I use about 30-pound hard leader type mono to attach bucktail flies to the gangion. This is lighter than my usual offshore deep water rock-codding rig, but since there aren't many big lings or cows in this area, it's plenty adequate for the fish here.

Huntington Beach Pier

The famous Huntington Beach Pier has gone through a number of incarnations in its long history. Originally built of wood in 1903, the pier collapsed twice and was eventually rebuilt of concrete in 1913. This pier was destroyed in 1923, and a new, longer pier was built in 1924. The end of the 1924 pier was damaged by a storm in 1939 and was repaired and reopened in 1940. During WWII, the Navy took it over as a submarine watch site, and it remained in military hands until the end of the war in 1945. The pier was heavily damaged by storms in 1983 and again in 1990, destroying the end third and the restaurant located there. In 1992, a totally new pier opened that is one of the largest in southern California and attracts many people, both tourists and fisher-

The Huntington Beach Pier is completely new
after storms destroyed the older, wooden pier.

men. It is open from 5:00AM until 1:00AM. The new pier has a lifeguard tower, a restaurant at the end, a bait and tackle shop, a snack shop, public restrooms, and a kite shop as well as fish cleaning stations situated in convenient locations along its length.

The end of the pier is diamond shaped, and the northern corner of the diamond points right to an underwater reef within easy casting distance from the pier. Sand bass, sculpin, and white croaker are fairly common catches near the reef. Schools of pelagic fish swim through at the end of the pier, mackerel are fairly common, along with the occasional bonito. Both bait and artificial lures are effective.

Halibut, shovelnose guitarfish, and jacksmelt make up the bulk of the fish caught at the pier's middle, which is the least productive area. Near the surf line, there are barred surfperch, corbina, and spotfin croaker, which probably offer the most productive fishing on the pier using sand crabs, ghost shrimp, or bloodworms. However, be careful of surfers, who consider "shooting the pier" or surfing between the pier pilings to be great sport, even though several young people die every year trying it. This is one of the most popular surfing spots in southern California. Around Labor Day, a pro surfing contest is held just south of the pier along with numerous skateboard, beach volleyball, and other sun and fun events. Because of the crowds during this type of event, it's best to fish elsewhere.

Downtown Huntington Beach is also located at the foot of the pier and has plenty of eateries, shops, watering holes, and movie theaters. You can park either in the lot just north of the pier or across from the Pacific Coast Highway in one of the two city parking structures.

The Buoys

A ring of mooring buoys is located just off the coast from the big Edison Electric Plant in Huntington Beach. These are used to moor tanker ships while they unload fuel for the power plant. Like any marine structure, these buoys and their chains provide a haven for baitfish, which, of course, attract game fish. Unlike the consistent fishing at Huntington Flats, the fishing here is often spotty—the bite is either heavy or not happening at all. Therefore, party boats often ignore this area for the more consistent and closer fishing at the Huntington Flats area. Nonetheless, I've hauled in plenty of great fish here. Most recently, I got a 20-plus-pound yellowtail on a blue and white jig, yoyoed deep. In spring and summer, sand bass, barracuda, bonito, and halibut also prowl here. An angler who is here at the right time with the right bait can really have some fun.

When birds are diving for baitfish near the buoys, the area is good for trolling. Troll right through the area with the most action, continually altering course to keep in the center of it if you have the luxury of being able to fish from your own boat.

Here's a productive and very fun technique for flyfishing the buoys: Cast a blue and white streamer fly right into the shadow of a buoy in the morning or evening hours when buoys cast a shadow (it doesn't work as well at midday). Then dart your fly with a ripping retrieve as fast as you can from the shadow into the light toward you. This simulates a baitfish making a run from shelter to get out of the area. If there's a big predator around, that will sure stimulate its strike instinct!

In the winter, I've successfully fished sculpin here with squid-baited shrimp flies in 1/0 size. They really snap them up at certain times of the year. I generally fish three flies on short 6-inch leaders from three-way swivels about 12 inches apart and using 2- to 4-ounce torpedo sinkers (depending on current). During winter there can be a substantial current here, so you need to adjust the amount of weight accordingly. When fishing this way, don't pull in a fish too hastily after it has hooked itself. The struggles of a hooked fish will impart far more action to the remaining two flies. Sometimes, you can't seem to catch just one fish, since getting the first one on is the hard part. Does this give you any ideas about the best way to fish shrimp flies?

Huntington Beach Artificial Reef

One of the earliest artificial reefs to be built in California, this reef is actually a whole series of quarry rock piles. There are four main reefs, each of which is approximately 3 acres and made from 1000 tons of rock. The reefs are located off the southern portion of Huntington Beach in 60 feet of water. From the Newport Beach Harbor jetty, a course of 261° magnetic for 6 miles will put you right in the midst of the reefs. The position of the four reefs is as follows: Reef #1—33°-37'-27" N × 118°-00'-04" W;

Barracuda are southern California's most widely caught pelagic fish. Most are caught on jigs, as was this "log" caught by Randy Lacko of Chino. Photo courtesy Captain Dave Bacon— Wavewalker Charters.

Reef #2—33°–37′–17″ N × 117°–59′-51″ W; Reef #3—33°-37′–09″ N × 117°–59′–17″ W; Reef #4—33°-36′–51″ N × 117°–58′–49″ W.

These reefs are home to plenty of sand bass, sculpin, and white croaker, with sheephead and calico bass thrown in for good measure. In spring and summer, schools of barracuda come here often to feed on the bait that are found at reefs such as this. In warmer years, an occasional bonito or yellowtail swims by, also. All in all, this reef is a great place to fish.

The bottom here is productive year-round. If the current is minimal, a Carolina rig with a sliding egg sinker and live bait is always very effective. Bass, sculpin, and deep-swimming barracuda all take this type of bait. If there are many barracuda around, you might want to switch to wire leaders to prevent one from biting off the

*Frank Selby of His &
Her Fly Fishing Shop in
Newport Beach conducts
one of his flyfishing the
surf classes at the mouth
of the Santa Ana River.
Photo courtesy
Frank Selby—His & Her
Fly Fishing Shop.*

leader. If the current is heavier, a torpedo sinker held above the bait on a dropper loop is better. If you find your bait getting stolen too often or that you're just plain missing when setting the hook, switch to cut up strip squid. Fish tend to inhale it instead of manipulating it around to swallow headfirst.

During warmer months, both hard metal jigs and rubber swimbait artificial lures work well. Work them near the bottom for best results unless there is a lot of bird action, which usually means the game fish are herding baitfish into balls. When this is the case, keep your retrieves in the midwater and surface areas for best results.

Santa Ana River Mouth

The famous Santa Ana River begins in the High San Gabriel Mountains and runs through Redlands, Riverside, Corona, where it is partially dammed by the Prado Dam, and then proceeds to Anaheim, where much of its remaining water is captured in percolating ponds to keep the Orange County aquifer filled. It then winds itself through Santa Ana, passing through Fountain Valley, and finally ending up as the dividing line between Newport Beach and Huntington Beach. The river only flows on the surface in the winter and spring when there's enough rain or snowmelt to fulfill the upstream water needs. The river's mouth is only about 75 yards wide most of the time but shrinks to less in late summer, especially at low tide, and swells up when snowmelt is at its peak.

I saw one of the most interesting and comedic wildlife events I have ever had the joy to experience here. A seal (actually a California sea lion) and a medium-sized dog were squaring off against each other in fairly shallow water. The seal lunged at the dog and barked at it in seal fashion. The dog backed up into very shallow water

A deceiver fly deployed in the shadow of an offshore oil rig just off Huntington Beach in Orange County brought in this big calico bass. Photo courtesy Frank Selby—His & Her Fly Fishing Shop.

where its footing was more secure, allowing more maneuverability. Then it was the dog's turn to bark and lunge at the seal, which was then at a disadvantage because it was mostly out of the water. So the seal backed down into deeper water, and once the water got deep enough, the dog lost its footing. Once again in its own element, the seal took the offensive. Back and forth they went, in and out of the water, never coming particularly close and never yielding until each was in the other's element. I had to pull off the highway because I was laughing so hard that I was afraid I might have an accident. They must have made six or seven trips back and forth before both animals decided it was futile and went their respective ways.

Where the Santa Ana River dumps into the ocean, a silt bar has built up where many surf fish come to feed. This is where many an aspiring saltwater flyfisherman first comes to try his hand at casting into the ocean. The sandbar at the entrance on the south side of the river is ideal for pitching a fly into the transition area between saltwater and freshwater. Barred surfperch, halibut, spotfin croakers, corbina, yellowfin croakers, white croakers, and even a striped bass this past year have been caught right at this sandbar.

Regina Scott of Mike Scott's Hackle, Tackle and Flies flyfishing shop in Orange, California, shows how saltwater fly-fishing is done by landing this nice dorado. Photo courtesy Mike & Regina Scott— Mike Scott's Hackle, Tackle & Flies.

For flyfishing, a bigger green woolly bugger or anchovy-imitating streamer fly are mighty effective, along with a number of pink, orange, and red shrimp or crab-imitating flies. Take a wide variety of flies, because you never know what they might hit. It all depends on the clarity of the water and what sort of critters are on the water. This is more like flyfishing for trout, where you match the hatch, as opposed to using the same old baitfish-imitating flies that most saltwater flyfishermen rely on.

Fishing the river mouth with bait is also effective. Bloodworms, ghost shrimp, mussels, clam siphons, and sand crabs are all effective. I prefer a Carolina rig for this type of fishing as opposed to the traditional surf style terminal tackle arrangement. I find it allows fish to pick up the bait and run with it because it doesn't feel the resistance of the weight until after the hook is set. Instead of a long surf rod and spinning reel, I usually use my calico bass rig here, because it isn't necessary to cast very far—about 30 yards is plenty.

Access to Seal Beach and Huntington Beach

Getting to the productive fishing at Seal and Huntington Beaches couldn't be easier. The famous Pacific Coast Highway runs right through the center of these cities as it follows the coast. From the north (Los Angeles), take Interstate 405 (San Diego Freeway) to the Seal Beach Boulevard Exit. Follow it west until it ends up right at the foot of the Seal Beach Pier. To get to Huntington from Seal Beach Boulevard, simply follow the Pacific Coast Highway south. From the south (San Diego, Orange County Airport), take Brookhurst Street west from Interstate 405. Brookhurst goes all the way to the Pacific Coast Highway in the southern part of Huntington Beach.

To fish this area by party boat, the Seal Beach Pier offers a sportfishing landing: Seal Beach Big Fish Sportfishing (24-hour information: 562-5698-6300, reservations 562-598-4700). Tickets can be obtained on the pier, and the boats leave from a ramp on the pier. These boats often fish the Huntington flats. Boats from Newport Beach often make the trip to the flats, as do boats from the many Long Beach and San Pedro (Los Angeles County) landings (check those sections for contact information).

Huntington Harbor is an excellent small craft harbor that is ideal for the trailer boat enthusiast. There are two excellent launch ramp facilities in the harbor. The closest to the ocean is at the foot of Edinger Street. From the south, take Edinger west from Interstate 405. From the north, take the Valley View/ Bolsa Chica exit from the Interstate 405/CA 22 fork. Follow it to Edinger and turn right. There is a small charge to use the ramps.

The other launch ramp is located at the intersection of the Pacific Coast Highway and Warner Avenue. This launch facility is free, but you have to pay for parking. It takes longer to get through the harbor to open ocean, but this can also be an interesting part of your trip.

As a word of caution, the Navy uses the outer part of Huntington Harbor, called Anaheim Bay, as a munitions loading area. There is often a destroyer or some other type of ship at the wide pier taking on munitions. A friend of mine who loaded ammunition onto a destroyer during the Vietnam War can attest that more than a few explosive devices ended up in the bay.

You are required to stay in the channel and not to fish or anchor in the outer bay. Rowboats, sailboats under sail, and personal watercraft are not allowed in this harbor. Only powered boats heading directly through the area are permitted to pass.

Newport Coastline

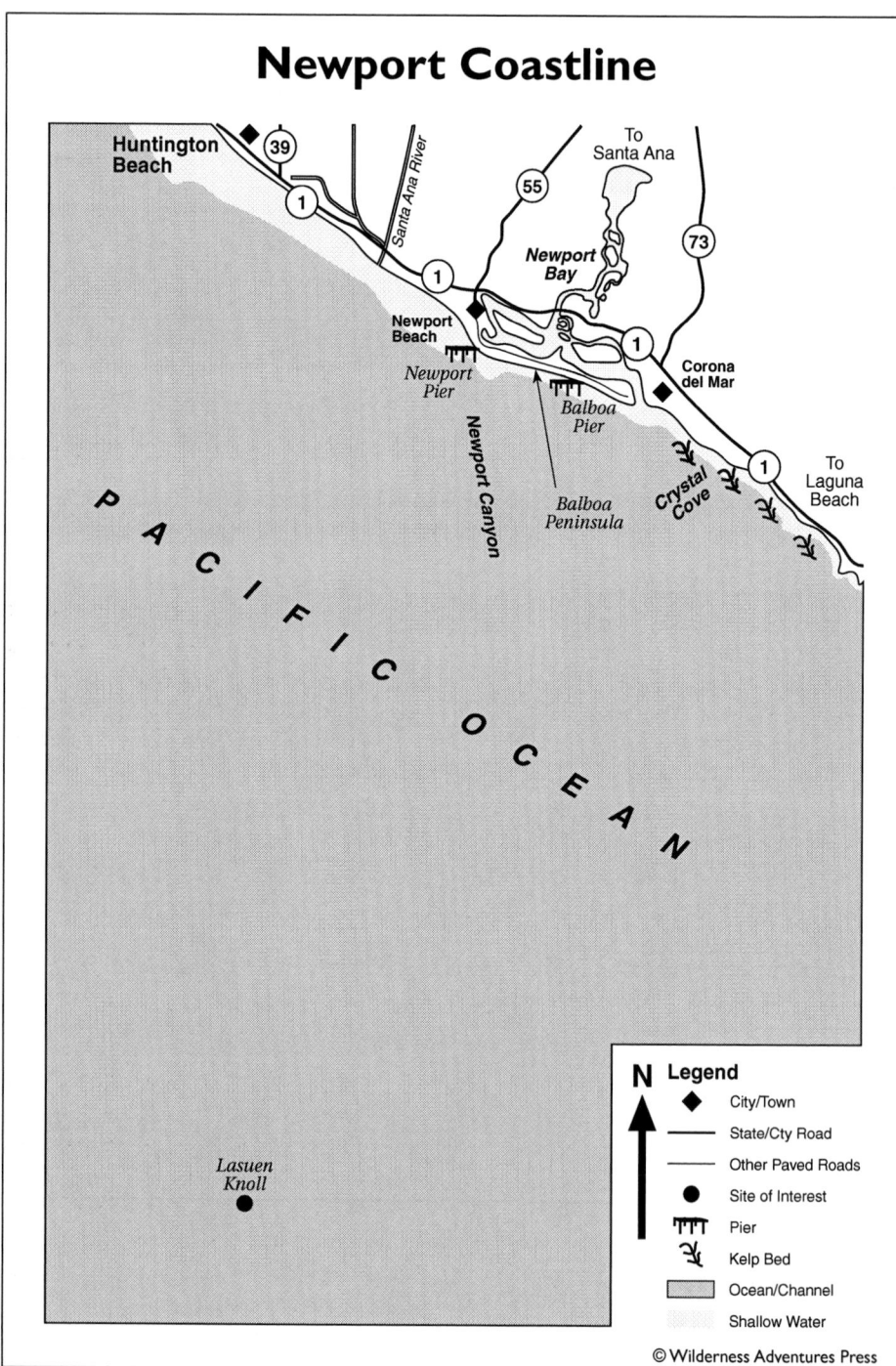

Legend

- ◆ City/Town
- State/Cty Road
- Other Paved Roads
- ● Site of Interest
- ⊤⊤⊤ Pier
- ⤸ Kelp Bed
- ▨ Ocean/Channel
- Shallow Water

© Wilderness Adventures Press

The bridge and channel just inside Huntington Harbor also requires boaters to remain alert. Stay in the clearly marked channel since many of the mudflats are exposed at low tide, which makes running aground a real possibility for the inattentive boater. In addition, the Pacific Coast Highway Bridge that separates Huntington Harbor from Anaheim Bay is low and requires that most sailboats lower their masts to get through.

Private boaters will also find this area very accessible from either Long Beach Harbor or Newport Harbor, being only 5 or 6 miles from either. With the mild weather common to this area and generally excellent visibility, especially in summer, these voyages are uncomplicated and enjoyable.

The Newport Coastline

The Newport coastline is generally considered the most desirable place to live in Orange County. Homes run from expensive to "you're kidding!" Nonetheless, it's a beautiful area, with a wonderful climate, stunning scenery, and some of the most elegant living to be found anywhere. There are enough world-class hotels, restaurants, major shopping centers, and enough quaint, seaside atmosphere to satisfy even the pickiest visitor to the Newport coast.

Newport Bay has one of the finest yacht harbors in California. It's loaded with things to do and see, from multimillion-dollar homes with their own private docks on islands in the harbor to the Balboa "Fun Zone," a teenager's delight. Two sportfishing landings are in the bay, along with several sportfishing charter operations. In addition, boat rentals, yacht charters, and several clubs offer boats that range from simple fishing skiffs to grand yachts, sailing lessons, and just about anything in the way of saltwater enjoyment. Kayaks, dive charters, surfing, boogie boarding, parasailing, jet skis, sail boarding, you name the water sport—you can do it in Newport Bay.

Newport's coast is also unique for its unusual deep water dropoff very near the coast. Within a mile of the shore in some places, the water can get 1500 feet deep. This often brings bigger, pelagic species close to the coast and makes the fishing, especially in summer, excellent. The fact that most of the sportfishing boats travel north to Huntington in the winter to fish the artificial reefs and Huntington Flats demonstrates the area's lack of reef habitat to support the year-round resident species. An exception to this is Lasuen Knoll, often called the 14 Mile bank. This is one of the prime, near-shore rock cod fishing spots in Orange County.

Shore fishermen enjoy a wide variety of options here. There are two excellent fishing piers, jetty fishing at the Newport bay entrance, great surf fishing along the beaches, bay fishing, and even rocky shoreline fishing. You can probably catch more species of fish from shore here than anywhere else in the area. In all, the Newport coast is an excellent fishing destination, whether you plan just a few hours of surf-casting or charter a big sportfishing boat to fish for the deep water pelagic species. If you are on a family vacation, Newport is an especially good place when other family members want to do something besides fish.

Some of the better spots to fish around Newport include:

Newport Canyon

Like a great gash slicing across the shallow plain that forms most of north Orange County's near-shore, subsea terrain, Newport Canyon is a major underwater geological feature that provides a sheltered habitat for many bottom-dwelling species. This area has always been and continues to be a very good bottom species hole. Sablefish, sometimes erroneously called hake or black cod, live in this area in good numbers. These are good eating fish, although they spoil easily. This is the bottom of their range, though I once caught one at La Jolla in San Diego County. These are a more northern fish and are esteemed in British Columbia for their light, flaky meat, which is often served smoked.

In addition to sablefish, Newport Canyon is home to red rock cod, bocaccio, bank rockfish, and chilipeppers. All of these fish hit on cut squid, squid-baited shrimp flies, or anchovies sent down among the deep rocks, although I prefer bucktail flies. You should fish at least 500 feet deep, but 600 is better yet for the quality species. But there are times, especially in winter or early spring and particularly if there has been a good squid run, when shallower water, 300 to 400 feet, is sometimes the best place, because the fish come up to feed on spawning squid. When this is the case, fish during the full moon because the squid are very active as well as helpless during the spawn.

Balboa Peninsula Beaches

Between the Newport and Balboa Piers, the sandy beaches of the Balboa Peninsula have been a classic surf caster's delight for over a century. Since people first started coming to Newport for recreation, this stretch of beach has been known as a fishing beach. Now lined with houses, it still receives its fair share of both fishermen and fish. Parking is often readily available along Balboa Boulevard, only a short block to the sand to make a few casts and enjoy a fresh summer morning. It's a great way to start the day (or end it for that matter!).

The usual surf species are found here, and corbina, spotfin croaker, and barred surfperch are caught most often. During the past few years, corbina have been making a recovery here. Whether from a reduction in pollution or the elimination of the near-shore net fisheries (I suspect a little of both), the return of this California classic game fish is to be heralded. To encourage this recovery, please release your catch so we can continue to enjoy this West Coast tradition for many years to come. Corbina love sand crabs, bloodworms, and ghost shrimp (in about that order), and any of these are the most effective bait here. In the winter months, a green rubber grub is powerful medicine when barred surfperch run along the coast.

Newport Pier

One of the finest fishing piers all along the coast, Newport Pier is situated at the north end of Balboa Peninsula separating Newport Bay from the ocean. The pier was originally built in 1888 and used as a commercial freight loading and unloading facility. It was purchased in 1922 by the city of Newport Beach and converted for use

Live squid are the hot ticket for white seabass, a favorite southern California game fish. Louie Orozco of Chino proudly displays his keeper-sized white. Photo courtesy Captain Dave Bacon— Wavewalker Charters.

as a public facility. At the foot of the pier, the famous Newport Beach Dory Fleet still goes out every morning to catch fish, returning to sell to the many local people who like to buy their fish fresh.

Newport Pier is unique because it was built at the very end of Newport Canyon, the undersea gorge that offers habitat for many species of deep water fish. Occasionally, there are squid runs very near the pier, sometimes even giant squid.

Upper Newport Bay is a great place to flyfish and can turn up plenty of spotted sand bass (sometimes called bay bass). This one, though, is too small to keep.
Photo courtesy Frank Selby—His & Her Fly Fishing Shop.

Not only are squid fun to catch and good to eat, bigger game fish that love squid, too, chase them into the shallows to feed. Yellowtail, bonito, white seabass, and even deep water sablefish (black cod) find squid an irresistible meal. Tuna boat fishermen often call squid "candy" because of the way big fish seem to jump on it.

On a typical day, though, the usual catch isn't yellowtail—it is most likely white croaker, sculpin, sanddab, or sometimes bass, jacksmelt, and surfperch. Near the end of the pier, you can also catch pelagic species, such as mackerel, barracuda, and bonito, especially in summer. A shiny spoon or bonito feather jig is just the ticket on balmy summer days. Keep your eyes out for bait schooling near the pier and cast into the thickest part of the school. Near the end or midpier area, fish the bottom with strip bait, either anchovy strips or cut squid. Another effective technique is jigging a Lucky Joe or Lucky Laura bait rig to get queenfish or jacksmelt to bite. Near the surf line, corbina, spotfin croaker, and barred surfperch can be caught when fished with sand crabs, ghost shrimp, or bloodworms.

Newport Pier is also one of the better shark and ray fishing piers. A hammerhead shark of 200-plus pounds and a 176-pound bat ray have both been caught at the pier. The best shark fishing is done at night using dead bait on the bottom, but be careful because some of these fish can be dangerous. A stingray can inflict a painful wound with a slash of its snakelike tail, and a leopard shark is flexible enough to reach around and bite your hand as you hold it by the tail. I guess I don't have to mention what a 200-pound hammerhead shark can do with its many rows of razor sharp, inch-long teeth.

The pier features restrooms, a bait and tackle shop at the foot, and a small restaurant at the end. There are also benches, lights, and fish cleaning stations situated around the pier, making it very convenient for anglers. There is plenty of metered parking if you arrive early in the morning or late in the afternoon. It can be pretty crowded at midday on a summer weekend. A row of shops, restaurants, and drinking establishments are located at the foot of the pier for your post-fishing pleasure. The pier is open 24 hours a day.

Balboa Pier

Balboa Pier is just south of the Newport Pier by a couple of miles. It is less crowded than Newport and often has very good fishing. The pier and the Balboa Pavilion across the peninsula on the Newport Bay side were built in 1906.

The beach's slope is fairly steep, and the water at the end of the pier is deep. Some of the better mackerel, bonito, and barracuda fishing from any pier in California is available at the end of the pier. The best option is to use live anchovies, but you will have to get them across the peninsula at Davy's Locker since they aren't available at the pier itself. To keep them alive, you will need a battery-powered aerator. Hardware, small jigs, spoons, and feathers also produce at the pier's end.

With live anchovies, the midpier area can produce for halibut, white croaker, and sculpin. Using a Lucky Laura or Lucky Joe in the midpier area can produce jacksmelt, some surfperch, and queenfish. Near the shoreline, the usual surf fish bait will entice these species.

Like Newport Pier, Balboa Pier is open 24 hours a day. A parking lot that charges by the hour is located at the foot of the pier, and plenty of parking is available, even on summer weekends when crowds show up in force. The pier features restrooms, benches, lights, and fish cleaning stations. There are no bait and tackle shops, but frozen bait is available across the peninsula at Davy's. For those who don't fish, there's plenty to do—the main downtown section is only a block away, and the Balboa Fun Zone only one block farther.

Newport Bay

Fishing in Newport Bay is a great way to break into ocean fishing for anglers who haven't previously fished saltwater. The bay is home to many species of fish that are usually found in open ocean and offers a sheltered, public setting for anyone from neophytes to old pros to spend a few enjoyable hours basking in California's sunshine while chasing fish.

The western breakwater at the end of Balboa Peninsula is one of the more popular spots to fish. In warmer months, two species of surf fish, croakers and surfperch, are abundant, along with sand bass, an occasional calico bass, and even bottom dwellers, such as halibut and sand sharks. A shore fisherman who comes equipped with the different tackle and bait needed to target the variety of species here can come up with a real mixed bag of fish. Drifting this area in a small boat is also a productive way to pick up fish. Be careful while boating because the harbor is crowded with both sailboats and powerboats in a seemingly endless procession, especially on warm summer weekends.

Farther up the bay, near the Balboa Pavilion where Davy's Locker is situated, the channel's bottom fishing can be especially productive. Plenty of bigger halibut prowl the bottom, and live bait fishermen can do very well fishing with anchovies on a Carolina rig sent down to the bottom. Davy's Locker rents fishing skiffs complete with live bait tanks for just this purpose.

Throughout the many fingers and channels of the bay, especially near the pilings of the docks and piers, perch of various types are common. Entice them with small pieces of cut squid or mussels on tiny hooks or small rubber grub-shaped lures. Also common along the bay's silty bottom are flatfish, sand sharks, and different types of rays. Live anchovies are the ticket for flatfish, while the sharks and rays prefer a variety of cut fish or squid bait, especially when fished at night when these creatures prefer to feed.

Lasuen Knoll

Lasuen Knoll is also known as the 14 Mile Bank because of its location 14 miles off the coast. Lasuen Knoll is named for George C. Lasuen (1883-1959), who was one of the most innovative and skilled anglers of the early 1900s. He invented kite fishing for marlin and bested huge tuna and marlin from rowboats using the thumb drag systems on old-fashioned reels. Early in 1999, he was inducted into the IGFA fishing hall of fame in Dania Beach, Florida. The Knoll was named for Lasuen because he discovered its unique fish habitat that attracts game fish from all over the southern California range.

Lasuen Knoll is a huge, round-topped undersea mountain standing in a deep flat plain. Like a landbound mountain deflecting winds over itself, a subsea mount like Lasuen Knoll deflects passing currents over itself. This creates upwellings where deeper, nutrient laden water is drawn upward on the upcurrent side of the knoll, while surface water is pulled downward on the lee side. This creates fertile conditions in which microscopic plants and free-swimming animals thrive. These, in turn, attract huge schools of small baitfish to graze on this bounty. Of course, where there's bait ... you know the rest.

During summer, both yellowtail and tuna are drawn to Lasuen Knoll to feed on the plentiful bait. The secret to fishing Lasuen from late spring to late fall is to look for two things: kelp paddies—the broken-off patches of kelp floating free offshore; or where birds are diving for bait, a sure sign of feeding game fish. This type of fishing always seems to be better during the new moon phase. I'm not sure why, but my guess is that the fish don't eat at night during this phase because there's not enough light to see their prey and are thus simply hungrier at daybreak. Whether this is true or simply the conjecture of a simplistic fisherman, I do know that the fishing has usually been better when fishing at daybreak during the new moon phase.

Trolling is the primary way to locate schools of pelagic fish during summer at Lasuen Knoll. Use trolling feathers near kelp paddies or areas where birds are active.

Gary Quon of Lakewood, CA, with this jackpot-winning yellowtail. Photo courtesy Gary Quon.

Upon hookup, chum the fish into a feeding frenzy and break out the bait or jigs. Plenty of yellowtail in cooler water years and dorado, yellowfin tuna, and skipjack in warmer water years have been yanked from the water around Lasuen in this way.

Lasuen Knoll is probably the Orange County coast's premier rock cod bank. Fishing is good year-round, but most anglers only target rock cod when nothing else is biting. This is really a shame, since rock cod fishing, while more work than surface fishing, is probably more productive and is quite interesting because of the unique tactics and techniques required. The knoll rises to a depth of 450 feet below the surface. While fishing is decent on top of the knoll, fishing the many cuts and canyons along the sides in 600 to 900 feet of water is the most productive and results in the highest percentage of quality species in the mix. Reds, cows, and boscos are available in good numbers in the deeper areas, while chilipeppers, bocaccios, and

Walt Starkey of Yorba Linda, California, has something to be happy about after catching this nice white seabass. Photo courtesy Matt Starkey.

bank rockfish inhabit the shallower depths. Typical 80-pound test gangions with squid-baited 4/0 to 5/0 shrimp flies are the hot ticket here. A 9/0-sized reel with 80-pound test is best, but a 6/0 with 60-pound also works well. Long, stiff, poles make handling the long gangions easier.

Jigfishing the deep water is also a productive technique at Lasuen. This can be quite a workout but is also a lot of fun. The new extra heavy yoyo style jigs in orange- or brown-spotted white bodies seem to work very well along with the orange and red jigs. Heavy chrome spoons and chrome kite-style jigs also perform, along with round bar and hex bar classic style rock cod jigs.

Crystal Cove Kelp

A dense kelp forest, which is prime habitat for calico bass, lies just off the south point of the beautiful Crystal Cove. This is classic kelp bed fishing in every way. All of the bass techniques are productive here. At certain times of the year, barracuda, the occasional bonito, and more recently, yellowtail, have frequented the kelp beds to chase bait. Work the edges of the kelp with live anchovies, but keep a jig stick handy with a blue and white jig just in case you see surface boils. Then pitch the iron into the path of the feeding fish.

White seabass have been showing up in increasing numbers here due in no small part to the excellent breeding program now in place in southern California. Fishing the midwater, especially with live squid, is an excellent way to entice these huge croakers to bite. Otherwise, rubber swimbaits with a squid strip scent enhancer or white jigs, yoyoed deep, can be productive techniques at times.

The rocky reef at the bottom attracts many kelp forest bottom dwellers, such as sheephead and treefish. For a change of pace, be sure to check the bottom if the surface bite slows down—this could round out your bag with different species. I use head-on shrimp, squid strips, squid-baited bucktail shrimp flies, or nose-hooked live anchovies.

Crystal Cove Beach

The beautiful Crystal Cove Beach is a state park. It has good fishing for the usual surf species, such as corbina, spotfin croaker, and barred surfperch. The bottom falls off fairly quickly here, so it also attracts some species not normally found in the surf, such as halibut, whitefish, and white croakers. Use sand crabs, bloodworms, and ghost shrimp for surf species, while cut squid, dead anchovies, or clams entice the other fish.

Excellent facilities are available at Crystal Cove, including parking, restrooms, and a snack bar that is very close. It's a popular tourist stop, so you might find yourself overrun with children playing in the surf on a Sunday afternoon. Stick to the early morning high tides to avoid hooking a not-so-rare, two-legged beach fish.

Access to the Newport Coastline

The Newport coastline is readily accessible via CA 55 (Newport Freeway). Simply take the Freeway south until it ends on Newport Boulevard. Another mile or so farther, Newport Boulevard crosses the Pacific Coast Highway, where you can turn south to the southern part of Newport Bay or the beaches to the south or go straight to Balboa Peninsula, where the two piers and the business end of Newport Bay are found.

Launch ramps for trailer boats are located in the back bay. Take the coast highway south from Newport Boulevard through the "Mariner's Mile" district and go over the bridge that crosses the channel. Take the first left turn to get to the back bay recreational area. This is an exceptional facility with plenty of parking and amenities. Its only disadvantage is the fairly long run from the launch ramp to open ocean. Throughout the bay, boats are restricted to no-wake speed due to the close proximity of the many boats and yachts moored throughout the bay. An RV park is also located in this area.

Two major sportfishing landings that offer half-day to overnight trips are located at Newport Bay. Both of these are located in the Balboa Pavilion area:

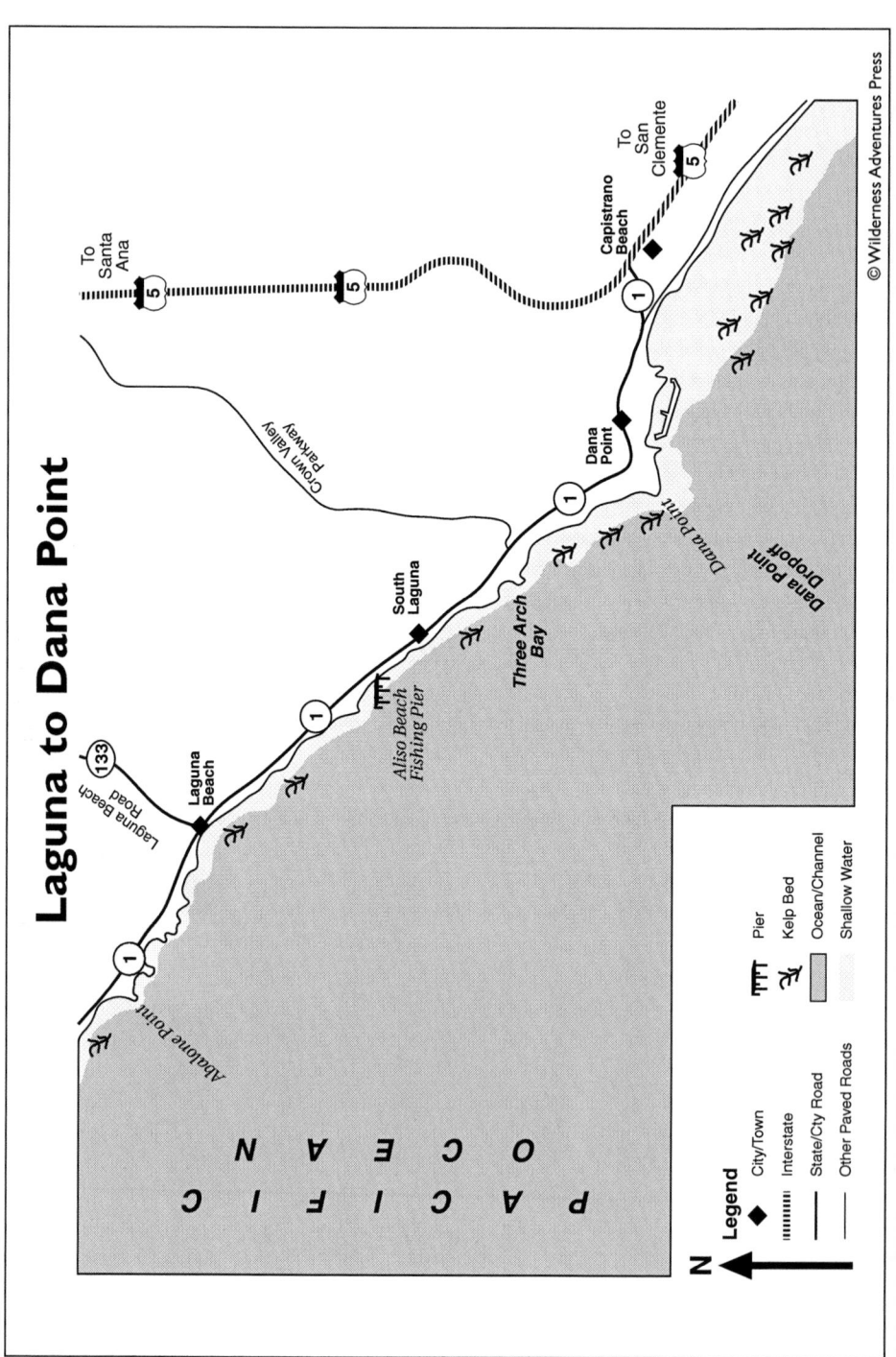

Laguna to Dana Point

To Santa Ana

To San Clemente

Capistrano Beach

Crown Valley Parkway

Dana Point

South Laguna

Dana Point

Dana Point Dropoff

Three Arch Bay

Aliso Beach Fishing Pier

Laguna Beach

Laguna Beach Road

Abalone Point

PACIFIC OCEAN

Legend

◆ City/Town

▬▬ Interstate

— State/City Road

— Other Paved Roads

Pier

Kelp Bed

Ocean/Channel

Shallow Water

N

© Wilderness Adventures Press

Davey's Locker Sport Fishing
400 Main Street
Newport Beach, CA 92661
949-673-1434
www.daveyslocker.com

Newport Landing Sport Fishing
309 Palm Street #F
Newport Beach, CA 92661
949-675-0550
www.newportlanding.com

A major fishing charter operation with three luxury boats is also here:

Bongos Sport Fishing
2140 Newport Boulevard
Newport Beach, CA 92663
949-673-2810
www.bongossportfishing.com

In addition, fishing skiffs for use in the bay only are available for rent at:

Balboa Pavilion
400 Main Street
Newport Beach, CA 92661
949-675-9444
www.balboapavillion.com

Laguna to Dana Point

Laguna Point to Dana Point is one of the most beautiful coastlines in the world. Tall mountains plunge into the sea with both rocky points and sandy coves. The stunning vistas from the shoreline make this an extremely desirable place to live. Couple this with Laguna's art colony atmosphere and throw in multitudes of world class restaurants, five star hotels, and resort class amenities, then cap it off with probably the finest weather in the entire United States—300 days of sunshine and an equal number of days in the low 70s—and light sea breezes, and you'll know why people stay here.

Dana Point was named after Richard Henry Dana, writer of the classic novel, *Two Years Before the Mast*. If you haven't read it, you owe it to yourself to spend a few enjoyable hours reading about a California yet to be discovered by the masses. His view of California before the Gold Rush is one you'll not soon forget: San Francisco as a minor trading center with only 400 people, San Diego's harbor devoid of construction and used as a cowhide loading port, and Santa Barbara as a predominantly Indian and missionary settlement. The book will give you a whole new perspective on this wonderful state.

The near-shore subsea terrain generally mimics the terrain of the dry land that abuts it, and here at Laguna, this is particularly true. The ocean bottom consists of steep dropoffs, deep canyons, and rugged rocky reefs. Kelp forests need a rocky bottom in which the giant kelp can anchor, and there's plenty of rocky bottom at Laguna where kelp forests flourish. Where there's kelp, you always find prime fishing, and the Laguna Coast is no exception. Some of the better places include:

Laguna Kelp

From Crystal Cove to the foot of Laguna Canyon Road, there are acres of kelp beds. Homes, restaurants, and hotels overlook this rocky, craggy bottom area from the cliffs above the shoreline. Kelp tends to be closer to shore here since the bottom falls away to 300 feet deep within a half-mile from the beach and to about 1800 feet within a mile. When navigating around the points, keep on the lookout for numerous boiler rocks.

The Laguna kelp beds are particularly good for calico bass. There generally isn't heavy fishing pressure since party boats from Newport tend to go north and those from Dana Point generally go south. Since many private boaters follow the party boats, this leaves the Laguna area overlooked as a primary fishing spot. That's all right with me, and you can guess where I like to go when I'm in that area.

Work the edges for calico bass using typical kelp bed fishing techniques. Yellowtail, barracuda, and bonito also frequent the area during the summer months. White seabass have been known to prowl the reefs, especially in winter and spring. Hardware (jig) fishing is my favorite method here and usually lands the biggest fish.

Though I've never tried it, flyfishing ought to be excellent here. Calicos and other game fish here are responsive to bait-imitating artificial lures, so a blue and white, green and white, or crystal flash all white streamer fly should knock them dead. Be prepared for some big fish here, though. It's easy to become complacent and step down to lighter tackle when the just barely legal calicos start getting boring on your 12-weight. Murphy's Law seems to go into effect at these times, because all too often when you have just put in your lightest rig, a big white seabass happens to be passing by and notices your fly.

With its rocky, craggy bottom, the area is also excellent for bottom fishing. Be sure to send down squid or bait on a sinker for sheephead, whitefish, treefish, or other types of rockfish that inhabit the reefs. Sometimes shrimp baits or rubber swimbaits are just the thing, too.

Laguna Beaches

The beaches in Dana Point, though generally small and surrounded by rocky points, attract their fair share of surf species. In fact, they might even be better than some of the more traditional wide and open beaches like Huntington. The fish all funnel into one area to feed on sand zone critters that get churned up by the high tide wave action. The main beach at Laguna at the foot of Laguna Canyon Road is just such a beach.

For the best results, catch this beach during the off hours when it isn't packed with people. Ideally, high tide at early morning or sunset is a great time to fish here. Plenty of surfperch are on the offing throughout the year. In the warmer summer months, spotfin croakers, yellowfin croakers, and corbina also come to these beaches to feed.

Clams and mussels are usually the better bait for Laguna. I suspect this is simply because there aren't as many sand crabs and ghost shrimp found here, and the fish are more naturally attracted to shellfish. Bloodworms also produce on these species, and, as always, the fresher the bait, the better.

Recent years have seen a return of southern California's most sought-after game fish, the yellowtail. Here, Sean Starkey of Yorba Linda, California, shows off a deckload, caught aboard the Hook Charters six-pack boat from Dana Point. Photo courtesy Matt Starkey.

Aliso Beach Fishing Pier

Aliso Beach is a small but very nice recreational facility in south Laguna. The beach features a short (only 620 feet long) but quite productive, diamond-shaped fishing pier. This is a really nice design, allowing fishing in the center of the diamond in the midst of all the pilings, where fish that like structure prefer to hide.

The usual surf species can be found near the shoreline, and mussels, bloodworms, and sand crabs are the best producers. The pier's end is best for pelagic species, such as mackerel, barracuda, and bonito. But the real fun at Aliso Beach is fishing the center, where both kelp bass congregate, especially when kelp becomes trapped in the pier, a common summer occurrence. In addition, bottom species, such as sculpin, halibut, and sometimes sheephead, can be caught in the center. Another fun thing to do while fishing at Aliso is to fish the center for surfperch of various types. Halfmoons, walleye surfperch, blacklip surfperch, and rubberlip surfperch can all be caught in the center near the pilings using tiny hooks, light leaders, and small cut bait, especially mussels.

This yellowfin croaker fell for a fly in Dana Harbor.
Photo courtesy Frank Selby—His & Her Fly Fishing Shop.

Or try a Lucky Laura rig and add jacksmelt, shiner surfperch, and walleye surfperch to your catch. This is quite a list of species for one small pier.

There are benches and a fish cleaning station on the pier, which is well lit for night fishing. Ample metered parking is available on both sides of the Pacific Coast Highway. Restrooms and a bait and tackle shop that also sells snacks are located at the foot of the pier for the convenience of fishermen. In all, it's a very pleasant place to visit and fish.

Dana Point Kelp

Stretching from Abalone Point, at the south end of Emerald Bay, to Dana Point, an excellent string of kelp forests blankets the coastline. These kelp beds have good numbers of calico bass and other kelp bed species. While fairly heavily fished due to the proximity to Dana Point Harbor, a very popular fishing port for both party boats and private boaters, these kelp beds seem to keep on producing in spite of the pressure. Sportfishing here is truly a sustainable fishery. Just as many fish seem to be born as are taken, seemingly affected only by natural seasonal variations.

In spring and early summer, barracuda schools circle the area in search of bait. Looking for bird action and tossing iron (fishing with jigs) will yield these toothy marauders of the California coast. In summer, yellowtail join in the feeding orgy. Many a new ocean fisherman has caught his first yellowtail right here at Dana Point.

From Dana Harbor, private boats, party boats, or charter boats can provide easy access to Dana Point. Don't forget to try saltwater flyfishing here. Blue and white bucktail streamers are probably the most effective and will entice calicos, yellowtail, barracuda, or the occasional bonito to your fly. But you have to pick your days since the wind can often pick up, especially on summer afternoons. Early morning or right at sunset are often the best times to flyfish, anyway, because the wind is lowest at these times.

Don't forget to check out the midwater and bottom fishing here. There's a grow-out facility for hatchery white seabass in Dana Harbor, and you can bet these fish head for the nearest kelp when they're released. Look for the population of these huge croakers to increase greatly as the hatchery fish begin to spawn in bigger and bigger numbers. On the bottom, you'll also find whitefish, sculpin, sheephead, and rockfish, especially among the craggy reefs associated with the area's bottom structure.

Dana Point Dropoff

A major subsea canyon is located right off Dana Point. This is a cut in the nearly vertical cliff that drops from the 300-foot-deep shelf adjacent to the coast to Catalina Channel's 2000-foot-deep bottom. Rockfish love this type of structure because it affords them plenty of nooks, crannies, and crevasses in which to hide and spawn. The best results here are found in deeper water (600-900 feet), where more hookups and larger fish of the quality species (reds, boscos, and cows) are possible. You can fish the shallower areas in the 400- to 500-foot range, but expect more chilipeppers and bocaccios. Not that they aren't excellent, very desirable fish, but the fish that inhabit the deeper waters have a higher table fare appeal.

The usual squid-baited bucktail flies in 4/0 or 5/0 size are the top producers in these canyons. Other good producers include dead anchovies, squid strips, and cut mackerel strips, especially when fished on a circle hook. Another technique that works here is to fillet a smaller rockfish, such as a chilipepper, but leave the tail, belly, and skin attached. Fish this on a 16/0 circle hook. As the swells cause the gangion to move up and down, the bait's tail waves around, which is irresistible to bigger rockfish.

Capistrano Beach

Capo Beach is another surf angler's paradise. Because it's a popular beach, it should be fished only in the early morning or late evening hours. Barred perch are plentiful here, and the minimal surf makes it easy to sense strikes, especially for smaller perch. At other beaches where the surf is high, you might not be able to feel a hit. Mussels and bloodworms are the hot ticket, but green rubber grubs on light leaders also produce well, especially in winter.

Capistrano is also a great place to take a fly rod, but watch out for other people on the beach. A big green woolly bugger is a good choice to start fishing. If that doesn't produce, switch to a red and orange bucktail fly to fool them into thinking they have a sand crab or shrimp in their sights.

Now that's a calico bass! These great-eating grouperlike fish haunt the many kelp beds of southern California.
Photo courtesy Bob Halal.

Doheny Flats and Kelp Beds

There's nothing finer than relaxing on a Sunday afternoon drifting the flats, and Doheny Flats is a wonderful place to do just that. Plenty of halibut, whitefish, sand sharks, sculpin, and sand bass in season call these flats home. There are several reefs here that sport dense patches of kelp during cooler water years. This, of course, attracts pelagic fish in summer and gives resident calico bass, white seabass, and sheephead a place to call home.

As with all flats fishing, live bait is king, and nose-hooked anchovies on a Carolina rig is the most effective way to present the bait. A good second choice is cut squid, also Carolina-rigged. If artificial lures are your thing, try 1/0 bucktail flies enhanced with a tiny strip of cut squid for scent. Rubber swimbaits are another winner that do well with scent enhancement. Greens, reds, root beer, or blue shad colors all seem to produce well, which one is preferred has more to do with the amount of

Dana Point Harbor's busy but high capacity boat launch facilities.

light present than whether the fish have a preference. As the light changes through-out the day, try other colors to keep the action hot.

Near the kelp areas at Doheny, surface plugs, flies, or metal jigs also produce, especially in the hotter summer months when fish seem to be gorging themselves on the bait bounty that moves into shallower water because of offshore fish pres-sure. Pay particular attention to areas where boiling fish can be seen or birds are working the bait.

Access to the Laguna to Dana Point Coastline

This productive stretch of coastline is readily accessible via the Interstate 405 or 5 freeways. To get to Laguna, take the Laguna Canyon west offramp from either 5 or 405 to the Pacific Coast Highway. From the south, take the Dana Point/Pacific Coast Highway west offramp from Interstate 5, then turn left at the Marina. Between Laguna and Dana Point, the coast highway is the main transportation corridor.

Dana Point Harbor serves this area well and is an excellent facility for boat launching or party boat fishing. Excellent launch ramps, parking, and facilities are available here. A number of excellent six-pack charter boat operations offer some-thing a bit nicer and more luxurious than the slightly crusty atmosphere surround-ing most party boats—of course, luxury comes at a price.

The major sportfishing landing in Dana Point is:

San Clemente and San Onofre Coastline

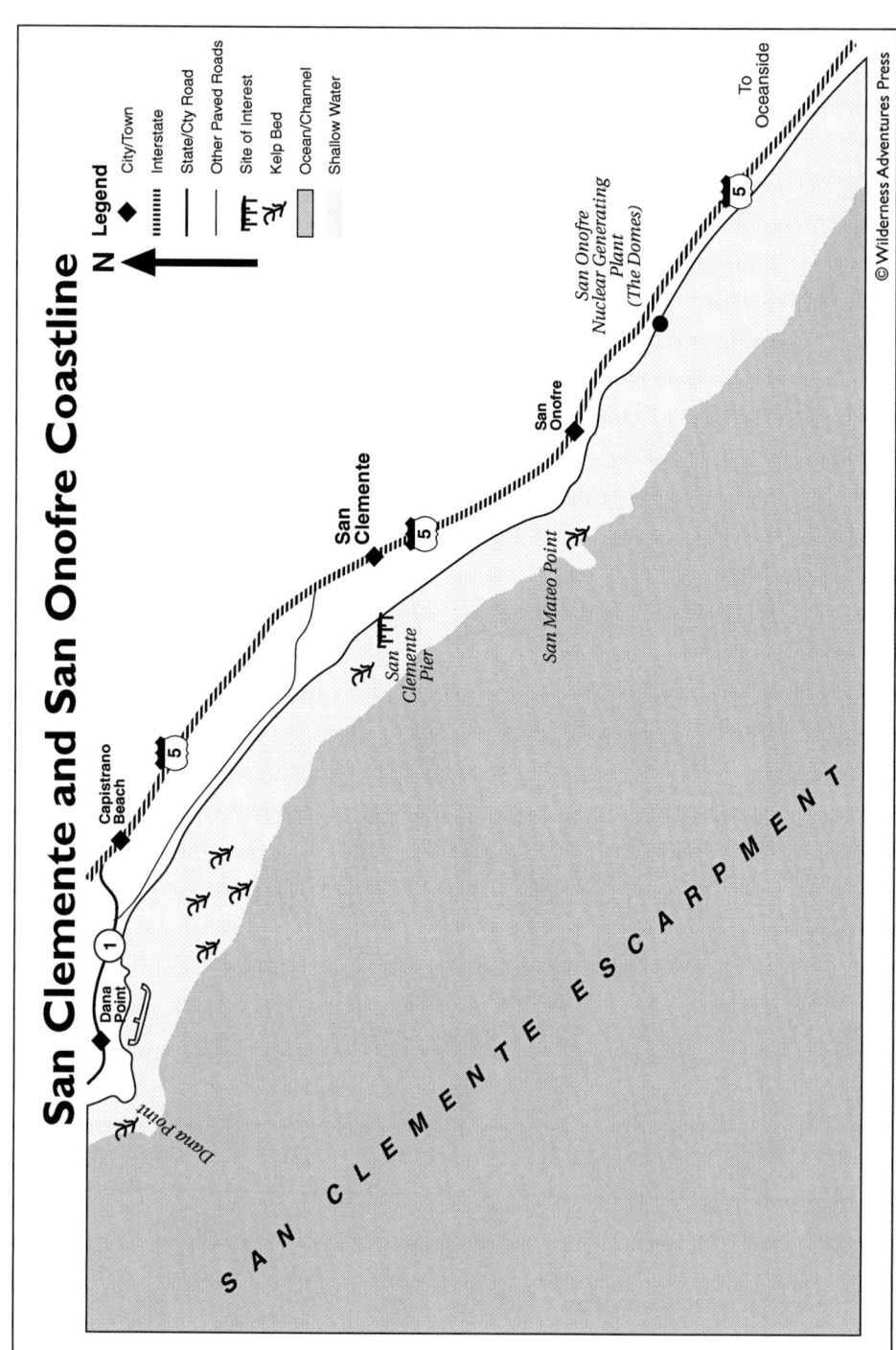

N

Legend

◆ City/Town

▦▦▦ Interstate

— State/Cty Road

— Other Paved Roads

♈ Site of Interest

🗻 Kelp Bed

⬜ Ocean/Channel

⬜ Shallow Water

Capistrano Beach

Dana Point

Dana Point

San Clemente

San Clemente Pier

San Mateo Point

San Onofre

San Onofre Nuclear Generating Plant (The Domes)

To Oceanside

SAN CLEMENTE ESCARPMENT

© Wilderness Adventures Press

Dana Wharf Sportfishing
34675 Golden Lantern
Dana Point, CA 92629
(949) 496-579
www.danawharfsportfishing.com

Some of the many excellent 6-pack charter boats include:

Stimulator Sportfishing
Dana Point, California
949-240-7226

Doctor's Orders Charters
Dana Point, California
949-287-8983

Hook Sport Fishing Charters
Dana Point, California
800-583-8133

You can rent boats in Dana Point at:

Capo Beach Water Craft Rental
34512 Embarcadero Place
Dana Point, CA 92629
949-661-1690

San Clemente and San Onofre Coastline

Just south of San Juan Capistrano, where Interstate 5 jogs over to the coastline, the quaint beach town of San Clemente hugs Capistrano Bight. It is the southern-most city in Orange County and abuts the huge Camp Pendleton Marine Corps Base to the south. When traveling south from San Clemente, the next area with any services is Oceanside on the south edge of Camp Pendleton, 17 miles away.

San Clemente was made famous during the 1960s as Richard Nixon's "Western White House." It's a delightful beach town, with ample services, a quaint, friendly atmosphere, and incredible southern California beach weather. This is predominantly a bedroom community, with homes ranging from tiny cottages to incredible mansions with fabulous ocean vistas.

The coastline here is mountainous with cliffs, gorges, and hills. This creates sandy beaches, rocky points, and stream outlets along the beach and offers a wide variety of habitats for many different fish species. Whatever your fishing preferences, the San Clemente area offers it. Some of the better areas to fish include:

San Clemente Beaches

The beaches north of the San Clemente Pier are sometimes very good fishing beaches, particularly in summer. These beaches are generally small and often rocky since the coast here is fairly mountainous, which makes it excellent territory for various surfperch. They tend to school over sand bottoms within a short sprint from shelter in case trouble brews. Fishing the surf with tiny pieces of bloodworms on #4

The San Clemente Pier offers several restaurants, family fun, and of course, great fishing.

to #6 hooks with a Carolina rig is one of the better techniques. Another is to use dark green rubber grubs on special hooks intended just for this purpose.

Lately flyfishermen have discovered the joys of surf fishing. More and more lake and stream flyfishermen are trying out their tackle and techniques in the surf and discovering how much it is to flyfish the beaches. Green woolly buggers or sand crab-imitating flies on a shooting head, sinking fly line is the best bet, and this is one of the better places to get started.

San Clemente Pier

One of the nicest piers along the Orange County coast, the San Clemente pier stretches out 1200 feet into the blue Pacific and is a popular strolling pier for tourists and locals. Two very good restaurants with attached drinking establishments reside on either side of the pier's foot.

Surf fish action is generally very good, especially in summer. Spotfin croakers, corbina, and yellowfin croakers are fairly common here. To fish for these, use mussels, bloodworms, or sand crabs and fish just outside the breaking waves. Barred surfperch are also frequent visitors here and can be caught the entire year.

In the midpier area, especially at night, the sand shark fishing is very good. Quite a number of bat rays, some exceeding 100 pounds have been landed here. At night, defrosted anchovies torn in half (don't cut them) seem to work best. They put out a good scent and blood trail that is easily followed by the ultrasensitive noses of sharks and rays.

Pelagic fish are also on tap at the San Clemente Pier, but their numbers are not generally as good as some of the piers that stretch out into deeper water. The Wildlife Conservation Board built a reef out near the end of the pier to attract resident and pelagic species to the area. This often attracts species that aren't generally associated with pier fishing, such as sculpin and sand bass, at times.

The pier is open 24 hours a day and has a bait and tackle shop out near the end. The pier has benches, fish cleaning stations, good lighting, and public restrooms. A parking lot is just north of the pier with 6- and 10-hour coin meters for parking convenience.

San Clemente Kelp

A rocky reef right off the San Clemente Pier grows an excellent, thick blanket of kelp in years with cool water. With the kelp come excellent schools of calico bass. The San Clemente kelp is one of the better close-in areas to kelp bed fish. It's a mere 5 miles or so from the Dana Point harbor entrance, and while it isn't as productive as the Domes kelp area, it has the advantage of being close, easy to find, and still a great place to fish.

In addition to calicos, the San Clemente kelp attracts pelagic species: Barracuda, bonito, and occasionally, yellowtail frequent this area in respectable numbers. Excellent catches are possible for anglers who visit here. Typical kelp bed techniques should be employed. Since many shallow reef fish call this area home, don't forget to check out the bottom when fishing here to add variety to your catch.

San Onofre Beach

San Onofre is one of the traditional "long board" surfer beaches, where surfers with plenty of gray hair are seen using those boat-sized boards from the 50s and 60s that were made popular by the beach movies of that era. San Onofre Beach has just the right characteristics to make it a long boarder's paradise. It features a wide beach and very shallow slope out to deep water. This means the surf builds slowly and breaks slowly for a long distance, which is why it is excellent for long surfboards.

The same characteristics that make San Onofre a great surfing beach make it a great surf-fishing beach. A very wide surf zone gives surf-feeding species a lot of area to browse in search of food and gives the surf fisherman a wide area to fish. Fishing the huge schools of barred surfperch that inhabit the area is a great and productive sport. In summer, corbina also love to scour the San Onofre beach in search of food. Sometimes, while feeding in very shallow water, they can be seen with their backs literally out of the water. It's great fun to toss sand crab or ghost shrimp-imitating flies right in their path.

Flies or bait are both effective at San Onofre. Ideally, look for a high tide in early morning or early evening to optimize your fishing fun and minimize the possibility of hooking one of the many beach-goers that flock to this popular tourist beach throughout the summer. I like tossing pieces of bloodworms on a Carolina rig out into the surf for a good chance to hook a perch, corbina, or spotfin.

San Clemente Escarpment

As with much of the Orange County Coast, the San Clemente sea bottom slopes slowly to form a coastal flat, then at about 150 feet, it drops steeply to the Santa Catalina Channel bottom at 2500 feet deep. Like the geological formations on land, steep, almost clifflike slopes underwater are also covered with irregular, erose features, such as gorges, caves, and rough surfaces. All of these features form excellent habitat for the rock cod that inhabit the deep reef. The San Clemente Escarpment is no exception.

Bocaccios, reds, and chilipeppers are the mainstay of the San Clemente Escarpment. You can start fishing in 80 fathoms (480 feet), but the best quality fish are usually found below 100 fathoms (600 feet), where there is a higher percentage of red rock cod and bigger fish. Occasionally, a big cowcod in the 20-pound class can be hauled up from the deeper water—your best chance for a cow is to fish 700 to 900 feet. Squid-baited bucktail flies are, by far, the best medicine for all the fish here. A 5- to 8-hook gangion, sent down with 3 to 5 pounds of lead, will bring the most successful catches.

The Domes

Called the domes because of the two huge dome-shaped nuclear power plant buildings on shore at San Onofre, this area is unique because of the warm water outfall from the reactor. Reactors are notoriously inefficient thermally, and huge quantities of water are used to take the heat away from the steam condensers. This is why reactors are always built either next to the ocean or on a large, flowing river. The warm water supports rapid algae growth that attracts tiny creatures, which attract baitfish, which, of course, attract game fish.

A reef just offshore from the power plant grows a kelp bed of several acres most years. This is one of the finest-producing kelp forests in the area, especially for yellowtail, calico bass, and barracuda. In recent years, giant black sea bass have made a remarkable return in this area. On a recent trip there, I hooked six big blacks, which are illegal to keep, but are so big and powerful, the thrill of the fight makes them an exciting prey. In addition, the bottom features many excellent resident reef fish, such as sheephead, sculpin, treefish, sand bass, and other smaller fish. The sandflats surrounding the reef are also excellent for halibut, leopard sharks, sanddabs, and other flats species. Even surfperch, opaleye, halfmoons, white croaker, and other small game fish abound here. It would not be an unusual summer day to catch 10 different species here.

An early morning pier fisherman enjoys solitude as he gazes over the blue Pacific.

One of the best ways to fish the Domes is with jigs. To discover the major species and at what depth they're feeding, toss jigs around the edges of kelp, then let them sink to various depths before your retrieve. Rubber swimbaits fished at various depths also yield exceptional results. Don't be surprised to haul up a big yellowtail, white seabass, or giant black sea bass from the deep using a rubber swimbait. I like green and white single-tails, brown and white single-tails, or green twintails for this type of fishing. Cast them a short distance, let them sink, and then give them an erratic, twitchy retrieve to stimulate the maximum pounce instinct in bigger game fish.

Calicos abound at the Domes, and often a light 8- or 10-pound test bass rig used to flyline live anchovies can yield hours of fun with these kelp bass. You can also try hard swimming lures, the kind used for bass in lakes, for a different slant on taking these excellent eating residents of the kelp. Even an anchovy-imitating fly will get snapped at with glee here at the Domes. Some days, you simply can't make a cast near the kelp without a calico grabbing at your bait.

Don't forget to get in on the spring and early summer barracuda action at the Domes. Jigs or bait are both equally effective. Work a dozen yards outside the edges of the kelp rather than the fringes and you'll not search long for these toothy torpedoes. If mackerel attack your bait, fish deeper—barracuda are often below the mackerel. This applies whether you're fishing with a jig, lure, bait or fly—send it deeper to get to the barracuda below the macks.

COMMON GAME FISH AVAILABILITY BY MONTHS
ORANGE COUNTY

Species	Jan	Feb	Mar	Apr	May	Jun	Jul	Aug	Sep	Oct	Nov	Dec
Yellowtail					Good	Good	Excellent	Excellent	Good	Possible		
Barracuda			Possible	Good	Good	Excellent	Excellent	Excellent	Excellent	Good	Possible	
Bonito			Possible	Good	Excellent	Excellent	Excellent	Excellent	Excellent	Good	Possible	Possible
Calico Bass	Possible	Possible	Good	Good	Excellent	Excellent	Excellent	Excellent	Excellent	Good	Good	Possible
Sand Bass	Possible	Possible	Good	Excellent	Excellent	Excellent	Excellent	Excellent	Excellent	Good	Good	Possible
White Seabass	Excellent	Excellent	Good	Good	Possible	Possible	Good	Good	Possible	Possible	Possible	Possible
Halibut	Good	Good	Good	Good	Good	Good	Good	Good	Good	Good	Good	Good
Lingcod	Excellent	Excellent	Good	Possible	Possible	Possible	Possible	Possible	Possible	Good	Good	Excellent
Shallow-water Rockfish	Excellent	Excellent	Good	Good	Good	Good	Good	Good	Good	Good	Good	Excellent
Deep-water Rockfish	Excellent	Excellent	Good	Good	Good	Good	Good	Good	Good	Good	Good	Excellent
Sheephead	Possible	Possible	Good	Good	Good	Excellent	Excellent	Excellent	Excellent	Good	Good	Possible
Sculpin	Good	Good	Good	Good	Good	Good	Excellent	Excellent	Good	Good	Good	Good
Blue Perch	Possible	Possible	Good	Good	Excellent	Excellent	Excellent	Excellent	Good	Good	Possible	Possible
Opaleye		Possible	Possible	Good	Good	Excellent	Excellent	Excellent	Good	Good	Possible	
Whitefish	Excellent	Excellent	Good	Good	Good	Good	Possible	Good	Good	Good	Good	Excellent

Legend: ☐ Not Available ▨ Fish Possible ▩ Good Fishing ▪ Excellent Fishing

Access to the San Clemente Coast

The San Clemente coast is readily accessible via Interstate 5 (San Diego Freeway) and the many San Clemente exits. All east/west streets end at the ocean. To get to the pier, take Del Mar Street from the center of downtown.

From Dana Wharf Sportfishing in Dana Point (see the Laguna Beach to Dana Point section), party boats often travel to this area to take advantage of the excellent fishing here. Three-quarter-day boats fish the Domes area often, especially in the productive spring and summer seasons. Six-pack party boat charters often go to this area, especially those chartered for half day, three-quarter day, or full day trips.

For the private boater, Dana Point's excellent marina facilities are ideal for either overnighting in transient slips or launching trailer boats at the modern launch ramp facilities. Ample parking is available at the launch ramps. These are very popular and heavily used, particularly in summer. Live bait is available at the Dana Point channel entrance barge.

Orange County Bait and Tackle Shops

Norms Big Fish Bait & Tackle
1780 Pacific Coast Hwy
Seal Beach, CA 90740
(562) 431-0723

A Fishermens Connection
7672 Alhambra Drive
Huntington Beach, CA 92647
(714) 848-6516

Charkbait Sportfishing Supplies
16732 Algonquin Street
Huntington Beach, CA 92649
(714) 846-6452

Fishermens Hardware
16942 Gothard Street
Huntington Beach, CA 92647
(714) 841-6878

Rod & Reel
7071 Warner Avenue
Huntington Beach, CA 92647
(714) 847-6053

Sport Chalet
16242 Beach Boulevard
Huntington Beach , CA 92647
(714) 848-0988
www.sportchalet.com

Bight Fishing Products
5880 Garden Grove Blvd
Westminster, CA 92683
(714) 899-9955
www.kickerjigs.com

Turner's Outdoorsman
18808 Brookhurst
Fountain Valley, CA 92708
(714) 965-5151
www.turners.com

The Longfin
2730 E Chapman Ave
Orange, CA 92869
(714) 538-8010
www.thelongfin.com

Turner's Outdoorsman
1932 N. Tustin
Orange, CA 92865
(714) 974-0600
www.turners.com

Anglers Marine
3475 E La Palma Ave
Anaheim, CA 92806
(714) 666-2628
www.anglersmarine.com

Dolphin Tackle Co.
883 S Rose Pl
Anaheim, CA 92805
(714) 687-9160

Melton Intl. Tackle
2600 E Katella Ave Suite B
Anaheim, CA 92806
(714) 978-9192 or (800) 372-3474
www.meltontackle.com

Taka's Bait and Tackle
2707 W Lincoln Ave
Anaheim, CA 92801
(714) 527-2920
www.takastackle.com

Fisherman's Access
1021 E Imperial Hwy Suite G2
Brea, CA 92821
(714) 674-0064

Sport Chalet
2500 East Imperial Highway #150
Brea , CA 92821
(714) 255-0132
www.sportchalet.com

Bob Marriott's Fly Fishing Store
2700 W Orangethorpe Ave
Fullerton, CA 92833
(714) 525-1827
www.bobmarriotts.net

Glenn's Tackle Shop
1145 Baker St Ste A
Costa Mesa, CA 92626
(714) 957-1408
www.glennstackle.com

The Grant Boys
1750 Newport Blvd
Costa Mesa, CA 92627
(949) 645-3400
www.grantboys.com

His & Her Fly Fishing Store
1566 Newport Blvd
Costa Mesa, CA 92627
(949) 548-9449
www.hisherflyfishing.com

JDS Big Game Tackle
Balboa Island
Newport Beach, CA 92660
(949) 723-0883
www.jdsbiggame.com

Whiteys Custom Tackle and Angler's
Center
419 North Newport Boulevard
Newport Beach, CA 92663
(949) 642-6662

Sport Chalet
2983 Michelson Drive
Irvine , CA 92612
(949) 476-9557
www.sportchalet.com

Sport Chalet
26532 Towne Centre Drive, Suite A
Lake Forest , CA 92610
(949) 588-6044
www.sportchalet.com

Sport Chalet
27551 Puerta Real
Mission Viejo , CA 92691
(949) 582-3363
www.sportchalet.com

Sport Chalet
27080 Alicia Parkway
Laguna Niguel , CA 92656
(949) 365-0342
www.sportchalet.com

The Jig Stop
34186 Pacific Coast Hwy
Dana Point, CA 92629
(949) 496-0960
www.jigstop.com

Get Reel
555 El Camino Real
San Clemente, CA 92672
(949) 498-0052
www.getreelfishing.com

Travelers Information for Orange County

As with all the counties in Southern California, Orange County hosts every conceivable convenience for the traveling angler. There is a world of things for nonfishermen to do, from theme parks to concerts, theaters to museums, professional sports to relaxing on the beach. The shopping is incredible, and the visitor will soon find there's far more to do than time to do it. For more information on the various coastal cities, contact their visitors bureaus. Most have free guides to their cities and area to give you more vacation ideas than you could ever need.

Anaheim-Orange County Visitor
& Convention Bureau
800 West Katella Avenue
Anaheim, CA 92802
714-765-8888
Fax: 714-991-8963
Website: www.go-orange.com

Corona Del Mar Chamber of Commerce
2843 East Coast Hwy
Corona Del Mar, CA 92625
949-673-4050

Costa Mesa Chamber of Commerce
1700 Adams Avenue
Costa Mesa, CA 92626
714-885-9090

Costa Mesa Tourism Council
P.O. Box 5071
Costa Mesa, CA 92628-5071
800-399-5499
Website: www.costamesa-ca.com

Dana Point Chamber of Commerce
24681 La Plaza, #115
Dana Point, CA 92629
949-496-1555

Huntington Beach Chamber
of Commerce
2100 Main Street, #200
Huntington Beach,CA 92648
714-536-8888

Huntington Beach Conference
& Visitors Bureau
417 Main Street
Huntington Beach CA 92648
800-729-6232 or 714-969-3492
Fax: 714-969-5592
Website: www.hbvisit.com
Email: hbvisit@ix.netcom.com

Laguna Beach Chamber of Commerce
357 Glenneyre Street
Laguna Beach, CA 92651
949-494-1018

Laguna Beach Visitors Bureau
252 Broadway
Laguna Beach, CA 92651
800-877-1115 Ext. 0
Fax: 949-376-0558
Website: www.lagunabeachinfo.org

Newport Beach Chamber of Commerce
1470 Jamboree Road
Newport Beach, CA 92660
949-729-4400

Newport Beach Conference
& Visitors Bureau
3300 West Coast Hwy
Newport Beach CA 92663
800-94-COAST
Fax: 949-722-1612
Website: www.newportbeach-cvb.com

Orange County Visitor Marketing
Consortium
888 West Katella Avenue
Anaheim CA 92802
877-GO-ORANGE
Fax: 714-765-8864
Website: www.go-orange.com
Free brochure available

San Clemente Chamber of Commerce
1100 North El Camino Real
San Clemente, CA 92672
949-492-1131

San Juan Capistrano Chamber
of Commerce
31781 Camino Capistrano, #306
San Juan Capistrano, CA 92675
949-493-4700

Seal Beach Chamber of Commerce
311 Main Street, #14A
Seal Beach, CA 90740
562-799-0179

South Orange County Chamber
of Commerce
23166 Los Alisos Boulevard, #264
Mission Viejo, CA 92691
949-830-1100

Orange County Accommodations

The following is a sampling of lodgings that are close to port in Orange County. These range from basic to luxury, and you should keep in mind that nothing along the southern California coast, particularly anything close to the water, is inexpensive.

Newport Beach Harbor
Best Western Bayshores Inn
1800 West Balboa Boulevard
Newport Beach, CA 92663
949-675-3463

Doyman's Oceanfront Inn
2102 West Oceanfront
Newport Beach, CA 92663
949-675-7300

Newport Channel Inn
6030 West Pacific Coast Highway
Newport Beach, CA 92663
949-642-3030

Newport Classic Inn
2300 West Pacific Coast Highway
Newport Beach, CA 92663
949-722-2999

Portofino Beach Hotel
2306 West Ocean Front
Newport Beach, CA 92663
949-673-7030

Newport Beach Inn
6208 West Pacific Coast Highway
Newport Beach, CA 92663
949-642-8252

Dana Point

Best Western Marina Inn
24800 Dana Point Harbor Drive
Dana Point, CA 92629
949-496-1203

Blue Lantern Inn
34343 Street of Blue Lantern
Dana Point, CA 92629
949-661-1304

Dana Point Harbor Inn
25325 Dana Point Harbor Drive
Dana Point, CA 92629
949-493-5001

Doubletree Guest Suites
34402 Pacific Coast Highway
Dana Point, CA 92629
949-661-1100

Quality Inn & Suites
34280 Pacific Coast Highway
Dana Point, CA 92629
949-248-1000

San Diego County

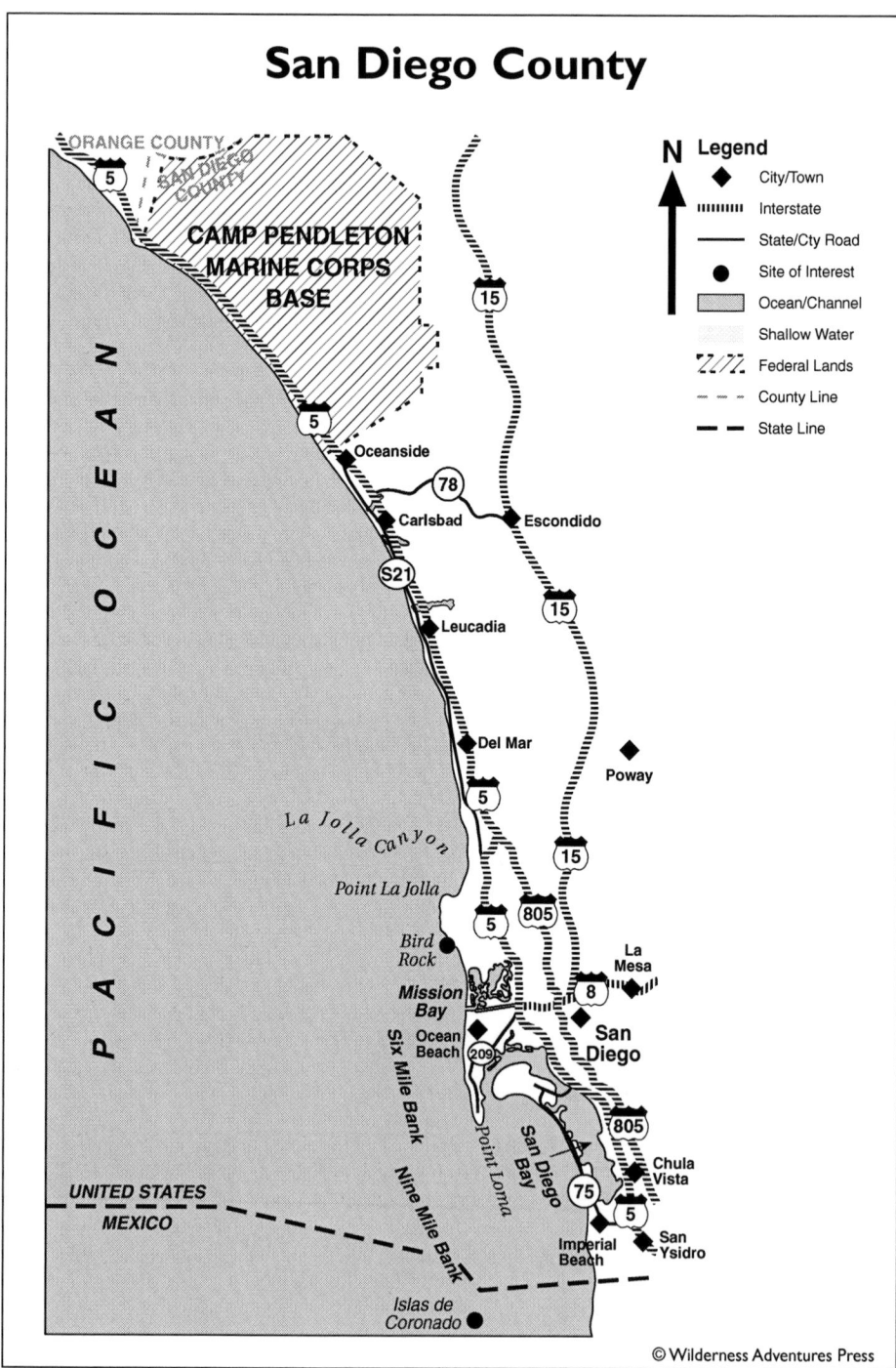

N

Legend

◆ City/Town

|||||||| Interstate

—— State/Cty Road

● Site of Interest

Ocean/Channel

Shallow Water

Federal Lands

– – – County Line

– – State Line

ORANGE COUNTY
SAN DIEGO COUNTY

CAMP PENDLETON
MARINE CORPS
BASE

P A C I F I C   O C E A N

Oceanside

Carlsbad

Escondido

S21

Leucadia

Del Mar

Poway

La Jolla Canyon

Point La Jolla

Bird Rock

La Mesa

Mission Bay

Six Mile Bank

Ocean Beach

San Diego

San Diego Bay

Point Loma

Chula Vista

Nine Mile Bank

UNITED STATES
MEXICO

Imperial Beach

San Ysidro

Islas de Coronado

© Wilderness Adventures Press

San Diego County

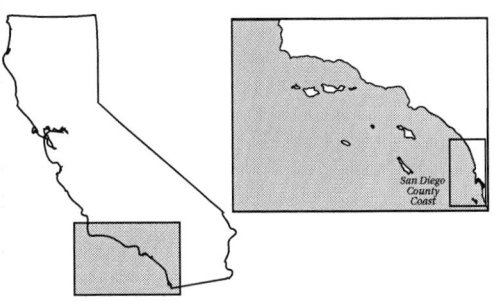

San Diego County is the south-western-most corner of the United States. It is bordered by Mexico on the south and the Pacific Ocean on the west. San Diego has some of the nicest weather in the entire country, with 300 days of sunshine, temperatures in the low 70s, and low humidity being the rule rather than the exception.

San Diego County is home to the sixth largest metropolitan area in the United States and the second largest in California. Many people are very surprised to find out that the Bay Area (metropolitan San Francisco) is not as large as San Diego. In the past, the San Francisco area has been one of the largest cities in California, even eclipsing huge Los Angeles. Huge migrations of people to California began right after World War II, when servicemen on their way to and from the fighting in the Pacific discovered the fabulous year-round weather and scenic beauty of southern California. Throughout the latter half of this century, southern California has had a strong attraction for people, whether from music touting "two girls for every boy" to depictions of lazing by the pool under palm trees in the movies. Because of recent migrations from the Northeast and Midwest, San Diego has become one of the most popular sunbelt destinations for people tired of shoveling snow and hibernating in the winter.

As a small boy living in Minnesota, I remember watching the Tournament of Roses parade and seeing baton twirlers in short skirts and spectators in golf shirts, while we huddled together in the living room during a blizzard, and wishing we lived out there in southern California.

San Diego has also become one of the premier resort cities in the United States. It has the greatest concentration of museums west of the Mississippi, a wide range of tourist activities, including wildlife parks such as Sea World, San Diego Wild Animal Park, and the world famous San Diego Zoo. Great golf courses, world class wineries, and of course, San Diego's fabulous beaches, are just a few of the many delights awaiting the tourist in San Diego.

Speaking of tourist destinations, care to venture a guess as to the most popular tourist destination in the entire world? Hawaii? Las Vegas? Disneyland? Nope, it's Tijuana, San Diego's mirror city just across the Mexican border. Over 15 million people per year cross the border to visit our neighbor to the south for shopping, food, and fiestas.

Of course, since you're reading this book, you're probably not as interested in wineries, museums, golf, or shopping as you are in fishing. If you like saltwater fishing, San Diego is your kind of place. Situated right on the Mexican border, San Diego County has the warmest ocean water, attracting the most warmwater game fish on

While southern California has many famous beaches, much of the coast is rocky, providing a variety of fish habitat and species for the shore angler.

the coast, and its surface fishing is the best in southern California. From tiny surfperch to huge bluefin tuna, the ocean here offers the most diverse species of fish and range of tackle and techniques to be found anywhere along the coast.

San Diego also has the biggest and most modern sportfishing fleet in the western United States. From 20-foot charter boats for two fishermen in the harbor to 120-foot long-range boats that are more like cruise ships than fishing boats, San Diego's fleet truly covers the entire spectrum of fishing. Fishing trips from four hours to 28 days long and ranging over 1000 miles from port can be booked here.

Excellent private boat facilities are available in the county for fishermen. Two beautiful, small watercraft ports and a major harbor, capable of handling all manner of crafts from kayaks to supertankers and aircraft carriers, are situated along the county's approximately 90 miles of coastline.

San Diego's huge, natural harbor offers fishermen excellent bay, pier, and shore fishing and has well-maintained extensive boat launching facilities. The harbor has a strong Navy presence, and every type of Navy vessel, from super carriers to fast attack submarines, can be seen cruising the bay. For many years, San Diego was primarily a Navy town, and this probably accounted for introducing tens of thousands of young men over the past century to this saltwater fishing paradise.

Some of the great San Diego County fishing areas include:

Camp Pendleton

Separating San Diego County from the huge Los Angeles/Orange/Ventura mega-metropolis is a 17-mile long stretch of land owned by the federal government and serving as one of the biggest Marine Corps bases in the western United States, Camp Pendleton. The Marine Corps has done an excellent job of keeping the land in its natural state and keeping developers from turning this last stretch of coastal wilderness into planned, gated communities. I sincerely hope the Marine Corps never abandons this base. It forms a wide and refreshing barrier that keeps Los Angeles and San Diego from merging into one 300-mile long super city.

Camp Pendleton is a very active base—nearly every day you can see troops training there as you drive through on Interstate 5. On occasion, all-out amphibious assaults are performed with sea, air, and armored equipment streaming ashore from ships sitting just offshore. It always makes me feel a little safer knowing the Marine Corps is there and prepared to defend us should they be called. This isn't intended as a patriotic sidebar, although that might apply. My intention is to convince you to stay out of the way when the Marines are doing their training exercises. The Coast Guard issues Notices to Mariners (NOTAMs) when the coastline will be closed for military activity. Read them. Know before you go. This is not something to trifle with.

Marines storming the beach aside, there are several excellent fishing destinations along the Camp Pendleton coastline. These include:

Pendleton Artificial Reef

An experimental artificial reef comprised of 10,000 tons of quarry rock covering a 3½-acre area was built in 1980 off Camp Pendleton. This reef is in 45 feet of water and is located 9.6 nautical miles from Oceanside on a 306° magnetic course or 12.4 nautical miles from Dana Point Harbor entrance on a 115° magnetic course at 33°-19'-30" N × 117°-31'-42" W.

Sand bass are the predominant species, with plenty of legal-sized fish available in late spring, summer, and fall into October. During spring, sculpin are attracted to the reef, and surfperch of various types are available year-round. Fish the reef with bait, especially if targeting bass. Rubber swimbaits also work well. I like to bring along a very light rig, usually 8-pound test and put tiny strips of cut squid on #6 hooks to bring home a mess of halfmoons (blue perch) for dinner.

The Barn Kelp

Why it's called the Barn kelp, I really don't know. Perhaps at one time there was a barn on the coast, but there hasn't been anything to identify this productive reef since I've been fishing the coast (late 60s to the present). The Barn kelp is always a consistent producer of calico bass, barracuda, and in warmer months, yellowtail. Boats often travel down the coast from Dana Point in Orange County or up from Oceanside to fish the area. This is especially true in spring when kelp beds closer to port haven't yet gotten consistent or when the barracuda begin to run.

Camp Pendleton

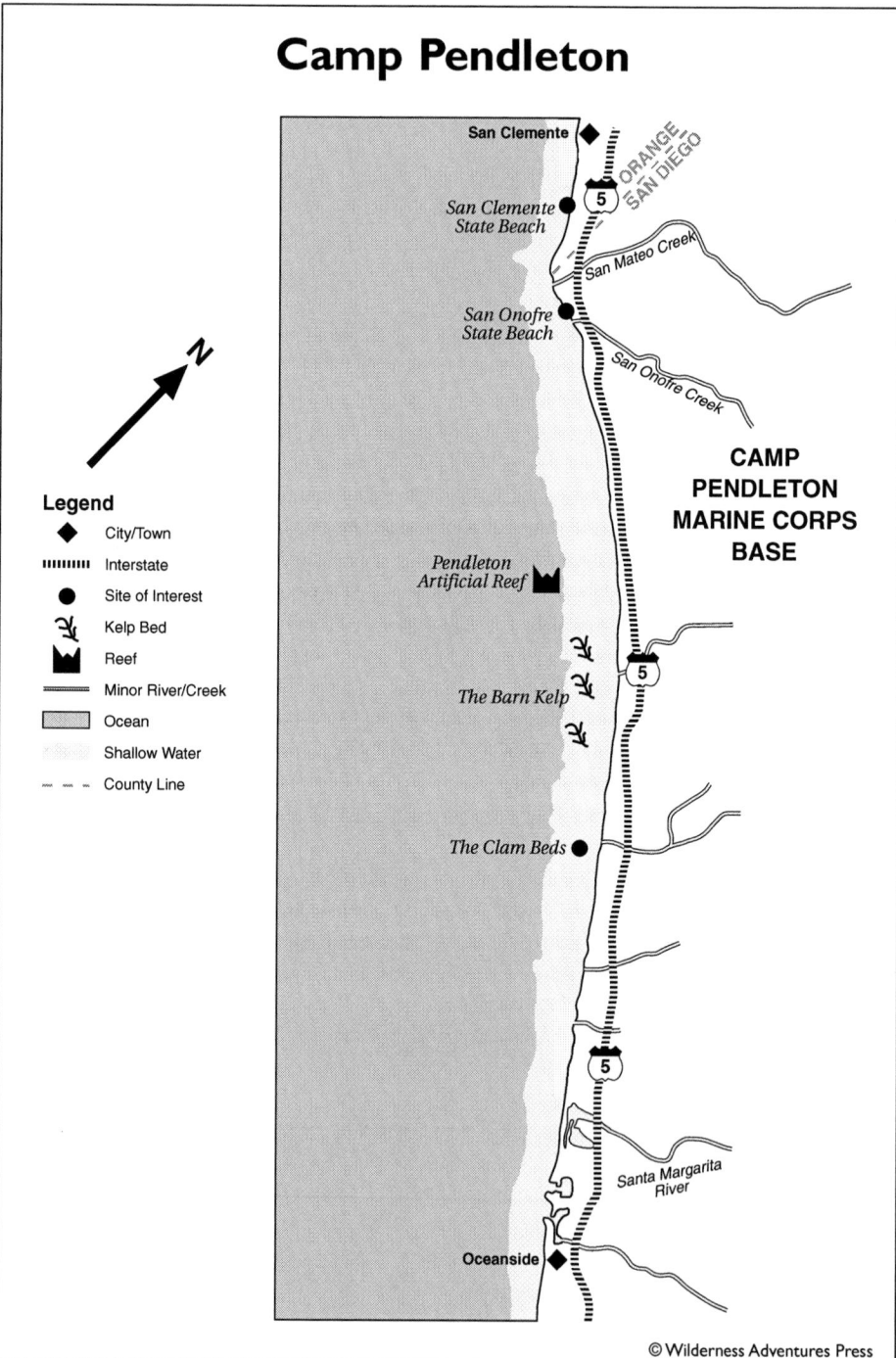

San Clemente

San Clemente
State Beach

San Mateo Creek

San Onofre
State Beach

San Onofre Creek

ORANGE
SAN DIEGO

CAMP
PENDLETON
MARINE CORPS
BASE

Legend
- ◆ City/Town
- ⦙⦙⦙⦙⦙ Interstate
- ● Site of Interest
- ⚘ Kelp Bed
- ♛ Reef
- ═══ Minor River/Creek
- ▨ Ocean
- ▨ Shallow Water
- ⚊ ⚊ ⚊ County Line

Pendleton
Artificial Reef

The Barn Kelp

The Clam Beds

Santa Margarita
River

Oceanside

© Wilderness Adventures Press

Fish the Barn as you would any kelp bed by working the edges of the visible kelp forest for calicos while keeping an eye out for moving pelagic fish. Jigs are often very effective. Smaller, barracuda-sized jigs in blue and white or green and yellow bone jigs are the hot ticket. As with any near-shore kelp bed, be sure to change the hooks on your jigs to single hooks if barracuda tend to run small. The Barn kelp can also be very productive as a flyfishing locale. Blue and white or green and white streamer flies produce the best, but as always, the color depends on the day.

The Clam Beds

Affectionately known as the Clam Beds, this area of the coast is prime yellowtail country. During the fabulous 1997 and 1998 El Niño summers, this area produced more yellowtail on a consistent basis than nearly any other in-shore fishing spot, but why this happened is a mystery. I don't know if the bottom is covered with clam beds or not, but you can bet there are plenty of forage fish attracted to this area that bring the big boys in.

Yellowtail in this area don't generally feed on the surface, so bigger bait, especially sardines, should be fished with a Carolina rig or dropper loop to get them down near the bottom. And hard jigs, fished deep, are always an excellent way to put a big yellowtail on the end of your line. Though most people never try it, a rubber swimbait is excellent for attracting yellowtail. Green sparkle twin-tailed scampi or single-tail purple or brown bait colored rubber seem to always do well, especially when the bite slows down on bait or bone jigs.

When yellowtail aren't home, many other species can be caught in the Clam Beds area, particularly flats fish, such as halibut, white croaker, sand bass, and sculpin. These are best fished with live bait, but the other techniques detailed in the flats fishing section are also effective.

Access to Camp Pendleton

Camp Pendleton's coastline is closed to the public since it's a working military installation. Often, the near-shore area is also closed during military training missions or other activities. When open, the beautiful coastline is accessible by private boat from either the Oceanside small craft harbor to the south or Dana Point harbor to the north. Both of these ports have excellent facilities, and the area's generally fair weather and good visibility make the short trip from these ports uncomplicated.

Sportfishing landings, both in Oceanside and Dana Point, have charters that visit the Pendleton coastline and its famous fishing. See those sections for landing information.

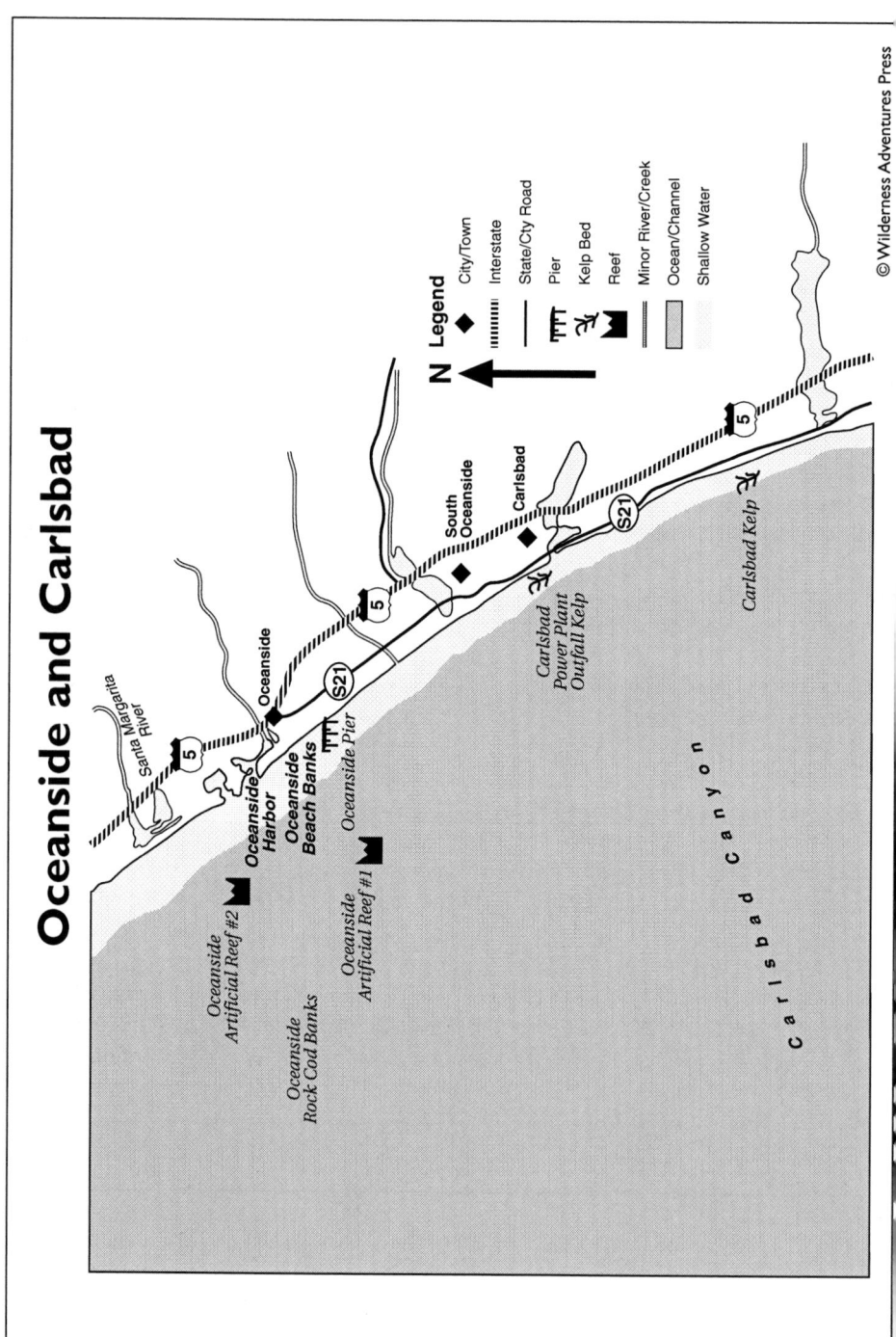

Oceanside and Carlsbad

© Wilderness Adventures Press

Oceanside and Carlsbad

These areas are very accessible via the small craft harbor at Oceanside. These are excellent fishing destinations, sometimes overlooked by fishermen eager to get as far south as possible. Oceanside is often shunned by tourists because of its reputation as a military town, situated as it is at the south end of Camp Pendleton. Nevertheless, Oceanside and Carlsbad offer fishing tourists plenty of excellent accommodations, services, and facilities at a cost generally much lower than some of the high-ticket places in San Diego. Some of the better places to fish in this area include:

Oceanside Beach Banks

Just south of Oceanside Harbor, sandy beaches invite the surf caster to ply his craft for the many surf species that feed along the beach. Barred surfperch, spot-fin croaker, and California corbina await the successful surf caster here. The best bait choice is probably ghost shrimp, with sand crabs, bloodworms, and razor clam siphons a close second.

The beach is fairly steep here, dropping off fairly quickly. It isn't necessary to cast out past the breakers when fishing for these species. The zone is between the breaking surf and the dry sand, and the best time is from two hours before high tide until one hour after.

Oceanside Rock Cod Banks

Right off the coast of Oceanside, a sharp dropoff, about 3 miles out, goes from about 100 feet to 3000 feet in a fairly short distance. This clifflike bottom formation is filled with cracks and crevasses, ideal cover for deep water rockfish. Although this cliff runs many miles up and down the coast, it is just north of Oceanside that a substantial gorge cuts into the cliff. This harbors excellent numbers of big bocaccio, along with chilipeppers and several other species of deep water rockfish.

As at Carlsbad Canyon, this area is best in deeper water. The techniques discussed in the Carlsbad Canyon section (below) are applicable to fishing this area.

Oceanside Artificial Reef #2

Probably due to the success of the first artificial reef in Oceanside (see below), a second reef of 10,000 tons of quarry rock was built in 1987. Rather than being placed in a single pile, a number of smaller piles were distributed over an area of about 250 acres. The reef is located 2 nautical miles from the Oceanside Harbor entrance on a 248° magnetic heading at 33°-12'-35" N × 117°-25'-48" W.

Like the first reef, the second is home primarily to barred sand bass. The trick here is to search the site, using a good fish finder, until feeding schools are located and then fish that area. Just because the reef is there doesn't mean the fish are feeding there. Since this reef is quite spread out, some closer inspection is necessary.

When you spot a school, fish the bottom with typical sand bass fishing gear and techniques and you won't be disappointed. Like the other Oceanside artificial reef,

Oceanside's beautiful, long pier is ideal for fishing and family fun with the parklike environment at its base.

other rock-type fish can be found here, so be prepared for different species and you should have no trouble filling your sack.

Oceanside Pier

This pier stretches out over 1900 feet into the Pacific and is one of the better fishing piers on the south coast. A quarry rock artificial reef was made out near the end of the pier, so you not only get the sandy species but also some rock-dwelling fish, such as rockfish and sculpin.

As with most piers, the surf line is the best place to catch such fish as corbina, spotfin croakers, and barred surfperch. When the Oceanside Harbor was built, much of the sand that was previously deposited here now gets deposited farther down the coast, so the pier isn't one of the best for near-shore species that prefer sandier habitats.

The midpier area is excellent for California halibut. Live bait is usually the best, but rubber swimbaits, cut squid, and frozen anchovies are the best approach in this area for flatfish. In addition to halibut, the midpier area offers up white croaker, guitarfish, jacksmelt, and walleye surfperch. Out near the end you'll find mackerel, barracuda, bass, and the occasional bonito. Because white seabass can often be

The fine boat launch facility at Oceanside Small Craft Harbor.

found near shore here, please be sure to return them so they can grow and eventually spawn.

The Oceanside Pier is open 24 hours per day and has excellent parking, a bait and tackle store, snack bars, and a restaurant. Plenty of benches and fish cleaning stations line the pier, as well as convenient restrooms. In all it's a very pleasant and productive place to fish.

Oceanside Artificial Reef #1

The first of the two very successful artificial reefs in the area is located only 1.75 miles from the channel entrance of Oceanside Harbor on a 202° magnetic course (33°-10-'-57" N × 117°-25'-00" W). This was originally a 4-acre site, built with 2000 tons of quarry rock in 1964. Since it was so successful, a load of scrapped concrete dock floats was added in 1987, increasing the site's size to over 60 acres.

This reef is inhabited by a healthy school of barred sand bass. These may be fished with live bait on Carolina rigs or on rubber swimbaits, which are especially effective when sweetened with strips of squid. The occasional white seabass also frequents the area, so be on the lookout when fishing for sand bass—you never know when you might be surprised by a 50-pound white.

Plenty of sheephead prowl the reef, too, so I usually make sure I have a few head-on shrimp baits to drop to the bottom and round out the catch when I'm there. Shallow water rockfish live in the reef year-round.

Carlsbad Kelp

This is the area's primary calico bass fishing spot and is situated right off the main part of the city of Carlsbad. These productive kelp beds can be fished nearly year-round. Here, swimming plugs, rubber swimbaits, and smaller spoons are an excellent supplement to live bait bass fishing.

These kelp beds also get their share of bigger, pelagic fish. Often, especially in spring, this area is full of barracuda, which are best fished with blue and white hard jigs in the smaller sizes. Please use single hooks so that the undersized by-catch can be returned to the water healthy and unmutilated.

Because the sea and weather are usually quite mild and pleasant, this is an excellent place to flyfish. In fact, just a couple of miles inshore from this area, the town of Vista boasts the best weather in the United States: The seasonal variation in average temperature is less than five degrees between winter and summer.

Carlsbad Power Plant Outfall Kelp

Anywhere there's a power plant, there's always an outlet for the warm water used to cool the steam condensers. In fact, all modern power plants, whether coal, oil, or nuclear, convert less than 7 percent of the total energy expended into electricity. The remainder is converted to heat and either expended up the smoke stack into the air or into the cooling water. This is not a bad thing for fish—the warmer water attracts many species normally inactive in the cooler months and provides a fishing bonanza for fishermen interested in pursuing these species.

The Carlsbad Power Plant kelp beds are not the best for calico bass but do attract plenty of yellowtail, bonito, and barracuda, along with the usual schools of mackerel. Fishing here is best done with live bait, hard jigs, or by trolling. During cooler water years, the kelp beds thicken up and also attract white seabass.

While fishing this kelp bed, don't forget to try the bottom. Surf-type fish, such as yellowfin croakers, spotfin croakers, and corbina, wandering around the flats can often be picked up. Sand sharks also frequent the area, and there's a good chance to catch a leopard shark or shovelnose guitarfish if you drift the area.

Carlsbad Canyon

Situated right off the coast of Carlsbad is a deep subsea gorge known as Carlsbad Canyon, prime habitat for many deep water rockfish species. Particularly plentiful here are bocaccio and chilipeppers, but numerous other species call this canyon home, too. The deeper you fish here, the larger the size and number of fish you'll likely catch. I like to fish at least 600 feet deep here and find it's almost a waste of effort to fish in less than 500 feet of water.

The canyon's steeper walls are the best place to fish. Work a depth line—steering the boat to follow a constant depth contour while keeping an eye on the bottom meter to find schools of feeding fish. Once you locate a likely school, move updrift (usually northwest here) and drop your lines so that they sink into the target area. Of course, on windier days, you need to move farther updrift, and on calm, balmy summer afternoons, you may not have to move much at all.

Shrimp flies, strip-baited with squid, are the best producer in this deep canyon. Red and pink, green and yellow, or blue and white are the best colors, with reds being my favorite here. In contrast to the deeper offshore banks, you don't need as much weight or as heavy line to fish here. A 4/0 reel with 30-pound test Dacron (or even better, 50-pound Spectra) and a pound of weight will suffice nicely here. I like to fish at least three hooks, but have used as many as five, especially if I have my 9/0 loaded with 80-pound test along.

Carlsbad Canyon can also be jigfished. I like to use the newer style in white, with brown- and orange-splotched rock cod jigs. I tie them to a 6-foot leader of 30-pound test mono and use a bucktail shrimp fly on a dropper loop about 4 feet above the jig as a teaser. I've brought up two fish on a rig like this. Once a fish gets hooked on one of the two lures, its thrashing motion gives lots of action to the other lure, which often gets snapped at immediately.

Access to Oceanside and Carlsbad

Oceanside and Carlsbad are situated just west of Interstate 5 (San Diego Freeway), about 30 miles north of San Diego. Oceanside Harbor is easily seen from the freeway and has its own exit. Oceanside Pier is located near the foot of Mission Street. The Pacific Coast Highway (Old Highway 101) follows the coastline more closely and is an excellent route to follow when checking out the beaches for prime fishing locales. Use the Hill Street exit from the north; from the south, take the La Costa exit west to the Pacific Coast Highway and follow it north along the coast.

Oceanside Harbor has a full-service sportfishing landing that runs half-day, three-quarter-day, and overnight trips that satisfy most demands, from casual tourists to serious, hardcore fishermen:

Helgren's Landing
315 Harbor Drive South
Oceanside, CA 92054
Harbor Drive and I-5
(760) 722-2133
www.helgrensportfishing.com

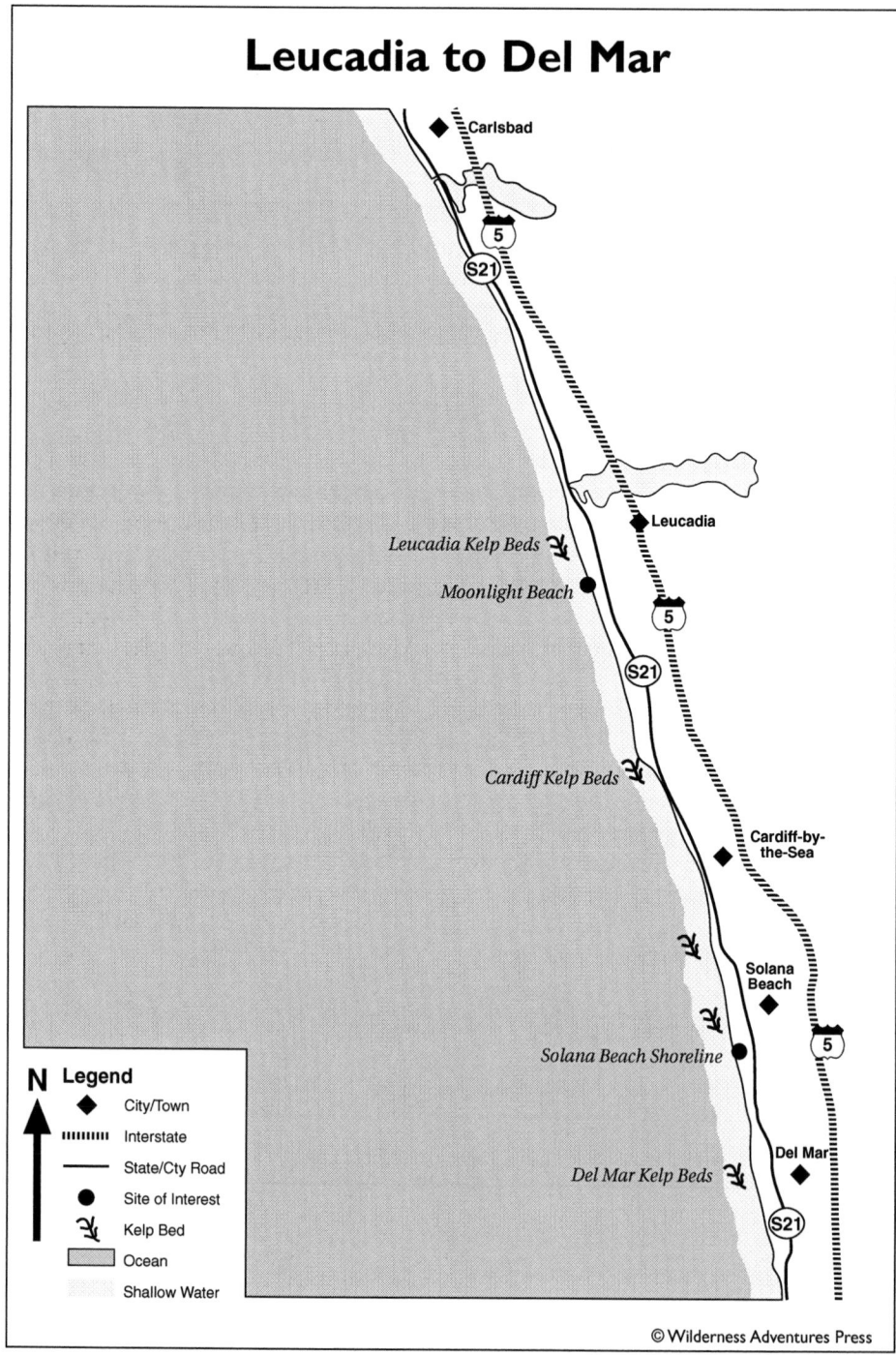

Leucadia to Del Mar

Carlsbad

5

S21

Leucadia

Leucadia Kelp Beds

Moonlight Beach

5

S21

Cardiff Kelp Beds

Cardiff-by-
the-Sea

Solana
Beach

Solana Beach Shoreline

5

Del Mar

Del Mar Kelp Beds

S21

N

Legend

◆ City/Town

||||||||| Interstate

—— State/Cty Road

● Site of Interest

🌿 Kelp Bed

▨ Ocean

▧ Shallow Water

© Wilderness Adventures Press

Leucadia to Del Mar

All along San Diego County's north coast, the terrain alternates between about a mile of sandy beach followed by a mile or so of rocky shoreline. This repeats quite a few times through the communities of Leucadia, Encinitas, Cardiff-by-the-Sea, Solana Beach, and Del Mar. When my parents moved to this area in the early 1970s, it was a fairly rural area, with sleepy beach towns separated by flower and vegetable farms. Now, it's covered with tract houses several miles inland from the beach. In addition, several major industries have relocated into this area, and industrial parks abound. Nonetheless, these communities remain one of the best areas in the United States to live. The climate is unsurpassed, with very mild winters and pleasant dry summers. The air is clean and the ocean remains both clean and filled with all manner of sea life.

Some of the better areas in this zone to fish are:

Leucadia Kelp Beds

The Leucadia kelp beds are probably a close second to the La Jolla kelp as the best near-shore surface fishing area in southern California. In the summer, yellowtail, bonito, and barracuda can be caught, as well as calico bass action year-round. In the winter, white seabass and sheephead can be found in the middle depths when fishing for calicos. In all, this is an excellent place to fish, though a bit distant from ports. The nearest port to the south is Mission Bay, about 18 miles away, and to the north, Oceanside, over 10 miles.

As with any kelp area, work the fringes with bait or lures to locate the most productive spots. You could also troll here, which is especially effective in midsummer when warmer water attracts yellowtail to the surface. Once you find a likely area, anchor up and switch to bait or hard jigs. Bonito and barracuda should also be available any time yellowtail are around.

This kelp bed is a topnotch place to fish for bass. Because of its distance from ports, it has minimal fishing pressure, although some three-quarter-day boats from Oceanside come down this far when the fishing holes closer to port aren't producing well. Work the fringes of the kelp with bait or lures, and you'll soon find your rod bending.

With plentiful fish and mild winds and currents, you'll find the Leucadia kelp beds a wonderful flyfishing destination. Fish here with an 8-weight when yellowtail aren't in season or a 10- to 12-weight in midsummer with a shooting head, fast sinking fly line having 8- to 12-pound test mono leader (there's no advantage to tapered leaders for this type of work). Blue and white or white and crystal flash streamer flies are the most effective. Cast the flies toward, but not into, the kelp. Let them sink a bit (the more overcast it is, the farther they need to sink), then use a ripping stop-and-go retrieve—your flies will get hit with amazing regularity.

One of the really fun aspects of flyfishing Leucadia's kelp beds is that you never know what you'll catch. From 10-inch calico bass and whitefish to 20-pound yellow-

This yellowfin croaker learned too late that fly-fishers also use kayaks. Photo courtesy Frank Selby—His & Her Fly Fishing Shop.

tail, this little patch of ocean has a wonderful variety of fish, both big and small. This is why you don't want to undergun yourself when fishing here.

Moonlight Beach

Moonlight Beach is found right at the foot of Encinitas Boulevard. Popular with surfers, the beach is one of the better surf fishing areas along the California coast yet remains largely undiscovered by fishermen. I love fishing Moonlight Beach when the evening high tide comes in. It always seems to produce just as the sun is setting into the Pacific and the full moon is rising.

Small green rubber grubs are excellent at Moonlight, and during winter, the little barred surfperch seem eager to sacrifice themselves for my dinner. Bloodworms, clam siphons, and mussel baits are also excellent at Moonlight and will get you plenty of surf feeders.

The beach drops off fairly quickly, and many a surf fisherman has reduced his chances by casting out too far. A 12-foot surf rod cast out 100 yards will put you way over the high tide feeding zone. I've seen corbina feeding with their backs out of the water. From where the waves are breaking to the sand is where you'll find these fish when the tide is high. Sometimes that's a band only a dozen yards or so wide.

Cardiff Kelp Beds

Right off the sleepy beach town of Cardiff-by-the-Sea, there are some very productive kelp beds. Producing excellent calico bass action, the Cardiff kelp is an excellent place to find resident species. Of course, larger pelagic species frequent the area, especially in the warmer summer months, but calicos, sheephead, and white seabass are the hot ticket year-round. The sandy bottom around the rocky reefs that provide anchorage for the kelp is also alive with resident fish, including sand bass and an excellent population of halibut. It is very likely the resident halibut are attracted to the area because of the San Elijo Lagoon outlet, a creek mouth and saltwater marsh area.

Drifting the flats that surround the kelp beds is a wise idea in addition to the usual kelp bed action. Cast diving swimming plugs around the fringes of the kelp bed to get into good bass action and send down rubber swimbaits to the rocky bottom for white seabass if they're in the neighborhood.

Another all-around option is to use live bait flylined in the warmer months or sent down with minimal weight during cooler months. From spring through fall, be on the lookout for yellowtail, bonito, and barracuda breezing by. During these months, it is always a good idea to keep an extra rod rigged with a metal bone jig in blue and white, green and yellow or a squid color in case you spot surface feeding action as schools of these fish travel through the area.

Solana Beach Shoreline

This shoreline is a wonderful place to fish: Its broad beaches attract plenty of barred surfperch, California corbina, and spotfin croaker, along with plenty of young people to enjoy the wonderful southern California sand, sea, and sunshine.

Ghost shrimp, bloodworms, razor clams, and mussel baits seem to produce the best here at Solana for croakers and corbina. It's often best to look for signs of these fish feeding in the surf and sight-cast toward them. In many areas, there are high hills above the coastline where you can scan with binoculars to see where the fish are feeding. If you don't get a hookup in a few casts, move up or down the beach. Keep trying—eventually you'll find where the fish are hanging out along the beach.

Del Mar Kelp Beds

The Del Mar kelp beds are prime calico bass habitat. Though not quite as productive for bigger pelagic species as the Leucadia kelp to the north or the La Jolla kelp to the south, the Del Mar kelp beds are nonetheless an excellent surface-fishing location. Resident bass are best enticed with live bait fished on the fringes of exposed kelp or with casting lures or rubber swimbait.

Access to the Leucadia to Del Mar Coast

From suitable harbors to the north and south, it isn't difficult to get to the ocean off this section of coast, and plenty of excellent fishing locations are found on the way. This is why it is underfished and usually produces excellent numbers and

Float tubers with fly rods catch spotted sand bass in the shadow of ritzy condominiums and yachts.
Photo courtesy Frank Selby—His & Her Fly Fishing Shop.

sizes of fish. Few party boats ever visit the area except for the northern edges of the Leucadia kelp, and then only when the Oceanside and Carlsbad kelp beds are not producing. Fishing this area usually requires a private boat.

Some people launch smaller boats through the surf to fish the Leucadia kelp. Canoes, kayaks, rubber boats, and even float tubes have all been employed successfully. The closest access to the Leucadia kelp beds is via the beach at the foot of Leucadia Boulevard, which is a popular surf destination. The downside to launching here is that you have to park up the hill and carry your boat down some stairs to get to the water. A more accessible launch spot is from the broad beaches just north of the town of Leucadia and then working your way south to the kelp beds.

The closest port for a trailered boat is Oceanside Small Craft Harbor. This excellent facility has all the amenities, including excellent launch ramps, live bait, tackle shops, and an excellent transient dock if you want to leave your boat in the water for a few days. Contact the Oceanside Harbor Master at 760-966-4570 for more information.

Torrey Pines State Beach to La Jolla

La Jolla is usually considered one of the best near-shore kelp bed fishing spots along the California coast. La Jolla (pronounced "la hoya") is probably the premier residential community in all of San Diego County. This is due, in no small part, to the mountainous projection of Point La Jolla into the Pacific Ocean. Where there is a mountainous rocky structure on shore, there is a rocky erose sea floor adjacent. La Jolla is no exception and features a deep canyon, stretching nearly 3 miles down within a very few miles of shore. The near-shore sea bottom is very erose and rocky, so plenty of submerged reefs, caves, and canyons are available to provide habitat for many species of fish.

A rocky bottom also provides a good anchoring point for kelp, and the La Jolla area is home to some of the broadest stretches of kelp forests in all of southern California. This also provides additional habitat for the major game fish species in the area.

Torrey Pines Artificial Reefs

Nestled below the cliffs of the beautiful Torrey Pines coastline, made famous for its tournament-caliber golf course, two artificial reefs were built to provide habitat for many fish species. The first of these, Torrey Pines Artificial Reef #1 was built in 1964 with about 1,000 tons of quarry rock. It covers a site about an acre in size but has since silted over substantially, and now only a very low relief of exposed rocks remains. Nonetheless, it still attracts and holds both baitfish and game fish on occasion, particularly calico bass and blacksmith perch. This reef is located 2.5 nautical miles on a 352° magnetic heading from the La Jolla tower in 67 feet of water at 32°-53'-12" N × 117°-15'-50" W.

The second reef was built in 1975 of 3,000 tons of quarry rock and augmented in 1979 with old concrete dock floats and provides a larger, more diverse habitat, including sheephead and some California lobster. It sits in only 44 feet of water, 3 nautical miles from the La Jolla tower on a 359° heading at 32°-53'-35" N × 117°-15'-35" W.

Fishing these reefs is like fishing any other shallow water, rocky-bottomed area. Live bait on a Carolina rig, shrimp flies, rubber swimbait, and hard jigs all produce fairly well. On those occasions when baitfish get driven to the surface by deeper predators, which for birds to locate the best fishing.

La Jolla Canyon

Just north of La Jolla Point, the extremely deep La Jolla Canyon rises from depths of nearly 3 miles deep just a few miles offshore and ends in La Jolla Cove. This fascinating piece of underwater topography brings nutrient laden water from deeper waters into La Jolla Cove, making it home to an amazing variety of life. La Jolla Cove itself is a marine sanctuary where it is not permitted to take any living organisms. With an almost tropical reef appearance teeming with different species of fish, shellfish, and marine plants, the cove is a favorite destination for snorkelers and scuba divers.

Torrey Pines State Beach to La Jolla

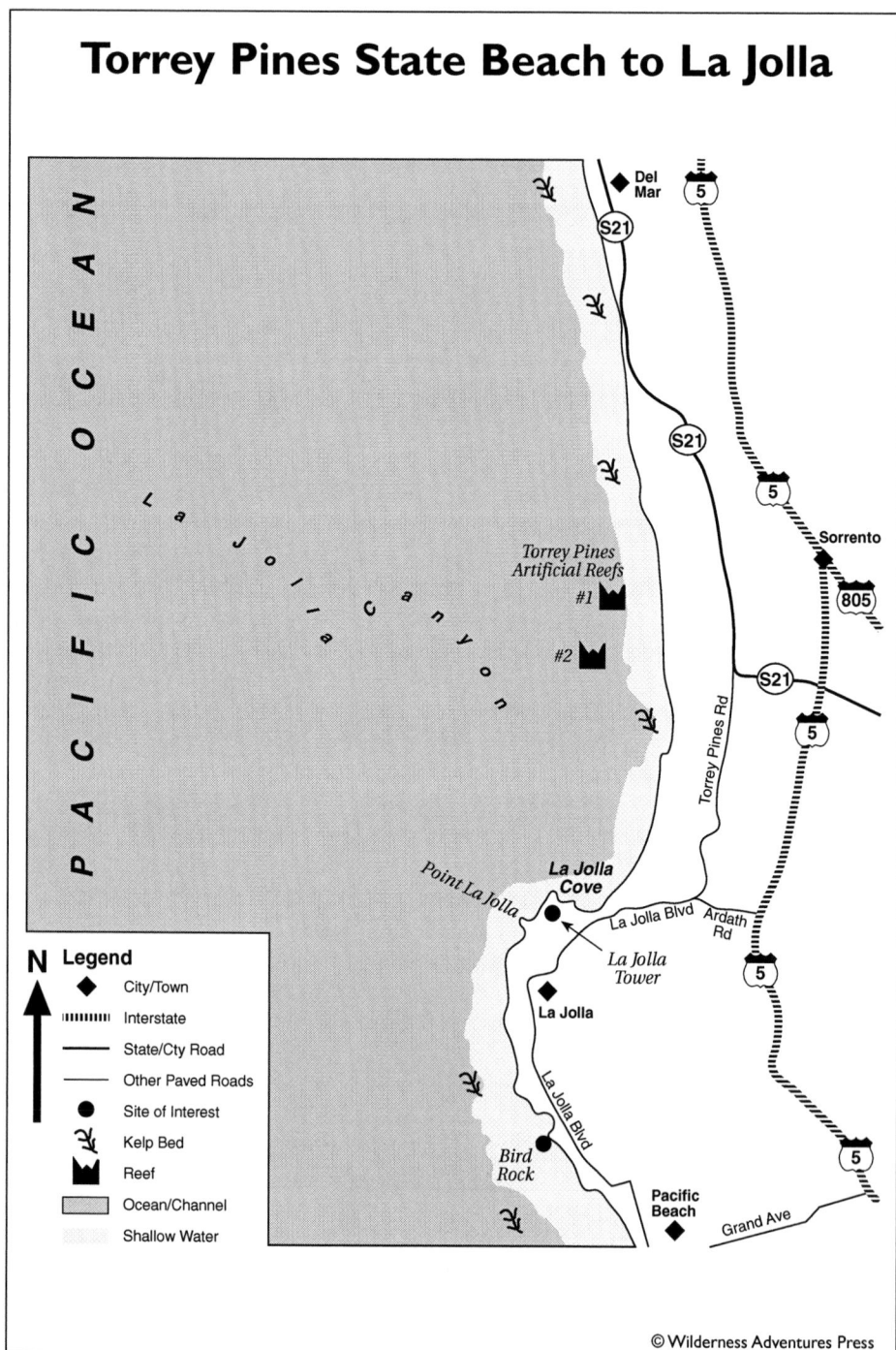

© Wilderness Adventures Press

Away from the Cove, outside the sanctuary, the steep walls of La Jolla Canyon are a fascinating place to catch deep water rockfish. Several species, very rare in southern California, such as sablefish (black cod), reside in the canyon along with the usual deep water rockfish.

There is no way to fish La Jolla Canyon without a good bottom meter. The steep-sided canyon means you could miss the water depth by thousands of feet with only a short surface displacement. You must meter the canyon walls for fish, dropping on the fish only when you find likely schools. Once you locate the schools, move updrift just a short distance and drop on the spots so that your lines will pass through the schools. Often the drift is north to south, so if you're fishing the south wall, you have very little time before the drift takes you much too high on the wall where you are in danger of losing your deep water tackle.

Good schools of reds (vermillion rockfish), chilipeppers, and bocaccios inhabit the canyon, but you're likely to find many other different species of deep water fish here. The usual anchovy-baited bare hooks, squid-baited shrimp flies, and other typical deep water gear all work just fine at the La Jolla Canyon.

La Jolla Kelp

The La Jolla kelp beds possibly offer the best-producing surface fish action all along the coast. To find better fishing grounds, you would have to venture south to the Islas Coronados or out to the offshore islands. At the age of 16 after having just moved to California from the Midwest, this is where I caught my first yellowtail, bonito, and barracuda. When my father and I graduated from the fishing barges and half-day boats to three-quarter-day boats fishing the La Jolla kelp beds, we thought we'd discovered Valhalla. It's also here that I broke my first fishing pole, got spooled for the first time, and discovered how to fish with conventional instead of spinning tackle without getting birdnest snags every time I tried to cast.

The kelp beds off Point La Jolla are thicker nearer shore, but this is not the best place to fish. Look for the deeper kelp just outside the thicker kelp, where you can fish freely without the annoyances of thick kelp bed fishing. The water is generally fairly clear, so the fishing can be downright exciting as you actually see your bait getting hit.

As it is with any kelp bed fishing, live bait is king at La Jolla. Hard jigs are a close second, with swimming plugs and rubber swimbaits following. On some days, it doesn't seem to matter what you have on the end of the line—it'll get hit. On other days, fish can be pickier.

La Jolla's kelp beds can be an excellent place to sight-cast. When you actually see a game fish, cast a plug or lure to entice the fish into a strike. Keep track of bait in the water, including chum, and you'll see plenty of opportunities for this type of fishing.

Speaking of sight casting, don't forget your fly rod at La Jolla! Blue and white streamer flies for calico bass, bonito, barracuda and yellowtail, or crystal and white flies for these species on brighter, sunny days are just the ticket to break into saltwater flyfishing. Once you land the fly in the fish's vicinity, use a fast, ripping retrieve to drive the game fish wild.

Bird Rock off the La Jolla coastline is a popular place to fish and dive, both from the shore and from boats—just watch out for boiler rocks if you approach by boat.

Bird Rock

Just off the beach, near the end of rocky Point La Jolla, lies a massive offshore exposed rock, covered with guano, called Bird Rock. It's probably less than an acre in size but it seems larger. Bird Rock is readily seen off La Jolla Village Drive, and the name has been used for many of the businesses along the drive.

The Bird Rock area can be fished from shore, from a boat out of Mission Bay, or even from a kayak or rubber raft launched from the beach. Plenty of shallow water rockfish call Bird Rock their home, and a variety of species can be caught from shore. Plenty of different species of surfperch inhabit Bird Rock, along with calico bass, sculpin (California scorpionfish), and sheephead. Even white seabass can be seen lurking around Bird Rock's craggy underwater structure in search of a tasty morsel.

Both live bait and other cut bait work well at Bird Rock. There's a predator for nearly any kind of offering you might use, including mussels, clams, shrimp, and cut squid. Rubber swimbaits seem to excel here as opposed to harder jigs. Fish deep structure to lure reef fish out of their holes and on to your bait. It is often best to keep the drag very snug for the initial run, since the fish's instinct is to head for a cave, often sawing the line off as it passes the rough entrance. Once the fish is headed your direction, you can back off the drag if your catch is heavier than your line strength.

Access for Torrey Pines to La Jolla

The offshore fishing spots in La Jolla are regularly visited by two sportfishing landings based in Mission Bay: Seaforth Sportfishing and Islandia Sportfishing, both described in the Mission Bay segment of this chapter. The three-quarter-day boats, particularly in the summer, almost always visit the La Jolla kelp beds to take part in the plentiful surface fishing action.

The short jaunt to the La Jolla area by private boat from Mission Bay is usually easy and uncomplicated, particularly in summer. The excellent visibility and minimal seas that prevail make it a reasonably easy trip for any seaworthy boat; however, I strongly suggest that you leave your lake boats at home unless you possess the knowledge, skill, and appropriate equipment to operate offshore because this is an ocean voyage.

The shore fishing area near Bird Rock is accessible from the north via La Jolla Village Drive from Interstate 5 and from the south via Garnet Street in Pacific Beach.

Pacific Beach and Mission Bay

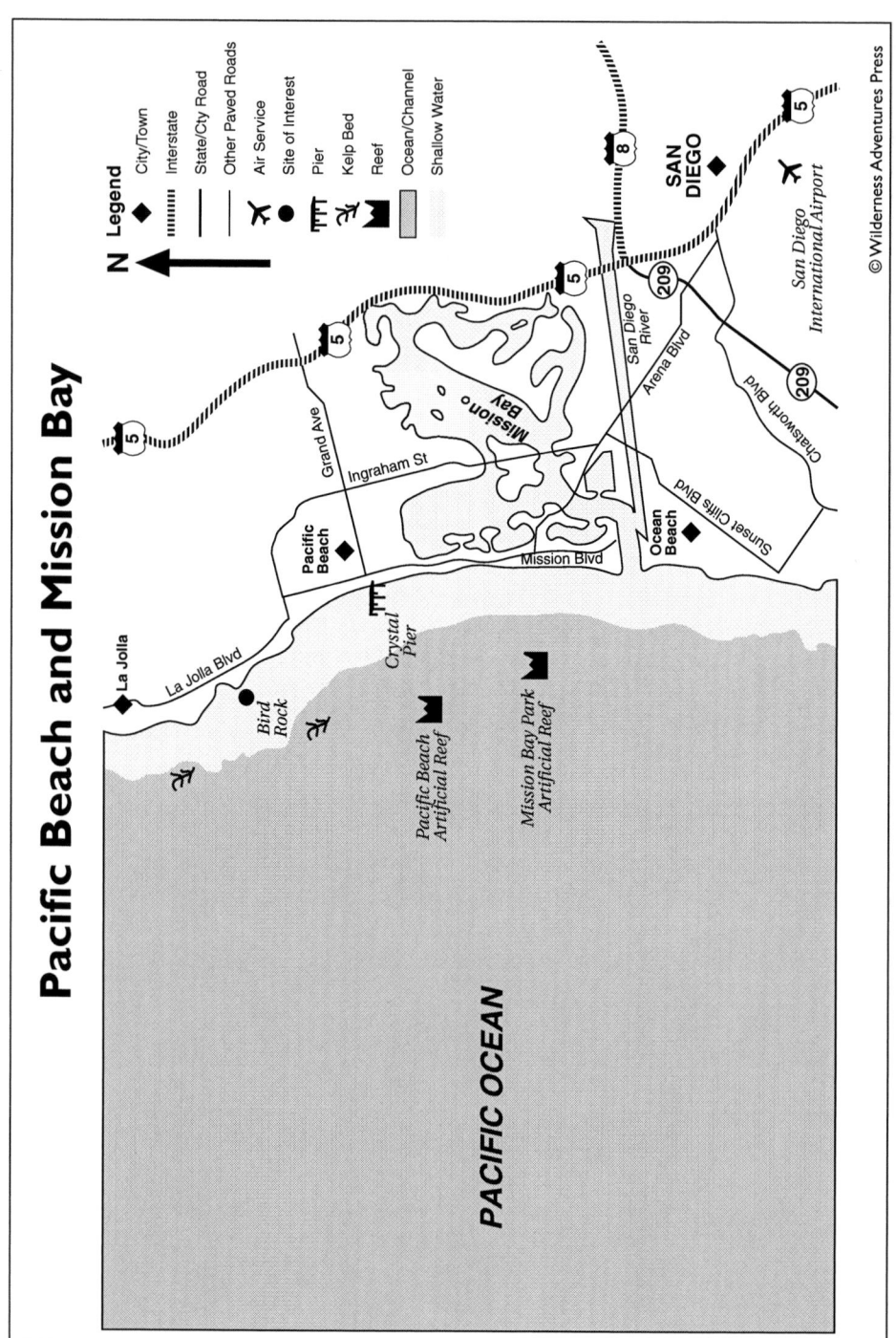

Legend

♦ City/Town
▬ Interstate
— State/Cty Road
✕ Other Paved Roads
● Air Service
⚲ Site of Interest
♒ Pier
⚓ Kelp Bed
▬ Reef
▒ Ocean/Channel
Shallow Water

N

PACIFIC OCEAN

La Jolla

Bird Rock

La Jolla Blvd

Crystal Pier

Pacific Beach Artificial Reef

Mission Bay Park Artificial Reef

Pacific Beach

Grand Ave

Ingraham St

Mission Blvd

Mission Bay

Ocean Beach

Sunset Cliffs Blvd

San Diego River

Arena Blvd

Chatsworth Blvd

209

209

SAN DIEGO

8

5

5

5

5

San Diego International Airport

© Wilderness Adventures Press

Pacific Beach and Mission Bay

Mission Bay is undoubtedly one of the finest yacht harbors in the world. Excellent facilities for every sort of water activity, particularly boating and fishing, are abundant. Originally a salt marsh, it was made into a bay back when it was considered progress rather than the destruction of a wetland. It is now a fabulous vacation destination area, including Sea World and all sorts of restaurants, hotels, and resorts along its beautiful shores.

Crystal Pier

Crystal Pier is unusual in that it offers motel rooms right on the pier. It's also one of the more consistent fishing piers in all of southern California. With some of the best pier fishing for barred surfperch, walleye surfperch (blue perch), and guitarfish, as well as pretty respectable halibut fishing, it's no wonder that this is a favorite spot for tourists and locals alike. There is also productive fishing for calico bass and sand bass at the pier's end, the center offers white croakers, and corbina and yellowfin croakers are found near the surf line in warmer months.

The pier is open from 7AM until 7PM for day visitors, but for those staying in the motel, it's open all night. It has restrooms, a fish cleaning station, benches, and lighting at night. Parking can be a problem, being limited to the metered curbside parking on the streets near the pier.

The best fishing is usually from the surf line to about halfway out, using bloodworms, sand crabs, ghost shrimp, clam siphons, anchovy pieces, or even cut squid. Some fishermen use drop nets to catch live bait, which works quite well and is probably the best way to get a halibut from the pier.

Pacific Beach Artificial Reef

Past the artificial reef in Mission Bay Park, another artificial reef is found two and a half miles from the Mission Bay channel entrance on a 324 magnetic course. This one is composed of 10,000 tons of quarry rock covering about 100 acres. While this doesn't attract as many divers as the closer, more interesting Mission Bay Park reef, it also has excellent sportfishing. Many sand bass, calico bass, and shallow water rockfish call this area home.

Mission Bay Park Artificial Reef

One nautical mile from the entrance to Mission Bay on a 324-degree (magnetic) heading lies an artificial reef made from the scuttled remains of three ships. The locals call it wreck alley, and it serves as a haven for many species of fish. It's a popular scuba diving spot as well, being so close to shore and the very popular Mission Bay small craft marinas. The site covers about 175 acres. Plentiful shallow water rockfish, calico bass, and pelagic species can be found nearby feasting on the bounty of small marine species seeking refuge from the open sea in the nooks and crannies of these sunken ships.

Pacific Beach Flats

Back in my college days, my father bought an 18-foot boat. It was home built and had a 50 HP Johnson Sea Horse engine that had to be at least 20 years old. I'm sure it was a good, reliable engine when new, but the engine probably hadn't had the kind of maintenance and attention it deserved, so it was a bit cantankerous, especially after warming up. We often headed to the La Jolla kelp beds to get in on the yellowtail action, but sometimes the old engine just decided it wasn't going to make it all the way up to La Jolla. Being the adaptable types, we opted to drift-fish out in front of the Mission Bay channel until the engine cooled down and we could restart it.

This was where I discovered the fun of flats fishing. This kind of sets me apart from a lot of fishermen, because I really like this type of fishing. It's relaxing, action-filled, and far less technique-oriented than kelp bed fishing. Basically, you bait up, drop to the bottom, and wait.

This is also where my mother caught an 8-foot thresher shark, which was also the first time I saw a big shark up close and personal—they're really something to see. We often caught sand bass, halibut, sanddabs, guitarfish, sculpin, opaleye, croakers, and surfperch at these flats. Part of the fun was never knowing what you might pull in. When fishing the kelp beds, you know instantly what type of fish you have by the strike, but on the flats, you almost never know what you have until you get the fish up to the boat.

The best bet to fish here is to use live bait. A Carolina rig that has just enough sinker to get to the bottom is the best rig, and the sinker should be at least 24 inches above the hook. I usually start with three-quarter ounce and adjust up or down from there. I use a #2 hook if the anchovies are running bigger or step down to a #4 in late summer when the anchovies are smaller.

Drop the bait to the bottom and let it sit for a bit, paying out line as the boat slowly drifts. When the line is out at about a 45-degree angle, lift the sinker off the bottom, crank the line in a few turns, then let it settle on the bottom again—then repeat. You should be able to feel the anchovy struggling at all times. If not, haul it in and rebait because the anchovy has expired. When you get hit, allow the fish to run with the bait for a slow three-count before engaging the reel and setting the hook.

This same technique can be used with a rubber swimbait. The old mojo and scampi lures work well in this kind of environment, especially when sweetened with a thin strip of cut squid. It gives the fish a natural odor to follow, important in a place like this where the water is often murky from the wave action on nearby beaches.

Fishing in Mission Bay

Mission Bay offers a variety of bay species and has some very good shark and ray fishing. Probably the best place to fish in the bay is Quivira Basin, where the bait barge is located—always a good place to find fish. Back when I fished Quivira Basin on an almost daily basis, I saw the biggest bat ray I'd ever seen lying on the bait

The convenient and well maintained boat launch ramps in Mission Bay.

barge. One of the deck hands had caught it early that morning. It must have weighed nearly 80 pounds and exceeded 5 feet from wingtip to wingtip—what a sight!

The main channel is another good place to fish. Although it is often crowded with boat traffic, the edges are the best places to fish anyway, either from a small boat or standing on the shore. The west end of Quivira Street is a particularly good place to drop a line, since you can fish the rocky edges for bass and other reef species or cast out into the deeper flats for sharks or flatfish. The northern jetty of the main channel is also accessible from the Pacific Beach side, and on a sunny summer Sunday, you'll likely see more than a few fishermen dropping a line from the rocks.

Fish where the rock jetties meet the bottom for calico bass, spotted sand bass, and several other species. Live bait is the best, but many types of rubber swimbaits, swimming plugs, and lures all have their days. For flats fish out in the channels, live anchovies or cut squid are both effective. Mussels and clams can be also used and often add some variety to the mixed bag of fish you're likely to encounter in Mission Bay.

After the tourists go home, the swimming beaches in Mission Bay are prime spots for leopard sharks. I used to go there often and had great fun hauling the sharks up on the beach. Dead anchovies and cut squid really got their attention. These sharks are bottom feeders, so a Carolina rig with a sliding egg sinker is the best bet. Cast out and slowly retrieve; then stop, retrieve and stop—when a 6-foot leopard pounces, you're sure you've been hit.

Access to the Pacific Beach / Mission Bay Area

Mission Bay is readily accessible from Interstate 5 (San Diego Freeway) or from Interstate 8. Just take the Sea World Drive exit west and you're there. Excellent launch facilities are located at:

Dana Landing Marina
2590 Ingraham Street
San Diego, CA
(Ingraham Street and
West Mission Bay Drive)
(619) 224-2513

South Shores Park
Along Sea World Drive
San Diego, CA
(619) 221-8901

De Anza Cove
De Anza Bay Drive
San Diego, CA
(Off North Mission Bay Drive)
(619) 221-8901

In addition, both Mission Bay sportfishing landings can be found in Quivira Basin:

Seaforth Sportfishing
1717 Quivira Road
San Diego, CA 92109
(619) 224-3383
www.seaforthlanding.com

Islandia Sportfishing
1551 West Mission Bay Drive
San Diego Ca 92109
(619) 222-1164
www.islandiasportfishing.com

These two landings offer full service sport fishing trips including local trips to the flats and kelp beds, with especially easy access to the excellent La Jolla kelp bed areas, and overnight trips for tuna and island fishing.

Ocean Beach and Point Loma

The guardian and protector of San Diego Bay is a huge mountain called Point Loma that keeps the prevailing northwesterly seas out of San Diego Harbor. It also holds fog banks at bay. I've often seen it foggy along the outer part of the point and blue skies and bright sunshine just inside the harbor. This is especially true in spring months when low clouds and fog, the so-called "Marine Layer," is an every morning and afternoon affair.

The coastline adjacent to Point Loma is a continuation of the mountain, with a craggy, rocky bottom and deep canyons—ideal habitat for growing kelp. One of the most productive kelp beds lies just outside San Diego Harbor next to Point Loma. There is also some excellent shore fishing along Point Loma's west-facing coast. This is rock and kelp type fishing as opposed to the usual California beach fishing and offers the shore angler a very interesting alternative to much of the usual beach fishing.

Ocean Beach Pier

This is a very good fishing pier, and its long length, almost 2000 feet, gets it out very near the northern edge of the Point Loma kelp bed. This means some kelp species, such as calico bass and barracuda, can be taken there. The end of the pier is a T-shape almost 400 feet wide. Though many people go there to fish, it's rarely crowded because of its huge size.

The pier is open 24 hours a day and features a free parking lot at its base, a bait and tackle shop, a snack shop, restrooms, and a number of fish cleaning stations—very well quipped for the fisherman.

Out at the ends, especially the south extension, kelp bass and sand bass are found from spring through fall. The ideal bait is a live anchovy, but they're not available at the pier. You could buy them in one of the bays and keep them alive in an aerated bait bucket, which is difficult and a bit expensive. Instead, use baitfish-imitating lures, such as blue rubber swimbaits and casting plugs.

Cut squid sometimes attracts bass, also. I've often used a small squid head with tentacles on a #2 hook with a half-ounce sliding sinker allowed to slide all the way to the hook to entice both calicos and sand bass. Sometimes, shrimp flies, baited with squid and sent down to the bottom with a sinker (don't take your fly rod on the pier!) also attract bass and other species, such as sanddabs, halibut, and sculpin.

A metal jig cast out and retrieved rapidly sometimes entices bass to hit when everyone else is using some other type of bait. You also have a good chance of hooking a barracuda or bonito this way because they love to hit jigs. Sight casting for bonito here can be a lot of fun. Watch for boils of these fish ripping through the schools of bait that sometimes hang around the pier. When you see this, cast a white and chrome bonito feather right in their path. Though this technique was more workable many years ago, it still works when these fish are around and shouldn't necessarily be shunned just because you can't do it every day. If you're there when the bonito are feeding, give it a try. The "dog days" of summer offer the most potential for sight casting to bonito.

Ocean Beach and Point Loma

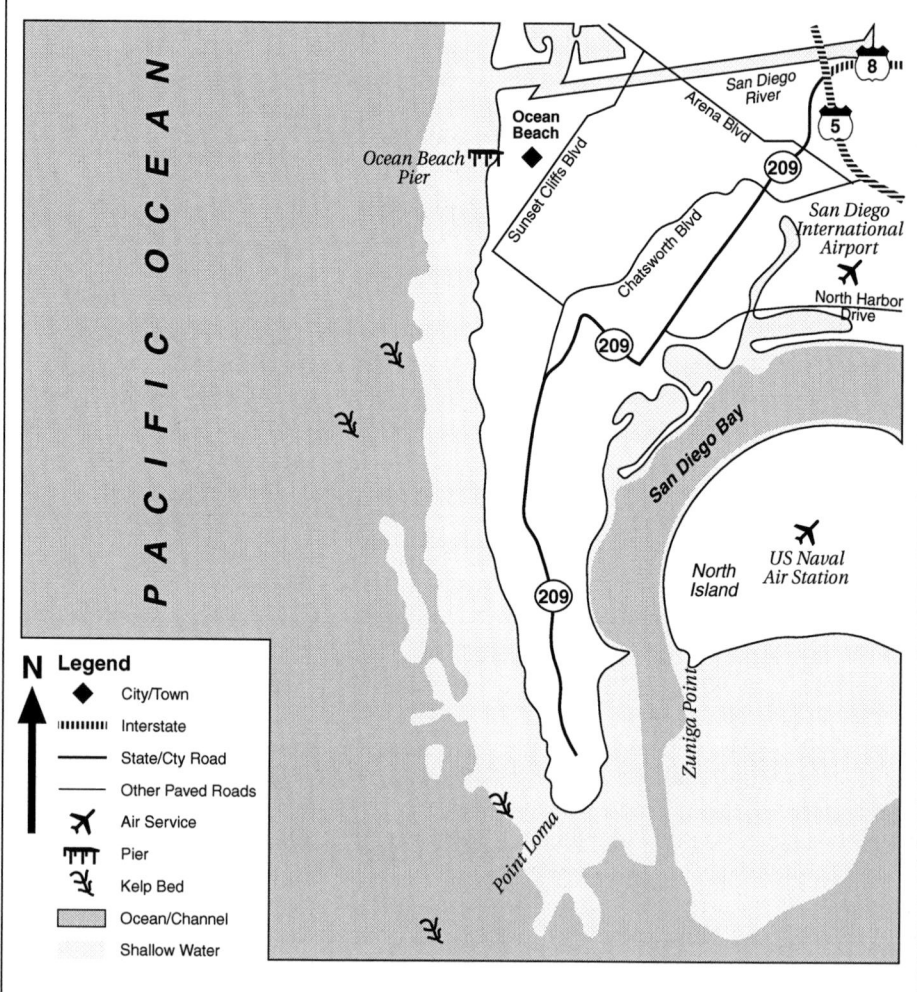

A rocky area near the foot of the pier's north side offers a variety of fish that isn't commonly found on California beach-style piers. In the right tidal conditions, opaleye, several types of perch, and even an occasional California lobster can be found. It's an experience not to be missed when fishing the pier.

The other surf species are also available: barred perch, corbina, and spotfins in the surf line, and sharks, jacksmelt, and white croaker along the middle of the pier.

Sunset Cliffs

Sunset Cliffs offers a number of places where the shore casting can be excellent. A number of species not ordinarily caught from shore are available here because it's possible to cast almost out to the kelp beds. Calico bass and shallow water rockfish are the mainstay of the Sunset Cliffs area, but occasionally barracuda, bonito, opaleye, and blue perch are possible. Fish this area as if you were fishing the edges of kelp beds using surface lures, cut squid bait, or rubber swimbaits. If there were a good way to get live anchovies here, it would prove a boon to fishing this area.

Ocean Beach

Known for its easygoing party lifestyle, Ocean Beach, with its white sand and warm sunshine, is a place everyone ought to visit at least once. Plenty of people come here and enjoy a variety of pastimes, so the best time to fish is early morning or evenings, when the beach has less activity, and especially when a high tide is happening.

Very good barred surfperch fishing, along with California corbina, spotfin croaker, and yellowfin croaker, is available along this stretch of beach. Occasionally, you can get a bite from leopard sharks, usually at night, and halibut during the day.

Ghost shrimp work best, but bloodworms, mussels, and clam siphons are also good surf fishing producers. This is a fairly flat beach and doesn't drop off very fast, so either cast well out or wade a bit to get the bait out to the surf line for best results.

Point Loma Kelp

All along Point Loma there is a thick, dense kelp forest, one of the largest along the southern California coast, known as the Point Loma Kelp. In some years, the kelp is so thick, it looks as though you could walk across it. This may be one of the best calico bass fishing areas on the entire coast. Big bull calicos have been the staple fish of this area for many, many years. Half-day boats go out daily to this kelp bed from San Diego Harbor, and only minutes out of port, both experienced and novice fishermen can be enjoying this plentiful fish. During warmer summer months, barracuda, bonito, and yellowtail call Point Loma home.

Flylining live bait is the best way to catch fish here. Bass eagerly snap at any frisky bait presented properly. Once, when fishing at Point Loma, I found a beautiful, 10-inch long brown bait (herring) mixed in with the usual anchovies. I waited until the bite was strong to load the herring on a hook and pitch it right to the edges of the kelp. I was sure I was in for a world record, or failing that, at least a magnificent

A fighting yellowtail can sure put a bend in a heavy, saltwater rod.
Photo courtesy Frank Selby—His & Her Fly Fishing Shop.

trophy-sized big bull calico. The bait was inhaled all right, not by my world record breaker but by an 11-inch calico. The calico ate bait that was nearly as long as it was. I didn't even have the privilege of filleting and eating that fish (the minimum size is 12 inches)—I had to toss it back.

The usual kelp bed fishing techniques apply at Point Loma. Trolling, casting flies, casting swimming plugs, and casting jigs all result in decent catches of typical kelp bed fish, such as barracuda, bonito, calico bass, and of course, the king of the kelp, yellowtail, when in season. Going to the bottom for white seabass, sheephead, sculpin, and rockfish is also an effective technique, especially when the surface bite is shut down due to weather, season, or if you simply want to round out your catch.

For an easy to reach, local spot, the Point Loma kelp offers consistent kelp bed fishing. In my opinion, only one area surpasses it, La Jolla, which is farther from a port and rather difficult to get to—an hour or two—unless you have a really fast boat. It's more of an all-day trip.

Access to Ocean Beach and Point Loma

Ocean Beach and Point Loma are readily accessible from either San Diego Harbor (Shelter Island launch ramps are the closest) or from Mission Bay, farther north. Mission Bay is an excellent, well-equipped small craft harbor with plenty of facilities, ranging from basic to luxurious. (See the section on Mission Bay.)

All the three major sportfishing landings in San Diego Harbor send half-day boats to the Point Loma kelp nearly year-round. In addition, many six-pack charter boats can be booked out of these fishing landings for those interested in a step up in comfort and luxury while fishing. These landings are:

Point Loma Sport Fishing
1403 Scott Street
San Diego, CA 92106-2767
Phone: 619-223-1627
Fax : 619-223-1591
www.pointlomasportfishing.com

Fisherman's Landing
2838 Garrison Street
San Diego, CA
619-221-8506
www.fishermanslanding.com

H&M Landing
2803 Emerson Street
San Diego, CA 92106
Voice: 619-222-1144
Fax: 619-222-0784
www.hmlanding.com

To get to Ocean Beach and the Ocean Beach Pier from the north, take Sea World Drive West off Interstate 5 to Sunset Cliffs Boulevard. Follow this to Newport Avenue, turn right and follow it to the pier parking lot. From the south, you can take Nimitz Boulevard off I-5 to Sunset Cliffs Boulevard and turn left on Newport. Continuing down Sunset Cliffs Boulevard takes you to the Sunset Cliffs area for shore fishing.

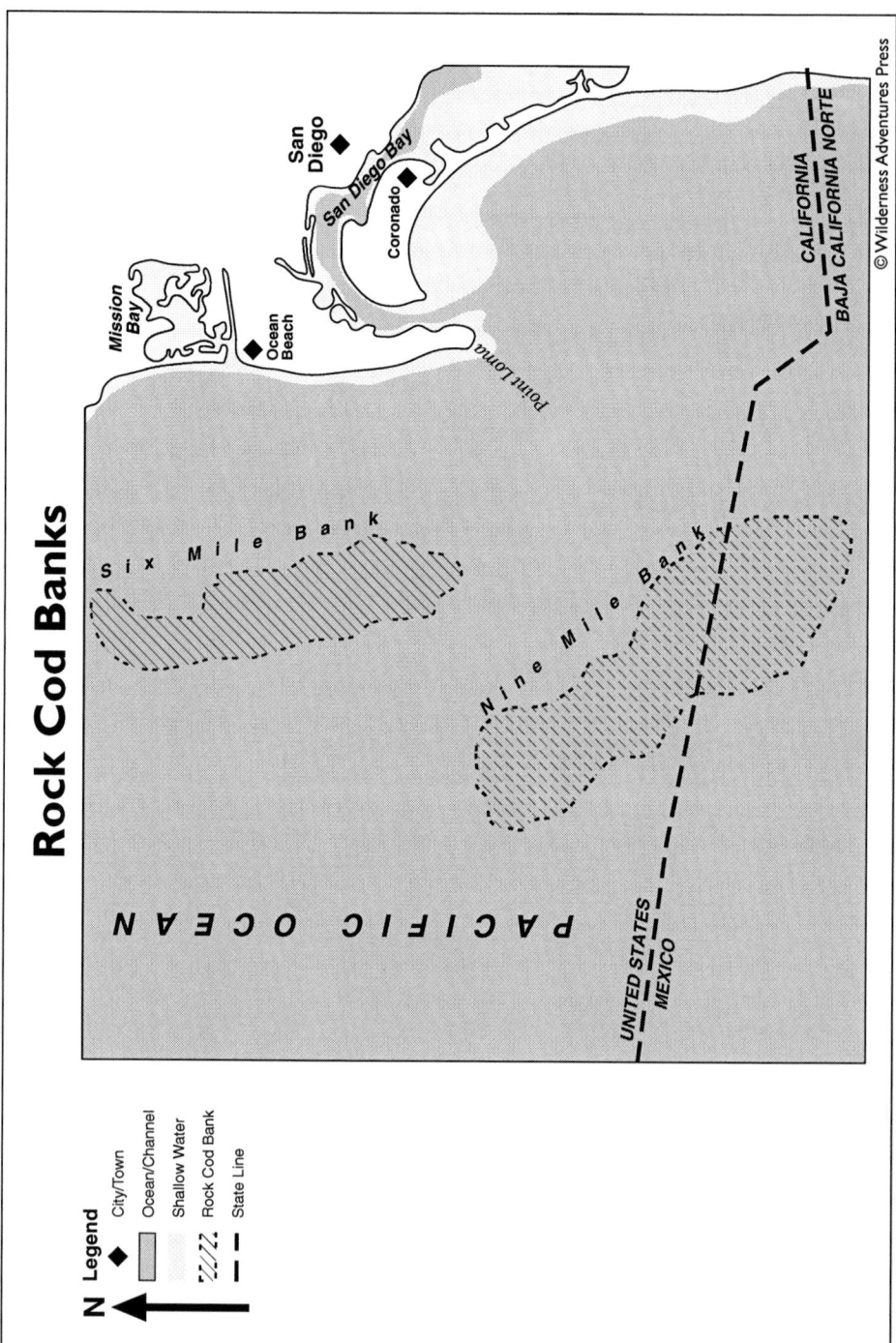

Rock Cod Banks

Rock Cod Banks

Two deep underwater banks that form two undersea mountain ranges are found just 6 and 9 miles off Point Loma. These formations are called, appropriately, Six Mile Bank and Nine Mile Bank. Though well fished, these two banks are capable of yielding up limits of deep water rockfish.

Fishing these banks requires more reliance on reading the fish finder than anything else. A well-executed search pattern is the best approach, keeping an eye on the depth sounder looking for fish. Once the school is spotted, a cloverleaf pattern is often driven to find the center of the school or highest point of the feeding fish. The boat is then maneuvered upcurrent of the school, and the lines are dropped and allowed to drift through the school.

Of course, the best option here is bucktail flies sent down in multiple hook gangions and baited with thin strips of cut squid. Other approaches include live bait, salted dead anchovies, and even jigs fished deep. Rock cod aren't particularly fussy about what they eat, but the right things on the right day yields the best quality fish and most consistent strikes.

Six Mile Bank

Six Mile Bank isn't really a bank—it's more like a dropoff from the shallow coastal plain to the valley lying between Six Mile Bank and Nine. While this area has been heavily fished for years, it still supports an excellent supply of deep water rockfish. The shallower parts of this area don't yield the size, number, and quality species that the deeper areas hold. In the deeper, rougher areas, reds (vermillion rockfish) and bocaccio are prevalent. In shallower water, chilipeppers become more common.

Six Mile Bank is best fished starting at about 450 feet. Follow the 450-foot line looking for schools on the bottom meter. If this doesn't produce, check the 500-foot line, and keep going deeper until schools are located. Once a school is located, drop squid-baited bucktail flies for best results or break out the jigs. Smaller 7X-sized jigs are the best performers on a 6-foot leader with a bucktail fly "teaser" about 4 feet above the jig.

Along the northern part of Six Mile Bank, almost directly west of the Mission Bay entrance, there's a big hole in the bottom in about 450 feet of water. An area about the size of a football field sinks to nearly 30 feet below the surrounding bank. The bottom of this hole is rocky and erose. Local fishermen call this the "Airplane Hole" and keep its location very quiet. It has been years since I fished this spot, but I always caught fish there. I fished there before the Global Positioning System was available and am unsure of its exact location, bit if you're out there metering fish and suddenly come to a sharp dropoff, then 50 to 100 yards later the bottom rises again, you've found the Airplane Hole.

Nine Mile Bank

Nine Mile Bank stretches from south of the Mexican Border nearly to Mission Bay. It rises in depth from about 1500 feet to less than 600 when approached from the east. The fishing at Nine Mile Bank is usually better than at Six Mile Bank. I'd suggest bypassing Six Mile for Nine Mile. Go back to Six Mile only if Nine Mile is barren.

Fish Nine Mile just as you would Six, but instead of starting at 75 fathoms (450 feet), start at 100 (600 feet). I actually prefer fishing even deeper, down to 1000 feet if given a choice. The fish are bigger and more plentiful. It is a lot of work, though, and you get a good workout just winching the gangions in.

Access to the Rock Cod Banks

The two deep water rock cod banks are best fished from private boats. They are equally accessible from either Mission Bay or from San Diego Harbor. Both of these facilities are very well equipped for trailer boats and feature extensive accommodations, dining, fishing tackle, bait, boat maintenance, fuel, and alternative activities. Either of these locales is excellent for family resort fun.

Without a boat, the only way to fish these banks is during winter. The sportfishing fleet based at Mission Bay makes trips here in winter only when other shallow water fishing has shut down. They may not go here every day of the week, either. You should call and ask if they're planning any deep water rock cod trips to make sure you show up with the right gear. Don't assume just because it's winter they'll be deep water rock fishing. They may drift the flats for sculpin and flatfish, or run to the artificial reefs for resident bass. If you're there with your 9/0 reel and 80-pound test, you won't have much fun watching everyone else catch fish.

The main two landings in Mission Bay are:

Islandia Sportfishing
1551 West Mission Bay Drive
San Diego, CA 92109
619-222-1164

Seaforth Sportfishing
1717 Quivira Road
San Diego, CA 92109
619-224-3383

San Diego Harbor

Within San Diego Harbor, some very good year-round fishing is available to almost anyone. Rocky shores, sandy beaches, piers, and breakwaters abound, as well as facilities for launching small craft, and even rental boats are available for some fun, productive fishing.

San Diego Harbor is a huge, natural bay, well protected from the northwesterly seas by the Point Loma Peninsula on the northwest and the Coronado/North Island Peninsula on the southwest. San Diego Harbor is an excellent deep water port and has been in continuous use for hundreds of years.

In 1867, a former New Englander named Alonzo Horton bought nearly 1000 acres of land along the harbor for about 27 cents per acre and offered the land free to anyone who would build on it. This spawned new growth in the harbor and gradually the city center shifted from the Old Town area to what is now downtown San Diego surrounding the scenic harbor. The majority of downtown San Diego is within sight of San Diego Harbor.

Right after the turn of the century, when the United States realized that it needed a military presence in the Pacific, San Diego became one of the most important naval ports on the West Coast. The excellent deep water harbor and mild climate were ideal for stationing a major Pacific fleet. With the growth of air power as an integral part of Navy operations, a major airfield was developed on the end of North Island, the Navy portion of Coronado Peninsula. This airfield still serves many of the Navy's fleet aircraft.

Since then, a fabulous resort city has grown up around the harbor, with beautiful hotels and an excellent airport, Lindbergh Field. This airfield is the home of Ryan Aircraft, manufacturers of the famous "Spirit of St. Louis," which carried Charles Lindbergh safely from New York to Paris in his famous 1927 flight. The airfield is now a major international airport, servicing the United States and many foreign destinations.

San Diego Harbor is a great place to fish. Both resident bay species and pelagic species range throughout the bay. Near the end of January, the San Diego Bass Tournament takes place. Every year, 200 two-person teams compete for cash prizes and gifts. Nearly every year, most teams manage to catch a limit of bass, which demonstrates the excellent year-round fishing available in the harbor.

Some of the better places to fish in the harbor include:

The South Jetty

Probably the best, most consistent fishing action in San Diego Harbor is found along the channel entrance. This area is known for producing not only good bass action but also such bigger pelagic species as yellowtail and white seabass, which have been known to frequent this area. The close proximity of the Point Loma kelp beds helps keep the area stocked with plenty of new fish every year. They wander away from the safety of the kelp while chasing bait and discover the excellent cover and plentiful food supply the rock wall has to offer.

San Diego Harbor

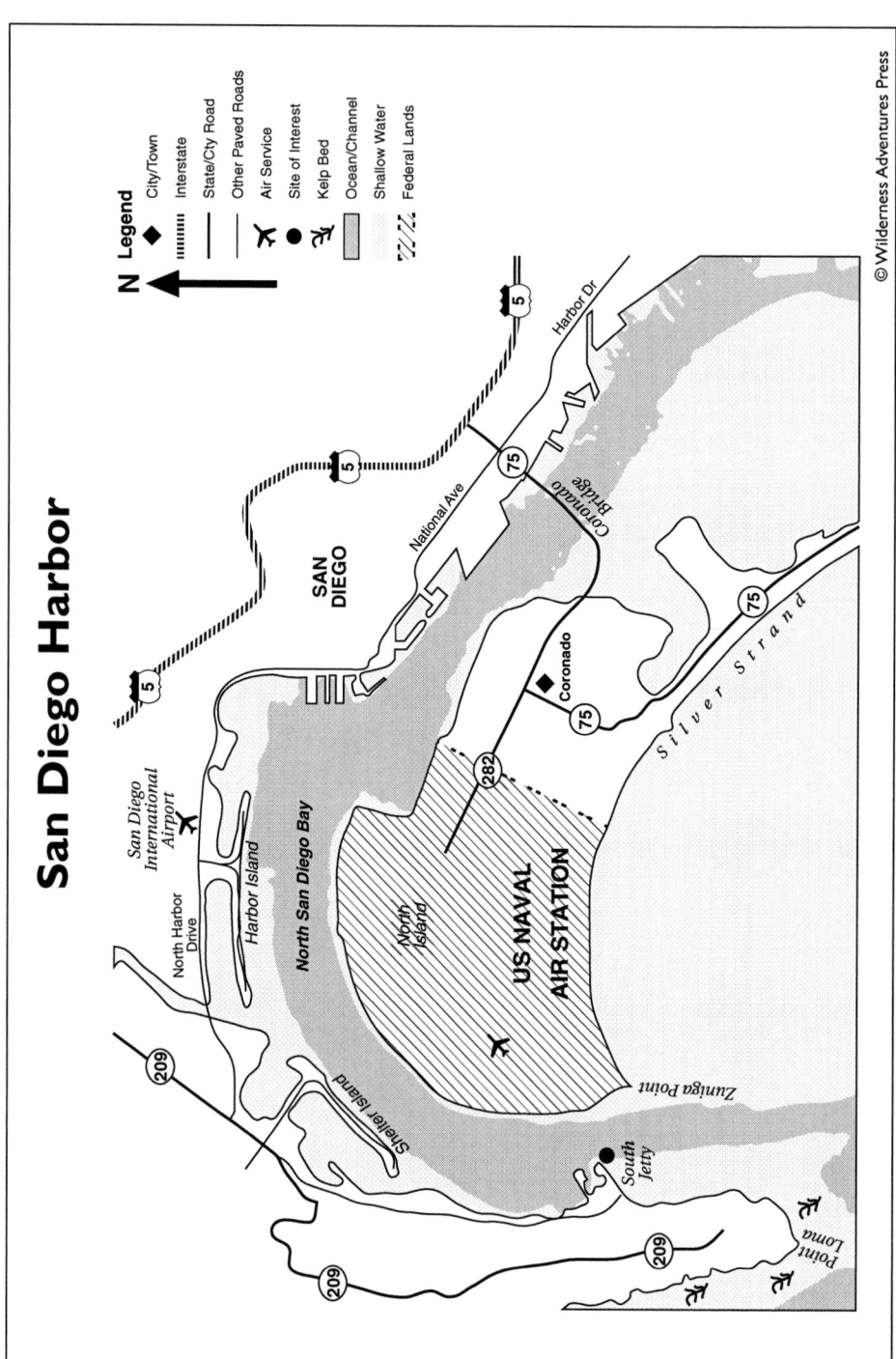

Just as in any area with structure, fish for bass by darting in and out of cover areas, especially where the jetty and mud bottom meet. Although you may be fishing for 12-inch calicos, a 20-pound yellowtail or 40-pound white seabass might grab your lure, so be prepared with the equipment to handle this possibility.

If bonito, barracuda, or yellowtail are around (nearly always a summer affair), live anchovies are the best draw. You can flyline or use just a slight amount of weight, like split shot, especially if there are mackerel around. Mackerel tend to feed higher in the water column, while barracuda and yellowtail work under the mackerel schools. This means you need to get your bait through the mackerel to the waiting game fish below.

When surface fish are around, jigs and bonito feathers also produce well. I tend to use a bit smaller jig in the bays than in blue water. The Tady #9 is my favorite size for this type of work, and similar jigs are available from nearly all jig manufacturers.

The South Jetty is also a great place to flyfish: It's convenient if you have a boat or rent one, and the flat water and usually very mild weather make it an easy place to fish. Work the jetty wall with blue and white or sparkly all white streamers in the sunshine and switch to green and yellow or purple and black flies when skies are overcast. Casting to the rocks with a fast, ripping retrieve induces bigger fish to strike. Trolling flies is another technique employed here at times. Although I love to troll with conventional tackle, I consider it a bit gauche to troll a fly with a fly rod. After all, why spend $50 plus for fancy fly line if you're just going to drag it through the water behind a powered boat.

Shelter Island Shoreline and Pier

Shelter Island is a manmade, T-shaped peninsula, originally designed to provide a protected area for small craft marinas. It has a full range of services, from fast food to restaurants to resort hotels. Wide, well-equipped launch ramps open into a small cove on the harbor side of the pier, and the main sportfishing fleet is based in the eastern cove made by the T-shaped, manmade peninsula.

All along the island's bay side, rocky walls provide excellent cover for calico bass and bay bass (spotted sand bass) Fish these areas just as you would the moorings for excellent action. From the shore you can also cast out into the midbay area and enjoy some of the better halibut, shark, and guitarfish fishing in San Diego Harbor.

A good number of pelagic species come within pitching distance of Shelter Island, including mackerel, barracuda, and bonito. A few tosses of a jig, particularly a shiny chrome one, out into the deeper areas can sometimes pay off big.

The excellent Shelter Island Fishing Pier stretches 500 feet out into the harbor and features a wide T-shaped end to accommodate quite a few fishermen. This pier is open from 6:00AM to 10:30PM. There's free parking, excellent restrooms, and a bait and tackle shop at the foot of the pier. This is one of the only piers where you can buy live anchovy bait, probably the best pier fishing bait there is.

Many fishermen who know this pier well use a high/low arrangement of hooks, putting one bait on the bottom and the other midway up the water column so they

The T-shaped Shelter Island Pier is wheelchair accessible and extends out into San Diego Bay, offering many pelagic fish in addition to the usual pier species.

have an opportunity for both the pelagic species and the resident bottom fish: halibut, sand bass, and calicos.

There are opportunities to catch several species of surfperch, including barred, as well as spotfin croakers, yellowfin croakers, and white croakers. Bottom fishing for these species is usually best at or near high tide.

This is a good pier for shark fishing. One as large as 125 pounds (bat ray) has been caught here. Some thresher sharks have been hauled in along this pier, but smaller leopard sharks, sand sharks, and guitarfish are more common. Locals favor strips of cut mackerel for shark bait.

I never take my flyfishing tackle to piers: There simply isn't enough room to really wind up and toss, especially not a fast-sinking fly line with a 2/0 fly on the end at times. Tourists are usually completely oblivious to what fishermen are doing and aren't aware of what can happen when a fly with a sharp hook comes whizzing by.

If you want to flyfish this area, stick to the rocky shoreline away from the main areas. There's a grassy separation between the road and the seawall that provides a bit of a buffer zone. But keep your eyes open for everything from toddlers with

*San Diego Harbor's boat launch facility at Shelter Island
is only a short run to the open ocean.*

helium balloons tied to their wrists to bicyclists to passing cars. I've never done it, but I'm pretty sure I never want to snag a passing Suburban mirror on the backcast with my 10-weight.

Harbor Island Shoreline

Harbor Island is also a manmade, T-shaped projection into San Diego Bay, designed to provide a sheltered marina for small craft. It's not really an island at all. Several large hotels are situated on the island and are very popular both for their terrific views of San Diego Harbor but also for their close proximity to San Diego's international airport. The island has easy parking and plenty of places to eat and stay.

The shore fishing from Harbor Island is always good. You can elect to cast out into the bay for typical mud bottom species, such as white croaker, halibut, sole, sand sharks, and rays, or work the rock wall and its junction with the bottom for calico bass and spotted sand bass.

For more relaxed fishing, cast anchovies, mussels, or cut squid bait on a weighted line as far as you can into the channel, flop down in a folding beach chair, and open a good book while you wait for something to swim by and eat your bait. The best fishing is around high tide, and sharks are the more prevalent species to be found during the night. Reverse that in the afternoons. For a little more activity while fishing, work the rock walls with rubber swimbait and casting plugs to pick up bass.

Flyfishing here is difficult because the tourist numbers are so high. You never know when Hiroshi and Mariko from Tokyo on their honeymoon, or Henry and Martha starting their retirement vacation from Oklahoma are going to sneak up behind you to see what that guy in the funny hat with the weird looking fishing pole is doing. One little girl on a pink bicycle with training wheels blindsided me once and ran right over my fast-sinking shooting head, 8-weight line. Stick to casting bait and lures here, and you'll have more fun with less worry.

The Moorings

Since bay bass like structure, the mooring near the Coast Guard helicopter station is an ideal place for them to hang out. There are plenty of places for fish to hide in this area's breakwater rocks and several sunken vessels. Fish the rock walls for calico bass and the bottom near structure for spotted sand bass.

Live bait, casting plugs, and rubber swimbait are the best choice in this area. Be patient and work all sides of any bottom structure in different tidal conditions to determine where and when fish are ready to strike. Once you find the combination for a particular day, plenty of bass will offer themselves up and reward your patience.

For the standing and waving types, flies presented close to either surface breaking structure or bottom structure, then erratically retrieved, will yield the best results. Calicos often stay near rock walls and find caves in which to hide while waiting for a tasty meal to cross their path—or at least a fur and feathers facsimile. Keep this in mind as you work the near-shore rocks.

This area also offers good fishing opportunities from shore. Remember the structure the fish prefer as you cast toward submerged moorings. Be on the alert for strikes just as you are bringing the bait back to shore and across the lairs where bass hide in the jetty rocks.

The Midbay

San Diego's midbay fishing area begins near the bait barges on the west end of Shelter Island and stretches all around the middle of the bay past the Coronado Bridge. Good to excellent halibut, shark, and ray fishing is available year-round here. The most effective technique is live anchovy bait drifted along the bottom. Rubber swimbaits can also be effective on these sand species.

You can anchor up in the bay, but it is far simpler and safer to just drift when fishing the center of the channel, because you can get moving with minimal effort. While the law says you have right of way when anchored up in a 16-foot fishing skiff, when a super carrier like the Enterprise comes home, the last place you want to be is between the ship and its dock. The carrier wharfs are located along North Island.

The midbay can have good fishing during warmer months, especially at the western end near the bait barges. From about May to October, plenty of mackerel, barracuda, and bonito inhabit the bay, and the occasional yellowtail wanders in, as well. Any of the surface fishing techniques work well, especially live bait, and shiny spoons and feathers, and baitfish-imitating flies also produce on these species.

Here's an ideal place to cut your teeth on saltwater flyfishing. Handling fast-sinking, shooting head 10- or 12-weight lines is nothing like presenting a double taper floating 4-weight line to trout in a babbling brook. Some practice is always a good idea before heading offshore for more serious fishing.

Access to San Diego Harbor

San Diego Harbor is easy to see, with the bulk of the city of San Diego lining its shore. Shelter Island is where both the boat launch ramps and rental boats are available. To get to Shelter Island from Interstate 5 (San Diego Freeway) or Interstate 8 (El Cajon Freeway), take the Rosecrans offramp (Highway 209) west for about 3 miles. Turn left on Shelter Island Drive and take it to the end. If you hear a splash and your car begins to fill with water, you've gone just a bit too far.

Shelter Island is brimming with fishing tackle shops, restaurants, several excellent resort hotels, and numerous boat and nautical shops. You can shop for multi-million-dollar yachts or have a fast food picnic on the grassy shoreline overlooking the bay. It has something for almost everybody.

If you want to rent a boat for use in San Diego Harbor, there are a number of places to do this including:

Shelter Island Boat Rental
2803 Emerson Street
San Diego, CA 92106
619-224-1681

Coronado Boat Rental
1715 Strand Way
Coronado, CA 92118
619-437-1514

Downtown Boat Rental
333 West Harbor Drive, Gate 1
San Diego, CA 92101
619-239-2628

South Beaches and Flats

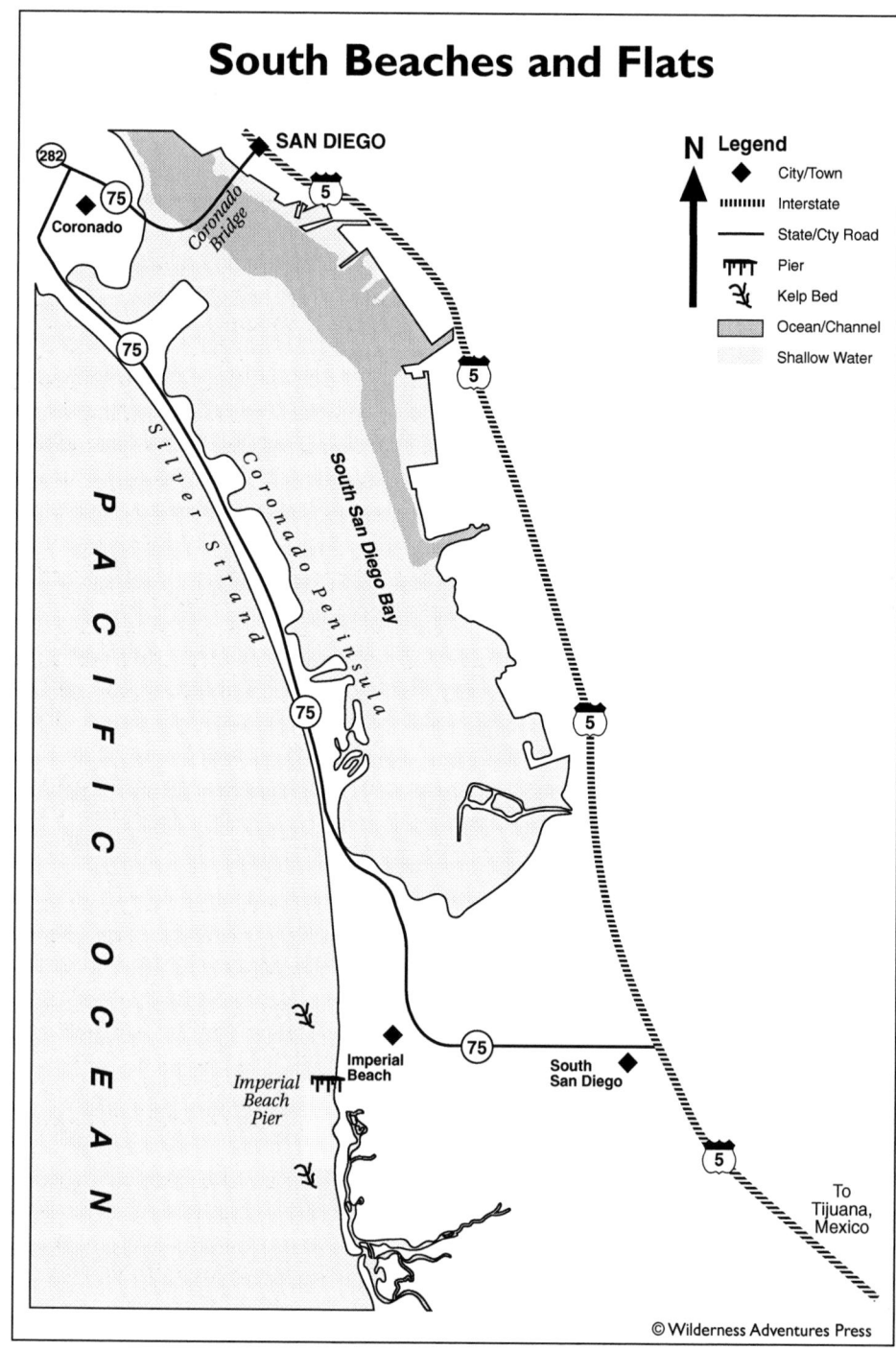

SAN DIEGO

Coronado

Coronado Bridge

Silver Strand

Coronado Peninsula

South San Diego Bay

PACIFIC OCEAN

Imperial Beach

Imperial Beach Pier

South San Diego

To Tijuana, Mexico

N Legend

◆ City/Town

▥▥▥ Interstate

— State/Cty Road

⊓⊓⊓ Pier

Kelp Bed

Ocean/Channel

Shallow Water

© Wilderness Adventures Press

South Beaches and Flats

The beaches bordering the Coronado Peninsula produce some excellent fishing action. Whether you like to fish off piers, surf cast, or fish from a small boat, this area is readily accessible by boat, car, and bicycle, or on foot. The mild weather and generally calm seas make this a year-round fisherman's paradise. Some of the better areas to fish are:

Coronado Flats and Beaches

The beautiful, wide sand beaches of the Coronado Peninsula are one of the premier surf fishing areas of southern California. California corbina, spotfin croaker, yellowfin croaker, and barred surfperch all frequent the area in good numbers and are willing to take a well-presented bait. Unlike the East or Gulf Coasts, it isn't necessary to cast a long way out to get these fish—right in the surf line is fine. I've even hooked them in ankle-deep water within a few feet of where I was standing. An 8-foot ocean-style spinning rod and reel with 15- to 17-pound test is plenty adequate for this type of fishing. When surfperch are running heavily in midwinter, I switch down to my 7½-foot graphite bass rod and reel with 10-pound test.

The traditional tackle setup uses a surf-style sinker on the end of the line, with a cut dropper loop tied to a bait-holder hook. This is fine when the surf is up and running, but on calmer days, I have found a simple Carolina rig with sliding sinker gets a higher percentage of hookups since the fish is able to run with the bait without feeling the weight of the sinker. If the surfperch are running small, I go to a very light leader, 6-pound test, and very small hooks, as small as #6, when using mussels or bloodworm bait.

If you have a choice, get a variety of bait. Sand crabs, ghost shrimp, bloodworms, mussels, and razor clams are all available and all work well in this area. I have to say that I have a preference for ghost shrimp as my first choice, with bloodworms a close second and razor clams third, especially in the fall when spotfin croakers are plentiful. They tend to have a preference for clams.

In midwinter, you can fish with rubber grubs and clean up on the surfperch here. Tie up a Carolina rig with a three-quarter ounce sliding egg sinker above a Teeny swivel with about 36 inches of very light leader (6- to 8-pound test). Use a somewhat small rubber worm type hook and a dark green or medium green and sparkle single-tailed rubber grub. Make sure you bury the point of the hook in the grub. Cast this rig out into the breaking waves and slowly retrieve through the whitewater, slowing up as the surge goes out and speeding up as it moves in. It shouldn't take too many casts before a tasty barred surfperch is on your hook, especially if you're fishing two hours before high tide until one hour after high tide.

Drifting in a small boat just outside the surf here is another excellent way to fish. In addition to the surf species, you can expect to catch white croaker, sanddabs, the occasional halibut, and shovelnose guitarfish. Even quite small boats from San Diego Harbor can reach the area very easily, and it is usually well protected with mild seas and weather.

Imperial Beach North Kelp

Just north of the Imperial Pier there is a rocky-bottomed area that is festooned with kelp beds during cooler water years. This area is ideal for calico bass, barracuda, bonito, and the occasional yellowtail in better years. Where kelp comes to the surface, fish the surface along the edges of the beds. In warm water years, look for rocky, erose bottoms on a depth sounder and fish deeper.

Imperial Beach Pier

Imperial Beach heralds itself as the most southwestern city in the United States, which it is, and it's also within walking distance to Mexico. It has wide sand beaches and an excellent fishing pier. The pier stretches 1500 feet out into the Pacific into water that's about 20 feet deep at the end and is managed by the city.

An artificial reef was created near the end of the pier to attract more fish, and it does attract plenty of undersized bass. Not many legal-sized bass are available, but if you're really persistent, you could take one home—but why bother when there's plenty of other species of fish available on the pier?

Newcomers invariably head out to the end of the pier to fish, but experienced pier fishermen know the surf line is the best place to get quality species. Sand crabs are probably the best bait, but ghost shrimp, mussels, and bloodworms also produce well. Barred surfperch, spotfin croakers, California corbina, and yellowfin croakers are all available at the pier using this bait. The best time to fish the surf line is within two hours before until one hour after high tide, especially if the tides are more extreme (new moons and full moons).

The middle zone of the pier offers white croaker, often called tomcod, and jacksmelt. These are midwater and bottom-feeding fish, so mussel bait on the bottom or in the midwater will have the most success. Another common mistake made by newcomer fishermen is to cast away from the pier. The fish generally hide under the pier amidst the mussel-encrusted pilings. Casting out into the relatively barren sand flats is not nearly as productive as keeping the bait close to the pier. This middle zone is also a good place to fish for sand sharks, rays, and guitarfish.

Out near the end of the pier is where to fish for pelagic species, such as mackerel and bonito and the occasional sand bass. Here, in addition to bait, bonito feathers or small shiny spoons can often be productive for these species.

This pier has a bait and tackle shop at the end, a restaurant, well-maintained restrooms, some benches, a fish cleaning station, and night lighting. It is open from 5am until 10pm. A curfew is enforced during closure. There is an excellent parking lot at the foot of the pier that charges $2 in the daytime or $1 at night. This pier offers an excellent way to spend an afternoon fishing.

Access to the Imperial Beach Pier is via Interstate 5. From the freeway take the Palm Avenue (Highway 75) exit west to where Palm Avenue and Highway 75 divide. Follow the Palm Avenue fork to Seacoast Drive, turn left on Seacoast, and follow it right to the pier.

The Imperial Beach Pier is the southernmost of California's piers and within sight of the Mexican border. It is also one of the more productive fishing piers.

Imperial Beach South Kelp

Just south of the Imperial Beach pier and lying close to shore is a kelp bed that attracts many of the kelp species, such as calico bass, bonito, barracuda, and yellowtail. On the rocky bottom, there are also treefish, starry rockfish, and sheephead prowling the reefs. While not as famous as some of the other excellent kelp fishing areas around San Diego, these beds are nonetheless very productive and easy to fish.

Flyline live anchovies for best results using bait. Fish with the reel declutched on conventional tackle or the bail open on spinning tackle and let those fish run with the bait for a full three seconds or so before setting the hook.

Surface swimming lures and diving lures also produce well here. Metal jigs also produce well and are good to have in your arsenal. Rubber swimbaits are good, as well, both retrieved near the surface or allowed to sink to the bottom and jigged. Here, experiment with a wide variety of techniques. Results vary depending on the water temperature, light conditions, tides, and I guess, how the fish just happen to feel that day.

The Imperial Beach kelp is an excellent place to flyfish on calmer days. Fish a shooting head, sinking fly line with a baitfish-imitating fly in blue and white, or a white and crystal streamer fly for best results. After casting near the kelp, just strip back line in erratic strokes for that frantic baitfish look, and it won't be long before your fly gets noticed.

Access here is by boat from San Diego Harbor and is a short, generally uncomplicated trip.

Southern Flats

About 5 miles due south of Point Loma (entrance to San Diego Harbor) a very productive flats area is found right on the Mexican border. This is a prime sand bass haunt, and from spring through midsummer, barred sand bass can be found here in substantial numbers. Even though this area has been fished for many, many years, the sand bass numbers continue to be strong. This is due in no small part to the 12-inch minimum size restriction and 10-fish bag limit. This allows all sand bass that make it to juveniles the ability to reproduce and maintain the fish stocks.

There are two schools of thought on fishing for sand bass in the open flats from a boat. One is to locate the fish by depth sounder, anchor up over the school and fish. The other is to drift through the flats, covering as much bottom as possible while fishing. I prefer the latter. Many of the flats fish are ambushers and remain motionless on the bottom awaiting food to come drifting by. Letting your bait or lures drift by is more what these fish expect in their natural setting, so they will be less suspicious.

To fish with bait here, a #4 hook with a Carolina rig (sliding egg sinker held 18 inches above the hook) provides the best chance of getting a bass to snatch the bait and get it deep enough in its mouth to set the hook. It's best to let them run a bit with the bait before setting the hook, or the bait will be pulled right out of its mouth.

Rubber swimbaits and deep sinking plugs are also productive in this area on the sand bass. In addition, sanddabs and sculpin abound here, so a squid-baited shrimp fly, skipped slowly along the bottom often gets inhaled by one of these species.

If you intend to fish here, it's an excellent idea to make sure you have both Mexican and Californian boat permits and fishing licenses. It's easy to drift across the border, especially since the international border makes a jog to split the difference between North Coronado and Point Loma. If the Mexican Coast Guard catches you boating without a permit, they will confiscate the boat; and if they catch you fishing in Mexican waters without a permit, they will fine you. The few dollars it takes to make sure everything is legal is well spent, even if only for your peace of mind.

This area is best reached by boat from any one of the San Diego Harbor launch ramps. The Shelter Island ramp is the most convenient and is described in greater detail in the San Diego Harbor section of this chapter. Few, if any, party boats fish this area, preferring to travel to the Coronado Islands or staying closer in near the Point Loma kelp beds.

Islas de Coronado

The Coronado Islands lie just 12 miles south of Point Loma in Mexican waters. They're just 7 miles offshore from the beaches of Mexico's Tijuana and Rosarito shorelines.

Few would disagree that the Coronado Islands are the premier yellowtail fishing spot in all of the southern California area. For many years, three-quarter-day party boats and private boats have traveled the short distance to the Coronados to feast on the bounty of the islands' plentiful game fish. In addition to yellowtail, the Coronados are famous for big bonito, barracuda, and at certain times of the year, white seabass, and halibut. Excellent rock cod fishing is also available near the islands.

The Coronados consist of a larger, southern island, called South Coronado, a smaller northern island, called (you guessed it) North Coronado, and two small rocky outcroppings, called Middle Coronado. There are no landing ports at the Coronados and no services, fuel, or water are available. There are several anchorages along the eastern shore of South Coronado where you could spend the night on the hook, but being only an hour out of San Diego Bay for even a slow boat, few private boaters elect to spend the night.

Following are some of the better locations around the islands:

Northern Flats

To the north and east of the islands there is a wide sandy flat harboring many different sandflat fishes. This area is often overlooked by anglers eager to catch yellowtail and other surface fish, so it can produce quite well for the angler interested in more fishing variety.

The flats are best fished by drifting bait or lures along the sandy bottom. Anchovies are the best live bait and are available from the bait receivers in San Diego Bay. A smallish hook (#4 to #2 depending on bait size) works best with nose-hooked anchovies. A 15-pound test rig is plenty for this type of fishing, but some elect to use heavier rigs just in case there are thresher sharks around. The smallest weight that will get the bait to the bottom at about a 45-degree angle is perfect for this type of fishing. I usually start with a three-quarter-ounce sliding egg sinker held 2 feet above the hook with either a split shot or "Carolina Keeper" flexible plastic bead designed specifically for this purpose. Fish this area with the reel in freespool and hold the line very lightly with just your fingertips so you can feel when something takes the bait. In the event of a hookup, let the fish run with the bait for several seconds before you snap the reel in gear and set the hook.

Instead of live bait, rubber swimbaits work very well here. You can fish them sweetened with either a small piece of cut squid or au natural. Shrimp flies sent to the bottom also do very well, especially for sanddabs and sculpin. I like to bait them with cut squid as well.

Many halibut come up off the bottom to chase a tasty looking morsel. Although I've never tried it here, I don't know why a deep diving plug wouldn't be productive

Islas de Coronado

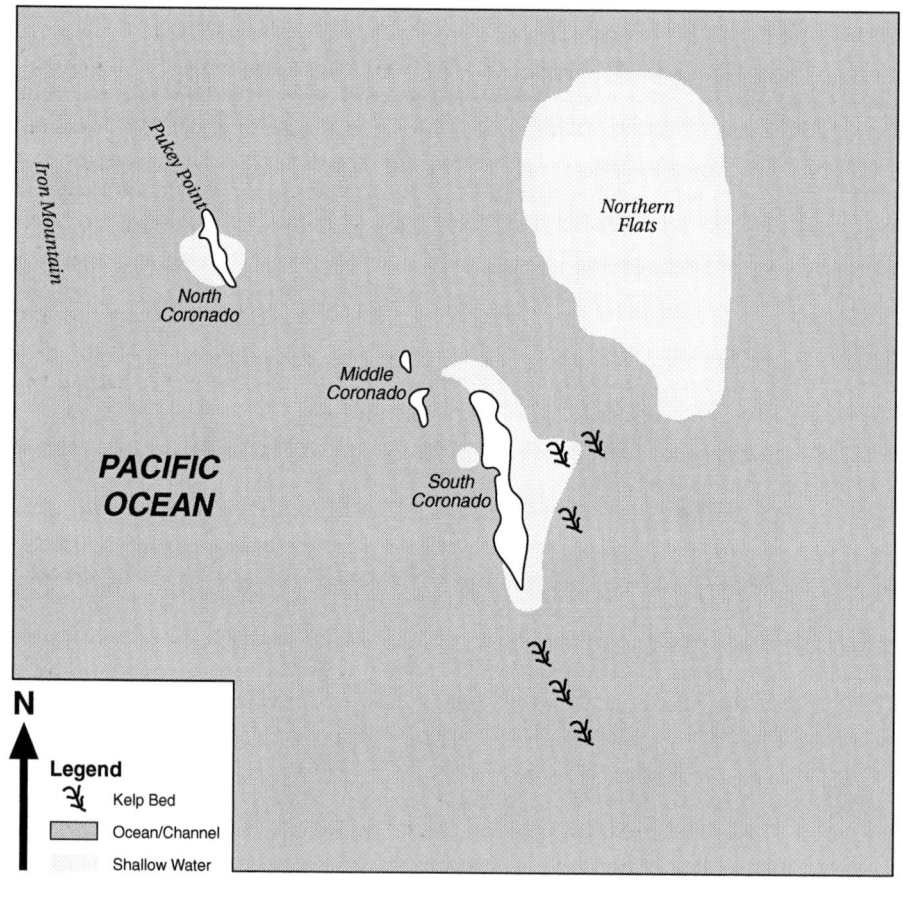

Pukey Point

Iron Mountain

Northern
Flats

North
Coronado

Middle
Coronado

PACIFIC
OCEAN

South
Coronado

N

Legend
Kelp Bed
Ocean/Channel
Shallow Water

© Wilderness Adventures Press

for bigger halibut. Send it to the bottom and give it an erratic retrieve to stimulate their strike instinct.

Halibut, sculpin, sanddabs, croakers, and sand bass, along with thresher and leopard sharks, occupy this area, and the same tackle and techniques may be used to catch any of these species here.

Pukey Point

Ungraciously dubbed "Pukey Point" by fishermen, this is North Coronado's northernmost point. This is often an excellent place to catch yellowtail but tends to be rough. Many a San Diego tourist on his first "deep sea" fishing trip has lost his or her lunch at Pukey Point. Fishing Pukey Point is a bit difficult and should be left to party boats and expert seamen. To fish the point, you need to anchor up about 300 yards off the point and back down with the stern of the boat facing the jagged cliffs of the island while the bow takes on the head seas. The seas smashing directly into the point throw up a substantial spray, and on anything but flat calm days, this maneuver can be downright dangerous. I've literally been within casting distance to the cliffs. In fact I once broke the hooks and hook loop off of one of my favorite jigs by bouncing it off the cliff in an overly energetic cast.

Pukey Point really can hold yellowtail, though. It's a bit unusual in that it either has lots of fish or none. I don't ever remember a scratch and pick time at Pukey Point. Either it was wide open or dead. The two primary methods to catch yellowtail here are by flylining live bait or by casting a metallic jig.

Iron Mountain

Iron Mountain refers to the sharp dropoff and deep gorge just 2 miles west of North Coronado. It has been named Iron Mountain because it has claimed so many boat anchors that the local skippers insist the bottom must be covered with a mountain of iron.

Iron Mountain is an excellent rock cod bank. The northern portion of the Baja Peninsula receives an upwelling of nutrient-laden water traveling up the submarine canyons. The rich nutrients attract plenty of microscopic life, which attracts everything else up the food ladder.

The bottom is the place to fish at Iron Mountain. Plenty of bocaccio, reds (vermillion rockfish), treefish, and bank rockfish await the angler. I use between 4 to 8 ounces of torpedo-shaped lead, tied with a weak link (about half the breaking strength of my line), and with three 1/0-sized long shank hooks on dropper loops spaced about 10 inches apart. You can nose-hook anchovies, use cut squid bait, or even use strips of cut mackerel. I like 1/0 bucktail shrimp flies baited with thin strips of squid.

To fish, drop the rig until it just touches the bottom, crank it up two to ten turns to keep it away from the jagged, tackle-stealing bottom, and wait. Periodically, declutch your reel and let the rig touch bottom again to make sure the current isn't pushing your rig upward.

You can fish the deeper parts of the canyon with good success for deeper water rock cod. Use heavier tackle and techniques as described elsewhere in this book for this type of action.

Middle Coronado Grounds

The middle grounds are probably the most popular area to fish. On a weekend day in the summer, you'll find at least several dozen private and party boats working this productive area. When there are several coldwater years in a row in southern California, kelp becomes thick in this area. In El Niño years, especially if there are two in a row as there were in 1993/1994 or 1997/1998, warmer water causes the kelp to die off. While there are still plenty of game fish to be caught, it's a bit harder to predict exactly where to find them.

This area experiences a lot of what are called "Breezers," small schools of 3 to 10 yellowtail moving (breezing) through while they chase scattered schools of baitfish. This is especially true when there is no kelp. If you're in a private boat, you can troll to increase your chances of picking up fish, but if you're on a party boat, you're pretty much stuck since these boats almost always anchor up and try to chum the fish in.

By throwing out plenty of chum—live anchovies—the boats hope to attract the schools. It works much of the time, but with 15 or 20 party boats all chumming, the schools just go from boat to boat, so the action might be fast and furious one minute and shut down the next. It's an interesting game and lots of fun.

In the middle ground, live bait and jigfishing dominate. Many really good jig fishermen simply wait, milling around and staring at the water for the slightest indication of fish, while the bait fishermen fish. If they see a boil, they launch their jigs right at it. For the bait fisherman, flylining in the summer and sinking to the bottom with whole squid in the colder times are the best strategies.

This area is also easy and productive to flyfish. Green and white streamer flies in 2/0 to 4/0 size tied on stainless steel hooks are my favorite. I like to add a bit of red sometimes, especially in the sunlight. It suggests the baitfish is bleeding. For bonito, use shinier flies, such as white, crystal flash streamers, or flies with lots of metallic artificial fibers in silver or gold.

The traditional white and chrome bonito feather still works wonders when bonito are cruising through the area. On a light line, tie the feathered jig directly to the line, cast it out, and use a fast, ripping style retrieve. Don't worry about pulling the lure in too fast, bonito can swim far faster than you can retrieve any lure, and they're used to their prey darting away at top speed. If anything it gets more strikes, as the predator is less wary of something fleeing really fast and strikes without close inspection, while lazily moving prey might draw more suspicion and warrant a closer look.

East Side of South Coronado

Productive kelp beds for surface fish can be found on the east side of South Coronado. These are in the lee of the island, so very calm water and light winds are the norm. If you're out to catch a yellowtail on a fly, here's a great place for it. Look for kelp patches extending up near the surface.

Check the area out first by trolling with green and yellow, red and white, or green and white feathered jigs. If you get strikes, stop and fish with bait, lures, or flies. Plenty of big bonito inhabit this stretch of water, too. When I was in high school, I picked up a 17-pound yellowtail here while fishing on a party boat with my father. It was by far the biggest fish on the boat and remained so for almost all of the afternoon. Just before leaving, a fisherman hooked a bonito that went 18 pounds to knock me off the jackpot. At that time, bonito were considered almost junk fish and often discarded. Having my first potential jackpot-sized beautiful, big yellowtail unseated by a bonito was agony! Those big bonito are still out there, too. Last year on a 6-pack trip to the Coronados, we ran into a school of huge bonito while trolling. They were really tasty, too!

Anyway, fish the east side kelp as you would any kelp bed, by flylining anchovies, casting plugs and lures, and occasionally dropping down to the bottom to see what you can find. If you see boiling fish, break out the jigs or flies and aim for the boilers.

South Kelp

A row of rocky reefs, well forested with kelp in cooler water years is found just south of South Coronado Island. In warmer water years, kelp doesn't normally appear on the surface. This area is referred to as the South Kelp and is one of the better yellowtail haunts in the islands. Bonito and barracuda can also be found here.

During a warm summer, flyline anchovies or sardines on the surface. Change the bait often to keep them fresh and lively. If you see boils or can chum the fish to the surface and get them chasing bait, switch to jigs. Blue and white or green and yellow jigs in the 6X size, retrieved quickly, will get the most attention. I used to have a green and black jig that also did well at times like that.

When the yellowtail are feeding deep, either live squid sent down into the reef or rubber swimbaits seem to be the best bet for hauling them up. Jigs, allowed to flutter all the way to the bottom and yoyoed, sometimes produce, too. During cooler months here, you also stand a good chance of enticing a white seabass with these techniques. Although there are a few calico bass present, not many are caught here or anywhere at the Coronados.

Access to the Coronado Islands

The Coronado Islands lie entirely within the borders of Mexico, and you are required to follow Mexican laws. If you are fishing from a San Diego-based party boat, you will be automatically issued a Mexican one-day fishing permit—it's included in the price of the trip. American skippers who frequent these waters keep current on the size and bag limits. Follow their suggestions. They'll keep you safely within the law.

On private boats, though, it's up to you to make sure all permits are carried. In Mexico, it is necessary for everyone aboard to have a fishing license, even if they don't fish. You're also required to have a boat permit. Unless you don't mind spending your vacation in an Ensenada prison with plenty of cucarachas to keep you company, make sure you follow Mexican laws to the letter. The Mexican government DOES patrol, DOES check, and DOES throw people in jail and confiscate their boats if they don't comply with the laws. Mexican permits are issued at the major sport-fishing landings in San Diego Harbor as well as the Mexican consulate and many travel offices. The Mexican Consulate's office in San Diego is:

Consulate General of Mexico
1549 India Street
San Diego, CA 92101
619-231-8414

The three major sportfishing landings in San Diego Bay offer both open party boats, six-pack charter boats, and larger party charter boats to fish the marvel-ous Coronado Islands. All three are located at the entrance to Shelter Island. Even though they all three have different street names, they share a common parking lot. They are:

Point Loma Sport Fishing
1403 Scott Street
San Diego, CA 92106-2767
Phone : 619-223-1627
Fax : 619-223-1591
www.pointlomasportfishing.com

H&M Landing
2803 Emerson Street
San Diego, CA 92106
Voice 619-222-1144
Fax 619-222-0784
www.hmlanding.com

Fisherman's Landing
2838 Garrison St
San Diego, CA
619-221-8506
www.fishermanslanding.com

Taking a private boat to the Coronado Islands isn't a difficult sea voyage, but it does require knowledge of seamanship and a reliable, well-equipped boat. On most days, the islands are clearly visible from the entrance to San Diego Harbor and Point Loma, and the entrance to the harbor is almost always clearly visible from the Coronados. The best place to launch a boat for a trip to the Coronados is at the Shelter Island boat ramps, a well-maintained, very wide, and easy-to-use facility located at the end of Shelter Island Drive. A prominent bait barge is located between Shelter Island and the harbor entrance, where bait can be purchased by the scoop. A boat equipped with a recirculating live bait system is required if you plan to fish with live bait. An aerator in a bucket just won't keep bait healthy enough to provide usable live bait once you make the trip across the border.

COMMON GAME FISH AVAILABILITY BY MONTHS
SAN DIEGO COUNTY

Species	Jan	Feb	Mar	Apr	May	Jun	Jul	Aug	Sep	Oct	Nov	Dec
Yellowtail												
Barracuda												
Bonito												
Calico Bass												
Sand Bass												
White Seabass												
Halibut												
Lingcod												
Shallow-water Rockfish												
Deep-water Rockfish												
Sheephead												
Sculpin												
Blue Perch												
Opaleye												
Whitefish												

Legend: ☐ Not Availabie   ▧ Fish Possible   ▨ Good Fishing   ■ Excellent Fishing

San Diego County Bait and Tackle Shops

Oceanside Bait & Tackle
250 North Pacific
Oceanside, CA 92054
(760) 966-1406

Pacific Coast Bait & Tackle
2110 South Coast Highway
Oceanside, CA 92054
(760) 439-3474
www.pacificcoastbiatandtackle.com

Tackle Town
1009 North Coast Highway
Oceanside, CA 92054
(760) 721-269

Boss Bait & Tackle
1998 Hacienda Drive
Vista, CA 92083
(760) 631-7417

California Tackle
123 S Santa Fe Ave
Vista, CA 92083
(760) 630-3474

Fishermans Wholesale Tackle & Supply
2503 South Santa Fe Avenue
Vista, CA 92083
(760) 598-8800
www.hotbite.com

P-Bods Fishing Tackle
1275 S Santa Fe Ave Ste 101
Vista, CA 92083
(760) 941-0143

Sport Chalet
40432 Winchester Road
Temecula , CA 92591
(951) 296-3001
www.sportchalet.com

Turner's Outdoorsman
2085 Montiel
San Marcos, Ca. 92069
(760) 741-1570
www.turners.com

Blue Water Tackle
124 Lomas Santa Fe Dr
Solana Beach, CA 92075
(858) 350-8505

Sport Chalet
4525 La Jolla Village Drive, Ste. D19
San Diego , CA 92122
(858) 453-5656
www.sportchalet.com

Turner's Outdoorsman
8199 Clairemont Mesa
Kearny Mesa, CA 92111
(858) 278-8005
www.turners.com

Anglers Choice and Lucs Custom Fishing
Rods
1910 Rosecrans
San Diego, CA 92106
(619) 223-2324

Dons Bait & Tackle
6407 Imperial Avenue
San Diego, CA 92114
(619) 263-1435

Hook Line & Sinker
1224 Scott Street
San Diego, CA   92106
(619) 224-1336
www.hlstackle.com

Mission Bay Deep Sea Fishing
1717 Quivira Road
San Diego, CA   92109
(619) 224-3383

Ocean Beach Pier Bait & Tackle
5091 Niagara Avenue
San Diego, CA 92107
(619) 226-3474

Outrageous Custom Rods
2207 Garnet Avenue
San Diego, CA 92109
(858) 483-6085

San Diego Fly Shop
124 Lomas Sante Fe Drive #208
Solana Beach, CA 92075
(858) 350-3111
www.sandiegoflyshop.com

Shelter Island Bait Tackle & Deli
1776 Shelter Island Drive
San Diego, CA 92106
(619) 222-7635

Sportman International
4315 Mayflower Way
San Diego, CA 92117
(858) 270-5732

Sport Chalet
3695 Midway Drive
San Diego , CA 92110
(619) 224-6777
www.sportchalet.com

Sport Chalet
1640 Camino del Rio North
San Diego , CA 92108
(619) 718-7070
www.sportchalet.com

Squidco Warehouse
1730 Kettner Boulevard
San Diego, CA 92101
(619) 238-0909

Taniguchi Inc Commercial & Sport
Fishing Supply
2272 Newton Avenue
San Diego, CA 92113
(619) 234-0431

L & M Bait & Tackle
1447 3rd Avenue
Chula Vista, CA 91911
(619) 691-1843

San Diego Information

Being one of the largest metropolitan areas in the United States, San Diego offers the traveler everything he could possibly want or need. With the incredible number of facilities available here, your best bet is to contact the visitors bureaus of the various cities in San Diego County to get the latest, up to date information on the many and varied things to do in San Diego. To contact some of these bureaus and information centers:

Alpine Chamber of Commerce
2157 Alpine Boulevard
Alpine, CA 91901
619-445-2722

Balboa Park Visitors Center
1549 El Prado
San Diego, CA 92101
619-239-0512

Border Station Parking and Tourist
Information Center
4570 Camino De La Plaza
San Ysidro, CA 92173

Carlsbad Convention
& Visitors Bureau
P.O. Box 1246
Carlsbad, CA 92018
760-434-6093

Chula Vista Visitors Information Center
750 E Street
Chula Vista, CA 91910
619-425-4444

International Visitor Information Center
11 Horton Plaza
San Diego, CA 92101
619-236-1212

Oceanside Visitor & Tourism
Information Center
928 North Coast Highway
Oceanside, CA 90254
760-721-1101

Poway Visitors Center
13172 Poway Road
Poway, CA 92064
619-748-0016

San Diego Convention & Visitors Bureau
401 B Street, Suite 1400
San Diego CA 92101
619-232-3101

San Diego East Visitors Bureau
4695 Nebo Drive
La Mesa, CA 91941
619-463-1166

San Diego North County Convention &
Visitors Bureau
720 North Broadway
Escondido, CA 92025
760-745-4741

San Ysidro Chamber of Commerce
663 East San Ysidro Boulevard
San Ysidro, CA 92173
619-428-1281

Travelers Aid Society
306 Walnut Avenue, #21
San Diego, CA 92103
619-295-8392

Any of these agencies are happy to provide all sorts of valuable visitor's information for the asking. Many have Internet web sites, also. Enjoy your fishing experience in San Diego by planning ahead. One very useful service available to visitors in San Diego is the Central Hotel Reservations Center. These helpful folks can book you into any of over 300 hotels. In addition they have discount tickets available for Sea World, the famous San Diego Zoo, the San Diego Wild Animal Park. Old Town Trolley Tours, Harbor Cruises, and Dinner Cruises. Best of all it's a free service and a toll free phone number at 800-434-7894.

San Diego County Accommodations

The following is a sampling of lodgings that are close to port in San Diego County. These range from basic to luxury, and you should keep in mind that nothing along the southern California coast, particularly anything close to the water, is inexpensive.

Oceanside Harbor
Days Inn at the Coast
1501 Carmelo Drive
Oceanside, CA 92054
760-722-7661

Oceanside Marina Inn
2008 Harbor Drive North
Oceanside, CA 92054
760-722-1561

Mission Bay
Hilton San Diego Resort
1775 East Mission Bay Drive
San Diego, CA 92109
619-276-4010

San Diego Paradise Point Resort
1404 West Vacation Road
San Diego, CA 92109
858-274-4630

Dana Inn & Marina
1710 West Mission Bay Drive
San Diego, CA 92109
619-222-6440

Hyatt Islandia
1441 Quivera Road
San Diego, CA 92109
619-224-1234

Best Western Blue Sea Lodge
707 Pacific Beach Drive
San Diego, CA 92109
858-488-4700

Crown Point View Suite Hotel
4875 North Harbor Drive
San Diego, CA 92109
858-272-0676

San Diego (Shelter Island Area)
Holiday Inn, San Diego Bayside
4875 North Harbor Drive
San Diego, CA 92106
619-224-3621

Best Western Posada
5005 North Harbor Drive
San Diego, CA 92106
619-224-3254

Humphrey's Half Moon Inn & Suites
2303 Shelter Island Drive
San Diego, CA 92106
619-224-3411

The Bay Club Hotel & Marina
2131 Shelter Island Drive
San Diego, CA 92106
619-224-8888

Shelter Pointe Hotel & Marina
1551 Shelter Island Drive
San Diego, CA 92106
619-221-8000

Vagabond Inn, Point Loma
1325 Scott Street
San Diego, CA 92106
619-224-3371

Point Loma Inn
2933 Fenelon Street
San Diego, CA 92106
619-222-4704

Offshore Islands

Offshore Islands

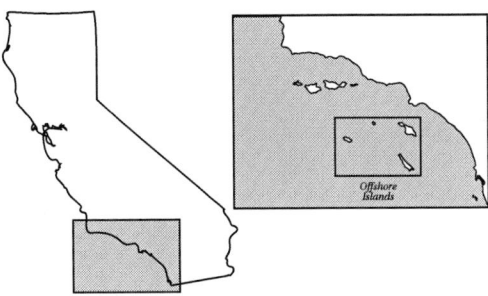

CATALINA ISLAND

"Twenty-six miles across the sea, Santa Catalina is the place for me," is the refrain from a 1930s song that comes to mind when talking about southern California's own resort getaway, just a few minutes by either airplane or boat from the hustle and bustle of southern California. Heading off to Catalina is like stepping back in time or maybe like the setting on some South Seas island. Because it is so different from the mainland, it seems that it should be much farther from the coast than it is. Catalina has a quiet, slow-paced small town resort atmosphere that many a southern Californian has grown to love.

Humans have occupied Catalina for over 7000 years. The Native Americans living here called the island "Pimu" and called themselves Pimugans. They were excellent seamen and paddled sturdy wooden canoes to the mainland and the other offshore islands to trade. Steatite, a rock that's easily carved and doesn't break or crack when exposed to the heat of a fire, was fashioned into artistic and useful cooking utensils. These items were also used to trade with Indians on other islands and the mainland. Although steatite occurs naturally only on Catalina Island, it has been found at archaeological sites in the Channel Islands and along coastal California, proving there was trade between the islands as well as the mainland.

When Juan Rodriguez Cabrillo made his famous journey up the West Coast of what is now the United States, he stopped and dropped anchor at the island on October 7, 1542. Pimugans paddled out to greet him in their canoes. Cabrillo named the island San Salvador after his ship's name. The island was left in peace after Cabrillo's visit for nearly 60 years until 1602, when the Spanish explorer, Sebastian Viscaino, sighted the island. He anchored up on November 24, the eve of Saint Catherine's day, and not knowing of Cabrillo's previous naming, called the island after Saint Catherine, Santa Catalina in Spanish, which it is still called today.

Spain had little ability to defend its enormous new world territories in the 1600s and 1700s. North America's western coast was so remote from Spain that few military expeditions could protect this territory from foreign smugglers and poachers. Russian, Yankee, and English ships were hiding at the island regularly while they

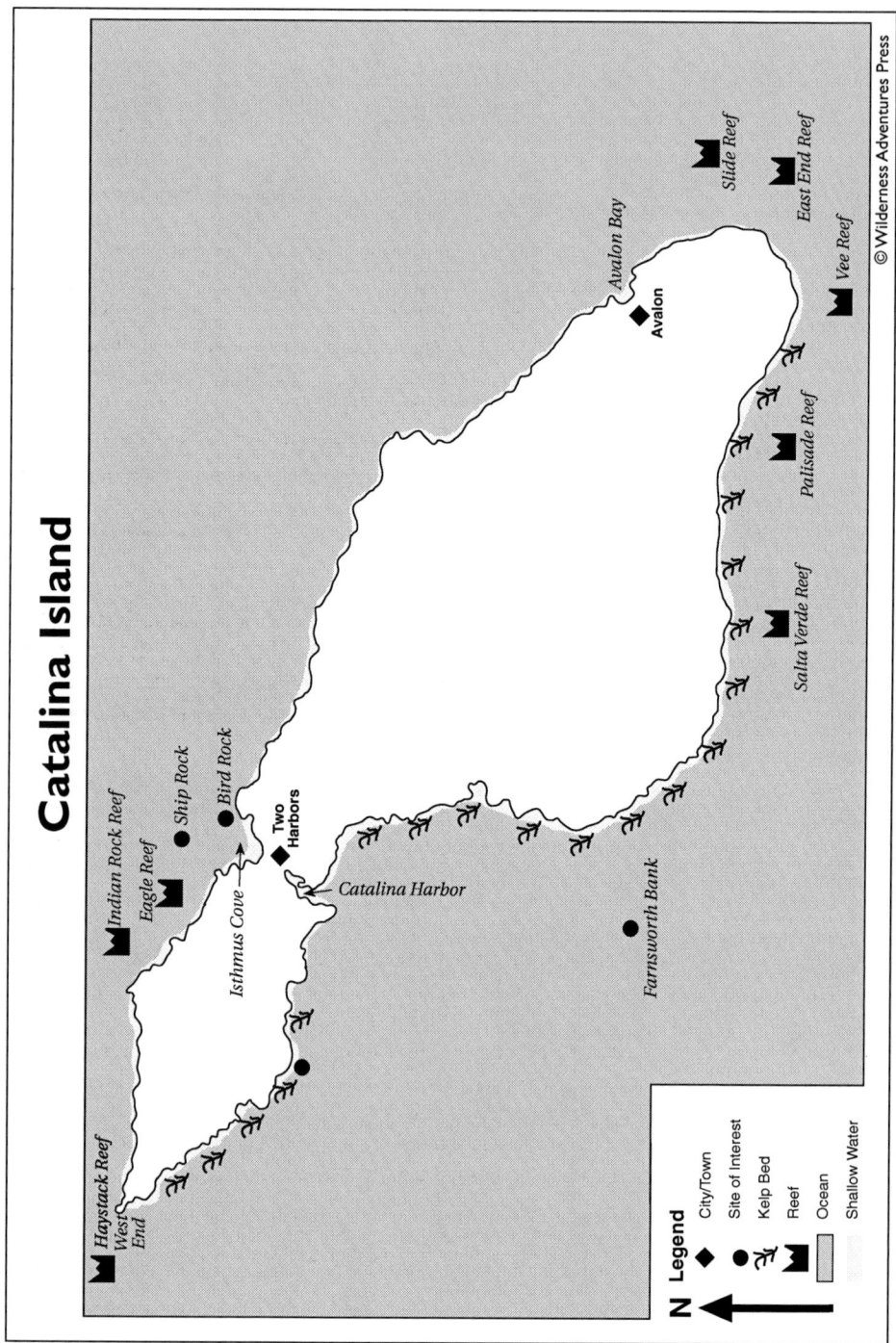

Catalina Island

Slide Reef
East End Reef
Vee Reef
Avalon Bay
Avalon
Palisade Reef
Salta Verde Reef
Indian Rock Reef
Eagle Reef
Ship Rock
Bird Rock
Two Harbors
Isthmus Cove
Catalina Harbor
Farnsworth Bank
Haystack Reef
West End

© Wilderness Adventures Press

Legend

City/Town
Site of Interest
Kelp Bed
Reef
Ocean
Shallow Water

N

traded illegally with the Alta-Californians. One of the favorite tricks of these semi legal smugglers was to unload most of their cargo at Catalina, then sail into San Diego and apply to the Spanish authorities to trade along the coast. Once they paid their tariff on only a fraction of the goods they actually intended to sell, they returned to Catalina to reload their cargo and begin trading with all permits dutifully signed and sealed.

The plentiful sea otters around Catalina were killed by poachers who sold the pelts for use in making coats, which were particularly in high demand in China. Russian otter hunters commonly visited the island and found the pickings easy. The Spanish forbade foreigners to hunt otters there, but there was little they could do to enforce the law. The otter hunters openly and defiantly ignored the Spanish laws.

By the early 1800s, the Pimugans had all either died from the new diseases the Europeans brought or had moved to the mainland and settled in the Mission San Gabriel area. After winning independence from Spain, Catalina Island, like all of California, came under Mexican rule. The island was granted to Thomas Robbins in 1846, just two years before the U.S. invaded California and took it from Mexico. Robbins was a naturalized Mexican citizen who was owed favors by the Mexican government. Robbins established a rancho on the island but lived there only four years, selling it in 1850 to Jose Maria Covarrubias.

After being annexed by the United States, the legality of Mexican land grants was often disputed, and squatters often challenged the ownership of land. Catalina had dozens of squatters staking claims on Catalina in the 1850s. Some of the coves and beaches still bear the names of these early settlers: Ben Weston Beach, Howlands Landing, Gallaghers Beach, Johnsons Landing. Later, it was decided that the original Mexican land grant to Robbins was legal, and James Lick of San Francisco purchased the island in 1867. The island then became a sheep and cattle ranch.

William Wrigley, Jr. (of chewing gum and baseball stadium fame) purchased Santa Catalina Island in the early 1900s. He began restoring the island to its original natural beauty. It had been scarred by over 200 years of mining and ranching. Ownership of most of the island has passed from the Wrigley family to the Catalina Island Conservancy in 1975, whose mission is: "Preserving one of the world's most magnificent islands for present and future generations to experience and enjoy."

The famous Tuna Club is located in the city of Avalon on Santa Catalina Island. It is the oldest sportfishing club in the world, founded in 1898. Many famous celebrities have been members of the Tuna Club, including Theodore Roosevelt, Winston Churchill, General George S. Patton, Cecil B. DeMille, Charlie Chaplin, and Bing Crosby. The Tuna Club is responsible for the development of the modern angling rules and sportsmanship that have been adopted by angling clubs the world over. The club is a California Historical Landmark and is on the National Registry of Historical Places.

Zane Grey, author of 89 books and a famous fisherman, built a pueblo-style home in Avalon. When Hollywood movie producers came to the island in 1924 to

Dorado are lots of fun to catch as well as great to eat. This one was caught from the Holly B *six-pack charter boat from San Pedro.*
Photo courtesy Kevin Rea---Holly B Sportfishing.

film one of his stories, they brought along 14 buffalo. The herd now includes over 200 animals that roam free on the island.

Today, Catalina boasts two towns, three excellent small craft harbors, a private airport, dozens of coves and anchorages, and just about anything a tourist could desire, from luxury resorts to exciting night life to warm sunny beaches. Of course, one of Catalina's greatest resources is its terrific fishing. Every fish that can be caught in southern California, from marlin to surfperch, can be found in excellent numbers at Catalina. If I could fish only one place in all of southern California, it would be here. A person could spend a lifetime exploring the Catalina coast and never stop discovering new places and techniques to add more enjoyment to his fishing experience. It is truly a fisherman's paradise.

There is good fishing everywhere around the island. To try to isolate productive spots is difficult, since the whole island seems to be teeming with sea life. Sometimes it seems that every line you drop, regardless of the bait being used, gets a nibble by some sort of fish. The following reefs, banks, and kelp beds are some of the more popular places to fish, and all seem to produce on a consistent basis:

West End Peninsula

West End Shelf

Catalina's west end receives the brunt of the prevailing weather. Nearly all of the weather in southern California comes from the northwest. On the mainland, the ring of islands and southern California's concave shape help minimize the weather's impact. But the islands have no such protection. Even when the weather is relatively mild on a summer afternoon, a stiff breeze can whip the sea surface into whitecaps, making for uncomfortable going on the water.

Lying northwest of the island's west end is a fairly large flats area with a scattered rocky bottom, generally referred to as the West End Shelf. Although this is mostly a bottom fishing area, it also attracts surface feeding pelagic fish at certain times of the year. The rocky areas along the shelf support good numbers of rock cod, and in winter, lingcod, calico bass, sand bass, sheephead, and even white seabass.

I like to use squid bait here, keeping it on or near the bottom. If you are positioned over the area's rocky parts, you'll have a chance at shallow rock species; if you are drifting over the hard, flatter bottom, you'll run across the flats fish mentioned above. If you drift across a sandy area, expect hits from sanddabs and halibut in addition to all of the above fish. If sanddabs are hitting, I immediately switch to small (1/0 hook) shrimp flies and load up. I love to eat those little guys and never miss a chance to take some home for dinner.

In spring, barracuda can be found herding schools of anchovies into tight balls, turning them into a buffet lunch out here along the shelf. You can spot these easily because of the agitated, frenzied birds diving into the water after the bait. If you spot such a baitball, drive right into it and get jigs out into the water. The frenzied fish will slash at almost anything shiny in this state, and you can land some fine school barracuda.

Haystack Reef

A series of rocks about a mile due north of West End Point forms what is generally known as Haystack Reef. I don't know if the name refers to a haystack on shore at one point or whether it's because several of the dome-shaped rockpiles look like a haystack. Either way, Haystack is a good place to fish the rocks for white seabass, probably the most sought after of all Catalina's game fish.

To fish Haystack Reef, send either live squid, dead squid, sardines, Spanish mackerel, or rubber swimbaits sweetened with a thin strip of cut squid down into the rocky reef. It's relatively easy to catch Spanish mackerel at Eagle Reef with a Sabiki, Lucky Laura, or Lucky Joe bait rig. Just jig them up and down in the midwater, and it'll soon fill up with baitfish that survive quite well in a bait tank. Probably the best bait is live squid, and if you can't buy it, you can catch it, especially during moonless nights in winter and spring. Just hang a light overboard at night and jig up and down with squid jugs, available at any bait and tackle store.

In addition to white seabass, Haystack also has many other bottom species, such as red rock cod, bocaccio, barberpoles, lingcod, sheephead, and whitefish. Sand

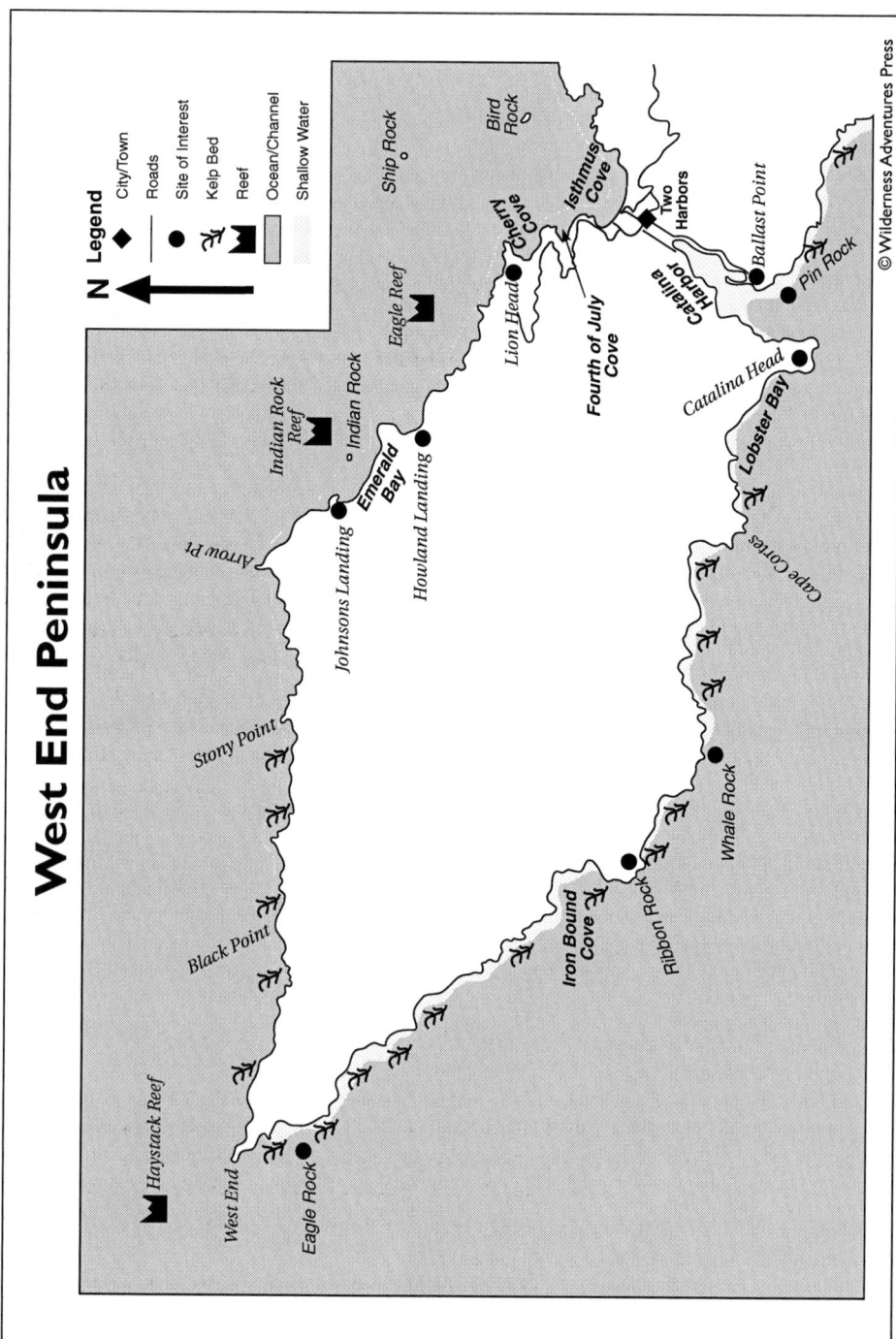

West End Peninsula

© Wilderness Adventures Press

bass, halibut, and sanddabs inhabit the areas between the rocks. This is why it is so much fun to fish—you never know what will be on your line. There tend to be quite a few black sea bass here, too, but make sure you return any to the water since they are protected.

Indian Rock Reef

Arrow Point is a prominent feature of the front side of Catalina's west end peninsula. About 1½ miles off Arrow Point is a series of submerged rocks, called Indian Rock Reef. These rocks lie in about 700 to 750 feet of water and hold rock cod. Indian Rock Reef is known as a great place for red rock cod (vermillion rock fish) and is one of the few really productive spots between Catalina and the mainland. In addition, bocaccio, barberpoles, chilipeppers, and occasionally lingcod and cowcod make this an excellent all-round deep water fishing spot. Standard deep water rock codding tackle and techniques are the best approach to fishing this area.

Eagle Reef

The front side of Catalina Island, the side facing the mainland, generally drops off quickly into relatively deep water very close to the island. Eagle Reef is a rocky projection from the island in this deep water. The inside edge is marked by a massive boiler rock that has claimed more than a few boats that blundered across the tidal surge and got pounded to bits on these sharp rocks. It is nonetheless a very popular place to fish—once you try it out, it becomes very obvious why. All sorts of fish, from blue perch to yellowtail, are plentiful along this reef. Because it's on the island's protected east side, the weather is generally quite mild. Even when winter seas are running big and the wind is blowing, it is close enough to the island that the high mountains protect the reef, making it fishable when the channel is barely crossable.

Just outside the boiler rock with its halo of kelp, calico bass are a staple of Eagle Reef. Of course, live bait is always a favorite of these California groupers, but they'll also take a swimming plug (one of my favorite places to pitch plugs) or rubber swimbait. The fish most often feed on the surface, so there's little need to use sinkers here for calicos.

At times during the year, particularly spring, huge schools of bonito mass around the reef. This reminds of a fishing trip I took the Saturday in 1991 that riots broke out after the Rodney King verdict. My friend and I were barely able to make it out of San Pedro Harbor on a three-quarter day boat. The original landing we had planned to use was closed, as were many Los Angeles businesses that Saturday. As it turned out, the boat had only about eight customers aboard, so everyone had plenty of elbow-room. We anchored up on Eagle Reef and couldn't get through the schooling bonito with live bait, jigs, or anything that flashed without hooking up. This continued for several hours, and the Captain finally moved the boat down the coast so we could have a chance at catching something besides bonito.

Barracuda, and sometimes yellowtail, are also frequent summer visitors to Eagle Reef. I fish almost exclusively with jigs for these fish but have hooked them on bait

A nice sand bass caught in the surf on a fly.
Photo courtesy Mike & Regina Scott—Mike Scott's Hackle, Tackle & Flies.

as well. While calico fishing, keep your eyes peeled for boiling fish surrounding the kelp and be prepared to pitch a jig in the event you see these bigger pelagic fish breezing through.

Eagle Reef is also prime white seabass country. Rubber swimbaits, particularly big, twin-tailed, squid-baited lures, are an excellent choice. Fish these in the mid-water, or if you're anchored up over the reef itself in water that's not very deep, try nearer the bottom. Big whites also love live squid if available. If you only have dead squid, try a whole dead squid jigged up and down near the bottom. An all white jig, yoyoed near the bottom, is another good technique to try here in white seabass season.

The biggest sheephead I've ever seen came from Eagle Reef. Whole, head-on shrimp, available at any oriental grocery store, are the best bait for these reef-dwelling wrasse. Also found on the bottom are bocaccio, sculpin, an occasional rock sole, and sometimes in winter, lingcod. Fishing live bait near the bottom will give you a shot at these species.

When I get bored hauling big fish in (yeah, right!), I take a light graphite spinning rod and reel. With 6-pound test, a number 6 hook, and tiny strips of cut squid, I have a blast with blue perch (halfmoons). They grow to a really nice size here, some in the 2-pound range. On light tackle they can be lots of fun and, of course, they're one of the best eating fish out there.

Main Island—East Side

Ship Rock to Bird Rock

Here is one of the few areas on the front (eastern) side of Catalina that has anything like a flat bottom. Between the two rocks, there is perhaps a square mile of water 100 feet deep with a rugged rocky bottom. Much of the bottom has kelp, but it is generally thin and easy to navigate. This entire area is ideal fish habitat, and every sort of southern California game fish, from resident species to the surface feeding pelagic species, all congregate in this area to chase around the schools of bait that also seem to gravitate here.

The best bet is to pick a likely spot by metering the bottom, drop anchor, and then test different depths until you find out what species are feeding and the best depth to catch them. The potential strike zone includes everything from the surface to the bottom, so stay alert.

Calico bass, bonito, barracuda, yellowtail, bocaccio, sheephead, white seabass, sculpin, and blue perch are all regular visitors to this area and are all a possibility when fishing here. It's best to anticipate bigger fish—start out with a 20-pound test rig until you're sure of what's biting

This area and Eagle Reef are excellent flyfishing spots. The island's tall mountains shelter the area from the prevailing winds, so casting is a breeze (no pun intended.) I like to start with my 12-weight with a shooting head, sinking fly line. A blue and white Clouser minnow is my favorite, but I sometimes like to switch to green, black, and white. A red and yellow shrimp fly gets lots of attention, especially in the warmer summer months when pelagic crabs (sometimes called tuna crabs or red crabs) are in the area. I've seen squid flies but have never tried one out, although I plan to as soon as I can. I'll bet it would be a wintertime killer.

Avalon

I have included Avalon Bay since nearly everyone can get to it easily, and weekenders often like to bring along their fishing rods for a few minutes of surf casting or pier fishing. Fishing around Avalon is a wonderful experience, much nicer than most of the mainland shore fishing. The scenic beauty and crystal clear water of Avalon lend an exotic quality to the fishing that you just can't seem to find at the graffiti-adorned rocks and seawalls around much of the Los Angeles area.

In Avalon Bay, the Green Pleasure Pier stretches out into the main part of the harbor. Although it's a small pier, don't overlook it if you find yourself in Avalon. From here, the water is as clear as glass, and all sorts of small game fish are available. Just a small piece of squid on a tiny hook, #6 or even #8, and you're all set up for some really fun fishing. You can catch calico bass, blue perch, opaleye, and many other types of fish. Be sure to return any undersized calicos (less than 12 inches) to the water and any garibaldi you might catch. The pier has bait, rental tackle, and is open 24 hours a day.

At the pier, you can rent small boats to take out in the bay. The catches are similar to the pier, but you're able to be more mobile. Some of the better places are out

Main Island—East Side

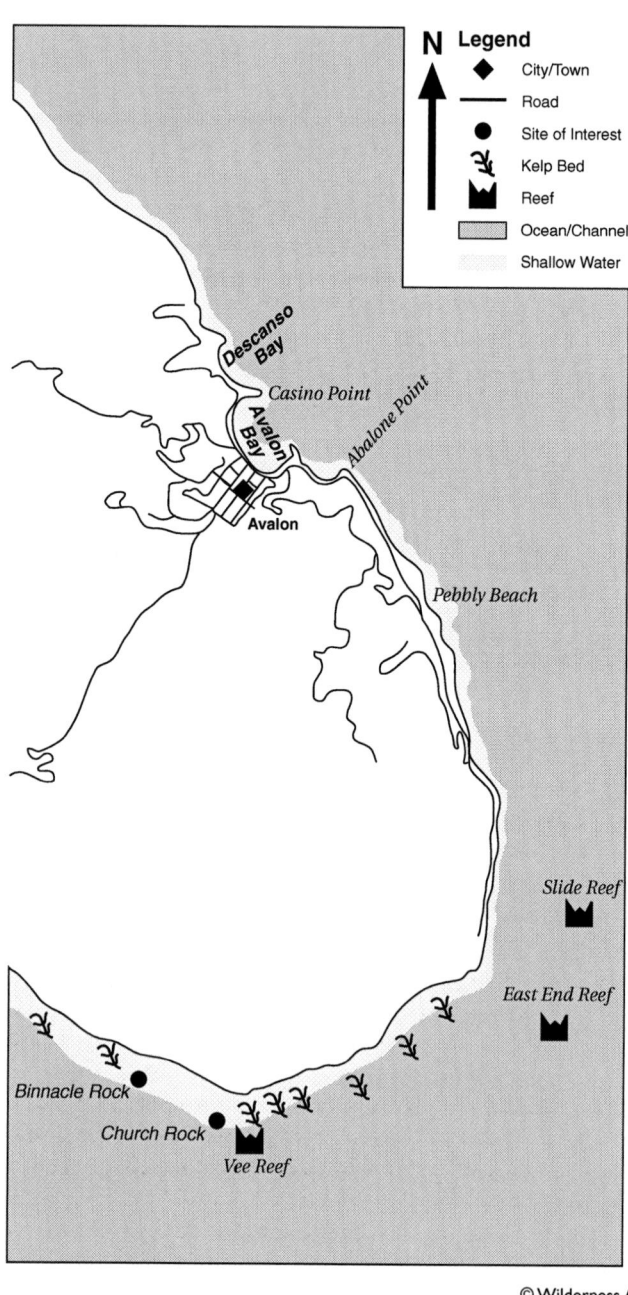

N

Legend

◆ City/Town

━ Road

● Site of Interest

🌿 Kelp Bed

♜ Reef

▨ Ocean/Channel

▨ Shallow Water

Descanso Bay

Casino Point

Avalon Bay

Abalone Point

Avalon

Pebbly Beach

Slide Reef

East End Reef

Binnacle Rock

Church Rock

Vee Reef

© Wilderness Adventures Press

among the boat moorings or near the bay's rocky banks. Just about anywhere you go, there are plenty of fish. If you decide not to rent a boat, you can also cast out to some excellent fish habitat from the rocky shoreline. It's a short and easy walk from the island's hotels and bed and breakfasts to get to the pier fishing and most of the bay's shoreline fishing.

Slide Reef

Named after the rock quarry on shore, Slide Reef is located just offshore from Catalina's east end. Along the shoreline are several exposed rocks, called Seal Rocks, and many years an excellent stand of thick kelp can be found just offshore. Sometimes, especially after two El Niño years in a row, there is practically no kelp. Whatever the case, there are several square miles of excellent fish habitat here.

Calico bass are Slide Reef's mainstay, but like most of the Catalina kelp beds, a number of different species either live here year-round or come to visit during the warmer summer months. Fish at different depths to discover the main species in the offing on the day you visit; then adjust your tackle and techniques to suit.

Breezers (bigger exotic fish) often visit these reefs looking for a meal. Look for yellowtail, dorado in warmer years, and an occasional bluefin tuna. Be prepared at all times with heavier tackle—30- or even 40-pound test in case tuna show up—or at least have a jig rigged to toss at any passers-by. With heavier bait fishing gear, it helps to have some Spanish mackerel in the bait tank. These can usually be caught with a Lucky Joe, Lucky Laura, or Sabiki bait rig, jigged up and down near the surface along the edges of kelp beds. Spanish mackerel are smaller and make better bait than the more common green-backed Pacific mackerel.

East End Reef

This reef is found just south of Slide Reef and extends farther offshore. This is actually a series of reefs with mud, shale, and sandflats in between. This is some of the best bottom fishing around the island, with the possible exception of the West End Shelf. Here you can go from rockpile to rockpile, catching calico bass, sheephead, white seabass (in season), and occasionally surface fish, such as bonito, barracuda, and yellowtail. When you drift away from the rocks, you're all set for halibut, sand bass, sculpin, and other flats species.

In addition to all of these, the East End Reef is a great shark fishing destination, with threshers, leopards, and rays on the bottom, and plenty of wandering blue sharks on the surface. Mako sharks periodically cruise through the area, and a fish in excess of 300 pounds isn't rare.

To fish, use traditional flats techniques around the reefs. Live squid or whole squid (live or freshly dead if you suspect white seabass are present) on a Carolina rig should be sent to the bottom with as little weight as possible to keep them down. For a change of pace, run a lead-headed rubber swimbait down amid the rocks or bounce it along the flats. Another useful technique is to use squid-baited shrimp flies in the flats and near the rocks. You'll get a chance at a wide variety of fish with these techniques.

The comeback of the white seabass through conservation and breeding efforts has become a model of sound fisheries management. Photo courtesy Bob Halal.

Vee Reef

Named for its V shape, Vee Reef is an often overlooked, smaller fishing spot that produces when no others seem to. It's a great place for wandering schools of pelagic fish to gather. Barracudas are the most frequently found denizens of Vee Reef, but bonito and yellowtail can be on the menu often, as well. The reef generally sports a small but usually thick stand of kelp forest where such resident species as calicos, sheephead, and white seabass generally abound.

I usually can't resist trolling past the Vee when traveling to or from the Farnsworth Bank. I usually get a jig stop and more often than not it is a big log barracuda. And where there's one barracuda, there are many others, so break out the jig sticks with blue and white or green hardware for some fun-filled barracuda action.

And don't ignore the reef's resident species: There are big white seabass here aplenty. In winter and spring, when squid are running on Catalina's backside, this reef can be extremely productive for these big croakers. You can usually catch bait while it's dark by using a powerful light and a squid jig—you then have a white seabass' favorite breakfast. Send them down on a Carolina rig into the reef and hang on, you won't be disappointed often. Winter yellowtail also go after live squid, and I've hauled some up from the deep in the off season enough times to make me certain it's not coincidence.

The kelp beds at Vee Reef are a great place to fish for calico in the warmer summer months. Live bait, swimming plugs, or rubber lures all work well. In the mornings, especially when the wind is minimal, some fun and productive flyfishing can also be done at this reef.

Steve Eckhardt with a nice yellowtail caught at Catalina Island. Photo courtesy Steve Eckhardt.

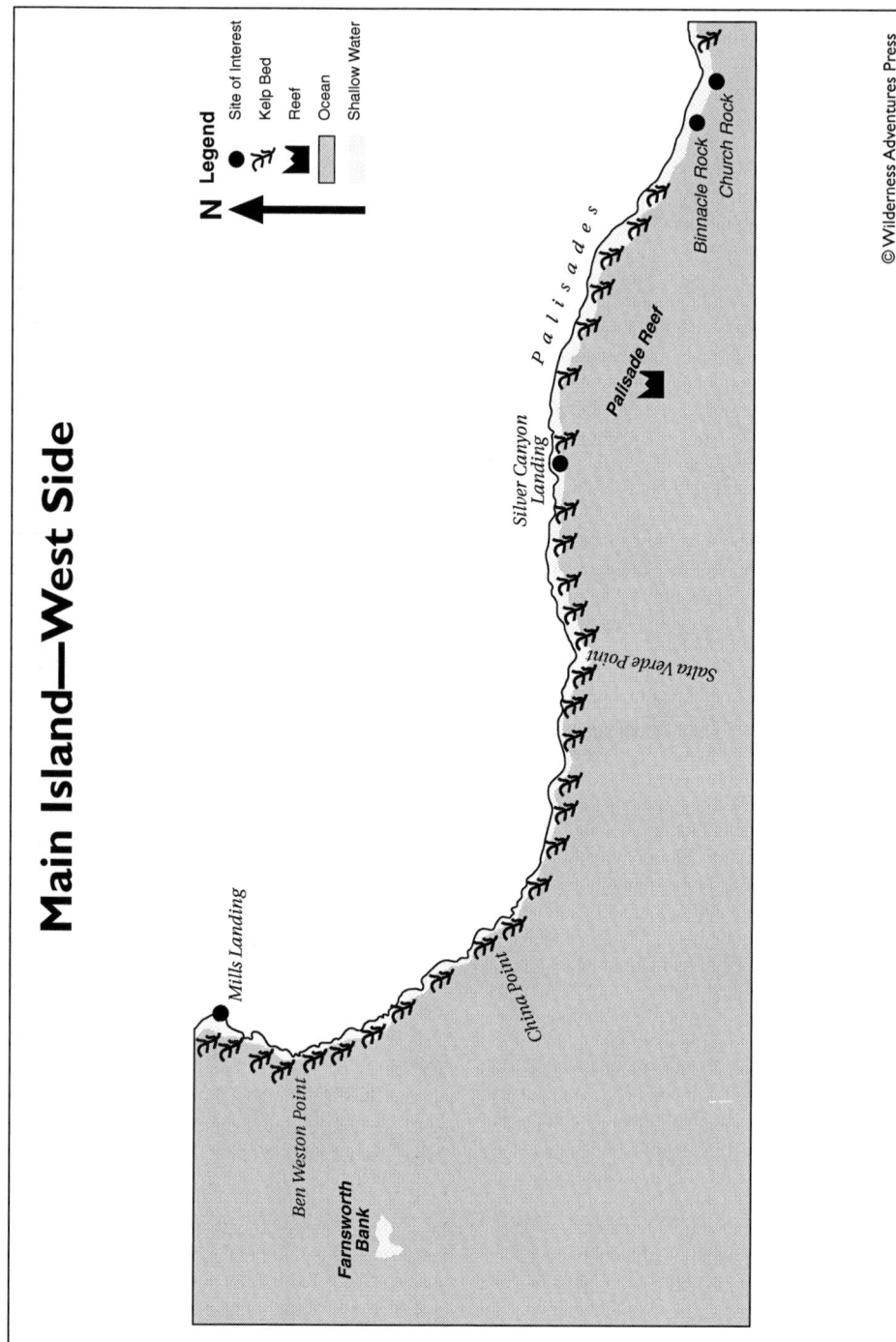

Main Island—West Side

Main Island—West Side

Palisades Reef

The Catalina Palisades plunge steeply down from about 1800 feet straight into the ocean. It looks like something from a 1930s monster movie—all that's needed is a castle on the top and a thunderstorm. In the light of day, however, the view is stunning, the colors vibrant, and the natural wonders of the place are more relaxing than forbidding.

Tucked in close to the shore at the Palisades are some rocky reefs, generally heavily festooned with kelp. This is one of Catalina's finest white seabass spots. Of course there are plenty more species of fish here, including calicos, sheephead, whitefish, barracuda, and bonito, so you can pretty much pick your poison. The traditional fishing techniques for these species all apply here.

Salta Verde Reef

Salta Verde Point is a prominent landmark along the island's back side. It marks the end of the mountain ridge that formed the Palisades. As this point plunges into the sea, a string of rocky reefs, called Salta Verde Reef, extend only a few hundred yards from the beach. Salta Verde Reef is generally covered with a thick blanket of kelp in most years, except exceptionally warm ones, so it has all the cover needed for excellent fish habitat.

The two main game fish here are calico bass and, in the cooler months, white seabass. Calicos generally feed at the surface here, so a flylined anchovy is often preferable to using a sinker for these kelp dwellers. I like a swimming plug here and have also had luck with a blue and white shad-shaped rubber lure. For bigger white seabass, a live squid is always the best bet. But many other techniques, including anchovies, sardines, or Spanish mackerel fished deep, and rubber lures or metallic bone jigs, fished from the midwater column to deeper water, all have their days and should all be considered when chasing these great-eating game fish.

Farnsworth Bank

Probably the best all-round fishin' hole at Catalina is the famous Farnsworth Bank. Esteemed by early sportfishing pioneers as a great place for catching bluefin tuna, Farnsworth still attracts tuna in the better years. It is also nearly synonymous with great yellowtail fishing and attracts bonito and barracuda, as well.

Trolling usually works for locating whatever schools of fish are in the area. And, as always, diving birds are an indication that big fish have chased bait to the surface.

If Farnsworth was only a pelagic fish bank, it would still be wonderful, but its secret is that it's a great bottom-fishing bank, too. There are probably more big white seabass caught here than anywhere at Catalina, and in winter, big lingcod come up from the depths until spring. Send down large sardines, small Spanish mackerel, or even double-hooked Pacific mackerel to entice these 50-pounders to strike. I like a big green, sparkly, twin-tailed scampi, baited with a thin strip of squid. I send it down on my jig stick with Spectra line so I can make it dance and twitch. It drives them wild!

You can also fish for rock cod at Farnsworth Bank. I use 4/0 marabou and bucktail shrimp flies, bait them with thin strips of cut squid, and send them down on 5- or 6-hook gangions into the rocky bottoms. It usually takes only a few drops to get a limit. Barberpoles, chilipeppers, bocaccio, and reds are all common at the bank. This bank is another of southern California's fine fishing spots.

Access to Santa Catalina Island

Situated only 22 miles from the Los Angeles Harbor San Pedro channel entrance, Catalina is readily accessible by passenger boat, helicopter, private aircraft, sportfishing boats, or private boats. Both Avalon and Two Harbors have overnight accommodations, and many camping facilities are available on the island. For information on travel and accommodations, contact the Catalina Island Visitors Bureau at 310-510-1520.

To travel by water, the Catalina Express operates from Long Beach, San Pedro, and Dana Point on the mainland to both Avalon and Two Harbors (the isthmus) on the island. Reservations are required, and the company can be contacted at 800-481-3470. Their schedule is on the Internet at http://www.catalina.com/express_outlink.htm.

Another passenger boat service is the Catalina Flyer, operating from Newport Bay at the Balboa Pavilion to Avalon Bay. They can be contacted at 949-673-5245. Reservations are also required. Another passenger ferry service is offered by Catalina Cruises out of Long Beach. They have several boats and boast the fastest boat to the island in addition to a classic fleet of boats. They can be contacted at 800-CATALINA or visit their website at http://www.catalina.com/cruises_outlink.htm, where a schedule is posted.

For the more adventurous, helicopter rides to Catalina are a faster and more exciting (though more expensive) way to cross the channel. The views are spectacular and are an experience of a lifetime. Island Express Helicopters operates from both San Pedro and Long Beach to the Catalina airport. From the island's airport, a shuttle bus is available to the city of Avalon.

For private pilots, Catalina has an excellent airport with a 3250-foot runway capable of handling almost all light aircraft up to and including DC-3s. There is no aviation fuel available, but the airport has all the other amenities, including a café. Overnight tie-down is available for a small fee. The airport, managed by the Catalina Conservancy, has a small landing fee to help pay for its maintenance. Call 310-510-0143 for general airport information or 800-255-8700 for weather information.

Most sportfishing landings offer Catalina fishing trips. To fish the backside, boats generally leave the night before, run overnight, make bait in the predawn darkness (you're expected to help) and fish from daybreak until midafternoon. Many of the landings at San Pedro, Long Beach, Newport Beach, and Dana Point offer these island overnight trips.

Three-quarter-day boats from San Pedro and Long Beach sometimes fish the near side of Catalina, usually only when local fishing is slow. You can call the landings and ask, but travel to the island is almost always at the discretion of the boat's captain.

For the private boater, Catalina is basically an uncomplicated sea trip, with minimal navigation difficulties and generally fair weather. However, it is an open sea voyage and should only be attempted by someone with the experience and confidence in his or her equipment to make the trip. Catalina offers two harbors, and Avalon has over 400 moorings. They're offered on a first-come, first-served basis, but you can bet that you will be out of luck on a Saturday night in summer. Avalon has fuel and a taxi service to the pier from moorings. Call 310-510-2683 or VHF channel 9 for more information.

The other main harbor is Two Harbors, a small, quaint village at the isthmus. The only boat moorage is by anchoring in the harbor and surrounding coves, and a taxi service is available through VHF Channel 9 or with three blasts of the boat horn. A dinghy dock is also available for tenders up to 13 feet. A gas and diesel dock is in the harbor and a mechanic is available. For more information, contact the Harbor Department on VHF Channel 9 or 310-510-COVE, or contact Two Harbors Visitor Information at 310-510-0303.

For most private boaters, Catalina is a day trip, but you can stay overnight and anchor up in any secluded cove on the protected front (mainland) side. Caution is advised because there are plenty of boiler and slightly submerged rocks near the coast. You have to pull right up close to the island to be in water shallow enough to get a good anchor set.

Back in my commercial fishing days, I had a favorite cove at Catalina where I used to stay on the hook. The area for an anchor set was quite small, and I usually let out 300 feet of line or so to get a good scope. Once set, the boat was actually over 200 feet of water. A commercial fishing boat always draws a crowd when anchored, since everyone else assumes the commercial fisherman knows what he's doing. Time after time, small boaters would pull up and drop their anchors, only to find out the anchor couldn't touch bottom and would then drift backward. They'd pull up again, try it again, and achieve the same results. Sometimes they'd try three or four times. Eventually, they'd be off to try someplace else, only to be followed by yet another boat trying to anchor next to me.

On the backside you have to be a bit choosier since the brunt of the northwesterly weather assaults this side of the island. Catalina Harbor, on the backside of the isthmus, is probably the best anchorage and has a good flat bottom for anchoring.

For most boaters, though, Catalina is a day trip, and most well built sea type 18 footers have little trouble making the trip. San Pedro is the closest port, but Long Beach, Huntington Harbor, Newport Beach, or Dana Point are all excellent ports for access to the island.

COMMON GAME FISH AVAILABILITY BY MONTHS
SANTA CATALINA ISLAND

Species	Jan	Feb	Mar	Apr	May	Jun	Jul	Aug	Sep	Oct	Nov	Dec
Yellowtail												
Barracuda												
Bonito												
Calico Bass												
Sand Bass												
White Seabass												
Halibut												
Lingcod												
Shallow-water Rockfish												
Deep-water Rockfish												
Sheephead												
Sculpin												
Blue Perch												
Opaleye												
Whitefish												

Legend:

☐ Not Available ▨ Fish Possible ▨ Good Fishing ■ Excellent Fishing

SAN CLEMENTE ISLAND

San Clemente Island is the southernmost of southern California's offshore islands. This long thin island is probably the best coastal fishing area in the whole region. Situated farther offshore, it receives fairly light fishing pressure as compared to the heavily fished shore side spots or the popular and closer Santa Catalina Island.

The Naval Ocean Systems Center occupies all of San Clemente Island, and the island's northern end has a permanent naval base. Though the Navy has an airfield on the base, it is not for civilian use, and anyone attempting to land there except in an extreme emergency would probably be in deep trouble. The Navy's primary harbor on the island, Northwest Harbor, is open to private boaters as a safe anchorage at night. In the northern part of the island along the east-facing coast, Wilson's Cove is an area where the Navy has sensitive underwater listening devices—you cannot anchor there. I choose to avoid the area entirely, since violators are given very little, if any, slack.

The southern half of the island is used as a target for naval aircraft and ships. Missile launches, shelling, and bombing runs are regularly practiced. Pyramid Cove, which is nearly the entire southern shore of the island, gets shelled frequently, and the Navy's security patrol force gets quite testy when an errant boater wanders into the shelling area or tries to cross under the shell's arc. Keep in mind that the ships tossing those shells toward the beach can be as much as 25 miles away. You never see them—all you see is the beach exploding and feel the concussion of tons of high explosives going off. Having experienced this first-hand from a distance of nearly 5 miles, I can assure you that you don't want to be any closer. The Coast Guard posts a Notice to Mariners when practice exercises are being planned. Be sure to check the latest notices before planning a trip to San Clemente. These are now also available online at the Coast Guard's Internet website: http://www.navcen.uscg.mil/

San Clemente Island is about 35 miles long and less than 5 miles wide throughout its length. The northwest corner is 48.9 nautical miles on a 213-degree course from Newport Harbor and 60.4 nautical miles from Oceanside along a 246-degree course. The southeastern corner, Pyramid Head, is 49.9 miles from Dana Point on a 206-degree course, and 57.2 nautical miles from Point Loma at the entrance to San Diego Bay.

Fishing San Clemente Island

San Clemente Island has everything a saltwater angler could want: kelp beds, reefs, rocks, deep water reefs, and sandflats. You can fish in well-protected waters or exposed to the open expanse of the Pacific. You can troll, drift-fish, or anchor up, and you can fish with bait, lures, or by casting flies. You name it—San Clemente Island has it. Since it's the farthest south of all the offshore islands, the bigger, pelagic game fish arrive sooner and leave later. It has the biggest population of yellowtail anywhere on the coast. In all, San Clemente is THE place for serious saltwater fishermen to get the most and biggest of southern California's marvelous array of game fish.

Excellent fishing can be found all around San Clemente, but some of the more famous spots and areas are as follows:

San Clemente Island

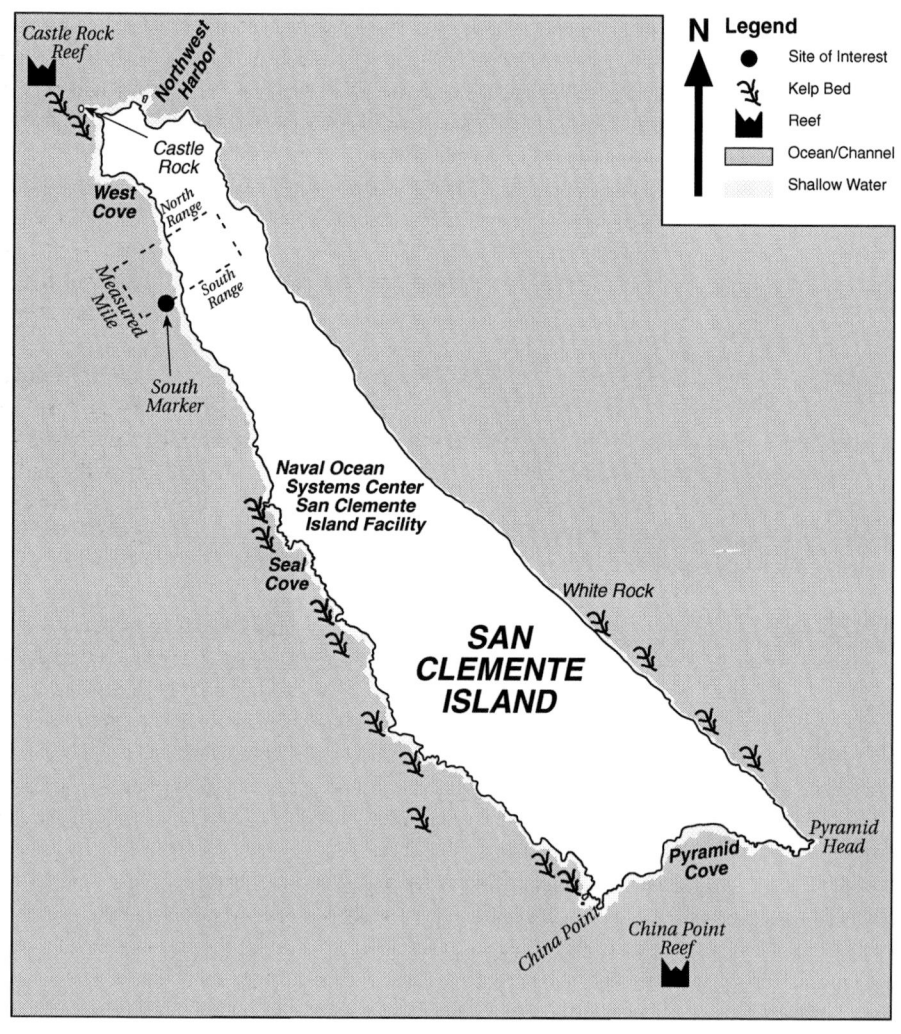

Legend

- Site of Interest
- Kelp Bed
- Reef
- Ocean/Channel
- Shallow Water

Castle Rock Reef
Northwest Harbor
Castle Rock
West Cove
North Range
South Range
Measured Mile
South Marker
Naval Ocean Systems Center San Clemente Island Facility
Seal Cove
White Rock
SAN CLEMENTE ISLAND
Pyramid Cove
Pyramid Head
China Point
China Point Reef

© Wilderness Adventures Press

White Rock to Pyramid Head

This is a prime area for most species near the kelp beds. The bottom drops off very quickly, and most fishing can be done very close to the island. The island's towering cliffs protect fishermen from wind, so flyfishing is excellent here. Look for the usual calico bass in the kelp forests—flipping swimbaits is very productive here. Good yellowtail action is sometimes witnessed, especially in spring and summer. During fall, fish seem to prefer the windward side of the island.

Many species of shallow water rockfish can be taken on the canyon walls. Drop bait, baited shrimp flies, or rubber swimbaits deep along the dropoffs to entice these species to bite. Keep a sharp eye on the current, since you'll be fishing within 100 feet or so from shore and anchoring will be difficult because of the dropoff.

China Point Reef

About 1½ miles south-southeast of China Point is a rocky reef that attracts a wide variety of both shallow water and deep water rockfish. This proliferation of life also tends to bring in bigger surface-feeding predators as well. You can catch yellowtail, barracuda, bonito, sheephead, red rock cod, lingcod, bocaccios, and many other species in this one area.

This reef is best fished with bone jigs or rubber swimbaits. You can bait either setup with thin strips of squid to enhance the scent. Cast out, let the lure sink until it hits bottom, then retrieve quickly for perhaps 30 to 50 cranks, then declutch and let the jig sink again. Repeat and you won't be disappointed. The fish often strike as the lure is fluttering down, so be alert to sudden changes in the way the line comes off on the sink. The water here is about 30 to 40 fathoms (180 to 240 feet) deep.

China Point to Seal Cove

Along the windward side, the fishing is great. Being farthest from the coast, it receives the least fishing pressure, and the windward side of the island is littered with rocks, reefs, crevasses, kelp beds, and all sorts of prime fish habitat. You can fish the kelp beds with bait or lures for chasing big bull calicos or switch to flies on less windy days or early in the day.

Plenty of yellowtail visit the area, and this is perhaps the hottest yellowtail area in all of southern California. Trolling, especially on warm summer days, works well to locate schools. Once a school is located, break out the bait, jigs, lures, or flies for lots of action. On cooler days or earlier in the season, let jigs, lures, or bait sink nearly to the bottom. You will be surprised at times to see how effective this can be. I've had people scoff at me when fishing the bottom with rubber scampi, thinking I was trying to catch lowly rockfish. They certainly switched tactics in a hurry when I started pulling up yellowtails that were 30 pounds and over.

This section of San Clemente holds a healthy population of white seabass. These huge croakers, sometimes in excess of 50 pounds, are a wintertime bonus for fishermen willing to brave the long crossing to Clemente. Live squid is best, and in winter it's usually not difficult to catch all you need in the predawn darkness using a bright light and squid jigs. Otherwise, bigger green sparkle twin-tailed scampi and mojo type jigs, sweetened with a thin strip of squid and sent down into the midwater or rocky reef is just the ticket for these big, hard-fighting game fish.

Seal Cove to the South Marker

Like the area below it, this stretch of San Clemente Island is also filled with reefs, kelp forests, and rocks. It is one of the best areas on the island for bass fishing. About a mile northwest of Seal Cove, just offshore from a rocky outcropping, there is a rocky reef rising to 4 fathoms (24 feet) from a bottom 12 to 20 fathoms deep. This is white seabass heaven in the winter and yellowtail alley in the summer. You won't go wrong fishing this area any time of the year.

Measured Mile Escarpment

From a small shelf that gradually slopes away from the island, the bottom takes a sudden dropoff from about 60 fathoms (360 feet) to 600 fathoms (three-quarters

Tom Bette of Western Outdoor News, *the most-read weekly periodical for southern California saltwater fishing, is all smiles as he hooks up on a fly. Photo courtesy Mike & Regina Scott—Mike Scott's Hackle, Tackle & Flies.*

of a mile deep) only about 3½ miles from the island. This undersea cliff is one of the best deep water rockfish areas around the island. The erose bottom keeps the commercial net fishermen away, and few San Clemente Island regulars seek out deep water rockfish in favor of shallower water species, so the big schools of red rock cod, cowcod, boscos, and other deep water fish thrive and prosper. There are plenty of big lingcod, also, in 800 feet of water or deeper in the summer but rising to the canyon rim in the winter.

West Cove

The cove area just south of the northwest end of San Clemente Island is a bit different than the rest of the island. There are the usual rocky bottoms, kelp beds, boiler rocks (BE CAREFUL), and shallow reefs near shore where the calico and barracuda fishing is prime, but just offshore is a broad flats area with plenty of whitefish, sanddabs, and big halibut on the prowl. In addition, springtime brings hordes of nesting sand bass for an angler's enjoyment.

Swimbaits are king in the West Cove area. Nearly every species will hit them with aplomb. Try darker colors, such as root beer and deep reds, on overcast days and greens or whites on sunny days. Single-tailed rubber baitfish imitators also work well in blue shad and brown bait colors, or sardine (green and yellow) colors. For some real fun, send down a three-hook gangion with 1/0-sized shrimp flies baited with tiny strips of squid. On many days, the sinker won't hit the bottom before all three hooks have sanddabs attached.

Castle Rock and the 7-Fathom Reef

Just off the northwest end of the island is Castle Rock. It is aptly named for its resemblance to a medieval castle with towers, spires, and parapets. This is the center of some excellent fishing in the many rocks and reefs surrounding the area. Most years, dense kelp forests blanket the area and make for excellent calico, barracuda, and bonito fishing, with plenty of yellowtail in the warmer months.

Don't forget about hitting the bottom and picking up some variety while you're there. A number of years ago, I caught a whitefish that had to be more than 2 feet long. I didn't know what it was at first, thinking I'd perhaps landed some sort of deformed yellowtail. All the whitefish I'd ever seen were in the 10- to 12-inch range, and here was this giant. Had I known at the time, I might have brought it home whole to see if it qualified for some sort of record. Instead, I just ate it—it was tasty, too.

About 0.85 nautical miles west-northwest of Castle Rock there is a great fishing reef, called the 7-Fathom Reef or sometimes the 9-Fathom Spot (don't ask me why). The reef rises to 7 fathoms (42 feet) and holds plenty of fish. The bottom is especially good for white seabass and shallow water rockfish in winter, and calico bass, yellowtail, barracuda, and bonito in summer. Work this reef as you would the edges of a kelp bed in the warm summer months and switch to bottom fishing techniques in the cooler water months.

Northwest Harbor

Believe it or not, Northwest Harbor is probably the most overlooked fishing ho' spot on San Clemente Island. Right in the center of the harbor is a sunken World War II destroyer escort named the Butler. It was sunk as a training exercise for Navy underwater demolition teams in 1970. The 306-foot-long ship lies in 80 to 90 feet of water and is in two pieces on the bottom. It's a popular scuba-diving destination since the water is generally calm in the harbor. The Butler is home to an enormous population of fish, from huge bull sheephead to bass, rockfish, and many other species.

A sandflat that is located just outside Northwest Harbor must have the biggest populations of flatfish anywhere in southern California. You can barely get a sinker to the bottom without getting hit by sanddabs. A barrel of fun awaits the light tackle fisherman dropping squid-strip-baited shrimp flies onto this flat.

Here's another secret about Northwest Harbor: Drop a crab net baited with the center of a fillet while anchored up during lobster season. You'll have a great dinner since there seem to be plenty of these tasty bottom dwellers here. However, be sure any lobsters are of legal size and taken in-season. The penalties are stiff, and it's just not kosher to violate the well-thought-out sportfishing rules.

Access to San Clemente Island

San Clemente Island is a popular spot at certain times of the year for overnight party boats based from San Diego to San Pedro. Check with local landings for trip information. Some overnight six-pack boats also travel to San Clemente. High-speed twin turbo diesel sportfishing boat charters can make it to the island and back for one-day trips, but expect to pay a healthy premium since these boats guzzle the fuel at an astounding rate. San Clemente Island is best fished from private boats.

San Clemente Island is a long way from land and can seldom be seen from land, nor can you see the mainland from the island. It takes real experience, a very reliable seagoing vessel, and the proper navigational equipment to make it. If you have the slightest doubt about any of the three, don't attempt the trip. Leave it to licensed, experienced charter captains. Fortunately, the island is big and awfully hard to miss if you can steer a moderately acceptable course, and the weather, especially in summer, is usually mild. But the ocean is unpredictable—just when you think everything is wonderful, it has a way of throwing a temper tantrum and putting you right in your place. I ran across a Hobie Cat one summer about 18 miles outside of San Diego Bay that was headed west in the late afternoon way out of sight of any land. I was on my way home from a few great days fishing at San Clemente Island. When I asked the two teenaged boys aboard where they were headed, they replied, "Back to San Diego."

I answered, "It's that way," pointing southeast.

They responded with a shrug and an, "Oh, OK," then started turning their boat.

I have no doubt if I hadn't come along, they would just be statistics by now. Don't make the same mistake.

COMMON GAME FISH AVAILABILITY BY MONTHS
SAN CLEMENTE ISLAND

Species	Jan	Feb	Mar	Apr	May	Jun	Jul	Aug	Sep	Oct	Nov	Dec
Yellowtail			Possible	Good	Possible	Excellent	Excellent	Excellent	Excellent	Excellent	Good	
Barracuda		Possible	Good	Excellent	Excellent	Excellent	Excellent	Excellent	Excellent	Good	Excellent	
Bonito		Possible	Good	Possible	Excellent	Excellent	Excellent	Excellent	Excellent	Excellent	Good	Possible
Calico Bass	Possible	Possible	Good	Good	Excellent	Excellent	Excellent	Excellent	Excellent	Good	Possible	Possible
Sand Bass	Possible	Possible	Good	Excellent	Excellent	Excellent	Excellent	Excellent	Good	Good	Possible	Possible
White Seabass	Excellent	Good	Good	Good	Possible	Possible	Possible	Possible	Possible	Good	Excellent	Excellent
Halibut	Good	Good	Good	Good	Good	Good	Good	Good	Good	Good	Good	Good
Lingcod	Excellent	Excellent	Good	Good	Possible	Possible	Possible	Possible	Possible	Good	Excellent	Excellent
Shallow-water Rockfish	Excellent	Excellent	Good	Good	Good	Good	Possible	Possible	Possible	Good	Excellent	Excellent
Deep-water Rockfish	Excellent	Excellent	Good	Good	Good	Good	Good	Good	Good	Good	Excellent	Excellent
Sheephead		Possible	Good	Possible	Excellent	Excellent	Excellent	Excellent	Good	Good	Possible	
Sculpin	Excellent	Good	Possible	Possible	Possible	Good	Excellent	Excellent	Excellent	Good	Good	Good
Blue Perch	Possible	Possible	Excellent	Excellent	Excellent	Excellent	Good	Good	Excellent	Excellent	Excellent	
Opaleye			Possible	Possible	Excellent	Excellent	Excellent	Excellent	Excellent	Excellent	Good	
Whitefish	Excellent	Excellent	Good	Good	Good	Good	Possible	Good	Excellent	Excellent	Excellent	Excellent

	Not Available		Fish Possible		Good Fishing		Excellent Fishing

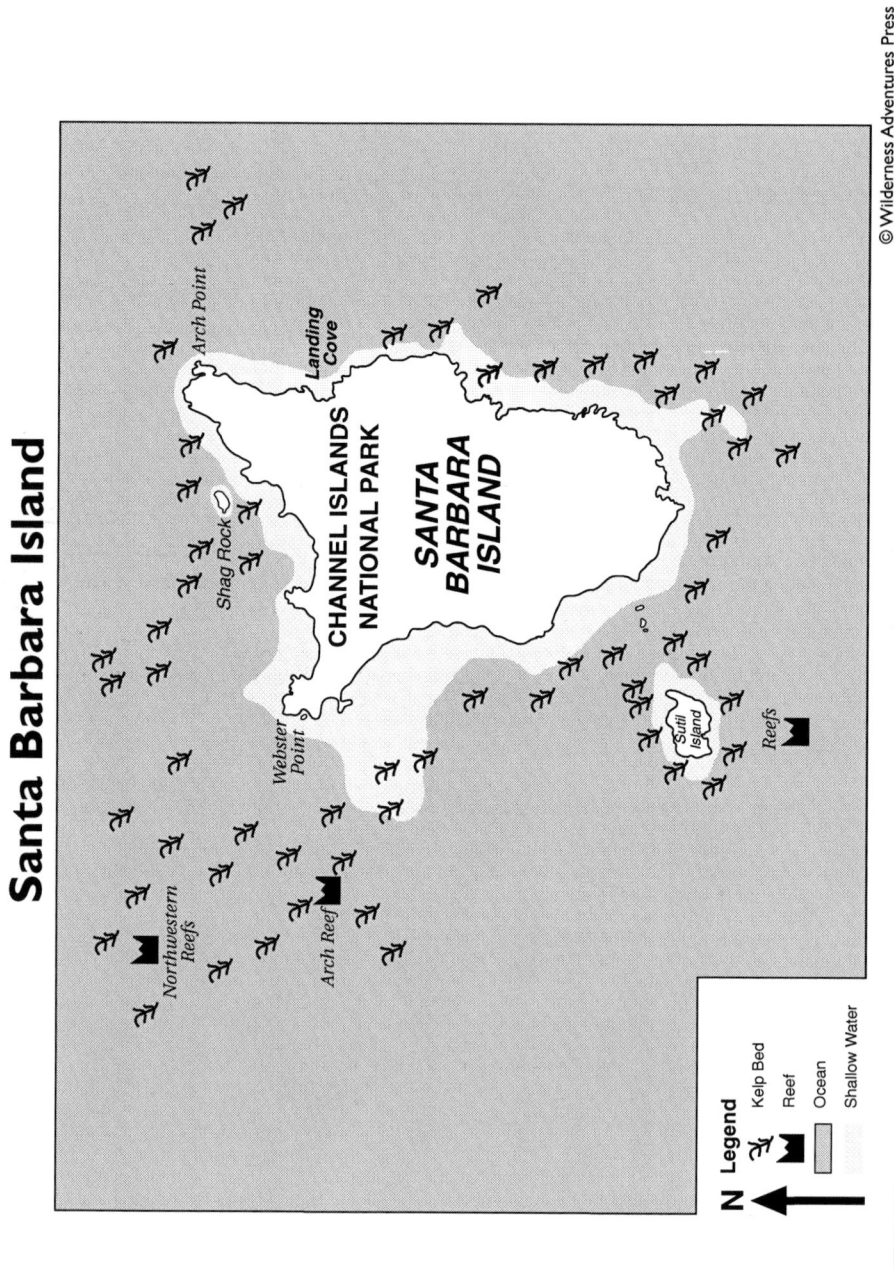

Santa Barbara Island

© Wilderness Adventures Press

Arch Point

Landing Cove

CHANNEL ISLANDS
NATIONAL PARK

SANTA
BARBARA
ISLAND

Shag Rock

Webster
Point

Sutil
Island

Reefs

Northwestern
Reefs

Arch Reef

N

Legend

Kelp Bed

Reef

Ocean

Shallow Water

Santa Barbara Island

Santa Barbara Island is a wonderful place to fish. This small, lonely island appears like a twin mountain rising from the sea when viewed from a distance. Closer, the marvelous details of towering cliffs with rocky textures are revealed as the scent of wild flowers and sagebrush greets the arriving fisherman. Since the island is quite a way offshore, it doesn't receive the fishing pressure of the near-shore fishing spots, so a wider variety and far less wary quarry await the fisherman able to make the journey from the coast.

Santa Barbara Island is part of Channel Islands National Park and is owned by the U.S. federal government. This is a small island, with the main island covering only 639 acres. Just to the southwest of the main island is a tiny island named Sutil Island. It has a wide variety of life in a number of diverse habitats. Most notable are the huge numbers of sea birds nesting on the island, safe from the wandering predators that are found at some of the larger islands and the mainland contain. Many sea mammals, seals, and sea lions, also make Santa Barbara Island their home.

Santa Barbara Island is 38 nautical miles west (221-degree course) from Redondo Harbor or 40.8 nautical miles on a 236-degree heading from the western Los Angeles harbor entrance. It is only accessible by boat. There are no aviation facilities on the island. In fact, there is only one manmade structure on the island: the national park ranger station located just a short walk from the best anchorage on the island, Landing Cove. The ranger station has a visitor contact station with a small museum showing the islands' varied wildlife. A campground with more than 6 miles of hiking trails makes the island an interesting outdoor adventure to explore.

Fishing Santa Barbara Island

Santa Barbara Island is a fisherman's dream. Wide fields of unmolested kelp forests harbor a strong population of calico bass for year-round fishing fun. During summer, barracuda, bonito, and yellowtail appear in significant numbers to feast on the huge schools of baitfish seeking shelter in the kelp. In winter, lingcod and white seabass come to feast on the cooler water squid populations spawning in the nighttime ocean around the island. All year, excellent catches of flatfish in the flat bottom areas, shallow water rockfish in the reefs and rocky areas, and deep water rockfish in the deeper reefs give fishermen plenty to target.

Just about anywhere around Santa Barbara Island can be successfully fished—especially areas with kelp beds nearby. Following are some suggested areas to target and methods to maximize your fishing fun and enjoyment:

Arch Point Area

The Arch Point area is prime fishing country for calico bass. Work the outer edges of the kelp beds with live bait, rubber "swim bait lures," hard casting lures, or bait fish imitating flies. Especially good are blue and white streamer flies or all white, flashy streamers imitating anchovies. A slow, erratic retrieve usually drives the kelp bass nuts and you'll quickly know if bass are about and hungry.

Certain times of the year, barracuda, bonito and, yellowtail cruise the outer edges of the Arch Point kelp and will strike baits or lures intended for calicos. If boils are seen (fish striking bait on the surface), floating bait fish imitations work best, or try metal bone jigs. Blue and white or green and yellow colors are summertime killers while green and black, purple squid or black and white "pissed off squid" color patterns work better in the cooler months.

On the bottom, you'll find rocky reefs and hard surfaces. Here, sculpin, whitefish, and sheephead are plentiful for the bait fisherman.

Southern Area

The southern area also has productive kelp beds, but the real game fish here are barracuda and bonito in the spring and summer and yellowtail in the summer and fall. The best bet is live bait fished with just enough lead to get it through the wandering schools of mackerel on the surface. Too many mackerel in the area, while fun to catch, don't allow you a chance to hook a more desired game fish. If all you can seem to catch is mackerel, move or switch to sinking jigs to get below the surface feeding macks.

There are some excellent flat fishing areas in the southern zone with ample supplies of good eating, easy to catch, sanddabs. They'll eagerly snap at multi colored shrimp flies either flyfished with a sinking, shooting head line, or sent down on conventional tackle with a sinker. Some bigger halibut inhabit the area also and will take a fly, a rubber swimbait, or a live anchovy fished on the bottom.

Sutil Island Area

There are good kelp areas for bass, along with plenty of bigger game fish to keep the fishing interesting. Work the outer edges of the kelp for bass while keeping your eyes peeled for bigger boils indicating yellowtail barracuda or bonito are in the area. Then switch tactics unless you have your heart set on filling a bag limit with calicos. This area is also a great area to troll. Use zucchini or purple/black feathers in overcast skies or Mexican flags (red, white, and green) or red/whites in the bright sun to find the schools, then break out the stationary fishing gear once productive areas are identified.

There are plenty of rocky reefs around Sutil Island, giving the angler a wide choice of species to target. White seabass, sculpin, sheephead, whitefish, blue perch, opaleye and sanddabs are just a few of the many fish you can find within a short distance from the island.

Webster Point

The Webster Point area is another kelp bed haven. Exposed to the prevailing northwest swells, this area is more difficult to fish, but can be more productive. Big calico bass fishing is the mainstay of Webster Point with wandering yellowtail, bonito, and barracuda during the spring, summer, and fall months keeping the bite interesting. As with other kelp areas, live bait will get you the most strikes but lures often attract bigger fish and have a better chance of bringing the fish to net.

Flyfishing at Webster Point is productive as long as the wind is not a major factor. Often afternoon breezes come up from the northwest, so mornings tend to be better. Be careful of fog. This area has plenty and there are enough boiler rocks to make it downright unsafe to attempt to navigate close to the island in the fog—even if your boat is radar equipped.

There is a substantial reef 900 yards west of Webster Point called Arch Reef. It comes within three fathoms (18 feet) of the surface and is probably the best spot in the whole area to fish. In addition to surface fish, all species of shallow water rockfish abound.

Northwestern Reefs

Several very productive reefs can be found about 1 to 1.2 miles northwest of Webster Point. These go by several names such as Hidden Reef, the 7½-fathom Spot, and Ten Spot. A detailed chart of the area along with a good, display type bottom meter will allow you to find these reefs with ease.

Some years these reefs harbor thick kelp forests while at other times, they may be devoid of kelp. As this book was being written, two years of extra warm El Niño water has killed off practically all the kelp. Not to worry, as with all cyclical events, the weather will return and plenty of kelp will come back. It will be great for bass fishermen but yellowtail fishermen might be disappointed.

Hidden reef is excellent for all species of surface or bottom fish. You could anchor up and catch almost any species of fish right here. Work the surface with flies, jigs or bait, then send rubber lures, bone jigs, baited shrimp flies or live bait to the bottom to add some variety to your catch.

Southern Deep Rocky Reefs

About 1 mile south of Sutil Island lies several rock pile reefs in about 55 fathoms of water. This is an excellent area for red rock cod (vermillion rockfish) and some other species of rockfish. Send down squid baited shrimp flies for best results. Heavier scampi and other rubber swimbaits work well also, especially when baited with a thin strip of cut squid. Live or dead anchovy baits also will produce well.

Certain times of the year, late fall until January, bigger lingcod move up from the depths to enjoy the shallower water bounty. When fishing during these months, try heavier chrome jigs or send down a whole mackerel and see if you can entice one of these toothy beasts.

Access to Santa Barbara Island

Santa Barbara Island is a popular spot for some overnight party boats. Check with the landings for schedules. The most probable landings that offer trips are Redondo Sportfishing in King Harbor or Marina Del Rey sportfishing. In addition, many six-pack charter boats, especially those with sleeping accommodations, are willing to make the trip to Santa Barbara. By far the easiest way to get there is by private boat.

Santa Barbara Island is a long way offshore for even experienced boaters. Going there without considerable sea experience, a proven sea boat, and redundant electronic navigational aids would be sheer folly. It is a very rare day, especially in the hazy summer months, when you can see any land from Santa Barbara Island or see the island from any other land. It's a small target in a big ocean, so for the occasional tourist, I'd suggest staying much closer to shore until you have the equipment, experience, and confidence to venture that far offshore.

COMMON GAME FISH AVAILABILITY BY MONTHS
SANTA BARBARA ISLAND

Species	Jan	Feb	Mar	Apr	May	Jun	Jul	Aug	Sep	Oct	Nov	Dec
Yellowtail			░	░	▒	▒	█	█	▒	░		
Barracuda		░	▒	▒	█	█	█	▒	▒	▒	░	
Bonito		░	▒	▒	▒	▒	█	█	█	▒	░	
Calico Bass	░	▒	▒	▒	█	█	█	█	▒	▒	░	░
Sand Bass		░	▒	▒	█	█	█	█	▒	░	░	
White Seabass	█	▒	▒	▒	░	░	░	░	░	▒	█	█
Halibut	░	░	▒	▒	▒	▒	▒	▒	▒	▒	░	░
Lingcod	█	▒	▒	░	░	░	░	░	░	▒	█	█
Shallow-water Rockfish	█	▒	▒	▒	▒	▒	▒	▒	▒	▒	█	█
Deep-water Rockfish	█	█	▒	▒	▒	▒	▒	▒	▒	▒	█	█
Sheephead	░	░	▒	▒	█	█	▒	▒	▒	░	░	░
Sculpin	▒	▒	░	░	░	░	░	░	█	█	▒	▒
Blue Perch	░	░	▒	█	█	█	▒	▒	░	░	░	░
Opaleye			░	▒	▒	█	█	▒	▒	░	░	
Whitefish	█	▒	▒	▒	▒	▒	░	░	▒	▒	▒	█

☐ **Not Available**   ░ **Fish Possible**   ▒ **Good Fishing**   █ **Excellent Fishing**

SAN NICOLAS ISLAND

San Nicolas is the most remote of the offshore islands in the southern California neighborhood. It is about 60 miles offshore from any port from Ventura to the Port of Los Angeles. Like San Clemente, San Nicolas Island is a U.S. Navy Reserve. A fully equipped naval base including an airfield capable of taking Navy jet and transport aircraft is situated on the island. The Navy performs weapons testing of many kinds on San Nicolas Island.

Keep close tabs on the Notices to Mariners for island closures and areas to steer clear of this place when the Navy says it's closed. I know it sounds fascinating to watch a missile launch or a Phalanx gun testing, but trust me, you don't want to wander down range when a Phalanx gun starts spitting out 6000 rounds per minute of 40 mm (1½-inch diameter) cannon fire at a passing drone or when a test missile goes out of control and has to be destroyed. Most likely, the Navy will stop the test and send a boat out to arrest you if you're in the area. I don't imagine that would be any fun either, so make sure you know what is going on when you're contemplating fishing San Nick.

San Nicolas Island lies 55 miles from Port Hueneme on a 169-degree course, 57 miles from Redondo harbor on a 217-degree course or 58 miles from the LA light entrance to LA harbor on a 227-degree course. The island is roughly 8 miles long and 3 miles wide. It is oriented in a northwest / southeast direction. The northwest point is usually referred to as the "West End."

Because San Nicolas is so far from the boat harbors of southern California and because of the Navy presence and frequent closings, San Nicolas receives very light fishing pressure. This means the fishing, especially for resident species, is excellent. Kelp bass, big sheephead, white seabass, and many other resident species thrive here and fishing for them here is reminiscent of the bounty available to the sport fisherman early in the 20th century all along the southern California coast. It is unlikely that heavy fishing pressure will ever fish out the island and our marvelous renewable resource of game fish is guaranteed for years to come. Don't take this to mean this island can be exploited, though. Practice catch and release wherever possible and only take those fish you plan to eat, and the island will remain the fisherman's heaven it is today.

Another of San Nicolas' wonderful traits is the abundance of shallow rocky reefs surrounding the island. This usually means an abundance of kelp forests to harbor both bait and game fish. The north end of the island is usually choked with many kelp forests extending out several miles from the land. In deeper water the erose, feature filled bottom provides plenty of structure to entice deeper water species to make San Nicolas their home while discouraging commercial trawler boats. To destroy their expensive nets trying to pull fish out of the deep underwater canyons, towering pinnacles, and constantly changing, rock strewn bottom, is simply not cost effective in the bigger picture, so they usually leave the island alone. This means there are plenty of fish just waiting for the sports fisherman to entice them to bite.

San Nicolas Island

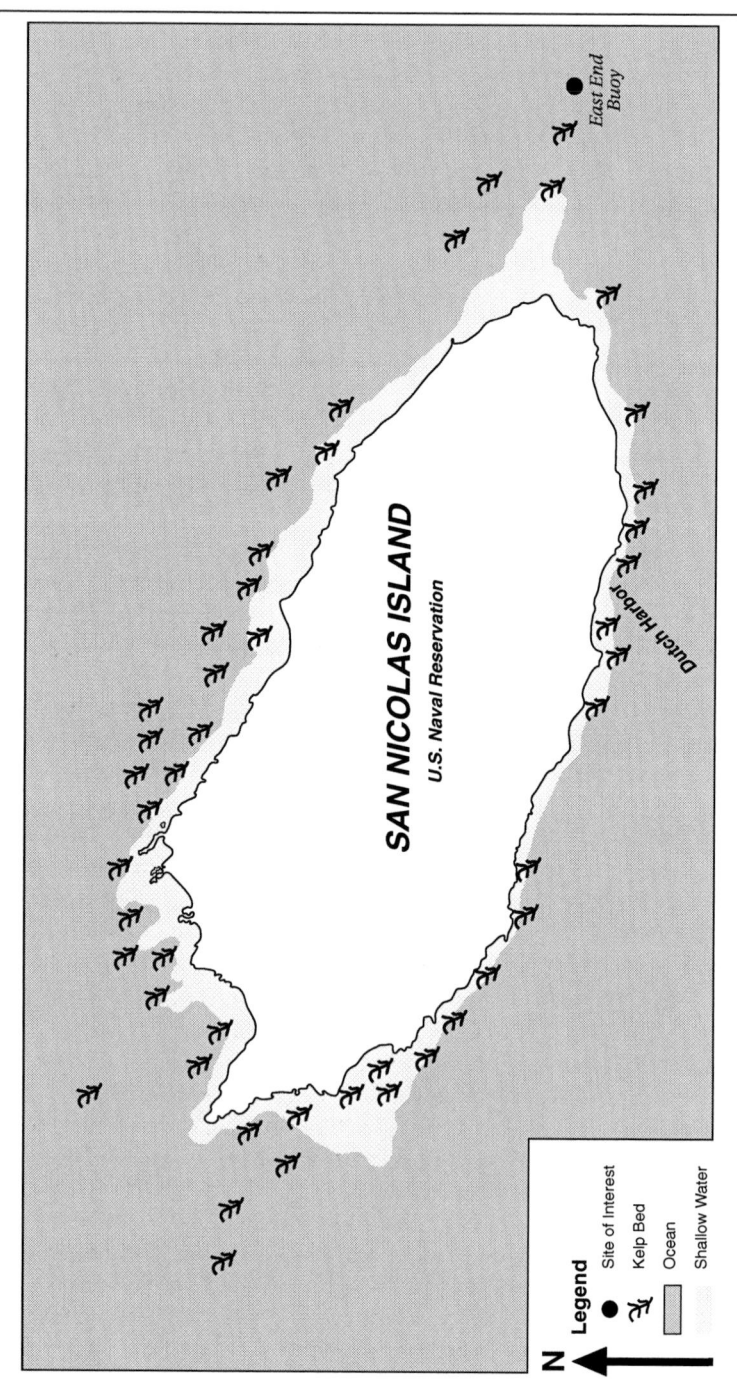

SAN NICOLAS ISLAND
U.S. Naval Reservation

Dutch Harbor

East End Buoy

Legend

● Site of Interest

 Kelp Bed

 Ocean

 Shallow Water

N

Fishing San Nicolas Island

San Nicolas Island is an outstanding fishing destination. Heavy kelp forests harbor a strong population of calico bass, barracuda, bonito, perch, and yellowtail. Near the bottom, plenty of sculpin, sheephead, whitefish, and other resident species abound. Lingcod and deep water rock cod are available over the deeper rocky reefs in warmer months and move to the shallower reefs in the winter. There are even lots of flatfish to catch in the sandy or muddy bottom areas. In all, San Nicolas Island is one of the best all around places to catch a wide variety of game fish.

Just about anywhere around San Nicolas Island can be successfully fished— especially areas with kelp beds nearby. Following are some suggested areas to target and methods:

Dutch Harbor to East End Buoy

This area is prime calico bass country. Plenty of fat, resident bass haunt these plentiful kelp beds. The best bet is live bait, flylined right on the edges of the kelp. If too many mackerel are about, add a small sinker to put the bait down into the thick part of the kelp to keep the surface feeding macks from stealing your bait. Rubber swimbaits are another good bet. Allow them to sink into the water column and retrieve them erratically for best results. Blues, greens, and root beer colors are all productive, depending more on the amount and direction of sunlight than anything else. This area produces best when there is a slight current allowing bait or lures to be drawn away from an anchored boat.

In summer, expect plenty of barracuda and bonito and, in the warmer water years, yellowtail prowling the edges of the kelp forests in search of food. If you suspect bigger predators are around, try switching to metal jigs. The smaller fish will leave them alone, and you'll fool the game fish into striking often and hard by using a rapid retrieve.

On calm wind days, this is a prime saltwater flyfishing area. Use a 10- to 13-weight sinking line, shooting head flyfishing rig and cast blue an white streamer flies or white crystal flash streamers for best results. I opt for the heavier line since many of these fish run for the kelp when hooked, which means you have to turn the fish before it has a chance to ball your line up in the weeds. If they make it, you've lost your fish and sometimes much of your line as well, so stay alert for strikes. In addition to calico bass, you might find yellowtail, bonito, and barracuda on the end of your fly line.

The bottom in this area is covered with rocky reefs, crevasses, and undersea caves, providing some excellent fishing action on the bottom. It may not be as glamorous as the surface bite, but the best eating fish come from the bottom, and I like to catch lots of different species when I fish. Fish the bottom with sliding sinker, Carolina rigs baited with live anchovies, squid-baited shrimp flies, whole shrimp, or cut squid. Rubber swimbaits, both single-tailed shad body lures or twin-tailed scampi type lures work fine. Bigger twin-tailed lures or live squid fished this way could entice bigger white seabass to your line. There are plenty of 50-pounders and bigger out there just south of San Nicolas Island.

North Side Kelp

The north side kelp beds are also great surface fishing locales. This area is more exposed to the prevailing winds and swells and can be a bit more difficult to fish than the sheltered southern kelp beds, however, at many times of the year, the extra effort pays off big.

When fishing, pay close attention to the drift and wind conditions so you can anchor up and allow the boat to ride on the hook just at the edges of the kelp beds. These beds produce plenty of bull calicos, yellowtail barracuda, and bonito. Bait, artificial lures, and flies all produce well in this area. It's best to flyfish early in the day, since the wind often blows up in the afternoon and makes flyfishing nearly impossible. Or for a change of pace, try flyfishing just after sundown, especially on nights when the moon is shining brightly. The wind almost always quits just after sunset and makes conditions perfect for tossing a fly. I like to tie a few flies with "glow-in-the-dark" phosphorescent hairs in the streamer. Charge these up by holding them under a strong light for a minute or two, then watch them glow as you present them to the fish. Often in summer, the water takes on a phosphorescent quality at night. This is due to microorganisms teeming in the water, so these are the best nights to fish with glow-in-the-dark flies.

Like the southern end of the island, the north side features a very irregular rocky bottom that is perfect for picking up shallow water rockfish and bigger white seabass. Fish it with live squid, live anchovies, or rubber swimbaits for some excellent and varied fishing.

West End Kelp and Rocks

The west end kelp beds and rocks are primarily a bottom fishing locale. Although the west end holds plenty of kelp beds and surface fish, the southern and northern kelp beds seem to be more consistent producers of surface fish. What the west end excels in is big white seabass. Plenty of these monsters inhabit the highly irregular bottom around the west end of the island.

There are also plenty of giant black sea bass in this area. Some of these fish can reach 400 pounds, but fish 100 pounds and up are common. It is illegal to take a black sea bass, punishable by a fine of up to $10,000 plus six months in jail, so make sure you can identify these fish (including the brick red juveniles) and release them immediately if you should catch one.

In late fall and winter, the middle depth reefs are excellent places to fish. Try rocky bottom areas in 150 to 250 feet of water. Jigs, bigger rubber swimbaits baited with squid strips, or large live baits (sardines or whole mackerel) sent down to these reefs often pay off big with larger white seabass and lingcod on the menu.

Be careful in these waters: There are many boiler rocks that are exposed only at low tides, and the wind and swells from across the wide Pacific have nothing to break their impact. If you break loose from your anchor and can't get your boat started quickly, neither your boat nor you will have much chance of surviving if the elements throw you onto the island's rocky shoreline. This area is for the most experienced only.

Sean Starkey of Yorba Linda, CA, showing a fine calico bass. Photo courtesy Matt Starkey.

Begg Rock

About 7 miles from the west end of San Nicolas Island lies a guano-covered islet called Begg Rock, surrounded by smaller rocks and boilers. Just north of the rock, a lighted buoy warns passing ships of the danger of running aground. The rocky reefs around Begg Rock and the irregular boulder-strewn bottom between Begg Rock and the main island are prime shallow water rockfishing areas.

The undersea crevasses, canyons, and rockpiles form prime habitat for white seabass, big sheephead, whitefish, bocaccio, sculpin, and other shallow water rockfish. There are also plenty of great eating rock sole haunting the bottom. The area's remoteness and sheer vastness make it one of the most productive and interesting places to fish. Squid-baited shrimp flies, rubber swimbaits, and live baits sent down among the rocks will almost always assure action.

Just north of Begg Rock in 50 to 65 fathoms of water (300 to 390 feet), there is a broad undersea plain of green mud and shale. This area is prime flatfish area, and plenty of California halibut and sanddabs call this area home. Though it is fished more than the shallower rocky areas, it is still very remote and the fishing is excellent. Drifting these flats with baited shrimp flies or live baits sent down to the bottom will yield plenty of chances to hook one of several different species available here.

Access to San Nicolas Island

San Nicolas Island is rarely visited by most party boat operators, but occasionally a trip is arranged from some of the more northern sportfishing landings—check with the landings for schedules. The most probable landings to offer trips are Redondo Sportfishing in King Harbor, Marina Del Rey Sportfishing, or Port Hueneme Sportfishing. There are also many six-pack charter boats (especially those with sleeping accommodations) that make the trip to San Nicolas Island. But the easiest way to get to San Nicolas is by private boat.

San Nicolas Island is the most remote of southern California's offshore islands. There is plenty of water to cross outside the normal shipping and boat traffic lanes. Consider suitable only to the most experienced boaters. There are no anchorages due to Navy restrictions, and the island is fully exposed to the brunt of the prevailing west winds, weather, and swells. I'd strongly suggest staying much closer to shore until you have the equipment, experience, and confidence to venture that far offshore.

COMMON GAME FISH AVAILABILITY BY MONTHS
SAN NICOLAS ISLAND

Legend: blank = Not Available · P = Fish Possible · G = Good Fishing · E = Excellent Fishing

Species	Jan	Feb	Mar	Apr	May	Jun	Jul	Aug	Sep	Oct	Nov	Dec
Yellowtail			P	P	G	G	G	E	E	G		
Barracuda		P	G	G	G	E	E	G	G	G	P	
Bonito		P	G	E	E	E	E	E	G	P	P	
Calico Bass	P	G	G	G	G	E	E	E	G	G	P	P
Sand Bass	P	P	G	G	E	E	E	G	G	G	P	P
White Seabass	E	E	E	E	G	G	G	G	G	G	G	E
Halibut	G	G	G	G	G	G	G	G	G	G	G	G
Lingcod	E	E	G	G	G	G	G	P	P	P	E	E
Shallow-water Rockfish	E	E	G	G	G	G	G	G	G	G	E	E
Deep-water Rockfish	E	E	G	G	G	G	G	G	G	G	E	E
Sheephead		P	G	G	E	E	G	G	G	G	P	
Sculpin	P	G	P	P	G	G	G	G	E	E	G	G
Blue Perch	P	P	G	E	E	G	G	P	P	P		
Opaleye			P	G	G	E	E	G	G	G	P	P
Whitefish	E	G	G	G	G	G	G	P	G	G	P	G

Not Available   Fish Possible   Good Fishing   Excellent Fishing

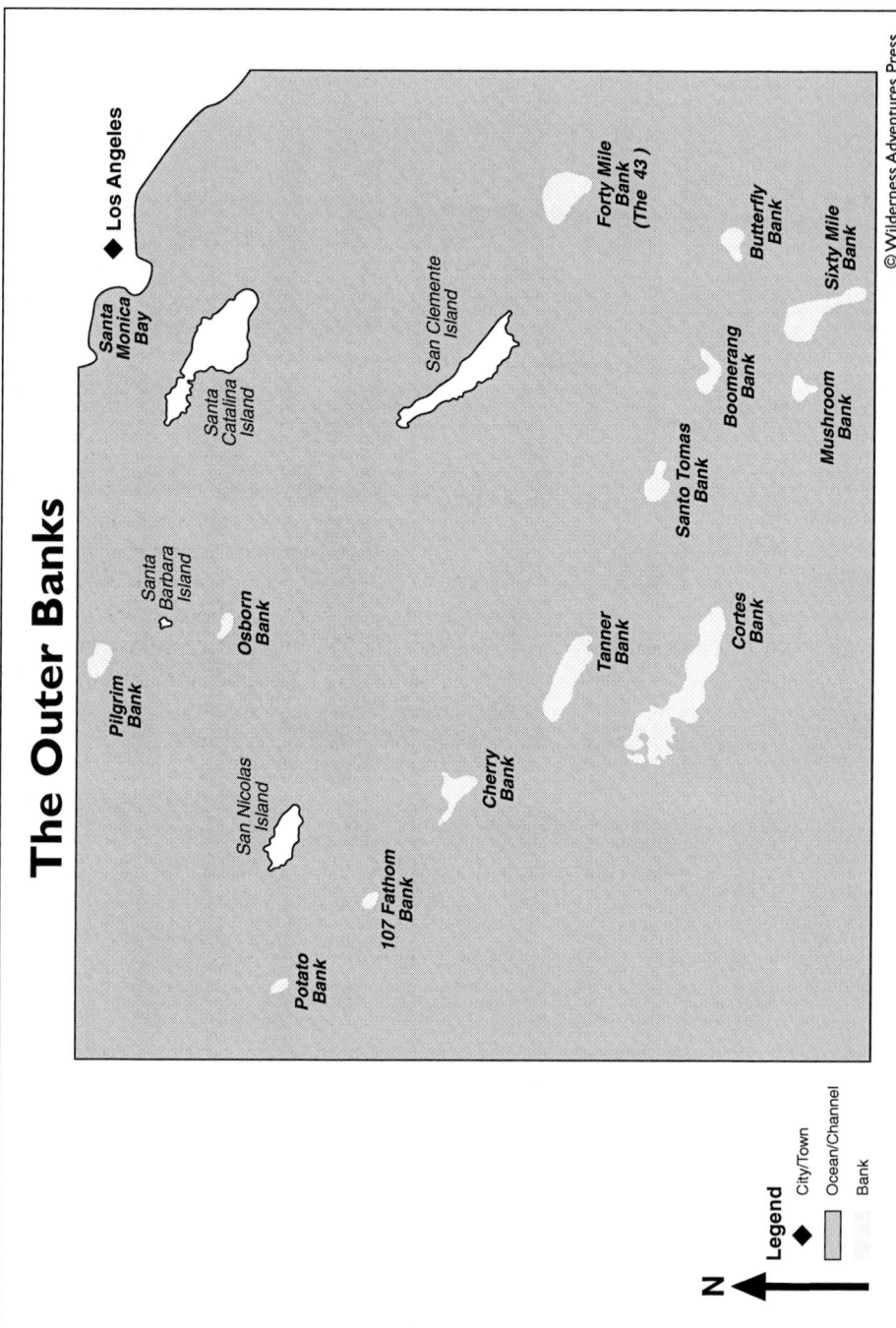

The Outer Banks

Los Angeles

Santa Monica Bay

Santa Catalina Island

San Clemente Island

Santa Barbara Island

Pilgrim Bank

Osborn Bank

San Nicolas Island

Cherry Bank

Tanner Bank

Cortes Bank

107 Fathom Bank

Potato Bank

Forty Mile Bank (The 43)

Butterfly Bank

Sixty Mile Bank

Boomerang Bank

Santo Tomas Bank

Mushroom Bank

© Wilderness Adventures Press

Legend

◆ City/Town

Ocean/Channel

Bank

N

The Outer Banks

The fact that surface feeding fish somehow manage to congregate over deep-sea, submerged mountains raises the question of why they do so. After all, I can't imagine something as primitive and instinctive as a tuna knowing whether it's in 2000 feet of water or 1200 feet.

The only likely answer is that is where the food is, and that begs the question of how the baitfish know what depth they are at. And the answer is the same: they go where they can find food. And the microscopic life forms that anchovies feed on are also there for the same reason. So how do the microscopic life forms get there? Now that's a fascinating tale.

The very same forces that affect the atmosphere influence oceans. The fact that air is much lighter means that outside forces can create greater effects. If the same forces that influence air also influence water, then it is easy to see why oceans are constantly in motion. When water encounters a submerged mountain range, well, it does exactly what moving air does when it encounters mountains—it travels around and over them. Water from deeper areas of the ocean is filled with nutrients that warmer water simply doesn't support. These nutrients are just the thing for tiny sea life, called diatoms, to live on. When deep-sea nutrient laden water is forced upward around undersea mountains, the diatoms in the area suddenly get fertilized. They bloom like weeds after watering and fertilizing a small patch of barren land. Diatoms and other microscopic life are food for the plankton that are food for small shrimps and other free swimming critters, and from there it goes all the way up the food chain.

When great schools of albacore arrive on the California coast in their annual migration, they stop and feed where the pickings are good: the Outer Banks. Also, in warmer water years, bluefin tuna, yellowfin tuna, bigeye tuna, dorado, and skipjack, wander up north from Mexico to take advantage of the good bait schools. The only difference is that albacore generally live in water that is 63 to 68 degrees, while the latter species are more tropical and prefer surface water temperatures in excess of 70 degrees. By the time the water gets that warm, albacore have generally migrated north. At times, the two temperatures can be found at different depths, so the yellowfin are in the warmer depth and the albacore in the cooler depth.

And the Outer Banks have yet another bonus: Since the underwater mountain ranges found at the Outer Banks are very rugged terrain, they abound in deep-water rockfish. Commercial trawlers are unable to drag their expensive nets through the rugged bottom, and since gill netting has been banned, the population of these bottom species has exploded. The only pressure these banks receive is the occasional commercial or charter hook-and-line boat. This fishing can't even begin to apply any significant pressure to the fish stocks found here. A bottom fishing trip to Potato, Cherry, 107, Tanner, or Cortes Banks can result in limits of quality fish in about an hour's fishing.

A word about traveling to these fishing spots—it's a long way out to sea and is not for the inexperienced! Because you made it all the way out to the Horseshoe Kelp

In some years, monster bigeye tuna migrate to southern California to the glee of local anglers. Photo courtesy Bob Halal.

and back a couple times doesn't mean you or your boat is ready for the extended off-shore journey that is needed to get to these spots. As much as 12 hours is needed each way to the banks—does your boat pack 24 hours worth of fuel? And the entire trip is out of sight of land. Even if you did get that spiffy $100 hand-held GPS for Christmas, it doesn't mean you're ready for this kind of trip.

More than one big macho guy with a big macho boat has perished every year venturing offshore in weather and conditions they were not equipped to handle. You need plenty of experience, a good seaworthy boat with a diesel engine or two, redundant electronics, as well as the experience and training to know how to find your way home when the electronics fail. Could you really find your way back home from 80 miles out, past an island chain, in dense fog with an electrical system failure (no radar, depth meter, GPS, Loran, VHF, CB)? If you have any doubts about your ability to do this, don't go. Have fun near shore or at the islands where you can pull

ito a cove and wait out heavy weather or flag down a passing boat (you'll see many
imes more inside the islands than outside), or at least plot a direct compass course
iome.

This isn't an attempt to scare anyone. By including this section, I'm sure I'll
empt some of you to try the fishing on the Outer Banks. I just don't want anyone
ieading out there half cocked in an 18-foot outboard just because they made it all
ie way to Catalina once or twice on a sunny days.

There are really only two types of fishing at the outer banks: bottom fishing
or rock cod and surface fishing for tuna, dorado, or yellowtail. At a couple of the
ianks that are closer in, you might also find bonito or barracuda, as well. I've gone
ito great depth about these techniques elsewhere, so I won't be redundant when
iscussing the individual banks. Suffice it to say that all of the Outer Banks I've
iescribed here are very productive places to fish. Several of them are too deep to
ven bottom fish. From north to south the primary outer banks fishing spots are:

Pilgrim Bank

I'm not sure if I should refer to Pilgrim as one of the Outer Banks. Although
hey're fairly far out, they really aren't outside the islands as are most of the other
ianks discussed in this chapter. Nevertheless, Pilgrim Banks are a substantial trip
rom any port and stand apart from any nearby islands. This bank is probably a
iunken island similar in form to the other islands off southern California. Judging
rom their rugged, erose shape, I feel it's fairly certain that it is the remnant of a long
igo extinct volcano.

Pilgrim Banks come to within 60 fathoms (360 feet) of the surface and can be a
iroductive rock cod fishing spot. Better results are gotten when fishing deeper than
100 fathoms here. The area also supports a healthy population of lingcod in winter
vhen they come out of their deep summer haunts to the shallower rocky reefs.

Surface fish also congregate at Pilgrim Banks, but it has to be an exceptional
ear for tuna or tropical species to appear here in fishable numbers. The great El
Jiño years of 1997 and 1998 brought plenty of dorado and yellowtail here.

Osborn Bank

Osborn is one of the most famous of the close-in fishing banks. It's generally
vithin sight of Santa Barbara Island (at least on clear days) and comes within about
'50 feet of the surface. It is a great rock cod bank if fished along the sides in deeper
vater. On the top of the hump, shallow-water rockfish species, such as sheephead,
iculpin, and the occasional white seabass, are also available.

Surface fishing for pelagic species is often quite good here. Barracuda, bonito,
ind sometimes yellowtail are the main species, unless you like to include mackerel.
The two main techniques to locate schools are by trolling and bird watching.

Potato Bank

Potato Bank is found just outside San Nicolas, the most remote of southern
California's offshore islands. It is also sometimes called the Nidever Bank (at least on

the charts; I've never heard a fisherman call it that). Potato is another sunken volcanic island and is separated from the shelf that San Nicolas sits on by a deep chasm.

Potato is both an excellent rock cod fishing bank and a good albacore bank when
the longfins are about.

107 Fathom Bank

This is an offshore troller's delight. It's more of a gently sloped ridge than a steep
vertical volcanic core. Marlin fishermen often come here to troll, but it is the area's
ability to draw tuna that makes it famous and popular. Albacore, bluefin, and in
warmer years, yellowfin, skipjack, and dorado are all drawn here to feed on the plentiful schools of anchovies and sardines this bank seems to attract.

Cherry Bank

Cherry Bank is the second best (behind Point Arguello Canyons) rock cod fishing spot in southern California. I used to fish with a group of guys who would charter a boat here about once every other month. I had plenty of big reds and cows in
my freezer in those days, and much of Orange County's Japanese community knew
when I went fishing because it meant plenty of fresh sashimi.

Cherry Bank is cowcod city—I've rarely made a trip there when I didn't catch at
least two or three cows in the 25-pound class. Big red rock cod, a few lings, and boscos filled out the limit from there. Of course, we never fished in water shallower than
700 feet, and 900 feet was more typical. On one trip to Cherry Banks, I remember
being nearly spooled on my 9/0 Senator with 100-pound test Dacron.

Cherry also gets its share of tuna when they're visiting the coast. It's one in a
chain of excellent banks to troll as you search for schools.

Tanner Bank

When I first fished commercially out of San Diego on a hook-and-line rock cod
boat, the mecca for rock cod was Tanner Bank. If you wanted to bring in a load
Tanner was the place to go. You never heard of Cortes, just a few miles away and
much bigger—Tanner was the place.

Of course, Tanner is about the farthest north of the really consistent tuna fishing banks. Most years, not just El Niño years, Tanner gets plenty of late action on
yellowfin, skipjack, and dorado. Bluefin and albacore also frequent the area, and the
occasional bigeye shows up with the yellowfin schools.

Cortes Bank

Cortes Bank is the only place where I have been able to catch tuna from an
anchored boat. I know they do it down in Mexico a lot, but tuna fishing north of the
border has always meant finding schools by trolling or dolphin chasing, then drifting and flylining, moving back to the school, and drifting again. At Cortes, you can
literally anchor up on the high spot and fish as if you were catching local fish. You
can send bait down with weights, cast jigs, or anything you want, and all without

School-sized yellowfin tuna can be a real challenge on light-tackle or flies. Photo courtesy Gary Quon.

having to worry if you drift away from the schools. I've caught yellowfin here as late as Thanksgiving weekend. It seems to have a magnetic attraction for these fish.

Cortes is also an excellent bottom fishing bank, as well. In the shallows, huge sculpin, sheephead, white seabass, and, in the winter, lingcod prowl the area, while in the deeper recesses of the bank, a wide variety of rock cod call the place home. I like to fish deep here, at least 600 feet, but there are plenty of fish available in the shallows, too. This area is so infrequently bottom fished that the fish are eager to snap at a bucktail shrimp fly, a piece of cut squid, or even a mangled dead anchovy.

Santo Tomas Bank

Between the southern edge of San Clemente Island and the southern tip of Cortes Bank lies a seamount that can be, at times, an excellent place to troll for tuna and other summer offshore fish. This is Santo Tomas Bank, which rises only to 300 fathoms (1800 feet) below the surface but nonetheless seems to attract considerable schools of bait. Keep your eyes peeled here for kelp paddies, bird action, or dolphin feeding action. Any of these three signals means there are feeding tuna or dorado.

Boomerang Bank

Named for its boomerang-shaped ridge, Boomerang Bank is somewhat shallower than many of the more obscure offshore banks. It rises to 150 fathoms below the surface (900 feet), so rock cod fishing is possible here. I've never tried it, however, and I know of no one who has. But I think it is quite possible to go there and get a limit of reds, cows, and boscos in no time flat since it probably receives zero fishing pressure.

As a surface fishing bank, however, Boomerang is another quite productive area. All of these remote, offshore banks have the ability to attract and hold good schools of tuna. It all depends on the water temperature patterns that change every year, so each has the potential to be barren or wide open on any given day.

Forty-mile Bank (The "43")

This famous bank was a staple for commercial rock cod fishermen out of San Diego for many years. In spite of having been fished for years by gill-netters, this bank still has an excellent population of bottom fish. Their recovery has been continual since the 1980s ban on this technique, and schools are now almost back to what they once were in the 1950s and 1960s. It's just another example of how resilient Mother Nature really is. All we have to do is quit doing whatever has been harming the habitat, and sure enough, it'll come back on its own. This is often called the "43" because the top of the undersea mountain ridge is 43 fathoms below the surface (260 feet).

Lately Forty-mile Bank has been a center for a great deal of surface fishing. During El Niño years and even some years with average water temperatures, schools of yellowfin, dorado, bigeye, and bluefin tuna have been reaching right into the Forty-mile Bank. I've been on boats at the Sixty-mile Bank in the morning and finding that we were too far out—the boats were scoring at Forty-mile, so we came in closer. It's an excellent place to fish.

Butterfly Bank

Butterfly is on a direct course between Sixty-mile Bank and Forty-mile Bank—maybe it should be called the Fifty-mile Bank. This is a surface fishing destination, where trolling is the usual the method for finding tuna schools. It's not necessarily any better than either Sixty-mile or Forty-mile, it just offers another hunting ground when the fishing is marginal. It is also shallow enough for rock cod fishing at about 90 fathoms (540 feet), but no one I know has ever tried bottom fishing there. I'll bet it's covered with big rock cod, though.

Sixty-mile Bank

Easily the most famous of the offshore banks for tuna and dorado, the banks gets its name because it lies 60 miles from the tip of Point Loma. Though it's shallow

*Jackpot Bob Schiffmacher and
a beautiful dorado caught offshore
in the warm summer ocean.
Photo courtesy
Jackpot Bob Schiffmacher.*

enough for rock cod fishing (50 fathoms—300 feet), I've never fished for bottom fish there and know of no one who has ever tried. It is famous as a tuna fishing spot.

Back when I was in high school, I made my first fishing trip to this bank for albacore. I wasn't sure what I expected to see when I got there, but I recall that when the skipper announced we were at the bank, I remember being let down. It reminded me of the old poem by Samuel Taylor Coleridge, "water, water everywhere..." How it could be recognizable was a mystery to me. Of course, that was before I had any knowledge of Loran, bottom sounding equipment, or other navigation aids.

If tuna are anywhere in the southern California range, they'll probably be at Sixty-mile Bank. Like all offshore banks, hopping the kelp with trolling gear is the best way to locate schools. Once you get a jig, stop and break out the live bait and start flylining. Other techniques that also work are following birds or dolphins and fish wherever the most commotion is taking place—old fashioned and a bit crude, but nonetheless effective techniques.

Mushroom Bank

Probably more of an extension to the Sixty-mile Bank ridge, this is a mushroom-shaped seamount lying about 10 miles due west from Sixty-mile Bank. It rises to about 150 fathoms (900 feet) and could be bottom fished, but it is generally a place to investigate as a tuna and surface fishing destination when fishing at Sixty-mile Bank.

Access to the Outer Banks

Unless you have plenty of experience and a big twin diesel sportfishing boat or yacht, leave trips to the Outer Banks to the pros. In summer, overnight trips from all the southern California landings, especially San Diego, visit the Outer Banks to catch the big, surface feeding summer visitors: tuna and dorado, as well as the yellowtail that are caught offshore around floating kelp paddies. In winter, many landings offer Outer Banks rock cod trips that are usually overnight ventures. Clients get on the boat the evening before, sleep all night as the boat travels to the distant bank, then fish all morning and into the early afternoon before the boat has to make the long trip back home. Contact the individual landings to find out when these trips are planned. Since there isn't nearly as much interest in winter fishing as there is in summer fishing, some boats only run out one or two days per week. There are also some long-range charters available. Check with the landings, listed elsewhere, for the latest information.

While the outer banks area in US waters used to be a popular spot for deep-water rock cod fishing, new regulations to protect a number of ground fish species have now closed them to rock fishing. Mexican territorial waters are still open to deep-water rock fishing, though. The California regulations are subject to change without notice. Be sure to consult the Department of fish & Game's web site at: www.dfg.ca.gov to be sure you're complying with current regulations before fishing there.

Planning a Fishing Trip on a Sportfishing Boat

Now that you know what species of fish to expect, when and how to fish for them, and specific techniques to use, it's time to help you plan a trip. The first thing to do is decide what kind of trip you want. The sportfishing industry in southern California is one of the best in the world. We have the nicest, best-equipped boats and plenty of them. Here is a sampling of some of the fishing trip options available at most landings:

Half-day Trips

Half-day trips are open party boats (open to anyone who shows up.) They generally have a maximum number of passengers but rarely leave the dock at maximum. Morning boats usually leave around 6:00am and return about noon. Afternoon half-day boats leave just after noontime and return about 5pm. Cost for these trips is around $25. These boats fish the local kelp beds, reefs, and flats near their home-ports. They rarely travel more than an hour away from port. Live bait is usually provided in a large bait tank in the center of the boat for everyone's use. Some also offer cut squid bait, but don't count on it. Unless I know for sure that a boat offers cut squid, I always take my own.

Twilight Trips

These are also half-day trips, except that they leave about 6:00PM and return about midnight. Most twilight trips only run during the summer months or when there's a major giant squid run. Other than that, they're the same as half-day trips and are usually done with the same kind of boats.

Three-quarter-day Trips

A step up from the half-day trips, these are also open party boats. They leave in early morning and return late in the afternoon. The cost is around $35. From any of the harbors, these longer trips allow you to fish the local kelp beds and flats. Some of these longer trips can also take you to the near side of Catalina from Long Beach and northern Orange County landings or the Coronado Islands from San Diego Harbor boats. As with half-day boats, bait is provided.

Island Overnight Trips

These are boats leaving in late evening and returning in the evening of the following day. They are also open party boats, and bunks are provided. You can show up alone or with a group of people. These cost around $75. You will be able to target surface fish or rock cod in the winter at the Outer Banks. Again, live bait is provided, but you may be responsible for making bait—catching some of your own bait, particularly live squid, in the predawn darkness to use when dawn breaks.

Tuna Overnight Trips

Overnight tuna trips leave in the late evening and return the evening of the following day, and bunks and bait are provided. Because this kind of trip requires more time and fuel than island overnight trips, they are more expensive, usually around $100. These trips offer fishing the Outer Banks for tuna and offshore species.

Limited Load Tuna Overnight Trips

When the tuna season is in full swing, some of the landings offer limited load tuna trips. These are the same as tuna overnight trips except the number of people is usually held to 24, depending on the boat. This is a much better deal if the fishing is hot and the boats are crowded. These trips cost around $150.

Long Range Trips

Many landings offer multiple-day trips. The landings farther to the south almost always head for Mexico's Baja California coast and the offshore islands. They spend from 2 to 28 days or more fishing. These boats are more like cruise ships, with air conditioned staterooms, gourmet meals, and the like. Bunks and food are provided. The cost is around $200 per day.

Six-pack Trips

These trips are available for charter, and the type of fishing is negotiable. The maximum load is six persons plus the crew. You'll be expected to have put together a load of six passengers, because the captains won't match up two from your party with three from another party, etc., and split the costs unless you make some kind of arrangement in advance. The cost ranges from $450 to $1500 per day, depending on the type of fishing, boat size, reputation, etc.

All of these boats feature galleys to prepare meals. On long-range boats and some six-pack boats, food is provided as part of the package, on others you have to pay. The food is generally so-so and ranges from the practically inedible to pretty darn good, depending on the cook. Galleys also sell coffee, sodas, beer, snacks, and candy. These days some sell water, but I'm in a habit of bringing my own bottled water, both to drink and to rinse my face off after a hard day of salt spray. Galleys also offer limited tackle sales in case you run out of hooks, jigs, or a special type of tackle you might need on the trip. Don't expect a full service tackle store when you get on—you'll just have to live with that old, rotten line until you get home. You're allowed to bring your own food if you wish, but hard liquor is forbidden, and you can't bring ice chests aboard.

Reservations are required when booking a trip and should be made well in advance. Unfortunately, some of the landings have taken after the airlines and started overbooking trips. They clearly state that the only reservations they are obligated to honor are those with a prepaid deposit. But I think it's unprofessional and rude to keep booking people and then cancel the reservation after a client has gotten up in the morning, driven to the landing, and waited in line, only to have the boat filled up on a first-come, first-served basis. Why bother with reservations? How

A typical six-pack charter boat, the Wave Walker
from Santa Barbara, with captain Dave Bacon at the helm.
Photo courtesy Captain Dave Bacon-—-Wavewalker Charters.

about a "standby" list? But on most days, particularly weekdays, you can get on just about any boat with minimal hassle.

The landings all rent fishing rods and reels to those who don't bring their own. They don't loan terminal tackle, but the landings are usually well equipped to sell you what you'll need. Ask the counter clerk in the landing's tackle shop, and he'll be happy to help you out with the hooks, sinkers, or lures you'll most likely need for the trip. If anything special comes up, the galley on the boat will usually be able to offer you what you need.

In addition to your fishing tackle, there are a few more items you don't want to be without. First is a light jacket or sweatshirt. Even in the warmest summer season, early morning and late evening are really chilly on the water. In winter, a coat is in order even if you don't need it on land. Trust me—on the water, it gets downright bone-chilling cold.

You'll also need sunblock. On sunny days in southern California (and that's 300 days per year), not many people have enough melatonin in their skin to avoid getting seriously burned by the sun. Don't think that a baseball cap will do. Your arms, hands, ears, and neck will receive plenty of direct and indirect solar radiation, because the water reflects the light even when you're standing in the shade. And while on the subject of hats—the bigger the better. A baseball cap is pretty good, but one with neck flaps (a la French Foreign Legion) or a broad-brimmed cowboy or farmer's hat is even better. Sunglasses are also important. In my tackle box, I keep two pairs of blue reflective clip-ons to go over my regular glasses.

Unless you're used to being out at sea, I strongly recommend you take something along for seasickness. Nothing can ruin a day faster than a seasick person. If you're not sure, plan on it. Newer seasick remedies are quite effective and have little or no side effects. Check with your doctor if you're not sure which to use. They are available over the counter in tablet form, with such names as Dramamine, Bonine, Marazine. There are also some patch forms that are available by prescription only.

Other than a valid California fishing license, that's about all you'll need. One-day or all-year fishing licenses are sold at the sportfishing landings.

For the best luck on the sportfishing boats, listen to the deck hands. Their advice usually means you'll catch more fish. Time after time, I see people ignore their advice and go empty handed. Those who listen to the deck hands' advice—cranking up when they say, changing bait, adding weights, fishing the surface, tightening the drag, or whatever their advice—usually catch more fish. It's also important to listen to the captain's orders on the loudspeaker. When he says wind 'em up, do so or you may find your line has been completely eaten off by a fast spinning prop. Always wait to drop until the captain says so. Everyone else may be casting out, but resist—sometimes he is just stopping for a moment to get a better look at the bottom, and then is off again. Sometimes he needs to swing the boat around to set the anchor well. Pay attention to what you're told, and you'll know when to drop for maximum results.

On the boat you will be offered a chance in the jackpot. The jackpot is a wager on the largest fish caught. Each person wanting to compete puts a certain amount of money in a pool, usually $3 or $5. The fisherman who catches the largest fish, which is actually the heaviest fish, wins the pot. Sharks and fish caught while trolling are excluded. I almost always let the deck hands keep the pot as a tip, some people deduct it from the trip cost, and some hog the whole thing. I figure I have had a lot of fun and it's worth the tip, since most of those deck hands don't make much at all.

After the jackpot call, the deck hands offer to clean or fillet fish. Most deck hands do a good job if your goal is to get bone-free fillets. They are a bit wasteful, though, and since I don't mind cutting them myself and using the whole fish when I cook it, I just get the fish gutted and gilled. This leaves the head on but removes the offensive internal organs. They'll also head and gut or even slab—fillet the fish but leave the bellies and skin on. The price usually varies but is generally about 50 cents per fish. I never pay just the asking price and usually take this opportunity to tip the deck hands.

The first couple of times you go on a party boat, you may not be able to follow all the activity, since it seems everyone is speaking in some sort of code. But after a short time, you'll get used to it and will probably meet many fun and interesting people. I've fished next to kids, beautiful blondes, 95-year-old retirees, construction workers, people who just got out of jail, tourists, and just about a hundred other different types of people. It's usually fun, fascinating, and a new experience every trip.

Important Phone Numbers

California Department of Fish & Game
Web Site: http://www.dfg.ca.gov/

Cal DF&G Marine Region
330 Golden Shore, Suite 50, Long Beach, CA 90802
Offshore Ecosystem Coordinator: Patricia Wolf (562) 590-5117
FAX (562) 590-5192

530 E. Montecito Street, Room 104, Santa Barbara, CA 93103
Public Information (805) 568-1231
FAX (805) 568-1235

4949 Viewridge Avenue, San Diego, CA 92123
Public Information (619) 467-4214
FAX (619) 467-4299

United States Coast Guard
Notices to Mariners Web Site: http://www.navcen.uscg.mil/lnm/d11/

Mexico Department of Fisheries
2550 Fifth Ave., Suite 101
San Diego, CA 92103
(619) 233-4324
FAX (619) 233-0344

National Marine Fisheries Service
501 W. Ocean Boulevard, Suite 4200
Long Beach, CA 90802-4213
(562) 980-4004
FAX (562) 980-4047
http://swr.ucsd.edu/index.htm

Pacific States Marine Fisheries Commission
45 SE 82nd Drive, Suite 100
Gladstone, OR 97027-2522
(503) 650-5400
FAX (503) 650-5426

United Anglers of Southern California
5046 Edinger Avenue
Huntington Beach, CA 92649
(714) 840-0227
FAX (714) 840-3146
http://www.unitedangler.com

San Diego County Fish & Game Association
2082 Willow Glen Road
El Cajon, CA
(619) 442-9971
http://www.sdfishgame.com/

San Diego County Fish and Wildlife Advisory Commission
5555 Overland Avenue, Building 3
San Diego, CA 92123-1292
(619) 694-3122
FAX (619) 565-7046
http://www.pottorff.net/fwac1.html

Sources for Nautical Charts
National Oceanic and Atmospheric Administration
Distribution Division, N/ACC3
National Ocean Service
Riverdale, MD 20737-1199
(800) 638-8972 or (301) 436-8301
http://www.noaa.gov/

Maptech Digital Charts
(888) 839-5551 or (978) 933-3000
http://www.maptech.com

Private Fishing Boats for Southern California

In general, the ocean off southern California is well protected from the brunt of the weather coming out of the northern Pacific basin because of its southwest-facing cove shape and by its string of protective islands. And because of the prevailing jet stream, an area of high barometric pressure usually sits right over southern California. This is what is primarily responsible for California's legendary sunshine. This means few storm fronts ever pass through, so the sea stays mild and pleasant.

The southern California ocean is crawling with tens of thousands of boats of all sorts, especially in the near-shore areas and between the coastline and the many offshore islands. This is especially true in summer. Plenty of traffic usually means that you can hail passing boats in the event you end up broken down or in trouble.

But that doesn't mean it's never a problem to be out there: oceans have a way of throwing curves at you and are not very forgiving to those unprepared for bad weather, unplanned breakdowns, or other troubles at sea. You need to be well equipped and well versed, both on the theoretical and practical aspects of seamanship, navigation, and small craft repair. If you are unwilling or unable to learn these skills, you'd be far better off going to your friendly local sportfishing landing and hopping on a boat where a professional, licensed captain takes you out fishing.

From car-top canoes to 100-foot-long motor yachts, there are as many different types of boats suitable for fishing in southern California as there are types of boats. Obviously, boat selection is as heavily dependent on your budget as it is on many other factors. Some of the other considerations include type of fishing, whether you're taking family aboard, whether you're planning any overnight stays in anchorages, economy of operation, and a host of others. Here are some of the different types of boats and their uses and limitations in southern California saltwater:

Small Outboard Skiffs

Ranging in size from about 12 feet to about 16 feet, small outboard skiffs are suitable only for fishing in harbors and bays. They're unsafe in even the mildest sea. Even when the seas are flat calm, a large boat or ship passing by can put out a breaking wake of several feet, capable of swamping small boats in this size range.

On the positive side, small skiffs are light, easily launched, easy to handle, and inexpensive. Considerable fun can be had with these small boats in southern California's harbors and. Bigger bays, such as Los Angeles Harbor and San Diego Harbor, have ample fishing opportunities and can produce large game fish in addition to the usual bay-dwelling small game fish.

Outboard Runabouts

Runabouts are a step up from outboard skiffs and are also suitable for bay and harbor fishing. They're generally easy to launch and handle, and having a covered foredeck and windshield, they offer more protection than a simple open boat. In the smaller size, they're suitable for protected waters in harbors and bays only, with occasional runs to near-port kelp beds and flats. Larger boats are suitable for more sustained operations in the ocean during fair weather, but their use should be restricted to local destinations that aren't far from port in the event some unexpected weather crops up. Runabouts used for water skiing are unsuitable for ocean use and should be limited to well-protected bays and harbors.

Center Console Fishing Boats

Ranging in size from about 18 feet to over 30 feet, center console fishing boats are the latest and greatest in modern ocean fishing craft. These boats are mostly outboard powered, but some inboard and stern drive models are available. They're generally very well equipped, with built-in bait tanks, insulated fish boxes, rod holders, and all the niceties. Many have a head compartment in the center console, another very welcome option.

In practice, most center consoles can operate safely all along the near-shore coastline, and most are capable of operating safely when crossing the channels between the coast and the near-shore islands. These are day-fishing boats only, since they don't have any accommodations for an overnight stay. Other than at Avalon on Santa Catalina Island, there are no marinas at the islands offering on-shore services, so use of these boats is limited to fishing for the day only.

Cuddy Cabin Fishing Boats

Because the southern California islands offer only anchorages in which to pull up and drop anchor, cuddy cabin boats are more popular here than in the East, where there are far more marinas with hotels at the more distant fishing destinations. Cuddy cabin boats are usually very similar to the center console boats, except they offer a small cabin, usually accommodating two people to spend the night. A head and small galley in the cabin are common features of many cuddy boats.

Most cuddy cabin fishing boats are offered with extensive fishing options, including live bait tanks, fish boxes, rod holders, and the like. Of these, the bait tank is the most important. These boats are usually powered by a single or twin outboard motors or inboard/outboard combinations. Modern outboard engines are reliable and economical to operate as compared to their ancestors. A considerable advancement in technology over the past 20 years or so has radically improved their performance, reliability, and economy.

Cuddy cabin fishing boats are suitable for fishing the near coastal waters, crossing the channels to the offshore islands, and fishing the closer banks. They're suitable for day or occasional overnight trips and range from 20 to 30 feet.

Cabin Cruisers

From about 22 to about 32 feet, cabin cruisers are a step up from cuddy cabin type boats. They offer more accommodations than their smaller cousins and are more suitable for overnight and multiple-day trips anchored along the lee side of offshore islands. Since these boats come equipped with all sorts of options and accessories, only those with very reliable power (dual gas engines, or single or dual diesels) and fully equipped modern and redundant electronics should be considered for extended offshore island use. Fuel capacity should be another major consideration for these boats if used for longer trips.

For inshore reef, flats, or kelp bed fishing, cabin cruiser type boats are a great choice. They offer some protection from the sun and weather and feature bunks, heads, and galleys for more comfort. The only downside is that it is somewhat difficult to pass around the cabin and get to the bow if you've hooked a bigger fish that wants to run forward, Center console and narrow cabin cuddy fishing boats are more "walk-around" friendly.

Trawler Yachts

Starting at about 32 feet and ranging in excess of 65 feet, a special class of offshore cruising boat called the trawler is another option to consider buying. Trawlers are usually slower than other types of boats, some cruising at less than 10 miles per hour. If you want to get somewhere fast, trawlers are not a good option. They are almost universally diesel powered, and what they lose in speed, they make up for in range, economy, and seaworthiness. These are all intended for extended cruising and are designed to handle storm seas with relative ease.

Trawler yachts generally offer very comfortable staterooms, salons, and galleys for extended cruising and long-range fuel capacity. This makes them suitable for all the fishing one might encounter in southern California. They're great for offshore banks fishing, offshore islands fishing, multiday trips to the islands, or any of the near coastal fishing. The only downside is their slow speed, which pretty much rules out even a weekend trip—you spend simply too much time getting there and home. The cockpits tend to be small, which is fine for one or two people, but not much room for a big gang.

Sportfishing Boats

Sportfishing boats are the hands-down preference of fishermen in offshore fishing boats. Most have diesel-powered twin engines, which are a step up in reliability and economy over gasoline engines. Most feature luxury accommodations, with staterooms, full galleys, salons, and well-equipped flying bridges. Live wells, fish boxes, rod holders, and all the fishing bells and whistles are usually offered as either standard or as options. They generally range in size from about 30 feet to 80 feet or larger.

Sportfishing boats are capable of fishing any water in southern California, from local kelp beds and flats to the offshore islands and outer banks, and are capable of making day, overnight, or multiple-day fishing trips. They're the ultimate for the salt-water angler, offering the ability to get to the fishing grounds fast and return fast, thus making all of southern California and the offshore islands within weekend range. The only downside is their relatively high purchase price and high operating costs.

Navigation Aids

A boat is just part of what you'll need to fish southern California's saltwater. To safely operate offshore and find fish, marine electronics are nearly as important as the choice of hull and engine. Navigation aids, communications systems, and bottom reading devices are all important if you are to have a safe, productive fishing trip. Some of these devices include:

VHF Radio

Being in touch with other boats and emergency services, such as towing services and the Coast Guard, are vitally important, and that means your radio is your single most important piece of electronic gear. While you may be able to get around a harbor without a radio, it's pure foolishness to venture anywhere out of port without the ability to call for help. Any boat venturing to the offshore islands or operating any distance from port should have two VHFs just in case one breaks down. Most commercial fishermen have two VHFs. They are available at any marine supply store for modest cost.

Depth Sounder

Knowing how deep the water is below the boat is not only important for locating schools of fish and underwater reefs, it's also an important navigation tool. I have used the depth meter when I was caught in fog without radar to locate the entrance to a channel. I simply followed a known depth line until I located a familiar buoy. I don't recommend this as common practice, but when the fog suddenly appears and you're not ready for it, it sure is nice to add this measure of certainty to your dead reckoning.

A depth sounder is also useful for locating schools of fish. If you select one for use in southern California saltwater, remember that the ocean is much deeper here than on the East and Gulf Coasts. You can get into 2000-foot deep water only 2 miles from shore, whereas in the East and Gulf, you might be in 200 feet of water 20 miles from shore. A unit that accurately sounds to 900 feet minimum is important, especially if you want to do some deep water rock codding.

Modern, sophisticated sideways and forward-looking sonar is a step up from a simple video bottom meter and allows more extensive searching for schools of fish. This equipment does cost quite a bit more than the standard depth meters that look only straight down and that cost only a few hundred dollars.

Loran and GPS

The older Loran system is being phased out, but the Loran C equipment is still very much a viable navigation tool. Loran systems operate by reading time delays from transmitted signals along the shoreline. An overprint of lines on nautical charts shows the various arced loran lines. A printout of the time delays on the face of the loran can be correlated with the lines on the chart and a position fix attained. They're quite accurate when operating properly but are a dying technology, so not much new research is being done with the system and if you have the choice, select the more modern GPS system.

The more modern GPS navigation devices use the Global Positioning Satellite "constellation" (group of satellites) to obtain a precise fix. The printout is usually in latitude and longitude. GPS devices also calculate courses, speeds, and direction to known locations, such as your homeport. Like most electronics these days, the costs are rapidly decreasing while the capabilities are increasing. The lower cost, hand-held units are as little as $100, but practical marine units in more rugged, saltwater resistant cases can cost substantially more.

A very practical and desirable feature, that some higher end marine GPS devices offer is a charting option. Built-in charts or those stored on a removable memory chip display your boat on a chart. Options include zooming and panning in north up or course up display and more. This is a highly desirable option, since all the navigation functions are there for you to view on a single display. On my ideal fishing boat, I would have two GPS devices: one that charts and the other a simple readout, just as a backup and to confirm the proper operation of the charting unit.

Radar

Another very handy navigation aid, radar enables you to see navigation aids, coastlines, and other boats during fog, haze, and nighttime. Though very useful, especially in the fog, it's not the panacea it's made out to be. Small boats are made of fiberglass and wood, not radar reflective materials, so while it's nice to avoid a passing tanker, you might not pick up a small boat. Nonetheless, radar is a quite powerful navigation aid, enabling you to spot landfalls, coastline shapes, and offshore islands long before you're able to see them, even when the weather along the coast is its usual best. A good radar set is an important addition to boats that are used for extensive offshore use and year-round conditions.

Catch & Release

Gone are the days when we can slaughter all the fish we want. The old pictures with the dozens or even hundreds of dead fish were taken at a time when conservation efforts weren't mentioned and everyone thought the bounty of the sea was limitless. Now we know better, having fished a number of species to the brink of extinction. These days, the fisheries are well understood and regulated by the Department of Fish and Game and size and bag limits are put into place to assure a sustainable fishery, that is a fishery where anglers may take fish within the limits of the restriction, and not have the population of fish decline as a result. This is an ideal situation, of course and it counts on not every angler catching a limit of fish every day.

In addition to reurning any undersized, illegal, or over limit fish to the water, it makes good sense to release any fish you do not wish to eat as well. For many, a single fish dinner is all they're looking for and the balance of the day's catch just taken for fun. Releasing fish not only allows them to be caught another day, it also allows them to continue breeding, the single, most important aspect of maintaining a sustainable fishery.

Releasing excess, unwanted or illegal fish is a simple task, particularly for surface feeding species. While the slow, careful revival usually depicted on the fishing shows on TV might pacify the PETA crowd, a much better way to release fish is to drop them head-first from several feet above the water. This forces water across the fish's gills and revives it instantly.

Extra care is sometimes called for when releasing deep dwelling fish. Some, like black seabass, have a swim bladder that overinflates when hauling the fish up from the depths; once inflated, the fish cannot resubmerge. Some advocate piercing the bladder with a needle to allow the trapped air to escape. This is workable, but a much better approach is to tie an 8 oz. to 1 lb sinker to a large (5/0 or bigger) hook with the barb flattened. Tie your fishing line to the curve of the hook rather than to the eye. With the hook stuck through the fish's lower lip, the weight allows the fish to be lowered and repressurized. Once on the bottom, a jerk on the line will pull the hook free.

Some fish that now must be released, like the fourth Boccacio under the new regulations, are hauled up from such depths that there is no hope of reviving the fish; it will already, or very shortly, be dead. It seems a wasteful regulation, but the hope is that if fishing an area with lots of Boccacio, the required discharge of a few dead fish will make the fishermen move to an area populated by other species of rock fish.

There's nothing wrong with killing some fish to eat, but there's plenty wrong with killing all you catch and have no intention of ever eating. Please practice catch and release whenever you can.

Public Health Advisories on Fish Consumption

from the California Department of Fish and Game

Twenty-four locations in southern California have been tested. No consumption advisories based on chemicals were issued for the following locations: Santa Monica Pier, Venice Pier, Venice Beach, Marina del Rey, Redondo Beach, Emma/Eva oil platforms, Huntington Beach, Laguna Beach, Fourteen Mile Bank, Catalina (Two Harbors), and Dana Point. Consumption advice for certain species of sport fish was issued for the other locations because of elevated DDT and PCB levels, as listed below. One meal is about six ounces. Consult current advisories to ensure up-to-date information.

CALIFORNIA COASTAL SITE	FISH SPECIES	RECOMMENDATION
Point Dume/Malibu	White Croaker	Do not consume
Malibu Pier	Queenfish	One meal a month
Short Bank	White Croaker	One meal every two weeks
Redondo Pier	Corbina	One meal every two weeks
Point Vicente/Palos Verdes	White Croaker	Do not consume
White's Point	White Croaker	Do not consume
	Sculpin	One meal every two weeks*
	Rockfishes	One meal every two weeks*
	Kelp Bass	One meal every two weeks*
Los Angeles/Long Beach Harbor	White Croaker	Do not consume
	Queenfish	One meal every two weeks*
	Black Croaker	One meal every two weeks*
	Surfperches	One meal every two weeks*
Los Angeles/Long Beach Breakwater	White Croaker	One meal per month*
	Queenfish	One meal per month*
	Surfperches	One meal per month*
	Black Croaker	One meal per month*
Belmont Pier	Surfperches	One meal every two weeks
Horseshoe Kelp	Sculpin	One meal per month*
Newport Pier	White Croaker	One meal per month*
	Corbina	One meal every two weeks

-Consumption recommendation is for all listed species combined.

Index